Sustainable Business Models

Sustainable Business Models

Special Issue Editor
Adam Jabłoński

MDPI • Basel • Beijing • Wuhan • Barcelona • Belgrade

Special Issue Editor
Adam Jabłoński
Institute of Management
WSB University Poznań
Poland

Editorial Office
MDPI
St. Alban-Anlage 66
4052 Basel, Switzerland

This is a reprint of articles from the Special Issue published online in the open access journal *Sustainability* (ISSN 2071-1050) from 2015 to 2016 (available at: https://www.mdpi.com/journal/sustainability/special_issues/sustainable_business_models).

For citation purposes, cite each article independently as indicated on the article page online and as indicated below:

LastName, A.A.; LastName, B.B.; LastName, C.C. Article Title. *Journal Name* **Year**, *Article Number*, Page Range.

ISBN 978-3-03897-560-1 (Pbk)
ISBN 978-3-03897-561-8 (PDF)

© 2019 by the authors. Articles in this book are Open Access and distributed under the Creative Commons Attribution (CC BY) license, which allows users to download, copy and build upon published articles, as long as the author and publisher are properly credited, which ensures maximum dissemination and a wider impact of our publications.

The book as a whole is distributed by MDPI under the terms and conditions of the Creative Commons license CC BY-NC-ND.

Contents

About the Special Issue Editor ix

Preface to "Sustainable Business Models" xi

Chih-Chao Chung, Li-Chung Chao, Chih-Hong Chen and Shi-Jer Lou
A Balanced Scorecard of Sustainable Management in the Taiwanese Bicycle Industry: Development of Performance Indicators and Importance Analysis
Reprinted from: *Sustainability* **2016**, *8*, 518, doi:10.3390/su8060518 1

Tuananh Tran and Joon Young Park
Development of a Novel Co-Creative Framework for Redesigning Product Service System
Reprinted from: *Sustainability* **2016**, *8*, 434, doi:10.3390/su8050434 22

Adam Jabłoński and Marek Jabłoński
Research on Business Models in their Life Cycle
Reprinted from: *Sustainability* **2016**, *8*, 430, doi:10.3390/su8050430 38

Nestor Shpak, Tamara Kyrylych and Jolita Greblikaitė
Diversification Models of Sales Activity for Steady Development of an Enterprise
Reprinted from: *Sustainability* **2016**, *8*, 393, doi:10.3390/su8040393 75

Andrea Sujova, Lubica Simanova and Katarina Marcinekova
Sustainable Process Performance by Application of Six Sigma Concepts: The Research Study of Two Industrial Cases
Reprinted from: *Sustainability* **2016**, *8*, 260, doi:10.3390/su8030260 94

Andrzej Bialas
Risk Management in Critical Infrastructure—Foundation for Its Sustainable Work
Reprinted from: *Sustainability* **2016**, *8*, 240, doi:10.3390/su8030240 116

Joanna Kurowska-Pysz
Opportunities for Cross-Border Entrepreneurship Development in a Cluster Model Exemplified by the Polish–Czech Border Region
Reprinted from: *Sustainability* **2016**, *8*, 230, doi: 141

Jinhuan Tang, Shoufeng Ji and Liwen Jiang
The Design of a Sustainable Location-Routing-Inventory Model Considering Consumer Environmental Behavior
Reprinted from: *Sustainability* **2016**, *8*, 211, doi:10.3390/su8030211 162

Adam Jabłoński
Scalability of Sustainable Business Models in Hybrid Organizations
Reprinted from: *Sustainability* **2016**, *8*, 194, doi:10.3390/su8030194 182

M. Isabel Sánchez-Hernández, Dolores Gallardo-Vázquez, Agnieszka Barcik and Piotr Dziwiński
The Effect of the Internal Side of Social Responsibility on Firm Competitive Success in the Business Services Industry
Reprinted from: *Sustainability* **2016**, *8*, 179, doi:10.3390/su8020179 217

Chia-Nan Wang, Xuan-Tho Nguyen and Yen-Hui Wang
Automobile Industry Strategic Alliance Partner Selection: The Application of a Hybrid DEA and Grey Theory Model
Reprinted from: *Sustainability* 2016, 8, 173, doi:10.3390/su8020173 232

Marzanna Katarzyna Witek-Hajduk and Piotr Zaborek
Does Business Model Affect CSR Involvement? A Survey of Polish Manufacturing and Service Companies
Reprinted from: *Sustainability* 2016, 8, 93, doi:10.3390/su8020093 250

Courage Matobobo and Isaac O. Osunmakinde
Analytical Business Model for Sustainable Distributed Retail Enterprises in a Competitive Market
Reprinted from: *Sustainability* 2016, 8, 140, doi:10.3390/su8020140 271

Elżbieta Izabela Szczepankiewicz and Przemysław Mućko
CSR Reporting Practices of Polish Energy and Mining Companies
Reprinted from: *Sustainability* 2016, 8, 126, doi:10.3390/su8020126 289

Barbara Kożuch and Katarzyna Sienkiewicz-Małyjurek
Inter-Organisational Coordination for Sustainable Local Governance: Public Safety Management in Poland
Reprinted from: *Sustainability* 2016, 8, 123, doi:10.3390/su8020123 306

Liliana Hawrysz and Joachim Foltys
Environmental Aspects of Social Responsibility of Public Sector Organizations
Reprinted from: *Sustainability* 2016, 8, 19, doi:10.3390/su8010019 327

Jingxiao Zhang, Haiyan Xie, Klaus Schmidt and Hui Li
A New Systematic Approach to Vulnerability Assessment of Innovation Capability of Construction Enterprises
Reprinted from: *Sustainability* 2016, 8, 17, doi:10.3390/su8010017 337

Ning Wang and Runlin Yan
Research on Consumers' Use Willingness and Opinions of Electric Vehicle Sharing: An Empirical Study in Shanghai
Reprinted from: *Sustainability* 2016, 8, 7, doi:10.3390/su8010007 362

Jeng-Wen Lin, Pu Fun Shen and Yin-Sung Hsu
Effects of Employees' Work Values and Organizational Management on Corporate Performance for Chinese and Taiwanese Construction Enterprises
Reprinted from: *Sustainability* 2016, 8, 16836–16848, doi:10.3390/su71215852 380

Chanwoo Cho and Sungjoo Lee
How Firms Can Get Ideas from Users for Sustainable Business Innovation
Reprinted from: *Sustainability* 2015, 7, 16039–16059, doi:10.3390/su71215802 393

Gianluigi De Mare, Maria Fiorella Granata and Antonio Nesticò
Weak and Strong Compensation for the Prioritization of Public Investments: Multidimensional Analysis for Pools
Reprinted from: *Sustainability* 2015, 7, 16022–16038, doi:10.3390/su71215798 414

Joanna Radomska
The Concept of Sustainable Strategy Implementation
Reprinted from: *Sustainability* 2015, 7, 15847–15856, doi:10.3390/su71215790 431

Jeng-Wen Lin, Pu Fun Shen and Bing-Jean Lee
Repetitive Model Refinement for Questionnaire Design Improvement in the Evaluation of Working Characteristics in Construction Enterprises
Reprinted from: *Sustainability* **2015**, *7*, 15179–15193, doi:10.3390/su71115179 . . . . **441**

Seungkyum Kim, Changho Son, Byungun Yoon and Yongtae Park
Development of an Innovation Model Based on a Service-Oriented Product Service System (PSS)
Reprinted from: *Sustainability* **2015**, *7*, 14427–14449, doi:10.3390/su71114427 . . . . **453**

Mateusz Lewandowski
Designing the Business Models for Circular Economy—Towards the Conceptual Framework
Reprinted from: *Sustainability* **2016**, *8*, 43, doi:10.3390/su8010043 . . . . **472**

About the Special Issue Editor

Adam Jabłoński is an associate professor Ph.D. at the WSB University in Poznań, Faculty in Chorzów, Poland, Institute of Management. President of the Board of the consulting company "OTTIMA plus" Ltd. Katowice and Vice-President of the Association Southern Railway Cluster. He holds a postdoctoral degree in Economic Sciences, specializing in Management Science. He is the author of a variety of studies and business analyses in the value management, risk management, balanced scorecard, and corporate social responsibility fields. He has also written and co-written several monographs and over 100 scientific articles in the field of management, published both in Poland and in abroad.

His scientific interests include issues of modern and efficient business model design, including sustainable business models and the principles of company value-building strategies that include the rules of corporate social responsibility. He is also interested in business models and their key attributes. He has explored various features of business models, especially focusing on the design and operationalization of business models in a network environment. He has studied the mechanisms that shape business models in a network environment, searching for universal principles, which are a source of further scientific exploration in this area.

Currently, he is also a member of Scientific Boards of International Journals and he is the scientific reviewer in 10 entities (USA, India, Denmark, Germany), and in Scientific Boards of National Journals he is a scientific reviewer in nine entities.

Preface to "Sustainable Business Models"

The dynamically changing world economy, which is in an era of intensive development and globalization, creates new needs in both the theoretical models of management and in the practical discussion related to the perception of business. Because of new economic phenomena related to the crisis, there is a need for the design and operationalization of innovative business models for companies. Due to the fact that in times of crisis, the principles of strategic balance are particularly important, these business models can be sustainable business models. Moreover, it is essential to skillfully use different methods and concepts of management to ensure the continuity of business. It seems that sustainable business models, in their essence, can support companies' effectiveness and contribute to their stable, sustainable functioning in the difficult, ever-changing market.

This Special Issue aims to discuss the key mechanisms concerning the design and operationalization of sustainable business models, from a strategic perspective. We invite you to contribute to this Issue by submitting comprehensive reviews, case studies, or research articles. Papers selected for this Special Issue are subject to a rigorous peer review procedure, with the aim of rapid and wide dissemination of research results, developments, and applications.

Adam Jabłoński
Special Issue Editor

Article

A Balanced Scorecard of Sustainable Management in the Taiwanese Bicycle Industry: Development of Performance Indicators and Importance Analysis

Chih-Chao Chung [1], Li-Chung Chao [1], Chih-Hong Chen [2] and Shi-Jer Lou [3,*]

[1] Institute of Engineering Science and Technology, National Kaohsiung First University of Science and Technology, Kaohsiung City 824, Taiwan; justin640513@yahoo.com.tw (C.-C.C.); chaolc@nkfust.edu.tw (L.-C.C.)
[2] Department of Modern Languages, National Pingtung University of Science and Technology, Pingtung 912, Taiwan; andrewchc@mail.npust.edu.tw
[3] Graduate Institute of Technological and Vocational Education, National Pingtung University of Science and Technology, Pingtung 912, Taiwan
* Correspondence: lou@mail.npust.edu.tw; Tel.: +886-8-770-3202

Academic Editors: Adam Jabłoński and Marc A. Rosen
Received: 5 February 2016; Accepted: 25 May 2016; Published: 28 May 2016

Abstract: The main purpose of this study is to investigate the development of the performance indicators of sustainable management in the Taiwanese bicycle industry and to perform an importance analysis. Based on the Balanced Scorecard concept, the framework of sustainable management is added. Ten experts evaluated the performance indicators of a sustainable Balanced Scorecard in the Taiwanese bicycle industry using five major categories: (1) Financial, (2) Customer, (3) Internal Business Processes, (4) Learning and Growth, and (5) Sustainable Development, and a total of 21 performance indicators were used. The analytic network process (ANP) was used to perform an importance analysis of the various performance indicators. Most of the experts suggested that for the introduction of a sustainable management strategy into the bicycle industry in Taiwan, it is necessary to include the definition of sustainable management and to improve five performance indicators: innovation process, customer satisfaction, operations process, after-sales service, and market share. According to the analysis results, this study proposed relevant management definitions and suggestions to be used as important references for decision-makers to understand the introduction of sustainable management strategies to the current bicycle industry in Taiwan.

Keywords: balanced scorecard; performance indicator; ANP; sustainable management; bicycle industry

1. Introduction

In today's complex and changing business environment, enterprises must carefully develop their business strategies to gain a competitive advantage over the long term. Therefore, how to plan and formulate strategies for enterprises plays a decisive role. With the development of environmental awareness and sustainability, market value is no longer dominated by a single performance indicator; instead, the triple bottom line (TBL) framework integrates economic, environmental, and social performance [1,2]. It has become an international focus to actively implement environmental protection and social responsibility. Therefore, the implementation of a new strategy in response to this trend is necessary for enterprises to remain competitive. Additionally, the issue of how to effectively integrate existing and future strategies to enhance competitiveness is an important issue that enterprises must consider.

Taiwan is known as the "Bicycle Kingdom" due to excellent manufacturing technology, successful market segmentation, and high profitability [3]. The current trends of global warming, environmental consciousness, sports and leisure activities, and high international oil prices are beneficial to the development of the bicycle industry. In view of these considerations, if the Taiwanese bicycle industry can conform to current environmental concerns, actively apply a sustainable business strategy, and maintain business leaders who assume industry responsibility, then the international image of Taiwan-made bicycles and industrial competitiveness would be enhanced.

Based on the Balanced Scorecard concept, this study includes the definition of sustainable management to develop performance indicators of a sustainable Balanced Scorecard for the bicycle industry. This study uses the characteristics of the ANP to perform an importance analysis of the priority of the various performance indicators in the bicycle industry. In addition, the study is intended to help decision-makers understand the focus of the introduction of a sustainable management strategy. Specifically, the research objectives concerning a sustainable Balanced Scorecard for the bicycle industry of Taiwan are as follows:

(1) to develop performance indicators;
(2) to investigate the importance analysis of the performance indicators;
(3) to summarize the management definition of the importance of the performance indicators.

2. Literature Review

The trends in sustainable management strategy will be reviewed and the application of a Balanced Scorecard will be discussed. The bicycle industry's current status and sustainability issues will be examined, and the application of the ANP will be illustrated.

2.1. Sustainable Management Strategy

The Report of the World Commission on Environment and Development states that humankind now faces economic, social, and environmental threats. Human beings must have the ability to continue to develop and to meet their actual needs, but humanity should not jeopardize the wellbeing of the next generation. This can be accomplished by applying the concepts of fairness, sustainability, and commonality [4]. However, the general measure of business performance can be broadly divided into three dimensions: financial performance, business performance, and organizational performance [5]. As the environment changes, companies should not pursue profit maximization as their primary goal; efforts should be made to meet the public's expectations of businesses, to enhance the corporate image, and to practice sustainable management [6]. To the stakeholders (consumers, shareholders, employees, communities, suppliers, and governments), organizations have a duty to maximize their positive impacts while minimizing the negative ones. Studies have suggested that in the future a multinational corporation will need to comply with more than 60 different environmental and societal norms [7]. Issues related to social aspects are gradually taken seriously. Many companies have been engaged in social responsibility and social welfare to strengthen their performance in terms of these social aspects. Moreover, the evaluation of business performance has gradually transformed into the triple bottom line framework, which consists of economic, environmental, and social performance [1,2]. The triple bottom line includes a financial baseline, an environmental baseline, and a social baseline. The financial baseline refers to a company's financial benefits, as shown by its financial report. The environmental baseline focuses on a company's performance in terms of sustainable management, which requires that the company not damage the sustainability of natural capital. Related environmental indicators include compliance with environmental laws and standards, environmental management systems, energy use, waste disposal, recycling, and the use of eco-technology. The social baseline focuses on social capital and the maintenance and development of human capital. Social capital includes the mutual trust between members of society and the co-operative relationship. Human capital includes staff education, investment in health and nutrition, and an emphasis on labor rights. Businesses can participate in meaningful work, such as the protection of human rights, the abolition of child labor, the protection of labor and women's rights, social care, education, and health care [8,9].

2.2. The Application of the Balanced Scorecard

The Balanced Scorecard (BSC) was developed by a one-year research project funded by the U.S. management consultancy firm Nolan, Norton & Co. (acquired by KPMG) in 1990 [10]. The program was created by David Norton, of Nolan–Norton, and Robert Kaplan, a Harvard University professor. The program aimed to explore "the future overall performance evaluation system of the organization". The strategy performance measurement system covered four dimensions: Financial, Customer, Internal Processes, and Learning and Growth; it is now known as the Balanced Scorecard [11–13]. The application of the Balanced Scorecard is widely employed. In response to different organizational patterns, characteristics, and life cycles, there are different focal points, including balanced financial and non-financial indexes, balanced internal and external composing factors, balanced lead–lag relationships of information, and balanced short-term performance and long-term value [14,15]. For example, there are benefits to linking activity-based costing regarding gross profit with the Balanced Scorecard after the Balanced Scorecard has been implemented [12]. Fletcher and Smith [16] discuss how, by integrating the analytic hierarchy process technique with the Balanced Scorecard, performance indicators can be established to objectively assess the performance of enterprises. In addition, the Balanced Scorecard can also be utilized in evaluating the performance of suppliers, particularly when choosing them [17,18]. The four dimensions are explained as follows.

(1) Financial perspective

The financial perspective is the ultimate goal of the four dimensions of the Balanced Scorecard; it represents the financial performance of its operations [11]. It is primarily the intersection between the interests of the shareholders and the financial impact of strategic objectives [19]. For most businesses, it is nothing more than the pursuit of revenue growth, increasing productivity, cost reduction, financial risk management, and other issues [10].

(2) Customer perspective

The customer perspective primarily concerns how the company can create major core values to the customer through policy and action [19]. The customer and market segments in which a business unit competes and the measures of the business unit's performance in these targeted segments are sources of revenue for the company to achieve its financial goals. [12]. The customer perspective can be categorized into market share, customer acquisition, customer retention, customer satisfaction, and customer profitability. Companies must amend the target based on the customers who will generate the most expected profit and the greatest potential for revenue growth.

(3) Internal business process perspective

The main difference between the Balanced Scorecard setting goals and traditional performance measurement systems is the inclusion of the internal business process. Kaplan and Norton state that before designing the internal processes of the measurable performance indicators, the business value chain should be analyzed. Based on the innovation process, the operation process, and post-sales service, the internal processes can be implemented such that customer needs are met in an optimal manner [20]. The beginning of the value chain of the internal business process perspective is the innovation process, which clarifies the current and future customer needs. New products are developed to meet and create customer needs. Next, the operation process focuses on providing products and services to existing customers. Finally, the post-sales service process, which includes defective products and returns, is accounted for.

(4) Learning and growth perspective

The Learning and Growth perspective is about how to improve the competitiveness of the organization and its human resources to accept the challenges to be faced in the future [19]. This perspective has three major core objectives—employee capabilities; information system capabilities; and motivation, empowerment, and alignment. The financial, customer, and internal business process perspectives of the Balanced Scorecard reveal gaps between the desired and actual ability of employees, systems, and procedures. To narrow these gaps, companies must invest to advance staff skills, strengthen information technology systems, and adjust organizational procedures and daily operations so that employee satisfaction is enhanced, and staff retention rates and employee productivity are maximized [11].

In summary, based on the structure of the Balanced Scorecard, there are implications for balancing the external metrics, such as stakeholders and customers, with the key internal metrics, such as internal processes, innovation and learning, and growth [21,22]. Because the Balanced Scorecard is an open system, when the interests of all stakeholders and institutions succeed as part of an integral strategy, these interests can be integrated into it [20]. Therefore, this study is based on the original structure of the Balanced Scorecard and therefore integrates the environmental and social perspectives to form new perspectives in order to achieve economic, social, and environmental objectives that also provide the possibility of sustainable development [21,23,24].

2.3. Current Status of the Bicycle Industry

The bicycle industry in Taiwan has been developing for the last 50 years. The foundation of the its industrial development was previous domestic transportation and loading operations. From 1971 to 1974, the bicycle industry in Taiwan has helped foreign manufacturers earn gross profits in the form of large ODM orders. Hence, a superb manufacturing technology and a supply chain network consisting of many small and medium enterprises has been developed [25]. With the collaboration of industry, government, academia, and research, the bicycle industry in Taiwan has moved toward the development of entrepreneurial firms. The title "Superior Bicycle Kingdom" was won by focusing on advancing quality and establishing domestic brands [26].

Since 2005, the government has proposed a transportation-industry promotion plan that targets the shaping of an international image of superior bicycles and the production of parts and components in Taiwan. Combined with industry, government, academia, and other research resources, the bicycle industry in Taiwan has been continuously developing new materials and innovative features that incorporate lightweight components, electronics, and ergonomics, as well as meet the demand for good-value and high-grade products [27].

By developing bicycle product design and research and development capabilities, new features of domestic products and the high-tech image have been enhanced. Therefore, the value added and product competitiveness has been increased. New features and new materials have been developed and integrated to create a technological environment able to promote product differentiation with the mainland products. With a leading position in bicycle stores, the bicycle industry in Taiwan has delivered more differentiated and innovative products in the international market [27,28]. The bicycle industry in Taiwan has successfully established a well-known international brand and marketing channels with the collaborative work of the government and private industry, and now strives to transform into an international high-quality research and development center and sales center [3].

In summary, the bicycle industry in Taiwan has gradually transformed from a manufacturing industry into one combined with a service industry. The market segments are targeted with the development of innovative, high-quality bicycle products and services compared with the bicycle industries of other countries. However, the bicycle industry's business strategy is less refined. Therefore, this study emphasizes that the bicycle industry must respond to the current trend, pay attention to the environment and sustainability issues, and create an excellent image with the superiority of a leading brand. To maintain the competitive advantage of the bicycle industry, a sustainable business strategy involving the image and products of the company must be actively initiated.

2.4. Analytic Network Process (ANP)

The analytic network process is a generalized model of the analytic hierarchy process; both were proposed by Thomas L. Saaty [29]. In recent years, the analytic hierarchy process (AHP) has been widely used in many problems involving system decision-making. This method concerns the division of system levels, considering one-way influence between the hierarchy, and assumes that elements of the same level are individually independent. However, there are many cases involving elements of interdependent and feedback relationships in decision-making problems; AHP cannot incorporate these connections [30]. Bentes, Carneiro, Silva, and Kimura [31] discuss the restrictions of an integration of BSC and AHP in the multidimensional assessment of organizational performance in a Brazilian telecom company. For example, there must be a hierarchical approach among the elements, assuming that there is no interaction between independent elements, or a sensitivity analysis cannot be performed to verify whether results are reasonably stable. Therefore, ANP, proposed by Saaty in 1996, included the characteristics of interdependence and feedback, enabling scholars and experts to apply it to a wide range of issues [32,33]. AHP is actually a special case of ANP; AHP assumes that there is independent influence between the relevant factors of an issue, while ANP assumes that there are mutually influential relations among factors [34]. ANP, like AHP, can reach a consensus of all decision-making through a specific method, but it has a relatively deeper level of consideration compared with AHP. The application of ANP consists of assessing the priority value of each object and establishing an interdependence relationship as well as a network between various objectives and guidelines. Accordingly, ANP not only considers the practical problems with dependent characteristics in programs and guidelines but also possesses a feedback mechanism to handle human society's real and complex problems [35].

The construction and the steps of implementing the ANP are as follows.

(1) The construction of decision problems system

By investigating the interaction between various criteria, the overall structure of the decision problem network map is constructed. If there is an influence of the criteria on the overall structure, it is an outer dependence; if there is an influence between the sub-criteria involved in each criterion group, it is an inner dependence.

(2) Pairwise comparisons between various groups and guidelines

After the relationship mentioned above is established, groups with dependencies or feedback relationships are pair-wise compared in the AHP methods with a comparison scale from 1 to 9 [36]. Questionnaires to all the experts are arranged as follows: by taking the geometric mean as the input value, the comparison matrices are compiled. Each comparison matrix is required for consistency analysis, and when the consistency ratio (C.R.) ⩽0.1, it can be accepted; the paired comparison questionnaires can be considered to be valid questionnaires [37,38]. Then,

$$C.R. = C.I./R.I. \qquad (1)$$

where *C.I.* is the consistency index and *R.I.* is random inconsistency.

(3) Building a super-matrix

After pairwise comparisons, the vector of each matrix can be calculated. All the vectors included within the matrix form the unweighted super-matrix. The weight of the same element within the unweighted matrix is multiplied by the relating number of community so that all straight fields add up to 1, resulting in the weighted super-matrix.

(4) The super-matrix of limiting calculation of decision problems

To obtain a state of long-term stability, the weighted super-matrix is multiplied by itself repeatedly until convergence, where in each column and field the numbers are equal; this can be expressed as the following limit of the weighted super-matrix:

$$W_{\lim} = \lim_{k \to \infty} \left(W_{weighted} \right)^k. \tag{2}$$

(5) The advantageous arrangement of feasibility plans

According to the various possible solutions and standards between each feature vector in the matrix to obtain the whole feature vector, one can find the best solution.

(6) Sensitivity analysis of the decision problem

The decision problem can be performed through sensitivity analysis to analyze the strength of the overall arrangement. This allows policy makers to see how the results change when a certain input value changes and to observe whether the result is stable after the order is changed. Therefore, policymakers can choose the proposed plan with more confidence.

ANP has a wide range of applications in addition to the use of multi-target and multi-criteria decision-making. It can access and evaluate the relative importance of a number of indicators to determine the most suitable solution and be an important reference for the organization's resource allocation and policy construction [39,40]. The main purpose of this study is to select the performance indicators of a sustainable strategy for the bicycle industry and to assess the relative importance of performance indicators. The bicycle industry can therefore adopt this model as an important reference for further sustainable decision-making.

3. Research Design and Methods

This study refers to *Incorporating Design Thinking into Sustainable Business Modeling* by Lehmann, Bocken, Steingrimsson, and Evans [41] to construct the bicycle sustainable management Balanced Scorecard performance indicators ANP assessment model. By integrating the value mapping tool [42] and different notions and concrete cogitations that focus the design process around the concerns, interests, and values of humans in an iterative and interactive way [43], the interaction design is assembled. This study design is divided into three stages. The detailed process of the study is shown in Figure 1, and the project team work is listed in Table 1.

The first stage is based on the four aspects of the Balanced Scorecard: the analysis of sustainable management and the literature review of the bicycle industry to summarize how the assessment dimensions and criteria can be incorporated into the bicycle industry's sustainable development strategy. The second stage is to draw on the experience and opinions of experts by using a questionnaire survey of the key elements of sustainable management strategies selected from all facets and important projects and to determine the correlation between the key elements as the basis for constructing the ANP evaluation model. The third stage is to construct the ANP evaluation model and to include analysis of the dependency of the relevance among the criteria. With the analysis of the ANP expert survey results, the relative importance of the key elements emerges to help policy-makers realize the relevance of sustainable management to Taiwan's bicycle industry.

Table 1. Timetable of project team and job description.

Stage		Date	Number of Participants and Category	Research Methods and Job Description
1st Stage	The initial stage	22 May 2015	3 senior managers in the bicycle industry, 4 research team members	Discussion on sustainable development, BSC and ANP, and other related documents; draw sustainable development goals for bicycle industry; making list of experts from industry, academia, research, *etc.*
	Setup of *ad hoc* group	19 June 2015	5 bicycle industry experts, 4 academic experts, 3 experts from research and development center, 4 research team members	Convening specialists of sustainable management from industry, academia, research, and the bicycle industry to from the *ad hoc* group
	The first meeting of the *ad hoc* group	26 June 2015	5 bicycle industry experts, 4 academic experts, 2 experts from research and development center, 4 research team members	Implementation of focus groups interviews to understand sustainable performance indicators in bicycle industry; making lists of indicators of sustainable development; draft expert questionnaire to be drawn; description and practice of BSC and ANP Research Tools
2nd Stage	The 2nd meeting of the *ad hoc* group	10 July 2015	4 bicycle industry experts, 4 academic experts, 3 experts from research and development center, 4 research team members	Implementation of expert questionnaire to determine the BSC sustainable development indicators in bicycle industry
	The 3rd meeting of the *ad hoc* group	31 July 2015	4 bicycle industry experts, 4 academic experts, 3 experts from research and development center, 4 research team members	Implementation of focus groups to understand the importance of performance indicators of sustainable management in bicycle industry and to determine the relevance; the construction of ANP model, and the development and drafting of an AHP experts questionnaire
	The 4th meeting of the *ad hoc* group	14 August 2015	5 bicycle industry experts, 4 academic experts, 2 experts from research and development center, 4 research team members	Implementation of experts questionnaire; consistency check of ANP experts questionnaire; verification of the relative importance of BSC sustainable development indicators of bicycle industry
3rd Stage	The 5th meeting of the *ad hoc* group	11 September 2015	4 bicycle industry experts, 4 academic experts, 2 experts of research and development center, 4 research team members	The proposal of importing sustainable development strategy in bicycle industry in accordance with the importance weight of sustainable development indicators
	Final report composing	30 October 2015	4 research team members	Final report composing in reference to the findings and recommendations of the experts

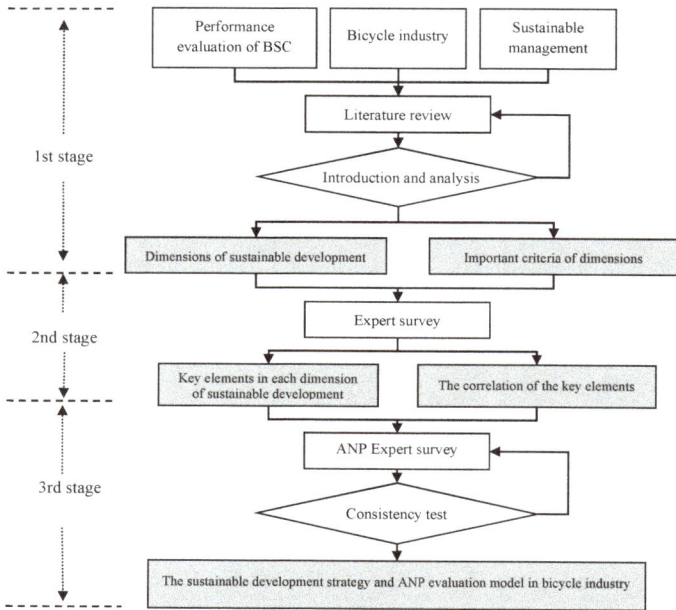

Figure 1. Research design flow.

3.1. Experts Survey

The opinions of experts on research and experience related to the bicycle industry and on sustainable management are assessed by the important criteria as summarized from the literature given importance ratings based on subjective value judgments. To obtain an expert rating for each project, an index of the questionnaire selection model is constructed on a scale of 0 to 1. The closer to 1, the higher importance the item holds. The opinions of industry, government, and academic experts are integrated to yield the analysis topics and construct the key factors in sustainable development in the bicycle industry.

3.2. The Analytic Network Process

This study adds a fifth dimension, the sustainable development aspect, into the traditional Balanced Scorecard. With the application of dependent characteristics of main criteria and sub-criteria among the decision problems of ANP elements, the relative importance criteria of sustainable management strategies and the bicycle industry are assessed by using Super Decisions software to analyze the results of the research. To increase the reliability of the results of the questionnaire analysis, the expert survey needs to be checked with consistency analysis. Those questionnaires that meet the standards are valid, and for those that do not meet the standards, the experts shall make further revisions. Finally, all valid expert questionnaire data are calculated by the geometric average number as a whole ANP expert questionnaire data.

3.3. Target Respondents

The perspective of sustainable management strategy in the bicycle industry is extensive, and there are different views from different angles. Therefore, in selecting target respondents, professional competence of the experts, the familiarity and authority of the study of topics are the considerations of the expert selection. The number of experts should preferably be five to 15 people because error can be reduced to a minimum with a group of at least 10 people, and the reliability is the highest [44].

This study requests 12 experts to participate in the expert survey and ANP questionnaire, with 10 questionnaires of effective recovery; the overall response rate was 83%. The background information of the interviewees is shown in Table 2. Professional fields are bicycle industry management, bicycle R&D, sustainable development, and corporate social responsibility. The target respondents adequately covered the scope of this study and hold at least eight years of experience in teaching or in industry to provide the most comprehensive and professional advice.

Table 2. Experts' background information.

Catalogue	Detailed Catalogue	A	B	C	D	E	F	G	H	I	J	Num.
Category	Industry	v	v	v	v							4
	Academia					v	v	v	v			4
	R&D Center									v	v	2
Educational background	Ph.D.					v	v	v	v			4
	Master's	v		v	v					v	v	5
	Bachelor's		v									1
Years	More than 15 years	v	v			v	v					4
	10 to 15 years			v	v			v		v	v	5
	5 to 10 years								v			1
position	General Manager/Professor	v	v			v	v					4
	Manager/Associate Professor			v				v				2
	Assistant Manager/Assistant Professor				v				v	v	v	4
Profession	Bicycle Industry Management	v	v		v	v	v	v				6
	Bicycle R&D	v	v	v			v	v	v	v	v	8
	Sustainable development			v	v	v			v		v	5
	Corporate Social Responsibility	v			v	v		v	v		v	6

4. Research Results and Analysis

According to the research aim and literature review, the results of analysis are to be made using the expert survey and the analytic network process. The analysis results are as follows.

4.1. The Analysis of the Expert Survey

This research is accomplished through a literature review examining how the bicycle industry is introduced to sustainable operation; also considered is the draft of the expert questionnaire design. According to the views and opinions of the industry experts, they amend and delete ambiguous pieces and other unsuitable measure of the effectiveness of sustainable projects in the questionnaire. Finally, four dimensions of the Balanced Scorecard, Financial, Customer, Internal Business Processes, and Learning and Growth, are collated and analyzed. Additionally, the Sustainable Development dimension is integrated as the fifth dimension. Along with 27 important projects, the five dimensions are incorporated into the expert questionnaire design and survey, and the score is calculated by the geometric mean (M value).

4.1.1. Selection of Key Elements of Sustainable Development

In this study, the result scores of 27 important projects under five dimensions are analyzed, as shown in Table 3. CS and LR have the highest score (0.864), followed by innovation processes, restructuring on employees' expertise, and industrial safety and health (0.826); productivity, cost management, customers' continuation rate, and employees' ability are in third place (0.792). The quartile scores of the 27 major projects are regarded as the basis of retention or deletion for sustainable management strategies. Six projects having a lower score than Q1 (Q1 = 0.706) were deleted after a careful assessment. Therefore, by the collection of the expert questionnaire, 21 key projects are selected in the study.

Table 3. Analysis results of expert questionnaire.

Five Dimensions	Key Projects	M Value	Sequence	Remark
1. Financial	1-1 revenue growth (RG)	0.761	3	retain
	1-2 productivity (PD)	0.792	1	retain
	1-3 return on capital employed (RCE)	0.732	4	retain
	1-4 cost management (CM)	0.792	1	retain
	1-5 risk management (RM)	0.686	5	delete
	1-6 investment strategy (IS)	0.663	6	delete
2. Customer	2-1 customer satisfaction (CS)	0.864	1	retain
	2-2 customers continuation rate (CCR)	0.792	2	retain
	2-3 market share (MS)	0.706	3	retain
	2-4 customer profitability (CP)	0.645	5	delete
	2-5 customer retention rate (CRR)	0.686	4	delete
3. Internal Business Processes	3-1 innovation process (IP)	0.826	1	retain
	3-2 business processes (BP)	0.761	2	retain
	3-3 service (SV)	0.761	2	retain
	3-4 information system capabilities (ISC)	0.706	4	retain
	3-5 products database management (PDM)	0.663	5	delete
4. Learning and Growth	4-1 employee satisfaction (ES)	0.761	3	retain
	4-2 employee continuation rate (ECR)	0.732	4	retain
	4-3 employees ability (EA)	0.792	2	retain
	4-4 restructuring on employees' expertise (REE)	0.826	1	retain
	4-5 incentives and authorization (IA)	0.732	4	retain
	4-6 supplier management capabilities (SMC)	0.686	6	delete
5. Sustainable Development	5-1 environmental protection (EP)	0.710	4	retain
	5-2 industrial safety and health (ISH)	0.826	2	retain
	5-3 labor rights (LR)	0.864	1	retain
	5-4 protection of human rights (PHR)	0.761	3	retain
	5-5 social care (SC)	0.710	4	retain
	Q1 = 0.706			

4.1.2. The Correlation Analysis of Key Elements of Sustainable Development

Experts were invited to evaluate the relationship of mutual influence among various performance indicators, which were scored according to the level of correlation, as shown in Table 4. Statistical analyses was performed on the evaluation results of correlation of performance indicators. If the mean was ⩾3 and reached significant difference, there was a significant correlation between two performance indicators. The key project-related outcomes are as shown in Appendix A. Each facet of the key items is deemed as a relevant necessity in this study; for example, the key dimensions of Financial perspective, 1-1, 1-2, and 1-4, serve as a key project as the pairwise comparison of essential items in the ANP internal dependencies, which produce 21 comparison matrices. The external dependency of key projects between dimensions is regarded as the expert selection results. For instance, in the Financial performance, key item 1-1 is connected with 2-3, is associated with 3-1 and 3-2, is related to 4-1, 4-3, and 4-5, and is associated with 5-3. Therefore, in the ANP analysis stage, the project must be considered based on key 1-1 and should carry out pairwise comparison of key 3-1 and 3-2; 4-1, 4-3, and 4-5. As for 2-3 and 5-3, due to the dimension with only one key project associated with 1-1, there is no need for comparison. According to the external dependency of performance indicators of dimensions, 63 pairs of comparison matrices were generated.

Based on the above considerations, the experts evaluated the correlation of internal and external dependency of a total of 21 performance indicators in five major categories, and 84 pairs of comparison matrices were generated. These were used as the basis to develop the ANP evaluation model of introduction of Balanced Scorecard of sustainable management into the bicycle industry.

Table 4. Questionnaire of mutual influence and relationship on key projects.

	Very Irrelevant	Irrelevant	Fair	Relevant	Very Relevant	
1-1 revenue growth	▫ (1 point)	▫ (2 points)	▫ (3 points)	▫ (4 points)	▫ (5 points)	2-1 customer satisfaction

4.2. The Analysis of Analytic Network Process (ANP) Expert Questionnaires

Expert questionnaires are utilized to assess the key projects of the bicycle industry adaptation to the sustainable management strategies, including 27 important projects under five dimensions, and their relevance, to construct the ANP evaluation model. Statistics and analyses are performed by the use of expert questionnaires and Super Decisions software. The results are as follows.

4.2.1. The Construction of the ANP Evaluation Model

The ANP evaluation model was established; the goal of decision-making is the bicycle industry's adaptation to sustainable management strategies. The five dimensions of the impact to achieve the target are regarded as the main criteria in the ANP: Financial, Customer, Internal Business Processes, Learning and Growth, and Sustainable Development. These five main criteria have a relationship of interdependence and influence. Under each main criterion, 21 sub-criteria are included; these are key projects that are selected through expert questionnaires, as shown in Figure 2. Between each sub-criterion, the relationship of interdependence and influence are defined according to expert opinions.

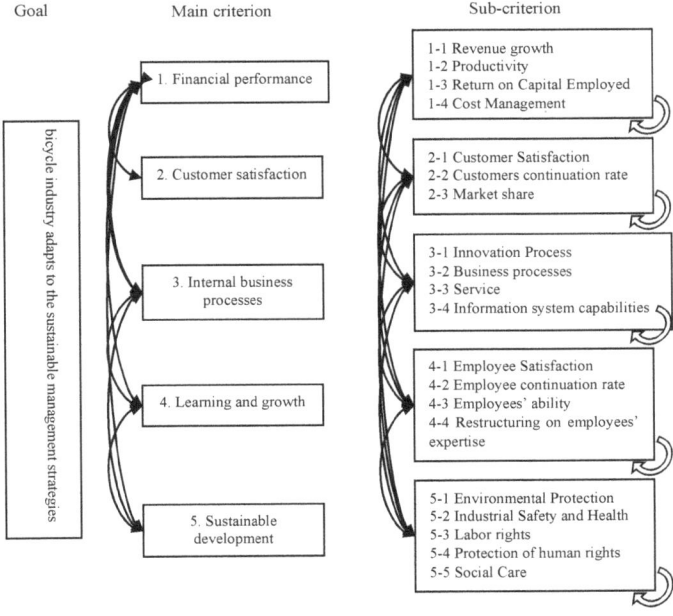

Figure 2. Mutual correlations of performance indicators of sustainable Balanced Scorecard.

4.2.2. Paired Comparison and Consistency Test

Based on the results of the ANP expert questionnaires, this study is examined for consistency with the advice of every expert included. Valid questionnaires are calculated with the use of the geometric mean to find the average. After the integration with the comparison matrix is obtained, the expert overall consistency test then followed. This study used Super Decisions software to obtain the weight and CI value of various matrices. The analysis results showed that the C.I. value of all the matrices was ⩽0.1, suggesting that there was a certain amount of consistency in paired comparisons obtained after experts' preference integration. The weights of various matrices were also highly reliable [36].

The eigenvectors obtained from various matrices were integrated to obtain the initial super-matrix assessed from the introduction of the sustainable management model into the bicycle industry; the unweighted super-matrix is shown in Appendix B. Because the unweighted super-matrix is composed of many paired comparison matrices, it is random. In other words, the total eigenvector of each row is not equal to 1. Therefore, it is necessary to adjust the unweighted super-matrix to conform to the basic principle of randomization of ANP theory.

In terms of the adjustment method, this study aligned the matrix of relative weights of various dimensions under the influence of various evaluation dimensions to obtain the complete cluster matrix, as shown in Table 5. Then, the cluster matrix was multiplied by the unweighted super-matrix to make the total of each row become 1 and form the weighted super-matrix, as shown in Appendix C. According to ANP theory, the continuous squaring of the weighted super-matrix can obtain a convergent extreme super-matrix, as shown in Table 6. At the same time, the weight of each indicator will be close to a fixed value. The final results of priority of importance of performance indicators obtained using the ANP and the analyses are summarized in the table.

Table 5. Cluster matrix.

Main Criteria	Financial	Customer	Internal Business Processes	Learning and Growth	Sustainable Development
Financial	0.151	0.161	0.193	0.135	0.187
Customer	0.265	0.248	0.251	0.251	0.176
Internal Business Processes	0.266	0.276	0.240	0.270	0.166
Learning and Growth	0.207	0.194	0.199	0.197	0.217
Sustainable Development	0.110	0.121	0.117	0.147	0.255

Table 6. Weights analysis table of sub-criteria to sustainable business strategy.

Main Criteria	Sub-Criteria	Weights	Sequence under Each Main Criterion	Overall Ranking
Financial	1-1 revenue growth	0.016	4	21
	1-2 productivity	0.039	2	11
	1-3 return on capital employed	0.062	1	6
	1-4 cost management	0.036	3	14
Customer	2-1 customer satisfaction	0.095	1	2
	2-2 customers continuation rate	0.035	3	15
	2-3 market share	0.074	2	4
Internal Business Processes	3-1 innovation process	0.106	1	1
	3-2 business processes	0.080	2	3
	3-3 service	0.063	3	5
	3-4 information system capabilities	0.036	4	13
Learning and Growth	4-1 employee satisfaction	0.055	1	7
	4-2 employee continuation rate	0.024	5	19
	4-3 employees' ability	0.040	3	10
	4-4 restructuring on employees' expertise	0.026	4	18
	4-5 incentives and authorization	0.046	2	8
Sustainable Development	5-1 environmental protection	0.039	2	12
	5-2 industrial safety and health	0.042	1	9
	5-3 labor rights	0.032	3	16
	5-4 protection of human rights	0.021	5	20
	5-5 social care	0.031	4	17

4.3. Analysis of the Relative Importance of Each Criterion Adapting to Sustainable Business Strategy

In addition, the key projects that further affect the bicycle industry adaptation to the sustainable management strategies are prioritized; both the analysis of the various dimensions of the main criteria and the overall analysis are clarified in detail.

4.3.1. Individual Analysis of Dimensions of the Main Criteria

As shown in Table 6, under the dimensions of the main criteria, the relative importance of sub-criteria is described below.

(1) Under the "Financial" main criterion, 1-3 "Return on Capital Employed" features the highest eigenvectors (0.062); 1-2 "productivity" followed (0.039). This shows that to improve financial performance of sustainable development, promoting the use of return on capital employed and productivity must be addressed.
(2) Under the "Customer" main criterion, 2-1 "Customer Satisfaction" features the highest eigenvectors (0.095), 2-3 "market share" followed (0.075). This shows that to improve customer satisfaction in sustainable management, sustainable concepts must meet customer requirements to advance customer satisfaction and market share.
(3) Under the "Internal Business Processes" main criterion, 3-1 "innovation process" features the highest eigenvectors (0.106), 3-2 "business processes" followed (0.080). This shows that internal processes under sustainable management must focus on changing the process of innovation and the nature of the enterprise, and then be implemented in the company's internal operational processes.
(4) Under the "Learning and Growth" main criterion, 4-1 "employee satisfaction" features the highest eigenvectors (0.055), 4-5 "incentives and authorization" followed (0.046). This shows that Learning

and Growth of enterprises under sustainable management must address employee satisfaction and emphasize employee incentives and sufficient authorization to improve the efficiency of learning and growth of the organization.

(5) Under the "sustainable development" main criterion, 5-2 "industrial safety and health" features the highest eigenvectors (0.042), followed by 5-1 "environmental protection" (0.039). The results show that under a sustainable management strategy, it is necessary to attach importance to the internal industrial safety and health of the company and to significantly reduce the use of various hazardous substances and energies, as well as to make products that are approved by various international green standard certifications, such as the IECQ QC 080000 hazardous substance management system standard, or the EU CE Marking to achieve the objectives of environmental protection and social care.

In summary, the application of ANP carries out an overall assessment to be more rational and more suitable for the company to determine the results [32]. When faced with the pressure of the international trend of sustainability, the Taiwanese bicycle industry has to adopt aggressive sustainable strategies, set up objectives as countermeasures, and use ANP to understand the importance of various indictors in various dimensions. In this way, the said information can be used as the basis for determining the priorities under limited resources in the organization. In addition, it can also be used to measure relative weights of company performance. Therefore, the bicycle industry can focus on the direction of execution of sustainable management strategies and assess the performance of execution of strategies to further improve strategy effectiveness.

4.3.2. Overall Analysis

From the overall analysis, most of the experts believe that the top five sub-criteria adapting to sustainable business strategy are innovation process (0.106), Customer Satisfaction (0.095), business processes (0.080), service (0.074), and market share (0.063), as shown in Table 6. The results show that to effectively achieve the overall effectiveness of the adaptation to sustainable management strategies, it is necessary to strengthen the application of the innovation process and the supply chain relationships, and mutual trust must be established with long-term interaction and cooperation [28]. Additionally, providing products to meet customer satisfaction is critical. For example, with the same products, there is now environmental consciousness in customers' choices, and they tend to buy products with eco-labels. Meanwhile, business processes within the enterprise must be implemented; otherwise, the effectiveness of the adaptation of sustainable management strategies will be greatly reduced [45]. Additionally, companies must plan sustainable services to meet customers' requirements for sustainable development, to increase market share, and to accomplish the goal of sustainable business strategies and benefits.

What is more, there is the added new dimension of the sustainability Balanced Scorecard—sustainable development, the five sub-criteria of which do not receive a higher rating from experts. They are: industrial safety and health (0.042), environmental protection (0.039), labor rights (0.032), social care (0.031), and protection of human rights (0.021). Nevertheless, they should be taken into account. According to Thomas Saaty, even the smallest factors, as long as they will have an effect, need to be included in the structure [38]. The results of this study show that most experts believe sustainable development strategy must be adapted from the comprehensive nature of system processes of the enterprise, rather than unilateral emphasis and promotion on individual indicators to achieve the overall effect.

Based on the above, this study used the characteristics of ANP to determine the priority of weights of each sub-criterion and reflect the current trend of sustainable issues of the bicycle industry in Taiwan. This study clarifies that with the adaptation of sustainable business strategies, it is also important to focus on the transformation of the company's internal systems. Under the premise of sustainable business strategies, innovative approaches are taken to improve enterprise business processes and to improve customer satisfaction and thus to achieve the goal of sustainable development [3,27].

5. Conclusions and Recommendations

In accordance with the purposes of this study, research and analysis are conducted; the conclusions, managerial implications, and suggestions are as follows.

5.1. Conclusions and Managerial Implications

(1) This study attempted to adjust and modify the traditional Balanced Scorecard framework and used an expert questionnaire to confirm that the introduction of sustainable management strategy into the bicycle industry should be from five major categories: Financial, Customer, Internal Business Processes, Learning and Growth, and Sustainable Development. With selection via a filtering mechanism, the five dimensions contain a total of 21 key projects. The results of the questionnaire show that the evaluations of the experts are highly consistent. On the managerial implications, these five dimensions can be regarded as the core of the bicycle industry's adaptation to sustainable management strategies, and according to the 21 key projects, the performance indicators are set correspondingly to measure the effectiveness of the adaptation of sustainable management strategies.

(2) From prioritizing key projects of various dimensions in the bicycle industry adaptation to sustainable management strategies, it is known that companies must focus on promoting the return on capital employed and productivity to improve financial performance. By achieving customer requirements for sustainable development, customer satisfaction and market share can be enhanced. The company must also focus on changing the process of innovation and the nature of enterprise, implemented in the company's internal operational processes. Furthermore, companies must pay attention to employee satisfaction and give emphasis to employee incentives and sufficient authorization to improve the efficiency of learning and growth of the organization. The company must start with industrial health and safety within and then broaden outward to the relevant interested parties to achieve the purposes of environmental protection and social care. In terms of managerial implications, the company can apply ANP to conduct the assessment on various dimensions, to obtain results that are more rational and more in line with the company's features. By confirming the relative importance of the various indicators as the performance measure in strategy implementation, the strategic direction of the company can be focused to enhance the effectiveness of the company's strategy execution.

(3) From the overall analysis of the bicycle industry adaptation to sustainable management strategies, the three key factors are innovation process, customer satisfaction, and business processes. The Taiwanese bicycle industry has responded to global sustainable environmental consciousness, as well as the highly competitive international business. To achieve the goal of sustainable development, the enterprise itself must have the forces of innovation and of research and development and be able to grow with trends and to create advantages. The company must also effectively take hold of the changing needs of customers and improve customer satisfaction. Moreover, when the industry adapts to the sustainable management strategies, the main point of implementation is to change the nature of the corporate business processes. As to managerial implications, if Taiwan's bicycle industry wants to possess a competitive advantage on the global stage, the results of this study should be heeded. Innovation process, customer satisfaction, and business processes must be emphasized to conform to the trend of the times and the environment. Innovative force must be restored in preparation for sustainable management strategies and to enable the brand leading the industry to grow.

5.2. Limitations of the Study and Recommendations

This study analyzes the assessment model of the bicycle industry's adaptation to sustainable management strategies, giving the practical applications to industry as well as directions for future research. The recommendations are as follows.

(1) Practical application to industry

This study analyzes and assesses only those strategies for the sustainable management of the bicycle industry; hence, the conclusions are not suitable to explain other industries. It is suggested that decision-makers from the bicycle industry can benefit from the results of this research, which are the Balanced Scorecard of sustainable management, the five facets, and a total of 21 performance indicators. They must merge and implement these tools with the company's sustainable management strategy. Additionally, performance evaluation is suggested to realize the current situation of the company as a basis for subsequent improvement.

Furthermore, the sustainable management BSC ANP assessment process in this study can also be referred to, to cope with external environmental factors and the company's attributes, as well as to reexamine and assess from a holistic perspective. By using ANP assessment to inspect the importance of each performance indicator and analyze its connotations for management wishing to create a concrete and feasible action plan, the implementation of performance indicators and the goal of sustainable development can be achieved.

(2) Future research

This study is primarily related to the bicycle industry; therefore, the conclusions give priority to the bicycle industry's sustainable development. Future research could incorporate the customer views into the bicycle industry to form the basis of strategic planning. In addition, the Balanced Scorecard of sustainable management mainly takes the entire bicycle industry as the research object to provide strategies of sustainable development. Follow-up studies could address individual bicycle businesses as a case study. Based on the attributes of the company, sustainable business performance assessment tools can be facilitated to design a more complete and detailed measure, and the performance of sustainable development strategy can be introduced to businesses so that they can perform quantitative analysis. In addition, in the current generation of shorter product life cycles, it is recommended to conduct a one-year period of dynamic monitoring.

The Balanced Scorecard assessment process proposed in this study can be taken into account for the assessment of future development in the bicycle industry, to manage the dynamics of the bicycle industry and therefore determine a company's business direction. Additionally, the bicycle industry trends and the status performance of the company can be compared to understand a company's advantages, disadvantages, and opportunities to better facilitate and make the most effective use of limited resources.

Acknowledgments: The authors would like to thank the reviewers for their thoughtful review and valuable comments.

Author Contributions: Shi-Jer Lou and Li-Chung Chao conceived and designed the experiments; Chih-Chao Chung and Shi-Jer Lou performed the experiments; Chih-Chao Chung and Chih-hong Chen analyzed the data; Chih-Chao Chung and Li-Chung Chao contributed reagents/materials/analysis tools; Chih-Chao Chung and Chih-hong Chen wrote the paper.

Conflicts of Interest: The authors declare no conflict of interest.

Appendix A

Table A1. Key interrelated projects for the bicycle industry's adaptation to sustainable management strategies.

No.	Key Projects	1-1	1-2	1-3	1-4	2-1	2-2	2-3	3-1	3-2	3-3	3-4	4-1	4-2	4-3	4-4	4-5	5-1	5-2	5-3	5-4	5-5	Comparison Matrix between Dimensions
1-1	RG		V	V	V				V	V			V		V		V			V			3
1-2	PD	V		V	V			V	V	V			V		V		V		V	V			4
1-3	RCE	V	V		V	V		V	V	V	V		V	V			V	V	V	V	V	V	5
1-4	CM	V	V	V		V		V	V	V					V		V		V				4
2-1	CS						V		V		V		V		V	V	V	V	V		V	V	5
2-2	CCR					V			V	V	V		V				V	V	V		V	V	4
2-3	MS					V	V		V	V	V		V				V	V	V				3
3-1	IP		V	V	V	V		V		V	V		V		V	V	V	V	V		V	V	5
3-2	BP		V	V	V	V	V	V	V			V	V		V		V	V	V		V	V	5
3-3	SV			V	V	V			V			V	V		V		V	V	V		V	V	3
3-4	ISC			V	V	V	V	V	V	V	V			V	V		V	V	V	V			5
4-1	ES	V		V		V		V	V	V					V	V	V	V	V	V	V	V	3
4-2	ECR			V					V	V	V	V	V		V	V	V	V	V	V	V	V	3
4-3	EA			V					V	V	V	V	V	V		V	V	V	V	V	V	V	3
4-4	REE								V	V	V		V	V	V		V		V	V			4
4-5	IA		V					V	V	V		V	V	V	V			V		V	V	V	4
5-1	EP	V	V			V			V	V		V	V	V	V				V	V	V	V	4
5-2	ISH					V		V	V	V			V	V	V	V	V	V		V	V	V	4
5-3	LR				V	V	V	V	V	V	V		V	V	V	V	V	V	V	V	V	V	4
5-4	PHR								V		V									V		V	4
5-5	SC								V		V										V		4
	Total																						84

Note: "V" means most experts identified a mutual influence between sub-criteria relationships.

Appendix B

Table A2. Unweighted super-matrix.

	Criteria	1. Financial				2. Customer			3. Internal Business Processes				4. Learning and Growth					5. Sustainable Development				
	Sub-Criteria	1-1	1-2	1-3	1-4	2-1	2-2	2-3	3-1	3-2	3-3	3-4	4-1	4-2	4-3	4-4	4-5	5-1	5-2	5-3	5-4	5-5
1.	1-1 RG	0	0.336	0.334	0.312	0	0	0	0	0	0	0	0	0	0	0	0	0.496	0	0	0	0
	1-2 PD	0.348	0	0.318	0.365	0.504	0	0	0.508	0.343	0	0	0.521	0	0	0	0	0	0.505	0	0	0
	1-3 RCE	0.312	0.306	0	0.323	0.496	0	0	0	0.315	0.482	0.478	0	0	0	1.000	0.509	0.504	0.495	1.000	1.000	0.502
	1-4 CM	0.340	0.358	0.348	0	0	0	0	0.492	0.341	0.518	0.522	0.479	0	0	0	0.491	0	0	0	0	0.498
2.	2-1 CS	0	0	0.508	0.512	0	0.540	0.507	0.531	0.515	0.512	1.000	0.515	0	0	0	0	0.524	0	0.528	0.387	0.513
	2-2 CCR	0	0	0	0	0.510	0	0.493	0	0	0.488	0	0	0	0	0	0	0	0	0	0.331	0
	2-3 MS	1.000	0	0.492	0.488	0.490	0.460	0	0.469	0.485	0	0	0.485	0	0	0	0	0.476	0	0.472	0.282	0.487
3.	3-1 IP	0.523	0.490	0	0.520	0.335	0.485	0.478	0	0.350	0.315	0.327	0.479	0.486	0.490	0.510	0.307	0.530	0.493	0.503	0.476	0.511
	3-2 BP	0.477	0.510	0.479	0.480	0	0	0	0.365	0	0.347	0.349	0.521	0.514	0.510	0.490	0.357	0	0.507	0.497	0	0
	3-3 SV	0	0	0.521	0	0.366	0.515	0.522	0.328	0.331	0	0.324	0	0	0	0	0	0	0	0	0.524	0.489
	3-4 ISC	0	0	0	0	0.300	0	0	0.307	0.319	0.338	0	0	0	0	0	0.337	0.470	0	0	0	0
4.	4-1 ES	0.340	0.309	0.332	0	0.340	0.487	0	0.324	0.327	0.340	0	0	0.273	0.246	0.257	0.251	0	0.524	0.352	0.367	0
	4-2 ECR	0	0	0.337	0	0	0	0	0	0	0	0	0.260	0	0.246	0.251	0.247	0	0.476	0.334	0.347	0
	4-3 EA	0.339	0.366	0	0.523	0.352	0	0	0	0.348	0.335	0.500	0.278	0.266	0	0.283	0.280	0	0	0	0	0
	4-4 REE	0	0	0	0	0	0.513	0	0.356	0	0	0	0.259	0.252	0.282	0	0.222	0	0	0.313	0.285	0
	4-5 IA	0.321	0.325	0.331	0.477	0.308	0	0.491	0.320	0.325	0.325	0.500	0.204	0.208	0.226	0.209	0	0	0	0	0	0
5.	5-1 EP	0	0	0.200	0	0.260	0.263	0.509	0.332	0.330	0.512	1.000	0.189	0	0	0	0	0	0.249	0.221	0.229	0.258
	5-2 ISH	0	0.510	0.229	0	0.259	0.264	0	0.363	0.369	0	0	0.228	0.492	0.499	0.490	0.375	0.271	0	0.294	0.285	0.251
	5-3 LR	1.000	0.490	0.210	0	0	0	0	0	0	0	0	0.221	0.508	0.501	0.510	0.323	0.264	0.276	0	0.269	0.249
	5-4 PHR	0	0	0.196	0	0.244	0.239	0	0	0	0.488	0	0.190	0	0	0	0	0.241	0.252	0.268	0	0.242
	5-5 SC	0	0	0.166	0	0.237	0.234	0.491	0.305	0.301	0	0	0.172	0	0	0	0.302	0.224	0.223	0.217	0.217	0

Appendix C

Table A3. Weighted super-matrix.

	Criteria		1. Financial				2. Customer			3. Internal Business Processes				4. Learning and Growth					5. Sustainable Development				
	Sub-Criteria	1-1	1-2	1-3	1-4	2-1	2-2	2-3	3-1	3-2	3-3	3-4	4-1	4-2	4-3	4-4	4-5	5-1	5-2	5-3	5-4	5-5
1.	1-1 RG	0	0.069	0.050	0.053	0	0	0	0	0	0	0	0.070	0	0	0	0	0.118	0	0	0	0
	1-2 PD	0.053	0	0.048	0.062	0.081	0	0	0.098	0.066	0	0	0	0	0	0	0.092	0	0.114	0	0	0
	1-3 RCE	0.047	0.063	0	0.055	0.080	0	0	0	0.061	0.093	0.092	0.065	0	0	0.180	0.089	0.120	0.112	0.187	0.187	0.120
	1-4 CM	0.051	0.074	0.053	0	0	0	0	0.095	0.066	0.100	0.101	0	0	0	0	0	0	0	0	0	0.119
2.	2-1 CS	0	0	0.135	0.153	0	0.159	0.195	0.133	0.129	0.128	0.251	0.129	0	0	0	0	0.118	0	0.093	0.068	0.115
	2-2 CCR	0	0	0	0	0.126	0	0.189	0	0	0.122	0.084	0	0	0	0	0	0	0	0	0.058	0
	2-3 MS	0.265	0	0.131	0.145	0.121	0.136	0	0.118	0.121	0	0	0.122	0	0	0	0	0.107	0	0.083	0.050	0.109
3.	3-1 IP	0.139	0.178	0	0.156	0.092	0.160	0.205	0	0.084	0.075	0.078	0.129	0.214	0.216	0.184	0.111	0.112	0.099	0.083	0.079	0.108
	3-2 BP	0.127	0.185	0.128	0.144	0	0	0	0.088	0	0.083	0.084	0.141	0.226	0.224	0.177	0.129	0	0.102	0.082	0	0
	3-3 SV	0	0	0.139	0	0.101	0.169	0.223	0.079	0.079	0	0.078	0	0	0	0	0	0	0	0	0.087	0.103
	3-4 ISC	0	0	0	0	0.083	0	0	0.074	0.076	0.081	0	0	0	0	0	0.121	0.099	0	0	0	0
4.	4-1 ES	0.070	0.087	0.069	0	0.066	0.113	0	0.065	0.065	0.068	0	0	0.087	0.079	0.067	0.066	0	0.138	0.076	0.080	0
	4-2 ECR	0	0	0.070	0	0	0	0	0	0.069	0.067	0	0.051	0	0.079	0.066	0.065	0	0.125	0.072	0.075	0
	4-3 EA	0.070	0.103	0	0.122	0.068	0	0	0	0.069	0.067	0.100	0.055	0.085	0	0.074	0.074	0	0	0	0	0
	4-4 REE	0	0	0	0	0	0.119	0	0.071	0	0	0	0.051	0.081	0.090	0	0.058	0	0	0.068	0.062	0
	4-5 IA	0.066	0.092	0.068	0.111	0.060	0	0	0.064	0.065	0.065	0.100	0.040	0.067	0.072	0.055	0	0	0	0	0	0
5.	5-1 EP	0	0	0.022	0	0.031	0.038	0.096	0.039	0.039	0.060	0.117	0.028	0	0	0.096	0.074	0.088	0.077	0.056	0.058	0.084
	5-2 ISH	0	0.077	0.025	0	0.031	0.038	0	0.043	0.043	0	0	0.034	0.118	0.120	0.100	0.064	0.086	0	0.075	0.073	0.082
	5-3 LR	0.110	0.074	0.023	0	0	0	0	0	0	0	0	0.033	0.122	0.120	0	0	0.078	0.085	0	0.069	0.081
	5-4 PHR	0	0	0.022	0	0.030	0.034	0	0	0	0.057	0	0.028	0	0	0	0.059	0.073	0.078	0.068	0	0.079
	5-5 SC	0	0	0.018	0	0.029	0.034	0.092	0.036	0.035	0	0	0.025	0	0	0	0	0.073	0.069	0.055	0.055	0

References

1. Elkington, J. Partnerships from cannibals with forks: The triple bottom line of 21st-century business. *Environ. Qual. Manag.* **1998**, *8*, 37–51. [CrossRef]
2. Hubbard, G. Measuring organizational performance: Beyond the triple bottom line. *Bus. Strateg. Environ.* **2009**, *18*, 177–191. [CrossRef]
3. Hu, M.-C.; Wu, C.-Y. Exploring technological innovation trajectories through latecomers: Evidence from Taiwan's bicycle industry. *Technol. Anal. Strateg. Manag.* **2011**, *23*, 433–452. [CrossRef]
4. Costanza, R.; Patten, B.C. Defining and predicting sustainability. *Ecol. Econ.* **1995**, *15*, 193–196. [CrossRef]
5. Venkatraman, N.; Ramanujam, V. Measurement of business performance in strategy research: A comparison of approaches. *Acad. Manag. Rev.* **1986**, *11*, 801–814.
6. Robbins, S.P. *Essentials of Organizational Behavior*; Pearson Higher Ed: Boston, MA, USA, 2013.
7. Robins, F. The future of corporate social responsibility. *Asian Bus. Manag.* **2005**, *4*, 95–115. [CrossRef]
8. Aaronson, S.A. Corporate responsibility in the global village: The British role model and the American laggard. *Bus. Soc. Rev.* **2003**, *108*, 309–338. [CrossRef]
9. Crook, C. The good company. *Economist* **2005**, *22*, 3–18.
10. Kaplan, R.S.; Norton, D.P.; Dorf, R.; Raitanen, M. *The Balanced Scorecard: Translating Strategy into Action*; Harvard Business School Press: Boston, MA, USA, 1996; Volume 4.
11. Kaplan, R.S.; Norton, D.P. Transforming the balanced scorecard from performance measurement to strategic management: Part I. *Account. Horiz.* **2001**, *15*, 87–104. [CrossRef]
12. Maiga, A.S.; Jacobs, F.A. Balanced scorecard, activity-based costing and company performance: An empirical analysis. *J. Manag. Issues* **2003**, *15*, 283–301.
13. Álvarez, C.; Rodríguez, V.; Ortega, F.; Villanueva, J. A Scorecard Framework Proposal for Improving Software Factories' Sustainability: A Case Study of a Spanish Firm in the Financial Sector. *Sustainability* **2015**, *7*, 15999–16021. [CrossRef]
14. Niven, P.R. *Balanced Scorecard Step-by-Step: Maximizing Performance and Maintaining Results*; John Wiley & Sons: New York, NY, USA, 2002.
15. Gibbons, R.; Kaplan, R.S. Formal Measures in Informal Management: Can a Balanced Scorecard Change a Culture? *Am. Econ. Rev. Pap. Proc.* **2015**, *105*, 447–451. [CrossRef]
16. Fletcher, H.D.; Smith, D.B. Managing for value: Developing a performance measurement system integrating EVA and the BSC in strategic planning. *J. Bus. Strateg.* **2004**, *21*, 1–17.
17. Bhattacharya, A.; Mohapatra, P.; Kumar, V.; Dey, P.K.; Brady, M.; Tiwari, M.K.; Nudurupati, S.S. Green supply chain performance measurement using fuzzy ANP-based balanced scorecard: A collaborative decision-making approach. *Prod. Plan. Control* **2014**, *25*, 698–714. [CrossRef]
18. Tjader, Y.; May, J.H.; Shang, J.; Vargas, L.G.; Gao, N. Firm-level outsourcing decision making: A balanced scorecard-based analytic network process model. *Int. J. Prod. Econ.* **2014**, *147*, 614–623. [CrossRef]
19. Epstein, M.J.; Wisner, P.S. Using a balanced scorecard to implement sustainability. *Environ. Qual. Manag.* **2001**, *11*, 1–10. [CrossRef]
20. Kaplan, R.S.; Norton, D.P. *The Balanced Scorecard: Translating Strategy into Action*; Harvard Business Press: Boston, MA, USA, 1997.
21. Möller, A.; Schaltegger, S. The Sustainability Balanced Scorecard as a Framework for Eco-efficiency Analysis. *J. Ind. Ecol.* **2005**, *9*, 73–83. [CrossRef]
22. De Felice, F.; Petrillo, A.; Autorino, C. Development of a Framework for Sustainable Outsourcing: Analytic Balanced Scorecard Method (A-BSC). *Sustainability* **2015**, *7*, 8399–8419. [CrossRef]
23. Epstein, M.J.; Research, I. *Measuring Corporate Environmental Performance: Best Practices for Costing and Managing an Effective Environmental Strategy*; McGraw-Hill: New York, NY, USA, 1996.
24. Schaltegger, S.; Burritt, R. *Contemporary Environmental Accounting: Issues, Concepts, and Practice*; Greenleaf Publishing: Sheffield, UK, 2000.
25. Chu, W.-W. Causes of growth: A study of Taiwan's bicycle industry. *Camb. J. Econ.* **1997**, *21*, 55–72. [CrossRef]
26. Yan, H.-D.; Hu, M.-C. Strategic entrepreneurship and the growth of the firm: The case of Taiwan's bicycle industry. *Glob. Bus. Econ. Rev.* **2008**, *10*, 11–34. [CrossRef]
27. Chen, Y.-S.; Lin, M.-J.; Chang, C.-H.; Liu, F.-M. Technological innovations and industry clustering in the bicycle industry in Taiwan. *Technol. Soc.* **2009**, *31*, 207–217. [CrossRef]

28. Brookfield, J.; Liu, R.-J.; MacDuffie, J.P. Taiwan's bicycle industry A-Team battles Chinese competition with innovation and cooperation. *Strateg. Leadersh.* **2008**, *36*, 14–19. [CrossRef]
29. Saaty, T.L. Fundamentals of the analytic network process-dependence and feedback in decision-making with a single network. *J. Syst. Sci. Syst. Eng.* **2004**, *13*, 129–157. [CrossRef]
30. Rossi, C.; Cricelli, L.; Grimaldi, M.; Greco, M. The strategic assessment of intellectual capital assets: An application within Terradue Srl. *J. Bus. Res.* **2016**, *69*, 1598–1603. [CrossRef]
31. Bentes, A.V.; Carneiro, J.; da Silva, J.F.; Kimura, H. Multidimensional assessment of organizational performance: Integrating BSC and AHP. *J. Bus. Res.* **2012**, *65*, 1790–1799. [CrossRef]
32. Saaty, T.L. *Theory and Applications of the Analytic Network Process: Decision Making with Benefits, Opportunities, Costs, and Risks*; RWS Publications: Pittsburgh, PA, USA, 2005; Volume 4992.
33. Staš, D.; Lenort, R.; Wicher, P.; Holman, D. Green Transport Balanced Scorecard Model with Analytic Network Process Support. *Sustainability* **2015**, *7*, 15243–15261. [CrossRef]
34. Biondi, S.; Calabrese, A.; Capece, G.; Costa, R.; Di Pillo, F. A New Approach for Assessing Dealership Performance: An Application for the Automotive Industry. *Int. J. Eng. Bus. Manag.* **2013**, *5*, 1–8. [CrossRef]
35. Chung, C.C.; Chao, L.C.; Lou, S.J. The Establishment of a Green Supplier Selection and Guidance Mechanism with the ANP and IPA. *Sustainability* **2016**, *8*, 259–282. [CrossRef]
36. Saaty, T.L. *What is the Analytic Hierarchy Process?*; Springer: Berlin, Germany, 1988.
37. Saaty, T.L. How to make a decision: The analytic hierarchy process. *Eur. J. Oper. Res.* **1990**, *48*, 9–26. [CrossRef]
38. Saaty, T.L. *Multicriteria Decision Making*; RWS Publications: Pittsburgh, PA, USA, 1996.
39. Karpak, B.; Topcu, I. Small medium manufacturing enterprises in Turkey: An analytic network process framework for prioritizing factors affecting success. *Int. J. Prod. Econ.* **2010**, *125*, 60–70. [CrossRef]
40. Abdi, M.R.; Labib, A.W. Performance evaluation of reconfigurable manufacturing systems via holonic architecture and the analytic network process. *Int. J. Prod. Res.* **2011**, *49*, 1319–1335. [CrossRef]
41. Lehmann, M.; Bocken, N.M.P.; Steingrímsson, J.G.; Evans, S. Incorporating Design Thinking into Sustainabl. Business Modelling. In Proceedings of the 2nd International Conference on Sustainable, Seville, Spain, 12–14 April 2015.
42. Bocken, N.; Short, S.; Rana, P.; Evans, S. A value mapping tool for sustainable business modelling. *Int. J. Effect. Board Perform.* **2013**, *13*, 482–497.
43. Meinel, C., Leifer, L., Plattner, H., Eds.; *Design Thinking*; Springer: Berlin, Germany, 2011.
44. Dalkey, N.; Helmer, O. An experimental application of the Delphi method to the use of experts. *Manag. Sci.* **1963**, *9*, 458–467. [CrossRef]
45. Bossidy, L.; Charan, R.; Burck, C. Execution: The discipline of getting things done. *Afp. Exchang.* **2004**, *24*, 26–29.

© 2016 by the authors. Licensee MDPI, Basel, Switzerland. This article is an open access article distributed under the terms and conditions of the Creative Commons Attribution (CC BY) license (http://creativecommons.org/licenses/by/4.0/).

Article

Development of a Novel Co-Creative Framework for Redesigning Product Service Systems

Tuananh Tran and Joon Young Park *

Department of Industrial and Systems Engineering, Dongguk University, Pil-dong, Jung-gu, Seoul 100715, Korea; meslab.org@gmail.com
* Correspondence: jypark@dgu.edu; Tel.: +82-222-603-714

Academic Editor: Adam Jabłoński
Received: 2 February 2016; Accepted: 28 April 2016; Published: 3 May 2016

Abstract: Product service systems (PSS) have been researched in academia and implemented in industry for more than a decade, and they bring plenty of benefits to various stakeholders, such as: customers, PSS providers, the environment, as well as society. However, the adoption of PSS in industry so far is limited compared to its potentials. One of the reasons leading to this limitation is that PSS design is tricky. So far, there are several methods to design PSS, but each of them has certain limitations. This paper proposes a co-creative framework, which is constructed using the concept of user co-creation. This novel framework allows designers to design PSS effectively in terms of users' perception of PSS value, design quality and evaluation. The authors also introduce a case study to demonstrate and validate the proposed framework.

Keywords: product service system; PSS; PSS design; co-creation; PSS redesign; PSS business model

1. Introduction

1.1. Product Service System

Before the 2000s, consumers were familiar with the paradigm in which companies sell tangible products to the market. For instance: Nokia provided mobile phones; Electrolux provided washing machines; HP provided printers, *etc.* Nowadays, the demands of customers become more and more diversified, and the business environment becomes more and more competitive. This leads to the fact that companies are having a difficult time competing with the conventional business model of selling purely tangible products [1,2]. There is a need for finding new ways to enhance competitiveness, to attract new customers, as well as to keep existing ones. This need is fulfilled by incorporating the concept of product service systems (PSS) [3–5]. These PSS are a form of servitization in which a combination of a tangible product and an intangible service, called a "PSS offering" or simply "PSS", is provided to the customers [6].

There are several examples of PSS in reality. According to Goedkoop *et al.* [7], PSS is "a marketable set of products and services capable of jointly fulfilling a user's needs". By this definition, the offering of an iPhone and the Appstore from Apple Inc. can be considered as a PSS. In the same manner, a car-sharing service, where the users check in and pick up a car at a station, use and return the car at another station, check out and pay per use, is also a PSS. In the car-sharing example, users do not buy the car; they buy the "mobility" or the use of the car. This new concept of buying is similar to a "functional economy" [8], where customers are interested in "hiring products to get jobs done" [3,9,10]. Baines *et al.* also introduced a well-known example of a PSS, which is the "document management solution" [11]. In this example, the customer does not buy a photocopier. Instead, the customer only buys its use. The company still owns the product and takes care of refilling, maintenance, replacing parts, *etc.*

Since the very first work by Goedkoop *et al.* nearly two decades ago, PSS has gone a long way with various research having been carried out by various researchers. The pioneering works also include the ones by Mont [8] and Morelli [12]. So far, PSS is classified into several types. According to Tukker [13], there are three types of PSS: product-oriented PSS, use-oriented PSS and result-oriented PSS.

1.2. Adoption of PSS in Industry

PSS brings benefits to various stakeholders, as studied in the literature [5,11]. For the customers, PSS provides flexible services with a higher level of personalization, better and continuously-improved quality and, finally, total satisfaction. For companies, thanks to the implementation of PSS, they gain the loyalty of customers, as well as better control of product quality, continuous improvement, chances for reducing costs, increasing knowledge and innovation. For society and the environment, PSS is also beneficial in terms of reducing materials' consumption through sharing their use, increasing the responsibility of manufacturers, expanding the lifecycle of the products and creating more jobs in the service sector.

PSS is now adopted more and more in industry. In order to promote the adoption of PSS, several challenges need to be resolved. These challenges were mentioned in various works by Mont [8], Baines *et al.* [11] and Beuren *et al.* [5]. The first challenge is that "ownerless consumption" is not familiar to the vast majority of customers. They are familiar with the concept of paying and getting "physical" items. Another challenge is for the manufacturers. They might have difficulties when making decisions on pricing, managing risks and changing the organization due to a changing business model. The major challenge for expanding PSS adoption is "PSS design". This is not an easy task, because PSS is a complicated system. In PSS, besides products and services, there are also other elements, such as the delivery network, stakeholders, value proposition, *etc.*

In order to design PSS, several methods have been introduced. Vasantha *et al.* reviewed eight well-known PSS design methods that have been implemented widely so far [6]. As will be analyzed in Section 2, there is still a lack of an effective method to design PSS collaboratively and practically. This lack somehow limits the expansion of PSS adoption in industry.

1.3. Motivation for This Work and Research Goal

This research is motivated by the following real-world scenario: Mulenserv is a company that provides various engineering services to customers in the industrial market. One of Mulenserv's services is a PSS, which leases technical manuals and books together with supporting services (lectures, application workshops, technical contests, *etc.*). Their target customers are engineering individuals, as well as small technical companies. This is a niche market, and the PSS is highly customized due to the diversified demands of various customers. After six months of the initial release, the response of the market was limited: acceptance of potential customers, as well as satisfaction of customers who purchased the PSS were lower than expected. The company needs to redesign to improve the PSS, so that the acceptance rate and customer satisfaction can be improved and the sales can be increased sustainably. In order to achieve this goal, they need an effective customer-centric framework to improve the PSS design, *i.e.*, redesign the new PSS starting from the existing one. According to Vezzoli *et al.* [14], most of the successful cases of PSS applications are from the B2B (business to business) sector, not B2C (business to consumer). Mulenserv is a typical B2C case, and a design solution is needed to help its PSS survive when being launched.

Since customer acceptance and satisfaction with the PSS is of critical importance to its success and this acceptance strongly depends on the perception of the users of the provided service [14], this paper aims to develop a co-creative framework that allows companies to redesign a PSS in order to improve the design of the PSS in terms of users' perception of its value, design quality and evaluation and, thus, leading to increasing customer acceptance and, therefore, increasing its success. In this work, we set the scope of the framework in a B2C environment. We construct this framework by incorporating the concept of user co-creation.

The next parts of this paper are organized as follows: Section 2 reviews existing literature that is related to the research topic. Section 3 analyzes solutions and proposes the framework. Section 4 introduces the case study, the experimental implementation, results and discussions. Section 5 draws concluding remarks and suggests future work.

2. Literature Review

2.1. Existing Methods to Design and Redesign PSS

PSS providers need tools, techniques and methods to design and enhance their PSS to satisfy their customers. There has been much research conducted to propose PSS design methodologies with similar intentions and different ideas [15].

Several methods for designing PSS have been introduced so far [1,2,11]. Beside case-specific methods, which were developed to design very specific PSSs [16,17], there are several generic methods that can be used to design various cases of PSS. These methods were summarized by Vasantha *et al.* [6]. Although being well known and widely implemented, these methods have limitations. One of them is the lack of user co-creation in the design processes [6]. These methods do not mention in detail the importance of co-creation, and there are no clear definitions of the roles of customers in the PSS design process.

More recently, Pezzotta *et al.* [18] proposed a framework to design and assess PSS from a service engineering approach. This framework utilizes computer-aided modeling tool for service design. It starts with functional analysis and the identification of customer needs, simulating and testing various scenarios to find out the best solution. Although being well structured, this method has little involvement in co-creation, and the case study provided in the work [18] is more like a B2B case.

Morelli [19] commented that design methods should identify who is involved in the design process and their roles, as well as possible scenarios that could occur. The need for implementing customer co-creation is also raised in the work of Beuren *et al.* [5]. Vezzoli *et al.* [14] implied that a design method should include details of where and when to involve stakeholders (producer/provider, customer, *etc.*) and to allow customers to customize a PSS according to their preferences.

Beside the lack of co-creation, existing PSS design methods provide little practical guidelines for practitioners (*i.e.*, companies) [2]. Incorporating incremental steps in a path or practice is necessary for a design method [14]. There is a lack of illustrating cases that can demonstrate and give insights into how PSS design methods work in various situations. This explains why existing methods are not effective in terms of practical implementation. Furthermore, Qu *et al.* [15] suggested that more quantitative works need to be conducted in the literature because these works are more objective and persuasive.

In summary, existing design methodologies have not considerably included co-creation in the design processes and are not effective enough to act as practical guidelines for practitioners. In this sense, the involvement of each stakeholder in the design phases is not clarified in detail, and the representation of PSS itself is complicated. There is a need for a new method that is co-creative with user involvement in the design process, better defined roles and responsibilities of stakeholders and a simpler PSS representation and that can provide practical guidelines. This method also need to be evaluable.

2.2. Value Perception

In a service-oriented system, like a PSS, value perception is a critical issue to decide the buying potential of customers, because the service part in PSS is intangible and its value is difficult to measure and estimate [9,11,12]. In order to increase the value perception of PSS, the value of the PSS needs to be visualized. One of the methods to visualize PSS value is communicating and demonstrating PSS to the customers [20]. The importance of PSS value and value proposition has been mentioned in several works [21–23]. In one of the PSS design methods reviewed by Vasantha *et al.* [6], the value proposition is considered as an important dimension that forms the PSS [24]. Value is claimed to be the differentiating factor that enables the success of a PSS, and new methods are needed to understand value perception in order to evaluate PSS performance [11].

There are also several notable works on PSS value visualization. The value proposition was emphasized in the PSS design method proposed by Morelli [12]. Several tools that support value visualization have been introduced, including the "PSS board" [9] and color-coded CAD models [25]. A framework to enhance value visualization and perception has also been proposed by Kowalkowski and Kindstrom [20]. The above works focus on either value perception of the company (instead of the customers) [9,12,25] or value perception particularly in industrial markets [20].

Vezzoli et al. [14] commented that because of the lack of understanding about PSS and the deep perception of its value, customers are not eager to adopt PSS solutions. This is a barrier for PSS application at the industrial scale. There is a need for new strategies and approaches to make consumers accept this new model of consumption.

In order to increase users' acceptance of PSS offerings, designers must find ways to increase users' perception of PSS value, and thus, the visualization of PSS becomes critical. In Section 3, the authors of this work propose a method to represent and present PSS to enhance the communication of PSS value to the users and enable user participation in co-creation.

2.3. Co-Creation in the Design Improvement and Evaluation of PSS

Steen et al. [26] identified three types of benefits of co-creation for the design project, the customers and the PSS provider. They did this by reviewing the literature and observing three service design projects. In that work, experimental results were not reported in terms of numerical data, and they also implied that there was a need for conducting another experiment and performing a numerical analysis to validate the effectiveness of user involvement in a service-oriented design project.

The design and development of PSS is a participatory process, and thus, co-creation has been mentioned in the literature as one of the success enabling factors for PSS [6,11]. Co-creation refers to the participation of customers or users in various phases of its lifecycle, such as ideation, design, development and implementation (i.e., use), etc. The role of user participation is critical to the success because of the importance of users in a PSS model. Users are among the most important stakeholders, and because of the presence of the "service" part in which users only buy or hire things that help them to get jobs done [3,9], users' voices deserve a deep consideration. As pointed out by Vansantha et al., to improve PSS design, co-creation is employed limitedly in existing PSS design methods [6].

PSS evaluation is an essential issue that has been mentioned by various researchers [9,27–30]. Especially, evaluation at the development stage can help companies to reduce the risks of PSS launching. Existing PSS design methods do not consider co-creation deep enough [6,11].

There are several works that dealt briefly with the evaluation issue in PSS design. A "lifecycle simulation" model was proposed by Komoto and Tomiyama [30] and was demonstrated with a maintenance service. The evaluation of PSS was also considered in the tool developed by Lim et al. [9]. Another approach to PSS evaluation through prototyping was proposed [28]. These works [9,28,30] focused on the evaluation of PSS mostly for companies, not for customers.

Customers can be used as a source of innovation by involving them in the PSS design process [1,11,31]. A PSS design process in which the participation of customers is used for evaluation was proposed by Shih et al. [27]. In other work, an algorithm for PSS evaluation was proposed by Yoon et al. [28]. However, still, in these works [27,28], customers are not the main drive for making a difference in the effectiveness of the evaluation result.

We aim to develop a novel co-creative framework that uses the co-creation of customers (i.e., users), has detailed defined roles, responsibilities and activities of stakeholders throughout the design process and includes a simple and clear PSS representation. This proposed framework is used to enhance the value perception, evaluation and design quality of PSS. It starts with the existing PSS or initial PSS conceptual idea and produces an improved PSS design as the outcome. The PSS that is developed using the proposed framework can be better accepted by customers. This leads to the success of PSS and encourage the application of PSS in industry.

3. Methodology

Figure 1 shows the research procedure of this paper. This explains how we construct this research. The authors analyze solutions to implement user co-creation and PSS representation. Based on those analyses and the sequence of co-creative design activities, the authors propose the framework. This framework is explained in detail and implemented in a case study as an experiment. The results were collected, analyzed and validated to evaluate the framework.

3.1. Implementation of the Co-Creation Concept

The co-creation of customers/users in the PSS design process can be enabled by the participation of users in various design activities. Previous research pointed out that allowing users to participate in the design process might make significant changes [32]. Users can participate in proposing ideas, suggesting design corrections or even generating new concepts.

As pointed out in a previous work [33], to make user participation become easy and effective, the co-creation tasks need to be clarified and simplified. In order to achieve this, we carefully train the participants about each task in which they are involved. We also use simplified PSS representation so that the users can contribute their innovation properly and systematically.

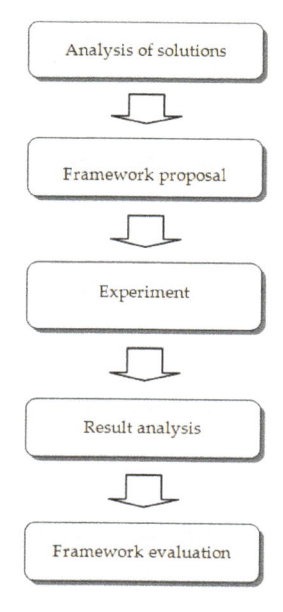

Figure 1. The research procedure.

3.2. Simplified PSS Representation

In order to simplify co-creation activity and maximize effective participation, we break down PSS into basic elements so that the representation of PSS can be in the simplest form. When being shown to the participants, the PSS will be represented as a combination of the following elements:

- Product: The tangible part of a PSS, for instance an iPhone.
- Service: The intangible part of PSS, for instance the Appstore

- Process: Serial and parallel activities happen inside a PSS. This describes the process of how a PSS is served to the customer.
- Parameters: The metrics of product and service features. For example: how long is the service time; how much is the charge per mile for a car sharing service, *etc.*
- Network: The infrastructure of PSS showing the interactions of products, services, users, *etc.* For example, to deliver technical support services to PC (personal computer) buyers, the company may use email, telephone, on-site, *etc.*
- Stakeholders: Companies, customers, suppliers, *etc.*
- Value proposition: Model that explains how PSS provides value to a customer, a company and other stakeholders.

A PSS can be represented in a simple form using a set of the above elements. Each representation is called a "PSS configuration" or "PSS design" in this work. The purpose of this simplification is to briefly represent a PSS as a combination of various "specifications", and thus, it allows users to suggest PSS designs easily by filling in the form with their favorite inputs for those specifications. We would like to note that this is for the convenience of user participation, and this simplification is used only within this work.

3.3. The Proposed Framework

Based on the analysis of solutions and the PSS design process, we propose a framework to enhance the value perception, evaluation and design quality of PSS. The proposed framework is shown in Figure 2.

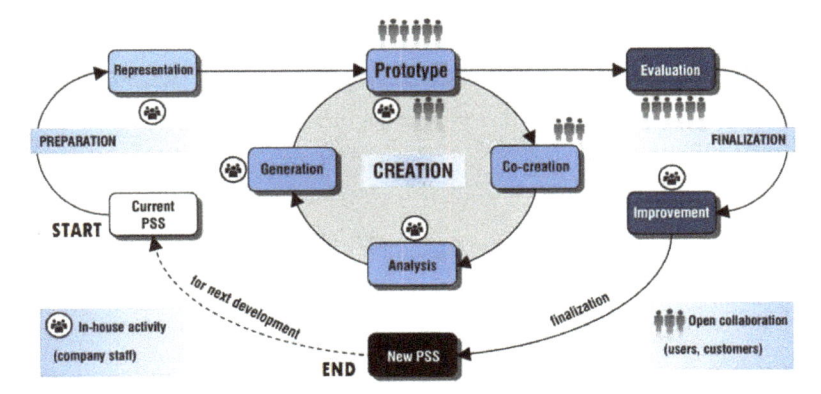

Figure 2. The proposed framework.

The proposed framework can be generally described as follows: The company wants to improve their current PSS by redesigning it with user co-creation. To do that, they first invite a group of users (Group 1) to participate. In order to make these users understand the PSS, the company represents the PSS in a simple form, and then, they prototype the PSS so that the users can actually see and experience the PSS. After that, these users co-create by suggesting various PSS options that they think might meet their needs. The company collects inputs from users, analyzes those inputs and produces new possible PSS designs. After new PSS designs are produced, the company invites another group of users (Group 2) to participate in prototyping and evaluating the newly-created designs. The designs will be evaluated by scoring along various criteria, and the one that gains the highest score will be selected as the winning design. The company will try to improve this design, if possible, and finally, they have a new PSS that is improved compare to the previous version. The detailed explanation of the proposed framework, its phases and corresponding methods can be found in Table 1.

Table 1. Working mechanism of the proposed framework.

Step	Tasks	Method	Implementation of Method
Preparation phase			
0	**Start** *Description*: The company has a PSS to be redesigned or a PSS idea to design further. *Purpose*: This step is the kickoff of the process.	N/A	N/A
1	**Representation** *Description*: The company breaks down a complex PSS into basic elements and prepares to communicate to users so that they can understand. *Purpose*: This step is the preparation for prototyping and user co-creation in the next phase.	*Method*: Simplified PSS presentation (Section 3.2) *Purpose*: This method is used to make users understand the PSS well, so that they can contribute their ideas effectively (Section 3.1).	A PSS is represented as a combination of elements, and the representation is summarized in a table (see Table 2 below).
Creation phase			
2	**Prototype #1** *Description*: The company demonstrates the prototype to a group of users. The users see and experience how the PSS works. This prototype can be presented in the form of a working prototype, such as: participatory prototyping or in the form of a storyboard, a simulation or any media-based illustration, depending on the type and characteristics of the PSS. *Purpose*: This step makes users (user Group 1) clearly understand what the PSS is like and how it might be provided. By understanding this, they can experience the PSS to some extent, and this allows them to contribute ideas more properly.	*Method*: Storyboard and participatory game *Purpose*: The storyboard explains briefly the PSS structure and mechanism, as well as elements and parameters, while the participatory game actually allows users to experience the PSS themselves by playing roles in the PSS process.	The PSS is introduced to the users firstly in the form of a storyboard, which explains what is included and how the PSS is provided (process, parameters, *etc.*). After that, the users are invited to participate in the participatory simulation of the PSS by playing roles.
3	**Co-creation** *Description*: The users participate actively to propose their own "PSS configurations" and customize the PSS design according to their own preferences. This can be done by inviting users, hosting participatory games or crowdsourcing. *Purpose*: This step allows users to contribute their ideas by directly inputting their desired parameters.	*Method*: User submission forms *Purpose*: These are forms that are created especially for collecting user inputs. The pre-defined forms helps to simplify the task for user submission and, thus, ensure effective contribution.	Users are asked to fill in a form with their desired parameters for the PSS. They are also asked to give comments and suggestions for the existing PSS, which was previously demonstrated in the "Prototype #1" step.
4	**Analysis** *Description*: The company analyzes user-generated PSS configurations and identifies the "favorite" configurations. *Purpose*: This step summarizes user inputs and analyzes how various alternatives of PSS options are favored by users. From this analysis, new PSS concepts might emerge.	*Method*: Simple statistical analysis *Purpose*: This method allows designers to collect and classify options to find "patterns".	Designers collect user input options and parameters, cluster them into segments of closely equivalent values, count frequencies and figure out the "favorite" configurations.

Table 1. Cont.

Step	Tasks	Method	Implementation of Method
Creation phase			
5	**Generation** *Description*: Based on the "favorite configurations" above, the company builds new PSS concepts, *i.e.*, "user-generated concepts". *Purpose*: This step makes new PSS concepts from users' favorite options and parameters.	*Method*: Concept generation *Purpose*: This method helps to generate various concepts or alternatives by combining various favorite options and parameters.	Designers combine various options and generate several alternatives that can be considered as user-generated concepts.
6	**Prototype #2** *Description*: The company demonstrates the prototypes of newly-generated concepts to a group of users so that they can evaluate them. *Purpose*: This step ensures that the users (user Group 2) understand the PSS thoroughly as, well as experience the PSS themselves, so that they can give a precise and proper evaluation.	*Method*: Storyboard and participatory game *Purpose*: The storyboard explains briefly the PSS structure and mechanism, as well as the elements and parameters, while the participatory game actually allows users to experience the PSS themselves by playing roles in the PSS process.	The PSS is introduced to the users firstly in the form of a storyboard that explains what is included and how the PSS is provided (process, parameters, *etc.*). After that, the users are invited to participate in the participatory simulation of the PSS by playing roles.
Finalization phase			
7	**Evaluation** *Description*: The evaluation criteria are explained to the users, and the users score to evaluate various concepts. Based on the evaluation results, the company can select the winning (*i.e.*, the best) concept. *Purpose*: This step collects the evaluation of users (user Group 2) for the newly-designed PSS, as well as the existing PSS, so that the performances of alternatives can be compared quantitatively.	*Method*: Multi-criteria scoring *Purpose*: This method allows users to evaluate the PSS along various criteria, and thus, a comprehensive evaluation can be achieved to give deeper insights and a precise comparison.	A list of criteria is proposed (Table 5) and a scoring scale of 1 to 5 is used to score PSS concepts. Scores are collected and calculated, and the results will be used to compare concepts to identify the best one.
8	**Improvement** *Description*: The company can improve the winning concept by selecting strong aspects of other concepts and implementing these aspects in the winning concept to achieve an "improved concept". *Purpose*: This step helps designers to exploit the best aspects of each concept to ensure that there is no waste of innovation.	*Method*: Manual improvement	Designers try to find strong aspects of low scored concepts and try to implement those aspects in the winning concept.
9	**End** The company achieves a new PSS design that is improved compared to the initial idea or the previous design.	N/A	N/A

Section 4 introduces a case study that is used to explain how the proposed framework can be used and validated.

4. Case Study and Validation of the Framework

4.1. Introduction to the Case

In Section 1, we mentioned Mulenserv and its PSS briefly. Mulenserv has a PSS called "N-Handbook", which is a book plus additional services for individuals and enterprises to learn new product development (NPD) at a professional level. The N-Handbook is a complex PSS offering, as shown in Table 2.

Table 2. Elements of the N-Handbook.

Element	Content
Product	<ul><li>A printed book</li><li>Optional additions: USB/DVD for lecture video storage, wooden box for keeping the book and accessories</li></ul>
Service	<ul><li>Lecture videos (YouTube channel)</li><li>Offline lectures</li><li>Additional documentation (tutorials, case studies, exercises, *etc.*, on closed discussion boards)</li><li>Questions and Answers (QnAs)</li><li>Offline seminars, examination and certification, project guidance, consulting</li></ul>
Process	<ul><li>Online/offline announcement</li><li>Customer consulting</li><li>Customer purchase + delivery</li><li>Customers use</li><li>Provide services</li><li>Feedback and prepare for next version</li></ul>
Parameters	<ul><li>Forms of support</li><li>Number of offline lectures</li><li>Length of each offline lecture</li><li>Availability of online lectures</li><li>Length of project practice</li><li>Availability of examination and certification</li><li>Recommendation for job seeking</li><li>Annual update frequency</li><li>Number of offline seminars/best practices</li><li>Renewal fee for new release</li><li>Price of the package</li></ul>
Network	<ul><li>Existing web systems of Mulenserv, social network, email, *etc.*, for delivering services</li><li>Offline network for delivering products (shops, post offices)</li></ul>
Stakeholders	<ul><li>The company (designers, staff)</li><li>Users</li><li>Suppliers (print shops, network providers)</li><li>Others</li></ul>
Value proposition	<ul><li>Bringing long-term benefits with flexible costs</li><li>Users make the most of the N-Handbook</li></ul>

4.2. Experimental Implementation of the Proposed Framework

In order to demonstrate, as well as to validate the proposed framework, we conduct an experiment with user participation. In this experiment, a group of users is asked to comment, suggest, give feedback to the existing design of the N-Handbook and to further ideate their own configuration of the N-Handbook. Details are as follows:

Step 0: Start

The company starts with the existing design of the N-Handbook, which is currently offered to customers. This design is denoted as D_0.

Step 1: Representation

The PSS is represented using a simplified representation.

In this experiment, assuming that the process, network, stakeholders and value proposition elements are fixed, the existing N-Handbook can be described as in Table 3.

Table 3. Details of the existing N-Handbook.

Element	Content
Product	• A printed book: black and white
Service	• Lecture videos: YouTube channel • Offline lectures: Yes • Additional documentation (tutorials, case studies, exercises, *etc.*, on closed discussion boards): Yes • QnAs: Yes • Offline seminars: Yes
Process	• Online/offline announcement • Customer consulting • Customer purchase + delivery • Customers use • Provide services • Feedback and prepare for next version
Parameters	• Forms of support (FOS): No • Number of offline lectures (NOL): 12 • Length of each offline lecture (LEL): 2 h • Availability of online lectures (AOL): Yes • Length of project practice (LPP): not available (N/A) • Availability of examination and certification (AEE): No • Recommendation for job seeking (RJS): No • Annual update frequency (AUF): 1 per year • Number of offline seminars/best practices (NOS): 1 per year • Renewal fee for new release (RFR): 50% discount (DC) • Price of the package (POP): 210 USD
Network	• Existing web systems of Mulenserv, social network, email, *etc.*, for delivering services • Offline network for delivering products (shops, post offices)
Stakeholders	• The company (designers, staff) • Users • Suppliers (print shops, network providers) • Others
Value proposition	• Bringing long-term benefits with flexible costs • Users make the most of the N-Handbook

Step 2: Prototype

The company communicates about the printed books and shows media about the additional services and explains the process, network, value proposition, parameters, *etc.*, of the N-Handbook in detail to a group of 21 participants (Group 1). These participants are selected from the database of individuals who showed interest in the N-Handbook, including the persons who asked for information and the persons who actually purchased. This is to ensure that the selected participants are enthusiastic enough about the future PSS and that we can keep them in the loop of participation.

Step 3: Co-creation

The participants are asked to give comments and suggestions for improving the existing design. The participants are also asked to propose their own preferences for the N-Handbook offering, including product, service and parameters. This is done by direct input to a pre-defined form.

Step 4: Analysis

The feedback (comments, suggestions) from the participants are collected and applied to improve the design of the existing N-Handbook.

The proposed preferences of the participants are collected and analyzed to find "favorite patterns" or the favorite PSS configurations. This is done manually by the designers by counting each and every proposed preference and making detailed statistics.

Step 5: Generation

The designers generate "new PSS designs" in this step. The design that is the result of implementing participants' comments and suggestions is called D_{0X}. There are three "favorite patterns" from participants' proposed preferences, and thus, the designers produce three more "new PSS designs", which are called D_1, D_2 and D_3. The details of D_{0X}, D_1, D_2 and D_3 can be found in Table 4 below.

Table 4. Comparison of various new N-Handbook designs.

Element	Content of N-Handbook Designs			
	D_{0X}	D_1	D_2	D_3
Product	Color printed book	Black and white printed book Wooden box USB DVD	Color printed book Wooden box DVD	Black and white printed book DVD
Service	YouTube channel Offline lecture Additional documentation QnAs Offline seminars	Offline lecture Additional documentation QnAs Offline seminars	Offline lecture Additional documentation QnAs Offline seminars	YouTube channel Offline lecture Additional documentation QnAs Offline seminars
Process	• Online/offline announcement • Customer consulting • Customer purchase + delivery • Customers use • Provide services • Feedback and prepare for next version			
Parameters	FOS: No NOL: 12 LEL: 2 h AOL: Yes LPP: 3 months AEE: Yes RJS: Yes AUF: 2 per year NOS: 2 per year RFR: 70% DC POP: 210 USD	FOS: Facebook NOL: 4 LEL: 2 h AOL: Yes LPP: 3 months AEE: Yes RJS: Yes AUF: 1 per year NOS: 4 per year RFR: 70% DC POP: 200 USD	FOS: Multi (*) NOL: 12 LEL: 2 h AOL: No LPP: 3 months AEE: Yes RJS: Yes AUF: 3 per year NOS: 3 per year RFR: 70% DC POP: 230 USD (*): Facebook, Boards, email, Mobile apps	FOS: Multi (*) NOL: 8 LEL: 2 h AOL: No LPP: 2 months AEE: Yes RJS: Yes AUF: 3 per year NOS: 2 per year RFR: 80% DC POP: 190 USD (*): Boards, email
Network	• Existing web systems of Mulenserv, social network, email, *etc.*, for delivering services • Offline network for delivering products (shops, post offices)			
Stakeholders	• The company (designers, staff) • Users • Suppliers (print shops, network providers) • Others			
Value proposition	• Bringing long term benefits with flexible costs • Users make the most of the N-Handbook			

Step 6: Prototype

The company demonstrates the prototypes of the PSS concepts to a new group of 65 participants (Group 2) who are selected from the database of individuals who showed interest in the N-Handbook, including the persons who asked for information and the persons who actually purchased.

Step 7: Evaluation

After explaining the four designs (i.e., D_{0X}, D_1, D_2 and D_3) thoroughly, the participants are asked to score each design along various criteria on a one to five scale. The scoring criteria are retrieved from the survey result from both groups of users before their participation. These are the most agreeable criteria to be used to evaluate the designed PSS among the participants. Details of the scoring criteria are provided below (Table 5).

Table 5. Scoring criteria.

Criteria	Description
Ease of access	How easily can the users access, use and leverage the package?
Applicability	Is this package applicable to the users' job?
Affordability	Is the price of the offering affordable (considering its content)?
Desirability	Do the users want to buy the package?
Necessity	Is this package necessary for the users' job?
Acceptance	If the users are offered this package, would they accept the offering?

Various designs are scored along the above criteria, and the results are recorded for further analysis. The analyzed results are shown in Section 4.3.

Step 8: Improvement

After scoring, the best design is identified, and the designers would try to improve it by trying to implement the strong aspects of other designs into it.

Step 9: End

The company achieves an improved PSS design with higher quality, user acceptance and satisfaction.

4.3. Experimental Results

After collecting the scores from participants, we calculate the mean values of scores for all 65 participants, as shown in Table 6.

Table 6. Mean values of scores for various designs along various criteria.

Criteria	Mean Value of Scores for Various Designs			
	D_{0X}	D_1	D_2	D_3
Ease of access	3.21	3.80	3.98	3.72
Applicability	3.18	3.74	3.90	3.97
Affordability	2.74	3.20	2.87	3.75
Desirability	2.70	3.13	3.38	3.44
Necessity	3.28	3.72	3.85	3.75
Acceptance	3.02	3.54	3.98	3.66

Figure 3 shows the data in Table 6 graphically.

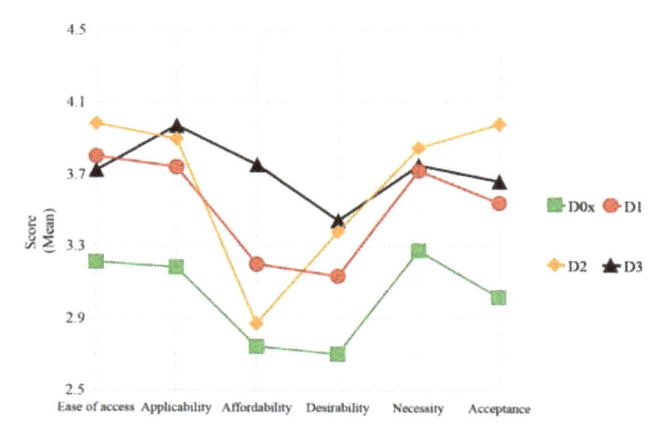

Figure 3. Visualized data showing the scores of various designs along various criteria.

Figure 3 shows that, for all criteria, designs that were suggested by users (*i.e.*, D_1, D_2 and D_3) perform better than the design that was developed solely by Mulenserv's designers (*i.e.*, D_{0X}, represented by the line with square points), especially in terms of "ease of access", "applicability" and "acceptance". This shows the outperformance of user-suggested designs, and thus, it shows the benefits of user co-creation and the use of the proposed framework.

4.4. Result Analysis and Validation

In order to validate the significance of experimental results to draw conclusions on the advantage of the proposed framework, the authors perform a *t*-test on the collected data of D_{0X} and D_2. The dataset for this *t*-test is collected from scoring results by all participants. This means that we use the result of the experiment performed at Mulenserv in the case study for this validation. The analysis results, which are rounded, are shown in Table 7.

Table 7. *t*-test analysis results.

Value	Ease of Access	Applicability	Affordability	Desirability	Necessity	Acceptance
Pearson correlation coefficients	0.257	0.317	0.403	0.391	0.390	0.0314
t-statistic	4.387	5.068	0.798	4.128	3.879	5.030
$P(T \leq t)$ one-tailed	2.191×10^{-5}	1.833×10^{-6}	0.214	5.399×10^{-5}	1.250×10^{-4}	2.111×10^{-6}
$P(T \leq t)$ two-tailed	4.382×10^{-5}	3.667×10^{-6}	0.428	1.080×10^{-4}	2.501×10^{-4}	4.221×10^{-6}

The reason why we choose D_2 to compare to D_{0X} is that D_2 performs the highest among the three user-suggested designs in terms of "acceptance", which is the most important criteria for a PSS.

Table 7 shows that, for almost all criteria, the differences between D_2 and D_{0X} are large enough to confirm the significance of the collected data because of the *t*-test result, $P(T \leq t) < 0.05$ for both one-tailed and two-tailed tests. There is only one exception for "affordability". For this criterion, the *t*-test result cannot ensure the real difference between D_2 and D_{0X}. Another *t*-test result shows that, in terms of "affordability", D_3, which was also suggested by the users, significantly outperforms D_{0X}. In order to improve D_2 to become even better, Mulenserv can consider applying D_3's pricing strategy to enhance D_2's "affordability".

Eventually, we can say that the experimental data are significant, the results are validated and the user-suggested designs perform better than the design that was solely developed by Mulenserv's team. This confirms the advantage of the proposed framework.

The key to successful implementation of this framework is user co-creation throughout the process. Users understand what they need the most and would be ready to accept offerings that are tailored to their needs. Two other important factors are the simplification of PSS configurations using elements and the demonstration of PSS prototypes so that the users can experience and understand the PSS before co-creation. The proposed framework is structured regarding all of those factors.

There are several issues when adopting the design process of conventional NPD (new product development) to the PSS context. In NPD, the company designs and develops products according to the requirements that were retrieved from customer needs and the results of competitive benchmarking. In some cases, the communication of customer needs to the design team is not done properly, and that leads to ineffective products. When being applied to PSS design, where user emotion, behavior and preferences are highly significant, conventional NPD processes may not work properly. These cases of designing PSS need a new approach, such as our proposed framework. On the other hand, if the design requires technical skills, such as engineering, drafting, manufacturing, *etc.*, the co-creation task may become difficult for users to participate in, and the model may not be applied effectively. In summary, the proposed framework can effectively deal with the designing of user-sensitive components, such as consumer PSS in a B2C environment (not industrial PSS in a B2B environment).

After proposing the framework and conducting the experiment, we gained more insights and experience of how users are actually involved in a co-creative design process. To gain the expected result for implementation, several guidelines can be found below:

- Prepare the scenario of implementing the framework in the case, and communicate necessary activities during the process to all design team members.
- Prototypes of PSS are very important. The prototypes help users to fully understand how the PSS works, allowing them to experience it so that they can generate and evaluate the PSS in a correct way.
- Representing of the PSS is also important. PSS representation needs to be simple, but thorough enough to cover all possible PSS elements and parameters. This allows users to co-create effectively in terms of quantity and quality.
- Selection of the right participants is essential. Since the participation to co-create in this process is time consuming and requires plenty of effort, only users who are enthusiastic enough can ensure effective participation.

4.5. Managerial Implications

As shown by the validation of the experimental data, proper implementation of the proposed framework can lead to better performance of the PSS. This suggests that the concept of co-creation and user involvement can be implemented to bring innovation and breakthroughs to PSS development. The proposed framework can also be used to estimate the response of potential users (buyers) to the "to be launched" PSS. Companies can customize the proposed framework for their specific PSS design projects while keeping the basic principles: the right users; simple representation; thorough prototypes; easy input forms; and comprehensive evaluation.

In the case study of this paper, we use an on-site participatory design for invited users. Other methods of involving users can also be used, such as crowdsourcing. In this case, we can use a website where we upload a call for participation, demonstrations of the PSS, guidelines for each and every step, *etc.* This is another option for PSS projects. As suggested in the "Tasks" column of each step (Table 1), companies can choose various tools to perform tasks in the process of the proposed framework.

5. Conclusions

In this work, the authors propose a co-creative framework for redesigning a PSS. For the first time, a framework for user co-creation in PSS design has been proposed, detailed and evaluated with experimental implementation.

Our work provides a practical guideline for developers in designing and redesigning PSS. It enhances the value perception, evaluation and design quality of PSS. The experimental implementation with the case study and the analysis of the experimental results shows that the proposed framework is valid.

The proposed framework can effectively deal with the designing of user-sensitive components, such as consumer PSS in a B2C environment. In cases that requires a high level of technical skills and knowledge or cases with complicated service processes, such as industrial PSS (in a B2B environment), this framework might not work effectively.

Whether PSS can lead to achieving sustainability depends on how the technical design and the business model are developed to address sustainable development criteria. One limitation of this work is that, due to its focus, there is a lack of such consideration. Therefore, this work cannot claim the possibility of achieving sustainability through PSS. In our following work, where the focus is more appropriate, we would consider this issue as a separate research topic.

Furthermore, for future work, in order to prove the advantages of the proposed framework, a comparison between its implementation results and those of other existing methods will be carried out. Furthermore, an architecture of a computer program (or a mobile application) that employs this framework as the backbone can be developed. This program can assist design teams to design PSS collaboratively within their own team and with innovative customers.

Acknowledgments: This research was supported by the Basic Research Program through the National Research Foundation of Korea (NRF) funded by the Ministry of Education (No. 2013R1A1A2013649).

Author Contributions: Tuananh Tran conceived of, designed and performed the experiments; Joon Young Park proposed and Tuananh Tran performed the analysis of the experimental data. Tuananh Tran wrote the initial manuscript. Joon Young Park corrected and revised the final writing.

Conflicts of Interest: There is no conflict of interest for this work.

References

1. Weber, C.; Steinbach, M.; Botta, C.; Deubel, T. Modeling of product–Service systems (PSS) based on the PDD approach. In Proceedings of the International Design Conference, Dubrovnik, Croatia, 18–21 May 2004; pp. 547–554.
2. Aurich, J.C.; Mannweiler, C.; Schweitzer, E. How to design and offer service successfully. *CIRP J. Manuf. Sci. Technol.* **2010**, *2*, 136–143. [CrossRef]
3. Bettencourt, L.A.; Ulwick, A.W. The customer—Centered innovation map. *Harv. Bus. Rev.* **2008**, *5*, 109–114.
4. Sakao, T.; Birkhofer, H.; Panshef, V.; Dorsam, E. An effective and efficient method to design services: Empirical study for services by an investment machine manufacturer. *Int. J. Internet Manuf. Serv.* **2009**, *2*, 95–110. [CrossRef]
5. Beuren, F.H.; Ferreira, M.G.G.; Miguel, P.A.C. Product-service systems: A literature review on integrated products and services. *J. Clean. Prod.* **2013**, *47*, 222–231. [CrossRef]
6. Vasantha, G.V.A.; Roy, R.; Lelah, A.; Brissaud, D. A review of product-service systems design methodologies. *J. Eng. Des.* **2012**, *23*, 635–659. [CrossRef]
7. Goedkoop, M.J.; van Halen, C.J.G.; te Riele, H.R.M.; Rommens, P.J.M. Product Service Systems, Ecological and Economic Basis. Report to Ministry of Housing, Spatial Planning and the Environment Communications Directorate, The Hague, The Netherlands. 1999. Available online: http://docplayer.net/334668-Product-service-systems-ecological-and-economic-basics.html (accessed on 29 April 2016).
8. Mont, O.K. Clarifying the concept of product-service system. *J. Clean. Prod.* **2002**, *10*, 237–245. [CrossRef]
9. Lim, C.H.; Kim, K.J.; Hong, Y.S.; Park, K.T. PSS Board: A structured tool for product-service system process visualization. *J. Clean. Prod.* **2012**, *37*, 42–55. [CrossRef]
10. Hussain, R.; Lockett, H.; Vasantha, G.V.A. A framework to inform PSS conceptual design by using system–in–use data. *Comput. Ind.* **2012**, *63*, 319–327. [CrossRef]
11. Baines, T.S.; Lightfoot, H.; Steve, E.; Neely, A.; Greenough, R.; Peppard, J.; Roy, R.; Shehab, E.; Braganza, A.; Tiwari, A.; *et al.* State-of-the-art in product service systems. *Proc. Inst. Mech. Eng. Part B* **2007**, *221*, 1543–1552. [CrossRef]
12. Morelli, N. The design of product/service systems from a designer's perspective. *Common Ground (Lond.)* **2002**, *18*, 3–17.

13. Tukker, A. Eight types of product-service system: Eight ways to sustainability? Experiences from SusProNet. *Bus. Strategy Environ* **2004**, *13*, 246–260. [CrossRef]
14. Vezzoli, C.; Ceschin, F.; Diehl, J.C.; Kohtala, C. New design challenges to widely implement 'Sustainable Product–Service Systems'. *J. Clean. Prod.* **2015**, *97*, 1–12. [CrossRef]
15. Qu, M.; Yu, S.; Chen, D.; Chu, J.; Tian, B. State-of-the-art of design, evaluation, and operation methodologies in product service systems. *Comput. Ind.* **2016**, *77*, 1–14. [CrossRef]
16. Luiten, H.; Knot, M.; van der Host, T. Sustainable product service systems: The kathalys method. In Proceedings of the 2nd International Symposium on Environmentally Conscious Design and Inverse Manufacturing, Tokyo, Japan, 11–15 December 2001; pp. 190–197.
17. Manzini, E.; Vezolli, C. A strategic design approach to develop sustainable product service systems: Examples taken from the "environmental friendly innovation" Italian prize. *J. Clean. Prod.* **2003**, *11*, 851–857. [CrossRef]
18. Pezzotta, G.; Pirola, F.; Pinto, R.; Akasaka, F.; Shimomura, Y. A Service Engineering framework to design and assess an integrated product-service. *Mechatronics* **2015**, *31*, 169–179. [CrossRef]
19. Morelli, N. Developing new product service systems (PSS): Methodologies and operational tools. *J. Clean. Prod.* **2006**, *14*, 1495–1501. [CrossRef]
20. Kowalkowski, C.; Kindström, D. Value visualization strategies for PSS Development. In *Introduction to Product/Service-System Design*; Sakao, T., Lindahl, M., Eds.; Springer: London, UK, 2009; pp. 159–182.
21. Sakao, T.; Shimomura, Y. Service Engineering: A Novel Engineering Discipline for Producers to Increase Value Combining Service and Product. *J. Clean. Prod.* **2007**, *15*, 590–604. [CrossRef]
22. Kim, Y.S.; Wang, E.; Lee, S.W.; Choi, Y.C. A Product-Service System Representation and Its Application in a Concept Design Scenario. In Proceedings of the 1st CIRP Industrial Product Service Systems (IPS2) Conference, Cranfield University, England, UK, 1–2 April 2009; pp. 32–39.
23. Maussang, N.; Zwolinski, P.; Brissaud, D. Product-service system design methodology: From the PSS architecture design to the products specifications. *J. Eng. Des.* **2009**, *20*, 349–366. [CrossRef]
24. Tan, A.R.; Matzen, D.; McAloone, T.; Evans, S. Strategies for Designing and Developing Services for Manufacturing Firms. *CIRP J. Manuf. Sci. Technol.* **2010**, *3*, 90–97. [CrossRef]
25. Bertoni, A.; Bertoni, M.; Isaksson, O. Communicating the Value of PSS Design Alternatives using Color-Coded CAD Models. In Proceedings of the 3rd CIRP International Conference on Industrial Product Service Systems, Braunschweig, Germany, 5–6 May 2011.
26. Steen, M.; Manschot, M.; De Koning, N. Benefits of co-design in service design projects. *Int. J. Des.* **2011**, *5*, 53–60.
27. Shih, L.H.; Hu, A.H.; Lin, S.L.; Chen, J.L.; Tu, J.C. ; Kuo T.C. An Integrated Approach for Product Service System Development: II. Evaluation Phase. *J. Environ. Eng. Manag.* **2009**, *19*, 343–356.
28. Yoon, B.; Kim, S.; Rhee, J. An evaluation method for designing a new product-service system. *Expert Syst. Appl.* **2012**, *39*, 3100–3108. [CrossRef]
29. Exner, K.; Lindow, K.; Buchholz, C.; Stark, R. Validation of Product-Service Systems-A Prototyping Approach. *Procedia CIRP* **2014**, *16*, 68–73. [CrossRef]
30. Komoto, H.; Tomiyama, T. Design of Competitive Maintenance Service for Durable and Capital Goods using Life Cycle Simulation. *Int. J. Autom. Technol.* **2009**, *3*, 63–70.
31. Dorst, K. The core of 'design thinking' and its application. *Des. Stud.* **2011**, *32*, 521–532. [CrossRef]
32. Kleemann, F. Un(der)paid Innovators: The Commercial Utilization of Consumer Work through Crowdsourcing Science. *Technol. Innov. Stud.* **2008**, *4*, 5–26.
33. Tran, T.; Park, J.Y. Crowd Participation Pattern in the Phases of a Product Development Process that Utilizes Crowdsourcing. *Ind. Eng. Manag. Syst.* **2012**, *11*, 266–275. [CrossRef]

© 2016 by the authors. Licensee MDPI, Basel, Switzerland. This article is an open access article distributed under the terms and conditions of the Creative Commons Attribution (CC BY) license (http://creativecommons.org/licenses/by/4.0/).

Article

Research on Business Models in their Life Cycle

**Adam Jabłoński * and Marek Jabłoński *

Department of Management, University of Dąbrowa Górnicza (Wyższa Szkoła Biznesu w Dąbrowie Górniczej), Zygmunta Cieplaka Str. 1c, 41-300 Dąbrowa Górnicza, Poland

* Correspondence: adam.jablonski@ottima-plus.com.pl (A.J.); marek.jablonski@ottima-plus.com.pl (M.J.); Tel.: +48-60-6364-500 (A.J.); +48-60-4538-566 (M.J.)

Academic Editor: Marc A. Rosen
Received: 18 January 2016; Accepted: 27 April 2016; Published: 30 April 2016

Abstract: The paper presents the results of theoretical discussions and research findings in the field of designing sustainable business models that support the creation of value at various stages of the business life cycle. The paper presents selected findings of extensive research into the business models of Polish companies listed on the Warsaw Stock Exchange. Companies which are at various stages of development should build and adapt their business models in order to maintain the ability to create value for stakeholders. Characteristics of business models at the early stages of development are different than at mature stages. The paper highlights the differences in business models in the context of the life cycle of companies and sustainability criteria. The paper presents research findings which show that the company's development can be seen from the point of view of the business model. Research on business models concentrated on identifying the key attributes and the configuration of the business models appropriate for the early stage of development as well as the maturity stage. It was found that the business models of companies at an early stage of the development of companies listed on the Warsaw Stock Exchange are oriented primarily to how the company shapes, delivers, and captures value from the market in order to generate profits for shareholders and increase the value of the company, while the business models of mature companies include the intentions of management used to balance objectives with respect to different groups of stakeholders, and to carefully formulate and implement business objectives with particular attention paid to preserving the sustainability of the business. The assessment of business models from the point of view of the life cycle proves that managers change their approach to configuring business models over time; at some point, they include management intentions aimed at a broader range of goals than merely generating profits. At the early stage, it is important to adapt the business model to the ability to create value for shareholders by actively searching for the optimal configuration of the business model. Here a component approach to making rapid changes in the structure of the business model is essential. The business model of mature companies is based on assumptions ensuring the long-term viability of the business and is holistic in nature. When the company moves from the stage of early development to the maturity stage, business models change in such a way that the assumptions of the Triple Bottom Line concept become increasingly important, as expressed in the joint implementation of Corporate Social Responsibility and Value-Based Management assumptions. At the early stage of development, the business model strengthens the need to create value for shareholders and is not as dependent on strong partnerships with a large number of stakeholders. At the maturity stage, it is important to balance the objectives of all stakeholders and to build long-term relationships with them. As regards relationships with the environment, business models at these two stages are different. The paper presents research on the business models of companies at their early stage of development as well as mature companies, taking into consideration the assumptions of the Sustainable Business Model.

Keywords: business model; company value; capital market; balance; a sustainable business model; life cycle of a business model; early stage of company development; maturity stage of company development

1. Introduction

Conducting business in the conditions of the economic crisis has given rise to a new perspective on the decision-making processes taking place in companies. Companies' ability to manage business continuity, including their abilities related to strategic revival or restructuring, is acquiring special significance which should contribute to ensuring the continued creation of company value. This is important in that the management mechanisms of the capital market are significantly influenced by changes in the macro-environment occurring at the same time, forces of sectoral determinants and internal decision-making processes in companies. One of the key strategic factors affecting these processes is to have the appropriate competencies related to company life cycle management using efficient business models. These models, which define and take advantage of the company's potential to compete, shape the image of the company in the market and are a source of competitive advantage which the company has and renews cyclically. It should be noted that, as [1] (p. 174) writes, a business model concept is based on economic sciences and paradigms related to conducting business. This insight allows a researcher to expand the scope of research into issues related to the active conduct of modern business. The authors hypothesize that the achievement of success by a company and its ability to build company value over a long period of time depends on having an efficient business model in each period of business activity using sustainability criteria. This model should be appropriate for the present market conditions and should allow the company to adjust to ever-changing needs by managing its configuration in such a way that the interfaces between its components provide a platform for the dynamic development and growth of the company at each stage of its operation.

The purpose of the paper is to present the research findings and discussions in the field of designing business models that contribute to the creation of value at various stages of the business life cycle, and indicates that a business model at the maturity stage of development has the characteristics of sustainability. The paper presents selected theoretical aspects and the findings of extensive research into the business models of companies listed on the Warsaw Stock Exchange, as published in works by M. Jabłoński [2] and A. Jabłoński [3]. The studies described in these publications have been selectively chosen for the purpose of this paper, as well as combined and interpreted in such a way as to cover all the stages of a company's life cycle. The same applies to studies and analyses and how they take into account the business models of both companies at the early stage of development and mature companies. Based on the data, the paper presents reflections on and analyses of business models in the life cycle in the context of business model development which fulfills the objectives of the sustainability concept. The managers of companies at the early stage of development focus their attention on designing, delivering scalability and dynamically adjusting the business model used. Conversely, in mature companies they significantly expand the understanding of the business model, adding management intentions to its attributes, based on balancing the interests of different groups of stakeholders and the coherent and coordinated use of assumptions of the Value-Based Management and Corporate Social Responsibility concepts, leading to the creation of the Sustainable Business Model. Business models examined by means of the criterion of the life cycle change due to the growing needs of stakeholders over time. As these needs and expectations are the greatest in the case of mature companies, it is therefore justifiable to create a category of a business model based on sustainability. The methodological objectives of the paper are based on the theory of a systems approach by L. von Bertalanffy [4], K.E. Boulding [5], R.L. Ackoff [6] and the approach of Resource Based View, Rumelt [7], E. T. Penrose [8], J. Barney [9–11], R. Amit, P., M. A. Peteraf [12], B. Wernerfelt 1984 [13], M. J. Dollinger [14], C. K. Prahalad and G. Hamel [15] (p. 81). The systems approach and resource-based view are suitable for the assessment of business models and company management in terms of the life cycle, as they take into account the pooling of resources in a relatively firm and unified whole. The business model is a system consisting of the fitting configuration of resources appropriate for a given situation.

This paper is structured as follows. After discussing the sustainability concept as a new way of understanding business sustainability (Section 2), business models are discussed in terms of the life cycle (Section 3). The literature on issues related to the life cycle and its reference to the concept of business models has been reviewed. Section 4 deals with the design of business models at the early stage of development, while Section 5 presents the design of business models at the maturity stage of development. These approaches to designing business models are slightly different as are the assumptions on which they are based. The research methodology is presented in Section 6, as well as the scope of research, research subjects, and hypotheses for both companies at the early stage of development and mature companies. The research findings are presented in Sections 7 and 8. The discussion is presented in Section 9. The conclusion in Section 10 summarizes the core findings of the paper and the core results of the analysis.

2. A Sustainable Business Model as a New Way of Ensuring Business Sustainability

The core premise underlying the concept of sustainability is related to the philosophy of the Triple Bottom Line [16] which increases the chances of survival in various conditions. Business model sustainability is now one of the key determinants of doing business. T. Dyllick and K. Muff define the evolution of sustainability according to three levels of Business Sustainability, the development of which is presented in Figure 1.

BUSINESS SUSTAINABILITY TYPOLOGY	Concerns (What)?	Value Created (What for)?	Organizational perspective (How)?
Business-as-usual	Economic concern	Shareholder value	Inside-out
Business Sustainability 1.0: Refined Shareholder Value	Three-dimensional concerns	Shareholder value	Inside-out
Business Sustainability 2.0: Triple Bottom Line	Three-dimensional concerns	Triple bottom line	Inside-out
Business Sustainability 3.0: True Business Sustainability	Starting with sustainability challenges	Creating value for the common good	Outside-in
The key shifts involved	1st shift: broadening the business concern	2nd shift: expanding the value created	3rd shift: changing the perspective

Figure 1. Business Sustainability: Typology with key characteristics and changes [17].

Figure 1 shows the evolution of the business sustainability concept, assuming that the formula of "Business Sustainability 3.0" is currently being developed, where the idea is action based on value creation by supplying goods and the organization's openness to the external environment. Different models, approaches and concepts presented in the literature make the concept of sustainability ambiguous and difficult to interpret. On the one hand, it mentions ensuring business sustainability, and on the other hand, a multidimensional look at the organization considering the interests of various groups of stakeholders. W. Stubbs and C. Cocklin express the view that, in relation to sustainable enterprise, the company should aim to generate income. Profits are used to pursue sustainable goals, as well as the mission and vision based on achieving social and economic objectives and financial performance [18].

S. Schaltegger and R. Burritt highlight the ambiguous impact of social and environmental attitudes on a company's financial performance, giving examples in which such attitudes have no effect on the economic success of the company [19].

T. Dyllick and K. Hockerts present a model based on the concept of corporate sustainability (balancing and integrating the company's activities) mapped in the form of a triangle. In the three corners of the triangle the focus is, respectively, on the business case, natural case and societal case [20]. W. McDonough and M. Braungart present the model of corporate sustainability in the form of a fractal triangle with ecology-ecology, equity-equity and economy-economy in its corners [21].

F. Boons and F. Lüdeke-Freund focus on linking the sustainability concept with innovation. In their opinion, the sustained success of an organization depends on innovation. Rules determining the functioning of a sustainable business model should be based on creating technological innovation that can create new markets after being commercialized [22].

The relationship between the concept of CSR (Corporate Social Responsibility) and financial management is highlighted by Archie B. Carroll and Kareem M. Shabana, who believe that generally, based on the review of practical business examples, CSR has a positive effect on company performance [23].

S. Schaltegger and R. Burritt show that applying the principles of corporate social responsibility and sustainability management uses the same assumptions, based on the integration of social, economic and environmental aspects [24].

Frank Boons, Carlos Montalvo, Jaco Quist, Marcus Wagner believe that sustainable business models should be supported by government agencies through appropriate policies. Companies and government should work together to create innovations implemented in sustainable business models [25].

A business case for sustainability according to S. Schaltegger, F. Lüdeke-Freund and E.G. Hansen is the interpretation which indicates that the key aspect differentiating classic business solutions between cases based on sustainability is a primary objective and incorporating smart solutions based on environmental and social factors affecting the economic success of the company into the business model [26]. J.G. York defines three conditions that guide the investors when they invest in sustainable business, namely the required increase in ROIC (Return on Invested Capital), the minimum value of the WACC (Weighted Average Cost of Capital) and an increase in the availability of capital. This approach is cost-effective and usable for startups [27].

S. Schaltegger, E. Hansen, and F. Lüdeke-Freund define a business model for sustainability as one which helps in describing, analyzing, managing, and communicating (i) a company's sustainable value proposition to its customers, and all other stakeholders; (ii) how it creates and delivers this value; (iii) and how it captures economic value while maintaining or regenerating natural, social, and economic capital beyond its organizational boundaries [28].

Nikolay Dentchev, Rupert Baumgartner, Hans Dieleman, Lara Johannsdottir, Jan Jonker, Timo Nyberg, Romana Rauter, Michele Rosano, Yulia Snihur, Xingfu Tang, and Bart van Hoof solicit inputs on the variety of organizational settings which support the implementation of sustainable business models.

- Do organizational and legal structures matter for the development of sustainable business models? If so, how does that help or hinder utilization of the new models?
- What are the drivers for profit-dominated organizations to engage in implementing sustainable business models?
- How does intrapreneurship impact the implementation of sustainable business models in multinationals?
- What is the role of the service sector in implementing sustainable business models, in addition to manufacturing or other types of industries?
- Are there conflicts of co-existence among multinational companies which are using sustainable and conventional business models?
- What are the dynamics of sustainable business model implementation in non-profit organizations and government-controlled organizations [29]?

N.M.P. Bocken, S.W. Short, P. Rana, and S. Evans believe that business model innovations for sustainability stand out from other concepts due to the fact that innovations based on reducing the adverse effects on the environment make it possible to effectively capture value from the market and increase the economic value of the company. At the same time, the product offer also changes [30].

Each approach indicates how interdisciplinary a sustainable business model concept is and how many interpretations it has. It is interesting to examine a sustainable business model from the point of view of the life cycle.

3. The Life Cycle of Business Models

The relevant literature proposes various definitions of business models. This concept is interpreted from different points of view. For example, according to R. Amit and C. Zott, "A business model describes the structure of transaction governance designed in such a way that value is created and all business opportunities are taken advantage of" [31] (p. 511).

The definition by R. Casadesus-Masanell and J.E. Ricart is based on identifying business logic in the context of creating value for stakeholders [32] (p. 196).

As far as preserving the continuity of the business in the long term is concerned, the definition of the business model was presented by B. Demil and X. Lecocq, who say that "a business model defines how the organization operates to ensure its stability" [33] (p. 231). An interesting definition has been presented by B. Mahadevan, who says that a business model is the unique configuration of three streams, namely a stream associated with customer service and cooperation with partners, a revenue stream, and a logistical stream [34] (p. 59).

D.J. Teece bases his definition on converting payments into profits [1] (p. 173).

An approach to business models based on the concept of innovation is presented by H. Chesbrough, who claims, based on joint works with R. Rosenbloom, that it is crucial for a business model to rely on assumptions resulting from presenting a value proposition, identifying market segments, designing the structure of the value chain, looking at the means of generating revenue, evaluating the cost structure, as well as describing the company's position in the value network. All this must be supported by an adequate competitive strategy [35] (p. 355).

E. Fielt highlights the description of business operation logic in terms of capturing value from the market [36] (pp. 91–92).

There are many definitions and approaches to business models and there is still no consensus on a universal definition. They are examined in terms of the essence of their definition, the use and the configuration of components. The proposed definition of the business model concept is interdisciplinary in its nature. They prove the broad extent to which the definitions of business models are examined in relation to many areas and perspectives. Some authors focus their attention on the strategic character of delivering value to a customer, others on the results such as profit, and still others on social aspects. The definitions presented emphasize other factors that distinguish them from one another. Undoubtedly, however, all of them focus on the logic of doing business, and thus on the assumptions on which the company has based its business. The distinct characteristics of various approaches to the issue discussed result from showing other features which can ensure the company's success. Life cycle is an important issue in terms of examining business models.

The issue of a company's life cycle is generally widely recognized in the literature. Authors who have contributed to the development of this issue include Chandler (1962) [37], Patton (1959) [38], Levitt (1965) [39], Cox (1967) [40], Churchill and Lewis (1983), Greiner (1972) [41,42], Hofer (1975) [43], Scott and Bruce (1987) [44], Quinn and Cameron (1983) [45], and Parnell and Carraher (2003) [46]. According to Levitt (1965) and Cox (1967), different strategies are adopted at different stages of the product life cycle. Thietart and Vivas (1984) [47] argue that strategies depend not only on the stage of the life cycle, but are affected by the company's strategic logic. In addition, the success of the strategy seems to be dependent on the sector and characteristics of the external environment.

In terms of the examination of the life cycle of companies in the context of the organization, from the point of view of business models, a cognitive gap can be observed in this area. To date, the issue of the life cycle of companies in terms of business model attributes and increasing the value of the company has not been widely discussed. The business model as an ontological being may also be examined from the point of view of the life cycle.

The authors highlight the research gap in existing studies, e.g., on strategic factors and interrelations, and derive their research questions. There is a significant research gap in management sciences in the scope of business models in the context of the life cycle, particularly in relation to the companies listed on the stock exchange applying the principles of sustainability.

As regards research into the life cycle of business models, D.R.A. Schallmo and L. Brecht show the relationship between the length of the life cycle and the application of corporate social responsibility principles, which, in a sense, is linked with the concept of sustainability. The authors suggest that the application of corporate social responsibility principles contributes to business model sustainability. These principles lengthen the life cycle of the business model [48].

Further research was done by M. de Reuver, H. Bouwman and I. MacInnes, who examined which types of external factors are most important from the point of view of the business model life cycle. They argue that, on the basis of 45 case studies from various sectors of the economy, the most important drivers of business model dynamics are technological factors. This is particularly important in the case of startups, where technological attributes should be supported by market needs, while for large companies this relationship is less important. External factors must be taken into account when designing the business model in various stages of development but also when modifying it [49].

As far as the business model at an early stage of development is concerned, some characteristics can be observed. A business model at an early stage of its development is shaped in the context of applying the effective configuration of components that constitute it, and which are conducive to the creation of value. A business model should be supported by the attributes related to the quality of the management team. This is particularly important as regards the quality of the management of companies at an early stage of their development. B. M. Martins Rodríguez [50] (p. 129) identifies a need to separate two key areas, namely the business model and the characteristics related to the top management team. A startup can succeed only if managers have high competencies and operational capabilities in terms of creating value.

A business model goes through the distinct stages of the idea, development and commercialization. Its shape is different from what it will be in the future, when, in order to maintain continuity of business, a company will need to use different methods and management concepts appropriate to the level of organizational development. The companies that are at an early stage of development and their business models should be geared to survival. However, the planning horizon in these companies is shorter due to a number of uncertainties. Young companies focus mainly on finding a viable, scalable and effective business model, which will allow the company to capture market value. Changes in such models as regards the company's configuration can happen very quickly—companies modify their business models throughout the life cycle. Survival is a goal for both young and mature companies, at which point stakeholders will play a greater role, expecting the distribution of the value produced. The final form of the business model will be based on balancing various areas of activity in the form of constructive comparison, which may be referred to as a sustainable business model. The concept of sustainability is understood as durability; sustainability is a relatively new concept not yet fully explored. W. M. Grudzewski, I.K. Hejduk, A. Sankowska, and M. Wańtuchowicz define sustainability as the company's ability to continuously learn, adapt and develop, revitalize, reconstruct and reorient to maintain a lasting and distinctive position in the market by offering buyers above-average value today and in the future (consistent with the paradigm of innovative growth) through organic variation constituting business models, and arising from the creation of new opportunities, objectives and responses to them, while balancing the interests of different groups [51] (p. 27). C. Kidd believes that the concept of sustainability derives from a broader look at this issue, in relation to balancing the influence of various political, social and scientific groups in time [52]. This means that there is a close correlation between the stability of the business and sustainable stakeholder relationship management. G. Svenson, G. Wood, and M. Callaghan also argue that a fundamental aspect of sustainability occurs when company expectations and ideas of the market and society affect the prevailing opinions of what can and cannot be done in sustainable business practice. In turn, stakeholders and their expectations help to answer this question [53] (p. 338). Relationships with stakeholders determine the shape and nature of the principles of sustainability in business. An interesting sustainable business model based on an original SMART concept (sustainability modeling and reporting system) has been developed by M. Daud Ahmed and D. Sundaram [54] (pp. 611–624). In this model, they defined the sustainability roadmap (sustainable business transformation roadmap) in which the key elements consist of design, transformation, monitoring and control, discovery, science and strategy. M. Yunus, B. Moingeon, and L. Lehmann-Ortega define the concept of a social business model, which can also be a sustainable business model, and have developed the foundations of building a social business model consisting of two areas also common to innovative models and areas specific to social models. They show similarities with conventional and innovative business models which include:

- the challenges of conventional knowledge and basic assumptions,
- the discovery of complementary business partners,
- undertakings in improving process experiments.

As regards the specific assumptions relevant to social business models, they show features such as:

- Encouraging social orientation in terms of profit for shareholders,
- Clear, specific objectives for profit for society.

The approaches presented show the essence of the sustainability concept and direct its attention to the continuous ability of the company to remain in the market when the condition of this goal is to have an effective business model at every stage of the life cycle. It should be largely oriented to social objectives without losing the features of a company focused on generating profit. The time taken from the stage of business model development to the achievement of a state characterized by features of a sustainable business model will depend on the particular character of the company, the sector which it operates in, and market volatility. Based on observations of the phenomena occurring in the economy, it can be said that this time grows ever shorter. The ability to understand the cycle designed in such a way allows managers to quickly detect weaknesses in the business model and adjust its configuration to ensure the constant ability to create value, at the beginning mostly only for shareholders, and later also for other stakeholders by adapting it to the expected value. It is possible that, at the initial stage of company development, a business model that has the features of a sustainable business model is built. However, it rarely happens in a free market economy. In its initial stage of development, the company focuses primarily on investing and multiplying profits for further expansion and development. At a later stage of development, the company can share what was gained in previous years. Figure 2 shows the change in the business model in the life cycle of the company. A business model at an early stage of development will be characterized by features other than a business model in its maturity stage of development. To ensure their usefulness and verify their effectiveness, different management methods and techniques will be used.

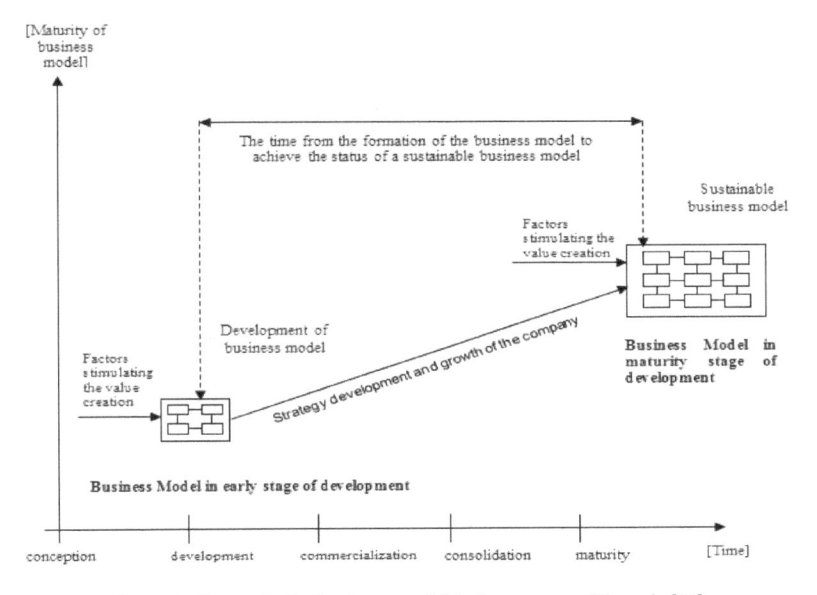

Figure 2. Change in the business model in the company life cycle [55].

Analyzing the approaches to and definitions of business models described in the literature, the authors adopt the approach by Ch. Zott and R. Amit in their reflections on further research. Their proposal is based on the fact that a business model is a package of specific actions performed in order to meet the needs of the market, in particular involving partnerships centered on the focal company and its partners [56]. The proposed approach requires a focus on how the business is conducted, on how value is created for all business participants and on identifying partners that can assist in performing actions important from the point of view of the business model. It is a holistic approach [57]. After analyzing the literature, the definition of a sustainable business model in the life cycle has been presented. A business model evolves during the life cycle of the company. In the authors' opinion, a sustainable business model in the life cycle is a business model that is capable of evolution throughout the life cycle, assuming an incremental increase in the value of the company when the principles of Corporate Social Responsibility and Value-Based Management are adhered to.

4. The Design of Business Models at the Early Stage of Development

Companies are increasingly competing not only on products and/or services, their quality or price, but on business models as well. A company with a profitable business model achieves higher market capitalization, is attractive to investors and stakeholders, and consequently has more market opportunities. Company value depends on the attractiveness of its business model and the skills to introduce dynamic changes therein, resulting from the needs of the environment. The proposed approach to the design of strategies and business models aimed at creating value is related to the configuration of the business model. This means a set of business model components that shape its whole, characterizing the essence of this model. The word "configuration" is used as business models can be altered by modifying their components, and even in some cases totally reconfigured. In this approach, the ontological essence is not so much the business model as this configuration. Dynamics of a business model means its ability to change, which leads to a higher company value than before the change, by using a different configuration of business model components. Issues pertaining to the level of technology, processes and strategies should be included in a measuring system used to monitor the process of creating value. Designing business models requires the ability to respond to any signals forecasting changes in the external and internal environment of the company; managers not taking them into consideration in the decision-making process can lead to economic losses. The business model constantly reacts to corporate strategy. The concept of strategy geometry developed by R.W. Keidal fulfills these expectations, making a clear distinction between elements of the complexity of formulating strategies in the context of the factors that influence them [58] (p. 6). Changing the business model can be natural (resulting from the company's flexibility in adapting to changes in its environment—a company changes when the business environment changes) or forced. Forced changes are often restructuring in their nature [59] (p. 36). This approach to management processes requires the implementation of a results-oriented organizational culture. Therefore, in the process of modifying business models quickly, it is essential to implement the concept of Strategic Performance Management. The assumptions of the concept have been presented by A. de Waal, who says that this is a process that requires company managers to regularly verify the mission, strategy and goals. As a result, these goals are measurable using key success factors and performance indicators to maintain the determined direction of the company's operations [60] (p. 19).

A dynamic aspect of business models exposes processes and value chains, but it also significantly affects the shape of organizational structures. The proposed approach should serve to quickly move from one model to another using a different business model configuration. One of the assumptions is considering business models from the perspective of seeking an effective configuration of the company strategic structure to identify such components of the business model that are crucial in the process of the creation of company value. Treating the concepts of business models, especially in the area of their configuration, jointly with the concept of value creation appears to be an important subject today, but one which is not fully recognized as yet, especially in the area of companies classified as innovative.

5. Design of Business Models at the Maturity Stage of Development

The dynamically changing global economy in the era of the intensive development of globalization creates new needs, both in theoretical management models as well as in practical discussions related to the perception of business. This is particularly important in the current economic and moral crisis, the effects of which are visible in most developed countries. It is important to find and/or use the existing management paradigms, the examination and codification of which will provide a platform for the development and growth of companies. By observing and analyzing business trends and the behavior of companies for the past few years, it can be concluded that many business orientations and concepts, whose roots and method of evaluation are often radically different, lead to similar business results. This has happened to the concepts of Value-Based Management, Corporate Social Responsibility, Shareholders, Stakeholders as well as Sustainable Business, and was significantly influenced by the globalized nature of world economies, which resulted in the creation of values on the basis of which corporate business models were built. The strategic behavior of companies and their intercultural exchange led to the creation of new sources and platforms for building competitive advantage, and consequently a stable source for building long-term value. The principles of sustainable development are increasingly appreciated, including in the United States. Transferred to the micro level in terms of the competitiveness of the company, its strategy and by following the principles of corporate social responsibility amid the global economic crisis, they resulted in the creation of a new management concept, namely Sustainability. This can be regarded as Sustainable Development aiming to simultaneously adhere to the principles of ethics, ecology and economy, and may also be understood as the ability of the company to manage quickly and flexibly, focusing on objectives and enabling the implementation of the company mission and vision, taking into account the establishment of competitive advantage on the market. This can be achieved by creating new products and/or services and implementing modern management methods and concepts, the source of which is scientific research and solutions to business practices. Sustainable business is business conducted when concepts of value-based management and corporate social responsibility are used in a systemic way, providing value for company stakeholders.

Sustainable business at all levels of management, which includes all of the factors and functions therein, ensures business continuity as well as the power to create value in the long term, and enables a sustainable dividend payout to shareholders and the generation of a social dividend to other stakeholders of the company. The combination of these factors and functions will result in the search for the most optimal business solutions. This can be done through the mutual, constructive comparison of resources and factors influencing the ability to increase company value. Therefore, the most important factor is to find such a balance that will ensure business continuity in the market, while achieving business results which guarantee the long-term value of the company. The balance ensuring the implementation of the sustainable business concept may result from building a sustainable business model connected with the principles of VBM (Value Based Management), CSR and the concepts of Stakeholders, Shareholders and Sustainable Business. This may lead to the continuity of the business in the volatile conditions of the market environment.

Therefore, considering the theoretical and practical dimensions of the above issues, it is important to answer the question, which as yet has not been fully answered in the literature: Which strategic factors and their interrelations in the adopted business models have the greatest impact on the long-term building of a socially responsible company? What should the design of such a business model be?

A premise which says that the subject is important, difficult and requires extended research and scientific discussions is that companies want to build long-term value, to operate successfully in the market, to ensure the continuity of the business, to renew (reconstruct, adapt) their business models, and finally to win. However, they are constantly looking for the optimal ways and mechanisms allowing them to do it effectively and efficiently. At the same time, signals from the market, economic impulses, the economic crisis, chaos in the market, public disappointment with the place and role of companies in the economy, and examples of business collapses all hinder the selection of the most appropriate way to manage companies.

Moving away from certain management concepts, changes in values, the occurrence of the rapid flow of not only capital but also information and knowledge and access thereto, changes in perceiving the nature of the business, and its place in the global ecosystem also resulted in a new dimension in using the strength of management sciences in global business.

According to the authors, new dimensions of business are responsible management, sustainable management, socially acceptable management and efficient and effective management. Such an effect can be obtained by applying sustainability principles in a socially responsible manner.

A socially responsible company is a company whose business model, in increasing its value, is built on the basis of strategic factors associated with corporate social responsibility and the principles of value-based management, while determining wise organizational behavior in the company, and wise market behavior towards company stakeholders, which are based on the principles of integrity, ethics and professionalism.

Strategic factors related to corporate social responsibility and value-based management are the factors associated with the functioning and behavior of the organization towards the external and internal environment, where an appropriate combination leads to sustainable value in terms of long-term operation on the market.

As a consequence of this approach, a holistic sustainable business model is created, reduced in its nature, becoming a platform for creating long-term, sustainable value for a socially responsible company.

A company that is responsible, to a limited extent, is a company that applies the principles of corporate social responsibility only sometimes, when it is clearly profitable. It adheres to these principles not on a voluntary basis, according to the organizational culture of the company, but in a forced way.

A socially irresponsible company is a company that—in its business activities—does not obey the principles of corporate social responsibility by, *inter alia*, failing to abide by applicable legal and other conditions, by organizational behaviors indicating discrimination, bullying, intimidation, and other pathological behavior towards staff and other company stakeholders (including suppliers, co-operators and others) and by treating the company and company personnel only as a tool for making profit. In view of the above discussions, it can be assumed that the main components of a sustainable business model built in the subject-object system are strategic factors related to:

1. A combined implementation of the concepts of corporate social responsibility and value-based management.
2. Balancing the potential of the company.
3. Combining the stakeholder concept and the shareholder concept, which are also strongly related to the concepts of corporate social responsibility (stakeholders) and value-based management (shareholders).
4. A sustainable dividend policy.

A holistic model of sustainable business creating company value in the long term can be built on the basis of the following driving forces that give it the proper dynamics.

1. Strength of conscious application of corporate social responsibility principles.
2. Strength of economic sustainability of the company.
3. Strength of conscious application of corporate governance principles.
4. Strength of stakeholder value and the dynamics of their migration processes.
5. Strength of the consensual relationship: company's board, shareholders, stakeholders.
6. Strength of implementing a sustainable strategy based on the principles of a balanced scorecard.
7. Strength of balancing intellectual capital of the company.
8. Strength of balancing fixed assets of the company.
9. Strength of balancing internal processes of the company.
10. Strength of the management style based on the logic of conscious decision-making [3] (p. 249).

6. Methodology of Research

As a research instrument, one basic method has been used, *i.e.*, analysis of the literature concerning the life cycle of business models from startup to mature company. The authors present the problem of creating the framework of business models in their life cycle. The level of sustainability depends on the stage of company development. For this purpose, the authors have used literature research, a sustained approach to shaping the attributes of business models, the features of companies at an early stage of development and mature companies, as well as the principles for building a sustainable business model at different stages of company development. The authors have adopted an interpretative approach as the methodology of scientific research, based on the literature and a systematic retrospective assessment of the business models of companies in the course of conducting their own business activity and during their consulting practice. As regards the companies at the early stage of development, the issue of which business model components are responsible for increasing shareholder value to the greatest extent is also important. They should, therefore, be a driver of adjusting business models, and changes aimed at building company value should focus on them. The scope of the issue presented in the paper represents an attempt to link the findings of the research in the context of the business life cycle criterion, namely at an early stage of company development, and at the maturity stage. Therefore, if we add the two scopes of research, quantitative research was conducted on a sample of 220 companies listed on the Polish Stock Exchange in Warsaw (48 New Connect companies, 44 Index WIG20, WIG40, WIGdiv, Respect Index, New Connect Lead companies and 128 companies taking part in the "Environmentally Friendly Company" national ecology competition). Qualitative research was conducted on a sample of 384 companies from the New Connect market and 10 selected companies taking part in the "Environmentally Friendly Company" national competition.

The research concentrated on the issue of shaping the business models of companies operating on the New Connect alternative trading system, organized by the Warsaw Stock Exchange, aiming to increase their value; its objective was to design the so-called sustainable business model of mature companies that build value over the long term and that operate on the Stock Exchange, in the following indexes: WIG20, WIG40, WIGdiv, Respect Index, New Connect Lead and companies participating in the "Environmentally Friendly Company" national ecology competition. To study companies at the early stage of development, the component approach by S.M. Shafer, H.I, Smith, I.C. Lander [61] (p. 202) and work by M. Jabłoński [62] (p. 39–47) were applied to shape the configuration of the business model. As far as the assumptions of the Value-Based Management concept are concerned, works by A. Rappaport [63] and T. Copelland, T. Koller and J. Murrin [64] were used. To study the business models of mature companies, the approach of combining VBM and CSR concepts promoted by J.D. Martin, J.W. Petty, J.S. Wallace [65] and work by A. Jabłoński [66] were used. The combination of these assumptions resulted in a coherent approach to examining business models from the point of view of the life cycle criterion. Business models change over time due to the influence of internal and external factors. In the relevant literature, the issue of business model changeability during the life cycle of the company has been studied broadly. Also, no extensive analyses have been conducted on transforming business models from the idea of building a business model configuration conducive to the creation of value, achieving scalability of the business model to obtaining the strategic balance of a holistic nature in relation to different areas.

The comparative table below shows the characteristics of a business model at the early stage of development and a sustainable business model. (see Table 1).

Table 1. Characteristics of a business model at an early stage of development and a sustainable business model.

Business Model Characteristic	Description of the Characteristic of a Business Model at an Early Stage of Development	Description of the Characteristic of a Sustainable Business Model
Recipients of a business model	Focus primarily on shareholders	Focus on shareholders and other stakeholders
Business perspective	Short-term	Long-term
The stage of the application of management methods and concepts	Initial	Advanced
Business model dynamics	Very high	Stable
Organizational culture	Changing significantly	Stable
Innovation	Very big	Stable
Access to capital	Difficult	Relatively easy
Possibility of bankruptcy	High	Low

The study process and its scope are presented in Figure 3.

The life cycle of a business model is graphically depicted. During initiation and growth, business models of the companies at an early stage of development, listed on the New Connect alternative Warsaw Stock Exchange market, were examined. The maturity stage was examined as regards the companies with a strong market position in WIG20, WIG40, WIGdiv, and the Respect Index indexes. For both research areas, *i.e.*, the early and mature stages of development, research hypotheses were formulated regarding the impact of various factors on building company value through developing business models. Research findings for both stages of company activity are presented below in Sections 7 and 8.

Figure 3

Life cycle of a business model	Profit / Initiation / Growth / Maturity / Decline / Time	
Research hypothesis	H1. Design of a business model conducive to the creation of value requires knowledge of how to configure each of its components, and awareness of the importance of these components, which are of particular significance for the creation of value. H2. Company value results directly from the effectiveness of the business model, its profitability and construction H3. It is necessary to adapt the business model to ensure the company's ability to create value, H4. There is a correlation between the effectiveness of the business model and the creation of value.	H1. The joint implementation of the principles of the CSR concept and Value Based Management balances the company's potential for building long-term value. H2. Combining the stakeholders concept with the shareholders concept affects the creation of the long-term value of the company. H3. Balancing the needs of different stakeholder groups has a positive effect on the processes of stakeholders' migration of high value. H4. Stakeholder value influences the company's ability to create company value
Stage of development	Initiation and Growth	Maturity
Research object	New Connect	Respect Index WIG 20, WIG 40

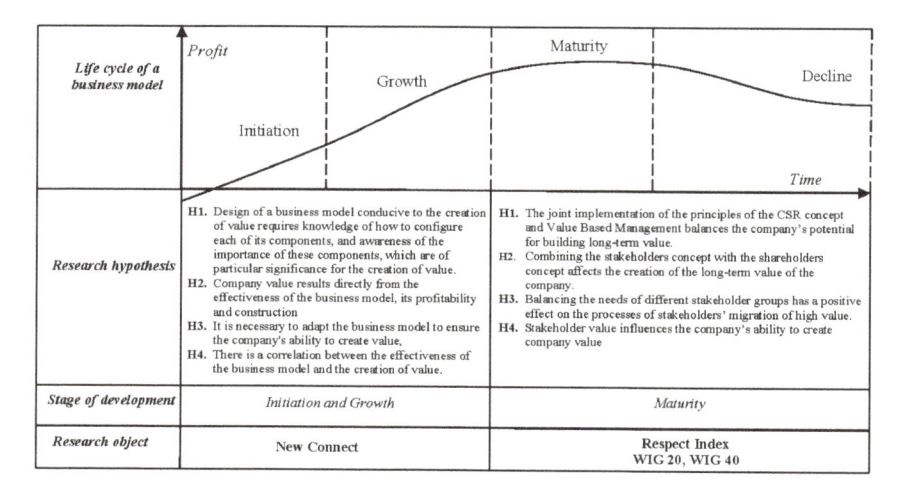

Figure 3. The structure and scope of the study.

7. The Findings of the Research on Business Models at an Early Stage of Development

Reviewing the trends in the Polish economy, the authors concluded that the most appropriate place where people use the idea of the business model is the Warsaw Stock Exchange. The New Connect alternative trading market is significant in the process of designing business models that create value in the initial stages of company development. The market has been operating in Poland since 30 August 2007, and commenced operations in a relatively difficult and deteriorating external environment. Despite the adverse conditions, the growth rate of IPOs (Initial Public Offerings) and the financing of their development was very high, through the market of both private and public offers prior to entry onto the New Connect market and thereafter [67] (p. 5). For the first few years of its operation, the market has produced satisfactory results. The measures of this are that of more than 400 companies listed on New Connect, about 20 companies have moved to the main market since the index was created; issuers in the alternative market have the choice of nearly 100 authorized advisers; the capitalization of all companies listed on New Connect is PLN 9.024 billion; investors may earn as much as 1875% on debut; the record drop in the share value of New Connect-listed companies to date is 99%; and there are three segments of issuers, namely ASO-NCLEAD, the best companies, NC HLR, companies with low liquidity, and NC SHLR, high-risk companies [68] (p. 37). Analyzing the data, it is possible to surmise that New Connect creates research conditions which facilitate a better understanding of the configuration of business models of Polish companies conducive to value creation. An examination of the business models of companies listed on New Connect in the context of the company value criterion is interesting, as such comprehensive studies have not been conducted to date. No recommendations on the development of these business models have been formulated, either.

It can be assumed that the configuration of business models determines their efficiency, and that skillful and rational management multiplies the wealth of investors. Managers of companies listed on New Connect should be aware of the strength of their business models on the path to the creation of value. They should also know the factors determining their design, modification and adjustment aimed at continually multiplying value for shareholders and the company, and should understand the rules affecting the ability to effectively manage business models. A business model is a kind of system which is composed of many elements, a proper configuration of which should facilitate the achievement of the ultimate goal, which is an increase in company value. The originally set goal has been expanded and new objectives have emerged during preliminary research, namely identifying the methods and tools used by the company in terms of monitoring the value creation process, the degree to which the company is results-oriented and the objective of building systems of value-based management.

The main purpose of the research was to assess the development of business models of Polish companies conducive to the creation of their value. In order to verify this relationship, it was necessary to formulate the following partial hypotheses:

The research sample was companies listed on New Connect at the time of conducting the research (desk research: 384 companies on New Connect), quantitative research (a research sample of 48 companies on New Connect) and qualitative research (12 companies selected from among the 384 companies listed on New Connect on 24 May 2012 which met the criteria of representative companies). Two case studies were developed. Research was conducted from November 2011 to May 2012, and research triangulation was applied. In terms of desk research, 384 companies listed on New Connect were studied. The research model adopted ensured the diversity of the research sample in terms of geography and the type of business. Furthermore, it ensured diversity among the business models used. Analysis was conducted based on public documents:

- the information document from the debut on New Connect,
- financial statements,
- financial analyses carried out by brokerage houses, investment houses and banks.

The analysis included an assessment of changes in the quotations of companies on the market. The companies were evaluated on the day of their debut, after 52 weeks of the floating date (if time of operation on the market was less than 52 weeks, its total operating time on New Connect was taken into account), and on the day the research was conducted. Within the framework of the quantitative research, the sample was selected in such a way that the objectives could be achieved. The companies surveyed were capital companies, mainly small- or medium-sized. Analyzing the territorial scope of activities of the surveyed companies, it should be noted that half of them operate on the international market, 37.5% operate on a national scale, while 12.5% only operate regionally. None of the companies operate only locally, which indicates the high potential and innovative character of their product offer. Therefore, the products and services they offer find both a national and international audience. As part of the qualitative analysis of business models, companies that achieved a positive return at the end of 2011 were selected (their rate of return at the end of the period was positive); moreover, the degree to which they fulfilled forecasts specified in the information document was not less than 90%. This criterion was adopted in order to select, out of all companies listed on New Connect, those companies that were the best in terms of the scope of value creation for investors and, at the same time, which demonstrated their effectiveness compared to their forecasts. A representative sample obtained in this way was used to prepare business models that were favorable to value creation. At the end of 2011, 338 companies in total were listed on the New Connect alternative market. During the period from 1 January 2011 to 31 December 2011, only 64 entities achieved a positive return at the end of the period. These companies accounted for only 18.9% of all listed companies. An additional criterion used in the analysis was the price-to-earnings (P/E) ratio and the price-to-book value (P/BV) ratio. The criterion for accepting companies for the research project was the requirement of positive values for both ratios. This additional criterion was fulfilled by 36 companies, accounting for 10.6% of all listed companies at the end of 2011. In particular, the assessment of indicators of the degree to which the net profit assumed in financial forecasts had been achieved was adopted. The indicators were compared with the annual updated rates of return. It was also assumed that the company should have been listed on New Connect for not less than six months—which means that its debut on New Connect was before 1 June 2011. In the original version of the concept of qualitative research on business models, it was assumed that the company should have been listed not less than 12 months prior (*i.e.*, its debut was before 1 January 2011). However, after preparing a sample meeting the proposed criteria, it turned out that only 14 companies fulfilled the criteria. It was agreed that this number was too small to conduct research reliably. Therefore, a decision was taken to accept companies with a shorter period of operation on New Connect. Presence on New Connect, which is characterized by very dynamic changes, for a period of six months, and maintaining investor confidence during this time (expressed in a positive rate of return), can provide a platform for formulating reliable conclusions in terms of the business model configuration, conducive to the process of company value creation. Out of all the companies listed on New Connect, 32 companies (accounting for 9.5% of all the listed companies at the end of 2011) fulfilled all the criteria to be accepted for analysis.

When the percentage share of these companies on New Connect at the end of 2011 was compared to the percentage share of companies examined in the NC Index (NewConnect Index), the total share of 32 companies in the NC Index was obtained, which amounted to 16.9%. The value of the percentage share in the NC Index was almost twice the percentage share in total. This means that the capitalization of New Connect companies meeting the criteria was above average. A total of 12 companies were selected for the qualitative analysis of business models, which accounts for 3.1% of all the companies listed on New Connect at the end of 2011. In order to assess the accuracy of the research sampling, the percentage share of those companies on the New Connect market at the end of 2011 was compared to the percentage share of the NC Index companies. In this way, the quantitative share was compared with the capitalization of companies. The total share of these 12 companies in the NC Index was 6.05%, and the value of the percentage share in the NC Index was almost twice the percentage share of the total. This means that the capitalization of New Connect companies meeting the criteria was above average. Being aware of the limitations resulting from the number of companies approved, they were accepted in terms of conducting the research. All 12 companies selected for qualitative research met the criterion of the degree of at least 90% net profit achieved when compared to that assumed in the financial forecasts (the level of 90% was established based on accepting 10% divergence from the expected result). Two examples were selected for the case study analysis: in the first one, an increase in company value was observed and the business model was not changed, and in the second, financial forecasts were not fulfilled and the business model had to be modified (strong pressure from investors and the Warsaw Stock Exchange Board), which resulted in the company changing its configuration and a significant increase in the share price.

There is no doubt that the business model of a company at an early stage of development is characterized by attributes other than a mature business model. Every company goes through different stages of development, which may change due to the specific nature of the business models. The stages may be as follows: conception, development, commercialization, consolidation, and maturity. At the initial stage of company operation are conception, development and commercialization. A business model should be designed in such a way that, at the expected stage of achievements, a unique combination of resources focuses on the value chain. It is also favorable to take an appropriate position in the value network in order to capture value. Moving from one priority to another in order to create value characterizes the dynamics of the business model. Managers' knowledge of the business model structure and ability to adapt it skillfully develops the ability to create value [2] (pp. 411–412). The configuration of the business model at the initial stage of company development is based on the basic attributes and is supported with management methods and techniques focused on the concept of project management. The simplicity of the business model should be its strength as, when combined with a unique configuration of attributes, it can lead to a company gaining competitive advantage, which can thus create value for shareholders. The research and analysis conducted allowed us to prove the main hypothesis: Company value is created by shaping the configuration of the business model components. All the hypotheses presented in Figure 3 are true. Figure 4 shows the results of research on shaping the business models conducive to the creation of value for companies in the early stages of development (companies listed on New Connect). The numerical values indicate the strength of the correlation between different components and value creation (or destruction). The proposed configuration of the business model components shown in Figure 3 is the result of extensive literature research related to identifying individual components constituting the structure for describing a business model. The final number of components is a result of the reduction of the components that, based on preliminary research, were not considered by respondents to have an impact on the creation of company value. The research findings indicate the components of the business model configuration that are of significance to the process of value creation for shareholders. The most important components include: customer relationships, value proposals for customers and brands, configuration of unique resources, quality of supplier products, and configuration of the value chain. These components of the business model configuration of companies at an early stage of development should be thoroughly evaluated and strengthened in order to increase the value of these companies. The stronger the correlation between the creation of value and the business model component, the bigger the effect on the increasing value. In addition, product and business model innovation increases the chances of creating value for shareholders. Companies whose business models are characterized by higher rates of innovation have a higher price-to-earnings ratio (P/E) and price-to-book value ratio (P/BV). The price-to-book value ratio shows the attractiveness of the business model used, meaning that the company has a business model with the potential for value creation. Companies that build dynamic measurement systems based on the defined key business model components control the company better in order to increase its value. Defined business model components determine the design of the indicators for monitoring company value. Companies that are characterized by the ability to obtain their net income forecasts achieve increased levels of P/E and P/BV as well as higher annual rates of return.

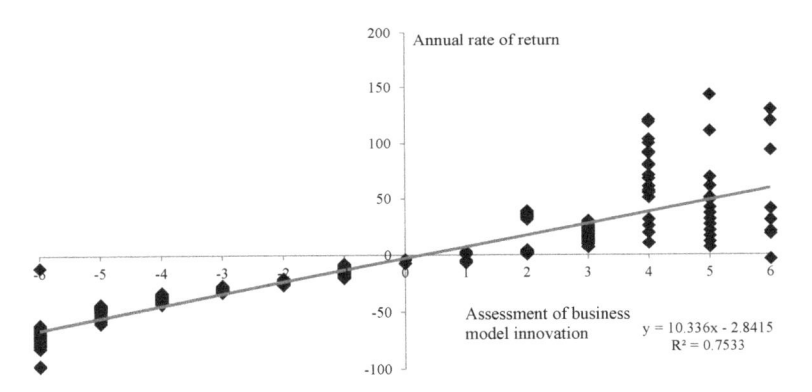

Figure 4. Relationship between a business model and the creation of value (in terms of value for investors)—correlation results [2].

In order to rate the relationship between a business model (described by means of business model innovation and product innovation) and the value of a P/E ratio and to rate the shape and strength between these characteristics, a statistical correlation was calculated.

Figure 4 shows the correlation results. In order to determine whether there is a correlation between a business model and a P/E ratio and, if so, how strong it is, Pearson's correlation coefficient (an unloaded estimate of the correlation coefficient r_{xy}) has been applied; the coefficient measuring the level of a linear relationship between the variables is $r_{xy} = 0.86$ for the variables tested.

The figure of 0.86 indicates that the correlation between a business model and a P/E ratio is strong. In addition, the significance of the correlation was determined by calculating the value of the function t for a correlation coefficient. The number of experimental points equals the number of companies listed on New Connect; it is 24.05.2012 and $n = 384$. We accept the hypothesis H_0, that there is a correlation between a business model and a P/E ratio, and the alternative hypothesis H_1, that there is no correlation between these characteristics. The value of the t-statistic, which has a Student's t distribution is $t = 1.9$. The level of significance is $\alpha = 0.05$ (standard for the population). We calculate a probability of $p = 0.07$. Since $p > \alpha$, we accept the null hypothesis, and we reject the possible alternative hypothesis—there is a correlation between the studied characteristics. (see Table 2).

Table 2. Relationship between a business model and the creation of value (in terms of value for investors) [2].

Statistical Value	Business Model/Value Creation
Pearson's r	0.86
Coefficient of determination R^2	0.7789
n	384

Figure 4 shows the data from the 384 companies listed on New Connect with a price-to-earnings ratio and the ranking of the attractiveness of business models in terms of an innovation criterion. It turns out that many companies have a high P/E ratio at a high ranking of the attractiveness of their business model, while conversely, a low ranking in terms of the attractiveness of a business model occurs in the case of many companies with a low or even negative P/E ratio. Therefore, it can be concluded that a price/earnings ratio is a good measure of business model attractiveness and can, in the long term, be used as an indicator thereof.

The result indicates that if we assume that a business model is effective when the degree of financial targets for the future in relation to the pursued strategy is at least 90%, a strong correlation, obtained as a result of research, between the extent to which the forecast net profit is achieved and an updated annual rate of return proves the relationship between a business model and an increase in value. It is possible to select such business models that enable the implementation of both forecasts and the achievement of positive returns.

To rate the relationship between business model components and an increase in company value (rated based on the answers chosen by managers in the survey), values of the mode, the median, and the arithmetic mean were determined for the factors studied. (see Table 3)

Table 3. Impact of business model components on an increase in value [2].

The Most Significant Business Model Component	Mode	Median	Arithmetic Mean	Standard Deviation
the customer	5	5	4.2771	1.0215
value proposition for the customer	5	4	4.1023	0.9586
competitive strategy	5	4	4.0448	0.9753
position in the value network	4	4	4.0089	0.9981
logic of generating income	5	4	3.9213	1.0269
organization of internal suppliers and their key capabilities	4	4	3.5474	1.4077

All business model components were then analyzed in terms of the influence of individual components from the subsystem on the business model (see Table 4). The following factors were rated:

- the customer,
- value proposition for the customer,
- logic of generating income,
- organization of internal suppliers and their key capabilities,
- competitive strategy,
- position in the value network.

The value of the t-statistic, which has a Student's t distribution, is $t = 2.01$. The level of significance is $\alpha = 0.05$ (standard for this population). We calculate the probability of $p = 0.06$. Since $p > \alpha$ we accept the null hypothesis, and reject the alternative hypothesis—there is the correlation between the studied criteria.

Table 4. Impact of business model components on the creation of value [2].

Component	Statistical Significance α	Pearson	Coefficients of Determination R^2	Relationship
Customer	0.05	0.81	0.77	Very strong
Value proposition for the customer	0.05	0.84	0.66	Very strong
Logic of generating income	0.05	0.74	0.64	Strong
Organization of internal suppliers	0.05	0.69	0.71	Strong
Type of strategy pursued	0.05	0.72	0.71	Strong
Position in the value network	0.05	0.73	0.79	Strong
Configuration of the value chain	0.05	0.82	0.56	Very strong

The test for the significance of the correlation coefficient proves the relationship between the studied criteria. The correlation is significant and strong, as indicated by the low probability coefficient. Correlations are statistically significant (at the level of $p < 0.1$).

The most important stakeholders are located by their impact on the value of the company and their importance for achieving long-term value.

By analogy, it is possible to adjust business models to market leaders (business model benchmarking). (see Figure 5).

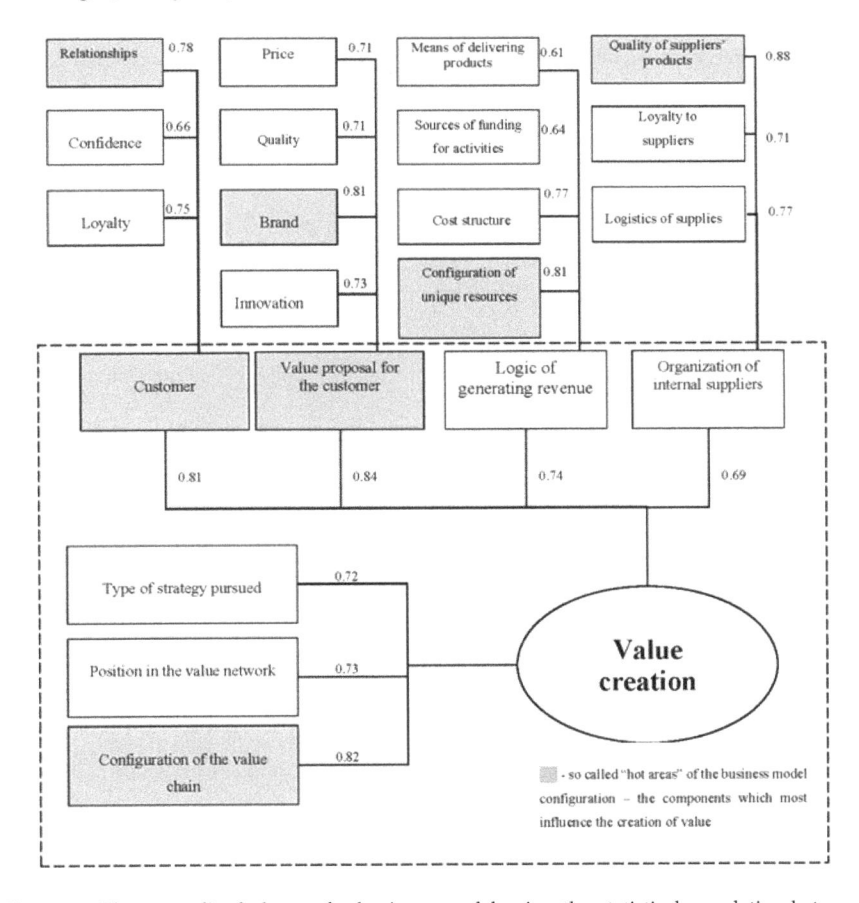

Figure 5. The generalized shape of a business model using the statistical correlation between components which ensure the creation of value for shareholders [2] (p. 337).

By making dynamic changes in the configuration of the business model, it is possible to adjust it to develop the ability to create value. The results have been analyzed based on this assumption.

Research and analysis conducted on business models of companies at an early stage of development in the context of activity on the capital market have allowed us to draw the following conclusions:

(1) Referring to the review of the relevant literature on business models and value-based management, a theoretical configuration of business models was developed. The results indicate that a business model should be a unique form of resources focused on the value chain. It is also favorable to take an appropriate position in the value network in order to capture value. Moving from one priority to another in order to create value characterizes the dynamics of the business model. Managers' knowledge of the business model structure and its skillful adaptation develops the ability to create value.

(2) Based on the research, the importance of the impact of individual components of the business model on company value was determined. The results allowed us to build a business model structure that indicates what the optimal configuration of the efficient and effective business model should be like. The main components were identified, which include the value proposition for the customer, the customer himself and the configuration of the value chain. The key subsystems of these components were also specified, which indicate what configuration, from among those proposed in the theoretical model, works best for managers, in the context of the criterion of company value. These include: in the area of the customer, relationships; in the value proposition for the customer, brand and innovation; in the area of revenue generation logic, the configuration of unique resources; in the area of organization of internal suppliers, the quality of provided services. The model presents the link between the components and their impact on the configuration of the business model conducive to the creation of value. The structure of a business model which is favorable to the creation of value should be consistent and should include the above-mentioned priorities. It depends highly on the configuration of the value chain.

(3) The analysis of the correlation of the degree to which the financial forecasts of net profit described in the annual information documents are fulfilled with the updated rates of return of companies listed on New Connect showed a high correlation coefficient at 0.79. If we assume that the efficiency of the business model is verified by the fulfillment of forecasts, the hypothesis that there is a relationship between the business model and the value increase can be proved. Business model configuration management aims to improve its effectiveness, including the fulfillment of expected forecasts, favors the creation of value and is verified with the values of return rates. Fulfilling forecasts, or failing to do so, significantly affects return rates.

(4) In order to assess the factors affecting the rate of company value growth, 23 factors were determined, of which the factors that are most important to New Connect companies include:

   (a) relationships with customers,
   (b) a full understanding of customer needs,
   (c) the ability to create unique value for the customer which is not offered by competitors.

(5) Having analyzed a designed portfolio of business model innovation and product innovation, it was concluded that as many as 63% of all companies listed on New Connect are characterized neither by an innovative business model nor by innovative products, which significantly affects the performance of these companies and, at the same time, their market value.

(6) Companies which were characterized by both innovative business models and innovative products, recognized as models of this market, accounted for only 10% of the New Connect index. If one looks at this phenomenon positively, in the future one in 10 companies on New Connect may, through capital gained on New Connect, build the elite class of companies changing the rules of the game in the sectors in which they operate.

(7) Comparing two extreme sets (the first characterized by an innovative business model and innovative products—only 10% of the companies surveyed; the second, characterized by an

unimaginative business model and products—63% of companies), the result is not promising. It is necessary to verify either the potential of the business model component configuration of these companies, or specify stricter criteria for floating on the New Connect market, which should include elements of innovation.

(8) During further research on the issue of whether there is a relationship between the business model and company value, it was concluded that there is a very strong correlation between the business model evaluated according to the criteria of innovation and the price/earnings ratio, at a figure of 0.86. The correlation between the degree to which financial forecasts of net profit are fulfilled and the average updated annual rate of return is strong and stands at 0.79. The results obtained give a strong message to theoreticians and practitioners of management that investment in innovation and diligent work towards fulfilling financial forecasts translate into the strong creation of value.

(9) There is strong pressure from investors and the board of the Warsaw Stock Exchange to ensure that the forecasts published by the companies are reliable, as this significantly affects the modification of business models used by these companies.

The results presented show that the principles of sustainability as regards the companies at an early stage of development and with respect to incorporating them into the genotype of business models of companies at an early stage of development are used inconsistently and only selectively. The situation is different for mature companies where sustainability is regarded as a value driver.

8. Research Findings on Business Models at the Mature Stage of Development

In conducting research on sustainable business models, the main hypothesis and 11 auxiliary hypotheses were proposed. The main hypothesis is that: the joint realization of the concepts of corporate social responsibility and value-based management affects the balance of the company's potential and how (and whether) the needs of different groups of stakeholders are fulfilled, which, as a result, translates into an increase in the long-term value of the company.

In the research conducted, in order to prove the proposed hypotheses, the principles of triangulation were used. The methodological triangulation applied covered three types of research: quantitative research, qualitative research and research based on the expert method.

The main objective of the research was to create a holistic sustainable business model contributing to building the long-term value of a socially responsible company. The scope of the research covered companies currently listed on the Warsaw Stock Exchange, on the following stock indexes: WIG20, WIG40, WIGdiv, Respect Index, New Connect Lead and companies participating in the "Environmentally Friendly Company" competition; 128 companies that adhered to the principles of corporate social responsibility with a strong theme of environmental responsibility participated in the first stage of the research, on the analysis of the results of the "Environmentally Friendly Company" ecology competition. In the second phase, survey questionnaires were sent to 100 companies listed on the Polish Stock Market Respect Index, WIG20, WIG40, WIGdiv and NewConnect Lead. In the first part, the companies completed a self-assessment questionnaire and underwent a competition audit, while in the second part, research surveys (questionnaires) were sent to the companies that voluntarily self-assessed by completing the questionnaires. The return rate was 44%, which is a satisfactory result. The research sample was selected so that it would fulfill the objectives included in the subject of the paper. The selection of the Respect Index companies, which included companies operating in accordance with best practices in information governance, corporate governance, investor relationships, CSR policy, environmental management, personnel policy, and management systems, aimed to receive answers from companies which consciously follow the principles of corporate social responsibility. The Respect Index companies satisfy the strict requirements of corporate social responsibility, pursue corporate responsibility strategies, or follow an orderly plan of action in terms of company social responsibility/sustainable development. This strategy is created based on business objectives, taking into account the key risks (specific and industry) and results from the need to examine the needs and expectations of significant stakeholder groups. It is pursued on the basis of the schedule adopted and performance measures (results, benefits). The Respect Index is an index of socially responsible companies in Central and Eastern Europe, which includes companies from the main market of the Warsaw Stock Exchange in its portfolio and is one of the indicators that builds their credibility in the eyes of investors. A key element of the business model of the Respect Index companies is an increase in their value, taking into account the principles of corporate social responsibility and the needs of stakeholders.

Questionnaires were also sent to the largest listed companies, that is WSE WIG20 and WIG40 companies, in order to examine these companies in terms of the application of corporate social responsibility and value-based management principles. To fully supplement the sample so that it met the criteria related to all hypotheses assumed, a survey questionnaire was also sent to WIGdiv companies, which is the revenue index (dividends and subscription rights taken into account). WIGdiv comprises the largest companies with high liquidity, which regularly pay dividends to shareholders. The index also includes certain WIG20 companies. The selection of companies in the index was determined by the specific character of these companies, namely that their business model is based on generating profit and regularly paying dividends to shareholders, and focuses on observing the rules of so-called sustainable dividends, which are consistent with the principles of sustainable business. Due to the fact that there is an important correlation between the adopted company business model and its stock index, companies of this index are also included in the research sample.

On the other hand, engagement in corporate social responsibility was also important in the selection of companies. Research was also conducted on 128 companies participating in the Environmentally Friendly Company ecology competition, which promoted the principles of environmental responsibility and sustainable development by creating effective strategies built on ecological criteria.

The research was extended further with the qualitative analysis of 10 companies whose profiles matched the companies from the area of quantitative research, *i.e.*, Respect Index, WIG20, WIG40, WIGdiv and New Connect Lead companies. Ten joint-stock companies were selected, all of which implement corporate social responsibility principles in order to increase competitive advantage and build long-term value. At the same time, these companies, in addition to fulfilling the criteria of ecological responsibility, met the fuller and broader criteria of corporate social responsibility.

The selection of the research sample was as follows:

To achieve the main objective of the study related to the achievement of the expected and assumed state, which is developing a holistic model of sustainable business contributing to building long-term value of a socially responsible company, surveys as well as expert studies were conducted using an evaluation questionnaire and analytical studies of existing documents related to the Respect Index stock exchange. A research criterion for choosing research companies was developed, and the analysis was conducted in terms of both subjective and objective criteria. As regards the subjective criterion, all forms of business activity in Polish legislation were analyzed: sole traders, partnerships, general partnerships, other partnerships, corporations (limited liability companies, joint stock companies). As far as an objective criterion is concerned, after reviewing the literature and business practices, evaluation criteria were defined that aim to properly select the profiles of the companies surveyed. These criteria include: company valuation (a company is subjected to valuation), the pattern of management "best practices" (it may be considered that the adopted management mechanisms, and the degree to which modern management methods and concepts are used, exceed standards in the Polish economy), a minimum market presence of 10 years (the maturity stage in business—in the author's opinion, a minimum 10-year presence in the market indicates that the company wants to continue its business activity, develop, gain competitive advantage, ensure business continuity and build the long-term value of the company), the principles of corporate governance are fulfilled (a company wants to operate in accordance with the standards of corporate governance, wants to conduct direct and indirect dialogue with shareholders through their representatives in the supervisory board of the company, wants to seek the most effective forms of communication, dialogue and relationships to achieve satisfactory performance), social responsibility is observed (a company which fulfills the principles of corporate social responsibility and includes them in the principles of doing business, wants to balance the interests of major groups of stakeholders and wishes to observe the law, follow core values, care for the environment, and generate profits for shareholders by building an organizational culture that helps achieve this goal), functions in various sectors of the economy and services (companies operate in different sectors, therefore the picture of the study will have a cross-sectoral dimension and the solutions developed during the study and the design of a business model have a chance to be applied in various sectors of the economy and services). (see Tables 5 and 6)

Table 5. Legal form of the winners of the three previous editions of the "Environmentally Friendly Company" (FBŚ) competition from 2006–2008 [3].

Legal Form	FBŚ 2006	FBŚ 2007	FBŚ 2008	Legal Form—FBŚ 2006–2008
Joint-stock company	7	16	17	40
Limited Liability Company	22	28	25	75
General Partnership	2	1	1	4
Other	4	3	2	9
Total	35	48	45	128

Table 6. Type of business activity of the winners of the three previous editions of the "Environmentally Friendly Company" (FBŚ) competition from 2006, 2007 and 2008 [3].

Type of Activity	FBŚ 2006	FBŚ 2007	FBŚ 2008	Type of Activity—FBŚ 2006–2008
Production	11	13	12	36
Services	14	22	21	57
Trade	1	1	2	4
Production and services	5	5	6	16
Production and trade	1	2	1	4
Production, services, trade	1	3	2	6
Trade and services	2	2	1	5
Total	35	48	45	128

8.1. The Company's Business Model Based on Fulfilling the Assumptions of the Concept of Corporate Social Responsibility

Companies' application of the assumptions of the concept of corporate social responsibility has its own internal reference because it is based on ethical principles within the organization, that on the one hand affect decision-making systems, and on the other hand the external environment of the company, shaping its social dimension and image in the market. The conscious application of CSR assumptions was the first area studied of the activity of companies that agreed to take part in research. (see Table 7)

Table 7. Impact of organizational cultures based on social responsibility and value-based management—statistical values [3].

Statistical Value	Value
Pearson	0.6599
Coefficient of determination R^2	0.4355
n	44.00

Figure 6 shows the correlation results. In order to determine whether the assumed correlation between organizational cultures based on CSR and VBM exists and whether it is strong, Pearson's coefficient was applied to the values (unloaded estimate of the correlation coefficient r_{xy}); it is a coefficient determining the level of a linear relationship between the variables. The calculated coefficient is $r_{xy} = 0.66$.

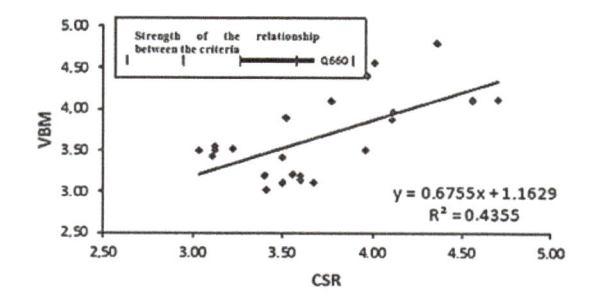

Figure 6. A graph showing the impact of organizational cultures based on social responsibility and value-based management [3].

It can be inferred from the calculation that the relationship is strong, but its significance is determined by the results of the t-test for the correlation coefficient. The number of experimental points is $n = 44$. We accept the null hypothesis H_0, that there is a correlation between CSR criteria and VBM, and the alternative hypothesis H_1, that there is no correlation between the criteria.

The value of the t-statistic, which has a Student's t distribution is $t = 2.3$. The level of significance is $\alpha = 0.05$ (standard for this population). We calculate the probability of $p = 0.06$. Since $p > \alpha$, we accept the null hypothesis, and therefore we reject the possible alternative hypothesis—there is a correlation between the studied factors.

The test for the significance of the correlation coefficient proved the relationship between organizational culture criteria based on social responsibility and value-based management. The correlation is significant and strong, as indicated by the low coefficient of probability. Correlations were statistically significant ($p < 0.1$).

Subsequently, a statistical relationship between corporate social responsibility and balancing the potential of the company was calculated, as well as between value-based management factors and balancing its potential. In order to determine whether a correlation exists and, if so, the strength thereof, Pearson's coefficient was applied to the values (unloaded estimate of the correlation coefficient r_{xy}); it is a coefficient determining the level of a linear relationship between the variables. The results of the calculations are presented in the table below (Table 8).

Table 8. Impact of organizational cultures based on social responsibility and value-based management on balancing the potential of the company [3].

Statistical Value	CSR/Sustainability	VBM/Sustainability
Pearson	0.409	0.508
Coefficients of determination R^2	0.17	0.26
n	44.00	44.00

For the correlation between the factors of social responsibility and balancing the potential of the company, the statistical value t is adopted, which has a Student's t distribution $t = 2.01$. The level of significance is $\alpha = 0.05$ (standard for this population). We calculate the probability of $p = 0.054$. Since $p > \alpha$, we accept the null hypothesis, and we reject the possible alternative hypothesis—there is a correlation between the studied factors.

For the correlation between the factors of value-based management and balancing the potential of the company, the statistical value t is adopted, which has a Student's t distribution $t = 2.01$. The level of significance is $\alpha = 0.05$ (standard for this population). We calculate the probability of $p = 0.054$. Since $p > \alpha$, we accept the null hypothesis, and we reject the possible alternative hypothesis—there is a correlation between the studied factors.

It can be inferred that there is no basis to reject the research hypothesis H_3, which says that the joint use of the concepts of corporate social responsibility (CSR) and value-based management (VBM) balances the potentials of the company.

Research clearly shows that most of the companies have an organizational culture based on organizational behavior deeply embedded in the joint implementation of the principles of corporate social responsibility and value-based management. The companies surveyed want to apply the principles of sustainable development and growth aimed at long-term functioning and continuous profit generation, limiting the possibility of uncontrolled risks and building a positive relationship with the environment. The value of the company depends on the skill of balancing its potentials (balancing a company's internal factors).

The most important elements of an organizational equilibrium concept are associated with the driving forces behind a sustainable business model and can be synthetically presented in the following relationships with sustainability related to:

- material balance (expressed as the strength of the economic sustainability of the company) and social balance (expressed as the strength of the conscious application of the principles of corporate social responsibility);
- internal balance, related to the strength of balancing the company's internal processes, and external balance, expressed as the strength of stakeholders.

As well as sustainability instruments related to:

- Strategy expressed as the strength of implementing a sustainable strategy based on the principles of a balanced scorecard.
- Procedures related to the strength of the management style based on the logic of conscious decision-making.
- Culture expressed as the strength of the conscious application of the principles of corporate governance.
- Structure expressed as the strength of a consensual relationship between company management, shareholders, stakeholders.

In order to test the strength of the relationships, the correlation between sustainability and sustainability instruments was analyzed. Balance has a material and social, internal and external dimension. Organizational balance (material, social) is based on the mutual adaptation of intraorganizational relationships and the relationship between the organization and the environment in a manner that satisfies the criteria of balance. It is associated with the strength of the conscious application of the principles of corporate social responsibility and the strength of economic sustainability.

Social imbalance is expressed primarily in the reduction of activities for the organization and the delegitimization of the organization and its activities in the environment; companies then reduce their commitment to social responsibility.

Material imbalance is expressed as reducing the economic efficiency of operations and reducing material resources provided by the organization environment. Thus, the strength of economic sustainability, related to value-based management (VBM), becomes an element requiring improvement.

Imbalance provides both a stimulus for change and innovation, transferring the imbalance to other areas, as well as for actions to regain balance and to re-define the company's criteria. The company has a number of sustainability instruments. The research examined sustainability instruments such as developing a strategy, procedures, programs, budgets, formal business structures, operating rules, procedures and systems, and organizational cultures, which aim to ensure organizational performance—this is expressed as the strength of the management style based on the logic of conscious decision-making.

The strength of the relationship between sustainability and sustainability instruments is related to the harmony between the four basic areas of balance—material, social, external and internal—where conflicts and contradictions may occur between balance requirements.

In order to determine whether there is a correlation between sustainability and sustainability instruments and, if so, whether it is strong, Pearson's coefficient (an unloaded estimate of the correlation coefficient r_{xy}) was applied to the values; it is a coefficient determining the level of a linear relationship between the variables. The calculated coefficient is $r_{xy} = 0.659$ (Table 9).

Table 9. Impact of organizational cultures based on social responsibility and value-based management—statistical values [3].

Statistical Value	Value
Pearson	0.659
Coefficient of determination R^2	0.511
n	44.00

Based on the calculation, it can be inferred that the relationship is strong, but its significance is determined by the results of a correlation coefficient t-test. The number of experimental points is $n = 44$. We accept the null hypothesis H_0, that there is a correlation between CSR and VBM criteria, and the alternative hypothesis H_1, that there is no correlation between the criteria.

The value of the t-statistic, which has Student's t distribution, is $t = 1.95$. The level of significance is $\alpha = 0.05$ (standard for this population). We calculate the probability of $p = 0.06$. Since $p > \alpha$, we accept the null hypothesis and we reject the possible alternative hypothesis—there is a correlation between the studied factors.

The test for the significance of the correlation coefficient proved the relationship between sustainability and sustainability instruments. This correlation is significant and strong, as indicated by the low probability coefficient. Correlations are statistically significant ($p < 0.1$).

Due to the fact that the selection of factors for the individual balance and sustainability components depends entirely on the market situational context, managers choose the most valuable current factors out of the package of corporate social responsibility and value-based management factors, which guarantee that the forecasted results are achieved in a defined time interval. This is in fact the creation of a sustainable business model that can be applied in various sectors of the economy. From this perspective, we talk about a cross-sectoral holistic sustainable business model. (see Table 10).

Trust has the greatest impact on value and sales growth in the company, and the least impact on investment in the company's working capital, as well as on investment in the company's fixed capital—the average weight of this factor is 4.3 (on a scale of 1 to 5). Corporate image and brand awareness have the greatest impact on the company's competitive advantage, and the least impact on investment in working capital, as well as on the company's fixed capital—the average weight of this factor is 3.9 (on a scale of 1 to 5). Competency—the average weight of this factor is 3.9 (on a scale of 1 to 5)—has the greatest impact on sales growth in the company and the company's competitive advantage, and the least impact on investment in the company's working and fixed capital. The principles of corporate governance have the greatest impact on the company's competitive advantage, and the least impact on two factors: investment in the company's working capital and investment in fixed capital—the average weight of this factor is 4.4 (on a scale of 1 to 5). Customer relationships have the greatest impact on sales growth and the company's competitive advantage. This factor has the least impact on investment in working capital and fixed capital—the average weight of this factor is 4.6 (on a scale of 1 to 5). The network of stakeholders has the greatest impact on sales growth and the company's competitive advantage. It has the least impact on operating profit margins, investment in working capital and fixed capital—the average weight of this factor is 4.6 (on a scale of 1 to 5). Company resources have the greatest impact on investment in working capital and investment in fixed capital, and the least impact on the company's value—the average weight of this factor is 4.3 (on a scale of 1 to 5). Social capital has the greatest impact on value and sales growth in the company, as well as the company's competitive advantage, while it has the least impact on investment in the company's fixed capital—the average weight of this factor is 3.4 (on a scale of 1 to 5). Customer relationships and the network of stakeholders are factors with the greatest impact in most areas. Expressed values, environmental products/services, and social capital are the least significant factors.

Table 10. Strength of the impact of factors [3].

	Mean Score						
	Has the Greatest Impact on Value	Has the Greatest Impact on Sales Growth in the Company	Has the Greatest Impact on the Company's Operating Profit	Has the Greatest Impact on Investment in the Company's Working Capital	Has the Greatest Impact on Investment in the Company's Fixed Capital	Has the Greatest Impact on the Company's Competitive Advantage	Mean Score
Trust	4.7	4.7	4.2	3.8	3.8	4.4	4.3
Corporate image and brand awareness	4.1	4.2	3.8	3.6	3.6	4.3	3.9
Competency	4.0	4.1	3.8	3.6	3.6	4.1	3.9
Principles of corporate governance	4.6	4.5	4.3	4.0	4.0	4.7	4.4
Customer relationships	4.8	5.0	4.6	4.1	4.1	5.0	4.6
Network of stakeholders	4.6	4.8	4.5	4.5	4.5	4.8	4.6
Company assets	4.1	4.3	4.3	4.5	4.5	4.2	4.3
Social capital	3.7	3.7	3.4	3.0	2.9	3.7	3.4

8.2. Research on the Fulfillment of the Needs of Different Groups of Stakeholders

In order to determine whether there is a correlation between balancing the needs of stakeholders and their migration processes and whether it is strong, Pearson's coefficient (an unloaded estimate of the correlation coefficient r_{xy}) was applied to these values; it is a coefficient determining the level of a linear relationship between the variables. The calculated coefficient is r_{xy} = 0.719. (see Table 11)

Table 11. Impact of organizational cultures based on social responsibility value-based management—statistical values [3].

Statistical Value	Value
Pearson	0.719
Coefficient of determination R^2	0.511
n	44.00

On the basis of the calculation it can be inferred that the achieved relationship is strong, but the significance of the correlation is determined by the results of a t-test for the correlation coefficient. The number of experimental points is n = 44. We accept the null hypothesis H_o, that there is a correlation between the criteria, and the alternative hypothesis H_1, that there is no correlation between the criteria.

The rating of the impact of the various stakeholder groups gathered around the organization on the value of the company is presented in Table 12. The results clearly indicate that the group of stakeholders that have the greatest impact (average above 4.51) on the value of the company are shareholders, followed by customers.

Table 12. Rating of the impact of the various stakeholder groups gathered around the organization on the value of the company [1].

	Mean Score													
	Impact on the Value of the Company?	Impact on Sales Growth?	Impact on Operating Profit Margins?	Impact on Investment in Working Capital?	Impact on Investment in Fixed Capital?	Impact on the Company's Cost of Capital?	Impact on the Efficiency of Enterprise Income Tax?	Impact on the Company's Competitive Advantage?	Which Stakeholder Demands the Most from the Company?	Impact on the Value of the Company	Profit from the Relationship with the Company?	Impact on the Company and Financial Results of the Company?	Impact on Business and the Company's Financial Performance? The Most Risky in terms of the Impact of the Risk on the Value of the Company?	The Greatest Ability to Reach a Compromise with the Company?	Mean Score
Shareholders, stockholders	4.88	4.88	5.00	4.8	4.9	4.8	4.89	4.79	4.89	4.8	4.99	4.56	3.79	3.48	4.68
Customers	4.7	4.89	4.9	4.1	5	4.9	4.9	4.36	5.00	5.00	4.98	4.56	4.88	3.49	4.67
Allies	4.31	4.35	4.39	4.29	4.01	4.56	3.89	4.21	4.31	4.01	4.78	4.56	3.79	2.79	4.16
Co-operators	3.88	4.11	4.22	4.39	4.13	4.27	4.55	4.52	4.31	4.01	4.29	3.99	3.79	3.51	4.14
Financial institutions, lenders	4.33	4.01	4.79	4.33	4.51	4.27	4.01	4.11	4.28	4.28	4.31	3.65	2.89	3.54	4.09
Employees	3.83	4.98	3.98	3.1	4.04	4.16	4.04	4.88	4.16	4.04	3.55	3.88	4.04	3.55	4.02
Board	3.98	4.04	4.15	4.24	4.14	4.04	3.99	3.1	3.55	4.01	3.99	3.1	3.05	4.1	3.82
Media	3.79	3.99	3.79	4.01	3.87	4.1	3.79	4.2	3.98	4.01	4.14	4.01	3.14	2.1	3.78
Government, state institutions	3.51	3.1	3.89	3.56	3.01	3.33	3.01	3.36	3.01	3.46	3.26	3.09	2.24	1.88	3.12
Suppliers	3.21	3.21	3.16	3.12	3.21	2.98	3.04	3.04	3.16	3.04	2.88	2.49	2.32	3.32	3.01
Local government institutions	3.02	2.8	3.4	3.26	3.15	3	2.89	2.9	3.2	3.16	3.1	3.01	2.55	1.8	2.95
Competitors	3.03	3.05	3.1	2.66	3.51	3.11	2.91	2.7	2.51	3.14	1.69	3.01	2.51	1.79	2.77
Business support organizations, chambers of commerce	2.28	2.6	2.1	2.55	2.13	2.16	2.56	2.98	2.71	2.66	3.21	2.25	2.55	3.2	2.59
Charities, sports, cultural organizations	2.11	2.15	2.02	2.36	2.56	2.1	1.9	1.89	2.11	2.15	2.22	2.14	2.5	1.5	2.12
National, international society	1.99	1.89	2.01	2.05	2.15	2.01	2.15	2.14	1.97	1.89	2.4	2.22	2.04	1.49	2.03

8.3. The Application of a Sustainable Dividend Policy

In order to ensure the company's liquidity and profitability today and in the future, companies pay a profit in the form of dividends, which are also sustainable: the allocation of one-third of the dividends to increase the company's equity in order to increase business credibility, also by increasing its debt-raising capacity; the allocation of one-third of the dividends for investments in tangible and intangible capital; and the allocation of one-third of the dividends for consumption by the company shareholders, who are the primary donors of cash for the development and growth of the organization and expect satisfactory return on capital employed in the reference period they establish.

It results in significant value added, arising from the application of the principles of social responsibility, and includes a financial dividend to shareholders paid in a sustainable manner and a social dividend, the beneficiaries of which are all company stakeholders.

A sustainable business model has been presented based on proving the hypotheses, as shown in Figure 5.

All the hypotheses are true. Quantitative research has been combined with qualitative research, which was supplemented with expert analysis. Methodological triangulation has been applied, *i.e.*, the use of many methods to examine a single issue. Raw data from empirical research has been used by means of a survey questionnaire as well as secondary data from analyzing the stock exchange and documents drawn up by companies related to applying the principles of corporate governance. The result of the research is a sustainable business model built on the basis of seven driving forces with marked correlations between its elements, between which the interactions occur. A holistic sustainable business model (Figure 5) shows the key statistical links that have particularly important implications for building the long-term value of the company. The correlations between variables (empirical research findings using questionnaires) that are considered important have been shown. The model is the result of empirical research with respect to the selected variables. The variables form the shape of relationships between determinants describing an eclectic sustainable business model. Not all variables correlate with other variables—only those that are important for building the long-term value of the company have been shown.

On the basis of the above design of a sustainable business model, its new definition has been developed using the proven hypotheses. The numbers in the figure indicate the statistical relationships between the different components of the proposed sustainable business model for mature companies. Where there are no numerical values, the relationship has not been studied and only the cause and effect relationships have been shown as it is necessary to show them for the applied holistic approach. A sustainable business model building the long-term value of a socially responsible company is the model built by the joint use of the corporate social responsibility and value-based management concepts which ensures that the needs of shareholders and other stakeholder groups are fulfilled through a skillful balancing of the company's potential towards generating value allocated in a sustainable way, enabling the continuity of company management.

A sustainable business model is a hybrid model, *i.e.*, a model built in the subject-object system. Components of this model include entities centered on the company, forming relationships, influencing the company value drivers and strategic factors connected with the theory of corporate social responsibility, value-based management, the theory of stakeholders and the theory of shareholders functioning in the mutual relationship based on the principles of sustainability. (see Figure 7).

This model is a holistic model of reduced nature, which could be applied in different sectors of the economy, treated as a subsystem of the entire ecosystem. This means that this model and its design are included in the middle-range theory. While determining the strategic options of the companies surveyed, enabling the design of an effective sustainable business model, boundary conditions which were defined in the course of constructing a 3S (Synergy, Symbiosis, Symmetry) triangle and DSB (Durability, Sustainability, Balance) triangle must be specified.

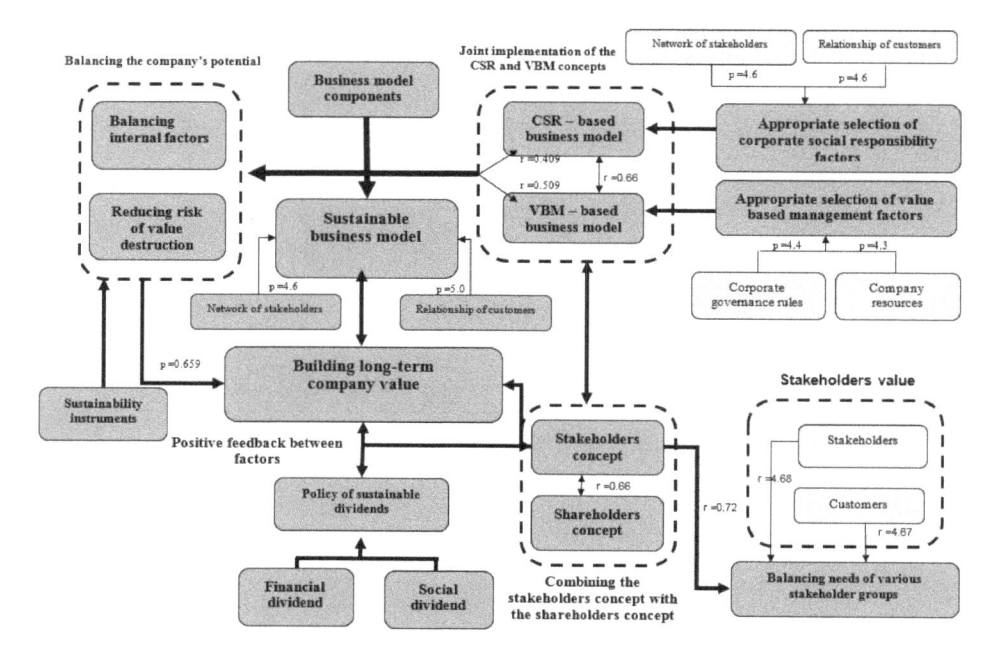

Figure 7. A holistic sustainable business model by A. Jabłoński [3] (p. 401).

The following are the definitions of the various elements of the triangle:

(1) Synergy—the joint use of corporate social responsibility and value-based management concepts, strengthening the company's financial and competitive strength, aimed at building its long-term value.
(2) Symbiosis—the co-existence of stakeholders gathered around the company, which excludes the uncontrolled loss of the value of certain stakeholders for the benefit of other stakeholders.
(3) Symmetry—the mutual, systematic development of the individual components of the company's potential, while maintaining the ability to move towards higher value inherent in the market and its stakeholder.
(4) Durability—the relationship between the strength of a consensual relationship between company management, shareholders, and stakeholders, and the strength of the conscious application of the principles of corporate governance.
(5) Balance—the relationship between the strength of the economic sustainability of the company, and the strength of balancing the intellectual capital of the company.
(6) Sustainability—the relationship between the strength of the conscious application of the principles of corporate social responsibility, and the strength of stakeholder value and the dynamics of their migration processes.

Below are presented key recommendation:

(1) As there is no clear definition and understanding of the concept of sustainability, the authors have developed their own definition of sustainability based on durability, sustainability and balance.
(2) Analyzing the behavior of companies based on research, making observations and reviewing the relevant literature, the authors have constructed a 3S triangle based on synergy, symbiosis and symmetry.
(3) In the DSB triangle, a balance point has been defined, located at the intersection of three triangle diagonals, understood as a place where the definition of sustainability in business developed by the authors is fully utilized.
(4) In the 3S triangle, a balance point has been defined, located at the intersection of three triangle diagonals, understood as a place where the principles of synergy, symbiosis and symmetry are fully used to build the long-term value of the company by means of the concept of sustainability.
(5) Overlaying two triangles on each other along with the results of the statistical analyses resulting from the research allowed the authors to determine the strategic options of the companies surveyed, which enabled the efficient design of a sustainable business model.
(6) From among the strategic options of the company presented, they choose the option which is the best, in their opinion, from the point of view of resources, business life cycle, and market relationships. (see Figure 8)

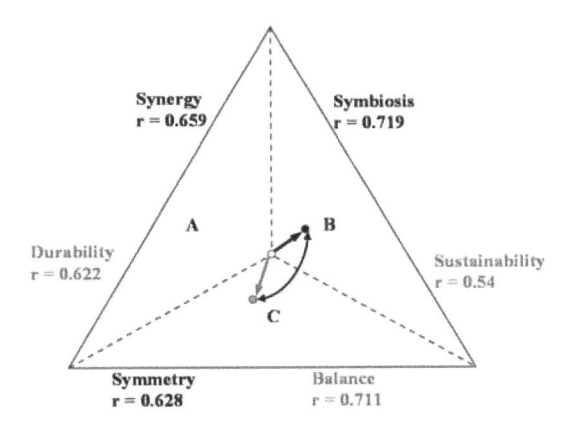

Figure 8. The imbalance gap between the 3S triangle and DSB triangle parameters by A. Jabłoński [3], (p. 393).

When the triangles overlap and are analyzed, a new triangle, which the authors call a SS (sustainability strength) triangle, is formed. In the SS triangle, the position of two points deviated from the balance point—red for the deviation from balance in the 3S triangle and green in the DSB triangle—is essential to determine the appropriate strategic options for the company. Table 2 shows the possible strategic options for the position of these points in the SS triangle. (see Table 13)

Table 13. Possible strategic options for the positions of points of deviation from balance by A. Jabłoński [3] (p. 391–392).

No.	Deviation in the 3S Triangle	Deviation in the DSB Triangle	Description of the System
1	A—Synergy	A—Durability	A relationship between corporate social responsibility and value-based management in terms of balancing the company's potential (the joint use of the concepts of corporate social responsibility and value-based management reinforcing the financial and competitive strength of the company aiming to build its long-term value), strengthened by applying the principles of durability, that is the relationship between the strength of a consensual relationship of a company's board, shareholders, and stakeholders, and the strength of the conscious application of corporate governance principles.
2	A—Synergy	B—Sustainability	A relationship between corporate social responsibility and value-based management in terms of balancing the company's potential (the joint use of the concepts of corporate social responsibility and value-based management reinforcing the financial and competitive strength of the company aiming to build its long-term value), strengthened by applying the principles of sustainability, that is the relationship between the strength of the company's economic sustainability and the strength of balancing the company's intellectual capital.
3	A—Synergy	C—Balance	A relationship between corporate social responsibility and value-based management in terms of balancing its potential (the joint use of the concepts of corporate social responsibility and value-based management reinforcing the financial and competitive strength of the company aimed to build its long-term value), strengthened by applying the principles of balance, that is the relationship between the strength of the conscious application of corporate social responsibility principles and the strength of the stakeholders' value and the dynamics of their migration processes.
4	B—Symbiosis	A—Durability	Strength of stakeholders' value and dynamics of their migration processes (co-existence of stakeholders centered around the company, which excludes uncontrolled loss of value of some stakeholders for the benefit of other stakeholders), strengthened by applying the principles of durability, that is the relationship between the strength of the consensual relationship: the company's board, shareholders, and stakeholders, and the strength of the conscious application of corporate governance principles.
5	B—Symbiosis	B—Sustainability	Strength of stakeholders' value and dynamics of their migration processes (co-existence of stakeholders centered around the company, which excludes uncontrolled loss of value of some stakeholders for the benefit of other stakeholders), strengthened by applying the principles of sustainability, that is the relationship between the strength of the company's economic sustainability and the strength of balancing the intellectual capital of the company.
6	B—Symbiosis	C—Balance	Strength of stakeholders' value and dynamics of their migration processes (co-existence of stakeholders centered around the company, which excludes uncontrolled loss of value of some stakeholders for the benefit of other stakeholders), strengthened by applying the principles of balance, that is the relationship between the strength of the conscious application of corporate social responsibility principles and the strength of the stakeholders' value and the dynamics of their migration processes.
7	C—Symmetry	A—Durability	Balance between the inside of the company and its environment (regular development of individual components of the company's potential, while maintaining the possibility of shifting the company in a move towards higher value inherent in the market and its stakeholders), strengthened by applying the principles of durability, that is the relationship between the strength of a consensual relationship: the company's board, shareholders, and stakeholders, and the strength of the conscious application of corporate governance principles.

Table 13. Cont.

No.	Deviation in the 3S Triangle	Deviation in the DSB Triangle	Description of the System
8	C—Symmetry	B—Sustainability	Balance between the inside of the company and its environment (regular development of individual components of the company's potential, while maintaining the possibility of shifting the company in a move towards higher value inherent in the market and its stakeholders), strengthened by applying the principles of sustainability, that is the relationship between the strength of the company's economic sustainability and the strength of balancing the company's intellectual capital.
9	C—Symmetry	C—Balance	Balance between the inside of the company and its environment (regular development of individual components of the company's potential, while maintaining the possibility of shifting the company in a move towards higher value inherent in the market and its stakeholders), strengthened by applying the principles of balance, that is the relationship between the strength of the conscious application of corporate social responsibility principles, and the strength of stakeholders' value and the dynamics of their migration processes.

The research and analysis on sustainable business models of companies in terms of activity on the capital market resulted in the following conclusions:

Companies should choose one of nine strategic options, the most appropriate to their current business context, depending on, *inter alia*, resources available, their relationships with stakeholders and their structure, the life cycle of the company, their location in the sector, and competitive, economic and intellectual strength:

- The A-A strategic option is most appropriate for joint-stock companies that operate in the securities market. The joint implementation of corporate social responsibility and value-based management concepts, including compliance with the rules of corporate governance and the skillful interaction of key actors creating business, results in satisfying the requirements of the capital market as regards fulfilling the needs of shareholders and ensuring the company's business security.
- The A-B strategic option is most appropriate for creative businesses operating, for example, in high technology sectors. These companies create value in a responsible way through the dynamic development of intellectual capital, possessing financial capital at the same time.
- The A-C strategic option is most appropriate for companies that operate in sectors where stakeholders strongly influence the market and products or services have an economic and social dimension (e.g., energy, public utility, water and sewage, or service sectors based on creating value for retail customers). Combining the principles of corporate social responsibility and value-based management with the strength of stakeholders can create new instruments for building competitive advantage while exchanging values and creating various kinds of values.
- The B-A strategic option is the most appropriate for joint-stock companies operating in the securities market whose products and services have an economic and social dimension, and the creation of value proposition through products and services requires strong cooperation, alliances or presence in the network structures. Symbiosis between all significant stakeholders and mutual reinforcement of their value while applying the principles of corporate governance can ensure the stability of the business, strengthen its brand value, its reputation and the positive image of the company on the market.
- The B-B strategic option is the most appropriate for companies that offer products and/or services rich in knowledge, the reception of which has a strong social dimension. Combining stakeholders' value with the company's economic and intellectual dimension can be a highly effective resource in achieving dynamic financial performance, taking into account the experience curve.

- The B-C strategic option is most appropriate for business and social enterprises which strongly influence society and its behavior. This is the most extensive model, as it applies not only to capital companies (operating in the capital market and outside), but also to non-profit and not-for-profit organizations. Orienting the strategy to fulfilling the needs of stakeholders is associated with the concept of social entrepreneurship, where value has not only a financial dimension (financial dividend), but also a social one (social dividend).
- The C-A strategic option is most appropriate for companies operating in relatively stable sectors of the economy, where the market growth rate is not high. By using creative comparison, the company may try to match its internal potential to relevant market expectations, following the principles of economic sustainability. Companies applying an evolutionary model in management can develop in a sustainable way and maintain their ability to effectively and efficiently manage business and social risk.
- The C-B strategic option is most appropriate for stable companies that create products and/or services rich in knowledge, based on the mechanisms of incremental innovation. They modify the products and/or services they offer, based on the continuous study of customer needs, market observations, flexibility and changes in the area—the inside of a company—the market.
- The C-C strategic option is most appropriate for companies operating in a stable market with the clearly defined, changing needs of customers and other stakeholders in a sustainable way. Stakeholders appreciate the stable state of the company operating in a stable market and seek to join the course of mutual value exchange. As a result, the value of the company increases, as well as the value of its stakeholders.

The above strategic options show the trends in the creation of sustainable business models for companies at the maturity stage of development.

9. Discussion

The assumptions of sustainability are achievable through the entire life cycle of the company—from the stage of incubation to maturity. Discussion of the results in terms of contribution to sustainability in the life cycle requires defining at least two extreme stages, the early stage of company development and the maturity stage. At each stage, the assumptions of the base business model will be different. In each case, survival in different conditions, which is a prerequisite for long-term value creation for different groups of stakeholders, should be a key stimulator of business activity. The configuration design and its monitoring of the survival strategy of business models at an early stage of development and business models operating in the market for a long time is the underlying assumption of creating value in the long term. The business model must change due to the changeable internal and external environment based on the capabilities inherent in its potential. Skillfully making changes to the business model during its life cycle enables it to survive. Therefore, survival is determined by the ability to modify the business model throughout the life cycle of the company, applying the solution appropriate for the situation in the sphere of business models. We believe that the concept of sustainability, which is based on configuring the business model in terms of its variability in the context of the company's life cycle, is subject to interpretation. Both young and mature companies want, first of all, to be able to survive to create maximum value for stakeholders in good times. The pillars of survival will be generally the same, even though they will be different at each stage. Whether a model is sustainable depends on the ability to reconfigure the business models at different stages of development. A sustainable business model, by the criterion of the company's life cycle, is understood as the development of a model configuration such that it will allow the company to survive on the market under all circumstances. Such logic implies that, at various stages of the company's life cycle, managers are able to configure their business models with business model components adequate for meeting the needs of the market. The resulting business model canvas will continue to evolve by changing the components that have been fully exploited and replacing them with those that will be able to further create company value and achieve high performance. As a result, the company still has an efficient business model. That efficiency translates into achieving appropriate rates of return from the business model. The accepted methodology of business model development will then be realized.

As a result, further research and work on application should be a contribution to creating other solutions in this respect. It is also interesting to examine this issue from the point of view of the network economy. In this way, a new approach to business models has been presented, which should contribute to the development of the sustainability issue from the point of view of the company's life cycle.

10. Conclusions

The functioning of companies in the Polish capital market in times of crisis determines new mechanisms not only of competing, but mainly of developing rules of conducting business. Companies which are at various stages of development and at different stages of functioning in their sector must design business models that can provide a platform for stability of the defined and used components, constituting an efficient business model. In order to be able to do it, they should make strategic decisions relevant to the life cycle they are in. Only such a design of the business model and strategy that is consistent with a given stage of company development may ensure an acceptable level of growth and development of the company, providing the basis for managing and maintaining its continuity over a long period of time, using sustainability principles. The assessment of business models can take into account the following factors:

- developed in other stages of the company life cycle
- requiring other methods and management concepts appropriate to the level of company maturity, supporting the process of value creation
- if the company is a participant in the capital market it may be listed in other indices (a company at the initial stage of its development in the New Connect Index, for example, and a mature company in the Respect Index)
- an emphasis on the creation of value in the short and long term
- an emphasis on the creation of value mainly for shareholders and/or the concept of value creation for the company through a dialogue with stakeholders as the conditions of implementing the principles of sustainability

Research included both companies at an early stage of development and mature companies. The data of companies listed on the Stock Exchange in Warsaw in the indices relevant to their specific character were used. Using the theoretical assumptions related to the concept of the component approach to building the business model configuration of companies at an early stage of development and stakeholder theory and the joint use of the CSR and VBM concepts for mature companies, two models have been developed relating to two extreme stages of development, the stage of shaping the business model for the objective of developing the company's ability to create value for shareholders and the stage of ensuring the long-term value of the company in the case of mature companies. In this way, individual attributes and their combinations for business models that are at two extreme stages of development have been identified. The first group of the surveyed companies was IPO companies, while the second was companies that had been listed on the Stock Exchange for a long time and that are governed by the principles of corporate governance. Thus, their business models are different. As shown in this paper, managers in start-ups focus their attention on designing, delivering scalability and dynamically adjusting the used business model, while in the case of mature companies they expand the understanding of the business model, adding management intentions to its attributes based on balancing the interests of different groups of stakeholders and a coherent and coordinated use of assumptions of the concepts of value-based management and corporate social responsibility, resulting in the creation of a sustainable business model. Business models examined using the criterion of the life cycle change due to the growing needs of stakeholders over time. As these needs and expectations are the greatest in the case of mature companies, the creation of a category of a business model concentrated on sustainability is therefore justified. In the case of companies at an early stage of development, it is also important to take into account which business model components are responsible for increasing shareholder value to the greatest extent. They should therefore be a driver of adjusting business models, and changes aiming to build company value should focus on them. Directions for further research may include the further development of the concept of business models of the early and mature stages of company development; mechanisms for creating, delivering and capturing value at various stages of the life cycle of the company; shaping networked business models in the life cycle; and the methods of achieving business model scalability at various stages of company development.

Prospects for further scientific research may include:

(1) The further development of the concept of a business model in the life cycle from the point of view of its sustainability.
(2) Building sustainable business models based on the network paradigm.
(3) Making changes in the configuration of business models on different levels of development.
(4) Studying the scalability of sustainable business models in hybrid organizations.
(5) Searching the impact of cooperative behaviors in building business models.

Several issues limiting research and analysis have been selected. The subject of studying business models in their life cycle is relatively new and not fully developed. Therefore, there are not many comparable studies that may provide a reference point for the research findings. There are a small number of scientific studies on business models examined in terms of the life cycle, which also makes it difficult to explore this issue. The limitations can also include problems resulting from the research sampling. The authors intend to develop the research issue and conduct further research on the subject for different groups of companies, not only capital market participants.

Author Contributions: Adam Jabłoński and Marek Jabłoński contributed equally to the research design, data collection and the composition of the paper.

Conflicts of Interest: The authors declare no conflict of interest.

References

1. Teece, D.J. Business models, business strategy and innovation. *Long Range Plan.* **2010**, *43*, 172–194. [CrossRef]
2. Jabłoński, M. *Kształtowanie Modeli Biznesu w Procesie Kreacji Wartości Przedsiębiorstw (Designing Business Models in the Process of Company Value Creation)*; Difin: Warszawa, Poland, 2013. (In Polish)
3. Jabłoński, A. *Modele Zrównoważonego Biznesu w Budowie Długoterminowej Wartości Przedsiębiorstw z Uwzględnieniem ich Społecznej Odpowiedzialności (Sustainable Business Models in Building Long-Term Value, Taking Their Corporate Social Responsibility into Account)*; Difin: Warszawa, Poland, 2013. (In Polish)
4. Von Bertalanffy, L. *General System Theory*; George Braziller: New York, NY, USA, 1969.
5. Boulding, K.E. *Economic Analysis*; Harper and Row: New York, NY, USA, 1966; Volume 1.
6. Ackoff, R.L. Towards a system of systems concept. *Manag. Sci.* **1971**, *17*, 661–671. [CrossRef]
7. Rumelt, R.P. How much does industry matter? *Strateg. Manag. J.* **1991**, *12*, 167–185. [CrossRef]
8. Penrose, E.T. *The Theory of the Growth of the Firm*; Wiley: New York, NY, USA, 1959.
9. Barney, J.B. Firm resources and sustained competitive advantage. *J. Manag.* **1991**, *17*, 99–120. [CrossRef]
10. Barney, J.B. Is the resource-based "view" a useful perspective for strategic management research? Yes. *Acad. Manag. Rev.* **2001**, *26*, 41–56.
11. Barney, J.B.; Clark, D.N. *Resource-Based Theory: Creating And Sustaining Competitive Advantage*; Oxford University Press: Oxford, UK, 2007.
12. Peteraff, M. The cornerstones of competitive advantage: A resource-based view. *Strateg. Manag. J.* **1993**, *14*, 179–191. [CrossRef]
13. Wernerfelt, B. A resource-based view of the firm. *Strateg. Manag. J.* **1984**, *5*, 171–180. [CrossRef]

14. Dollinger, M.J. *Entrepreneurship. Strategies and Resources*; Prentice Hall: Upper Saddle River, NJ, USA, 2001.
15. Prahalad, C.K.; Hamel, G. The Core Competence of the Corporation. *Harv. Bus. Rev.* **1990**, *18*, 79–91.
16. Elkington, J. *Cannibals with Forks: The Triple Bottom Line of Twenty-First Century Business*; Capstone: Mankato, MN, USA, 1997.
17. Dyllick, T.; Muff, K. Clarifying the meaning of sustainable business: Introducing a typology from business-as-usual to true business sustainability. *Organ. Environ.* **2015**. [CrossRef]
18. Stubbs, W.; Cocklin, C. Conceptualizing a "sustainability business model". *Organ. Environ.* **2008**, *21*. [CrossRef]
19. Schaltegger, S.; Burritt, R. Business cases and corporate engagement with sustainability: Differentiating ethical motivations. *J. Bus. Ethics* **2015**. [CrossRef]
20. Dyllick, T.; Hockerts, K. Beyond the business case for corporate sustainability. *Bus. Strateg. Environ.* **2002**, *11*, 130–141. [CrossRef]
21. Mc Donough, W.; Braugnart, M. *The Next Industrial Revolution*; The Atlantic Monthly: Washington, DC, USA, 1998.
22. Boons, F.; Lüdeke-Freund, F. Business models for sustainable innovation: State-of-the-art and steps towards a research agenda. *J. Clean. Prod.* **2013**, *45*, 9–19. [CrossRef]
23. Carroll, A.; Shabana, K. The business case for corporate social responsibility: A review of concepts, research and practice. *Int. J. Manag. Rev.* **2010**, *12*, 85–105. [CrossRef]
24. Schaltegger, S.; Burritt, R. Corporate sustainability. In *The International Yearbook of Environmental and Resource Economics. 2005/2006: A Survey of Current Issues*; Folmer, H., Tietenberg, T., Eds.; Edward Elgar: Cheltenham, UK, 2005; pp. 185–222.
25. Boons, F.; Montalvo, C.; Quist, J.; Wagner, M. Sustainable innovation, business models and economic performance: An overview. *J. Clean. Prod.* **2013**, *45*, 1–8. [CrossRef]
26. Schaltegger, S.; Lüdeke-Freund, F.; Hansen, E. Business cases for sustainability: The role of business model innovation for corporate sustainability. *Int. J. Innov. Sustain.* **2012**, *6*, 95–119. [CrossRef]
27. York, J.G. Pragmatic sustainability: Translating environmental ethics into competitive advantage. *J. Bus. Ethics* **2009**. [CrossRef]
28. Schaltegger, S.; Hansen, E.; Lüdeke-Freund, F. Business models for sustainability: Origins, present research, and future avenues. *Organ. Environ.* **2015**. [CrossRef]
29. Dentchev, N.; Baumgartner, R.; Dieleman, H.; Jóhannsdóttir, L.; Jonker, J.; Nyberg, T.; Rauter, R.; Rosano, M.; Snihur, Y.; Tang, X.; et al. Embracing the variety of sustainable business models: Social entrepreneurship, corporate intrapreneurship, creativity, innovation, and other approaches to sustainability challenges. *J. Clean. Prod.* **2015**. [CrossRef]
30. Bocken, N.M.P.; Short, S.W.; Rana, P.; Evans, S. A literature and practice review to develop sustainable business model archetypes. *J. Clean. Prod.* **2014**, *65*, 42–56. [CrossRef]
31. Amit, R.; Zott, C. Value creation in e-business. *Strateg. Manag. J.* **2001**, *22*, 493–520. [CrossRef]
32. Casadesus-Masanell, R.; Ricart, J.E. From strategy to business models and onto tactics. *Long Range Plan.* **2010**, *43*, 195–215. [CrossRef]
33. Demil, B.; Lecocq, X. Business model evolution: In search of dynamic consistency. *Long Range Plan.* **2010**, *43*, 227–246. [CrossRef]
34. Mahadevan, B. Business models for internet-based ecommerce: An anatomy. *Calif. Manag. Rev.* **2000**, *42*, 55–69. [CrossRef]
35. Chesbrough, H. Business model innovation: Opportunities and barriers. *Long Range Plan.* **2010**, *43*, 354–363. [CrossRef]
36. Fielt, E. Conceptualising business models: Definitions, frameworks and classifications. *J. Bus. Models* **2013**, *1*, 85–105.
37. Chandler, A. *Strategy and Structure: Chapters in the History of Industrial Enterprise*; Doubleday: New York, NY, USA, 1962.
38. Patton, A. Stretch your product's earning years: Top management's stake in the product life cycle. *Manag. Rev.* **1959**, *48*, 9–14.
39. Levitt, T. Exploit the product life cycle. *Harv. Bus. Rev.* **1965**, *43*, 81–94.
40. Cox, W.E. Product life cycles as marketing models. *J. Bus.* **1967**, *40*, 375–384. [CrossRef]
41. Churchill, N.C.; Lewis, V.L. The five stages of small business growth. *Harv. Bus. Rev.* **1983**, *61*, 30–50.
42. Greiner, L. Evolution and revolution as organizations grow. *Harv. Bus. Rev.* **1972**. [CrossRef]

43. Hofer, C.W. Toward a contingency theory of business strategy. *Acad. Manag. J.* **1975**, *18*, 784–810. [CrossRef]
44. Scott, M.; Bruce, R. Five stages of growth in small business. *Long Range Plan.* **1987**, *20*, 45–52. [CrossRef]
45. Quinn, R.E.; Cameron, K. Organizational life cycles and shifting criteria of effectiveness: Some preliminary evidence. *Manag. Sci.* **1983**, *29*, 33–51. [CrossRef]
46. Lester, D.L.; Parnell, J.A.; Carraher, S. Organization life cycle: A five-stage empirical scale. *Int. J. Organ. Anal.* **2003**, *11*, 339–354. [CrossRef]
47. Thietart, R.A.; Vivas, R. An empirical investigation of success strategies for businesses along the product life cycle. *Manag. Sci.* **1984**, *30*, 1405–1423. [CrossRef]
48. Schallmo, D.R.A.; Brecht, L. Business model innovation in business-to-business markets—Procedure and examples. In Proceedings of the 3rd ISPIM Innovation Symposium: Managing the Art of Innovation: Turning Concepts into Reality, Quebec City, QC, Canada, 12–15 December 2010.
49. De Reuver, M.; Bouwman, H.; MacInnes, I. Business model dynamics: A case survey. *J. Theor. Appl. Electron. Commer. Res.* **2009**, *4*, 1–11. [CrossRef]
50. Rodríguez, B.M.M. A new insight into the valuation of start-ups: Bridging the intellectual capital gap in venture capital appraisals. *Electron. J. Knowl. Manag.* **2003**, *1*, 125–138.
51. Grudzewski, W.M.; Hejduk, I.K.; Sankowska, A.; Wańtuchowicz, M. *Sustainability w Biznesie Czyli Przedsiębiorstwo Przyszłości, Zmiany Paradygmatów I Koncepcji Zarządzania*; Wydawnictwo Poltext: Warszawa, Poland, 2010.
52. Kidd, C.V. The evolution of sustainability. *J. Agric. Environ. Ethics* **1992**, *5*, 1–26. [CrossRef]
53. Svenson, G.; Wood, G.; Callaghan, M. A corporate model of sustainable business practices: An ethical perspective. *J. World Bus.* **2010**, *45*, 336–345. [CrossRef]
54. Ahmed, M.D.; Sundaram, D. Sustainability modelling and reporting: From roadmap to implementation. *Decis. Support Syst.* **2012**, *53*, 611–624. [CrossRef]
55. Jabłoński, A.; Jabłoński, M. Modele biznesu w cyklu życia przedsiębiorstwa—Wyzwania strategiczne (Business models in the company life cycle—Strategic challenges). *Prz. Organ.* **2013**, *9*, 17–21. (In Polish)
56. Zott, C.; Amit, R. Business model design: An activity system perspective. Special Issue on Business Models. *Long Range Plan.* **2010**, *43*, 216–226. [CrossRef]
57. Zott, C.; Amit, R.; Massa, L. The business model: Theoretical roots, recent developments, and future research. Available online: www.iese.edu/research/pdfs/di-0862-e.pdf (accessed on 22 April 2016).
58. Keidal, R.W. *The Geometry of Strategy, Concepts for Strategic Management*; Routledge Taylor & Francis Group: New York, NY, USA, 2010.
59. Jabłoński, M. Geometria strategii a procesy kreacji wartości przedsiębiorstwa (The Geometry of strategy and processes of company value creation). *Prz. Organ.* **2011**, *4*, 36–41. (In Polish)
60. De Waal, A. *Strategic Performance Management, a Managerial and Behavioral Approach*; Palgrave Macmillan: New York. NY, USA, 2007.
61. Shafer, S.M.; Smith, H.I.; Lander, I.C. The power of business models. *Bus. Horiz.* **2005**, *48*, 199–207. [CrossRef]
62. Jabłoński, M. Geometria modeli biznesu. *Ekon. Organ. Przeds.* **2011**, *4*, 39–47. (In Polish)
63. Rappaport, A. *Creating Shareholder Value: The New Standard for Business Performance*; Free Press: New York, NY, USA, 1986.
64. Copeland, T.; Koller, T.; Murrin, J. *Valuation: Measuring and Managing the Value of Companies*; John Wiley & Sons: New York, NY, USA, 1994.
65. Martin, J.D.; Petty, J.W.; Wallace, J.S. *Value Based Management with Corporate Social Responsibility*; Oxford University Press: Oxford, UK, 2009.
66. Jabłoński, A. *Corporate Social Responsibility in Value Based Management*; Wyższa Szkoła Biznesu: Dabrowa Górnicza, Poland, 2009.
67. New Connect after One Year, Raport z Dojrzewania (A Maturity Report), Warszawa, Poland, 2008. Available online: http://www.newconnect.pl/pub/dokumenty_do_pobrania/Raport_NC.pdf (accessed on 22 April 2016).
68. Niedzielska, J. A Guide to 5 Years of New Connect, New Connect.info, Warszawa, Poland, 2012. Available online: http://www.newconnect.info/przewodnik/przewodnik_zwiastun.pdf (accessed on 22 April 2016).

© 2016 by the authors. Licensee MDPI, Basel, Switzerland. This article is an open access article distributed under the terms and conditions of the Creative Commons Attribution (CC BY) license (http://creativecommons.org/licenses/by/4.0/).

Article
Diversification Models of Sales Activity for Steady Development of an Enterprise

Nestor Shpak [1], Tamara Kyrylych [1,*] and Jolita Greblikaitė [2,*]

1. Department of Management and International Business Undertakings, Economics and Management Education Research Institute, National University "Lviv Polytechnic", Metropolitan Andrey street 3, 79013 Lviv, Ukraine; dida_05@ukr.net
2. Faculty of Economics and Management, Business and Rural Development Management Institute, Aleksandras Stulginskis University, Studentu str. 11, Akademija, 53361 Kaunas, Lithuania
* Correspondence: povstenkot@mail.ru (T.K.); jolita19@gmail.com (J.G.);
  Tel.: +38-666-575-299 (T.K.); +37-061-644-615 (J.G.)

Academic Editor: Adam Jabłoński
Received: 10 December 2015; Accepted: 18 April 2016; Published: 21 April 2016

Abstract: The paper substantiates the importance of the optimal directionality choice of sales activity as one of the main lines of enterprise activity, the functioning of which should be complete, synchronous and complementary. Diversification is one of the powerful instruments to ensure the steady development of the sales activity of an enterprise. Three models of sales activity diversification of an enterprise are developed. The first model is based on unveiling the potential of sales channels and allows us to show the peculiarities of their use. The second model of the optimal quantitative distribution of production between sales channels is based on profit maximization. This approach not only takes into account the evaluation of the prescribed parameters of sales channels, but also provides the high profitability of each assortment item and of the whole enterprise. The third model of the optimal distribution of production between sales channels accounts for the experience of collaboration between the enterprise and sales channels during the past period and ensures the minimal risk and appropriate profitability for each sales channel. The proposed models are tested and compared to actual data of the enterprise; the advantages and peculiarities of each model are discussed.

Keywords: sales activity; diversification; optimal production distribution; sales channels; profitability; business risk

1. Introduction

Market fluctuations are noticeably observed in modern conditions of uncertainty, disbalance and disproportions between the expected and actual state of the market. A reaction of enterprises on these processes is manifested by the adaptation to such conditions, an active search for new instruments and methods, which allow a company to ensure steady development, to confine the competitive positions and to reduce exogenous and endogenous risks appearing during the economic activity of market entities. One of such instruments providing the steady development of an enterprise consists of diversification, which is directed toward expanding the domain of company operation. Diversification of sales activity is a process of extended use of innovative tools, mechanisms, methods and models for achieving marketing goals and determining optimal sales channels and the optimal distribution of products in each sales channel. Diversification provides an instrument for varying the enterprise operation and constructive optimal decision-making to improve enterprise conditions.

Today, more and more companies choose multichannel distribution systems; the use of such systems has increased greatly in recent years [1]. It was emphasized in [2] that the increasing complexity of the competitive environment requires new approaches to stating company strategy and tactics. Enterprises diversify their sales activities to vary the use of distribution channels and to reduce a risk of profit deficiency caused by exploiting only a few sales channels or by cooperation with undisciplined intermediaries.

In this paper, we present three models of sales activity diversification of a company. Section 2 includes a review of existing approaches to the selection of sales channels, the conceptual discussion and presentation of models. The potential of sales channels and the peculiarities of their use are discussed in Section 3. The second approach to the optimal quantitative distribution of production between distribution channels based on profit maximization is considered in Section 4. The third model of the optimal distribution of production between distribution channels based on risk minimization is described in Section 5. The proposed models are tested and compared to actual data of the company; a comparison of predicted income is presented in Section 6. The advantages and peculiarities of each model are discussed in Section 7. Conclusions are reported in Section 8.

2. Theoretical Framework

The problem of the optimal selection of sales channels has attracted considerable interest of many researchers. Coughlan et al. [3] discussed the structure, function, framework, development, maintenance and management of distribution channels to attain significant competitive advantages. Developing relationships between sales channels and control mechanisms in such channels was reviewed in [4,5]. Nevin [5] emphasized that to be effective in designing channels, marketing managers need to understand the alternative mechanisms for controlling the individual channel members. Different kinds of consumers and their behavior on a market to provide the effective selling distribution were analyzed in [6,7]. Various aspects of sales channels choice by consumers have also been studied in [8–10]. Sutton and Klein [11] considered the optimization of marketing instruments to drive profitable sales channels of an enterprise. They underlined the need of optimizing the performance of each marketing channel (which channels perform better than others?) and of identifying risks and critical success factors to hit performance targets. Ingene and Parry [12] analyzed channel performance, channel strategy and mathematical models of sales channels. Evaluating channel choice, Magrath and Hardy [13] considered three groups of criteria: efficiency (cost, capacity), effectiveness (coverage, control, competence) and adaptability (flexibility, vitality). Criteria characterizing producers, markets, purchasing peculiarities, goods, intermediaries, customers, behavior of sales channels participants, *etc.*, were examined in [14–18]. Kotler [19] described economical, control and adaptive criteria of channels' evaluation. Criteria for selecting and evaluating intermediaries in indirect sales channels were discussed in [19–21]. Rolnicki [22] provides a comprehensive list of channel member selection criteria, including reputation, business and managerial stability, financial strength, type of market coverage, sales competency, *etc.* Various aspects of the sustainability of distribution channels were discussed by Dent [23]. Different profit-maximization models for distribution channels were proposed in [24]. Several examples of using the linear programming methods in management were presented by Anderson et al. [25]. A game-theoretical approach to modeling distribution channels was used in [26,27].

At the present time, the problem of selecting the best sales channels and arranging the movement of goods in them is still investigated incompletely, especially taking into account the specificity of Ukrainian economic relations. This determines the need of system research ensuring the steady development of sales activity of enterprises based on diversification principles. Choosing optimal sales channels, enterprises have to deal with a set of questions and problems. To solve these problems, the authors have proposed three approaches to the diversification of sales activity of a company. The presented complex of criteria has been formulated by the authors based on the large amount of literature on this topic, taking into account the practice of sales activity in Ukraine and previous authors' investigations. Three models considered in the paper present a new solution of a problem of sales channels' selection using the present-day mathematical technique. The mathematical tools are known in the literature, but the authors have implemented and adapted these models to existing conditions of enterprise functioning and development taking into account special features of proposed qualitative and quantitative characteristic criteria for comparing direct and indirect sales channels.

The choice of a model depends on the production type, the product life cycle stage, the goals of an enterprise (maximal profit or minimal risk) and other parameters. The model of determining the sales channel potential assumes comparing the sales channels based on qualitative and quantitative characteristic criteria, which reflect the peculiarities of cooperation between a company and intermediaries or take into account the sales results of individual direct sales channels. The second model of the optimal quantitative distribution of production between sales channels is based on profit maximization. This approach not only takes into account the evaluation of the prescribed parameters of sales channels, but also provides the high profitability of each assortment item and of the whole enterprise. The third model of the optimal distribution of production between sales channels accounts for the experience of collaboration between the enterprise and sales channels during the past period and ensures the minimal risk and appropriate profitability for each sales channel.

3. The Model of Determining the Sales Channel Potential

Based on the research mentioned above, the practice of economic entities and our own study [16], the qualitative-quantitative criteria were elaborated for evaluating and comparing the direct and indirect sales channels. The importance of elaborating such criteria was also emphasized by Magrath and Hardy [13]: "Products or services must be graded, assembled, bundled, converted, augmented, promoted, displayed, sold, warranted, repaired, transported, and so on. Any channel of distribution can be compared in terms of its inherent ability to fulfill such functions".

As an example, Svitovyr, LLC (Lviv, Ukraine), was considered. The characteristic criteria of comparing direct sales channels are presented in Table 1. We also give recommendations for their calculation. The obtained criteria will be used to compare the direct channels' potentials using the improved radar method (see Figure 1a).

Recommendations for the calculation of the qualitative and quantitative characteristic criteria for direct channels:

(1) The channel having the largest total production turnover gets 10 points; the points of other channels are calculated proportionally to the leading channel.
(2) The channel having the largest increase of sales volume gets 10 points; the points of other channels are calculated proportionally to the leading channel.
(3) $\frac{\text{The sum of strengths and opportunities positions}}{\text{The sum of weaknesses and threats positions}}$. The direct channel having the maximum value of the ratio gets 10 points; the points of other channels are calculated proportionally to the leading channel.
(4) Independent experts interview top-management representatives of direct sales channels forming the expert opinion according to a 10-point grading scale.
(5) The direct channel having the lowest markup rate gets 10 points. Points for other channels are calculated subtracting 0.5 points for every additional 5% of markup rate.
(6) The direct channel having the shortest period of goods delivery from the producer to a consumer gets 10 points. Points for other channels are calculated subtracting 0.5 points for every additional day.
(7) A secret shopper evaluates sales personnel according to the 10-point grading scale.
(8) $\frac{\text{Total population of settlements, where production is presented}}{\text{Population of Ukraine}}$.
(9) The leading direct channel gets 10 points; the points of other channels are calculated proportionally to the leading channel.
(10) $\frac{\text{The number of months in use}}{\text{The number of months of company existence}}$.

Table 1. Characteristic criteria of comparing direct sales channels of Svitovyr.

No	Criterion Weight	Characteristic Criteria for the Selection of a Direct Sales Channel	Actual Value of a Characteristic of a Direct Channel		The Number of Points of Each Sales Channel (According to a 10-Point Scale)		The Number of Points for Each Sales Channel Corrected by the Weight	
			ES	IS	ES	IS	ES	IS
1	0.20	Year turnover of a sales channel	29,000 UAH	21,000 UAH	10	7.24	2	1.45
2	0.13	Increase of sales volume	5%	3%	10	6	1.3	0.78
3	0.11	Enterprise efficiency index according to SWOT analysis	1.4	1.1	10	7.86	1.1	0.86
4	0.11	Competence and professionalism of management personnel	-	-	7.8	9	0.86	0.99
5	0.10	Markup rate	19%	10%	9	10	0.9	1
6	0.09	Averaged velocity of commodities circulation from the producer to a consumer	At once	At once	10	10	0.9	0.9
7	0.08	A level of service and a level of production presentation by sales personnel	-	-	8.4	9.5	0.67	0.76
8	0.08	Territorial coverage	0.22	0.09	2.2	0.9	0.18	0.07
9	0.05	The number of visitors (the number of customers in a database)	19,000 visitors	16,000 visitors	10	8.42	0.5	0.42
10	0.05	Using period	1	0.2	10	3	0.5	0.15

Abbreviations: ES, Exhibition Sales; IS, Internet Sales.

The qualitative and quantitative characteristic criteria of comparing indirect sales channels of Svitovyr, LLC (Lviv, Ukraine), are presented in Table 2. We briefly characterize these criteria and give recommendations for their calculation. It should be emphasized that the number of qualitative and quantitative characteristic criteria for indirect distribution channels should be substantially larger than that for direct channels, as the manufacturer has less possibilities of control and influence on the intermediary behavior. The obtained criteria will be used to compare the indirect channels' potentials using the improved radar method (see Figure 1b).

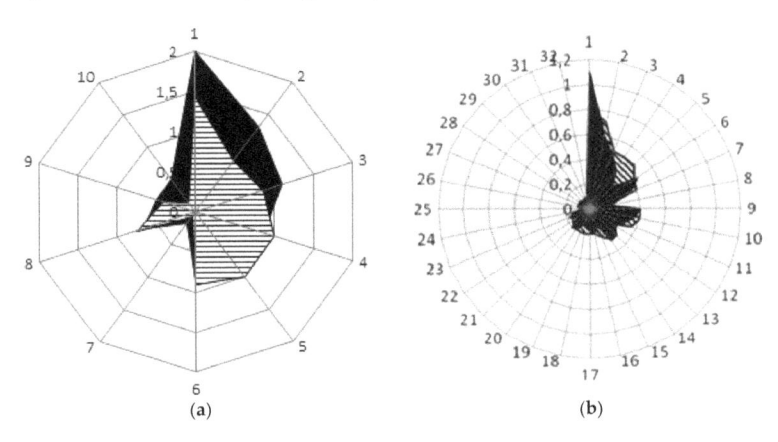

Figure 1. Graphical interpretation of the evaluation of direct (**a**) and indirect (**b**) sales channels for Svitovyr using the improved radar method (data from 2014). Nomenclature for Figure 1a: ■, internet sales; ≣, exhibition sales; nomenclature for Figure 1b: ◆, specialized hypermarket; ■, distribution network.

Recommendations for the calculation of qualitative and quantitative characteristic criteria for indirect channels:

(1) The intermediary having the largest year turnover of the producer production gets 10 points; the points of other indirect sales channels are calculated proportionally to the leading channel.
(2) Data from the last two years are compared. The intermediary having the largest sales increase gets 10 points; the points of other indirect sales channels are calculated proportionally to the leading channel.
(3) The intermediary having the least credit debt gets 10 points. For each additional 1000 UAH, 0.5 points are subtracted.
(4) The direct channel having the maximum value of the ratio gets 10 points; the points of other indirect sales channels are calculated proportionally to the leading channel.
(5) The intermediary having the largest increase in sales gets 10 points; the points of other sales channels are calculated proportionally to the leading channel.
(6) The intermediary having no debts during the last year gets 10 point. 0.5 points are subtracted for each debt month.
(7) Independent experts give the number of points according to a 10-point grading scale.
(8) $\frac{\text{Total population of settlements, where production is presented}}{\text{Population of Ukraine}}$.
(9) The indirect sales channel having the lowest markup rate gets 10 points. Points for other channels are calculated subtracting 0.5 points for every additional 5% of markup rate.
(10) The intermediary having the lowest discount gets 10 points; 0.5 point are subtracted for each additional percentage.

(11) Independent experts interview top-management representatives of an indirect sales channel forming the expert opinion according to a 10-point grading scale.
(12) Independent experts give the number of points according to a 10-point grading scale.
(13) The intermediary having the lowest freight charges gets 10 points; 0.5 point are subtracted for each additional 1000 UAH.
(14) The intermediary with the largest year turnover gets 10 points; the points of other indirect sales channels are calculated proportionally to the leading channel.
(15) A secret shopper evaluates sales personnel according to a 10-point grading scale.
(16) The intermediary having the largest frequency of promotions gets 10 points; the points of other sales channels are calculated proportionally to the leading channel.
(17) The intermediary having the least increase in sales of the analogical production of competitors gets 10 points. The points of other channels are calculated subtracting 0.5 points for each additional 5% increase.
(18) The duration of intermediary activity is compared; the leading indirect channel gets 10 points; the points of other indirect sales channels are calculated proportionally to the leading channel.
(19) The part of producer's costs in joint promotions is compared to that of the intermediary. The channel in which the part of producer's costs is the lowest gets 10 points; the points of other indirect sales channels are calculated proportionally to the leading channel.
(20) The intermediary having the shortest period of product delivery from the producer to a consumer gets 10 points. Points of other channels are calculated subtracting 0.5 points for each additional day.
(21) $\frac{\text{Turnover of producer production}}{\text{Total turnover of the intermediary}}$. The indirect channel having the largest ratio gets 10 points; the points of other indirect sales channels are calculated proportionally to the leading channel.
(22) The Marketing Department and Sales Department give the number of points according to a 10-point scale.
(23) Independent experts give the number of points according to a 10-point grading scale.
(24) Independent experts give the number of points according to a 10-point grading scale.
(25) $\frac{\text{The number of months in use}}{\text{The number of months of company existence}}$.
(26) The dates of the last investment in fixed assets are compared. The indirect channel with the last investment gets 10 points. The points of other channels are calculated by subtracting one point for each year earlier than the leading channel.
(27) The use of ecological modes of transport and the use of rendering plant facilities are estimated. The indirect channel having at least one of the abovementioned items gets 10 points.
(28) The indirect sales channel having no returns gets 10 points. The points for other channels are calculated subtracting one point for each return.
(29) Independent experts give the number of points according to a 10-point grading scale.
(30) $\frac{\text{The number of nonstandard situations solved positively}}{\text{The number of nonstandard situations}}$.
(31) The dates of the last purchase are compared. The indirect channel with the latest purchase gets 10 points. The points of other channels are calculated subtracting 0.5 points for each month earlier than the leading channel.
(32) Volumes of the last purchase are compared. The indirect channel with the largest purchase volume gets 10 points; the points of other indirect sales channels are calculated proportionally to the leading channel.

Table 2. Qualitative and quantitative characteristic criteria of comparing indirect sales channels of Svitovyr.

No	Criterion Weight	Characteristic Criteria for the Selection of an Indirect Sales Channel	Actual Value of a Characteristic of an Indirect Channel SH	Actual Value of a Characteristic of an Indirect Channel DN	Points (According to a 10-Point Scale) SH	Points (According to a 10-Point Scale) DN	The Number of Points Corrected by the Weight SH	The Number of Points Corrected by the Weight DN
1	0.11	Year turnover of a sales channel	16,200 UAH	19,100 UAH	7.5	10	0.825	1.1
2	0.07	Increase of sales volume of producer production	14%	12%	10	8.6	0.7	0.602
3	0.05	The quantity of credit debt	1000 UAH	2200 UAH	10	9.4	0.5	0.47
4	0.05	Enterprise efficiency index according to SWOT analysis	0.95	0.7	10	7.4	0.5	0.37
5	0.05	Increase of total sales volume	6%	3%	10	5	0.5	0.25
6	0.05	Exact time payment for shipped production	3 months	2 months	8.5	9	0.425	0.45
7	0.05	Consistency between a target consumer of the intermediary and the producer	-	-	8	7	0.4	0.35
8	0.05	Territorial coverage	0.22	0.32	2.2	3.2	0.11	0.16
9	0.04	Markup rate	29%	32%	10	9.8	0.4	0.392
10	0.04	Discount for production	6%	8%	10	9	0.4	0.36
11	0.04	Competence and professionalism of management personnel	-	-	9	7	0.36	0.28
12	0.04	Existence and quality of marketing strategy	-	-	5	6	0.2	0.24
13	0.03	Freight charges	7500 UAH	8000 UAH	10	9.8	0.3	0.294
14	0.03	Total year turnover of the indirect channel	144,000 UAH	153,000 UAH	9.4	10	0.282	0.3
15	0.03	A level of service and a level of production presentation by sales personnel	-	-	8	5	0.24	0.15
16	0.02	Frequency of joint promotions	2 times a year	2 times a year	10	10	0.2	0.2
17	0.02	Increase in sales of the analogical production of competitors	11%	17%	10	9.4	0.2	0.188
18	0.02	Duration of intermediary activity	1.9 year	1.4 year	10	7.4	0.2	0.148
19	0.02	Participation in joint promotions	26%	41%	10	6.3	0.2	0.126
20	0.02	Averaged velocity of goods circulation from the manufacturer to a consumer	3 days	2 days	9.5	10	0.19	0.2
21	0.02	A part of the turnover of producer production in the total turnover of the indirect channel	0.11	0.12	9.2	10	0.184	0.2
22	0.02	Elasticity in decision-making	-	-	8	6	0.16	0.12
23	0.02	Quality of promotions	-	-	7	9	0.14	0.18
24	0.02	Existence and quality of the review of branch markets for a channel	-	-	7	6	0.14	0.12
25	0.02	Using period	0.3	0.3	3	3	0.06	0.06
26	0.01	Date of the last investment in fixed assets	2010	2010	10	10	0.1	0.1
27	0.01	Ecological compatibility of commodity circulation	-	-	10	10	0.1	0.1
28	0.01	Merchandise returns	-	2007	10	9	0.1	0.09
29	0.01	Image, professionalism and reputation	-	-	10	8	0.1	0.08
30	0.01	Elasticity and accommodation of sales channel personnel to nonstandard situations	0.7	0.9	7	9	0.07	0.09
31	0.01	Date of the last purchase	8 July 2013	5 October 2013	7	10	0.07	0.1
32	0.01	The last purchase volume	100 items	110 items	9.1	10	0.091	0.1

Abbreviations: SH, Specialized Hypermarket; DN, Distribution Network.

On the basis of the described criteria, the direct and indirect channels' potentials will be compared. The existing radar method [28,29], which does not account for the criterion weights, involves building a circle with a radius equal to 10 conventional units. Next, a graphical cyclogram is constructed at the radial axis at which the criteria values are marked. These marks are connected creating a polygon (the number of axes is equal to the number of criteria). The proposed improved radar method [16] consists of building a circle with a radius equal to the maximum value of all of the criteria, sorting the criteria into groups according to the weight decrease and according to points adjusted by the weight coefficient. It should be mentioned that the recommended values of criteria weights reflect their significance and are set based on the experience of enterprise activity. At the radial axis of the graphical cyclogram, the criteria values corrected by their weights are marked. The area S_p^* of the obtained polygon is determined as follows:

$$S_p^* = \sin\left(\frac{2\pi}{n}\right) (a_1 \times \gamma_1 \times a_2 \times \gamma_2 + a_2 \times \gamma_2 \times a_3 \times \gamma_3 + a_3 \times \gamma_3 \times a_4 \times \gamma_4 + \ldots + \\ + a_{n-1} \times \gamma_{n-1} \times a_n \times \gamma_n + a_n \times \gamma_n \times a_1 \times \gamma_1) \times 0.5 \quad (1)$$

where n is the number of criteria, α_i is the value of the i-th characteristic criterion and γ_i denotes the weight coefficient of the i-th criterion.

Comparison of sales channels is carried out using the generalized characteristic index Y_k^* which is calculated as:

$$Y_k^* = \frac{S_p^*}{S_c^*} \quad (2)$$

In this equation, S_c^* is the area of a circle with a radius equal to the maximal value of all of the weighted criteria ($r = \max(a_i * \gamma_i)$). The greater is the value of Y_k^*, the more profitable is the sales channel (see Figure 1).

Based on graphical evaluation of the direct and indirect sales channels of Svitovyr, using the improved radar method, the correspondence between the actual and reference values of the characteristics of sales channels are presented in Table 3.

The analysis of the obtained results for Svitovyr allows us to conclude that exhibition sales has the largest potential among the direct sales channels, as its level of correspondence between the actual and reference values of the characteristics is equal to 0.125. According to this model, specialized hypermarket has the largest potential among the indirect sales channels, as its level of correspondence between the actual and reference values of the characteristics is equal to 0.067.

The recommended percentage of production distribution between the direct sales channels calculated on the basis of generalized characteristic indices is the following: 55% for exhibition sales and 45% for internet sales; whereas the recommended percentage of production distribution between the indirect sales channels is the following: 67% for specialized hypermarket and 33% for distribution network.

Actual values of income per unit and actual sales volumes of three-phase and single-phase transformers for direct and indirect distribution channels of Svitovyr, LLC (Lviv, Ukraine), are presented in Table 4.

The recommended sales volumes for the three-phase and single-phase transformers obtained on the basis of the considered model are shown in Table 5.

Table 3. The results of evaluation of direct and indirect sales channels for Svitovyr using the improved radar method (data from 2014).

The Names of Parameters		Types of Sales Channels	Parameter Values
Reference saturation of the characteristics of the sales channel, S_c^*	Direct channels	Exhibition Sales	6.602
		Internet Sales	12.56
Actual saturation of the characteristics of the sales channel, S_p^*		Exhibition Sales	0.821
		Internet Sales	1.266
A level of correspondence between the actual and reference values of the characteristics (the generalized characteristic index), Y_{kj}^{*dir}, $j = 1, 2$		Exhibition Sales	0.125
		Internet Sales	0.101
Reference saturation of the characteristics of the sales channels, S_c^*	Indirect channels	Specialized Hypermarket	2.137
		Distribution Network	3.799
Actual saturation of the characteristics of the sales channel, S_p^*		Specialized Hypermarket	0.143
		Distribution Network	0.124
A level of correspondence between the actual and reference values of the characteristics (the generalized characteristic index), Y_{kj}^{*indir}, $j = 3, 4$		Specialized Hypermarket	0.067
		Distribution Network	0.033

Table 4. The values of income per unit and actual sales volumes of direct and indirect sales channels of Svitovyr in 2014.

Production Items	Sales Channels / Parameters	Exhibition Sales	Internet Sales	Specialized Hypermarket	Distribution Network
Three-phase transformer	Income per unit	164.35	140.20	153.90	115.78
	Actual annual sales volume, Q_{1j}, $j = \overline{1;4}$	1890	2050	1820	3290
Single-phase transformer	Income per unit	161.13	152.46	166.71	101.42
	Actual annual sales volume, Q_{2j}, $j = \overline{1;4}$	1680	1658	1403	1779

Table 5. The recommended sales volumes of direct and indirect sales channels of Svitovyr in 2014 following from the model of determining the sales channels' potential.

Production Items	Sales Channels / Sales Volumes	Exhibition Sales	Internet Sales	Specialized Hypermarket	Distribution Network
Three-phase transformer	Recommended annual sales volume, $Q_{1j}, j = \overline{1;4}$	2167	1773	3424	1686
Single-phase transformer	Recommended annual sales volume, $Q_{2j}, j = \overline{1;4}$	1836	1502	2132	1050

The actual annual income of Svitovyr from sales of two types of transformers is 2,196,843 UAH; after redistribution of production between sales channels, it will be 2,313,626 UAH, i.e., it will be larger by 116,783 UAH or by 5.32%. The advantage of such a redistribution for the three-phase transformer will be also discussed in Section 6. It should be mentioned that the model of determining the sales channels' potential does not assume the redistribution of the product from direct channels to indirect and *vice versa*. The models discussed below allow such a redistribution.

4. The Model of the Optimal Distribution of Production between Sales Channels Based on Profit Maximization

The model of determining the sales channel potential described in the previous section can be used for further investigation of sales activity diversification of an enterprise. The results obtained for the generalized characteristic indices will be used to formulate the constraints in the linear optimization problem discussed in this section. The objective function of the optimal distribution of production between sales channels should guarantee the maximal profit:

$$\sum_{i=1}^{m}\sum_{j=1}^{n} G_{ij} = \sum_{i=1}^{m}\sum_{j=1}^{n} [P_{ij} \times \frac{(100 - \gamma_j)}{100} - (S_i + W_{ij} + U_{ij} + A_{ij} + C_{ij})] \times Q_{ij} \to \max \qquad (3)$$

where:

G_{ij} is the profit for the *i*-th assortment item using the *j*-th sales channel;
P_{ij} is the price of the production unit for the *i*-th assortment item with the use of the *j*-th sales channel;
γ_i denotes the discount for the intermediary when the *j*-th sales channel is used, %;
S_i is the prime cost of the *i*-th assortment item;
W_{ij} are the costs of warranty repair and guarantee maintenance of the production unit guarantee for the *i*-th assortment item when the *j*-th sales channel is used;
U_{ij} stands for expected logistics costs per *i*-th output unit with the use of the *j*-th sales channel;
A_{ij} are the administrative costs for the *i*-th assortment item when the *j*-th sales channel is used;
C_{ij} denotes the stimulation costs of intermediary for the *i*-th assortment item in the *j*-th sales channel;
Q_{ij} is the production volume of the *i*-th assortment item when the *j*-th sales channel is used;
m is the number of assortment items;
n is the number of sales channels.

Now, we formulate a system of constraints of the linear optimization problem:

(1). In the proposed optimization model, the planned output volume of every assortment item is equal to or less than the initial output one W_i^{beg} as its increase leads to the corresponding cost increase. Hence:

$$\sum_{j=1}^{n} Q_{ij} \leqslant W_i^{beg}, \ i = \overline{1,m} \qquad (4)$$

(2). Expert interview of sales channels managers of Svitovyr has shown that the channels will continue the collaboration with this enterprise under conservation of at least 25% of actual sales volume. Such a constraint is written as:

$$Q_{ij} \geq 0,25 \times U_{ij}^{beg}, i = \overline{1,m}; j = \overline{1,n} \qquad (5)$$

where U_{ij}^{beg} is the actual sales of the i-th assortment item in the j-th sales channel.

(3). To take into account the potential of each direct and indirect sales channel, we use the results of their evaluation obtained in Section 2 by the improved radar method, which allows us to calculate the profitability of each channel. Mathematically, this constraint has the following form:

$$\sum_{i=1}^{m} Q_{ij} = \lambda_j \sum_{i=1}^{m} \sum_{j=1}^{\alpha} Q_{ij}, j = \overline{1,\alpha}, \sum_{j=1}^{\alpha} \lambda_j = 1 \qquad (6)$$

$$\lambda_j = \frac{Y_{kj}^{*dir}}{\sum_{j=1}^{\alpha} Y_{kj}^{*dir}}, j = \overline{1,\alpha} \qquad (7)$$

where λ_j is the ratio of the generalized characteristic index Y_k^{*dir} of the direct sales channel (see Equations (2) and (7)); α is the number of direct channels.

Similarly, for indirect sales channels, we have:

$$\sum_{i=1}^{m} Q_{ij} = \mu_j \sum_{i=1}^{m} \sum_{j=\alpha+1}^{n} Q_{ij}, j = \overline{\alpha+1,n}, \sum_{j=\alpha+1}^{n} \mu_j = 1 \qquad (8)$$

$$\mu_j = \frac{Y_{kj}^{*indir}}{\sum_{j=\alpha+1}^{n} Y_{kj}^{*indir}}, j = \overline{\alpha+1,n} \qquad (9)$$

where μ_j is the ratio of the generalized characteristic index Y_k^{*indir}.

(4). The standard constraint of the optimization problems of such a type is the requirement of the non-negativity of sales volumes:

$$Q_{ij} > 0 \qquad (10)$$

Actual data necessary for formulating and solving the corresponding optimization problem for direct and indirect sales channels of Svitovyr can be found in Table 4. Based on these data, the objective function is stated as:

$$\begin{aligned} 164.35 \times Q_{11} + 140.20 \times Q_{12} + 153.90 \times Q_{13} + 115.78 \times Q_{14} + 161.13 \times Q_{21} \\ + 152.46 \times Q_{22} + 166.71 \times Q_{23} + 101.42 \times Q_{24} \rightarrow \max \end{aligned} \qquad (11)$$

The constraints are the following:

$$Q_{11} + Q_{12} + Q_{13} + Q_{14} \leq 9050, \qquad (12a)$$

$$Q_{21} + Q_{22} + Q_{23} + Q_{24} \leq 6520, \qquad (12b)$$

$$Q_{11} + Q_{21} = 0.45 \times (Q_{11} + Q_{12} + Q_{21} + Q_{22}), \qquad (12c)$$

$$Q_{13} + Q_{23} = 0.33 \times (Q_{13} + Q_{14} + Q_{23} + Q_{24}), \qquad (12d)$$

$$Q_{11} \geq 473, \qquad (12e)$$

$$Q_{12} \geq 513, \qquad (12f)$$

$$Q_{13} \geq 455, \tag{12g}$$

$$Q_{14} \geq 823, \tag{12h}$$

$$Q_{21} \geq 420, \tag{12i}$$

$$Q_{22} \geq 415, \tag{12j}$$

$$Q_{23} \geq 351, \tag{12k}$$

$$Q_{24} \geq 445. \tag{12l}$$

The solution of the optimization problem Equations (11) and (12) ensuring profit maximization was obtained using the simplex method realized by the computer program [30]. The solution results are presented in Table 6.

Table 6. The values of optimal sales volumes of direct and indirect sales channels of Svitovyr obtained in the profit maximization model.

Production Items	Parameters	Sales Channels	Exhibition Sales	Internet Sales	Specialized Hypermarket	Distribution Network
Three-phase transformer	Optimal annual sales volume, $Q_{1j}^*, j = \overline{1;4}$		5487	1916	455	1192
Single-phase transformer	Optimal annual sales volume, $Q_{2j}^*, j = \overline{1;4}$		420	5304	351	445

The actual annual income of Svitovyr from two analyzed types of transformers is 2,196,843 UAH; after optimization, it will be 2,358,439 UAH. The proposed redistribution of production between the sales channels allows the enterprise to raise the annual income by 161,596 UAH, *i.e.*, by 7.35%.

5. The Model of the Optimal Distribution of Production between Sales Channels Based on Risk Minimization

The model considered in the previous section takes into account only the last annual income, but it is worthwhile to account for annual incomes for several previous years, as the experience of preceding years may be essential for decision-making. Every enterprise tends to maximize its income, but there appears the admissible risk that the company owner is ready to incur. According to [31,32], risk is incorporated into different types of decision models, and there are different types of risk management strategies: risk sharing, risk pooling and risk diversification. Some enterprises are of the opinion that it is better to restrict slightly their income to a certain level, but to minimize their risks ("safety first" objectives [31,32]).

In this section, we investigate the diversification of marketing activity from the viewpoint of minimal risk and formulate the new model of the optimal distribution of product between the sales channels based on risk minimization. Steady development of an enterprise is also possible under the use of such a strategy. The solution of the formulated problem can be obtained by adapting Markowitz's portfolio theory [33,34] to risk estimation under conditions of using the specified sales channels. This approach allows us not only to compare the sales channels from the viewpoint of their profitability, but also to investigate their risk level.

To illuminate the proposed approach, we present the information of Svitovyr about the profitability of three-phase transformer (Table 7) and single-phase transformer (Table 8) in direct (exhibition sales, internet sales) and indirect (specialized hypermarket, distribution network) sales channels during 2010–2014.

The use of Markowitz's portfolio theory for the investigation of the optimal integration of sales channels based on risk minimization is motivated by its origin approach to the mathematical formulation of the relation between profitability and risk.

Table 7. The values of profit per production unit (UAH) for the three-phase transformer in the sales channels of Svitovyr.

Years	Sales Channels	Exhibition Sales	Internet Sales	Specialized Hypermarket	Distribution Network
2010		107.90	100.20	102.00	101.70
2011		134.02	102.70	130.90	114.81
2012		165.72	128.16	145.45	154.47
2013		172.13	135.50	147.98	145.80
2014		164.35	140.20	153.90	115.78
The mean profit value per production unit during 2010–2014		148.82	121.35	136.05	126.51

Table 8. The values of profit per production unit (UAH) for the single-phase transformer in the sales channels of Svitovyr.

Years	Sales Channels	Exhibition Sales	Internet Sales	Specialized Hypermarket	Distribution Network
2010		117.50	126.20	127.75	109.00
2011		124.44	162.97	154.22	105.78
2012		132.15	170.16	178.40	129.65
2013		175.27	172.35	187.45	133.80
2014		161.13	152.46	166.71	101.42
The mean profit value per production unit during 2010–2014		142.10	156.83	162.91	115.93

The general stages of implementation of the optimal production distribution between sales channels based on risk minimization are the following:

(1) Gathering data about profitability $P_i^{(k)}$ of the selected assortment item in the i-th sales channel within the span of some period.
(2) Determining the mean value of profitability r_i of every sales channel.
(3) Calculating the covariance between profitability of sales channels:

$$\text{cov}(P_i, P_j) = \frac{1}{N-1} \sum_{k=1}^{N} (P_i^{(k)} - r_i)(P_j^{(k)} - r_j), \, i = \overline{1,n}, \, j = \overline{1,n}, \quad (13)$$

where N is the number of periods (years).

(4) Arranging a symmetric covariance matrix of the profitability of sales channels:

$$\mathbf{A}(\text{cov}) = \begin{pmatrix} A_{11} & A_{12} & \ldots & A_{1n} \\ A_{21} & A_{22} & \ldots & A_{2n} \\ \ldots & \ldots & \ldots & \ldots \\ A_{n1} & A_{n2} & \ldots & A_{nn} \end{pmatrix} \quad (14)$$

where $A_{ij} = \text{cov}(P_i, P_j)$.

(5) Finding the inverse matrix $\mathbf{A}(\text{cov})^{-1}$.
(6) Calculating the mean squared deviation based on the percentage relation between the sales channels. The essence of the considered model of the optimal production distribution between the sales channels consists of risk minimization. If x_i denotes the part of the production distributed

using the i-th sales channel, then the mean squared deviation, which reflects the risk level of the sales channel, is written as:

$$\sigma = \mathbf{X} \cdot \mathbf{A}(\text{cov})^{-1} \cdot \mathbf{X}^T, \tag{15}$$

where $\mathbf{X}$ is the vector with components x_i; $\mathbf{X}^T$ is the transpose of the vector $\mathbf{X}$; $\mathbf{A}(\text{cov})^{-1}$ denotes the matrix inverse to the covariance matrix.

The problem formulation, including the objective function and constraints according to the Markowitz model [35]:

$$\begin{array}{l} \sigma = \mathbf{X} \cdot \mathbf{A}(\text{cov})^{-1} \cdot \mathbf{X}^T \to \min, \\ \sum_{i=1}^{n} x_i = 1, \\ x_i \geqslant 0, \ i = \overline{1, n}. \end{array} \tag{16}$$

(7) Solving the optimization problem (finding the optimal production distribution between sales channels that ensures minimal risk).

We will illustrate the described approach by the study of the profitability of sales channels for Svitovyr. The necessary input data for the formulation of the optimization problem are presented in Table 9 for the three-phase transformer.

Table 9. Covariance of profitability of sales channels for Svitovyr (sales of the three-phase transformer).

Sales Channels	Exhibition Sales	Internet Sales	Specialized Hypermarket	Distribution Network
		Covariance		
Exhibition Sales	740.9	469.8	545.9	486.0
Internet Sales	469.8	349.3	346.4	251.0
Distribution Network	545.9	346.4	433.8	301.6
Specialized Hypermarket	486.0	251.0	301.6	505.4

The covariance matrix takes the form:

$$\mathbf{A}(\text{cov}) = \begin{pmatrix} 740.9 & 469.8 & 545.9 & 486.0 \\ 469.8 & 349.3 & 346.4 & 251.0 \\ 545.9 & 346.4 & 433.8 & 301.6 \\ 486.0 & 251.0 & 301.6 & 505.4 \end{pmatrix} \tag{17}$$

The inverse matrix is calculated as:

$$\mathbf{A}(\text{cov})^{-1} = \frac{1}{10^8} \cdot \begin{pmatrix} 33.62 & -14.05 & -23.01 & -11.62 \\ -14.05 & 7.25 & 8.54 & 4.81 \\ -23.01 & 8.54 & 16.97 & 7.76 \\ -11.62 & 4.81 & 7.76 & 4.36 \end{pmatrix} \tag{18}$$

The objective function of the optimization problems is written as:

$$\sigma = (x_1, x_2, x_3, x_4) \cdot \begin{pmatrix} 33.62 & -14.05 & -23.01 & -11.62 \\ -14.05 & 7.25 & 8.54 & 4.81 \\ -23.01 & 8.54 & 16.97 & 7.76 \\ -11.62 & 4.81 & 7.76 & 4.36 \end{pmatrix} \cdot \begin{pmatrix} x_1 \\ x_2 \\ x_3 \\ x_4 \end{pmatrix} \to \min \tag{19}$$

or:

$$\begin{array}{l} \sigma = 33.62x_1^2 - 28.10x_1x_2 - 46.02x_1x_3 - 23.24x_1x_4 + 7.25x_2^2 + \\ +17.08x_2x_3 + 9.62x_2x_4 + 16.97x_3^2 + 15.52x_3x_4 + 4.36x_4^2 \to \min. \end{array} \tag{20}$$

The constraints are the following:

$$x_1 + x_2 + x_3 + x_4 = 1 \qquad (21)$$

$$x_1 \geq 0, \; x_2 \geq 0, \; x_3 \geq 0, \; x_4 \geq 0 \qquad (22)$$

The convexity property of a quadratic form ensures that any local minimum must be a global minimum. A quadratic optimization problem is convex if and only if the inverse covariance matrix in the objective function is positively defined, *i.e.*, its eigenvalues are positive. In our case, the characteristic polynomial of the inverse covariance matrix:

$$\lambda^4 - 62.20\lambda^3 + 171.32\lambda^2 - 73.18\lambda + 3.63 = 0 \qquad (23)$$

has the following roots:

$$\lambda_1 = 0.05707 > 0, \; \lambda_2 = 0.45535 > 0, \; \lambda_3 = 2.35422 > 0, \; \lambda_4 = 59.33336 > 0. \qquad (24)$$

Hence, the objective function is positively defined.
The problem is solved using the Lagrange multipliers: to find the minimum of the function:

$$L = 33.62x_1^2 - 28.10x_1x_2 - 46.02x_1x_3 - 23.24x_1x_4 + 7.25x_2^2 + 17.08x_2x_3 + \\ + 9.62x_2x_4 + 16.97x_3^2 + 15.52x_3x_4 + 4.36x_4^2 - \lambda(x_1 + x_2 + x_3 + x_4 - 1) \to \min. \qquad (25)$$

The conditions of existence of an extremum read:

$$\begin{array}{l}
\frac{\partial L}{\partial x_1} = 67.24x_1 - 28.10x_2 - 46.02x_3 - 23.24x_4 - \lambda = 0, \\
\frac{\partial L}{\partial x_2} = -28.10x_1 + 14.50x_2 + 17.08x_3 + 9.62x_4 - \lambda = 0, \\
\frac{\partial L}{\partial x_3} = -46.02x_1 + 17.08x_2 + 33.94x_3 + 15.52x_4 - \lambda = 0, \\
\frac{\partial L}{\partial x_4} = -23.24x_1 + 9.62x_2 + 15.52x_3 + 8.72x_4 - \lambda = 0.
\end{array} \qquad (26)$$

From system Equation (26), we obtain:

$$x_1 = 11.14\lambda, \; x_2 = 7.12\lambda, \; x_3 = 8.14\lambda, \; x_4 = 7.48\lambda \qquad (27)$$

Inserting these values of x_i in the constraint Equation (21), we get that $\lambda = 0.0295$; hence, the optimal production distribution (for the three-phase transformer) between the sales channels of Svitovyr will be the following:

$$x_1 \approx 0.33, \; x_2 \approx 0.21, \; x_3 \approx 0.24, \; x_4 \approx 0.22, \qquad (28)$$

i.e., 33% for Exhibition sales, 21% for internet sales, 24% for specialized hypermarket and 22% for distribution network. Based on data presented in Table 7, a similar optimization problem can be also solved for the single-phase transformer.

6. Comparison of Predicted Income

Analyzing three models of the diversification of sales activity shows that every model gives the possibility to optimize the product distribution between sales channels. The owner or top-managers, which have the right of decision-making, decide about the global strategy of enterprise development taking into account the peculiarities of the competitive position, the market environment situation, *etc.* Table 10 shows the prediction results for sales of the three-phase transformer on the bases of the three discussed models of distribution channels' diversification.

Table 10. Results of the diversification of sales channels for Svitovyr using different models (sales of the three-phase transformer).

Model	Recommended Sales Volume for Sales Channels								Total Income, UAH
	Exhibition Sales		Internet Sales		Specialized Hypermarket		Distribution Network		
	Pieces	%	Pieces	%	Pieces	%	Pieces	%	
Determining sales channel potential	2167	24	1773	20	3424	38	1686	18	1,326,880
Optimal production distribution between sales channels based on profit maximization	5487	61	1916	21	455	5	1192	13	1,378,446
Optimal production distribution between sales channels based on risk minimization	2986	33	1901	21	2172	24	1991	22	1,322,058
Actual sales volume (2014)	1890	21	2050	23	1820	20	3290	36	1,259,046
Actual profitability per production unit, UAH (2014)	164.35		140.20		153.90		115.78		

As can be seen from the presented calculations, all three models predict the excess of the total income in comparison with the actual income (by the example of the three-phase transformer); this testifies that every model can be used. The largest total income is predicted by the model based on profit maximization, whereas the model based on risk minimization predicts the least total income (though larger than the actual one). The model of determining sales channels potential predicts that the product redistribution between sales channels allows the firm to increase the annual income by 67,834 UAH or by 5.39%. According to the model based on profit maximization, the annual income will increase by 119,400 UAH or by 9.48%. The model of optimal production distribution between sales channels based on risk minimization forecasts the increase of annual income by 63,012 UAH or by 5%.

7. Verification and Comparison of Models

The model of determining the sales channel potential is a general-purpose tool for all kinds and types of enterprises (large, medium, small). This model is simple in use, reveals the sales channel potential, covers a wide spectrum of estimated parameters and takes into account the weight of each parameter. The use of the model lays down no special technical requirements. The processing of results is conducted by simple analytical methods using graphical tools (Excel environment or some analogue). The considered model includes qualitative and quantitative characteristic criteria. We have proposed the quantitative measurement of qualitative criteria using expert estimation. Such an estimation assumes that independent experts synthesize information by quantitative evaluation of a criterion that characterizes the compared sales channels. For example, a level of service and a level of production presentation by sales personnel is evaluated by a secret shopper according to the 10-point grading scale. Similarly, the competence and professionalism of management personnel is estimated on the basis of the interview of top-management representatives according to a 10-point grading scale. For Svitovyr, LLC (Lviv, Ukraine), such an estimation was carried out in 2014. The shortcoming of this model consists of the possibility of giving rise to inadequate or "warped" information; the more so as the data volume required for getting relevant data in each sales channel is sufficiently large. To ensure a well-grounded and balanced management decision, such studies should be conducted systematically, in the dynamics, immediately determining undesirable changes in sales channels.

The model of the optimal distribution of production between sales channels based on profit maximization ensures the maximal profit of an enterprise by choosing the most profitable sales channel. The advantages of this model are the following: the accuracy of the obtained results, a high level of their processing, the possibility of formulating additional constraints according to the needs and interests of a company, the possibility of comparing current and potential sales channels, the possibility of changing undisciplined intermediaries and redistributing production into more profitable direct and indirect sales channels. The shortcomings of the considered model are connected with the need to have specialists in linear programming, the risk of sales channel "overestimation" and the failure to take account of dynamic conditions.

The model of the optimal distribution of production between sales channels based on risk minimization is helpful for enterprises of those countries, the economy of which develops under indeterminate and chaotic conditions. This model can also be used when the product life cycle is at an initial stage and when an enterprise tries to enter into a new market where gathering information is complicated and there is high probability of product "aversion" by customers. The advantages of this model consist of the balance of risks and profits in the selection of the optimal sales channel and in elimination of the influence of subjective factors. The shortcomings of this model are connected with the threat of profit deficiency due to "underestimation" of the future sales channel potential and with the need of invoking experts-mathematicians to formulate a one-off optimization problem or the need for employing one's own specialists in this field.

8. Conclusions

Steady development of an enterprise is ensured by harmonious, synchronous and complementary realization of all of the directions of company activity. Our paper is devoted to one of such directions: sales activity. Mathematical modeling provides the tools for the optimal choice of sales channels based on diversification. Three models of such a choice have been proposed: the model of determining sales channels' potential, the model based on profit maximization and the model of the optimal production distribution between sales channels based on risk minimization. The first model allows us to throw light on the potential of sales channel, to show the peculiarities of its use and to introduce the qualitative and quantitative characteristic criteria for comparing direct and indirect sales channels.

To ensure steady development of a company, it is necessary not only to determine the key parameters of sales channels, but also to provide high profitability of every assortment item, as well as high profitability of the whole enterprise. The second model solves this problem as a problem of linear optimization. At the same time, the second model takes into account only current profitability and does not consider the comparison with the previous periods. This aspect is investigated by the third model based on accounting for the experience of the previous periods and risk minimization. The use of every model forecasts larger income than that brought by the current product distribution. The proposed models can be used by individual enterprises, as well as by consulting companies that offer facility for analysis and optimization of sales activity.

Author Contributions: All authors contributed equally to this work for drafting the paper, reviewing relevant studies, compiling and analyzing the data. All authors wrote, reviewed and commented on the manuscript. All authors have read and approved the final manuscript.

Conflicts of Interest: The authors declare no conflict of interest.

References

1. Kotler, P.; Armstrong, G. *Principles of Marketing*, 12th ed.; Prentice Hall: Upper Saddle River, NJ, USA, 2008.
2. Lambin, J.J.; Schuiling, I. *Market.-Driven Management: Strategic and Operational Marketing*, 3rd ed.; Palgrave Macmillan: London, UK, 2012.
3. Coughlan, A.T.; Anderson, E.; Stern, L.W.; El-Ansary, A.I. *Marketing Channels*, 7th ed.; Prentice Hall: Upper Saddle River, NJ, USA, 2006.

4. Weitz, B.A.; Jap, S.D. Relationship marketing and distribution channels. *J. Acad. Mark. Sci.* **1995**, *23*, 305–320. [CrossRef]
5. Nevin, J.R. Relationship marketing and distribution channels: Exploring fundamental issues. *J. Acad. Mark. Sci.* **1995**, *23*, 327–334. [CrossRef]
6. Jobber, D.; Lancaster, G. *Selling and Sales Management*, 8th ed.; Prentice Hall: London, UK, 2009.
7. Trenz, M. *Multichannel Commerce: A Consumer Perspective on the Integration of Physical and Electronic Channels*; Springer: Heidelberg, Germany, 2015.
8. Gupta, A.; Su, B.; Walter, Z. Risk profile and consumer shopping behavior in electronic and traditional channels. *Decis. Support. Syst.* **2004**, *38*, 347–367. [CrossRef]
9. Konuş, U.; Verhoef, P.C.; Neslin, S.A. Multichannel shopper segments and their covariates. *J. Retail.* **2008**, *84*, 398–413. [CrossRef]
10. Verhagen, T.; van Dolen, W. Online purchase intentions: A multi-channel store image perspectives. *Inf. Manag.* **2009**, *46*, 77–82. [CrossRef]
11. Sutton, D.; Klein, T. *Enterprise Marketing Management: The New Science of Marketing*; John Wiley & Sons: Hoboken, NJ, USA, 2003.
12. Ingene, C.A.; Parry, M.E. *Mathematical Models of Distribution Channels*; Kluwer Academic Publishers: Boston, MA, USA, 2005.
13. Magrath, A.J.; Hardy, K.H. Selecting sales and distribution channels. *Ind. Mark. Manag.* **1987**, *16*, 273–278. [CrossRef]
14. Hertsyk, V.A. *Distribution Management of Enterprise Production*; Volodymyr Dahl East Ukrainian National University: Luhansk, Ukraine, 2011. (In Ukrainian)
15. Kovalchuk, S.V., Ed.; *Marketing Innovations in Economics and Business*; Poligrafist-2: Khmelnytskyi, Ukraine, 2013; pp. 1–321. (In Ukrainian)
16. Shpak, N.; Kyrylych, T. Sales channels selection for small industrial enterprises based on qualitative-quantitative characteristic criteria. *Int. Quart. J. Econ. Technol. New Technol. Model. Process.* **2013**, *2*, 79–88.
17. Shpak, N.O.; Kyrylych, T. The method of optimal planning of distribution activity for small industrial enterprises. *Econ. State* **2014**, *4*, 15–22. (In Ukraininan)
18. Emrich, C. *Multi-Channel Communications- und Marketing-Management*; Gabler Verlag: Wiesbaden, Germany, 2008.
19. Kotler, P. *Marketing Management: Millenium*, 10th ed.; Prentice Hall: Upper Saddle River, NJ, USA, 2000.
20. Capon, N.; Capon, R.; Hulbert, J.M. *Managing Marketing in the 21st Century: Developing & Implementing the Market. Strategy*; Wessex: Bronxville, NY, USA, 2009.
21. Kotler, P.; Armstrong, G.; Harris, L.C.; Piercy, N. *Principles of Marketing*, 6th European ed.; Pearson: Harlow, UK, 2013.
22. Rolnicki, K. *Managing Channels of Distribution: The Marketing Executive's Complete Guide*; AMACOM: New York, NY, USA, 1998.
23. Dent, J. *Distribution Channels: Understanding and Managing Channels to Market*; Kogan Page: London, UK, 2008.
24. Chen, J.M.; Chen, T.H. The profit-maximization models for a multi-item distribution channel. *Transp. Res. Part E Logist. Transp. Rev.* **2007**, *43*, 338–354. [CrossRef]
25. Anderson, D.R.; Sweeney, D.J.; Williams, T.A.; Camm, J.D.; Martin, K. *An. Introduction to Management Science: Quantitative Approaches to Decision Making*; South-Western Cengage Learning: Mason, OH, USA, 2011.
26. Park, S.Y.; Keh, H.T. Modelling hybrid distribution channels: A game-theoretical analysis. *J. Retail. Consum. Serv.* **2003**, *10*, 155–167. [CrossRef]
27. Dong, Y.; Shankar, V.; Dresner, M. Efficient replenishment in the distribution channel. *J. Retail.* **2007**, *83*, 253–278. [CrossRef]
28. Kuz'min, O.Y.; Chernobay, L.I.; Romanko, O.P. Methods of analysis of the enterprise competitiveness. *Sci. Bull. Ukr. Natl. Forest. Univ.* **2011**, *21*, 159–166. (In Ukrainian)
29. Kalashnik, O.V.; Omelchenko, N.V.; Tovt, V.M. The use of graphical models for evaluating the competitiveness of goods. *Commod. Res. Innov.* **2011**, *3*, 234–241. (In Ukrainian)
30. Library of Practical Software Open Access "Optimizing Resources with Linear Programming". Available online: http://www.phpsimplex.com/en/index.htm (accessed on 27 April 2011).
31. Robinson, L.J.; Barry, P.J. *The Competitive Firm's Response to Risk*; Macmillan: New York, NY, USA, 1987.

32. Tsay, A.A. Risk sensitivity in distribution channel partnerships: Implications for manufacturer return policies. *J. Retail.* **2002**, *78*, 147–160. [CrossRef]
33. Markowitz, H.M. *Portfolio Selection. Efficient Diversification of Investments*; John Wiley & Sons: New York, NY, USA, 1959.
34. Fabozzi, F.J.; Markowitz, H.M. *The Theory and Practice of Investment Management*, 2nd ed.; John Wiley & Sons: Hoboken, NJ, USA, 2011.
35. Zakharin, S.V. Economic diversification as an efficient mechanism of ensuring enterprise development. *Bull. Kyiv Nat. Univ. Technol. Design* **2012**, *1*, 139–145. (In Ukrainian)

© 2016 by the authors. Licensee MDPI, Basel, Switzerland. This article is an open access article distributed under the terms and conditions of the Creative Commons Attribution (CC BY) license (http://creativecommons.org/licenses/by/4.0/).

Sustainable Process Performance by Application of Six Sigma Concepts: The Research Study of Two Industrial Cases

Andrea Sujova *, Lubica Simanova and Katarina Marcinekova

Department of Business Economics, Technical university in Zvolen, T.G.Masaryka 24, 96053 Zvolen, Slovakia; lubica.simanova@tuzvo.sk (L.S.); xmarcinekovak@is.tuzvo.sk (K.M.)
* Correspondence: sujova@tuzvo.sk; Tel.: +421-45-5206-438; Fax: +421-45-532-811

Academic Editor: Adam Jabłoński
Received: 22 December 2015; Accepted: 7 March 2016; Published: 10 March 2016

Abstract: The current approach to business management focuses on increasing the performance of business processes. To achieve the required processes performance means to ensure the required quality and capability of processes. The partial aim of this paper is to confirm the positive effects of the Six Sigma methodology (SSM) on the corporate performance in the Slovak Republic and an investigation of the dependency of SSM implementation on the certified quality management system (QMS) as a set-forward condition via a questionnaire survey carried out in Slovak industrial enterprises. The survey results confirmed the above-mentioned assumptions. The SSM using DMAIC (Define-Measure-Analyze-Improve-Control) was applied in real conditions of two manufacturing enterprises with a different level of quality management system. The results of the research study proved a possibility to implement SSM and to use the same methods in enterprises aside from a level of QMS. However, more remarkable results were achieved by the enterprise which introduced QMS. The first application of SSM in enterprises within specific conditions of furniture production processes can be considered to be a contribution of the research study, as well. The result of the work is the model including the methodology and the appropriate combination of methods and tools for assuring the sustainable performance of the business processes.

Keywords: process performance; Six Sigma; sustainable improvement; furniture manufacturing

1. Introduction

Due to the increased pressure of globalization upon the world market, business competitiveness is currently dependent upon the innovative abilities of companies, not only in the area of products but also in processes. One modern approach is based on corporate performance measurement by means of internal process performance measurements. Companies are, therefore, shifting more and more of their attention from the quality of products to the performance and quality of internal business processes.

The performance of business processes represents achieving the required results in a given process, and its size is expressed by the difference between the actual and the required results. The performance of the process is evaluated by comparing actually achieved and required value of the stated index of the process, which can be the duration of the process, costs for the process, the quality of the process, added value, the number of skills, and the number of innovations.

To make the required process performance sustainable their capability must be assured, *i.e.*, the required process quality. Correct decisions play an important role in the quality assurance process and they shall be based on the situation analysis using appropriate tools and methods of operational management and quality improvement. The Six Sigma methodology (SSM) is used as the process quality assurance and improvement method, as its implementation has achieved significant cost reductions, mainly in the machine, automotive, and electric and technical industry.

Successful results in an automotive industry after implementation of the Six Sigma methodology (SSM) are presented in studies [1–3]. Benefits of using SSM in achieving the required process capabilities improvement, hence improving the system stability, were presented by Al-Agha et al. [4]. The highly useful role of Six Sigma for small and medium enterprises was justified by Kaushik et al. [5]. The main idea of successful leadership to achieve sustainable competitive advantage to ensure the quality of service by using SSM was reviewed in the paper of Rabeea et al. [6].

Six Sigma has been applied not only in the industrial enterprises but also in the area of the services, health, and public administration, both in the private and public field, where there is a strong orientation on the customer, quality, time, and performance [7].

Six Sigma originated in the 1980s as a corporate strategy containing a set of techniques for improvement of manufacturing processes and the elimination of defects in the Motorola company. The main goal of the strategy was to minimize the dispersion of the characteristics critical for quality of the manufactured products and performed processes and setting of the average values approaching the target values defined by the customers. The application of SSM brought about changes within a short time, leading to the reduction of defects in the products using the same labor, technology, and design, while consuming less cost. Thanks to the strategy, Motorola gained the leading position in the area of the quality and was awarded the Malcom National Quality Award. Many worldwide enterprises like Toyota, Ford, BMW, Hilti, Shell, General Electric, Honeywell International, Caterpillar, Raytheon, and Merril Lynch have successfully applied this methodology [4]. General Electric was one of the first companies adopting the SSM from Motorola and in the three years since introduction they calculated that the method had saved them $750 million, net, after subtracting all costs, including the cost on the method.

Based on a case study done by Nilmani and Shidhar in a firm producing automotive components, the company was able to improve the process yield from 44% to 90% after applying SSM [8]. The process capability sigma level improved from 2.91 to 4.43 sigma [9]. According to Gibbons, by applying Six Sigma in a well-known manufacturing company in the United Kingdom, overall equipment effectiveness improved significantly from 40% to 85% [10]. He also concluded that using the DMAIC (Define-Measure-Analyze-Improve-Control) approach provided a systematic improvement and problem-solving process. Moreover, this kind of process improvement approach resulted in a sustainable and stable process.

Experience of Slovak and Czech enterprises has proven that, for example, processes in manufacturing companies in the automobile industry with an already established quality assurance system are at an average level of around 3.5 to 4 sigma. In this case, an improvement in the firm's processes by 0.2 sigma represents economic benefits in the amount of 1% of company income.

Six Sigma processes show a proven approach for businesses and organizations to improve their performance and that sustainability programs are in need of this operational approach and discipline. Six Sigma helps a business leader design a sustainable program for value creation [11].

Research from several authors, as well as experience from companies, have shown that Six Sigma provides process performance on a high and sustainable level. The authors of the paper have chosen, out of all existing concepts, just this one to create a model of sustainable process performance.

The first aim of the work was to prove the positive effects of the Six Sigma concept on the corporate performance of the enterprises in the Slovak Republic and investigate the dependency of SSM implementation on the implementation of a quality management system as a set-forward condition. To meet the purpose, a primary quantitative survey using a questionnaire method was carried out. The aim resulted from several studies dealing with effects of SSM on corporate performance [12,13] and investigating the relationship between certified QMS and SSM [14–16]. The results of the studies were the inspiration behind our research hypotheses.

The goal of the paper is to introduce the Six Sigma concept in the companies with a different level of quality management system and find out the effect of the process performance. The result of the work is a model, including the methodology and the appropriate combination of the methods and tools for assurance of the sustainable performance of the business processes.

2. Material and Methods

The purpose of this study has arisen by the idea how to ensure sustainable quality and improvement of production processes. The first step was the study of the theoretical and latest scientific knowledge. Based on the study, the goal and methodology of the primary research was stated. The research results led the authors to create the purpose and procedure of the application in the real conditions of enterprises.

2.1. Literature Review

The name of the "Six Sigma" methodology comes from statistics where σ means standard deviation. The term "Six Sigma" refers to the ability of highly-capable processes to produce output within specification. In particular, processes that operate with six sigma quality produce at defect levels below 3.4 defects per (one) million opportunities [4]. According to [2–6] a Six Sigma is a statistical measure of process capability, which is equivalent to 99.99966% of good parts.

According to Töpfer et al. [17], Six Sigma has two dimensions which are:

- Six Sigma, as project management, with sound statistical foundations and effective quality management tools, which contain:
    - systematic methodology—DMAIC and DMADV (Define-Measure-Analyze-Design-Verify),
    - project and process management,
    - a set of tools—process analysis for resolving problems, statistics,
    - philosophy and quality culture at a zero defect level.
- Six Sigma, as a statistical concept for measurement, is based on the principle that there are no more than 3.4 errors in the process per million chances, whilst taking into account the complexity of products and processes.

There exist several definitions of Six Sigma, as a concept, which were summarized in the paper by Simanova [18]. Based on studies of the opinions of individual authors of Six Sigma methodology, we may state a concordance of opinions that Six Sigma is an approach or system which, by combining the use of statistical methods, understanding customer requirements, and decreasing the variability of processes, leads to an improvement in processes and increases their level of perfection which is expressed by a maximum number of 3.4 faults per million chances.

The literature review of a lean six sigma for the manufacturing industry was provided by Albliwi et al. [19]. It is based on a review of papers published in the top journals, which resulted in definitions of limitations and impending factors before starting an implementation process of SSM.

Limitations and impending factors before starting a SSM implementation process were also presented in [20,21]. According to Kuvvetli et al. a project selection and its scope, quality culture, and defining and measuring metrics were determined as the top factors that affect success levels of six sigma projects [20]. The study of Arumugam et al. has shown that technical and social supports jointly affect the success of Six Sigma implementation [21].

The relationship between certified quality management system and SSM was investigated in the studies [14–16]. The results of literature review performed by Karthi et al. point to little work carried out on integrating Six Sigma and ISO 9001 standards. The synergy of implementing ISO 9001 standards and Six Sigma has been eluding contemporary organizations [14]. The work of Chiarini deals with differences between requirements of ISO 13053 aimed to standardizing SSM implementation and the actual practises of companies by implementing Six Sigma [16].

If we compare the contribution of Six Sigma from various sources [1–6,9,22–25], it is clear that deployment of this methodology in companies brings increased performance, increased productivity, increased competitiveness, and growth in market share, whilst retaining loyal customers and obtaining new, decreased production costs by decreasing the proportion of costs for repairs and disposal of non-conforming products, new product designs, and, growth in the qualifications and professional level of employees. The study by Aldowiasan, focusing on Six Sigma performance for non-normal processes, showed that less variation reduction was required to improve exponentially distributed processes [26]. Chao-Ton and Chia-Jan classified the benefit of SSM into hard saving involving tangible outcomes in relation to cost and revenue, and soft savings, involving actual improvements in efficiency, quality, and cash flow [27].

Six Sigma has two key methodologies: DMAIC and DMADV. DMAIC (Define-Measure-Analyze-Improve-Control) is used to improve an existing business process, and DMADV (Define-Measure-Analyze-Design-Verify) is used to create new product or process designs for predictable, defect-free performance [28].

DMAIC procedure has been described in several studies concerning application of Six Sigma methodology [1–11]. Steps of DMAIC procedure endeavor to adopt a smarter way of doing things so as to minimize the occurrence of errors. It emphasizes doing things right the first time, rather than spending effort on correcting errors [29].

The tools used by this procedure focus on minimizing the general causes of errors, increasing the quality of process outputs, decreasing operational costs, increasing process performance, and eliminating faults caused by other factors. It also involves the use of statistical methods, quality improvement techniques, and the scientific method, as well [30]. The study of Prashar deals with the use of non-statistical Shainin DOE (Design of Experiments) tools to simplify the quality improvement initiative and its incorporating within SSM [31]. The suggestion to implement Poka–Yoke technique in DMAIC phases is the result of the work done by Vinod *et al.* [32].

The summary of the most often used methods and tools in the methodology Six Sigma with classification to individual phases of the improvement model DMAIC in accordance with the recommendation of the authors [1–4,17,27–33] was made. It can be found in Table A1 in Appendix of this paper.

2.2. Analysis of the Current Situation in Slovak Enterprises—Methodology of the Research

The current situation in the area of process performance management has been analyzed through primary quantitative research in Slovak enterprises using the questionnaire method. The main research objective was the analysis of using traditional and modern methods and tools for process performance management and measurement in Slovak enterprises from selected industrial branches.

In the first step a database of enterprises data has been created. The information sources came mostly from the Internet databases and Statistical Bureau. The database size comprised 2235 enterprises from branches of engineering, construction, automotive, and wood-processing industries. By means of Internet applications an online questionnaire has been created and distributed to 1500 enterprises.

Questionnaire questions were divided into three areas: common characteristics (branch, region, ownership, number of employees, activity orientation, type of production organization), financial results (turnover, indicator ROE), and area of internal processes, production, and quality. Questions concerning internal processes were as follows:

- What qualitative level corresponds with implementation of processes in your company?
- What level of elaborated process map does your company have?
- What methods are used in process management in your company?
- What indicators for production process performance measurement are used in your company?
- What indicators for evaluation of employee performance in processes are used in your company?

- What internal processes and their indicators are regularly measured and evaluated in your company?
- What certification of quality management system has got your company?

Data collection was carried out in the first quarter of 2013 and an online database for data collection was created. Number of returned questionnaires was 164, which is a representative sample in the research. Selected results have been published by authors [34–36].

One of the research objectives was the analysis of using the methods and tools for securing of process quality (capability) in Slovak enterprises from selected industrial branches.

The following hypotheses were set for the questionnaire survey:

- H1: There is a positive dependence between the application of Six Sigma and the amount of return on equity (ROE).
- H2: There is a positive dependence between the application of Six Sigma and the implementation of quality management systems (QMS) according to the standards of ISO 9001.

Investigation of a dependency between SSM and QMS according to the standards ISO 9001 was suggested after the assumption that QMS according to the standards ISO 9001 is focused on ensuring and improving the process quality and it creates the basic prerequisites and necessary conditions for implementation of Six Sigma. The next reason was finding if enterprises without certified QMS have implemented the Six Sigma concept.

Results of the survey were processed by the application of several scientific methods of analysis, synthesis, deduction, and comparison. Another group of applied methods include mathematical methods focusing on the calculation of absolute, relative, and cumulative frequencies of the answers. Cross-tabulations were used for the structural analysis of the relations and causalities.

The chi-square independence test (χ^2) was used for hypotheses verification. It is necessary to create alternative hypotheses alongside with the principal hypotheses for testing:

- $H0_1$: "There is no dependence between the application of Six Sigma and amount of the return on equity ROE."
- $H0_2$: "There is no dependence between the application of Six Sigma and implemented QMS."

For independent phenomena it is applicable: A, B applies to $P(A \cap B) = P(A) P(B)$; therefore, it is inevitable to compare the empirically-determined frequencies n_{ij} with expected frequencies.

Estimated theoretic frequencies:

$$\hat{\pi}_{i.} = n_{i.} \div n \qquad (1)$$

$$\hat{\pi}_{.j} = n_{.j} \div n \qquad (2)$$

and estimated theoretic compound probability:

$$\hat{\pi}_{ij} = \hat{\pi}_{i.} \times \hat{\pi}_{.j} = n_{i.} \times n \times n_{.j} \times n = n_{i.} \times n_{.j} \times n^2 \qquad (3)$$

Therefore, the estimation of theoretic frequency is:

$$n'_{ij} = \hat{\pi}_{ij} = (n \times n_{i.} \times n_{.j}) \div n^2 = (n_{i.} \times n_{.j}) \div n \qquad (4)$$

Equation (4) shall be interpreted as a rule used for the calculation of the expected values:

$$\text{Expected frequency} = \text{sum in column} / \text{total sum} \times \text{sum in line} \qquad (5)$$

Test statistics were calculated according to the following formula:

$$\chi^2 = \sum_{i=1}^{r} \sum_{j=1}^{s} \frac{(n_{ij} - n'_{ij})^2}{n_{ij}} \qquad (6)$$

under the assumption of the independence of symbols X and Y, for sufficiently high n, the approximate Pearson χ^2 (ν) is a distribution with degrees of variance $\nu = (r-1)(s-1)$. (n_{ij} are empirical frequencies, n'_{ij} are theoretical, *i.e.*, expected frequencies). We decline the hypothesis about the independence of the symbols X and Y if:

$$\chi^2 \geq \chi^2_{1-\alpha}(\nu), \text{ where } \nu = (r-1)(s-1) \tag{7}$$

2.3. Application Proceeding of Six Sigma Conception in Enterprises

The choice of enterprises for application of the Six Sigma concept resulted from findings in the questionnaire survey. The focus was on industries where enterprises do not use the SSM and achieve a low performance (ROE). To verify the generality of the SSM, regardless of the level of quality management system, the enterprises with a different level of quality management were chosen.

For the proposed elaboration on how to implement the Six Sigma methodology, the DMAIC phases were followed. In the respective phases of the DMAIC procedures, we carried out a selection of the methods and tools so that all members of the project team would be able to apply them and no special training or methods would be necessary for respective kind of production [18]. The key components of the DMAIC cycle can be seen in Figure 1.

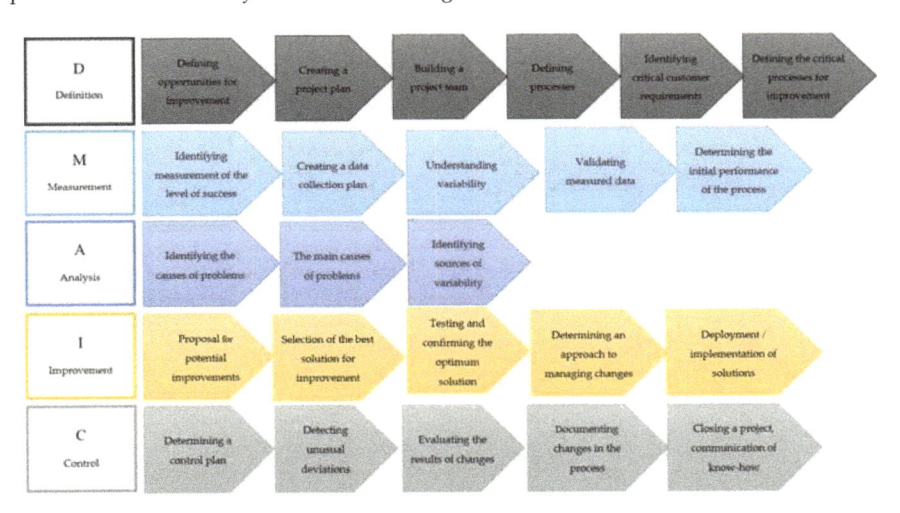

Figure 1. Key components of the DMAIC cycle.

In the ***Definition*** phase it is necessary to identify the problem, the connection of the process with the requirements of the customer, form a project team and define goal and target level of critical characteristics of the process quality.

A critical process and a specific problem in the process were identified by the defect analysis in the process. Defects were divided into material and technological. The DPMO value, the process efficiency as a total output revenue, and a level of Six Sigma were calculated. *DPMO* (Defects Per Million Opportunities) denominates the number of defects that occur per one million opportunities at the development or manufacturing of a product and can be calculated according to the following formula:

$$\text{DPMO} = \frac{\text{number of defect products}}{\text{total number of products} \times \text{number of opportunities per defect}} \times 10^6 \tag{8}$$

PPM (Parts Per Million) denominates *defects rate*, *i.e.*, the numerically-identified number of defects, and those that really occurred, after manufacturing. Defects rate (PPM) is expressed by complementary quantity, thus, by the proportion of units without defects to the value one.

OFD (Opportunities For Defects) is a probability of defects of one unit, which describes how many places defects can occur.

Measurements of the defect frequency, according to the DPMO, and Sigma criteria can distinguish the level of the process in regard of the defect frequency at the output and identify critical, bottleneck points in the processes.

Subsequently, a critical process map, SIPOC, was elaborated (Suppliers-Inputs-Process-Outputs-Customers). SIPOC is a process map that helps understand and identify process boundaries and key processes to ensure focus only on the customer [9].

The target of the defined critical process and the final level of Six Sigma was determined in the project charter proposal. The project charter contains an outline for the problem definition, project team, time duration, and project target.

The objective of the phase *Measurement* is to gain relevant data about critical processes by measurement of the key process attributes so that the problem area could be defined. In this phase, potential sources for non–conformity in the process are identified. In the first phase, the quality index of the critical process was determined and a number of measurements were done to find out the capability of the process. The following methods were used:

- The measurement plan by Pande *et al.* [22]: five-phase methodology for measurement plan.
- Capability indexes C_p and C_{pk}: critical process capability evaluation in terms of keeping specified or expected limits and an average value (see [4,18,37]).
- Histograms as a visual synthesis of frequency distribution and process variability.

Modules of descriptive statistics, industrial statistics, and Sigma process analysis were used for the calculations.

In the phase *Analysis*, the attention is given to the data analysis and dependence verification of type cause and effect, process comprehension with the objective to find out the key problem causes. The following methods were used at the application in enterprises:

- Brainstorming: looking for causes of critical process incapability.
- Diagram of causes and effects—Ishikawa diagram: graphical visualization of coherence between the problem and causes or possible solutions.
- Method FMEA (Failure Mode and Effect Analysis): analysis of the occurrence of failures, possible causes and effects for the customer.

In the phase *Improvement*, solutions to eliminate problem causes are proposed, carried out and verified. The applied methods:

- An action plan and diagram: solutions to eliminate the identified cause of failures and an improvement of the critical process.
- Repetitive measurement of the critical process and the calculation of process capability indexes.

In the final phase *Control*, the results from the previous phases are evaluated, processes are continually followed and the process control is carried out so that any variation from the target value would be corrected before the effect of failure (non-conformity) occurs. The appropriate implementation of the changes and improvements with the objective of the sustainable improved condition is controlled. The applied methods include:

- QFD method (Quality Function Deployment): customer requirements are deployed into the product characteristics and critical process outputs.
- Affinity diagram serves for identification of logical or causal connections between the problem elements [13].

The applied procedure of the SSM in the companies was verified by the efficiency evaluation of Six Sigma in the companies with a different level of quality management. For that purpose, the hypothesis was tested: "Implementation of Six Sigma methodology would decrease the cost on claims and non-conformities by at least 10%". Verification of the hypothesis was carried out through economic evaluation of the proposal based on the calculation of the cost of defects and through the calculation of DPMO, process efficiency, and Sigma level after the application of the model. We used the method of economic results comparison to compare the original and current situation of the critical processes.

3. Results and Discussion

3.1. Questionnaire Survey Results

This part presents the questionnaire survey results that show the rate of Six Sigma utilization in the enterprises in Slovakia structured according to the industrial branches, company sizes, and product types.

Cross-tabulation (Table 1) depicts the absolute and relative frequency of the utilization of the Six Sigma method in individual groups divided according to the following factors: production type, the number of employees, implemented quality management system according to ISO 9001 standard, and the application of process management in the industrial branch.

Table 1. Cross-tabulation for Six Sigma and chosen variables.

		Using Six Sigma			
		yes		no	
	Frequency	absolute	relative	absolute	relative
Production type	mass	2	1.22%	29	17.68%
	Job-work	0	0.00%	36	21.95%
	Small-lot	2	1.22%	16	9.76%
	Non production activity	0	0.00%	58	35.37%
	batch	6	3.66%	15	9.15%
Employees	1–10	0	0.00%	50	30.49%
	11–50	0	0.00%	47	28.66%
	51–250	1	0.61%	32	19.51%
	over 250	9	5.49%	25	15.24%
QMS	yes	9	5.49%	62	37.80%
	no	1	0.61%	92	56.10%
Process management	yes	10	6.10%	113	68.90%
	no	0	0.00%	41	25.00%
Industry	Automotive	4	2.44%	12	7.32%
	Pulp and Paper	1	0.61%	1	0.61%
	Woodworking	0	0.00%	21	12.80%
	Electrical	1	0.61%	7	4.27%
	Construction	0	0.00%	15	9.15%
	Engineering	2	1.22%	28	17.07%
	Wood cutting	0	0.00%	5	3.05%
	Furniture	0	0.00%	11	6.71%
	Other	2	1.22%	54	32.93%

Source: own processing.

The results show that only 10 enterprises out of 164, which is 6.1%, utilize Six Sigma methodology at the process management level since all those companies apply a process approach towards management. 40% of all companies utilizing the Six Sigma method belong to the automotive industry branch, whereby this industrial branch is one of the most productive within the Slovak market. The majority of the companies (60%) utilizing the Six Sigma method have a serial production. 90% of them employ more than 250 employees and have implemented ISO 9001 standards.

Tables 2 and 3 demonstrate the measured and expected frequencies in the respective groups to verify H1 hypothesis: there is a positive dependence between the application of Six Sigma and amount of the return on equity ROE.

Table 2. Empirical frequencies for ROE.

		Using Six Sigma			
		yes		no	
	Frequency	absolute	relative	absolute	relative
ROE over 7%	yes	5	3.05%	26	15.85%
	no	5	3.05%	128	78.05%
Total		10	6.10%	154	93.90%

Source: own processing.

Table 3. Expected frequencies for ROE.

		Using Six Sigma			
		yes		yes	
	Frequency	absolute	relative	absolute	relative
ROE over 7%	yes	1.89	1.15%	29.11	17.75%
	no	8.11	4.95%	124.89	76.15%
Total		10	6.10%	154	93.90%

Source: own processing.

The data were processed by Statistica 10 software (Prague, the Czech Republic), which created results of the Chi-square test presented in Table 4. Based upon the data, we can state that the value p is lower than the level $\alpha = 0.05$; therefore, we decline the null hypothesis about the independence with 95% probability and accept the H1 hypothesis; thus: *"There is statistically relevant dependence between the application of Six Sigma and amount of the return on equity ROE"*.

Table 4. Results of Chi-square test for ROE.

	Chi-square statistics	Variance rate	Value p
Pearson's chi-square test	6.718157	1	0.00954
M-V chi-square test	5.312536	1	0.02117

Source: own processing.

Tables 5 and 6 present the measured and expected frequencies of the groups to verify H2 hypothesis: "There is a positive dependence between the application of Six Sigma and implemented quality management system according to the standards ISO 9001".

Table 5. Empirical frequencies for QMS.

		Using Six Sigma			
		yes		yes	
	Frequency	absolute	relative	absolute	relative
Implemented QMS	yes	9	5.49%	62	37.80%
	no	1	0.61%	92	56.10%
Total		10	6.10%	154	93.90%

Source: own processing.

Table 6. Expected frequencies for QMS.

		Using Six Sigma			
		yes		yes	
	Frequency	absolute	absolute	absolute	absolute
Implemented QMS	yes	4.33	2.64%	66.67	40.65%
	no	5.67	3.46%	87.33	53.25%
Total		10	6.10%	154	93.90%

Source: own processing.

For the calculation of the value p, Excel software was used, which uses formulas for the Pearson Chi-squared test. Test significance (value p) is on the level 0.002096317, which is lower than $\alpha = 0{,}05$, and proves the statistic dependence of variables. The Chi-squared test can be applicable when all table cells are filled, at least 80% of the theoretical frequencies apply to $n'_{ij} \geqslant 5$, and the remaining theoretical frequencies are $n'_{ij} > 1$. However, in this case, the conditions of good approximation were not kept and, at the same time, it is not possible to join the groups; therefore, it is necessary to complete the research with further data so that hypothesis H2 would be confirmed. It is not possible to confirm statistically relevant dependence among the searched variables. Nevertheless, the value p indicates a possibility to examine this dependence using a major sample of respondents. The cross-tabulations show that in 90% of the variables, Six Sigma is applied in those companies which have certified QMS according to the standards ISO; on the other hand, this shall not be a condition for Six Sigma utilization.

3.2. Results of Six Sigma Application in Real Conditions of Enterprises

Six Sigma methodology, according to the DMAIC phases, was applied in two enterprises dealing with furniture production with a different quality management system (QMS): a company with a certified QMS according to the ISO 9001:2008 standard (hereafter, the Company) and a firm without a certified QMS (hereafter, the Firm). The Company belongs among large companies with a series production and is a part of a multinational concern. The Firm belongs to smaller enterprises with the custom production of interior bespoke furniture.

The enterprises from the furniture industry were chosen from several reasons. According to the results of the primary research, no furniture company uses SSM, enterprises reach the lowest performance among analysed industrial branches, and most furniture companies are micro- and small-sized without certified quality management systems.

The specific features of furniture production process had to be considered by proposal of SSM implementation procedure. From the technologic-organizational view the process of furniture production is divided into two phases bounded by a buffer store. The buffer store has a control and organizational function. The first phase includes a production of particular furniture parts. Inputs of this phase representing primary inputs for the whole production process are wood-based panels, sawnwood, and decoration materials. Materials are divided to dimension timber, which are synchronized with forms of parts. The next step is a form and construction treatment involving pressing, sanding, and milling. The last step of the first phase is a surface preparation. The second phase of production process is represented by joint of two groups of operations: surface finishing and furniture assembly. The basic model of production can have more variants in dependency on type of production input materials, technology, and product.

Having analyzed the input conditions in the enterprise and the options of usage of individual methods, the results of the applications were as follows:

3.2.1. Phase D—DEFINE

The critical process was identified by the defect analysis in the production process. The calculations of DPMO, process efficiency, and a sigma level were applied. The defects which appeared in the processes were divided into material and technology defects.

The worst values in the Company occurred in the process of pressing which was identified as critical. The efficiency of the pressing process range from 81.0165519% to 92.7540334% and the sigma level moves from 2.38 to 2.96 which means the process is not stable. The average values are given in Table 7. The defects in the pressing process were caused mostly during glue application representing 70.84% from the total defect number.

Table 7. Average values of DPMO, efficiency, and sigmas of selected processes in the Company.

Process	DPMO	Efficiency in %	Sigma
Pressing	107,536.58	89.2666268	2.7
Side gluing	2802.89	99.7348749	4.3
Surface finish	1429.76	99.8600916	4.7
Assembly and manipulation	7764.59	99.2360674	4.1

Source: own processing.

The worst values in the Company's parameters occurred in the process of sanding. According to DPMO 197,629.13 defects per million opportunities resulted, with the output value of the sanding process expressed as the average value of efficiency was 80.23% and achieved the average sigma value of 2.36. The average values are given in Table 8. The most numerous group of defects at sanding were material faults, which occurred before the procedure of primer varnish coating and represented 71.5% out of the total number of defects.

Table 8. Average values of DPMO, efficiency, and sigmas of selected processes in the Firm.

Process	DPMO	Efficiency in %	Sigma
Sanding	197,629.13	80.2370870	2.36
Side gluing	49,407.28	99.7361300	5.48
Surface finish	26,388.71	97.3611296	3.47

Source: own processing.

Next SIPOC diagrams of the critical process were created for the process of pressing in the Company, and for the process of sanding in the Firm. Lastly, the proposal of the project charter was formulated. The selection of the project was based on the requirements of the enterprises to stabilize and improve the process which is the most defective and where the enterprise can save at least 10% of costs on defective products. The primary aim of the projects in both enterprises was to state the decrease on the defective products. The basic information from the project charter for the Company for the critical process of pressing, and for the Firm for the critical process of sanding, are stated in Table 9.

3.2.2. Phase M—MEASURE

In the phase of measuring, the quality measure was defined in the due critical process and series of measurements (12 series by 10 measurements) was carried out. Variability of critical processes via capability index calculations was found out by measuring the defined quality measure.

In the Company, in the operation of gluing within the critical process of pressing, the weight of a glue layer on one side of a part in grams was, consequently, calculated to g/m^2 was defined as the quality measure. Measured values of weights of glue coating were used to state the process variability by calculation of capability index C_p and capability index C_{pk}, where the upper standard level (USL) of the weight of the glue coating was defined as 56 g/m^2 and the lower standard level (LSL) of the weight of the glue coating as 48 g/m^2. Figure 2 shows the distribution of interval frequency of weights of glue coatings in the sets of measurements D1 to D12 which shows heterogeneity signs. The values of weights exceeded the upper standard level of 56 g/m^2 in 120 cases in the interval of 56–58 g/m^2. The excess of the lower standard level occurred in 28 cases.

Table 9. Basic data of the project charter.

	Company	Firm
Critical process	Pressing	Sanding
Problem identification	Number of nonconforming parts in the process is 5875 pcs	Number of nonconforming parts in the output of the processes 593 pcs
Problem relations	Nonconforming parts in the process relate to the glue coating	Nonconforming parts in the process relate to the quality of DTD and technical condition of the production equipment—the sanding machine
Objective definition	Lowering the number of nonconforming parts and costs of nonconforming parts by 10%	Lowering the number of nonconforming parts and costs of nonconforming parts by 10%
Target Sigma Level	2.85	2.7
Target non-conformity cost ratio	10%	2%

Source: own processing.

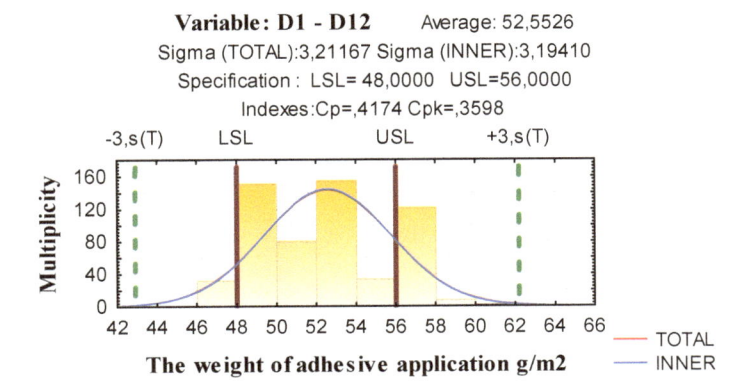

Variable: D1 - D12   Average: 52,5526
Sigma (TOTAL):3,21167 Sigma (INNER):3,19410
Specification : LSL= 48,0000 USL=56,0000
Indexes:Cp=,4174 Cpk=,3598

Figure 2. Measuring the weight of adhesive application D1–D12.

The comb distribution points out that process variability is high and is not caused by a natural fluctuation of variability in the process. The values of the capability indexes are also low; the overall coefficient $C_p = 0.4174$ and the overall coefficient $C_{pk} = 0.3598$. Both coefficients are less than 1. Therefore, and also based on total results, we can state that this production process is not capable.

In the Firm, in the critical process of sanding, a thickness of a part was stated as a quality measure. Measured values of furniture parts thicknesses were used for calculations of capability index C_p and capability index C_{pk}, where the upper standard level was defined as 19.3 mm and the lower standard level was as 18.7 mm. As it can be seen in Figure 3, distribution of the interval frequency of part thicknesses are rather variable.

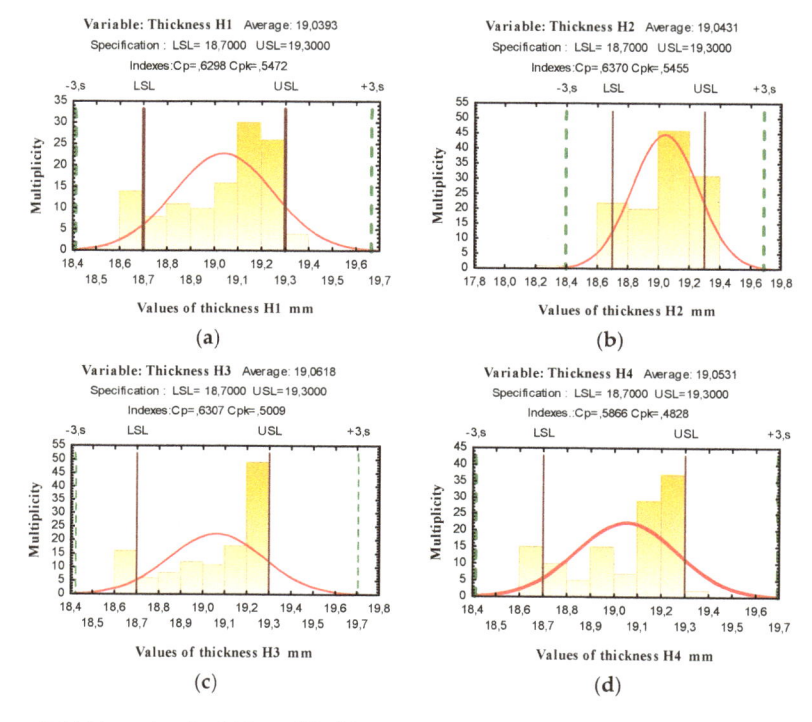

Figure 3. (**a**) Measuring the thickness H1; (**b**) measuring the thickness H2; (**c**) measuring the thickness H3; and (**d**) measuring the thickness H4.

As it can be seen in Figure 3, the shapes are asymmetrical, with comb ones which suggest that variability in the process is quite high. Another factor supporting the concept of high variability are the values of capability coefficients C_p, which ranged from 0.5866 to 0.6370. The values of capability coefficient Cpk ranged from 0.4828 to 0.5472. Both coefficients in individual measurements accounted for values less than 1. Therefore, we can state that the production process is not capable.

3.2.3. Phase A—ANALYZE

Based on the data gained by measurements, we focused on identification of the main problem, sorting the possible causes, and identification of non-conformity causes which imposed the variability of the critical process. This was used for brainstorming a method and, consequently, creating an Ishikawa diagram. The first stage of possible cause occurrence was divided into five categories in both enterprises: input materials, work conditions, operation equipment, employees, and technological conditions.

In the Company, in the process of pressing—gluing, these causes of high process variability were identified:

- Non-working control of technical parameters of the glue, such as temperature and viscosity, which have the primary effect on the weight of glue coating on the parts of chipboard.
- Failures in compliance with technological discipline by the operator of the gluing machine, mainly during the adjustment of glue thickness.

In the Firm, in the process of sanding, the following causes of incapability of the process were recognized:

- Insufficient input control of technical parameters of input materials of chipboard during the delivery.
- Incorrect choice of sandpaper grit.
- Insufficient clean-up of the production facility.
- Lack of attention during taking over the information from order schedules.

3.2.4. Phase I—IMPROVE and Phase C—CONTROL

To eliminate the causes of a non-conformity occurrence, a so-called "reaction plan", which was also depicted as a regulation diagram, was designed.

In the Company for the process of pressing—gluing, the reaction plan contains a graphic illustration of the placement of values of glue coat weights in the individual phases of the regulation diagram and adjustment, measurement, control, and the relegation of information for an operational procedure.

In the Firm, the reaction plan focused on improvement of the sanding process. It contains the span of setting and technological interval 19 ± 2 mm, a graphic illustration of the placement of measured data, simple description of duties for the personnel at the control and service of the production facility.

Based on the instructions stated in the reaction plan, the repeated measurements were carried out to verify the measures designed to decrease non-conformity.

In the Company, the measurement focused on the weight of glue coating as the main cause of the high variability of the process of pressing. The asymmetric histogram in Figure 4 shows that variability of the process compared to the original measurements decreased after corrective measures had been carried out. The values of capability coefficients increased, which is well-proven by the increase of the variability coefficient C_p from 0.4174 to 0.8313, and the value of coefficient C_{pk} increased from 0.3598 to 0.8061. After the reaction plan had been introduced, no excesses of upper and lower standard levels occurred.

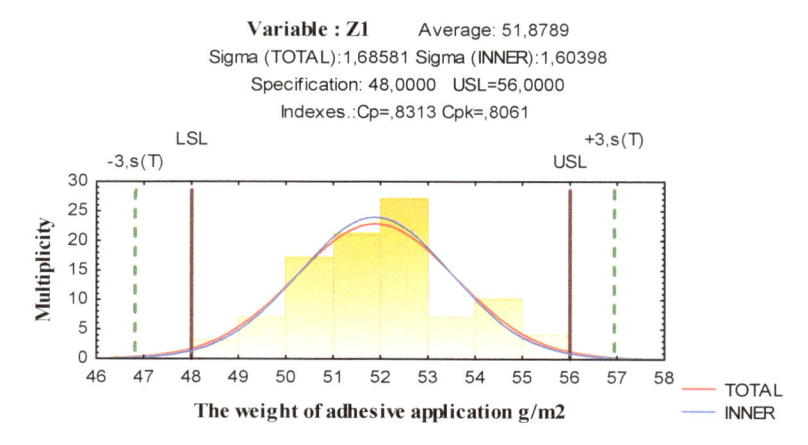

Figure 4. Repeated measuring of the weight of adhesive application.

In the Firm, verification of the solution design was carried out by the measurement of 24 parts of veneered chipboard in the 96 valid measurements in the process of sanding. The results of the measurements are shown in Figure 5. The truncated shape of the histogram in Figure 5 proves that variability of the process of sanding, compared to original measurements, decreased after the corrective measures were carried out. The values of capability coefficients increased, represented by the increase of C_p from the lowest value of 0.5866 to 0.7383 and the value of C_{pk} increasing from 0.48288 to 0.6911. Evident improvement of the process occurred in compliance with standard levels after the introduction of the reaction plan into the process of sanding. In check measurements, the upper and lower standard levels were not exceeded.

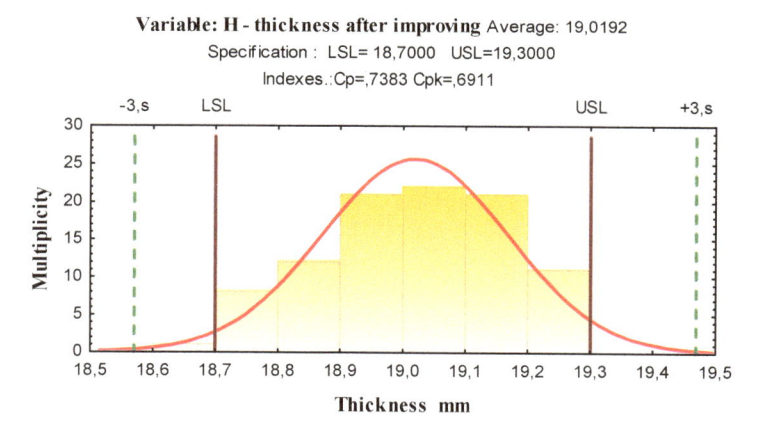

Figure 5. Measuring the thickness of the panels following corrective actions.

In the Control phase, the particular corrective measures to improve variability in the identified critical processes were recommended based on the achieved results. The QFD method was suggested and implemented in the Company. The matrix diagram was created by transforming customer's requirements in the specification of the product—a cupboard/cabinet. In the Firm, the proposal of measures to sustain the permanent quality of processes was presented via an affinity diagram.

3.3. Impacts of Implementation of Six Sigma Methodology in Enterprises

Verification of the hypothesis which assumes decreasing the costs on claims and non-conforming products by 10% via implementation of Six Sigma was performed by comparison of the original and the current state of the process, which were assessed as critical and by economic assessment of decreasing costs of non-conformity.

Basic data to perform an economic assessment of the design were the numbers of non-conforming products divided according to the kind of defects and the price of a part in € in the critical process before and after implementation of Six Sigma.

In the Company, as is obvious from Table 10, we can see that total value of non-conforming products in the process decreased. It can be stated that after implementation of suggestions to improve quality by the Six Sigma methodology there was a decrease in the costs by 12.97%, which met the aim outlined by the project charter.

Table 10. Economic assessment of the proposal in the Company—the process of pressing.

State	Number of non-conformities in pcs	Price in €/pcs	Total sum in €	% share of non-conformities in production volume
Original	5879	8.23	34,277.95	3.40
Current	5324	8.23	29,833.75	2.18

Source: own processing.

An improvement can be also seen in the DPMO categories, which also decreased and the value of effectiveness increased. The sigma value increased from 2.75 to 2.95. The sigma level was set to increase from 2.75 to 2.85 in the aims of the project charter. The overview of the original and current DPMO, efficiency, and sigma levels is presented in Table 11. On the basis of the mentioned analysis, we can declare that the charter aim for the critical process of pressing was fully met. Based on the above-mentioned results of the analyses in the process of pressing in the Company with a certified system of quality management, the hypothesis can be confirmed.

Table 11. Values of DPMO, effectiveness, sigma level in the Company—the process of pressing.

State	DPMO	Effectiveness in %	Sigma
Original	107,536.58	89.2463424	2.75
Current	73,261.27	92.9700000	2.95

Source: own processing.

In the Firm, the number of non-conforming products was counted before and after the implementation of improvement proposals by the price of a part in € after sanding, before the primer coat. As we can see in Table 12, there was a decrease in the total value of non-conforming products, representing 8.25% of the total value of non-conforming products in the process of sanding caused by faults in sanding before the primer coat. The aim set in the project charter was not achieved.

Table 12. Economic assessment of the proposal in the Firm—the process of sanding.

State	Number of non-conformities in pcs	Price in €/pcs	Total sum in €	% share of non-conformities in production volume
Original	424	11.36	4816.64	3.40
Current	389	11.36	4419.04	2.18

Source: own processing.

Table 13 gives the overview of the original and current DPMO values, the value of effectiveness, and sigma levels in the process of sanding in the Firm. The improvement appeared in the values of DPMO categories, effectiveness, and the sigma level, which increased from 2.36 to 2.60. The aims of the project charter proposed an increase of the sigma level from 2.36 to 2.7. Referring to the analysis, we can declare that the aim of the project charter was not achieved at 100%. Referring to the results of the analysis in the process of sanding in the Firm, which does not have a certified quality management system, the hypothesis was not confirmed.

Table 13. Values of DPMO, effectiveness, sigma level in the Firm—the process of sanding.

State	DPMO	Effectiveness in %	Sigma
Original	197,629.13	80.237087	2.36
Current	134,753.36	86.520000	2.60

Source: own processing.

3.4. The Model of Ensuring Sustainable Processes Performance via the Six Sigma Concep

The model describes essential activities according to DMAIC, methods, and tools of how to ensure activities to improve quality of processes from the viewpoint of decreasing non-conformity and DPMO, increasing effectiveness and sigma level, decreasing process variability, their stabilization, the search, and analysis of causes of non-conformity occurrence, proposals to eliminate the causes of non-conformity occurrence, process control, a procedure of the measurements and verification of corrective measures, process management, the usage of methods and tools of descriptive statistics, the usage of modules of industrial statistics, and Six Sigma modules.

The model introduces one cycle of improvement of process performance via the improvement of an identified critical process, which can be constantly repeated and, so, constantly increased process performance. It is illustrated in Figure 6.

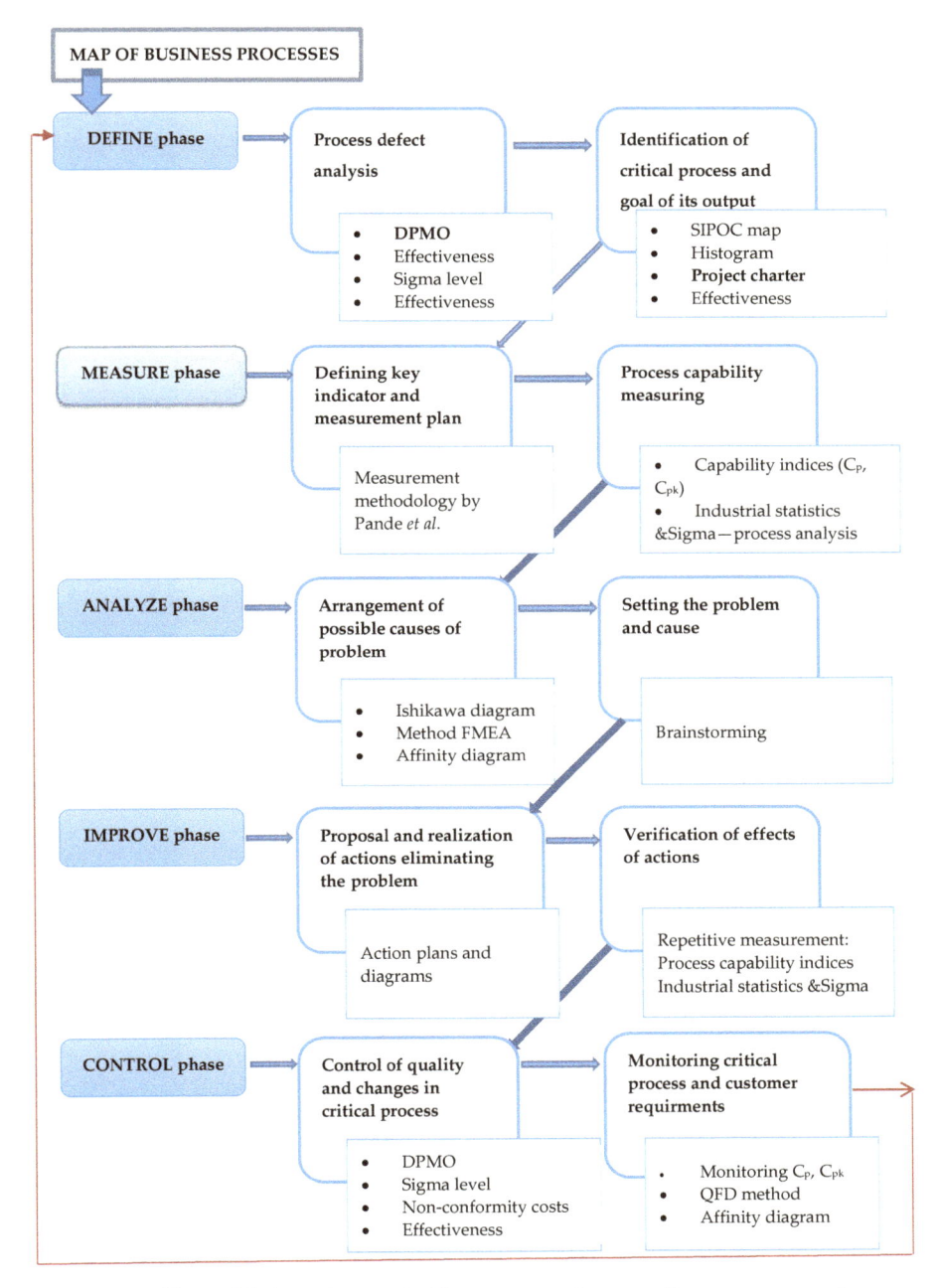

Figure 6. The model of ensuring sustainable processes performance. Source: own processing.

4. Conclusions

The results of the survey of the Slovak enterprises confirmed positive effects of the Six Sigma methodology presented in the studies of several foreign authors. Slovak enterprises which use the methodology achieve not only higher performance of business processes, but also higher corporate performance. Moreover, the dependency of achieved corporate performance on the use of Six Sigma was statistically confirmed. The application of Six Sigma methodology in practical conditions of Slovak enterprises producing furniture confirmed achievement of better results in the field of ensuring and improving the quality of production processes, an increase of savings on costs of claims and nonconforming products, and a possibility to implement measures to eliminate causes of non-conformity occurring in a process.

The limitations of the research study consist in the insufficient statistical confirmation of dependency on SSM on a certified quality management system because of a small number of investigated enterprises with an implemented Six Sigma concept. The next part of the work was focused on two specific cases: two furniture manufacturing enterprises from 500 existing furniture companies in Slovakia. Therefore, a generalization will require further careful investigation.

Despite the above-mentioned limitations, the research study proved a possibility to implement the Six Sigma methodology and to use the same methods in enterprises, aside from a quality management system, such as quality management under certification according to ISO 9001 standards or only utilizing the basic tools of quality management.

The results of the study further showed that better results were achieved in the enterprise which has introduced a quality management system. Therefore, we may claim that quality management systems form better grounds to implement Six Sigma and the achievement of higher benefits.

The results of this work develops contemporary knowledge in assumptions and limitations by the application of Six Sigma methodology and its tools in connection with quality management systems and they indicate a direct dependence with a level of corporate performance. The contribution of the research study can be considered in the first application of SSM in enterprises within specific conditions of furniture production processes.

The practical implications of the research can be seen in the suggested model, including procedures, suitable methods, and tools for implementation and permanent utilization of SSM in manufacturing enterprises. The suggested model of sustainably ensuring the required performance of processes enables monitoring and unveils the critical moments of processes, constantly, and eliminate them, subsequently. The model presents a never-ending cycle, which ensures sustainable process performance. The SSM and a suitable selection of tools are the means of a constant assurance and increase of business processes performance. Six Sigma provides a permanent improvement of processes by the effective use of methods, tools, techniques, and procedures, particularly by decreasing variability and variance of processes, by an increase of capability of processes.

Further research will be focused on the utility of other modern methods and tools by ensuring a sustainable process performance and its continual improvement with higher effects than SSM, especially in enterprises without a certified quality management system. The research work will also deal with other aspects of process improvement, such as process economic efficiency and lean processes leading to the suggestion of a methodology for complex improvement of the process.

Acknowledgments: This article has been supported by funds of the project No. 1/0286/16 under VEGA agency, Slovakia for covering the publishing costs.

Author Contributions: Andrea Sujova designed the study and conducted literature review. Lubica Simanova performed case study in enterprises. Katarina Marcinekova processed research data and performed statistical analyses. The first author wrote the manuscript and all authors read and approved the final manuscript.

Conflicts of Interest: The authors declare no conflict of interest.

Appendix

Table A1. The use of methods and tools in the steps of DMAIC procedure.

Method	D	M	A	I	C
Affinity diagram	o	o	o	o	o
FMEA—Failure Mode Effect Analysis	o				o
CBA—Cost-Benefit-Analysis		o	o		
FTA—Failure tree analysis		o			
MSA—Measurement system analysis		o			
Analysis of measurement systems R&R	o				
Audit	o		o	o	
Affinity diagram	o	o	o	o	o
Benchmarking	o		o		
Benwriting	o	o	o	o	o
Techniques of data collection		o	o		
Cause and effect diagram	o		o		
QFD—Quality Function Deployment		o	o	o	o
Histogram	o				
IPO diagram	o	o			
Control diagrams (tables)					o
Scatter diagram	o	o	o	o	
Pareto diagram of a Lorentz curve				o	o
Method of error avoidance Poka–Yoke		o			
Flow chart		o	o	o	
DOE—Design of Experiments		o	o		
Control chart		o	o		
Run chart			o	o	
Regression analysis	o				
Table SIPOC (Suppliers-Inputs-Process-Outputs-Customers)	o	o	o	o	o
SOP—Standard Procedures	o				o
VOC—Voice of customer		o	o	o	o
Stratification	o	o	o	o	o
SWOT Analysis		o			
T-test		o		o	
Six Sigma matrix	o				o
TOC—Theory of containts		o			
X^2 test	o	o	o	o	o
Methods of risk analysis		o	o	o	
Process capability		o	o		
Reliability/Item Analysis		o	o		
Root Cause Analysis			o		
Method 5 Why			o		
SI—System engineering			o	o	o
VA—Value Analysis		o	o		
VS—Value steam mapping				o	
Modelling and simulation				o	
Method Global 8D				o	
TPM—Total Productive Maintenance				o	
SMED—Single Minute Exchange of Dies				o	
Method 5S				o	
KAIZEN				o	
Pull management systems				o	
SPC—Statistical Process Control	o	o	o		o
Workshops		o	o	o	o
Management by Objectives					o

Source: [1–4,17,27–33].

References

1. Carvalho, G.; Christo, E.S.; Costa, K.A. Application of Six Sigma Methodology in Improving of the Industrial Production Processes. *Appl. Mech. Mater.* **2014**, *9*, 327–331. [CrossRef]
2. Ev, G.; Scaria, J. Reducing rejection and rework by application of Six Sigma methodology in manufacturing process. *Int. J. Six Sigma Compet. Advant.* **2010**, *1*, 77–99.
3. Korenko, M.; Uhrin, P.; Kaplík, P.; Foldešiová, D. Application of Six Sigma Methodology in Production Organization. *Adv. Mater. Res.* **2013**, *9*, 87–94.
4. Al-Agha, O.; Alzubaidi, A.J.; Al-Agha, M.I. Implementing Six Sigma Methodology in Industrial Control Systems. *Int. J. Comput. Appl. Technol.* **2015**, *5*, 2229–6093.
5. Kaushik, P.; Khanduja, D.; Mittal, K. A case study: Application of Six Sigma methodology in a small and medium-sized manufacturing enterprise. *TQM J.* **2012**, *1*, 4–16. [CrossRef]
6. Rabeea, O.; Al-Mfraji, M.; Almsafir, M.K. Sustainable Competitive Advantage Using Six Sigma Methodology: Review. *J. Mod. Mark. Res.* **2012**, *1*, 10–26.
7. Schroeder, R.A. *Six Sigma: The Breakthrough Management Strategy Revolutionizing the World's Top Corporations*; Currency: Sydney, Australia, 2006.
8. Sahu, N.; Sridhar, N. Six Sigma Implementation using DMAIC approach: A case Study in a Cylinder Linear manufacturing Firm. *Int. J. Mech. Product. Eng. Res. Dev.* **2013**, *4*, 11–22.
9. Ng, K.C.; Chong, K.E.; Goh, G.G.G. Improving Overall Equipment Effectiveness (OEE) through the six sigma methodology in a semiconductor firm: A case study. In Proceedings of International Conference on Industrial Engineering and Engineering Management, Selangor, Malaysia, 9–12 December 2014; pp. 833–837.
10. Gibbons, P.M. Incorporating six sigma thinking and asset management strategy performance indicators into the overall equipment effectiveness measure. In Proceedings of the second European Research Conference on Continuous Improvement and Lean Six Sigma, Bristol, UK, 18 January 2010.
11. Kadri, S. Six Sigma Methodology for the Environment Sustainable Development. In *Mechanism Design for Sustainability*, 1st ed.; Luo, Z., Ed.; Springer: Berline, Germany, 2013; pp. 61–76.
12. Sin, A.B.; Zailani, S.; Iranmaneshb, M.; Ramayah, T. Structural equation modelling on knowledge creation in Six Sigma DMAIC project and its impact on organizational performance. *Int. J. Product. Econ.* **2015**, *168*, 105–117.
13. Jacobs, B.W.; Swink, M.; Linderman, K. Performance effects of early and late Six Sigma adoptions. *J. Oper. Manag.* **2015**, *36*, 244–257. [CrossRef]
14. Karthi, S.; Devadasan, S.R.; Murugesh, R.; Sreenivasa, C.G.; Sivaram, N.M. Global views on integrating Six Sigma and ISO 9001 certification. *Total Qual. Manag. Bus. Excell.* **2012**, *23*, 237–262. [CrossRef]
15. Chiarini, A. Relationships between total quality management and Six Sigma inside European manufacturing companies: A dedicated survey. *Int. J. Product. Qual. Manag.* **2013**, *11*, 179–194. [CrossRef]
16. Chiarini, A. A comparison between companies' implementation of Six Sigma and ISO 13053 requirements: A first investigation from Europe. *Int. J. Process Manag. Benchmarking* **2013**, *3*, 154–172. [CrossRef]
17. Töpfer, A. *Six Sigma*, 1st ed.; Computer Press: Praha, Czech Republic, 2008; p. 287.
18. Simanova, L. Specific Proposal of the Application and Implementation Six Sigma in Selected Processes of the Furniture Manufacturing. *Procedia Econ. Financ.* **2015**, *34*, 268–275. [CrossRef]
19. Albliwi, S.A.; Antony, J.; Lim, S.A.H. A systematic review of Lean Six Sigma for the manufacturing industry. *Bus. Process Manag. J.* **2015**, *21*, 665–691. [CrossRef]
20. Kuvvetli, Ü.; Firuzan, A.R.; Alpaykut, S.; Gerger, A. Determining Six Sigma success factors in Turkey by using structural equation modeling. *J. Appl. Stat.* **2016**, *43*, 738–753. [CrossRef]
21. Arumugam, V.; Antony, J.; Kumar, M. Linking learning and knowledge creation to project success in Six Sigma projects: An empirical investigation. *Int. J. Product. Econ.* **2013**, *141*, 388–402. [CrossRef]
22. Pande, P.S.; Neumann, P.R.; Cavanagh, R.R. *Zavádíme Metodu Six Sigma*, 1st ed.; TwinsCom: Brno, Czech Republic, 2008.
23. Fan, J.J.; Fan, J.; Qian, C.; Yung, K.; Fan, X.; Zhang, G.; Pecht, M. Optimal Design of Life Testing for High-Brightness White LEDs Using the Six Sigma DMAIC Approach. *IEEE Trans. Device Mater. Reliab.* **2015**, *15*, 576–587. [CrossRef]
24. Dora, M.; Gellynck, X. Lean Six Sigma Implementation in a Food Processing SME: A Case Study. *Qual. Reliab. Eng. Int.* **2015**, *31*, 1151–1159. [CrossRef]

25. Ericsson, E.; Gingnell, L.; Lillieskold, J. Implementing Design for Six Sigma in large Swedish product developing organisations-an interview study. *Total Qual. Manag. Bus. Excell.* **2015**, *26*, 648–660. [CrossRef]
26. Aldowaisan, T.; Nourelfath, M.; Hassan, J. Six Sigma performance for non-normal processes. *Eur. J. Oper. Res.* **2015**, *247*, 968–977. [CrossRef]
27. Chao-Ton, S.; Chia-Jan, C. A Systematic Methodology for the Creation of Six Sigma Projects: A Case Study of Semi-conductor Foundry. *Expect Syst. Appl.* **2008**, *34*, 2693–2703.
28. Pyzdek, T.; Keller, P. *The Six Sigma Handbook*, 4th ed.; McGraw-Hill Professional: London, UK, 2014.
29. Okpala, K.E. Total Quality Management and SMPS Performance Effects in Nigeria: A Review of Six Sigma Methodology. *Asian J. Financ. Account.* **2012**, *2*, 363–378. [CrossRef]
30. Sanchez, J.; Valles, A. Successful Projects from the Application of Six Sigma Methodology. In *Six Sigma Projects and Personal Experiences*; InTech: Rijeka, Croatia, 2011; pp. 91–116. Available online: https://www.researchgate.net/publication/221913365 (accessed on 19 November 2015).
31. Prashar, A. Using Shainin DOE for Six Sigma: An Indian case study. *Product. Plan. Control* **2016**, *27*, 83–101. [CrossRef]
32. Vinod, M.; Devadasan, S.R.; Sunil, D.T.; Thilak, V.M.M. Six Sigma through Poka-Yoke: A navigation through literature arena. *Int. J. Adv. Manuf. Technol.* **2015**, *81*, 315–327. [CrossRef]
33. Nenadál, J.; Plura, J. *Moderní Management Jakosti*, 1st ed.; Management Press: Praha, Czech Republic, 2008; pp. 348–354.
34. Sujova, A. Business Process Performance Management—A Modern Approach to Corporate Performance Management. In Proceedings of International Conference Liberec Economic Forum, Liberec, Czech Republic, 16–17 September 2013; pp. 542–550.
35. Sujová, A.; Marcineková, K. Modern Methods of Process Management Used in Slovak Enterprises. *Procedia Econ. Financ.* **2015**, *23*, 889–893. [CrossRef]
36. Marcineková, K.; Sujová, A. The Influence of the Process Control Level on the Enterprises' ROE. *Procedia Econ. Financ.* **2015**, *34*, 290–295. [CrossRef]
37. Simanova, L.; Gejdos, P. The Use of Statistical Control Tools to Quality Improving in Furniture Business. *Procedia Econ. Financ.* **2015**, *34*, 276–283. [CrossRef]

© 2016 by the authors. Licensee MDPI, Basel, Switzerland. This article is an open access article distributed under the terms and conditions of the Creative Commons Attribution (CC BY) license (http://creativecommons.org/licenses/by/4.0/).

Article

Risk Management in Critical Infrastructure—Foundation for Its Sustainable Work

Andrzej Bialas

Institute of Innovative Technologies EMAG, 40-189 Katowice, Leopolda 31, Poland; andrzej.bialas@ibemag.pl; Tel.: +48-32-200-77-00; Fax: +48-32-200-77-01

Academic Editors: Adam Jabłoński, Giuseppe Ioppolo and Marc A. Rosen
Received: 24 October 2015; Accepted: 26 February 2016; Published: 4 March 2016

Abstract: The paper concerns research related to the European project CIRAS and presents a validation experiment with the use of a risk management tool adapted for critical infrastructures. The project context and state of the art are discussed. The adaptation of the risk management tool is performed according to previously elaborated requirements which consider interdependencies, cause-consequences analysis, risk measures and risk register implementation. A novel structured risk management method was proposed how to deal with internal and external impacts of a hazardous event which occurred in the given CI. The method is embedded into the critical infrastructure resilience process. These requirements can be implemented on the ready-to-use software platform for further experiments. The experimentation results are used as the input for CIRAS. The discussed tool can be applied as the risk reduction component in the CIRAS Tool, and the validation process presented here is the basis to elaborate two project use cases.

Keywords: critical infrastructure; risk management; bow-tie concept; software tool; interdependencies

1. Introduction

The paper concerns the risk management issue in critical infrastructures. Today's societies are based on products and services provided by large-scale technical infrastructures of such sectors as energy, oil, gas, finances, transport, telecommunications, health, *etc*. These infrastructures, when disrupted or destroyed, have a serious impact on health, safety, security or well-being of the society or effective functioning of governments and/or economies, therefore they are called critical infrastructures (CIs). Smooth functioning of the CIs builds right relationships between the citizens and governments. Modern societies are very sensitive to any disturbances in critical infrastructures. The CI disturbances or damages hamper the economic growth, social prosperity and sustainable development of our civilization. For this reason, it is very important to mitigate any negative impact on critical infrastructures. Risk management, which plays the key role in the CI protection, still remains a challenge due to many unresolved problems. This was the author's motivation to undertake research in this field.

CI is identified as a very complex socio-technical system, sometimes called a system of systems. The system of systems (SoS) consists of multiple, heterogeneous, distributed, occasionally independently operating systems embedded in networks at multiple levels, which evolve over time [1]. To function properly, CIs include many diversified components (technological, IT hardware, software, environmental, personal, organizational) and complex processes interrelated with other processes across different economy sectors.

In such environments different kinds of threats and hazards may occur, such as: natural disasters and catastrophes, technical disasters and failures, espionage, international crime, physical and cyber terrorism. To avoid disturbances in CIs and to minimize possible consequences of threats, critical infrastructure protection (CIP) programmes are implemented, which specify a consistent set of diversified security measures applied for the given CI: technical, organizational and procedural. The measures should properly affect the identified risk. The measures selection is based on risk management principles.

1.1. Resilience and Risk Management in Critical Infrastructures

Risk management is a continuous process including the identification, analysis, and assessment of potential hazards in a system or hazards related to a certain activity. Based on the recognized risk picture, the risk control measures are proposed to eliminate or reduce potential harms to people, environment, or other assets. The risk management process encompasses risk monitoring and communication. ISO 31000 [2] is the basic risk management standard. Examples of the most recognized risk management methods and techniques are included in IEC 31010 [3].

The risk management issue in critical infrastructures has a specific character because CIs are very complex, diversified and there are mutual interrelations between different infrastructures. Because of relationships between infrastructures, the state of each infrastructure influences or is correlated to the state of the other. They are called interdependencies [4–7] and can be divided to four categories: physical, cyber, geographical and logical interdependency. The effects of an incident may propagate across CIs with dire consequences. The paper takes into account interdependencies, however the complex interdependencies issues are not the basic topic of the paper.

Well-secured CIs can resist external and internal disturbances and are able to work on an acceptable efficiency level even when these disturbances occur. To improve the CI resilience is the main objective of CI stakeholders. The CIs resilience is an effective, sustainable use of critical infrastructures by stakeholders to perform tasks for the economy, government and citizens. "The concept of resilience can be seen as a superset in which typical risk assessment is a complementary part" [6]. The following activities leading to the CI resilience are proposed in this publication:

- preparing the CI specification based on the structural analysis—the most critical elements, the most vulnerable points, dependencies and interdependencies are identified; please note: dependency defines a unidirectional relationship between infrastructures, while interdependency defines a bidirectional relationship;
- running the dynamic analysis to identify the most dangerous risk scenarios—generally the subject of analysis or simulation are: propagation of dire effects of CIs phenomena, identification of the threats impact, analyses of common failures, system response to a failure or an incident, recovery process, *etc.*
- the most dangerous risk scenarios, prioritized, are taken into account later during the risk management process.

1.2. Research Related to the CIRAS Project

The critical infrastructure protection is recognized in European Union (EU) as one of the key issues. The CIP related needs on the EU and member-state levels are expressed in the European Council (EC) Directive [8]. It specifies rules of the CI identification based on the casualties, economics and public criteria, as well as the risk analysis issues and management programmes. In 2006 the European Programme for Critical Infrastructure Protection (EPCIP) was issued. A revised version is included in the EC document [9].

The CIP programmes encompass diversified (physical, technical, organizational) countermeasures, applied on the basis of risk. The risk management issue in CIs is extremely important and has not been fully solved so far. There are several dozen EU or worldwide CIP R&D projects, either already completed or currently running (Framework Programmes—FP6 and FP7, Horizon 2020, The Prevention, Preparedness and Consequence Management of Terrorism and other Security-related

Risks Programme—CIPS). Most of them deal with risk management methodologies and their supporting tools. The CIRAS (Critical Infrastructure Risk Assessment Support) project [10] is one of them.

The paper concerns a preliminary research of the CIRAS project. CIRAS was launched by the international consortium comprising:

- ATOS Spain SA (ATOS),
- Center for European Security Strategies from Germany (CESS),
- Institute of Innovative Technologies EMAG from Poland (EMAG).

The CIRAS objective is to develop a methodology and tool to support decision makers in the security measures selection for critical infrastructures. The CIRAS approach to security management in critical infrastructure protection takes into account typical CI phenomena like interdependencies, cascading and escalation of incident impacts.

The novelty of the CIRAS approach lies in a holistic assessment of all aspects of CIs security measures, including the expected risk reduction and its cost, financial benefits, as well as many vague socio-political factors to be considered in the security planning process. To select the right security measure (countermeasure) according to the CIRAS methodology, the decision maker should select a countermeasure that:

- properly reduces the risk volume to ensure security on an accepted level and to bring benefits for CI stakeholders,
- is cost-effective during implementation and operation,
- is free of social, psychological, political, legal, ethical, economical, technical, environmental, and other limitations; these vague factors in the project are called "qualitative criteria".

To support the decision making process, these issues are solved by three separate pillars, implemented as the key software components of the CIRAS Tool:

- a Risk Reduction Assessment (RRA) component,
- a Cost-Benefit Assessment (CBA) component,
- a Qualitative Criteria Assessment (QCA) component.

The CIRAS approach is based on the methodology elaborated in the FP7 (Seventh Framework Programme) ValueSec project [11]. Both the ValueSec and CIRAS methodologies support the decision making process using these three pillars, but the domains of applications and the pillars implementation approaches are different. Please note that the critical infrastructure domain, due to its specific phenomena caused by interdependencies, is much more complex than the ValueSec application domains (mass event security, mass transportation security, communal security planning, air transport security, protection against cyber-attacks on a smart grid). The CIs complexity influences the shape of the RRA, CBA and QCA components as well as the components collaboration within the framework implemented in the CIRAS Tool.

Research was performed by the project team members to elaborate the CIRAS methodology and to design and implement it in the CIRAS Tool. The project uses four main inputs:

- an extensive review of the state of the art of risk management, cost-benefits, and decision support methodologies and tools, especially those for critical infrastructure protection,
- conclusions from the CIRAS stakeholders' workshops,
- experience gained by the CIRAS team members from the ValueSec project, particularly concerning the pillars implementation.

This paper deals with a part of this research focused on the RRA component implementation. The problems addressed are:

- how to find and adapt a tool to be the RRA component,

- how to develop a new tool, according to the project requirements, if the above is not possible.

The RRA component should satisfy the project requirements:

- the basic requirements for CI risk management tools identified in [12], and
- the project specific requirements identified by the consortium with the stakeholders' help, *i.e.,* RRA should be able to properly manage the risk in critical infrastructures by selecting security measures with the right cost-benefits parameters and free of vague restrictions, should be able to easily integrate with other CIRAS components of the tool, and should be relatively simple.

The research presented in this article was focused on the feasibility of the OSCAD-based RRA. OSCAD (proprietary name) [13] is a ready-made software platform to be adapted and configured to different domains of application. The CIRAS consortium considered it a candidate for the RRA component.

This paper presents research which allowed to assess whether OSCAD can fulfil the project requirements and whether it can be used as the RRA component of the CIRAS Tool.

As a result of the experiment a novel approach is proposed how to deal with internal and external impacts of a hazardous event which occurred in the given CI. It allows to distinguish three main categories of impacts: direct CI damages, event escalation by breaching internal security barriers and causing secondary damages, event escalation from the given CI on the dependent CIs. The elaborated structured risk management method for critical infrastructures is embedded into the CI resilience process. The method is implemented in the OSCAD-CIRAS experimental tool. The tool allows to assess critical infrastructure damages in several time horizons and to assess several security measures alternatives with respect to the risk reduction and cost-benefits parameters.

1.3. State of the Art

During the CIRAS project a review [4,14–16] of laws, standards, frameworks, methods and tools was performed and summarized in [17].

The review confirms that the risk management issue in critical infrastructures is much more complicated than in other domains of application. It is specific due to the following factors:

- unprecedented CIs complexity, even when compared to very large business organizations or technical facilities,
- continuous evolution and enhancement of critical infrastructures,
- mutual interrelations between different infrastructures (interdependencies),
- problem diversity—the risk management issue is related to many other issues, like: complex systems architectures, interdependencies, complex interactions, behavioral aspects, reliability theory, vulnerability analysis, resilience, emerging behavior,
- knowledge of architecture and functioning principles of complex systems is fuzzy and the data incomplete,
- different abstraction levels applied to manage CIs and cross-sectoral relations,
- high-impact and low-probability events may occur,
- increased needs for communication and coordination among the CI operators.

The review shows that a significant number of risk assessment methods and tools can be applied in the critical infrastructure domain. Usually, they were developed for different organizations to solve their technical or organizational risk-related problems within the limited environments, and initially they were not dedicated to critical infrastructures. Later, many of them were adapted to CI needs. Usually, they are very mature, sector-specific, represent the detailed approach to the risk issue and can be easily applied on the lower level of the CI hierarchy. Their basic features are: threats and vulnerabilities categorization and identification, and the evaluation of impacts. Only few tools are able to operate on the higher CI hierarchy level. This group is still extended.

Risk management methods are very diverse and their shapes and abstraction levels depend on the levels of CIs where they are used. For example, a CI operator needs a more detailed approach than a policy maker working on the system-of-systems level, and the tool implemented for the CI asset level is more detailed than the tool for the CI operator. Generally, a higher CI level requires a more general approach.

The asset level methods and tools are adapted to higher levels but this generates problems how to handle cross-sectoral dependencies. This issue has been examined by many researchers. The challenge is how to adapt risk assessment methods used on the CI lower level to the higher level (complex system) needs.

The interdependency methodologies, supporting risk management methodologies, are growing in a parallel manner to each other. They are based on modeling and simulation techniques [6]. They are crucial to ensure the CI resilience, and in this sense they also support risk management methodologies. Many general purpose risk managers are not able to use input from the interdependencies analysis.

The review confirms that it is very hard to point out a tool which can be applied in the CIRAS Tool. There are many tools which satisfy certain basic requirements and are able to assess and manage the risk in critical infrastructures, however they do not address sufficiently the CIRAS project requirements, especially those related to the following issues:

- cross-sectoral risk management,
- cooperation with the CBA and QCA components (using cost, benefit, and vague factors in the risk management process),
- operations on the alternative packages of countermeasures,
- easy integration (connectivity, source code availability, commonly used technologies).

During the review the OSCAD was analyzed in comparison with other tools. This is a general purpose tool (software platform) which, when developed, was not intended especially for CIs. The tool is very flexible. Its functionality satisfies the basic CI risk management requirements and there is also a chance to meet the CIRAS project requirements. The paper presents research allowing to explain these issues.

1.4. Paper Content

The paper presents the following: a risk management study (Section 2) including the experimentation platform requirements, risk assessment method description, implementation of the requirements on the ready-made software platform, experiment plan workout, and the experimentation process. Section 3 includes the experimentation summary, and Section 4—the paper summary.

2. Risk Management Case Study

The case study is focused on the analysis how particular project requirements can be fulfilled by the OSCAD-based RRA, and shows step by step how this component has been developed according to the proposed risk management method.

2.1. General Requirements for Experimental Risk Manager

Basic requirements for the CI risk management tool were discussed in [12]. Summarizing this discussion, the following requirements were proposed:

(1) The CI specific phenomena, such as common cause failures, cascading and escalating effects, as well as interdependencies between CIs [5] should be considered in the risk management process.

(2) The bow-tie risk concept [4,18] is recommended for implementation as the conceptual model of the risk assessment tool. It embraces both causes of the given hazardous event and its diversified and multidirectional consequences.

(3) The CI risk register, as the managed inventory of hazardous events used in CIP programmes, should include at a minimum: related hazards/threats, corresponding hazardous event, probability of the event and its consequences. There are some other data associated with the risk register items, such as assets, societal critical functions, vulnerabilities, countermeasures, *etc.*

(4) Risk measures and the assessment process should be defined for the given application domain. A common method is to assess the likelihood (probability, frequency) of a hazardous event, and to assess the consequence severity in different dimensions. Risk is the function of both, usually expressed by a risk matrix.

The following issues are relevant with respect to the CIRAS project requirements:

(1) The RRA component should be able:

- to assess risk before a measure is implemented and reassess the risk for a certain number of security measures alternatives considered for implementation,
- to consider cross-sectoral dependencies,
- to take into account cost-benefits factors and qualitative criteria dealing with the security measures alternatives.

(2) RRA should exchange information with the CBA and QCA components during the decision process dealing with the security measures selection.

(3) RRA component should consider the CI specific phenomena, analyze causes and impacts of hazardous events, and manage the risk register data.

The data exchange between the components cannot be fully demonstrated, because the components have not been integrated yet.

2.2. Implementation Platform

The OSCAD software platform was chosen as the research platform [13]. Initially, this platform was designed to support business continuity management in accordance with ISO 22301 and information security management in accordance with ISO/IEC 27001. The software can identify different disturbances of business processes and/or breaches of information assets in different companies and organizations. OSCAD helps to reduce their losses, caused by incidents, and can support the recovery process too. OSCAD is an open and flexible tool, therefore it can be adapted to protect assets or processes in different application domains, e.g.,: flood protection [19], railway safety management systems [20] and coal mining [21]. The risk management functionality of OSCAD is of key importance to the protection of critical infrastructures.

OSCAD is equipped with risk assessment tools which analyze the causes of hazardous events (pairs: threat-vulnerability with respect to the asset or process):

- Asset Oriented Risk Analyzer (AORA),
- Process Oriented Risk Analyzer (PORA).

AORA is used to calculate risk levels of critical assets and risk reduction levels after security measures implementation. The analysis is conducted for the given asset with the related threats which exploit the asset vulnerabilities. The impact and likelihood values of threats and the current values of security measures are used to determine the inherent risk level. After applying new security measures, the risk level is reassessed and the gain in risk reduction can be determined. The PORA analysis is similar, however, it is focused on causes of the processes disturbances.

Moreover, OSCAD is equipped with tools which are able to analyze multidimensional impacts of hazardous events:

- Asset Oriented Business Impact Analyzer (ABIA),
- Process Oriented Business Impact Analyzer (PBIA).

ABIA is used to assess possible impacts of assets loss for an organization (here CI). The assessment is made according to different loss categories such as: fatalities and qualitative costs (political, social, legal), damages of infrastructure, revenue loss, external costs in other organizations. High loss levels indicate that security measures should be applied to reduce risk. PBIA is similar, however it concerns impacts for an organization (here CI), when the processes are disturbed.

As a result of the adaptation, the OSCAD-CIRAS tool prototype was developed [22]. The OSCAD adaptation performed by the author encompasses the elaboration of the domain specific system dictionaries, e.g., assets, threats, vulnerabilities, countermeasures, risk measures, software configuration, *etc*. OSCAD-CIRAS can be used as an experimental tool to acquire knowledge and experience which will then be used as an input to the CIRAS project.

2.3. Requirements Implementation on the Ready-Made Software Platform

The paper extends the works presented in [23] and deals with risk management experiments conducted with the use of the ready-made open OSCAD software platform, which was adapted to fulfill the basic CIs requirements with respect to risk management. It was assumed that one OSCAD-CIRAS instance, at minimum, can be implemented in one infrastructure. OSCAD-CIRAS is able to co-operate with similar systems working in other infrastructures. This co-operation is focused mainly on communication during the risk management process [2]. The presented experiment concerns the railway transport CI co-operating with the electricity CI. To simplify the experiment, both CIs are implemented in one OSCAD-CIRAS.

Risk management items implemented in OSCAD-CIRAS comply with the taxonomy included in the EC Directive [8], which distinguishes two groups of CIs: ECI (European CI), embraced by the EC Directive, and others (non-ECI). Assets and other items belonging to the given CI are preceded by a label being the abbreviation of a CI name: Ele (Electricity), Oil (Oil), Gas (Gas), RoT (Road Transport), RaT (Rail Transport), AiT (Air Transport), IWT (Inland Waterways Transport), Sea (Ocean and Short-Sea Shipping and Ports).

Based on the discussed below requirements a structured risk management method was developed and presented in Subsection 2.4 (Figure 6).

2.3.1. Interdependencies and CI-specific Issues—Input from Resilience Analysis

Critical infrastructure is a complex socio-technical system which interacts with similar systems working in other application domains. These interactions are considered on different layers (e.g., on the CI operator layer, sector layer, intra sector layer) [6].

The risk management process should be extended beyond a single infrastructure, because a hazardous event occurring within the given CI impacts this CI but may also cause problems for other interacting CIs, and similarly, the given CI may be impacted by hazardous events which occurred in external CIs. The risk management process should be able to consider interdependencies. This issue still remains a challenge.

OSCAD-CIRAS does not have a specialized functionality to analyze resilience, including interdependencies, and for this reason it should be supported externally to get the relevant information. The resilience analysis, producing necessary input, precedes and supports the risk assessment process.

The first kind of input concerns information about interdependencies obtained from the resilience analysis, more specifically from its static part focused on the system of systems analysis. During the dependency analysis [6], the following factors are taken into account:

- shared resources, shared services,
- common assets, components, policies,
- common causes of potential impacts, like: fire, flooding, virus attack, network attack, communication unavailability.

Diagrams, called dependency networks are obtained in the course of the interdependency analysis. The dependency network diagram represents homogenous dependencies between input and output. It will be shown in Figure 1 by an example related to the CIs presented later in the case study. The left part presents a scheme of collaborating infrastructures—rail transport (RaT), electricity (Ele) and others.

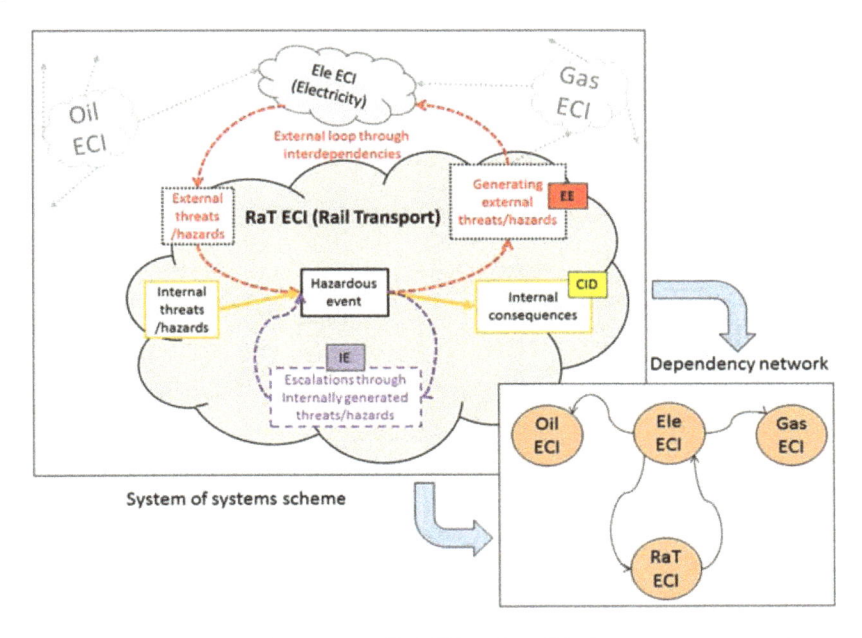

Figure 1. Two collaborating infrastructures (RaT, Ele) as the validation context—system-of-systems scheme and dependency network diagram.

The example of a dependency network, presented in the right part of Figure 1, shows that RaT ECI depends on Ele ECI and *vice versa*, and, additionally the Gas and Oil infrastructures depend on Ele.

The objective of the method presented here is to distinguish three main categories of impacts (Figure 1):

- CID (CI Degradation) category—different kinds of damages within the given CI;
- IE (Internal Escalations)—new internally generated threats or new or increased vulnerabilities which influence the considered CI, caused by the hazardous event; this allows to consider secondary effects of the given event;
- EE (External Escalations)—generated threats which impact the external CIs, or new or increased vulnerabilities in the external CIs, caused by the hazardous event.

Please note that the EE category impacts propagate across infrastructures due to existing dependencies. For example, an impact can propagate from RaT to Ele, from Ele to Gas and to Oil.

The second kind of input from the resilience analysis concerns information about critical risk scenarios. Please note that the paper presents the typical approach to risk assessment, including the identification and prioritization of threats, identification of vulnerabilities relevant to these threats and the impact assessment. This is a relatively simple approach, but it can be unsuccessful if all possible scenarios are taken into account in the risk management process—only the most critical scenarios are selected. The dynamic resilience analysis [6], preceding the risk management process, returns these very critical scenarios, such as the CI collapsing scenarios. It is assumed that to identify these scenarios, structural analyses of the collaborating CIs and dynamic resilience analyses were made.

It is assumed for the presented method and tool that the critical scenarios and interdependencies are known prior to initiating the risk assessment.

Apart from critical scenarios and interdependencies, the resilience analysis provides information about the most critical nodes, the most vulnerable nodes, strength of coupling between the nodes, and a lot of other information useful in the risk management process.

2.3.2. Bow-Tie Risk Assessment Concept Implementation

The bow-tie conceptual model [18] embraces both multiple and complex causes of the given hazardous event and its diversified and multidirectional consequences (impacts). It means that it is composed of two elements: causes analysis and consequences analysis. These features are the basis for the method presented here.

The consequences analysis part of the bow-tie model is implemented on the ABIA or PBIA basis. Later, they are called BIA (in short). For a given asset (process), which is under the hazardous event, impact can be assessed with the use of the loss matrix.

In OSCAD-CIRAS two causes analyses are possible: AORA or PORA, later called RA (in short). AORA allows to analyze each threat-vulnerability pair which can breach the given asset, while PORA does the same with respect to the given process. First, the BIA type analysis is performed, next the RA analysis (Figure 6).

2.3.3. Critical Infrastructure Risk Register and Related Issues

OSCAD-CIRAS distinguishes primary assets which are to be protected and secondary assets related to them. For example, RaT:Node, representing the railway node, can be considered a primary asset. It can be impacted when a hazardous event occurs, for this reason it should be protected. This complex asset embraces many diversified secondary assets (rails, level crossings, buildings, signaling equipment, ICT equipment, people, countermeasures, *etc.*).

The asset destruction implies multidirectional impacts on the CI where the event occurs and on other, dependent infrastructures. This is a subject of the BIA analysis. For the given protected asset there are threats and vulnerabilities considered, because they imply hazardous events which may cause full or partial damages on an asset. This is a subject of the RA analysis.

The risk register contains information about assets (and/or processes) impacted during a hazardous event, consequences, event frequency, threats, vulnerabilities, and assessed multidirectional impacts.

2.3.4. Risk Measures and the Assessment Process

The measures of multidimensional impacts of the hazardous event, used during BIA analyses, encompass three above mentioned main categories of impacts (CID, IE, EE). For each of them several loss categories are defined (four for CID, two for IE, and two for EE—eight categories in total)—see Figure 2. All categories and their number are user-defined.

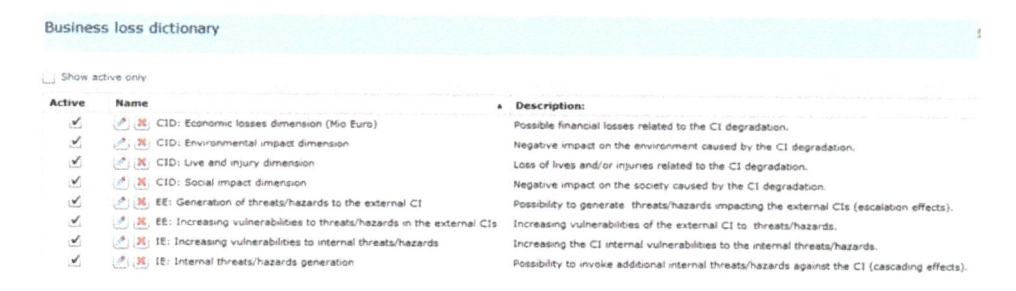

Figure 2. Event multidirectional impacts measures (CID, IE, EE) in OSCAD-CIRAS [23].

For all loss categories the same number of loss levels are defined (here: five): from Level 1 (the lower level) to Level 5 (the upper). Each level gets a clear interpretation. This way the loss matrix, *i.e.*, the basic BIA tool, is defined and shown in Figure 3. The "CID: Economic losses dimension (Mio Euro)", "CID: Live and injury dimension" and "CID: Social impact dimension" loss categories were defined according to the propositions from [4], others by the author.

Business loss category	Level1	Level2	Level3	Level4	Level5
CID: Economic losses dimension (Mio Euro)	< 0.1	[0.1-1)	[1, 100)	[10-100)	≥ 100
CID: Environmental impact dimension	No impacts or not significant impacts (surrounding area, recovery < 1 year)	Minor impacts (limited area, recovery time < 5 years)	Major damages (considerable area, e.g. plant area, recovery time 5-10 years)	Severe damages (broad area, e.g. region, recovery time 10-20 years)	Very large area impacted, e.g. country, recovery time > 20 years)
CID: Live and injury dimension	< 4 injured /seriously ill	4-30 injured /seriously ill	1-2 fatalities, 31-100 injured /seriously ill	3-20 fatalities, 101-600 injured /seriously ill	> 20 fatalities, > 600 injured /seriously ill
CID: Social impact dimension	None or not significant	Minor social dissatisfaction	Moderate dissatisfaction, possible episodic demonstrations	Serious dissatisfaction, possible demonstrations, strikes, riots	Migration from the affected area or country
EE: Generation of threats/hazards to the external...	Negligible. No threats/hazards generated	Minor damage. 1-2 threats/hazards influence a single external CI	Major damage. 3-5 threats/hazards influence a single external CI	Severe loss. 6-10 threats/hazards influence 1 or 2 external CIs	Catastrophic. More than 10 threats/hazards influence more than 2 external CIs
EE: Increasing vulnerabilities to threats/hazards i...	Negligible No influence on the external CIs vulnerabilities	Minor damage Increased 1-2 vulnerabilities of a single external CI	Increased 3-5 vulnerabilities of a single external CI	Increased 6-10 vulnerabilities of 1 or 2 external CIs	More than 10 increased vulnerabilities of 2 or more external CIs
IE: Increasing vulnerabilities to internal threats/h...	Negligible No influence on the internal CI vulnerabilities	Minor damage Increased 1-2 vulnerabilities of the considered CI	Increased 3-5 vulnerabilities of the considered CI	Increased 6-10 vulnerabilities of the considered CI	More than 10 increased vulnerabilities of the considered CI
IE: Internal threats/hazards generation	Negligible No threats/hazards issued	Minor damage 1-2 threats/hazards of the 1st generation issued for the	Major damage 3-5 threats/hazards of the 1st generation issued for the	Severe loss 6-10 threats/hazards of the 1st generation issued for the	Catastrophic More than 10 threats/hazards of the 1st generation issued for the considered CI OR more than 5 threats/hazards of the 2nd generation issued for the considered CI OR the 3rd or next threats/hazards

Figure 3. Business loss matrix used for BIA analyses.

The BIA analyzer operates on three main categories of impacts (CID, IE, EE) and their loss categories shown in Figure 3. For each CID, IE, EE impact category the worst case value of loss categories is selected as a partial BIA result, marked as CIDval, IEval, and EEval. The BIA aggregated result, depending on the chosen calculation model, is defined by very simply functions:

- for the worst case model (WCM):

$$BIAvalue = Worst\,Case\,of\,(CIDval,\ IEval,\ EEval) \qquad (1)$$

- for the total model (TM):

$$BIAvalue = CIDval + IEval + EEval \qquad (2)$$

- for the product model (PM):

$$BIAvalue = CIDval \times IEval \times EEval \qquad (3)$$

In the example discussed in the paper, BIA considers three main categories of losses (CID, IE, EE) and five levels of losses (1 to 5). It means that the range of the BIA aggregated results can be: 1 to 5 for WCM, 3 to 15 for TM, and 1 to 125 for PM. The kind of the calculation model is configurable. The WCM model is chosen due to its simplicity.

For the RA analysis the risk value is expressed as:

$$\text{Risk} = \text{Event likelihood} \times \text{Event consequences} \qquad (4)$$

The RA "Event likelihood" measures, based on [12,18], are presented in Table 1, and their implementation in the OSCAD-CIRAS dictionary is shown in Figure 4. The number of likelihood measures is fully configurable – here five levels are assumed.

Table 1. Event likelihood measures.

Level of measure	Frequency per year	Description
Fairly normal 5	1–10	Event that is expected to occur frequently
Occasional 4	10^{-1}–1	Event that may happen now and then and will normally be experienced by personnel
Possible 3	10^{-3}–10^{-1}	Rare event, but will be possibly experienced by personnel
Remote 2	10^{-5}–10^{-3}	Very rare event that will not necessarily be experienced in a similar plant
Improbable 1	0–10^{-5}	Extremely rare event

Event likelihood dictionary

Name	Description:	Value
Fairly normal	Event that is expected to occur frequently. Frequency per year: 1 - 10	5
Occasional	Event that may happens now and then and will normally be experienced by personnel. Frequency per year: 0.1 - 1	4
Possible	Rare event, but will be possibly experienced by personnel. Frequency per year: 0.001 - 0.1	3
Remote	Very rare event that will not necessarily be experienced in a similar plant. Frequency per year: 0.00001 - 0.001	2
Improbable	Extremely rare event. Frequency per year: 0-0.00001	1

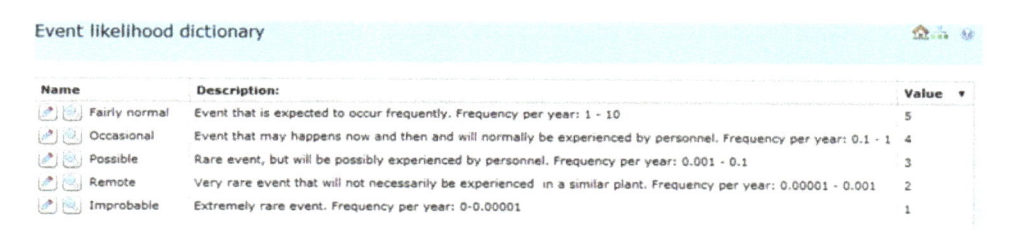

Figure 4. Event likelihood measure in OSCAD-CIRAS [23].

The RA "Event consequences" measures are derived from the loss matrix categories. It is possible because the BIA analysis precedes the RA one, and the measures of both are harmonized. Table 2 is an example of mapping the BIA aggregated results (BIAval) on the RA consequences measures with respect to the used calculation model.

Table 2. The RA consequences derived from BIA aggregated results depending on the used BIA calculation model (an example).

RA consequences	Mapping the BIA Aggregated Results on the RA Consequences for Different Calculation Models		
	for Worst Case Model (WCM)	for Total Model (TM)	for Product Model (PM)
Negligible damage 1	1	3–5	1–25
Minor damage 2	2	6–8	26–49
Major damage 3	3	9–10	50–80
Severe loss 4	4	11–13	81–100
Catastrophic 5	5	14–15	101–125

The contents of Table 2 are implemented in the consequences dictionary (Figure 5). For further BIA examples the measures with the "WCM_" prefixes are used, and the RA consequences are measured in the range from 1 to 5.

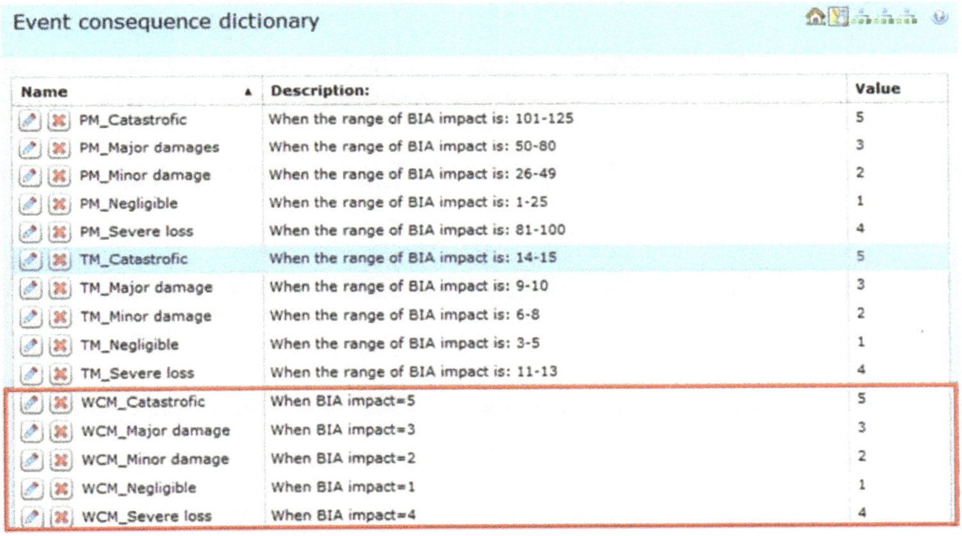

Event consequence dictionary

Name	Description:	Value
PM_Catastrofic	When the range of BIA impact is: 101-125	5
PM_Major damages	When the range of BIA impact is: 50-80	3
PM_Minor damage	When the range of BIA impact is: 26-49	2
PM_Negligible	When the range of BIA impact is: 1-25	1
PM_Severe loss	When the range of BIA impact is: 81-100	4
TM_Catastrofic	When the range of BIA impact is: 14-15	5
TM_Major damage	When the range of BIA impact is: 9-10	3
TM_Minor damage	When the range of BIA impact is: 6-8	2
TM_Negligible	When the range of BIA impact is: 3-5	1
TM_Severe loss	When the range of BIA impact is: 11-13	4
WCM_Catastrofic	When BIA impact=5	5
WCM_Major damage	When BIA impact=3	3
WCM_Minor damage	When BIA impact=2	2
WCM_Negligible	When BIA impact=1	1
WCM_Severe loss	When BIA impact=4	4

Figure 5. Event consequences measures for different BIA calculation models implemented in the system dictionaries.

2.4. Risk Assessment Method Implemented in OSCAD-CIRAS

The risk assessment method proposed in the paper takes into account previously specified requirements, including the CIRAS RRA requirements, and the abilities of the OSCAD software platform [13].

This method is embedded into the process, which ensures the resilience of the given CI, e.g., RaT ECI. The general scheme of the risk assessment process is presented in Figure 6. The risk assessment processes run concurrently in each of the collaborating infrastructures.

The risk assessment process running in the given CI gets from the resilience analysis a set of basic critical risk scenarios, dependency network diagram and any other risk-relevant information. There are three risk scenarios repositories:

- for basic risk scenarios, obtained from the resilience analysis;
- for externally generated hazards for the given CI; the EE-related risk scenarios are identified outside the CI;
- for internally generated hazards for the given CI, causing secondary impacts (the IE-related risk scenarios).

The assessment process starts from the basic scenario of the highest criticality obtained from the resilience analysis. First, BIA (a consequences analysis) is performed, and its results encompass the following:

- CI internal damages (CID)—CIDval,
- generated internal hazards (IE)—IEval,
- generated external hazards (EE)—EEval.

The aggregated BIA result is identified as the function of CIDval, IEval, EEval, according to the calculation model (here, for WCM: BIA result is the maximal value of CIDval, IEval, EEval).

Next, RA (a causes analysis) is launched to identify threat/vulnerability pairs leading to the hazardous event. Their likelihood is assessed. OSCAD requires the event consequences input as well. In this case, the BIA-derived value is introduced by default. During the risk management process, the risk is reassessed after the countermeasure implementation (the risk after), and if the countermeasure affects the event consequences, e.g., data backup, the default value (from BIA) can be corrected manually.

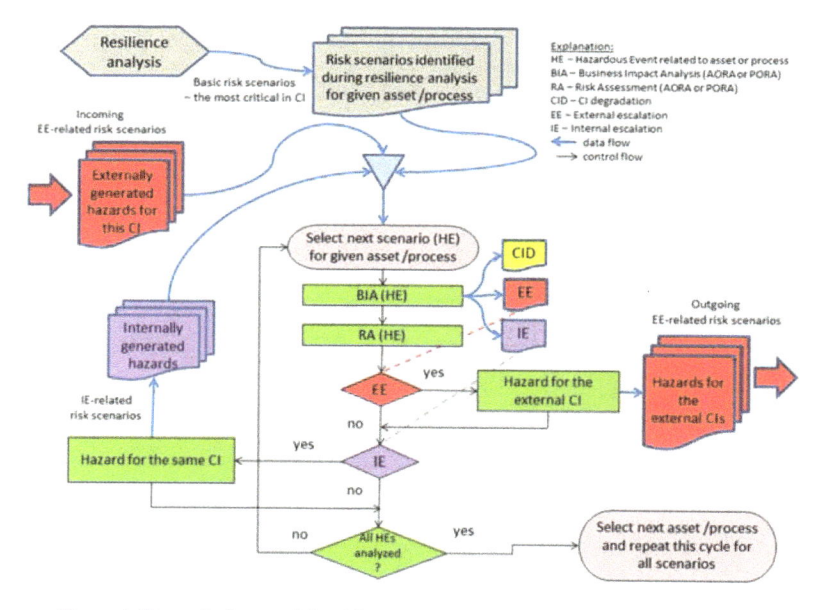

Figure 6. General scheme of the risk assessment process in a critical infrastructure.

After completing the BIA/RA pair, its results are analyzed. When the EE impact occurs, the warning about the generated hazard (embracing causes and consequences: new threats and/or increased vulnerabilities, external impact, risk and impact values, *etc.*) is formed as the EE-related risk scenario and sent to the potentially impacted CI to be considered in the risk assessment process. The risk communication process (an important part of the whole CIs risk management framework) is responsible for exchanging such warnings between the collaborating and dependent infrastructures. This EE-related risk scenario is placed in the external hazards repository of the warned CI.

Next, the IE impact is analyzed. When the impact occurs, the IE-related risk scenario is defined (a record embracing the causes and consequences: new threats and/or increased vulnerabilities within the considered CI, secondary impact, risk and impact values, *etc.*) and added to the internal hazards repository. Moreover, this newly generated internal hazard is assessed (BIA-RA). This secondary effect may cause new secondary internal damages (CID), an external impact (an additional EE-related risk scenario) as well as a new IE-related risk scenario, which is placed in the repository and then analyzed (BIA/RA). These analyses focus on internal escalation and are repeated until no internal secondary effects occur. Then, the next basic risk scenario is taken into account and analyzed in the same way. When all basic scenarios are finished, next the hazards externally generated for this CI are analyzed similarly as the basic ones. The whole process stops when all basic and externally generated for this CI are analyzed.

2.5. Scenario of the Validation Experiment

The validation deals with the railway and energy collaborating infrastructures and encompasses one basic risk scenario: a catastrophe in an important railway node. To simplify the experiment, both CIs are analyzed in the same OSCAD-CIRAS. They are distinguished by prefixes RaT and Ele. Let us assume that this critical risk scenario is downloaded from the basic repository for the risk assessment process.

Figure 7 shows four pairs of analyses of the validation experiment. Each pair, composed with BIA-RA, represents a bow-tie idea. The following numeration rule of the particular pairs of analyses is assumed: the basic scenario (called here the 1st iteration) has no postfix, for the second, third, *etc.*, expressing the escalated impacts, the iteration number is followed by a postfix expressing the kind of impact (ie, ee), *i.e.*, 1, 2ie, 2ee, and 3ee.

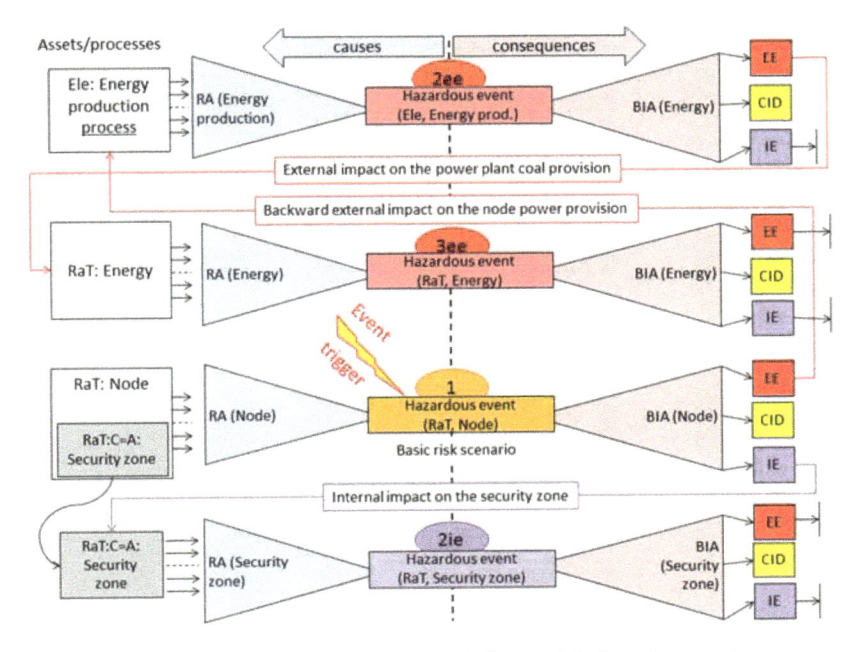

Figure 7. Validation scenario shown with the use of the bow-tie concept.

The scenario is initiated by the event trigger which occurred in the RaT:Node (please note the naming convention: CIname:AssetName) primary asset and caused a hazardous event, e.g., intentional derailment seriously impacting the railway node area.

1st iteration

The "1 BIA(RaT:Node)" analysis identifies multidimensional impacts of this event. Please note that the impacted asset or process is within the brackets. The internal degradation (mostly financial consequences) which is caused by an intentional derailment is assessed (CID). BIA proves that this event:

- impacts the external infrastructure Ele as the coal transport for the power plant is stopped for a long time (EE-related risk scenario generated); normally this should imply sending this scenario to OSCAD-CIRAS working in Ele CI, but here both CIs are simulated in one OSCAD-CIRAS instance;
- breaches the security zone (countermeasure) which is a secondary asset of RaT:Node; IE-related risk scenario is generated and placed in the internal repository.

The "1 RA(RaT:Node)" analysis identifies causes of the hazardous event and the related risk. Because secondary effects are revealed, they should be further analyzed, causing the next iteration, instead of taking a new basic scenario.

2nd iteration

Due to the external escalation (EE), extra analyses for Ele CI (energy production in the power plant) are performed:

- "2ee BIA(Ele:Energy)" identifies the CI degradation caused by an externally generated threat; it does not identify any internal impacts (IE), but identifies backward external impacts to the RaT infrastructure (energy provision for the RaT:Energy); this implies the 3rd iteration;
- "2ee RA(Ele:Energy production process)" identifies how coal delivery disturbance impacts the energy production process (here the process-oriented approach is applied).

Due to the internal escalation (IE), extra analyses of the security zone are needed:

- "2ie BIA(RaT:Node→Security zone)",
- "2ie RA(RaT:Node→Security zone)".

Please note that a secondary asset is preceded by "→". The related BIA identifies secondary CI degradation caused by a breach in the security zone (here: theft) but does not identify any further IE or EE impacts.

3rd iteration

Due to the external threat generated by Ele for RaT:Energy, two extra analyses are performed:

- "3ee BIA(RaT:Energy)",
- "3ee RA(RaT:Energy)".

The additional CI internal degradation is assessed, and no internal/external escalations are detected. In the 3rd iteration both RaT and Ele infrastructures achieve a stable state and therefore no further analyses are needed. Particular analyses were performed during the validation process.

2.6. Running the Validation Experiment

The validation experiment embraces eight analyses (four BIA, four RA) performed in OSCAD-CIRAS according to the scenario shown in Figure 7.

The left side of Figure 8 presents the OSCAD-CIRAS menu/submenu depending on the context of the operation, here: risk analyses. The right part shows all performed analyses, their status, and risk acceptance parameters (not discussed here). It is an entry point to view/modify the details of each analysis.

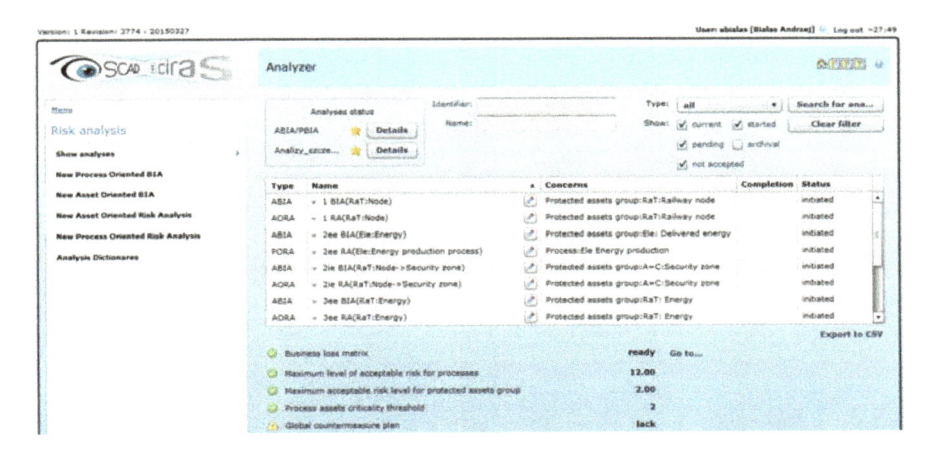

Figure 8. OSCAD-CIRAS presenting performed analyses.

The four of eight performed analyses are exemplified in the following subsections.

2.6.1. Identifying Impact of the Railway Node Crash—"1 BIA(RaT:Node)"

This BIA analysis assesses multidirectional impacts when the railway node crashes. "1 BIA(RaT:Node)" embraces three main impact categories, represented by three OSCAD-CIRAS tabs: CID (Figure 9), EE (Figure 10), IE (Figure 11).

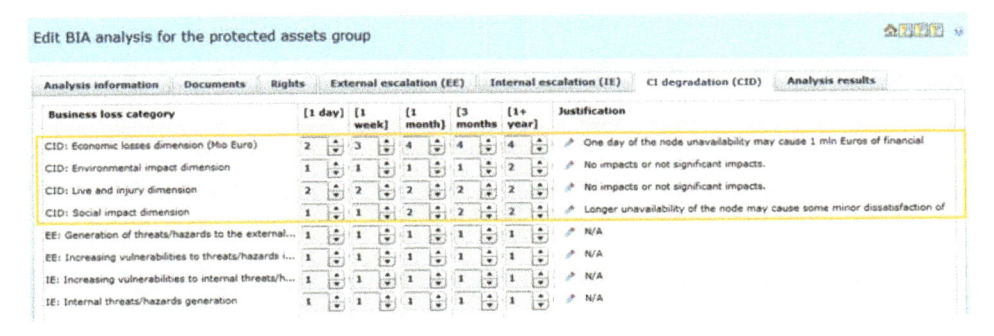

Figure 9. The BIA analysis for the railway node—internal degradation tab.

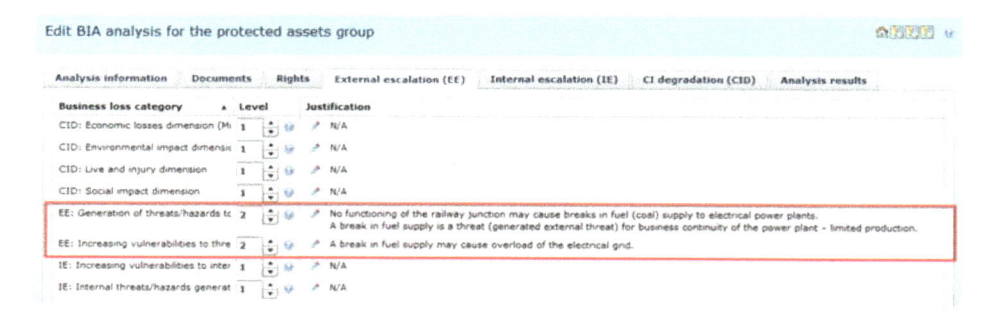

Figure 10. The BIA analysis for the railway node—external escalation tab.

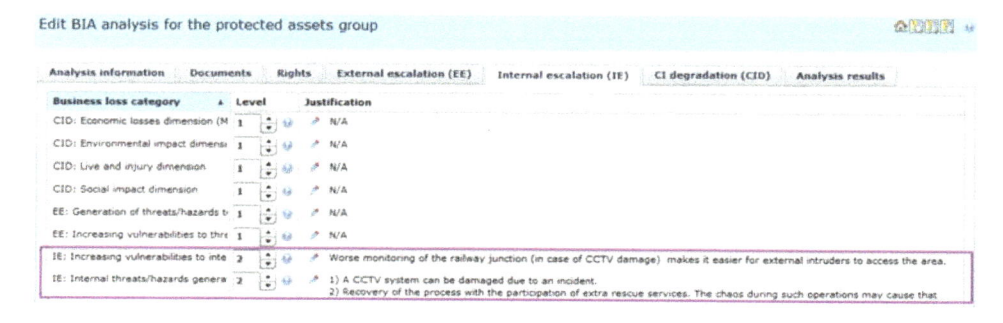

Figure 11. The BIA analysis for the railway node—internal escalation tab.

The tool offers a possibility to assess CID-type losses in a certain number (here: five) of time horizons (Figure 9). Please note that CIDval = 4 (worst case value).

Figure 10 presents the assessment of the external impact of the crash in the railway node. The disturbance in the Ele critical infrastructure is possible because coal transport failed (limited production, network overloading). Please note that EEval = 2.

Figure 11 presents the assessment of the internal impact of the crash in the railway node. The crash may breach the node protection system (security zone, CCTV) raising vulnerabilities to other threats. This may cause negative secondary effects. Please note that IEval = 2.

Assuming that the worst case model is used, BIAvalue = max(4,2,2) = 4.

2.6.2. Causes of the Railway Node Crash—"1 RA(RaT:Node)"

Figure 12 exemplifies the "1 RA(RaT:Node)" analysis, mentioned in the validation scenario (Figure 7). Apart from the train derailment (a green frame), some other node risk scenarios are listed, like: manipulation in the train depot, power supply failure, theft of equipment, but they are not discussed here.

Figure 12. The RA analysis for the railway node.

The event triggered in the railway node is classified as "intentional derailment". The derailment is possible due to the following exploited vulnerabilities:

- "Large areas and facilities" of the railway node – difficult to monitor,
- "Insufficient infrastructure protection",
- "Low awareness".

For each pair threat-vulnerability the risk is assessed. Each pair has consequences from BIA (BIAvalue = 4). Please note the pair: "Derailment—intentional"—"Large areas and facilities". The implementation of the countermeasures package (security zone, CCTV cameras, additional fences, police guards), not shown here, decreases the likelihood from "Possible" (3) to "Remote" (2), with the same consequences (4), and the risk from 12 to 8 (max. value is 5 × 5 = 25.0). Please note that the countermeasures cost rises from 69,000 Euros to 212,000 Euros (for the given package of countermeasures the cost is assigned).

Certain parameters, like countermeasure class or implementation level, are not used in the paper.

2.6.3. Causes of Breaching the Node Security Zone—"2ie RA(RaT:Node→Security Zone)"

During the IE assessment (Figure 11) a breach of the node security zone was identified implying two analyses:

- "2ie BIA(RaT:Node → Security zone)"—to assess impact related to this event, like: "Significant financial losses possible in case of long-lasting disturbance in functioning of security zone", neither IE nor EE are detected—BIA not shown;
- "2ie RA (RaT:Node → Security zone)"—presented in Figure 13.

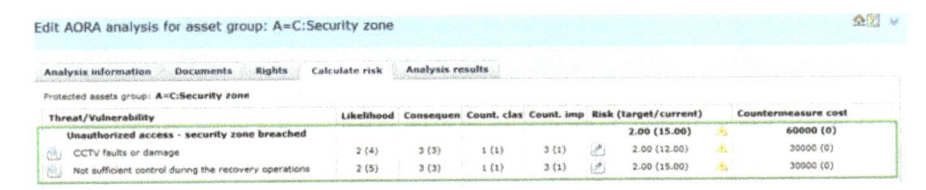

Figure 13. The RA analysis for the breached security zone.

The breached security zone becomes more vulnerable because the CCTV system was damaged and the node was not properly watched due to the recovery process in the node (resources shortage). For this reason, unauthorized access is more realistic.

Please note that the security zone plays twofold role, therefore in the system dictionary a special category A = C (Asset as countermeasure) was defined.

The security zone is a barrier, a countermeasure, and an asset belonging to the set of assets representing the railway node. In OSCAD-CIRAS it is possible to asses risk for this node similarly to other assets.

2.6.4. Identifying Impact of Energy Delivery Disturbance—"2ee BIA (Ele:Energy)"

While EE was assessed for the basic scenario (Figure 10), the disturbance of the fuel (coal) delivery for the power plant was detected, implying two other analyses to be done for the Ele infrastructure:

- "2ee BIA(Ele:Energy)" was made, which revealed the possibility of the energy delivery problem (Figure 14); this may impact railways, therefore "3ee BIA(RaT:Energy)" and "3ee RA(RaT:Energy)" are launched (not shown).
- "2ee RA(Ele:Energy)"; the process-oriented risk analysis (PORA) is applied to exemplify that the process approach is possible in OSCAD-CIRAS; the analysis is focused on the causes of the "Energy production process in the power plant" disturbance.

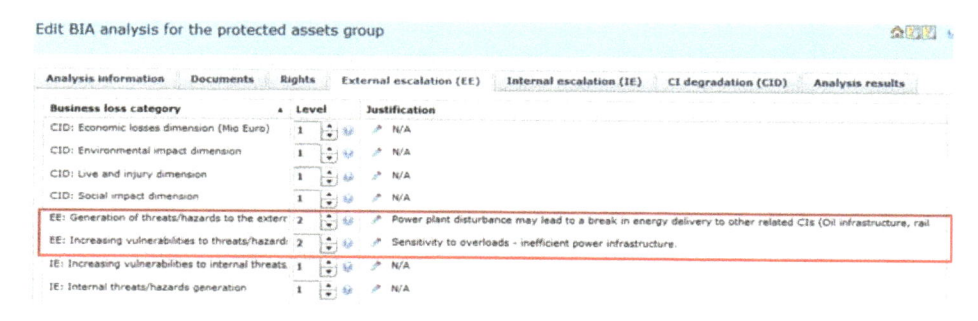

Figure 14. BIA for the energy asset provided by the power plant (EE tab).

The implied, but not shown here "3ee BIA (RaT:Energy)" and "3ee RA (RaT:Energy)" conclude that the disturbance of the railway energy system can be serious, still the probability is low thanks to the implemented redundancy.

Please note that the event "Energy delivery problem" can be considered a common cause event, because it impacts all energy dependent infrastructures. The validation scenario is simplified and considers only one dependent infrastructure (RaT).

3. Results and Discussion

The paper presents the validation experiment related to risk management in critical infrastructures with the use of the ready-made OSCAD software platform adapted for this application domain as the OSCAD-CIRAS tool.

To develop this CI-dedicated experimental tool, the following input was considered:

- the general requirements for the CI risk manager [12], elaborated on the basis of publications, laws, standards and tool reviews,
- the CIRAS project requirements.

The objective was to perform a case study and to acquire knowledge for the CIRAS project. The question is to what extent the requirements are satisfied by OSCAD-CIRAS, i.e., whether OSCAD-CIRAS is able to work as the risk reduction assessment (RRA) component within the CIRAS Tool. The ready-made OSCAD was configured, equipped with the domain data (dictionaries, measures, different parameters, *etc.*), and the validation was performed according to the elaborated plan. As a result, the OSCAD-CIRAS experimentation tool was worked out.

3.1. Meeting Basic Requirements

Reviewing the basic requirements (Section 2.1.), the following conclusions are possible.

(1) OSCAD-CIRAS takes into account the CI specific phenomena, such as common cause failures, cascading and escalating effects, as well as interdependencies between CIs, though OSCAD-CIRAS should be supported by a resilience analysis. During the validation experiment it was shown that OSCAD-CIRAS is able to consider the following:

- common cause initiating events; for the given hazardous event BIA is able to detect hazardous events, that are implied by the given hazardous event, in all dependent infrastructures by generating many outgoing EE-related risk scenarios; this possibility was mentioned in Figure 14 (Ele => RaT, Ele => Oil, Ele => Gas) but was shown only for one dependency path (Ele => RaT);
- cascade initiating events; apart from internally triggered hazardous events, the RA analysis considers external triggers incoming from other infrastructures as the incoming EE-related risk scenarios; the considered impacted CI depends on infrastructures which generate these scenarios; this possibility is represented by the following analyses:
  - "2ee RA(Ele:Energy)"—a coal delivery problem may disturb the energy production process;
  - "3ee RA (RaT:Energy)"—an energy delivery problem may disturb railway transport;
- cascade resulting events; BIA is able to detect any hazardous event resulting from the original event which impacts a dependent infrastructure; this was represented by: "1 BIA(RaT:Node)"/Figure 10, "2ee BIA(Ele:Energy)"/Figure 14 and "3ee BIA (RaT:Energy)" (not shown);
- escalating events; BIA performed in the first infrastructure is able to detect a hazardous event in the second impacted dependent infrastructure, and BIA performed for the second impacted infrastructure is able to detect a hazardous event in the third infrastructure, and so on; this was exemplified by the analysis chain for RaT => Ele => RaT (Figure 7—a red line).

(2) The bow-tie concept embracing the analysis of consequences and causes was implemented as the pairs of the RA-BIA analyses. It was exemplified by the analyses chain shown in Figure 7. Usually BIA precedes RA.

(3) The risk register is represented by the OSCAD-CIRAS data (assets—primary and secondary, processes, threats, vulnerabilities, risk scenarios, countermeasures, *etc.*)—some data are predefined (dictionaries), some created during the performed analyses.

(4) Risk measures are configurable: categories of losses, number of loss levels and their interpretation, number of time horizons, likelihood levels and their interpretation, e.g., in the frequency domain, calculation models and formulas for risk assessment.

3.2. Meeting CIRAS Project Requirements

As for the CIRAS project requirements (Section 2.1), the following conclusions are possible.
(1) OSCAD-CIRAS is able:

- to assess risk before a measure is implemented and reassess the risk for a certain number of security measures alternatives considered for implementation,
- to take into account cost-benefits factors and qualitative criteria dealing with the security measures alternatives.

The validation scenario, simplified for the purposes of this article, was focused on the risk assessment before the countermeasure was implemented. However, the selection of measures in OSCAD-CIRAS, which is a part of the risk management process, needs additional explanation.

Figure 15 shows an example of security measures selection (the example slightly differs from the validation example) for the given threat-vulnerability pair. It is assumed that the "risk before" the measures implementation was assessed earlier (Current state tab). The decision maker who selects countermeasures for implementation may define several security measures alternatives (here three, marked A, B, C). Each alternative represents a coherent package of countermeasures, with their risk, cost, benefits, qualitative criteria and other parameters. Then the most advantageous alternative is selected for implementation.

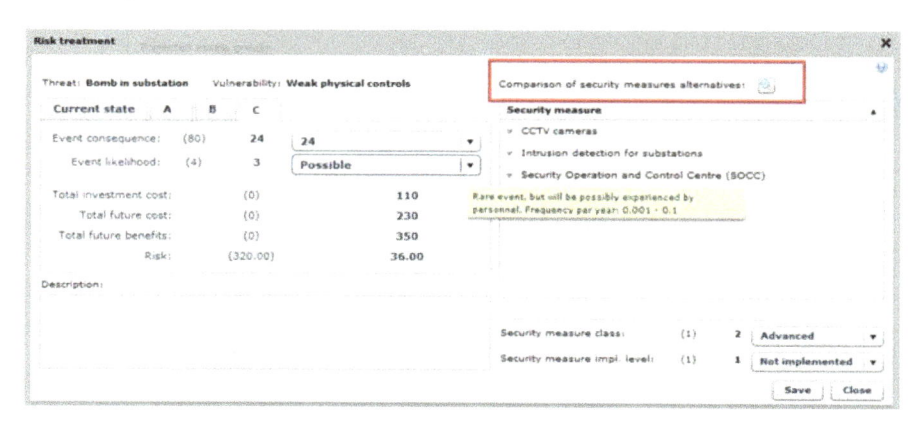

Figure 15. OSCAD-CIRAS risk manager—considering security measures alternatives.

To support the decision maker in this process, some aggregated data from RRA, CBA and QCA are available on diagrams (note the button "Comparison of security measures alternatives", marked by the red frame). An example of a diagram, related to CBA parameters, is shown in Figure 16. Please note other tabs.

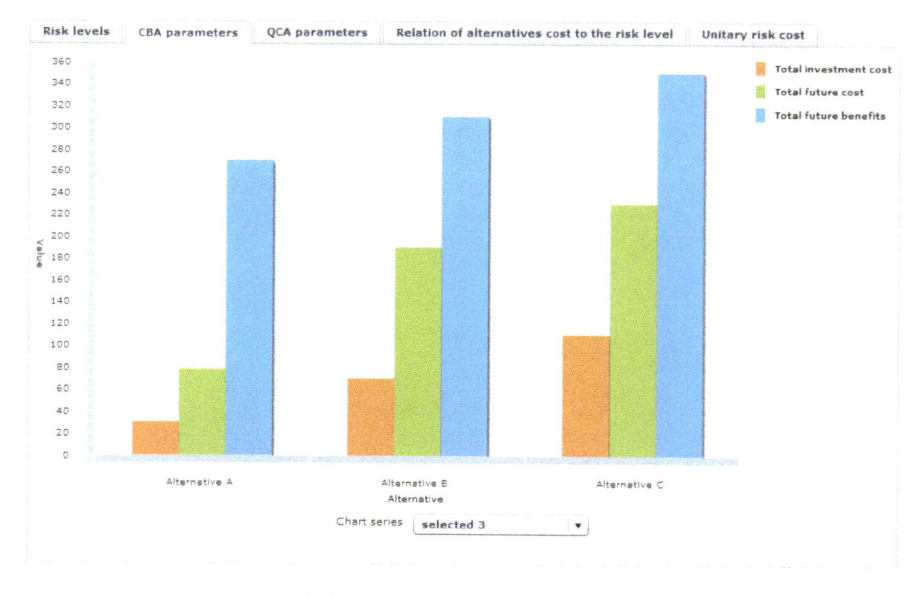

Figure 16. OSCAD-CIRAS risk manager—considering external cost-benefit parameters.

More detailed graphs, tables, reports related to particular alternatives will be available from the CIRAS tool level. Currently they are under development. OSCAD-CIRAS is able to exchange (through developed web services) information with the CBA and QCA components during the decision process dealing with the security measures selection

(2) Other issues related to the project requirements were discussed previously, like the ability to consider the CI specific phenomena and cross-sectoral dependencies, to analyze causes and impacts of hazardous events, and to manage the risk register data.

Reassuming, the validation process is based on the planned scenario which encompasses two critical infrastructures: railway transport (RaT) and electricity provision (Ele). Two kinds of escalation effects are demonstrated:

- those propagated through a CI internal path,
- those propagated through a path crossing one or more CIs.

The consequences of hazardous events in a given CI can impact the same CI again and/or the neighboring CIs, creating a complex sequence of impacts. The presented method allows to identify:

- direct consequences occurring within the considered infrastructure (called here: CI degradation);
- secondary effects caused by breaching internal barriers (CI safeguards) and occurring in this CI as the consequences of a hazardous event (called here: internal escalation); this escalation can propagate further causing additional hazardous events—internal or external;
- secondary effects occurring in the external CIs as the consequences of a hazardous event (called here: external escalation); they can propagate further, impacting other CIs or generating internal escalations.

The scenario depends on the new risks identified during the analysis. The presented method assumes (in the loss matrix for BIA analyses) that a new hazardous event (internal or external) can be triggered as a consequence of a previous hazardous event. Internally triggered events result from breaching the CI internal barriers. Events triggered within the external CIs can propagate thanks to existing CI interdependencies. The risk assessment results give information if the hazardous event will propagate internally and/or externally, or nowhere. It means that each risk situation may drive quite a different scenario in the same set of infrastructures. If, during the analysis of infrastructure A, it was detected that a breach in infrastructure B is possible (EE), then the risk analysis in infrastructure B is needed and will be added to the risk analyses scenario. Otherwise, the analysis in infrastructure B will not be added to this scenario. If, during the analysis of infrastructure A, it was detected that a security barrier can be breached (IE), then the analysis in infrastructure A is needed and will be added to the risk analyses scenario. Otherwise, it will not be added to this scenario.

For this reason, each scenario is here called a risk-driven scenario. It is assumed that interdependencies are known—all paths with possible propagation of impacts are known.

4. Conclusions

The objective of the paper is to develop a structured risk management method for critical infrastructures, embedded into the CI resilience process (Figure 6). The method distinguishes three categories of impacts composed into the BIA loss matrix:

- CID (direct CI degradation),
- IE (escalation by breaching internal security barriers),
- EE (escalation by breaching security barriers in external CIs).

The method is based on the commonly used risk management methodology, though it was enhanced by three above mentioned features which allowed to take into account the following issues (Section 3):

- how a hazardous event which occurred in the given CI impacts the dependent CIs; this allows to consider common cause initiating events, cascade resulting events, externally escalating events;
- how a hazardous event which occurred in external CIs impacts the given CI; this allows to consider cascade initiating events, externally escalating events;
- secondary impacts of a hazardous event which occurred in the given CI and lead to an internal escalation; this allows to analyze breaches in the multilayered protection system.

There are some extra features which make it possible to assess a critical infrastructure degradation in several time horizons (CID-type consequences). In addition, they can assess several security measures packages with respect to the risk reduction ability.

To elaborate, implement and validate this method, the research includes as well:

- the identification of CI domain-related data, like assets, processes, threats, vulnerabilities, common used countermeasures, *etc.*, and put them into the OSCAD system dictionaries,
- the risk parameters definition, *i.e.*,: scales of measures for likelihood, consequences, impacts categories and levels, loss matrix, calculation formulas configuration,
- the planning of the validation scenario (to be simple enough and be able to exemplify all features of the elaborated method),
- performing validation to assess the feasibility of the proposed solution.

The paper gives substantial contribution to the CIRAS project. The aim of the research presented in the paper is to acquire knowledge about the shape of the key component responsible for risk assessment (RRA) of the CIRAS Tool. The case study was based on the ready-made business continuity/information security management OSCAD software. During the research this software was adapted to the critical infrastructure application domain, according to the identified requirements. This way the dedicated OSCAD-CIRAS tool was developed. The near real data were prepared for the critical infrastructure domain and the software was configured. According to the planned validation scenario, the risk assessment within two collaborating infrastructures (railway, energy) was studied. The case study gives information how to use OSCAD-CIRAS in the CIRAS project. The results of research confirm that OSCAD-CIRAS can be applied as the RRA component.

The acquired knowledge was used by the CIRAS project team. Currently all components (RRA, CBA, QCA) are integrated into the CIRAS Tool. The case study described in the paper is the basis for two CIRAS project use cases.

The CIRAS project considerably extends the risk reduction assessment by additional CBA (cost-benefits) and QCA (vague factors) assessments to obtain a full risk picture for the decision maker.

Acknowledgments: The author thanks his Colleagues from the CIRAS project consortium for reviewing this paper and discussing the presented concept. The author is grateful for their assistance during the OSCAD customization (installation, logo edition, preparing the OSCAD dictionaries).

Author Contributions: The presented validation experiment represent the author's own research.

Conflicts of Interest: The author declares no conflict of interest. The OSCAD is owned by the Institute of Innovative Technologies EMAG. This project has been funded with support from the European Commission. This publication reflects the views only of the author, and the European Commission cannot be held responsible for any use which may be made of the information contained therein (obligatory for each paper concerning CIRAS).

References and Notes

1. Eusgeld, I.; Nan, C.; Dietz, S. "System-of-systems" approach for interdependent critical infrastructures. *Reliab. Eng. Syst. Saf.* **2011**, *96*, 679–686. [CrossRef]
2. ISO. *Risk management—Principles and guidelines*; ISO 31000:2009; International Organization for Standardization: Geneva, Switzerland, 2009.

3. IEC/ISO. *Risk Management—Risk Assessment Techniques*; IEC 31010:2009; International Electrotechnical Commission (in cooperation with ISO): Geneva, Switzerland, 2009.
4. Hokstad, P.; Utne, I.B.; Vatn, J. *Risk and Interdependencies in Critical Infrastructures: A Guideline for Analysis, Reliability Engineering*; Springer-Verlag: London, UK, 2012.
5. Rinaldi, S.M.; Peerenboom, J.P.; Kelly, T.K. Identifying, Understanding and Analyzing Critical Infrastructure Interdependencies. *IEEE Control Syst. Mag.* **2001**, *21*, 11–25. [CrossRef]
6. Giannopoulos, G.; Filippini, R. Risk Assessment and Resilience for Critical Infrastructures. In Proceedings of Workshop Proceedings, Ispra, Italy, 25–26 April 2012; Available online: http://publications.jrc.ec.europa.eu/repository/handle/JRC71923 (accessed on 29 February 2016).
7. Min, H.-S. J.; Beyeler, W.; Brown, T.; Jun Son, Y.; Jones, A.T. Toward modelling and simulation of critical national infrastructure interdependencies. *IIE Trans.* **2007**, *39*, 57–71. [CrossRef]
8. The Council of the European Union. Council Directive 2008/114/EC—on the identification and designation of European critical infrastructures and the assessment of the need to improve their protection. 2008. Available online: http://eur-lex.europa.eu/legal-content/EN/TXT/?uri=CELEX%3A32008L0114 (accessed on 29 February 2016).
9. European Commission. Commission Staff Working Document—on a new approach to the European Programme for Critical Infrastructure Protection Making European Critical Infrastructures more secure. 2013. Available online: https://ec.europa.eu/energy/sites/ener/files/documents/20130828_epcip_commission _staff_working_document.pdf (accessed on 29 February 2016).
10. CIRAS project web site. Available online: http://cirasproject.eu/content/project-topic (accessed on 22 December 2015).
11. ValueSec FP7 project web site. Available online: www.valuesec.eu (accessed on 22 December 2015).
12. Bialas, A. Critical infrastructures risk manager—the basic requirements elaboration. In *Theory and Engineering of Complex Systems and Dependability*; Zamojski, W., Mazurkiewicz, J., Sugier, J., Walkowiak, T., Kacprzyk, J., Eds.; Springer-Verlag: Cham, Switzerland; Heidelberg, Germany; New York, NY, USA; Dordrecht, The Netherland; London, UK, 2015; pp. 11–24.
13. EMAG. OSCAD project web site. Available online: http://www.oscad.eu/index.php/en/ (accessed on 21 December 2015).
14. Giannopoulos, G.; Filippini, R.; Schimmer, M. *Risk Assessment Methodologies for Critical Infrastructure Protection—Part I: A State of the Art*; Publications Office of the European Union: Luxembourg, 2012.
15. European Commission. EURACOM Deliverable D20: Final Publishable Summary, Version: D20.1. 2011. Available online: http://cordis.europa.eu/result/rcn/57042_en.html (accessed on 21 December 2015).
16. ENISA. Inventory of Risk Management/Risk Assessment Methods and Tools. Available online: http://rm-inv.enisa.europa.eu/methods (accessed on 21 December 2015).
17. Baginski, J.; Bialas, A.; Rogowski, D.; Flisiuk, B.; (Institute of Innovative Technologies EMAG, Katowice, Poland); Martin, J.; Garcia, A.; (ATOS S.A., Madrid, Spain); Klein, P.; (Center for European Security Strategies, Munich, Germany). State of the Art of Methods and Tools. 2015.
18. Rausand, M. Risk Assessment: Theory, Methods, and Applications. In *Statistics in Practice*; Wiley: Hoboken, NJ, USA, 2011.
19. Białas, A. Risk assessment aspects in mastering the value function of security measures. In *New Results in Dependability and Computer Systems*; Zamojski, W., Mazurkiewicz, J., Sugier, J., Walkowiak, T., Kacprzyk, J., Eds.; Springer-Verlag: Cham, Switzerland; Heidelberg, Germany; New York, NY, USA; Dordrecht, The Netherland; London, UK, 2013.
20. Bialas, A. Computer support for the railway safety management system—first validation results. In *Advances in Intelligent Systems and Computing*; Zamojski, W., Mazurkiewicz, J., Sugier, J., Walkowiak, T., Kacprzyk, J., Eds.; Springer-Verlag: Cham, Switzerland; Heidelberg, Germany; New York, NY, USA; Dordrecht, The Netherland; London, UK, 2014.
21. Białas, A. Business continuity management, information security and assets management in mining. *Mechanizacja i Automatyzacja Górnictwa* **2013**, *8*, 125–138. Available online: http://yadda.icm.edu.pl/yadda/element/bwmeta1.element.baztech-891910b0-6f4e-4dfb-8bc3-345d940cc88b?q=fd72cbbb-7631-435b-9e4e-cf0b5ebdcc38$4&qt=IN_PAGE (accessed on 29 February 2016).

22. OSCAD-CIRAS. Available online on request using the author's e-mail.
23. Białas, A. Experimentation tool for critical infrastructures risk management. In Proceedings of the 2015 Federated Conference on Computer Science and Information Systems (FedCSIS), Lodz, Poland, 13–16 September 2015.

© 2016 by the author. Licensee MDPI, Basel, Switzerland. This article is an open access article distributed under the terms and conditions of the Creative Commons Attribution (CC BY) license (http://creativecommons.org/licenses/by/4.0/).

Article

Opportunities for Cross-Border Entrepreneurship Development in a Cluster Model Exemplified by the Polish–Czech Border Region

Joanna Kurowska-Pysz

Management and Engineering Production Department, University of Dąbrowa Górnicza, Str. Cieplaka 1c, 41-300 Dąbrowa Górnicza, Poland; jkurowska@wsb.edu.pl; Tel.: +48-602-231-123

Academic Editor: Adam Jabłoński
Received: 31 December 2015; Accepted: 18 February 2016; Published: 2 March 2016

Abstract: The subject of the paper is the analysis and evaluation of cross-border entrepreneurship development opportunities on the basis of cross-border cooperation, which has gradually evolved from consisting of bilateral partnerships to a networking model or even a cluster. The study conducted at the Polish–Czech border area indicates that, in terms of the development of cross-border cooperation, the economic sphere is lagging far behind social activities such as culture, education and tourism. At the same time, Polish and Czech enterprises are not sufficiently mobilized to develop cross-border entrepreneurship, although a number of support instruments in this regard have been proposed. Sustainable development of the border should take into account both social and economic aspects. An important research problem therefore becomes determining the possibility of boosting the development of cross-border entrepreneurship on the basis of the existing forms of cross-border cooperation, including cooperation in the social sphere. The aim of this paper is to define the conditions and opportunities for the development of cluster cooperation in the area of cross-border entrepreneurship. The author has attempted to resolve whether the intensity of cross-border cooperation can be a factor which mobilizes companies to develop their cross-border entrepreneurship and whether cross-border entrepreneurship can be further developed within the cluster model.

Keywords: sustainable development of the border region; cross-border cooperation; cross-border entrepreneurship; partnerships; cluster

1. Introduction

Processes occurring in the world economy have a significant impact on the functioning of enterprises, regardless of the scale of their business activity. Increased globalization favours the expansion of large transnational corporations, whereas simultaneously in the economy, there are many mechanisms stimulating the development of small and medium-sized businesses. Smaller enterprises, mostly operating on a regional or local scale, also have good prospects on the market, and also show a tendency for integration (also with larger companies), for example as clusters [1]. Clusters are a form of partnership aimed at developing cooperation between enterprises, but also local governments, academic institutions and business environment institutions, located in immediate geographical proximity and representing related sectors. These two strategic conditions are necessary to form appropriately strong bonds between the participants of a cluster.

An impulse for the development of any form of cooperation, including cooperation within the clusters, can be both the needs and expectations of interested entities as well as external factors encouraging integration. Particularly favourable system conditions, aiding the development of cooperation, are created in border regions. In contrast to many well-developed border towns in

Western Europe or East Asia, Eastern Europe border regions are developing rather poorly, especially in economic and social terms. They are disadvantaged and at risk of marginalization, requiring special support. The reason is certainly the geopolitical situation in the communist bloc, which has pursued a specific policy of borderland development. Until the fall of the communist bloc, obtaining a passport was only possible for some citizens cooperating with the authorities. Until Poland and the Czech Republic joined the Schengen Zone on 21 December 2007, each crossing of the border was associated with the control of documents. Before freely crossing the border was allowed, the border area, as a militarily strategic zone, was excluded from priority economic and social investments, and it was patrolled by the army in the large part. In a social sense, crossing the border was seen as an extraordinary necessity, not as a privilege of border residents and other citizens. This possibility was exploited only in specific situations. The border was therefore divided and not united, which at present means the process of cross-border cooperation between Poland and the Czech Republic, despite its undeniable dynamism, is not progressing as fast as in other regions of the world.

Integration activities, stimulating the development of border areas, are undertaken both at the level of the European Union, as well as individually by neighbouring member states, which are in favour of cross-border business development and socio-economic integration of the neighbouring communities.

So far, in cross-border cooperation, both in terms of social as well as economic cooperation, bilateral partnerships are the dominant type of cooperation existing between local governments and NGOs, and occur much less frequently between enterprises. There is no doubt that bilateral cooperation between the same partners continuing for a long time strengthens cross-border relations, yet does not fully serve the development of border areas. In order to effectively counteract the development-related problems of these areas, it is both necessary to form new partnerships between entities that have not worked together before as well as develop networking opportunities. Currently, most examples of networking occur in the social sphere whereas at the economic level they occur only occasionally. In order to balance this trend, it is necessary to define mechanisms to encourage cross-border entrepreneurship development and economic cooperation of a networking nature that could develop as clusters.

Analysis of cooperative relations occurring in the borderland has encouraged the author to consider the opportunities for cluster cooperation development in these areas. It is fostered by both a natural tendency for cross-border integration, as well as the external conditions, resulting among other factors from the socio-economic policy of neighbouring border regions and the European Union's system support, e.g., in the form of the INTERREG VA 2014-2020 funds [2].

The aim of the paper is to define the conditions and possibilities for the development of cluster cooperation in the area of cross-border entrepreneurship. An example of Polish–Czech cross-border cooperation between Silesian Voivodeship (Poland) and the Moravian-Silesian Region (Czech Republic) was used to measure the level of development of cross-border entrepreneurship. The author has attempted to resolve whether the intensity of cross-border cooperation can be a factor that mobilizes businesses to develop their cross-border entrepreneurship and whether cross-border entrepreneurship can thrive in the cluster model.

In the studied area, qualitative research was conducted: desk research and quantitative research involving IDI, CATI, CAWI and CATI and PAPI data collection methods. In this paper, the author used qualitative research (IDI), implemented in 2014 by the TRITIA association and the Regional Development Agency in Ostrava, on a sample of 30 Polish and Czech companies. Research topics related to the motives and the process of the development of cross-border entrepreneurship and other conditions related to their activities at the border. As part of this study, several case studies were undertaken of companies developing their cross-border entrepreneurship, including the company run by the author in the field of consulting. In addition to these studies, the author has used her own research conducted by means of the CATI method with 14 companies from the voivodeship of Silesia and the Moravian country, identifying their level of interest in cross-border entrepreneurship, as well as their opinions about the barriers and benefits related to it. In order to identify potential regional specializations which can form the basis for the development of future cross-border clusters, the author also used her own qualitative research conducted in the years 2014–2015, including:

- survey methods such as: CATI, CASI and CAWI on a group of 466 Polish local government units and 199 Czech local government units for assessing the current state of Polish–Czech border cooperation, identification of factors shaping the development of this cooperation, the projected directions of this cooperation and the main actors of this cooperation,
- survey using PAPI method, giving the possibility of creating in Polish-Czech Euroregion Cieszyn Silesia—of a cross-border cluster in cultural and creative industries, which covered a total of 40 entities from Poland and the Czech Republic, declaring their intention to strengthen cross-border cooperation, including 18 Polish and Czech companies. These studies related to the nature and extent of cooperation with the entities in the neighboring country, the key benefits of cluster cooperation in the field of culture and creative industries as well as barriers to this process.

Conclusions from the study will serve as recommendations for entities responsible for cross-border cooperation policy (e.g., regional governments, business environment institutions) whose task is to create good conditions for the development of cross-border entrepreneurship.

2. Cross-Border Territorial Partnerships as a Form of Inter-Organisational Cooperation in the Border Regions

Territorial partnership is voluntary and is based on the agreement between at least three partners representing at least two of the three sectors: public, private and non-governmental. These partners maintain autonomy and jointly implement long-term measures for the benefit of a specific region. Within the framework of cooperation, they improve and monitor the partnership and maintain the principle of equality in the sharing of resources, responsibilities, risks and benefits [3]. The development of territorial partnerships in the 1980s contributed to the popularization of the local resources management model, involving—among others—the creation of more or less formal organizations uniting representatives of public, private and non-governmental sectors in a specific area [4,5]. Partnerships also developed through the process of European integration and the support of cross-border cooperation, as well as the pursuit to strengthen the competitiveness of peripheral and marginalized areas. Territorial partnerships bear a reference to cross-border cooperation.

The definition of cross-border cooperation was provided in the European Charter for Border and Cross-Border Regions (1981) [6], the European Outline Convention on Transfrontier Cooperation between Territorial Communities or Authorities (1980) [7] and the European Charter of Regional Self-Government (1997) [8]. Generally, it can be stated that cross-border cooperation is one of the forms of territorial cooperation of different types of units in the border regions, which might be related to all areas, including entrepreneurship. A common historical origin and other important similarities between neighbouring areas on the borderland (e.g., linguistic, cultural, constitutional, social or economic) may aid in joining forces to achieve common development goals.

Cross-border cooperation applies equally to the activities of local authorities at various levels, as well as to joint initiatives, e.g., non-governmental organizations or businesses. It aims to create cooperation networks at local and regional levels, as a result of which cooperation on economic matters can be fostered, while cultural and social barriers in local communities disappear [9].

The issue of partnerships was recognized, among others, in the regulation of EU structural funds [10]. Traditionally, partnerships are a mechanism for the transfer of development policy to lower levels of the hierarchy (top down policy). Partnerships are also agreements of entities at different levels of the hierarchy, providing interested parties with influence and participation in the development processes, both initiated at the lowest levels of cooperation (bottom up policy), as well as arranged at higher levels (as mentioned above, top down policy) [11].

The principles of entering into cross-border partnerships have been stipulated in the Council Regulation (EC) No. 1083/2006. Each country, depending on its needs and legislative capabilities, enters into partnerships with public authorities at various levels, or with other entities, including NGOs, which can act as economic and social partners [12].

Currently, partnership is most commonly associated with various forms of cooperation between institutions, entities and individuals in the implementation of common social, economic or environmental goals. The essence of partnership consists in finalizing an agreement (but also civil law or association agreement) by entities, institutions, organizations and individuals aimed at engaging all the concerned parties in actions aimed at optimal use of the available resources and stimulating multi-dimensional development, using various tools and cooperation mechanisms. The consequence of the concluded agreement is to undertake joint ventures (projects, programs) of a different nature, enabling achievement of common objectives.

An example of cross-border partnership are Euroregions—associations operating in the borderlands of two or more countries, specializing in cross-border cooperation [13]. The main aim of their activities is the removal of socio-economic inequalities, solving the problems of disadvantaged and peripheral areas, building mutual trust and cooperation across borders [14] as well as promoting cross-border entrepreneurship development and integration in other fields, e.g., education [15]. Such goals are pursued by Euroregion Cieszyn Silesia. This forum of cooperation covers the border areas of the Silesian Voivodeship (Poland) and the Moravian-Silesian Region (Czech Republic). In the Polish and Czech part, there are two associations whose members are municipalities, NGOs and enterprises engaged in Euroregion activity. Both active associations and their members have undertaken a series of cross-border projects, some of which were carried out with the support of European Union structural funds [16]. However, in the period following the completion of these projects, cooperation was continued and further developed [17]. An example of such integration trends, based on the implementation of earlier EU projects may be, among others, interest in creating a cross-border culture cluster in the Euroregion Cieszyn Silesia. It is one of the examples of partnership activities, consisting in the creation of local network structures or a cluster, based on the cooperation of persons, entities and institutions interested in the development of a given territory.

However, increasing trends to further strengthen cross-border relations to form a cluster can be observed, which allow for a departure from bilateral cooperation to multilateral interaction between the main actors in the cluster. Sectoral clusters are among the inter-organizational networks, which involve the transfer of knowledge [18] and other flows (material or information), as well as the development of relationships (formal and informal), of which the most important are social. In the networks of cooperation, the participation of enterprises, research units, administration [19], civil society and those responsible for environmental issues [20] is necessary. Due to the institutional and social nature of clusters, official relationships overlap here both structurally (between the cooperating parties) and organically (between the people involved in the cooperation). Another aspect is that friendly, neutral as well as hostile or competitive relationships [21] can form in the cluster. The number of links, the types of actors and the industry specializations of the cluster have been captured by M. Hennning, J. Moodysson and M. Nilsson [22]. They emphasized how important it is to direct cross-organizational cooperation, including clustering, according to regional specializations. This leads to the involvement of entities responsible for shaping regional policy, going beyond the typical areas of clusters' operation. This coupling of actions drives the competitive advantage of the region, and various measures to strengthen inter-organizational cooperation in sectoral clusters were also included in this paper. The author focuses on the example of the eastern part of the Czech–Polish border, *i.e.*, Euroregion Cieszyn Silesia, where a clear regional specialization in the field of culture and creative industries is being established, and entities responsible for the regional policy of Poland and the Czech Republic as well as for cross-border policy (i.a. TRITIA) are involved in integration policy. An example would be, among others, interest in creating a cross-border cluster of culture and creative industries in the Euroregion Cieszyn Silesia.

3. Clusters as an Advanced Form of Cross-Border Cooperation Development

The territorial and integrative context of cluster activity is an important prerequisite to considering the possibility of cross-border cluster development in borderlands. Low levels of socio-economic development of border areas indicate the need for greater emphasis on the economic aspects of integration and cooperation, which so far have definitely been outweighed by the social aspects. Not only in borderland regions, an important feature of innovative and competitive organizations is their propensity for cooperation, including the development of various types of network relationships [23–25].

These are structures in which individuals and groups, acting independently, collaborate towards achieving a common goal [26]. This cooperation may take the form of various types of territorial partnerships, single and multi-sector, as well as networks and clusters [27,28]. The degree of institutionalization of clusters is varied [29]. They involve mainly businesses, but also institutions of operating in varied business environments, local governments at various levels, NGOs, local development agencies, schools, banking institutions and the R&D sector, including scientific bodies.

A cluster is a geographic concentration of interconnected enterprises, specialized suppliers, service providers, businesses operating in related sectors and associated institutions in particular fields, competing with each other but also cooperating [30]. The cluster can also be defined as geographically limited agglomerations of enterprises [31], together generating synergistic effects. There are many other similar definitions [32,33]

A cluster is defined by the following key elements: the cluster members and the relationships between them, generated knowledge and innovation, and the economic impact (economic effect) of cluster activities.

The process of cluster development in a border area can be considered as one of the new challenges of cross-border cooperation, which is currently evolving from consisting of bilateral partnerships towards a networking model. Clusters serve in the cooperation of entities within a certain geographical area, which provides the ability to initiate and develop direct contact between the participants in the network. Another premise is the possibility of achieving synergy through joint action for the benefit of the given community and territory. Clusters as a form of networks are often characterized by loose and voluntary relationships, involving the transfer of resources between individuals, including the transfer of information and knowledge [34]. Clusters are also characterized by specialization in a particular sector or industry, affinity of the technologies and skills used, consistency between objectives and products or services offered on the market [35].

In the long term, the success of the cluster is determined by the quality of internal collaboration and having common objectives among its participants. It is also important to appoint a leader who is able to animate and develop cooperative relationships within a cluster, despite many obstacles and restraints that constrain this process.

Natural tendencies for integration, the popularity of inter-organizational cooperation, as well as the availability of mechanisms supporting this cooperation (including structural funds) are certainly important factors conducive to the development of cluster structures in border regions, which concern external entities interested in the development of clusters and networks. The European Commission indicates that the regions which combine risk capital, competence and high quality research on a broad portfolio of clusters have a chance to become nodes of innovation [36]. Such development impulses are important in border regions, often peripheral and marginalized, mostly characterized by lower indicators of economic and social development, also with weaker potential than preferably located areas. For these regions, especially important is access to valuable knowledge and the ability to overcome various types of barriers to development, including barriers in cross-border relations, thanks to which economic and social cohesion of borderland is fostered. In the process of "learning" in border regions and developing cross-border cooperation, an important role might be served by clusters.

The location of the cluster in cross-border environments where various forms of cooperation are very popular, including cross-sector partnerships involving entities from neighbouring countries, could become a catalyst for closer relations between cluster members. In general, the scope and objectives of cooperation in the cluster are defined by partners themselves (entrepreneurs, local governments, NGOs, *etc.*), but in the border region the broader context of cluster activity should be taken into account—the desired and expected development of cross-border cooperation. Clusters have the chance to become effective, future-oriented forms of cross-border cooperation which will contribute to a better use of the diverse potential of the entire border, effectively overcoming barriers in building mutual relations between neighbouring communities, as well as achieving more dynamic development of the whole cross-border region. The development of cluster structures in the borderland contributes to overcoming the negative aspects of the peripheral location of border areas, the use of the development opportunities arising from the proximity of the neighbouring country, promoting the idea of European unity and international cooperation, the spreading of the socio-cultural influences and innovations, among other benefits

4. Cross-Border Entrepreneurship and Cross-Border Cooperation

Entrepreneurship is a result of the development of social relations. Entrepreneurs strive to create value [37] and to improve their own personal well-being, but also that of society [38,39], which is reflected in the wide economic development of the area in which they operate. The development of entrepreneurship can be one of the indications of cross-border cooperation, leading to the improvement of the socio-economic situation of marginalized areas. Social activities have an important role to play here as well (e.g., joint planning at a cross-border level, events, cultural activities, education, investment in infrastructure on both sides of the border, *etc.*), which makes the integration process more natural and versatile [40]. According to P. Drucker, entrepreneurship as a mode of behaviour, can be attributed to individuals, a team or institution [41]. Thus, in the regional system, the development of entrepreneurship is the resultant behaviour of many entities with different business objectives. In this sense, entrepreneurship refers not only to the business itself, but also to local governments, non-governmental organizations or other entities in the business environment [42]. Of great importance in the process of enterprise development are such factors as education and quality of intellectual capital, intensity and diversity of support for growing businesses, the activity of local and regional authorities in creating conditions conducive to economic revival, the social attitude of residents and the tradition of entrepreneurship in the given area.

Cross-border entrepreneurship concerns many indications of economic activity beyond borders, which usually include various forms of partnerships [43]. The cross-border location of economic entities means that it is often not necessary to register a business activity on the other side of the border, or else business activity is carried out there through another entity in the neighbouring border region.

The conceptual importance of cross-border entrepreneurship is thus determined by: the term cross-border, which means exceeding national borders; and its transboundary nature, which entails regular and continuous contact beyond national borders, with daily (institutionalized or not) cooperation in the areas on both sides of the border [44].

Cross-border entrepreneurship represents an opportunity both for the development of the regions as well as individual enterprises. The relationship between cross-border entrepreneurship and cross-border cooperation is interdependent. On the one hand, cross-border cooperation stimulates the development of entrepreneurship in marginalized regions, but at the same time, entrepreneurship expanding across national borders is also an impetus for closer cross-border cooperation.

Cross-border entrepreneurship has an influence on capital, supply and sales markets, the search for business partners, transfer of knowledge and know-how, acquiring staff and other resources of interest to the partners on both sides of the border [45]. Cross-border entrepreneurship can also include cross-border clusters and cooperation networks.

5. Conditions for the Development of Cross-Border Entrepreneurship in the Silesian Voivodeship and the Moravian-Silesian Region

The Silesian Voivodeship and the Moravian-Silesian Region are twin areas located on the Czech–Polish border, which for many years have been brought together through close cross-border cooperation. According to the data as of 31 December 2013, Silesian Voivodeship had a population of approximately 4.6 million and occupied an area of 12.333 km^2, while GDP per capita at current prices amounted to 44.960 PLN (approx. 11 thousand Euro). On the other hand, the Moravian-Silesian Region was inhabited by approx. 1.2 million people and occupied an area of 5427 km^2 and GDP per capita at current prices amounted to 325.963 CZK (12 thousand Euro) [46]. Despite the differences in the level of population and surface area, the economic potential of both regions is similar. In the report "Doing Business 2015", in terms of the conditions for conducting business, Poland was ranked 32nd place, while the Czech Republic 44th place for 189 countries assessed, while in terms of barriers in starting up a business, Poland was classified 85th, while the Czech Republic was ranked at 110th place [47].

In both countries, there exist similar business solutions. A comparative analysis shows that both in the Silesian Voivodeship, as well as in the Moravian-Silesian Region, a number of institutions operate which support developing companies. These are mainly technology parks and entrepreneurship incubators, as well as loan and delivery funds. In both regions, there are also grants from structural funds available, and additionally in these areas, there is the possibility of tapping into EU funds intended specifically for the development of borderlands which come from the Operational Programme of Cross-Border Cooperation Czech Republic—Republic of Poland 2007–2013 and the Operational Programme INTERREG VA Czech Republic-Poland 2014–2020. There are also funds available that are intended for other entities, e.g., local governments, NGOs, labour market institutions, *etc.* which are aimed at the development of cross-border entrepreneurship, among other goals.

Both regions (together with Opole Voivodeship—Poland and the Local Government Žilina Region—Slovakia) are members of the European Grouping of Territorial Cooperation TRITIA (TRITIA), which was established in 2013. In 2013, the implementation of the strategy for the system cooperation of the regions forming the European Grouping of Territorial Cooperation TRITIA was conducted, in which economic goals and the main tasks for achieving cross-border cooperation in the field of entrepreneurship were established [48].

The objectives and activities that foster the development of cross-border entrepreneurship are included in Table 1.

Table 1. Objectives and actions supporting the development of cross-border entrepreneurship initiated by European grouping of territorial cooperation TRITIA, Ltd. TRITIA.

Kind of Objectives/Support	Discription of Activities
Overall objective	Creating an environment for employment growth and the development of cross-border economic space based on entrepreneurship, geographic location, local human resources, common history and the complementary strengths of all the regions
Specific objectives	1. Establishing conditions for the development and institutionalization of the different elements of cooperation leading to the establishment of cross-border economic space 2. Supporting the development of human resources and administrative/institutional potential of the cross-border region 3. Supporting cross-border initiatives in research, development and innovation.

Table 1. Cont.

Kind of Objectives/Support		Discription of Activities
Selected forms of support	1.	Pooling and cooperation of cross-border clusters
	2.	Cooperation of universities
	3.	Meetings institutionalisation of entrepreneurs from the participating regions—brokerage event
	4.	The creation of cross-border economic forum TRITIA—supporting the development of the business community on the border
	5.	Promoting financial tools to support the SMEs sector and institutions supporting entrepreneurship, enhancing the attractiveness of the business environment and a culture of innovation, together with raising the quality of public services addressed to entrepreneurs
	6.	Cross-border development of the labour market
	7.	Coordination of cooperation of entities supporting entrepreneurship, e.g., regional development agencies, chambers of commerce, *etc*.
	8.	Activities undertaken within cross-border cooperation of entities involved in R & D and the entrepreneurs sector, aimed at developing an innovative environment
	9.	Cooperation in the creation of cross-border products supporting a culture of innovation (e.g., education activities, academic entrepreneurship, cross-border innovation portals, joint actions aimed at implementing innovation strategies, *etc*.).
	10.	Investment in public infrastructure necessary to ensure the development of entrepreneurship and innovation (science and technology parks, entrepreneurship incubators, industrial parks, innovation centres, *etc*.).
	11.	Cooperation in other areas of R & D (research and development), including fostering the integration of academic and commercial spheres.

Source: own elaboration based on information about the project.

In 2014, TRITIA and the Regional Development Agency from Ostrava conducted a qualitative study of 30 young companies (15 Czech and 15 Polish companies, each of which have been in operation on the market for less than three years) among small and medium-sized enterprises in the Silesia Voivodeship and Moravian-Silesian Region. The study was conducted as part of the project "Sustainable economic activity", co-financed by the Operational Programme of Cross-Border Cooperation Czech Republic–Republic of Poland 2007–2013. Respondents for the study were recruited from among the companies leading innovation-oriented development activities and interested in developing cross-border business, benefiting from the support of entrepreneurship incubators, technology parks and other business institutions on the border. The research involved the development of case studies examining the company's development path with reference to cross-border interest in entrepreneurship and integration with other companies operating on the border. In-depth personal interviews (IDI) were also conducted as part of the study, and the respondents were asked, among others, questions regarding the following issues:

- the process of creating companies and business conditions in the market,
- the scope of the offer and its development,
- the main market, including the market focused on cross-border cooperation,
- interest in the development of intellectual capital in their companies,
- cooperation with universities,
- interest in the sectoral integration and cross-border cooperation,
- recommendations on the stabilization of the company on a cross-border market.

The results of this study are shown in Tables 2–6.

Table 2. Structure of cooperation.

Structure of Cooperation	
Silesian Voivodeship (PL)	**Moravian-Silesian Region (CZ)**
2/3 of the surveyed companies were established using a grant enabling unemployed people to start a company. This implies the need to respect business plans and running business activities mainly as a self-employed person or hiring a few persons. Thus the development of cooperation with other entities is progressing rather slowly, as companies try to act based on their own resources. The use of domestic subsidies often restricts development cooperation. Most companies have not given priority to acquiring enterprises for cooperation purposes from cross-border market so far.	For small businesses the biggest expense are wages, and therefore they restrict employment to a minimum, while they still prefer close relationships with regular suppliers and close associates. In this way permanent cooperative groups of enterprises are formed whose business activity is a part of a common product or service. Until present, this cooperation has been focused on the regional market, companies are not looking for business partners on cross-border market, but some companies are already present in this market as producers.

Source: own elaboration based on data from the project.

Table 3. The scale of business activity.

The Scale of Business Activity	
Silesian Voivodeship (PL)	**Moravian-Silesian Region (CZ)**
In foreign markets, 6 companies operate (more than 1/3 of respondents), and for one of them exports account for 90% of revenue. Three companies operate on a cross-border market, the remaining three are suppliers for Czech companies. In the vast majority, however, the domestic market is their dominant market, although all Polish respondents are interested in the Czech market. Most companies declare that they are too weak to compete in the cross-border market.	In the foreign markets, 7 companies operate, 1 company already operates on a cross-border market, others are investigating this market. The companies claim that at the first stage of development they want to focus on the domestic market since they do not feel strong enough to enter foreign markets, including the cross-border market.

Source: own elaboration based on data from the project.

Table 4. Development of human resources.

Development of Human Resources	
Silesian Voivodeship	**Moravian-Silesian Region**
Most respondents have used specialist training in their field and entrepreneurship before starting their business. These people have gained expertise before they established the company. More than 1/3 of companies intend to continue specialist trainings also in the scope of business activity.	Undertaking business activity was mainly driven by the competence of the respondents and not different types of incentives to establish a business. Despite the wide range of courses, trainings, *etc.* self-education is the dominant mode, as well as investing in language learning. Companies are also willing to benefit from the offer of free consultations, conferences and meetings funded by, among others, cross-border funds.

Source: own elaboration based on data from the project.

Table 5. Collaboration with universities.

Cooperation with Universities	
Silesian Voivodeship	Moravian-Silesian Region
1/5 of respondents cooperate with universities in projects, R&D services, and vocational education of students. Much more popular is the cooperation with NGOs offering companies specific advisory support regarding business development, consulting and training. Universities lack such an offer. Through these forms of cooperation, respondents have contact with cross-border partners, since universities and non-governmental organizations often rely on cross-border funds.	Nearly 2/3 of respondents cooperate with universities with regard to research or educational activities, e.g., organization of apprenticeships and traineeships. No concrete results of this collaboration have been indicated. Cooperation with universities, which are beneficiaries of cross-border projects gives businesses access to partners from the border area.

Source: own elaboration based on data from the project.

Table 6. Willingness to integrate.

Willingness to Integrate	
Silesian Voivodeship	Moravian-Silesian Region
The vast majority of respondents declare membership or cooperation with trade or business associations, or even clusters (1 company).	Only one company is a member of a trade association, and the others did not have such a need or did not realize there was such a possibility.

Source: own elaboration based on data from the project.

The selected research findings presented above, because of the sampling mode (non-random), reflect only indicative trends in the development of young companies operating in the Silesian Voivodeship and Moravian-Silesian Region. The results indicate that the presence of the enterprise in the border area market does not mean that it automatically treats the neighbouring market as a natural expansion area. Awareness of the border is very strong among novice entrepreneurs. As companies are focused on overcoming the initial challenges in starting up their business and gaining the nearest market (mostly local), the prospect of cross-border market is quite remote for them. However, the tendency to cooperate with universities and the development of human resources, which contributes to improving the quality of human capital in the region, should be assessed positively [49].

In these studies, the author took personal part, since her Polish consulting company develops cross-border entrepreneurship in three aspects: by serving Czech customers, through the procurement of the suppliers from the Czech market and through the Polish–Czech consortium in which large orders are provided. In addition to the cited studies, in 2015, the author conducted her own qualitative research based on interviews with 14 companies (seven Polish and seven Czech companies) from the provinces of Silesia and Moravia that maintain business relationships across the border. The conclusions from the study are as follows:

- companies are interested primarily in acquiring specific cooperation partners (suppliers, customers) in the area of industry in which they specialize, they attach less importance to networking;
- companies expect cross-organizational cooperation, which will allow them to find market niches and will quickly manifest in their revenues and profits, and they are less interested in the exchange of knowledge, information, joint promotion, *etc.*;
- companies expect governments, scientific institutions and other business entities to take a partnership approach in the development of cross-border entrepreneurship, but in this field, the integration is still too weak and is characterized by differing interests;

- companies indicate that the purchasing power of borderland residents is weak and competition in the market large, and therefore entering the same sector on the other side of the border can be afforded by only the most competitive enterprises,
- as a great aid in the development of cross-border entrepreneurship, companies point to direct contacts on the other side of the border, e.g., Polish–Czech staff, participation in the Polish–Czech Chamber of Commerce, participation in trade missions, participation in EU projects *etc.*
- as the key barriers to the development of cross-border entrepreneurship, companies point to: the lack of an effective system of support for such operations on the border, the lack of sufficient knowledge about the partner's market, currency risk, a similar structure of demand on both sides of the border and difficulties in producing a unique product, the bureaucracy, and the divergence in regulations.

The above-described attitude of the surveyed companies represents a big contrast to the above-mentioned actions supporting cross-border entrepreneurship which have been declared by TRITIA and Regional Development Agency of Ostrava. Similar projects supporting the development of Polish–Czech business have been undertaken by Czech-Polish Chamber of Commerce in Ostrava, Regional Development Agency in Ostrava, Innovation Support Centre VSB of Technical University in Ostrava, Entrepreneurs Club in the Castle of Cieszyn, Regional Chamber of Commerce and Industry in Bielsko-Biala and many other public and social entities, as well as local governments and their associations. Analysis of the initiatives undertaken by these entities indicates that many companies are monitoring the cross-border market, but do not have the courage to enter it. A meeting of Czech and Polish entrepreneurs, sponsored by the Czech-Polish Chamber of Commerce in Ostrava, is held annually in Ostrava and involves at least 150–200 companies from both countries, but it has not focused on the development of specific business investments. Similar opinions can be found among users of the Polish-Czech portal [50] which is a services platform in the field of cross-border economic cooperation for small and medium-sized enterprises. Another portal [51] dedicated for the inhabitants of the Polish–Czech border has a similar function. The development of cross-border business might be perceived by businessmen as an innovation in approaching the market, for which they are not yet ready. For many companies, innovative business solutions and the accompanying changes bring uncertainty which is difficult to deal with [52].

While cross-border cooperation is for many local governments and other organizations on both sides of the border a statutory requirement and a natural course of action, for other entrepreneurs it is meaningful only when real profits can be generated. In contrast to public or social bodies, entrepreneurs focus their activities primarily on the profit maximization of their own company, and only later on the interests of entities in their surroundings.

It should be noted, however, that despite general declarations about the need to support cross-border business, local governments do not see economic issues as a key area of cross-border cooperation. In 2015, the author conducted on the Czech–Polish border a comprehensive study assessing cross-border cooperation among a group of 466 Polish local government units and 199 Czech local government units (differences in the number of respondents are due to the size of the areas studied). The study was carried out by means of CATI, CAWI and CASI interviews. The elected results of this study are presented in Table 7.

Table 7. Evaluation of Polish–Czech border cooperation by local authorities in the border area.

Respondents form the Polish Part of Border Area (PL)	Respondents from the Czech Part of Border Area (SK)
Assessment of cross-border cooperation in selected areas	
- culture 76.37% of positive answers - sport, recreation, tourism 76.64% of positive answers - town-twinning 64.92% of positive answers - safety 54.38% of positive answers - environmental protection 50.76% of positive answers - **economic cooperation 38.55% of positive answers**	- culture 53.36% of positive answers - sport, recreation, tourism 49.03% of positive answers - town-twinning 44.34% of positive answers - security 35.89% of positive answers - environmental protection 30.13% of positive answers - **economic cooperation 22.92% of positive answers**
Selected factors shaping the development of cross-border cooperation	
- the quality of interpersonal relations 77.02% of positive answers - joint acquisition of EU funds 80.92% of positive answers - historical affinity and geographical proximity 47.04% of positive answers - **the economic interests 24.30% of positive answers**	- the quality of interpersonal relations 65.97% of positive answers - joint acquisition of EU funds 50.53% of positive answers - historical affinity and geographical proximity 59.76% of positive answers - **the economic interests 22.85% of positive answers**
The projected growth rate of the Polish–Czech border cooperation in the next 10 years	
- cooperation will continue to develop—53.33% of positive answers - cooperation will remain at a similar level—39.36% of positive answers - cooperation will disappear—4.37% of positive answers - there will be no cooperation—2.94% of positive answers	- cooperation will continue to develop—49.95% of positive answers - cooperation will remain at a similar level—38.80% of positive answers - cooperation will disappear—7.90% of positive answers - there will be no cooperation—3.36% of positive answers
Projected development directions of Polish–Czech border cooperation in the next 10 years	
- sports, recreation and tourism 21.48% of positive answers - culture 16.48% of positive answers - education and higher education 5.19% of positive answers - economic cooperation 5.81% of positive answers	- sports, recreation and tourism 15.89% of positive answers - culture 18.05% of positive answers - education and higher education 10.47% of positive answers - economic cooperation 3.47% of positive answers
The dominant partners in the cross-border cooperation for local governments	
- local governments 45.79% of positive answers - NGOs 18.17% of positive answers - **enterprises 4.83% of positive answers**	- Local governments 62.99% of positive answers - NGOs 10.50% of positive answers - **enterprises 2.96% of positive answers**

Source: own elaboration based on data from the project.

The above data indicates that economic relations occupy a marginal position in cross-border relations as developed by the Polish and Czech local governments. Similar results were obtained for the Polish-Belarusian-Ukrainian border area [53]. This is in contrast to the main assumptions of this paper concerning the development of border areas. Sustainable development of the border should take into account both social and economic aspects; meanwhile, currently cross-border cooperation focuses primarily on social issues. This is evident both in terms of the leading areas of cooperation (culture definitely outweighs the economy), as well as in the factors which are indicated as determinants of development of cooperation. In this case, the historical relationship or the quality of human relationships play much greater roles than common economic interests. The economy was also not listed among the most frequently indicated directions of development of cross-border cooperation in the next 10 years. It was outrun by sport, culture, tourism, *etc.* The study findings indicate that nearly half of the surveyed local authorities stated that cooperation would continue to develop. The dominant model of cross-border cooperation for the coming years will be primarily based on public partnerships and public–social partnerships, based on local governments and non-governmental organizations, whereas cooperation with enterprises attracts relatively little interest.

The results presented above indicate that young companies located on the Czech–Polish border are not sufficiently mobilized in the integration and development of cross-border entrepreneurship. At the same time, it is clear that in certain areas that cross-border cooperation is developing very dynamically (e.g., culture, recreation, tourism), which also points to the economic potential of these industries. In 2014, the author conducted research on the possibility of establishing in Polish-Czech Euroregion Cieszyn Silesia a cross-border cluster of culture, which would have a sectoral nature [54,55]. In this cluster, the participation of governments, NGOs, scientific institutions and companies operating in the broadly defined field of culture, including creative industries (enterprises were the least represented in this group). Qualitative research (CAWI interviews) consisted of 20 entities from Poland and the Czech Republic, which fulfilled the requirements of participation in the potential cluster and declared their willingness to strengthen cross-border cooperation in the field of culture. Studies have shown that a key prerequisite for integration measures are the benefits which the respondent can derive from this cooperation. Nearly 68% of respondents said they are interested in cooperation in the field of culture and creative industries within the transboundary cluster, about 7% were not interested and 25% had no opinion on this subject. According to the study, despite the fact that in this area creative industries are developing rapidly, cultural cooperation associated more with the social rather than the economic sphere might become a platform for the further development of clusters. The establishment of such clusters is dependent of the potential cluster participants finding some distinct advantages in this form of integration.

This is confirmed by the opinions of the companies, extracted from the above studies by the author, in the sector of culture and creative industries (18 entities, including cinemas, theatres and cabarets, studios of design arts, museums and regional chambers, design studios, graphic and advertising studios, computer game developers, craftsmen, folk artists, media). These entities were asked about the following issues:

- the nature and extent of cooperation with entities of the neighbouring country,
- key benefits of cluster cooperation in the field of culture and creative industries as well as barriers to this process.

According to those narrowly focused studies, potential participants in the cluster of culture and creative industries work mainly with local governments and public cultural entities, which are often the recipients of their offerings. This explains the important role of local governments and cultural bodies in the potential development of a cluster for culture and creative industries. Some of these entities also cooperate with NGOs working in related industries, as well as with the media (these tendencies are stronger on the Polish side than on the Czech side). This fact also bodes well in terms of other potential clusters.

Greater interest in entering into clusters exists on the Polish side, where this form of cooperation is more popular, and also more companies declare interest in the Czech market and its customers. Therefore, efforts to strengthen cross-border cooperation in the form of a cluster would require more support from the Czech side for the very idea of further integration, and perhaps a better understanding of the meaning and purpose of such measures. A prerequisite for mobilizing cluster cooperation should be a better understanding of its benefits for each party.

The studied entities were asked questions about the evaluation of the benefits which can be accrued from closer cooperation in the sector of culture and creative industries within the cluster. The respondents answered that these might include the following benefits:

- better joint promotion of the offer among customers around the border and reaching new groups of recipients,
- the possibility of joint acquisition of EU funds for cross-border projects,

- mutual compensation of resources and other forms of mutual assistance within the framework of ongoing business operations,
- joint training of staff and improving of standards of operation and exchange of know-how in the cultural and creative industries,
- optimization of the costs of economic activity.

The key barriers to cluster cooperation included:

- lack of funds for projects in the cluster,
- differences in the goals of individual parties' activities,
- low level of knowledge of potential partners and lack of confidence in them,
- the lack of real involvement of partners in the activities of the cluster.

6. Prospects for the Development of Cross-Border Entrepreneurship in the Cluster Model

As indicated by the above-described study, cross-border entrepreneurship is developing much more slowly than cross-border cooperation in social areas such as culture, sports, tourism or education. Efforts to expand the transboundary market are much weaker among companies, and the trend for integration of border communities at various levels is only indirectly related to the economy. It seems, however, that economic issues which are seemingly distant from social issues in practice are interconnected, as can be demonstrated, among other factors, by the cross-border cultural cluster mentioned above, also encouraging cooperation between entrepreneurs from the creative industries.

Assuming that a cross-border cluster should be cross-sectoral and, therefore, should integrate both businesses as well as local governments, non-governmental organizations and scientific bodies, a thesis can be put forward that the areas in which cross-border entrepreneurship may develop in a cluster model are those forms of cross-border cooperation that are developing most dynamically at present on the border. Cross-border cooperation in the form of various types of partnerships could therefore be the basis for further integration within the cluster model. Owing to extended cross-border cooperation, entities operating on the border understand the importance and benefits of integration activities. They can use this mechanism to achieve their own benefits, and thus for meeting the development needs of the whole border area. It can therefore be concluded that cluster initiatives on the Czech–Polish border, which immediately precede the formation of a cross-border cluster, should have their origin in cooperation of a social nature (e.g., in the fields of culture, sports, tourism, *etc.*). This is due to the fact that, in this area, the strongest integration processes take place, which can become a catalyst for the future development of the cluster. For the currently dominant, solid bilateral partnerships, cooperation development will be represent much added-value, mobilizing efforts to establish a cluster.

While companies do not feel strong enough to independently develop cross-border entrepreneurship, in these areas where the activities of companies on the border are connected with cross-border cooperation of a social nature, further integration is possible.

The economic development of the border region should be attended to by all the key stakeholders of the two neighbouring countries. The creation of a cross-border cluster should involve primarily entities conducting business activities (including companies, social organizations, public and government institutions providing some paid services and some schools and the media); there is also a place for institutions and non-profit organizations and the broad business- and social-related environment. Without a doubt, the formation of the cluster should be based on the specializations relevant to the border region, because in this way the economic interests of its constituent bodies go hand in hand with the interests of the region. Such a cluster can seek support in the regional environment and can draw on various types of support mechanisms of a systemic or individual nature [56]. Currently, by the example of the Czech–Polish border, and especially the voivodeship of Silesia and the Moravian-Silesian country, culture and creative industries can be pointed to as two key areas of integration. As mentioned above, the tendency for cluster cooperation on the Czech–Polish border is mainly centred on the Polish side, but more and more also Czech entrepreneurs are gaining interest. Two cluster initiatives are already in place, the so-called Silesian Cluster of the Design in Cieszyn and the Locomotive of Culture in Bielsko-Biala [57] which intend to open up cross-border cooperation. An exemplary model of cluster cooperation in the sector of culture and creative industries is shown in Table 8. In Table 9 we can find recommended market segmentation and description of the role of participants in the cross-border cluster of culture and creative industries.

Table 8. Proposed areas of cross-border cooperation and cross-border entrepreneurship possible for the development of a cluster in the cultural sector.

Cultural Cluster			
Public Sector	**NGO Sector**	**Scientific Sector**	**Commercial Sector**
Local governments, community centres, theatres, museums, libraries, cinemas, art schools, points of cultural information and virtual platforms of cultural information etc.	NGOs operating in the sphere of culture, e.g., music and dance groups, associations cultivating folklore and folk culture, associations of amateur artists etc.	Research units conducting research and training in the fine arts, humanities and social sciences	The media, commercial cultural institutions, companies from the creative industries sector, event companies, artistic management companies etc.

Source: own elaboration based on data from the project.

Table 9. Recommended market segmentation and the role of participants in the cross-border cluster of culture and creative industries.

Group	Description of the Group
Freelancers	Independent developers, not employed on a full-time basis in culture or in the creative industries, e.g., actors, dancers, musicians, sculptors, painters and writers. This group plays an important role in the cluster, since it creates a crude substance (e.g., manuscript), which may subsequently be processed (e.g., in the form of a book). Cooperation within the cluster can help them in the dissemination of work to a wider audience.
Micro Businessmen and Industry giants	In the sector of culture and creative industries, there are many small and large companies, few middle-size ones. This is due to the specificity of the industry. Small companies usually invest in niches, while the largest companies operate in sectors oriented on typically commercial activities, e.g., music, publishing, television or IT and often create powerful multi-sectoral, international conglomerates. Cooperation in the cluster can help smaller entities to compete with the "industry giants". The key is to engage in joint activities with appropriate partners, having complementary competencies and resources.
Centres of creative education	Centres shaping the knowledge and competencies of creative people, educating personnel for companies (from the creative sectors, and not only), creators and performers of culture as well as teaching staff, who communicate their knowledge and skills to the next generation. An important role is played here by academic centres educating professional artists and different kinds of entities operating to stimulate the creativity of society (e.g., courses in design, sewing, etc.).

Table 9. *Cont.*

Group	Description of the Group
Public cultural institutions	Museums, cultural centers, libraries, theaters, cinemas, concert halls, galleries and historic buildings, conducting a whole spectrum of socio-cultural activities, providing visitors a variety of cultural forms of entertainment (e.g., the performances, festivals, music concerts), acquiring knowledge and new skills (e.g., craft workshops, drawing), as well as developing their creative expression. Their offer attracts residents, domestic and foreign tourists, as well as artists looking for possibilities of establishing contacts with other artists or just inspiration for the development of their own work.
Gatekeepers	Persons or entities that determine which products is launched on the market, e.g., art gallery manager, chief editor of the publishing house, the artistic director of the theatre, *etc*.
Creative hidden people	Talented people, who use their talent to work for entities outside the creative industries. They occupy positions in the project departments (designers, architects), marketing (copywriters, graphic designers), IT (IT specialists), as well as in other spheres, where their creative abilities are used.
Non-governmental organizations (NGOs)	Organizations of authors, but also those who want to work to strengthen these sectors in the region. These organizations are often involved in the development of socio-cultural heritage of the given region, including support of cooperation and integration in the environment of creators, promoting the work of young talents, supporting public participation in culture and its activity with respect to fostering national heritage, promotion of cultural heritage of a region in the country and abroad.
Public authorities	Public authorities can initiate and support the development of creative industries in the region in many different ways, both directly (e.g., through financing or co-financing of business, science and culture-related activities) as well as indirectly, reinforcing the environment in which these entities operate.

Source: own elaboration [57].

Cooperation of organizations, commercial entities and institutions within the cluster of culture and creative industries fits perfectly with the determinants of cross-border cooperation as well as cross-border entrepreneurship. In terms of cross-border cluster operation, one can talk about further integration within a specific industry, sector e.g., culture, as well as the creation of mechanisms to encourage improvement of competitiveness and development of entities operating within a cluster. So far, there are not many examples of networking available. This may be due to many reasons: too strong an impact of barriers hindering this type of cooperation in the border area, and insufficient awareness of the benefits, advantages and conditions of networking cooperation.

Although the issue of partnership and sustainable cooperation is not an unfamiliar subject to any of the entities operating on the border (e.g., due to the large number of cross-border projects in different areas), among the companies there is a lack of spontaneous tendency to develop cross-border entrepreneurship. While the majority of surveyed companies declare that they are interested in such cooperation, they do not take any actions towards its effective establishment. It is a large dissonance compared to the intensive cross-border cooperation occurring in the social sphere in terms of culture. As the author recommends, it is therefore possible to draw on the good cooperation that exists between local governments in order to intensify economic relations. Such opportunities have emerged on the basis of previous studies on the establishment of transboundary cultural clusters. Research cited in this study confirms the important role local governments and the non-governmental sector has in the cross border development entrepreneurship of which can be transferred to enterprises. Extremely important is the education of potential participants of networks and clusters in terms of the specifics of this form of cooperation.

7. Conclusions

Cross-border entrepreneurship is an important aspect in the development of cross-border cooperation, which should contribute to ensuring there are equal development opportunities in peripheral areas at risk of marginalization. It is favoured by both natural integration trends in the border regions as well as the high availability of EU funds from the INTERREG program for the development of cross-border cooperation. In the studied area of the Czech–Polish border, effects of cross-border cooperation are clearly visible in the social sphere, primarily in the fields of culture, education, sports and tourism, administration, *etc*. However, this cooperation has developed to a much lesser extent in the economic sphere. For most companies operating in border regions, the markets of neighbouring countries are treated equally to other, much more distant foreign markets. It is difficult to identify clear trends for economic cooperation here.

The results of research and several years of involvement by the author in cross-border entrepreneurship, from a scientific and practical point of view, show that the development of cross-border cooperation—supported by local authorities—is limited to bilateral contact and projects. It is difficult to indicate a direction that allows for further strengthening of cooperation in the economic field, although further cluster cooperation seems a natural path.

Despite a series of actions aimed at systematic promotion of economic cooperation on the borderline, it is difficult to identify a significant number of such examples in Silesia Voivodeship and the Moravian-Silesian Region. This is in contrast to the strategy of cross-border cooperation for the border area, which has been implemented since 2013. In this document, economic cooperation is of key importance. Another real problem of cross-border cooperation is the stability of partnerships and lack of tendency to transform bilateral cooperation into networking cooperation. This means that cooperation between the same partners strengthens, but it does not expand to other entities. In these circumstances, cluster cooperation can be a model especially worth promoting among all entities interested in border development, among local governments as well as non-governmental organizations and entrepreneurs.

Although sustainable development of the border should be based on both social and economic processes, the sphere of entrepreneurship is now clearly ignored. It can be seen i.a. in the results of research carried out among local governments. They do not appreciate the economic aspects of cross-border cooperation, and the most promising directions of further integration are considered to be culture, education, tourism, *etc*. These sectors, however, also have certain economic potential, which means that there are opportunities for the involvement of entrepreneurs in cross-border cooperation in these areas.

The study results confirmed that between the Polish and Czech companies operating in the border area, there are differences in developmental processes, approaches to businesses, types of offerings, *etc*. This is not conducive to the natural processes of integration. It can therefore not be said that the chances of economic integration in each of the branches are identical.

In trying to solve the research problem relating to the possible development of cross-border entrepreneurship on the Polish–Czech border, the author turned to the concept of cluster cooperation, which has been more developed on the Polish side. Prospects for the development of clusters on the Polish–Czech borderland have been linked with the sectors that are developing most quickly in this area, *i.e.*, the sector of culture and creative industries. As the second criterion, the author took into account the involvement of partners from different sectors: administration and local government, science and non-governmental organizations from both sides of the border. The studies conducted in this field have shown that culture and creative industries is the sphere where the entities of the Polish and Czech border areas see the greatest opportunities for further integration.

In the opinion of the author, the catalyst for cross-border entrepreneurship, at least in some sectors (e.g., in the field of creative industries), may centre on the very sophisticated cross-border cooperation at the public and social levels (*i.e.*, the cooperation of local governments and non-governmental organizations), in which enterprises operating on each side of the border can be engaged. It also gives impetus to further expansion of this cooperation and transforming bilateral relationships to ones based on networking and clustering. Such opportunities have already been verified by the author in previous studies analysing the conditions conducive to the emergence of cross-border cultural clusters.

According to the author, in the study area, it is difficult to extract natural tendencies and the desire of companies to develop cross-border entrepreneurship, but a factor that can boost economic integration is rapidly developing cross-border cooperation in the social field, e.g., in culture [47,48] *etc*. Although it is not a universal solution that can be applied to any industry, at least in sectors distinguished by intense cross-border relations, including business entities in this cooperation can bring measurable results, reflected also in the development of the border area. The condition for this mechanism is the awareness of the benefits which both parties can gain from the development of co-operation, also including entrepreneurs. Another important consideration affecting the efficiency of cross-border cooperation that determines the participation of entrepreneurs is the creation of mechanisms for its further development, including the gradual transformation of bilateral agreements into networking and clustering cooperation.

In conclusion, as long as the sectors such as culture and creative industries (or other sectors in other border regions) will be indicated directly or indirectly according to regional specializations, whose development is supported by all stakeholders of cross-border cooperation (including i.a. governments, research bodies, NGOs and entrepreneurs), then the cross-border cooperation can be transformed into that of clusters. This cooperation has its origin in typically social activities (as mentioned above, EU bilateral projects implemented mainly by local governments and non-governmental organizations), but under favorable conditions, it can also extend to business activities that generate economic benefits and contribute to the development of cross-border regions by strengthening regional specializations.

Conflicts of Interest: The author declares no conflict of interest.

References

1. Bleeke, J.; Ernst, D. The way to win in cross-border alliances. *Harvard Bus. Rev.* **1991**, *69*, 127–135.
2. Program INTERREG VA Czech Republic-Poland 2014–2020. Available online: https://www.ewt.gov.pl/media/5504/Program_INTERREG_V_A_Czechy_Polska.pdf (accessed on 15 November 2015).
3. The OECD Study on Local Partnerships, OECD, Paris 1990. Available online: http://www.oecd.org/cfe/leed/theoecdstudyonlocalpartnerships.htm (accessed on 20 November 2015).
4. Ray, C. Neo-endogenous Rural Development in the EU. In *Book Handbook of Rural Studies*; Cloke, P., Marsden, T., Mooney, P., Eds.; Sage: London, UK, 2006; pp. 278–291.
5. Simard, J.F.; Chiasson, G. Introduction: Territorial Governance—A New Take on Development. *Can. J. Reg. Sci.* **2008**, *31*, 471–485.
6. European Chapter of Border and Cross-Border Regions. Available online: http://www.aebr.eu/files/publications/110915_Charta_EN_clean.pdf (accessed on 15 November 2015).
7. European Outline Convention on Transfrontier Co-operation between Territorial Communities or Authorities. Available online: https://rm.coe.int/CoERMPublicCommonSearchServices/DisplayDCTMContent?documentId=0900001680078b0c (accessed on 15 November 2015).
8. European Charter of Regional Self-Government. Available online: http://www.cvce.eu/en/obj/draft_european_charter_of_regional_self_government_5_june_1997-en-78ae4dcf-6346-4aa8-8474-7535e4091bf7.html (accessed on 15 November 2015).

9. Perkowski, M. Współpraca transgraniczna. Available online: http://www.prawoipartnerstwo.pl/stara/publikacje/Wspolpraca.pdf (accessed on 15 November 2015). (In Polish)
10. Rozporządzenie Rady z 21 Czerwca 1999 r.; Wprowadzające Ogólne Przepisy Dotyczące Funduszy Strukturalnych nr 1260/1999/WE. Available online: http://ec.europa.eu/regional_policy/sources/docoffic/official/regulation/content/pl/02_pdf/00_1_sf_1_pl.pdf (accessed on 15 November 2015). (In Polish)
11. Geddes, M. *Partnership Making Policy, Report: Enhancing the Capacity of Partnerships to Influence Policy*; Available online: http://www.oecd.org/cfe/leed/36279186.pdf (accessed on 15 November 2015).
12. Rozporządzenie Rady z 11 lipca 2006 r. nr (WE) nr 1083/2006, Ustanawiające Przepisy Ogólne Dotyczące Europejskiego Funduszu Rozwoju Regionalnego, Europejskiego Funduszu Społecznego Oraz Funduszu Spójności i Uchylające Rozporządzenie (WE) nr 1260/1999. Available online: http://www.oecd.org/cfe/leed/36279186.pdf (accessed on 16 November 2015). (In Polish)
13. Lepik, K. Euroregions as mechanisms for strengthening cross-border cooperation in the Baltic Sea region. *Trames* **2009**, *13*, 265–284. [CrossRef]
14. Kramsch, O.; Hooper, B. *Cross Border Governance in the European Union*; Routledge: New York, NY, USA, 2004.
15. Perkmann, M. Policy Entrepreneurship and Multi-Level Governance. A Comparative Study of European Cross-Border Regions. *Environ. Plan. C Gov. Policy* **2007**, *25*, 861–879. [CrossRef]
16. Harguindéguy, J.; Bray, Z. Does cross-border co-operation empower European regions? The case of INTERREG III-A France-Spain. *Environ. Plan. C Gov. Policy* **2009**, *27*, 747–760. [CrossRef]
17. Kurowska-Pysz, J. Problem trwałości klastrów dofinansowanych ze środków Unii Europejskiej w aspekcie nowych uwarunkowań wdrażania projektów w latach 2014-2020. In *Book Zarządzanie i inżynieria produkcji. Wybrane zagadnienia*; Kurowska-Pysz, J., Ed.; Wydawnictwo Naukowe Wyższej Szkoły Biznesu w Dąbrowie Górniczej: Dąbrowa Górnicza, Poland, 2015. (In Polish)
18. Trott, P. *Innovation Management and New Product Development*; Pearson Education Ltd.: Edinburgh, UK, 2008.
19. Etzkowitz, H. The triple helix. In *University-Industry-Government Innovation in Action*; Routledge: London, UK, 2009; pp. 15–22.
20. Carayannis, E.; Barth, T.; Campbell, D. The Quintuple Helix innovation model: Global warming as a challenge and driver for innovation. *J. Innov. Entrep.* **2012**. [CrossRef]
21. Olesiński, Z. *Zarządzanie Relacjami Międzyorganizacyjnymi*; Wydawnictwo CH Beck: Warszawa, Poland, 2010. (In Polish)
22. Henning, M.; Moodysson, J.; Nilsson, M. Innovation and Regional Transformation. In *From Clusters to New Combinations*; Region Skane: Malmö, Spain, 2010.
23. Lazerson, M.; Lorenzoni, G. The Firms that Feed Industrial Districts: A Return to the Italian Source. *Ind. Corp. Chang.* **1999**, *8*, 235–265. [CrossRef]
24. Bathelt, H. Cluster Relations in the Media Industry: Exploring the "Distanced Neighbour" Paradox in Leipzig. *Reg. Stud.* **2005**, *39*, 105–127. [CrossRef]
25. Sheppard, E. Positionality and globalization in economic geography. In *The Changing Economic Geography of Globalization: Reinventing Space*; Giovanna, V., Ed.; Taylor & Francis: Oxfordshire, UK, 2005.
26. Lipnack, J.; Stamps, J. The age of network. In *Organizing Principles for the 21st Century*; Oliver Wight Publication: Gloucester, UK, 1994.
27. Pachura, P. Analiza potencjału budowy efektywnych struktur transgranicznych sieci innowacyjnych na przykładzie województwa śląskiego oraz regionów Czech i Słowacji, Ministerstwo Rozwoju Regionalnego, Częstochowa 2009, 9. Available online: https://www.ewaluacja.gov.pl/Wyniki/Documents/2_059.pdf (accessed on 30 November 2015). (In Polish)
28. Brito, C.; Correia, R. Regions as networks. Towards a conceptual framework of territorial dynamic, Research Work in Progress. 2010, 357, pp. 20–23. Available online: http://www.fep.up.pt/investigacao/workingpapers/10.01.18_wp357.pdf (accessed on 30 November 2015).
29. Fromhold-Eisebith, E.; Eisebith, G. How to institutionalize innovative clusters? Comparing explicit top-down and implicit bottom-up approaches. *Res. Policy* **2005**, *34*, 1250–1268. [CrossRef]
30. Porter, M. *The Cooperative Advantage of Nations*; Harvard Business Review: New York, NY, USA, 1990; Available online: http://dl1.cuni.cz/pluginfile.php/50387/mod_resource/content/0/Porter-competitive-advantage.pdf (accessed on 30 November 2015).
31. Rosenfeld, S.A. Community College/Cluster Connections: Specialization and Competitiveness in the United States and Europe. *Econ. Dev. Q.* **2000**, *14*, 51–62. [CrossRef]

32. Almodovar, J.; Teixeira, A. Conceptualizing clusters through the lens of networks: A critical synthesis. *FEP Working Papers*, 2009. Available online: http://www.fep.up.pt/investigacao/workingpapers/09.07.15_wp328.pdf (accessed on 20 December 2015).
33. Maskell, P.; Kebir, L. What qualifies as a cluster theory? Available online: http://www3.druid.dk/wp/20050009.pdf (accessed on 30 November 2015).
34. Lepik, K.L.; Krigul, M. Cross-border cooperation institution in building a knowledge cross-border region. *Probl. Perspect. Manag.* **2009**, *7*, 33–45.
35. Rialland, A. *Cluster Dynamics and Innovation*; IGLO-MP2020 Working Paper; Norwegian University of Science and Technology: Trondheim, Norway, 2009.
36. Ketels, C.; Lindqvist, G.; Sölvell, Ö. Strengthening Clusters and Competitiveness in Europe. The Role of Cluster Organisations, the Cluster Observatory, 2012. Available online: https://www.google.com.hk/url?sa=t&rct=j&q=&esrc=s&source=web&cd=1&ved=0ahUKEwjatNi3wp7LAhVBhSwKHa9HCWcQFggbMAA&url=http%3a%2f%2fwww.clusterportal-bw.de%2fservice%2fpublikationen%2fclusterpolitik-und-clusterpolitische-massnahmen%2fpublikation%2fPublikationen%2fdownload%2fdokument%2fstrengthening-clusters-and-competitiveness-in-europe%2f&usg=AFQjCNGM483M6JL2-3T08HLuEWhUYNqvAA&sig2=lS6kD_sy6cBB-vSU0J6lXw (accessed on 21 November 2015).
37. Hisrich, R.D. Entrepreneurship/intrapreneurship. *Am. Psychol.* **1990**, *45*, 209–222. [CrossRef]
38. Burns, P. *Entrepreneurship and Small Business*; Palgrave MacMillan: Houndmills, UK, 2007.
39. Davidsson, P. The domain of entrepreneurship research: Some suggestions. In *Book Cognitive Approaches to Entrepreneurship Research*; Katz, J.A., Shepherd, D.A., Elsevier, J.A.I., Eds.; Book Series: Advances in Entrepreneurship, Firm Emergence and Growth, Emerald Insight; Available online: http://www.emeraldinsight.com/doi/book/10.1016/S1074-7540(2003)6 (accessed on 21 November 2015).
40. Schuler, R.S.; Tarique, I.; Jackson, S.E. *Managing Human Resources in Cross-Border Aliancess, Advances in Mergers and Acquisitions (Advances in Mergers and Acquisitions, Volume 3)*; Emerald Group Publishing Limited: Bingley, UK; pp. 103–129.
41. Drucker, P. *Innovation and Entrepreneurship, Practice and Principles*; Harper&Row: New York, NY, USA, 1985.
42. Ābele, L.; Līduma, D.; Leitāne, I.; Mežinska, A. Analysis of factors forming competitive business environment in cross-border region. *Econ. Manag.* **2012**, *17*, 1308–1313. [CrossRef]
43. Smallbone, D.; Welter, F. Cross-border entrepreneurship. *Entrep. Reg. Dev. Int. J.* **2012**, *24*, 43–63. [CrossRef]
44. Reśko, D. Przedsiębiorczość transgraniczna w wybranych jednostkach terytorialnych pogranicza polsko-słowackiego. *Stud. Reg. Lokalne* **2010**, *2*, 121–131. (In Polish).
45. Smallbone, D.; Welter, F.; Xheneti, M. *Cross-Border Entrepreneurship and Economic Development in Europe's Border*; Edward Elgar: Cheltenham, UK; Northampton, MA, USA, 2012.
46. The project "Sustainable economic activities", co-financed by the Operational programme of cross-border co-operation Czech Republic—Poland 2007–2013. Available online: http://www.egtctritia.eu/pl/projekty/nasze-projekty/zrownowazona-dzialalnosc-gospodarcza (accessed on 21 December 2015).
47. Report doing business, World Bank Group 2015. Available online: http://www.doingbusiness.org/ (accessed on 21 December 2015).
48. The project "Strategies for System Cooperation of Public Institutions of Moravian-Silesian Region, the Voivodeship of Silesia and Opole" co-financed by the European Regional Development Fund under the Operational Programme of Cross-Border Cooperation Czech Republic - Republic of Poland 2007–2013. Available online: http://www.slaskie.pl/strona_n.php?jezyk=pl&grupa=9&dzi=1312275679&art=1312275911&id_menu=455 (accessed on 21 December 2015).
49. Szczepańska-Woszczyna, K. Rola edukacji w rozwoju regionu, Polityka gospodarcza gminy (rozwój Zagłębia Dąbrowskiego wczoraj i dziś). *Zeszyty Naukowe WSB* **2001**, *2*, 149–159. (In Polish)
50. Services platform for cross-border cooperation between Czech and Polish SME. Available online: http://www.cespolgroup.com/pl/ (accessed on 21 December 2015).
51. Platform for cooperation of Polish-Czech societies. Available online: http://www.anotak.info/pl/biznes (accessed on 21 December 2015).
52. Szczepańska-Woszczyna, K. Innovation process in the social space of the organization. *Reg. Form. Dev. Stud.* **2014**, *3*, 220–229.

53. Klimczuk., A.; Klimczuk-Kochańska, M.; Plawgo, B. Współpraca transgraniczna małych i średnich przedsiębiorstw jako czynnik rozwoju regionalnego na przykładzie podregionu białostocko-suwalskiego i podregionu krośnieńsko-przemyskiego w Polsce, obwodu Zakarpackiego na Ukrainie oraz obwodu grodzieńskiego na Białorusi. In book *Współpraca transgraniczna małych i średnich przedsiębiorstw jako czynnik rozwoju regionalnego*; Plawgo, B., Ed.; Białostocka Fundacja Kształcenia Kadr: Białystok, 2015; Available online: http://ssrn.com/abstract=2604198 (accessed on 21 December 2015). (In Polish)
54. Kurowska-Pysz, J. Assessment of trends for the development of cross border cultural clusters. *Forum Sci. Oecon.* **2014**, *3*, 31–51.
55. Kurowska-Pysz, J. Proces zarządzania wiedzą w klastrach—Kluczowe uwarunkowania. *Mark. I Rynek* **2015**, *12*, 17–23. (In Polish)
56. Thissen, M.; Oort, F.; Diodato, D.; Ruijs, A. *Regional Competitiveness and Smart Specialization in Europe*; Edward Elgar Publishing Limited: Cheltenham, UK, 2013.
57. Szultka, S. *Klastry w Sektorach Kreatywnych—Motory Rozwoju Miast i Regionów*; Polska Agencja Rozwoju Przedsiębiorczości: Warszawa, Poland, 2012. (In Polish)

© 2016 by the author. Licensee MDPI, Basel, Switzerland. This article is an open access article distributed under the terms and conditions of the Creative Commons Attribution (CC BY) license (http://creativecommons.org/licenses/by/4.0/).

Article

The Design of a Sustainable Location-Routing-Inventory Model Considering Consumer Environmental Behavior

Jinhuan Tang [1,*], Shoufeng Ji [2] and Liwen Jiang [2]

1 School of Economics and Management, Shenyang Aerospace University, Shenyang 110136, China
2 School of Business Administration, Northeast University, Shenyang 110169, China; sfji@mail.neu.edu.cn (S.J.); 1310514@stu.neu.edu.cn (L.J.)
* Corresponding: jinhuan_tang@sau.edu.cn; Tel.: +86-151-4016-3732

Academic Editors: Adam Jabłoński and Giuseppe Ioppolo
Received: 12 January 2016; Accepted: 19 February 2016; Published: 29 February 2016

Abstract: Our aim is to design a sustainable supply chain (SSC) network, which takes into consideration consumer environmental behaviors (CEBs). CEBs not only affect consumers' demand for products with low carbon emissions, they also affect their willingness to pay premium prices for products with low carbon emissions. We incorporate CEBs into the SSC network model involving location, routing and inventory. Firstly, a multi-objective optimization model comprised of both the costs and the carbon emissions of a joint location-routing-inventory model is proposed and solved, using a multi-objective particle swarm optimization (MOPSO) algorithm. Then, a revenue function including CEBs is presented on the basis of a Pareto set of the trade-off between costs and carbon emissions. A computational experiment and sensitivity analysis are conducted, employing data from the China National Petroleum Corporation (CNPC). The results clearly indicate that our research can be applied to actual supply chain operations. In addition, some practical managerial insights for enterprises are offered.

Keywords: sustainable supply chain network; consumer environmental behaviors; location-routing-inventory; MOPSO

1. Introduction

Along with the heightened concerns over the past few decades relating to sustainable supply chains (SSC), governments, enterprises and consumers are becoming increasingly aware of the need to reduce carbon emissions. Governments have introduced a number of regulations, such as carbon taxes, cap-and-trade mechanisms and carbon constraints to mandate carbon emission reductions in SSC management [1]. In addition, a few socially responsible enterprises have engaged in voluntary emission reduction programs. Companies such as BP and Nike have taken actions to reduce emissions in order to improve their public image. Wal-Mart and Tesco require their suppliers to reveal their carbon emissions on product labels, where they can be seen by consumers and society. In addition, consumers with higher levels of environmental consciousness are willing to pay a premium price for low carbon products [2–5]. The demand for low carbon products has become greater and greater [6–8]. It can be safely assumed that low carbon products will become more competitively priced in the future. Clearly, the drive for environmental improvement is increasing.

Traditionally, a supply chain network design problem focuses on minimizing the fixed and operational costs that companies directly incur. Only recently, however, have some studies started taking carbon emissions into account [9–11]. Many studies indicate that there is a trade-off between the environment and economics in a supply chain [12–14]. However, it is possible to significantly reduce carbon emissions without greatly increasing costs, using proper supply chain operations [15,16]. In general, there is a paradox between cost and carbon emissions in SSC management.

Companies are never going to reduce their carbon emissions until factors such as cost, profits, brand awareness and consumer pressure are involved. Currently, the main drive for carbon emission reduction can be classified into two categories. The first is mandatory emission reductions, which includes features such as carbon taxes and carbon cap policies [17]. This approach to carbon emissions is punitive. The alternative method is to encourage enterprises to voluntarily reduce their carbon emissions. This encouragement, in turn, can take the form of two types of motivation. One type is through policies such as carbon allowances and cap-and-trade mechanisms. The second type takes on board market considerations. For example, studies have shown that green products have the marketing potential to endow an enterprise with a good public image, which in turn can improve the relevant products' pricing structure or increase consumer demand [8,18]. Looking further into the future, the effects of exploiting the marketing potential of products with low carbon emissions will increase substantially. Creating a SSC network is both a challenge and an opportunity. Presumably, the information already available to society at large has made consumers more environmentally mature, and these mature consumers would like to purchase products with smaller carbon footprints. In this study, we propose the design of a SSC network from a market-driven perspective. Specifically, the purpose of this study is to optimize the profitability of a company through CEB. We decide on the design of the SSC network after considering the number and location of warehouses, the routes from manufacturers to warehouses and from warehouses to retailers, and the inventory polices of the various facilities. Firstly, a multi-objective model is constructed to create a trade-off between cost and carbon emissions. Then, a general revenue objective factoring in CEBs is modeled, based on the relationship between cost and carbon emissions. This study allows us to achieve the best of both worlds, *i.e.*, maximizing the profits of companies, while reducing carbon emissions as much as possible. These achievements also represent the main points of innovation in this paper.

The remainder of the paper is organized as follows: Section 2 reviews the relevant literature. Problem descriptions and assumptions are presented in Section 3. Section 4 describes the multi-objective model that creates the trade-off between cost and carbon emissions, and then constructs the general revenue objective function taking CEBs into consideration. The approach used as a solution for the model is given in Section 5. Results of the computational experiment and a sensitivity analysis are conducted in Section 6; the managerial insights are also illustrated in this section. Finally, our conclusions are presented in Section 7.

2. Literature Review

A key driver of any supply chain is its distribution network. This network, however, is generally also the main source of carbon emissions. The operations of a supply chain network consist of three major components, namely location, routing and inventory (LRI). However, most existing literature integrates only any two of the above, *i.e.*, location-routing problems [19], inventory-routing problems [20], and location-inventory problems [21], as their target topics. Ahmadi-Javid and Azad [22] presented for the first time a model to simultaneously optimize location, routing and inventory decisions in a supply chain network. Ahmadi-Javid and Seddighi [23] studied a ternary integration problem that incorporated location, routing and inventory decisions in designing a multi-source distribution network. They then solved the model using a three-phase heuristic. On the whole, very few researchers have studied the ternary integration LRI problem, and fewer still have incorporated carbon emissions into an LRI problem when designing a supply chain network. This is a very important issue, which has unfortunately been largely ignored.

Numerous studies concentrate on the trade-off between the environment and the economy in supply chain management [12,24]. According to the most recent papers, three types of research have been conducted and corresponding suggestions made: (i) Translate carbon emissions into cost by introducing carbon regulations, such as a carbon tax, cap-and-trade mechanisms, *etc*. Kroes *et al.* [25]

investigated the relationship between a firm's environmental performance compliance and their marketing success in the context of stringent cap-and-trade regulations. Benjaafar *et al.* [12] presented a cost optimization model via translating carbon emissions into unit costs by carbon price. The two studies proved that there is a close relationship between economic costs and carbon emissions. Similar research was conducted by Hua *et al.* [24], which studied managing carbon footprints in an inventory system under a carbon emission trading mechanism. (ii) A mandatory carbon cap is used to reduce emissions. This policy specifically prohibits companies from emitting any carbon emissions in excess of their carbon cap. Diabat *et al.* [26] proposed a mixed-integer program model with carbon cap constraints when designing a supply chain network. A carbon-constraint economic order quantity (EOQ) model was provided to reduce emissions by properly adjusting order quantities [16]. The effects of carbon-constraint measures are significant. However, it is relatively difficult to implement such policies, as they are currently unacceptable to many companies. Businesses, which are profit-driven, lack the motivation to participate in this non-profitable activity. (iii) Provide a set of Pareto solutions, which shows the trade-off between cost and carbon emissions. The advantage of this method is that it can give a set of non-dominated solutions. In addition, the decision makers can choose their preferred configuration. Wygonik and Goodchild [27] presented trade-offs between cost, service quality and the carbon emissions of an urban delivery system. Wang *et al.* [28] provided a bi-objective optimization model for a green supply chain network design. One of the two objectives was cost minimization; the other was to minimize carbon emissions. The Pareto results showed that the bi-objective model is an effective tool for solving this kind of problem. However, the terminal decision will be made by managers, and thus, personal preferences will inevitably be involved.

The worldwide reduction framework would involve drawing more companies into carbon reduction activities and also into assuming social responsibilities. In order to determine how to make enterprises voluntarily reduce emissions in the context of an earnings-dominated market, it is first necessary to learn how best to improve the potential motivation for corporations to reduce their carbon emissions. The use of carbon labeling is an effective means to encourage consumers to buy environmentally friendly products. There is, however, a definite need to better understand consumers' responses to eco-labels [28]. Consumers' willingness to pay a premium price for products with lower carbon emissions has been shown to be increasing [4,29]. Vanclay *et al.* [30] defined three levels of carbon labeling (from low to high) as green, yellow and black. They then found that after labeling, the black-labeled (highest carbon emission) product sales decreased by six percent, while green-labeled product sales increased by four percent, when all other conditions were basically unchanged. These results imply that the potential effectiveness of carbon labels in emission reductions is significant. However, green products usually cost more than conventional products, which in turn makes green goods more expensive [3].The key issue is whether consumers will be willing to pay a premium price for the green goods. If not, governments may have to subsidize producers who manufacture green products [5]. Some studies have shown that the higher the CEBs, the higher the price consumers are willing to pay for environmentally friendly products [2].

Economic globalization and rapid high-tech development have intensified market competition to unprecedented levels. New patterns of product competition will emerge over the next few years, and the manufacture of green products as part of that competition is an irresistible trend. Conrad [3] studied the effects of consumer environmental concerns on price, choice of product and market share in the context of duopoly. Liu *et al.* [8] proved that, as consumers' environmental awareness increases, retailers and manufacturers with superior eco-friendly operations will benefit in the long run. A model considering the effect of environmental conscious consumers on firms' adoption of cleaner technologies showed that, as pollution intensifies, consumers play a much more positive role in the companies' environmental activities. The consumers' attitudes encourage firms to reduce carbon emissions, even in the absence of emission regulations [7]. However, many studies focus on emission reduction through governmental regulations, and rarely through market forces [31]. Actually, consumer response and preference for greener products, as well as market competition, combine to strongly encourage companies to adopt environmentally friendly operations.

By reviewing previous studies, we find that very little research has been conducted on LRI optimization as a means to minimize carbon emissions. Fewer still have incorporated CEBs into a revenue model. Indeed, most studies fail to properly integrate market-driven factors—in particular CEBs—and LRI operations and revenue objectives with cost-environment trade off. In this paper, we make the following contributions: (i) The concept of consumer environmental behaviors (CEBs) was proposed and incorporated into a revenue function. CEBs not only affect consumers' demand for low carbon emission products, but also their willingness to pay a premium price for low carbon emission products. (ii) A multi-objective mixed-integer formulation for the trade-off between cost and carbon emissions was presented first. The solution was then found using the multi-objective particle swarm optimization (MOPSO). Hence, a set of distributed Pareto optimal solutions can be obtained. On this basis, revenue function can be maximized. (iii) We conduct a computational experiment based on data from the China National Petroleum Corporation (CNPC) to test the presented models. Then, the Pareto solutions are presented. In addition, a number of sensitivity analyses are implemented on multiple variables. Hence, we obtain interesting managerial insights that may be of use to logistics service firms.

3. Description and Assumptions

3.1. Problem Description

For a supply chain network consisting of manufacturers (M), warehouses (W) and retailers (R), the location of warehouses is potentially significant. In addition, each warehouse has a specific capacity level, which makes the supply chain network more realistic. The goals of our model are to choose and allocate warehouses, schedule vehicle routes and determine an inventory policy to meet retailers' demands taking into consideration CEBs. The framework of the problem is depicted in Figure 1.

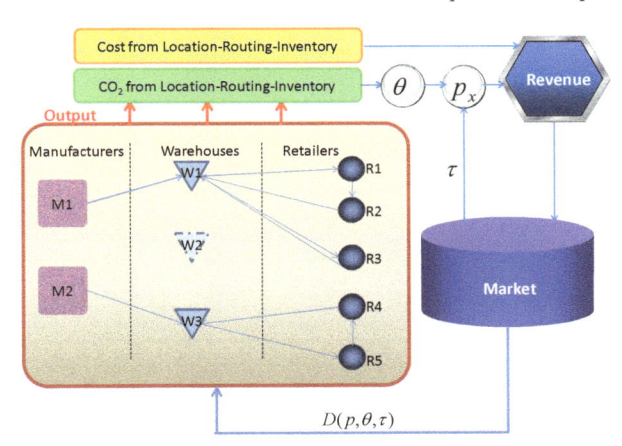

Figure 1. The framework of supply chain network.

In Figure 1, the operations generate cost and CO_2 in a supply chain network involving location, routing and inventory. θ is the green level coefficient of products, which is decided by the CO_2 emissions from the LRI operations, which can in turn be calculated by Equation (14); τ is the consumer environmental behaviors (CEBs), and a larger τ indicates that consumers are willing to pay a higher premium for greener products. CEBs can be calculated as $\tau = \int_{\underline{g}}^{\overline{g}} \tau(g)\beta$, where $\tau(g)$ is the CEBs of consumer group g, β is a correction factor of CEBs over time. We assume $\beta \geq 1$, because CEBs would not decrease over time; $\underline{g}$ is the consumer group with the worst CEBs, and $\overline{g}$ is the consumer group with the best CEBs. p is the price of the product, which is decided by θ and the CEBs τ. The market demand of a product depends on p, θ and τ. Conversely, operation-induced emissions and cost will be influenced by the market, which is important, especially in a situation of oversupply. To maximize profits, supply chain enterprises will certainly endeavor to meet consumers' preferences, so as to improve their businesses' performance.

3.2. Assumptions

We assume that the consumers are under symmetric information regarding products' carbon emissions. With the preferences displayed by CEBs, we aim to find the optimal supply chain network design and operational strategy.

(i) In this paper, the CEB choices focus on the carbon emissions from the LRI, including sourcing, production and/or recovery. It is reasonable to choose supply chain services as the study object, as they represent a major source of carbon emissions.
(ii) There is no difference among delivery routes, and the road conditions are nearly the same. In other words, the carbon emissions and costs are only affected by the distance travelled.
(iii) Each warehouse is assumed to follow a (Q, R) inventory policy. That is, when the inventory of a warehouse reaches the reorder point R, a fixed quantity Q is ordered from the upper stream plant.
(iv) The discussed products/services are in an oversupplied market. CEBs are in positive correlation with market demand. We assume the consumer demand function is expressed as:

$$D(p_x, \theta, \tau) = D_0 - \lambda_1 p_x + \frac{1}{2}\lambda_2 \tau \theta \qquad (1)$$

where D_0 is the initial demand without considering CEBs or a premium for greener products, λ_1 is the market inverse demand coefficient, λ_2 is the attraction coefficient with the environmentally friendly level of products, and τ is the consumers' environmental preference for low carbon products. Obviously, the market demand is a decreasing function of price, and an increasing function of θ and τ.

4. The Model

4.1. A Multi-Objective Model for Cost and Carbon Emissions

There is a trade-off between cost and carbon emissions in supply chain operations. Generally, a set of optimal Pareto solutions (c_x, e_x) can be obtained, and particularly, the extreme values on the Pareto curve are $(\underline{c}, \overline{e})$ and $(\overline{c}, \underline{e})$. The aim of this paper is to find the optimal solution (c_x^*, e_x^*) in the supply chain; one which will maximize profits while taking CEBs into consideration. For these operations, we should make the following decisions:

(i) Location decisions—how many warehouses should be opened, and where to locate the opened warehouses.
(ii) Routing decisions—how to assign the vehicle routes from manufacturers to warehouses (M-to-W) and from warehouses to Retailers (W-to-R).
(iii) Inventory decisions—what is the order quantity, and how many safety stocks should be maintained?
(iv) What is the most appropriate level of green to choose?

Thus, the decision variables can be denoted as

$$y_j = \begin{cases} 1, & \text{if warehouse } j \text{ is opened} \\ 0, & \text{otherwise} \end{cases}, j \in J$$

$$x_{ji}^r = \begin{cases} 1, & \text{if retailer } i \text{ is assigned to warehouse } j \\ 0, & \text{otherwise} \end{cases}, i \in I, j \in J$$

$$x_{kj}^p = \begin{cases} 1, & \text{if warehouse } j \text{ is assigned to manufacture } k \\ 0, & \text{otherwise} \end{cases}, j \in J, k \in K$$

$$z_{miv} = \begin{cases} 1, & \text{if } m \text{ precedes } i \text{ in the route of vehicle } v \\ 0, & \text{otherwise} \end{cases}, \forall m \in (I \cup J), i \in I.$$

Q_j is the order quantity of warehouse j.

The multi-objective function includes cost and carbon emissions from location, routing and inventory. First, the cost is composed using the following terms:

(i) Location cost. The cost of warehouse location is $\sum_{j \in J} f_j y_j$, where f_j is the single cost of opening warehouse j.

(ii) Routing cost occurs in the distribution from M-to-W and from warehouse to retailer (W-to-R), which are $\sum_{k \in K} \sum_{j \in J} t_1 d_{kj} x_{kj}^p$ and $\sum_{j \in J} \sum_{i \in I} \sum_{m \in (I \cup J)} t_2 d_{mi} z_{miv}$, respectively, where t_1 is the M-to-W routing cost per distance; d_{kj} is the distance from manufacturer k to warehouse j; t_2 is W-to-R routing cost per distance; and d_{mi} is the distance from warehouse j (or retailer k k) to retailer k'

(iii) Inventory cost. Working inventory is $\sum_{j \in J} \sum_{i \in I} (h_o \frac{\sum_{i \in I} \mu_i x_{ij}^r}{Q_j} + h_j \frac{Q_j}{2})$, and safety stock is $\sum_{j \in J} h_j z_\alpha \sqrt{L_j \sum_{i \in I} \sigma_i^2 x_{ji}^r}$ [22], where h_o is the ordering cost, μ_i is the demand by retailer i, h_j is the hold cost per unit; L_j is the lead time of DC j; z_α is left α-percentile of standard normal random variable Z, i.e., $P(Z \leq z_\alpha) = \alpha$ (α is the desired percentage of retailers' orders that should be satisfied); σ_i^2 is the variance of demand from retailer i.

The carbon emissions are composed of the following terms:

(i) Carbon emissions from facilities. The carbon emissions of a warehouse location can be denoted as $\sum_{j \in J} \hat{f}_j y_j$, where $\hat{f}_j$ is the carbon emissions of building warehouse j.

(ii) Carbon emissions from routing. The routing emissions from the M-to-W and W-to-R transportations are denoted as $\sum_{k \in K} \sum_{j \in J} \hat{t}_1 d_{kj} x_{kj}^p$ and $\sum_{j \in J} \sum_{i \in I} \sum_{m \in (I \cup J)} \hat{t}_2 d_{mi} z_{miv}$, respectively, where $\hat{t}_1$ is the M-to-W carbon emissions per distance, and $\hat{t}_2$ is the carbon emissions per distance from warehouse j (or retailer k) to retailer k'.

(iii) Carbon emissions from inventory. The inventory emissions come from the working inventory and safety stock, which are $\sum_{j \in J} \sum_{i \in I} \hat{h}_j \frac{Q_j}{2}$ and $\sum_{j \in J} \hat{h}_j z_\alpha \sqrt{L_j \sum_{i \in I} \sigma_i^2 x_{ji}^r}$, respectively, where $\hat{h}_j$ is the carbon emissions per holding inventory. It is worth mentioning that carbon emissions from inventory mainly refer to the energy consumption and product emissions during storage.

(iv) Other emissions, including emissions from purchasing, production and recovery. The purchasing emission is $Pur' \cdot \sum_{i \in I} \mu_i$, where Pur' is carbon emissions from purchase per unit. The production emission is $Pn' \cdot \sum_{i \in I} \mu_i$, where Pn' is carbon emissions from production per unit. The recovery emission is $Rcy' \cdot \sum_{i \in I} \mu_i$, where Rcy' is carbon emissions from recovery per unit.

The multi-objective problem is formulated as follows:

$$\min c_x = (\sum_{j \in J} f_j y_j + \sum_{k \in K} \sum_{j \in J} t_1 d_{kj} x_{kj}^p + \sum_{j \in J} \sum_{i \in I} \sum_{m \in (I \cup J)} t_2 d_{mi} z_{miv} + \sum_{j \in J} \sum_{i \in I} (h_o \frac{\sum_{i \in I} \mu_i x_{ji}^r}{Q_j}$$
$$+ h_j \frac{Q_j}{2}) + \sum_{j \in J} h_j z_\alpha \sqrt{L_j \sum_{i \in I} \sigma_i^2 x_{ji}^r}) / \sum_{i \in I} \mu_i \quad (2)$$

$$\min e_x = (\sum_{j \in J} \hat{f}_j y_j + \sum_{k \in K} \sum_{j \in J} \hat{t}_1 d_{kj} x_{kj}^p + \sum_{j \in J} \sum_{i \in I} \sum_{m \in (I \cup J)} \hat{t}_2 d_{mi} z_{miv} + \sum_{j \in J} \sum_{i \in I} \hat{h}_j \frac{Q_j}{2}$$
$$+ \sum_{j \in J} \hat{h}_j z_\alpha \sqrt{L_j \sum_{i \in I} \sigma_i^2 x_{ji}^r}) / \sum_{i \in I} \mu_i \quad (3)$$

$$\text{s.t.} \quad Q_j + z_\alpha \sqrt{L_j \sum_{i \in I} \sigma_i^2 x_{ji}^r} \leq N_j, \forall j \in J \quad (4)$$

$$\sum_{i \in I} \sum_{m \in (I \cup J)} \mu_i z_{miv} \leq V^c, \forall m \in (I \cup J) \quad (5)$$

$$\sum_{v \in V} \sum_{m \in (I \cup J)} z_{miv} = 1, \forall i \in I \quad (6)$$

$$\sum_{j \in J} \sum_{i \in I} z_{jiv} \leq 1, \forall v \in V \quad (7)$$

$$\sum_{m \in (I \cup J)} z_{miv} - \sum_{m \in (I \cup J)} z_{imv} = 0, \forall i \in I, \forall v \in V, \forall m \in (I \cup J) \quad (8)$$

$$R_{iv} - R_{mv} + (n_r \times z_{miv}) \leq n_r - 1, \forall i \in I, \forall m \in (I \cup J), \forall v \in V \quad (9)$$

$$y_j = \{0,1\}, \forall j \in J, \forall n \in N_j \quad (10)$$

$$x_{kj}^p = \{0,1\}, \forall k \in K, \forall j \in J \quad (11)$$

$$x_{ji}^r = \{0,1\}, \forall j \in J, \forall i \in I \quad (12)$$

$$z_{miv} = \{0,1\}, \forall m \in (I \cup J), i \in I, \forall v \in V. \quad (13)$$

Equation (2) minimizes the cost of the CLRIP, where the first three terms are the fixed location cost, inventory cost, and routing cost, respectively. Equation (3) minimizes the carbon emissions. Equation (4) restricts the inventory in warehouse j to remain within its capacity N_j. Equation (5) restricts the load of each vehicle to within its capacity V^c. Equation (6) ensures one and only one vehicle serves any retailer. Equation (7) requires that each vehicle serves no more than one warehouse. The flow conservation Equation (8) states that a vehicle entering a node must also leave the node, so as to ensure the route is circular. The sub-tour elimination Equation (9) guarantees that each tour contains a warehouse, from which the tour originates and some retailers [32], where R_{iv} is an auxiliary variable defined for retailer i for sub-tour elimination in the route of vehicle v, n_r is the number of retailers. Equations (10)–(13) enforce the decision variables to remain within their respective domains.

4.2. The Revenue Model Considering CEBs

This study focuses on the effects of CEBs on the task of designing a supply chain network, which includes making LRI decisions. CEBs not only affect consumers' willingness to pay premium prices for greener products, but they also affect the market demand for such products. This willingness to pay varies greatly across industries and consumer groups and also changes in intensity over time [4]. If anything, carbon emissions due to logistics operations have been a concern for a considerable length of time, as these operations are a major source of emissions. We are interested in determining how to maximize earnings, as well as how to improve competition, through the influence of CEBs in three supply chain network structures which include location, routing and inventory considerations.

As non-green products have already been in circulation for many years, the general optimal decision is based on cost minimization. In this study, however, in addition to cost, we also consider carbon emissions as a benchmark. There is a terminal consumer group with an average CEB in the market. The green level θ is closely related to the carbon emissions from the supply chain. It has been proven that the carbon emissions and cost are in negative correlation, and thus, we assume that the optimal cost corresponds to a poor performance in relation to carbon emissions, and vice versa. Specifically, with an operation map, we can connect inputs $[\underline{c}, \overline{c}]$ to corresponding outputs $[\overline{e}, \underline{e}]$. Then θ can be denoted as

$$\theta = \overline{e}/e_x \tag{14}$$

where e_x is the actual carbon emission, and thus $(\theta - 1)$ is the carbon abatement ratio. p is the price of non-green products, $(\underline{c}, \overline{e})$ represents the cost and carbon emissions, and p_x is the price with (c_x, e_x). As we know, the marginal cost of carbon reduction increases by degrees. The "low hanging fruit" effect also indicates that initial basic improvement is easier, but the cleanup is harder. Thus, the above situation is considered, and the price of a product with green level θ is

$$p_x = p\theta^2 \tag{15}$$

It is worth noting that product price is a quadratic function of θ, since the environmental improvement has an increasing marginal cost, and production price is worked out to the costing. The quadratic function is commonly used to describe the cost related to the product's environmental improvement. That is, each additional increment of emissions reduction is more difficult, and hence costlier to achieve [8]. Also, from the market's perspective, consumers with CEBs are willing to pay a premium price for green products. The greener the product, the more expensive it will be. In addition, for an advanced green product, too, even a small improvement will result in a significant price increase. This increase is deemed to be reasonable.

The aim is to find an optimal portfolio (c_x, e_x) under this context. The basic profit function can be defined as

$$\prod = (p_x - c_x - c_0)D - \varepsilon \tag{16}$$

where constant c_0 is the unit cost of raw materials, and ε is other expenditure, which can be ignored in most cases.

Substituting Equations (1)–(15) into Equation (16), then:

$$\prod = (p\theta^2 - c_x - c_0)(D_0 - \lambda_1 p\theta^2 + \frac{1}{2}\lambda_2 \tau\theta) \tag{17}$$

Based on Equation (17), if there is no CEB, the enterprise loses the motivation to reduce carbon emissions, which is consistent with the traditional model. We assume the traditional model has revenue of Π^C, with the only measure being the cost, and we mark it as model PC. In this condition, $\theta = 1$, $\tau = 0$, thus:

$$\Pi^C = (p - \underline{c} - c_0)(D_0 - \lambda_1 p) \tag{18}$$

Enterprises have an incentive to join in carbon reduction practices only when $\Pi - \Pi^c > 0$. c_0 is the same constant in Π and Π^c, and thus can be ignored. Then, enterprises will participate in carbon emissions when $(p\theta^2 - c_x)(D_0 - \lambda_1 p\theta^2 + \frac{1}{2}\lambda_2\tau\theta) > (p - \underline{c})(D_0 - \lambda_1 p)$, and thus $c_x < p\theta^2 - \dfrac{(p-\underline{c})(D_0 - \lambda_1 p)}{D_0 - \lambda_1 p\theta^2 + \frac{1}{2}\lambda_2\tau\theta}$. Actually, θ is a function of e_x; the relationship between c_x and e_x is important, and it will be solved in the next section.

5. Solving Approach

5.1. Particle Swarm Optimization Algorithm

The particle swarm optimization (PSO) algorithm was first proposed by Kennedy and Eberhart [32]. It is a population-based optimization technique and is becoming very popular, due mainly to its simplicity of implementation and ability to quickly converge to a reasonably good solution [33]. It has been extensively applied to many complex network optimization problems. In the PSO heuristic procedure, a swarm of particles is retained in the search process. Each particle follows a specific trajectory in the search space, and each step of the particle determines a trial solution. Each particle has knowledge of its previous best experience, as well as the best global experience of the entire swarm. The current best fitness of, *i.e.*, the best solution found so far by particle p is represented by $\mathbf{x}_{pbest_p}$, while the global best fitness among all particles is represented by $\mathbf{x}_{gbest}$. The velocity and position of particle p at iteration (time) t in dimension d are represented by $v_{pd}(t)$ and $x_{pd}(t)$, respectively. Each particle updates its direction at time t according to Equation (19) in the following [32]:

$$v_{pd}(t) = \omega v_{pd}(t-1) + c_1 r_1(t)(\mathbf{x}_{pbest_{pd}} - \mathbf{x}_{pd}(t)) + c_2 r_2(t)(\mathbf{x}_{gbest} - \mathbf{x}_{pd}(t)) \qquad (19)$$

where ω is the inertia influencing the local and global ability of the particle; usually a value between 0.2 to 0.6 is recommended; c_1 and c_2 are cognitive and social learning rates, respectively, and $r_1(t)$ and $r_2(t)$ are two uniform random numbers such that $r_1, r_2 \in [0,1]$.

The position of particle p is then updated according to Equation (20) in the following

$$x_{pd}(t) = x_{pd}(t-1) + v_{pd}(t) \qquad (20)$$

The update of velocity and the position process is repeated for every dimension and for all particles in the swarm. Eventually the swarm as a whole, like a flock of birds collectively foraging for food, is likely to move close to an optimum of the fitness function [33].

5.2. The Hybrid PSO

The multi-objective model contains location and routing assignments involving binary decisions. Multi-objective programming problems with binary variables cannot be directly processed using the Multi-objective Particle Swarm Optimization (MOPSO) heuristic procedure. Following Shankar *et al.* [33], the velocity of a particle should be modified if x_d is binary. The modified velocity can be updated as:

$$v_{pd}(t) = v_{pd}(t-1) + r_1(t)(x_{pbest_{pd}} - x_{pd}(t-1)) + r_2(t)(x_{gbest} - x_{pd}(t-1)) \qquad (21)$$

where $r_1(t)$ and $r_2(t)$ are two random numbers. The position of particle p can be updated as:

$$x_{pd}(t) = \begin{cases} 0, & \text{If } \rho_{pd} < s(v_{pd}(t)) \\ 1, & \text{If } \rho_{pd} \geq s(v_{pd}(t)) \end{cases} \qquad (22)$$

where ρ_{pd} is a uniformly distributed random number such that $\rho_{pd} \in [0,1]$ and $s(v_{pd}(t))$ is the probability threshold given by $s(v_{pd}) = \dfrac{1}{1+\exp(-v_{pd}(t))}$. In the MOPSO heuristic procedure, the velocity and positions of the continuous particles are updated according to Equations (19) and (20), respectively, while those of the binary variables are updated according to Equations (21) and (22), respectively.

5.3. An Improved Constraint of the MOPSO

In order to improve the ability of the heuristic procedure to search the edges crossing unconnected parts of the feasible region, and also to obtain global non-dominated solutions, some infeasible solutions that are near the feasible solutions are retained in the swarm at the beginning of the search process. A constraint that restricts the infeasibility degree of the constraints is used. At the end of the solution process, all particles retained in the swarm must be feasible. Any infeasible particles will be deleted from the external file gradually, throughout the progress of the search process. A dynamic self-adapting process is needed to control the infeasibility degree in the heuristic procedure. In the multi-objective programming model, the ℓth inequality constraint can be written as $g_\ell(\mathbf{x}) \leq 0$ and the ℓ'th equality constraint can be written as $h_{\ell'}(\mathbf{x}) - \delta = 0$. The infeasibility of a trail solution $\mathbf{x}$ can be quantized as follows:

$$C(\mathbf{x}) = \sum_{\ell} \max(g_{\ell}(\mathbf{x}), 0) + \sum_{\ell'} \max(|h_{\ell'}(\mathbf{x}) - \delta|, 0) \qquad (23)$$

In Equation (23), δ is a permissible deviation, such that $\delta > 0$ and is very small. If $\mathbf{x} \in X$, $C(\mathbf{x}) = 0$. A dynamic infeasibility threshold ε is used that guarantees the final solutions are all feasible. This threshold is defined as:

$$\varepsilon = \begin{cases} \varepsilon_0 \times (1 - 5t/4T), & \text{if } t \leq 0.8T \\ 0, & \text{if } t > 0.8T \end{cases} \qquad (24)$$

where ε_0 is the initial allowable deviation of all the constraints. Obviously, ε decreases with the increase in the number of evolutionary generations. In the searching process, the solution $\mathbf{x}$ is retained if $C(\mathbf{x}) \leq \varepsilon$; otherwise it is discarded.

5.4. Selecting the Optimal Particles

The solution of the MOPSO optimization problem is different from a single objective optimization problem. With a single objective problem, it is easy to know which particles are the personal best (pbest) and global best (gbest). With the MOPSO, however, it is difficult to judge which particles are pbest and gbest, because the particles are often non-dominate solutions. However, it is important to pick suitable pbest and gbest particles, since each particle must change its position, as guided by pbest and gbest. Each particle moves toward the non-dominated frontier during the search process [34].

The selection for pbest is relatively simple compared to gbest. A method called Prandom is used in this study, according to which a single pbest is maintained. Pbest is replaced if a new value < pbest, or else, if the new value is found to be mutually non-dominating with pbest, one of the two is randomly selected to be the new best [35]. Before the selection for gbest, there are still some works to illustrate. In the MOPSO algorithm, we usually store the non-dominate solutions in archive, and the archive has a limited capacity. Thus, in order to maintain the archive, the crowding distance should be measured as a base for reserving or discarding non-dominate solutions. The crowding distance dt_{ij} can be calculated as:

$$dt_{ij} = \sqrt{\sum_{l=1}^{k} f_l(X_i) - f_l(X_j)^2} \qquad (25)$$

where $f_l(X)$ denotes the objective functions in the dimension l. According to Equation (25), the crowding distance matrix can be indicated as:

$$DT = \begin{bmatrix} dt_{11} & dt_{12} & \cdots & dt_{1n} \\ dt_{21} & dt_{22} & \cdots & dt_{2n} \\ \vdots & \vdots & \vdots & \vdots \\ dt_{n1} & dt_{n2} & \cdots & dt_{nn} \end{bmatrix} \qquad (26)$$

where n is the number of non-dominate solutions in the archive. Set S and A represents the populations with particles and archive storing, non-dominate solutions. The particles in S can be divided into two types. One set (S1) is comprised of particles that are dominated by at least one of the non-dominate solutions in A. The other set (S2) is comprised of particles that are not dominated by any one solution in A. $S = S1 \cup S2$. In the same way, archive A can also be divided into three types. Set A1 is the non-dominate solutions, which dominate at least one of the particles in S. Set A2 is the non-dominate solutions which have the same position with the particles in S. Set A3 is comprised of the other non-dominate solutions. $A = A1 \cup A2 \cup A3$. Figure 2 shows the mapping relations of S and A.

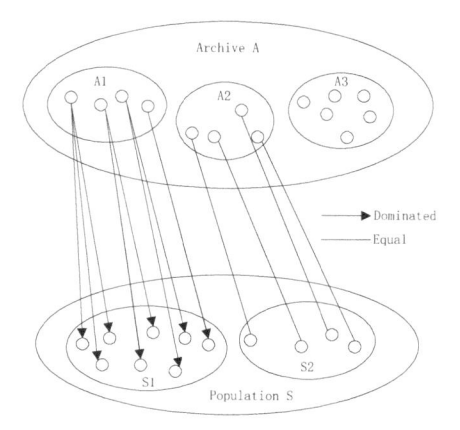

Figure 2. The mapping relationship of archive A and population S.

For the MOPSO algorithm, the diversity and convergence of population are contradictory issues. One contradiction is the diversity, which guarantees the global best while avoiding the local optimal. The other is the convergence, which promotes particles approaching the Pareto frontier as far as possible. Hence, for particles in S1, if we select non-dominate solutions in A1, which dominate the particles as gbest, the search engines would speed up. However, this can lead to a premature problem. For particles in S2, the global best selection strategy would lead those particles moving to less crowded regions to improve the capability of a global search.

Regardless, each non-dominate solution in the archive has its unique feature. To maintain the diversity of an algorithm, each should have a chance to become a global guide. When paired with these factors, two properties, f_{ri} and f_{pi}, are given for non-dominate solutions in the archive. f_{ri} denotes how often the non-dominate solution is selected as gbest, and f_{pi} denotes how many particles in the current population select the non-dominate solution as gbest. Generally, the size of f_{pi} should be restricted. If one gbest is selected by too many particles, the result would be particles converging to a limited region. Based on our experience, we use $f_{pi} \leqslant 0.05N$, where N is the number of particles [36].

Putting the above pieces together, the global best can be selected as follows:

(i) For each particle in S1, we select a non-dominate solution that randomly dominates the particle from A1 as gbest, but $f_{pi} \leqslant 0.05N$ is necessary. If no solution is found, the gbest should be selected from the A1 with greater crowding distance and smaller f_{ri}.

(ii) For each particle in S2, a random probability model is employed to select gbest from the A2 with greater crowding distance and smaller f_{ri}.

The pseudo-code of MOPSO algorithm depicting the entire process is given as follows:

(1) Initialize positions and velocities of all particles.
(2) Set the current particle position as Pbest.
(3) While (iter_count < T)
(4) for each particle (i = 1:n)
(5) Select a gbest from the archive.
(6) Update velocity and position.
(7) Evaluate the fitness values of the current particle i.
(8) Update the pbest of each particle by comparison criteria.
(9) End for
(10) Update archive by non-dominate solutions.
(11) For each particle in archive

(12) If $f_{pi} \leqslant 0.05N$
(13) Select a dominate solution with greater crowding distance and smaller f_{ri} from archive as gbest randomly.
(14) End if
(15) End for
(16) Output
(17) End while

6. Computational Experiment

In this section, we evaluate the presented model using a set of numerical data from a real case. The problem is solved by the MOPSO method with Matlab 7.01 on a PC with Intel core i5 and 2.4 GHz. Then, the effects of CEBs and green levels on the decision process are comprehensively analyzed. Finally, some managerial insights are presented.

6.1. Case Study

We consider the experiment based on a case study from the petrochemical industry. Specifically, data from the Northeast Chemical Sales Company of the China National Petroleum Corporation (CNPC) (Beijing, China) was studied. CNPC is a large group, and its supply chain network is responsible for transporting petrochemicals from plants, via warehouses, to retailers. This transportation operation involves location, routing and inventory decisions, as well as the creation of considerable carbon emissions. In this paper, a section of the operational data was analyzed. Specifically, this case study involves two plants, five potential warehouses with retailing functions and eight retailers. Each trajectory is relative to a routing cost and the amount of carbon emission. The routings and distances are shown in Figure 3. The parameters of the warehouses and retailers are listed in Tables 1–3. In addition, the market inverse demand coefficient is set as 5500, and the attraction coefficient with the environment level of products is set as 5000. CEB is 1, and the routing cost per distance of M-to-W and W-to-R are all equal to q. The order cost is 500, and the capacity of each vehicle is 1500. In addition, $\hat{f}_j^A = 29.3N_j$, the carbon emissions per distance are 0.17, and the carbon emissions per inventory are 0.00276.

Table 1. The parameters of potential warehouses.

	Beijing	Tianjin	Cangzhou	Jinan	Zhengzhou
Lead time(days)	3	5	6	4	8
Demand variance	12	14	9	11	8
Service level	95%	95%	95%	95%	95%

Table 2. The area and fixed location cost of potential DC.

	Area of Location (m^2)	Fixed Location Cost (¥)	Hold Cost (¥/ton Day)
Beijing	3000	2,000,000	0.3
Tianjin	3600	1,800,000	0.25
Cangzhou	4000	1,120,000	0.3
Jinnan	4200	1,560,000	0.25
Zhengzhou	5000	1,870,000	0.3

Table 3. The parameters of retailers.

	Beijing	Tianjin	Baoding	Cangzhou	Shijiazhuang	Jinan	Liaocheng	Linyi	Qingdao	Xinyang	Zhengzhou	Taiyuan	Yuncheng
Initial demand	430	416	463	577	506	509	522	439	536	696	589	554	694
Service level	92%	91%	95%	95%	90%	98%	91%	94%	95%	95%	95%	95%	90%
Demand variance	9	12	7	8	14	6	6	9	9	11	9	7	9

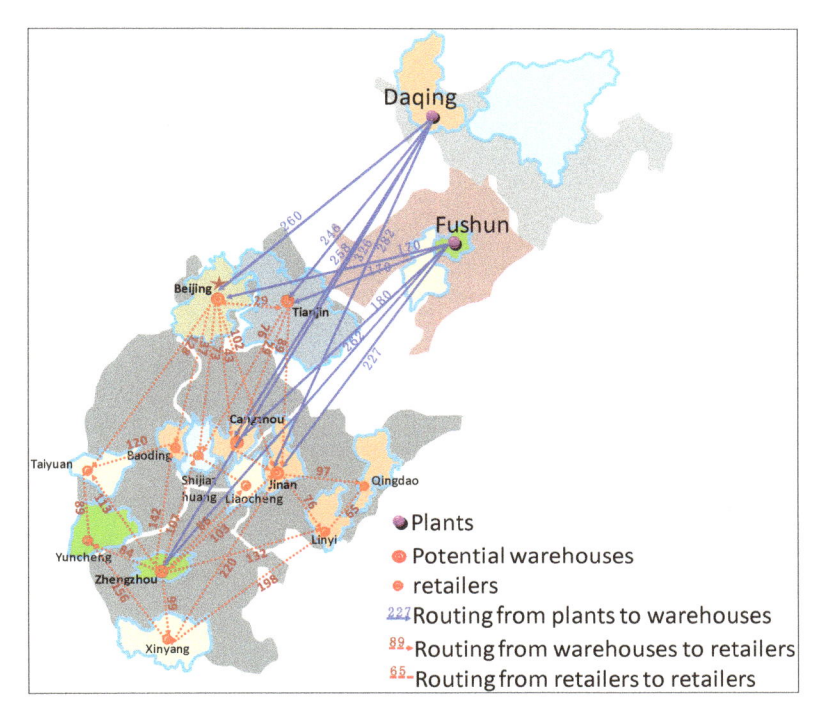

Figure 3. The network of two plants, five potential warehouses and 14 retailers.

6.2. Numerical Analysis

According to the above data and the approach used to solve the question in Section 5, the trade-off between cost and carbon emissions can be shown as Figure 4. The result provides decision makers with decidedly indifferent choices. In conclusion, all the points on the Pareto line are the solutions, but the managers themselves cannot directly decide. If CEBs are incorporated, the optimal solution is unique (Figure 5). Clearly, revenue first increases and then decreases with increasing carbon emissions. The increasing gradient is greater than the decreasing gradient. This result illustrates that a proper carbon reduction policy can improve corporate revenue, but excessive carbon reduction activities would have a negative impact. Figure 5 shows that the maximum attainable revenue is ¥601,230,000. The optimal configuration can be shown as follows: The location decision is to open Cangzhou, Jinan, and Zhengzhou. The routing decision is divided into two parts. (i) As regards the routing from plants to warehouses, the first decision is that Daqing serves Cangzhou and Jinan, while Fushun serves Zhengzhou. (ii) Considering transportation from warehouses to retailers, the routing schedule of the Cangzhou warehouse is Cangzhou-Tianjin-Beijing-Baoding-Cangzhou-Shijiazhuang-Taiyuan-Cangzhou. The routing schedule for the Jinan warehouse is Jinan-Liaocheng-Linyi-Qingdao-Jinan, and the routing schedule for the Zhengzhou warehouse is Zhengzhou-Xinyang-Yuncheng-Zhengzhou. The order quantities of the three warehouses are 4792, 3156 and 2834 tons, respectively.

We are interested in how CEBs affect companies' decision making. As we know, CEBs mainly affect demand. The effect of consumers' environmental preference on demand for products with different carbon emissions is shown in Figure 6. We vary the CEBs from 1 to 1.8 and obtain a series of demand *vs.* carbon emissions. Clearly, the curves move from left to right as the coefficient increases from 1 to 1.8, which implies that with the same carbon emission levels, larger CEBs lead to greater demand. This is due to the fact that when consumers pay closer attention to environmental protection, enterprises are more likely to take actions that will improve their environmental protection levels. Then, consumers with greater environmental awareness will buy more products from those enterprises with superior eco-friendly operations. This is a virtuous cycle. However, the marginal cost of implementing environmental improvements increases by degrees. As we know, the ultimate goal of enterprise management is to maximize benefits. Similarly, we adjust the carbon emissions variable to analyze the effect of CEBs on revenue (Figure 7). Clearly, revenue increases as the CEBs move from 1 to 1.8. However, the degree of revenue growth is clearly slower than the increasing CEBs. That is to say, the initial improvement brought about by the CEBs greatly affects the operation of supply chain enterprises, but this effect will weaken because of the high costs associated with further reductions of carbon emissions.

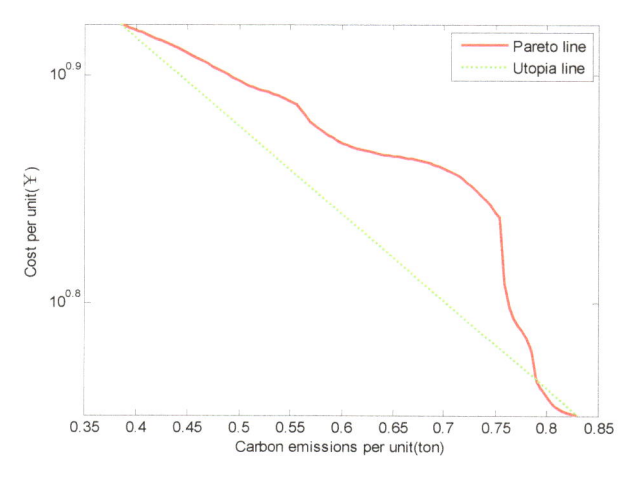

Figure 4. Pareto optimal curve between cost and carbon emissions.

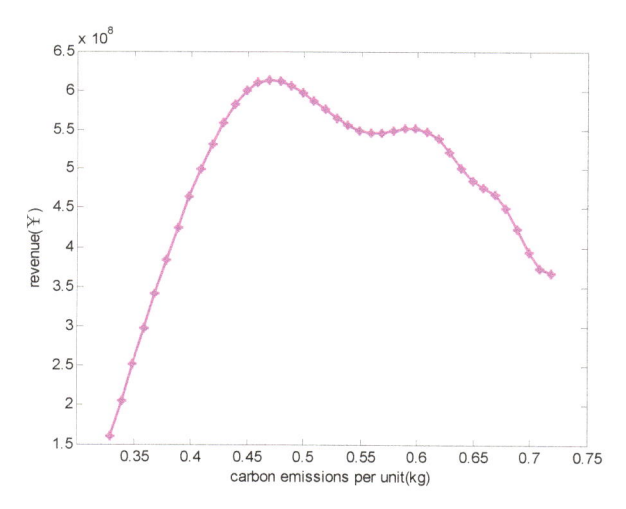

Figure 5. The relationship between carbon emissions and revenue.

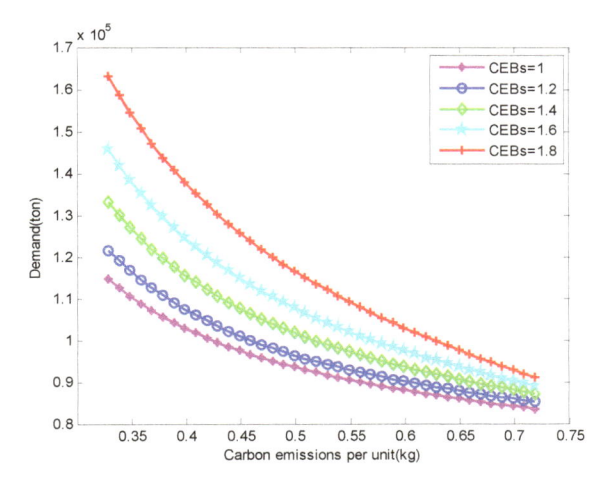

Figure 6. The demand in different consumer environmental preferences varying with carbon emissions.

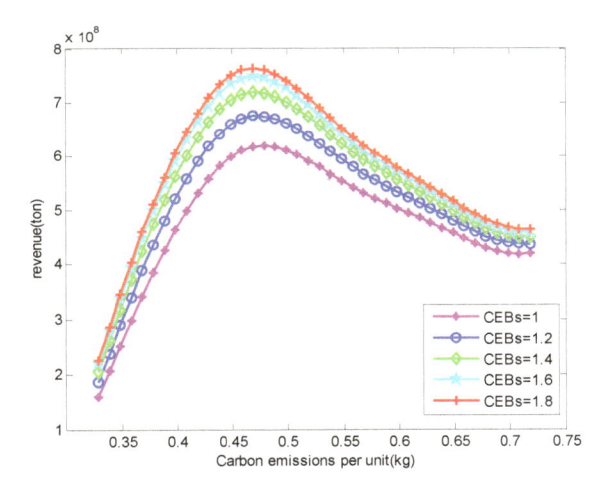

Figure 7. The revenue in different consumer environmental preferences varying with carbon emissions.

We assume that product pricing is a function of carbon emissions. However, it is not a hard and absolute fact that pricing is the single, key factor. Our analysis (Figure 8) shows that higher prices generate greater revenue. What is important is that the higher the price of a product, the bigger the revenue will be obtained with lower carbon emissions. This illustrates that a higher price for green products can stimulate a reduction in carbon emissions, but that higher price can also curb product demand (Figure 9). Clearly, product pricing is increasing with a reduction in carbon emissions. When the price increases, the product demand decreases. In this case, the consumer's willingness to pay is the most important factor. Hence, the enterprise should encourage consumers to improve their CEBs, and pay closer attention to purchasing green products.

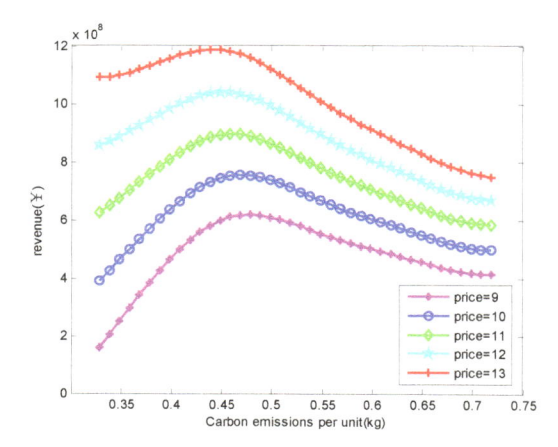

Figure 8. The revenue *vs.* carbon emissions in different product pricing.

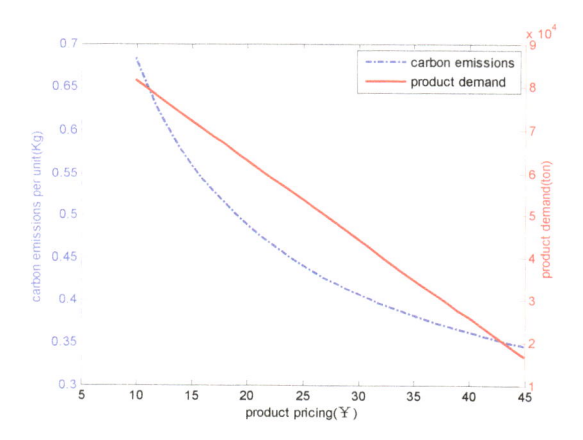

Figure 9. The relationship between product pricing -carbon emissions, and product pricing-product demand.

6.3. Managerial Insights

In the current business climate, enterprises and consumers have gradually come to recognize the importance of environmental protection. Both businesses and consumers are more inclined to make an effort to reduce carbon emissions. In particular, consumers with greater environmental awareness are happy to pay a premium price for low carbon emission products. This willingness, which is based on increased environmental awareness, provides an opportunity for logistics enterprises. Our study is consistent with the work of Liu *et al.* [8], which found that, with consumers' greater environmental awareness, more of them are willing to pay higher prices for low carbon emission products. In turn, the enterprises that produce those products can earn greater revenue.

In addition, the companies that produce low carbon emissions should also make a concerted marketing effort to shift consumers' traditional purchasing decision criteria and transform those buyers into a group with a preference for low carbon emission products and services. This study indicates that the returns can be substantial if consumers who are currently not interested in purchasing environmentally friendly products make even a little progress. Moreover, the results show that low carbon emission operations cost more than the operations that do not consider carbon emissions.

However, when the CEBs are positive, an optimal degree of carbon reduction will maximize revenue. Sadly, the unavoidable fact is that most consumers loathe paying to pay premium prices for low carbon emission products. If enterprises are going to implement sustainable decisions, they must be certain of CEBs.

7. Conclusions

This paper discussed the effects of consumer environmental behaviors (CEBs) on the design of a sustainable supply chain. CEBs not only affect consumers' willingness to pay premium prices for low carbon emission products, but also the overall demand for low carbon emission products. We introduced a sustainable supply chain network model based on the joint optimization of location, routing and inventory, taking carbon emissions into consideration. The distinguishing feature of our model is its consideration of the CEBs, which affect both carbon emission decisions and product demand.

First, a multi-objective model is constructed, which provides a trade-off between costs and carbon emissions. The MOPSO algorithm is used to solve the model, and then a Pareto optimal set can be obtained. After that, we model the revenue function based on the Pareto solutions. In the computational experiments, we test the model by the data from the Northeast Chemical Sales Company of CNPC. We first obtain the Pareto optimal curve, which provides a portfolio of configurations for decision makers. Then, we can use the same technique to obtain the revenue curves from different carbon emissions. Hence, the unique optimal revenue levels and the relevant decisions can be acquired. Finally, the sensitivity of the case study was analyzed. We are interested in the effects of CEBs on the demand and revenue in a three-level supply chain. The results show that more positive CEBs result in greater demand and higher revenue. We also observe that the pricing of low carbon operations is critical. Therefore, enterprises should make marketing efforts to strengthen consumers' environmental preferences. Companies should support their claims to consumers and ensure the degree of CEBs before implementing their carbon emission reduction policies.

Further research is required to determine more specific factors pertaining to CEBs in a supply chain (e.g., the decision makers' appetite for risk, the expectations of market development and the effects of government intervention via carbon emission reduction policies and legislation), so that the model will be more adaptive to real-life scenarios.

Acknowledgments: The authors would like to express our sincere thanks to the anonymous referees and editors for their time and patience devoted to the review of this paper. This work is supported by NSFC Grant (No. 71572031).

Author Contributions: Jinhuan Tang proposed the model, write and revise the whole paper. Shoufeng Ji contributes to join the research and give many valuable suggestions. Liwen Jiang is responsible for the solving method, especially in the game theory, she made an enormous contribution.

Conflicts of Interest: The authors declare no conflict of interest.

References

1. Hufbauer, G.C.; Charnovitz, S.; Kim, J. *Global Warming and the World Trading System*; Peterson Institute for International Economics: Washington, DC, USA, 2009.
2. Chistra, K. In search of the green consumers: A perceptual study. *J. Serv. Res.* **2007**, *7*, 173–191.
3. Conrad, K. Price competition and product differentiation when consumers care for the environment. *Environ. Resour. Econ.* **2005**, *31*, 1–19. [CrossRef]
4. Laroche, M.; Bergeron, J.; Barbaro-Forleo, G. Targeting consumers who are willing to pay more for environmentally friendly products. *J. Consum. Market.* **2001**, *18*, 503–520. [CrossRef]
5. Moon, W.; Florkowski, W.J.; Brückner, B.; Schonhof, I. Willing to pay for environmental practices: Implications for eco-labeling. *Land Econ.* **2002**, *78*, 88–102. [CrossRef]
6. Ghosh, D.; Shah, J. A comparative analysis of greening policies across supply chain structures. *Int. J. Prod. Econ.* **2012**, *135*, 568–583. [CrossRef]

7. Gil-Moltó, M.J.; Varvarigos, D. Emission taxes and the adoption of cleaner technologies: The case of environmentally conscious consumers. *Resour. Energy Econ.* **2013**, *35*, 486–504. [CrossRef]
8. Liu, Z.L.; Anderson, T.D.; Cruz, J.M. Consumer environmental awareness and competition in two-stage supply chains. *Eur. J. Oper. Res.* **2012**, *218*, 602–613. [CrossRef]
9. Elhedhli, S.; Merrick, R. Green supply chain network design to reduce carbon emissions. *Transp. Res. Part D* **2012**, *17*, 370–379. [CrossRef]
10. Paksoy, T.; Özceylan, E.; Weber, G.W.; Barsoum, N.; Weber, G.W.; Vasant, P. A multi objective model for optimization of a green supply chain network. *Glob. J. Technol. Optim.* **2011**, *2*, 84–96.
11. Paksoy, T.; Özceylan, E. Environmentally conscious optimization of supply chain networks. *J. Oper. Res. Soc.* **2013**, *65*, 855–872. [CrossRef]
12. Benjaafar, S.; Li, Y.; Daskin, M. Carbon footprint and the management of supply chains: Insights from simple models. *IEEE Trans. Autom. Sci. Eng.* **2013**, *10*, 99–115. [CrossRef]
13. Kim, N.S.; Janic, M.; Van Wee, B. Trade-off between carbon dioxide emissions and logistics costs based on multiobjective optimization. *Transp. Res. Rec. J. Transp. Res. Board* **2009**, *2139*, 107–116. [CrossRef]
14. Wang, F.; Lai, X.F.; Shi, N. A multi-objective optimization for green supply chain network design. *Decis. Support Syst.* **2011**, *51*, 262–269. [CrossRef]
15. Chaabane, A.; Ramudhin, A.; Paquet, M. Design of sustainable supply chains under the emission trading scheme. *Int. J. Prod. Econ.* **2012**, *135*, 37–49. [CrossRef]
16. Chen, X.; Benjaafar, S.; Elomri, A. The carbon-constrained EOQ. *Oper. Res. Lett.* **2013**, *41*, 172–179. [CrossRef]
17. Babiker, M.H.; Criqui, P.; Ellerman, A.D.; Reilly, J.M.; Viguier, L.L. Assessing the impact of carbon tax differentiation in the European Union. *Environ. Model. Assess.* **2003**, *8*, 187–197. [CrossRef]
18. Jabali, O.; Woensel, T.V.; de Kok, A.G. Analysis of Travel Times and CO_2 Emissions in Time-Dependent Vehicle Routing. *Prod. Oper. Manag.* **2012**, *21*, 1060–1074. [CrossRef]
19. Nagy, G.; Salhi, S. Location-routing: Issues, models and methods. *Eur. J. Oper. Res.* **2007**, *177*, 649–672. [CrossRef]
20. Dror, M.; Ball, M. Inventory/routing: Reduction from an annual to a short-period problem. *Naval Res. Logist. (NRL)* **1987**, *34*, 891–905. [CrossRef]
21. Shen, Z.J.M.; Coullard, C.; Daskin, M.S. A joint location-inventory model. *Transp. Sci.* **2003**, *37*, 40–55. [CrossRef]
22. AhmadiJavid, A.; Azad, N. Incorporating location, routing and inventory decisions in supply chain network design. *Transp. Res. Part E Logist. Transp. Rev.* **2010**, *46*, 582–597. [CrossRef]
23. Ahmadi-Javid, A.; Seddighi, A.H. A location-routing-inventory model for designing multisource distribution networks. *Eng. Optim.* **2012**, *44*, 637–656. [CrossRef]
24. Hua, G.W.; Cheng, T.C.E.; Wang, S.Y. Managing carbon footprints in inventory management. *Int. J. Prod. Econ.* **2011**, *132*, 178–185. [CrossRef]
25. Kroes, J.; Subramanian, R.; Subramanyam, R. Operational compliance levers, environmental performance, and firm performance under cap and trade regulation. *Manuf. Serv. Oper. Manag.* **2012**, *14*, 186–201. [CrossRef]
26. Diabat, A.; David, S. A Carbon-Capped Supply Chain Network Problem. In Proceedings of the IEEE International Conference on Industrial Engineering and Engineering Management, Hong Kong, China, 8–11 December 2009; IEEE press: Piscataway, NJ, USA, 2010; pp. 523–527.
27. Wygonik, E.; GooDChild, A. Evaluating CO_2 emissions, cost and service quality trade-offs in an urban delivery system case study. *IATSS Res.* **2011**, *35*, 7–15. [CrossRef]
28. Thøgersen, J. Promoting Green Consumer Behavior with Eco-Labels. In *New Tools for Environmental Protection: Education, Information, and Voluntary Measures*; Dietz, T., Stern, P., Eds.; National Academy Press: Washington, DC, USA, 2002; pp. 83–104.
29. Young, W.; Hwang, K.; McDonald, S.; Oates, C.J. Sustainable consumption: Green consumer behaviour when purchasing products. *Sustain. Dev.* **2010**, *18*, 20–31. [CrossRef]
30. Vanclay, J.K.; Shortiss, J.; Aulsebrook, A.; Gillespie, A.M.; Howell, B.C.; Johann, R.; Maher, M.J.; Mitchell, K.M. Customer response to carbon labeling of groceries. *J. Consum. Policy* **2011**, *34*, 153–160. [CrossRef]
31. Tang, C.S.; Zhou, S. Research advances in environmentally and socially sustainable operations. *Eur. J. Oper. Res.* **2012**, *223*, 585–594. [CrossRef]

32. Desrochers, M.; Laporte, G. Improvements and extensions to the Miller-Tucker-Zemlin subtour elimination constraints. *Oper. Res. Lett.* **1991**, *10*, 27–36. [CrossRef]
33. Kennedy, J.; Eberhart, R. Particle swarm optimization. In Proceedings of the IEEE International Conference on Neural Networks, Perth, Australia, 27 November–1 December 1995; pp. 1942–1948.
34. Shankar, B.L.; Basavarajappa, S.; Chen, J.C.; Kadadevaramath, R.S. Location and allocation decisions for multi-echelon supply chain network–a multi-objective evolutionary approach. *Expert Syst. Appl.* **2013**, *40*, 551–562. [CrossRef]
35. Everson, R.M.; Fieldsend, J.E.; Singh, S. Full Elite Sets for Multi-Objective Optimisation. In *Adaptive Computing in Design and Manufacture V*; Springer: London, UK, 2002; pp. 343–354.
36. Ling, H.F.; Zhou, X.Z.; Jiang, X.L.; Xiao, Y.H. Improved constrained multi-objective particle optimization algorithm. *J. Comput. Appl.* **2012**, *32*, 1320–1324.

© 2016 by the authors. Licensee MDPI, Basel, Switzerland. This article is an open access article distributed under the terms and conditions of the Creative Commons Attribution (CC BY) license (http://creativecommons.org/licenses/by/4.0/).

Article

Scalability of Sustainable Business Models in Hybrid Organizations

Adam Jabłoński

The Department of Management, the University of Dąbrowa Górnicza (Wyższa Szkoła Biznesu w Dąbrowie Górniczej), Zygmunta Cieplaka Str. 1c, Dąbrowa Górnicza 41-300, Poland; adam.jablonski@ottima-plus.com.pl; Tel.: +48-32-262-2805

Academic Editor: Giuseppe Ioppolo
Received: 21 October 2015; Accepted: 17 February 2016; Published: 23 February 2016

Abstract: The dynamics of change in modern business create new mechanisms for company management to determine their pursuit and the achievement of their high performance. This performance maintained over a long period of time becomes a source of ensuring business continuity by companies. An ontological being enabling the adoption of such assumptions is such a business model that has the ability to generate results in every possible market situation and, moreover, it has the features of permanent adaptability. A feature that describes the adaptability of the business model is its scalability. Being a factor ensuring more work and more efficient work with an increasing number of components, scalability can be applied to the concept of business models as the company's ability to maintain similar or higher performance through it. Ensuring the company's performance in the long term helps to build the so-called sustainable business model that often balances the objectives of stakeholders and shareholders, and that is created by the implemented principles of value-based management and corporate social responsibility. This perception of business paves the way for building hybrid organizations that integrate business activities with pro-social ones. The combination of an approach typical of hybrid organizations in designing and implementing sustainable business models pursuant to the scalability criterion seems interesting from the cognitive point of view. Today, hybrid organizations are great spaces for building effective and efficient mechanisms for dialogue between business and society. This requires the appropriate business model. The purpose of the paper is to present the conceptualization and operationalization of scalability of sustainable business models that determine the performance of a hybrid organization in the network environment. The paper presents the original concept of applying scalability in sustainable business models with detailed interpretation. The paper and its findings are based on longitudinal research with participant observation, bibliographic research and the author's own experience in the processes of building and implementing business models in the years 2005–2015. At the time, the author observed the conceptualization and operationalization of several business models of companies operating in the Polish market.

Keywords: scalability; sustainability; business models; hybrid organisations; network environment

1. Introduction

The dynamics of change in modern business create new mechanisms for company management to determine their pursuit and achievement of their high performance. This performance maintained over a long period of time becomes a source of ensuring business continuity by companies. An ontological being enabling the adoption of such assumptions is such a business model that has the ability to generate results in every possible market situation and, moreover, it has the features of permanent adaptability. A feature that describes the adaptability of the business model is its scalability. Being a factor ensuring more work and more efficient work with an increasing number of components, scalability can be applied to the concept of business models as the company's ability to maintain similar or higher efficiency through it. Ensuring the company's performance in the long term helps to build the so-called sustainable business model that often balances the objectives of stakeholders and shareholders, and that is created by the implemented principles of value-based management and corporate social responsibility. This perception of business paves the way for building hybrid organizations that integrate business activities with pro-social ones. The combination of an approach typical of hybrid organizations in designing and implementing sustainable business models pursuant to the scalability criterion seems interesting from the cognitive point of view. Today, hybrid organizations are great spaces for building effective and efficient mechanisms for dialogue between business and society. This requires the appropriate business model. The purpose of the paper is to present the conceptualization and operationalization of scalability of sustainable business models that determine the performance of a hybrid organization in the network environment. The paper presents the original concept of applying scalability in sustainable business models with detailed interpretation.

2. The Methodology of Research

The research phases focus on the following issues:

(a) the review of the relevant literature and its analysis covering domestic and foreign references as well as Internet sources,
(b) the practical analysis of research and its multidimensional synthesis aimed at scientific inference, including preliminary research and the main research,
(c) the development of a six-phase research model,
(d) the implementation of the analysis and inference process, completed with the development of a holistic sustainable business model in building the long-term value of a socially responsible company with a reduced character, possible for use in the further development of the theory of management science and applicable in the practice of modern business by company managers.

They are used to answer the following questions: Which strategic factors and their relationships in the adopted business models have the greatest impact on building the long-term value of a socially responsible company? What should the structure of such a business model be?

Research is expected to result in a sustainable business model becoming a source of building the long-term value of a socially responsible company.

In order to achieve the objective of the book and the defined objectives of the research, different research methods have been used after in-depth analysis, including both analysis and synthesis of primary and secondary data, including:

(1) Longitudinal research with participant observation conducted in the period of 2005 to 2015, when the author observed, in a continuous system, several business models of companies operating in the Polish market. These companies represented various sectors of the economy. However, it was important that these companies had a formal or semi-formal business model that could be assessed and verified.
(2) Bibliographic research—the literature studies on the evaluation of management in theory and practice: the concept of Network Environment, the concept of CSR (Corporate Social Responsibility), the concept of Value-Based Management, the concept of Shareholders and the concept of Stakeholders, the concept of Business Models, and the concept of Business Sustainability and Business Scalability.
(3) The experience of the author resulting from his long managerial, research and teaching work in the area of management theory and practice.
(4) Extended interviews revealing the specific character of the functioning of companies in today's market economy.

According to J.R. Kimberly [1] (p. 329), longitudinal organizational research consists of those techniques, methodologies, and activities which permit the observation, description, and/or classification of organizational phenomena in such a way that processes can be identified and empirically documented. Longitudinal research essentially investigates processes across multiple time periods. Since the time duration between data collection efforts is defined by the researcher and by the unit under investigation, the length of a longitudinal study and number of data collection periods vary across designs. Longitudinal designs vary along six parameters: length of study; duration between data collection efforts; number of data collection periods; method of data collection; research objectives; and unit of analysis [2]. Janson (1981) suggests two broad classes of longitudinal research, (1) correlative longitudinal research (including studies of both normal representative populations and non-representative populations); and (2) experimental manipulative research [3]. Longitudinal research is associated with the implementation of repeatable measurements of the same individuals or population over a long time, meaning a period of time that enables the detection of changes. Longitudinal research is often called prospective research. In longitudinal research, the author studied the cause and effect relationships occurring in the conceptualization and operationalization of the observed business models. The cause and effect relationships were mainly related to the attributes (components) of business models of the surveyed companies. The author studied and identified events important to the development of the processes of change and the development of company business models and their attributes to understand and explain the processes of business model configuration changes. The reflections contained in the paper are based, among others, on the author's own observations of the actual business models in business practice. They can therefore be used as a benchmark for the management mechanisms used by managers in the design and operationalization of sustainable business models of companies.

Bibliographic research involved a multidimensional review of the literature. Conducting bibliographic research, the author followed the assumptions defined by Z. Jourdan, R. Kelly Rainer, and T.E. Marshall [4].

The structure of bibliographic review and the framework of theoretical development followed the assumptions of M. Massaro, J. Dumay, J. Guthrie and included the following steps:

(1) Writing a literature review protocol.
(2) Defining the questions that the literature review is setting out to answer.
(3) Determining the type of studies and carrying out a comprehensive literature search.
(4) Measuring article impact.
(5) Defining an analytical framework.
(6) Establishing literature review reliability.
(7) Testing literature review validity.
(8) Coding data using the developed framework.
(9) Developing insights and critique through analyzing the dataset.
(10) Developing future research paths and questions [5].

The above methodological assumptions were necessary to effectively present the scientific argument of the author.

The assumptions of the literature review included, *inter alia*, defining actual economic mechanisms occurring in the macroeconomic, sectoral and microeconomic dimensions.

Due to this fact, this issue addressed according to the adopted methodology is particularly important in terms of the following assumptions describing actual economic mechanisms occurring in the macroeconomic, sectoral and microeconomic dimensions. Furthermore, an important factor in the development of this issue is the fact that two parallel streams of building sustainable business models develop. One concerns the creation of entities developing according to the sustainability business trend and the other one concerns the trend of building social organizations including non-profit entities.

In this context, economic entities aiming to make a profit try to balance their goals, processes and actions to maintain dynamic, strategic balance with reasonable profit and the other entities are determined to offer social services that follow the sustainability business principles. From this perspective, the following macroeconomic, sector and microeconomic assumptions determine the current dimension of the business.

Macroeconomic assumptions [6]:

In the situation of the global economic crisis and increased public awareness of the quality of life, professed values have changed significantly

Social inequality in the world results in waves of discontent and conflict.

(1) Access to knowledge, information and goods is very easy. The only limitation is money.
(2) Free movement of goods and services enables the migration of people in search of a better quality of life. This results in the intercultural and ideological exchange of the population.
(3) The aging of European society and the stronger role of Asian countries are changing views on the functions of companies in the economy.
(4) The global ecosystem of the world has a significant impact on the economic sub-systems of individual continents, regions and countries.
(5) The current world is the world of communication via the Internet and a network society.
(6) Civilization changes are creating new needs and conditions of business
(7) The network environment is a key business environment.
(8) Virtualization determines the development of contemporary business.
(9) Market mechanisms are global and unpredictable.
(10) Access to information, knowledge and many resources is simple and universal.

Sector assumptions [7–10]:

(1) The place and role of sectors and sectoral conditions in the economy are dramatically changing.
(2) In many cases, sectors are blurred and fragmented; they overlap, merge or are eliminated.
(3) Socially unacceptable economic sectors are supplanted by high technology sectors, and industrial sectors are turned into service sectors.
(4) Regions compete with each other and their value is built for society. As a consequence, local decision-making systems create a need for the emergence of new economy sectors.
(5) Classic sector analyses do not fulfill their role, because the life cycles of sectors become shorter and also because of the dynamics and unpredictability of the expectations that society has.

Microeconomic assumptions [11–19]:

(1) Currently, a company is not perceived only as a financial instrument, but as a source of social capital as well.
(2) A company becomes a tool for redistribution of value for its stakeholders.
(3) Autocratic management methods based on bloodthirsty maximization of value for shareholders are not accepted in many cases, both in companies and in society.
(4) A company plays an educational, cultural and economic role for the whole society.
(5) A company becomes a factor in population migration towards prosperity and better quality of life.
(6) A company becomes a source of permanent innovation. Without innovative products, processes and management methods, companies are not able to survive in the market.
(7) Mechanisms based on the symbiosis of many conflicting interest groups and their synergies towards ensuring business continuity determine the new areas of decision-making systems.
(8) Due to the uncertainty of the company towards individuals, mechanisms based on a system approach to management are playing a stronger role. Only tight management systems can

protect companies against risks caused by the company stakeholders (including hostile ones), as well as those caused by the unpredictability, asymmetry and arrhythmia of the external market.
(9) A company is now seen as the sum of its contracts over time [20–23]
(10) A company is a tool for value migration through network structures.
(11) A company is a place of intellectual and social capital development.
(12) A company is increasingly perceived and built by virtual dimensions.
(13) A company is a platform for developing many dimensions of ideas and innovation.
(14) The company's business model is determined by the network.

These assumptions can provide a platform for multidimensional scientific discussion about the search for the best possible solution for building effective business models. In the author's opinion, this solution may include seeking the scalability of sustainable business models in hybrid organizations.

Based on the above reflections, a research gap related to the lack of the sufficient amount of research on the scalability of sustainable business models of hybrid organizations in a network environment is noted.

A scientific problem has been presented, which says: Business model scalability affects the sustainability of the business model of hybrid organizations. The research problem is significant as there is currently very little research on business model scalability, particularly in a network environment. Simultaneously, the dynamically developing concept of sustainable business models is used for hybrid organizations. The interconnection of these two important subjects seems to be scientifically important and cognitively interesting.

In order to solve the scientific problem, the following hypotheses have been formulated:

Hypothesis 1. Scalability and sustainability are key determinants of building a business model of hybrid organizations embedded in a network environment.

Hypothesis 2. The network environment is favorable to building sustainable business models that are highly scalable.

Hypothesis 3. In order for a business model of the hybrid organizations to be sustainable, first of all it must be scalable.

The author proves the hypotheses based on the described research.

3. Network Environment

Changes in the world economy lead to new paradigms of management that create a new dimension of competing, creating value and achieving results. Currently, one of the key management paradigms changing the image of management science is the network paradigm, within which the network is the key element around which management takes place. The network may have many interpretations, which make the effective application of this paradigm in business practice complicated. Therefore, it is important to thoroughly understand the mechanisms applicable to a network approach.

According to M. Gorynia, the sources and origin of a network approach are related to the following research prospects:

- marketing, and in particular the relationship between the participants in the distribution channels (Hakanson, 1982) [24].
- a resource dependence model in analyzing the relationships between organizations (Pfeffer, Salancik, 1978) [25].
- the social exchange theory (Cook, Emerson, 1984) [26].
- the theory of industrial organization (Porter, 1980) [27].
- the new trend in institutional economics with the transaction costs theory (Williamson, 1975) [28].

It is worth highlighting the evolution of interest in the network approach in management science. In recent years, in management, as in many other disciplines, the amount of research on social networks has dramatically increased. The amount of literature about networks has risen exponentially, as shown in Figure 1.

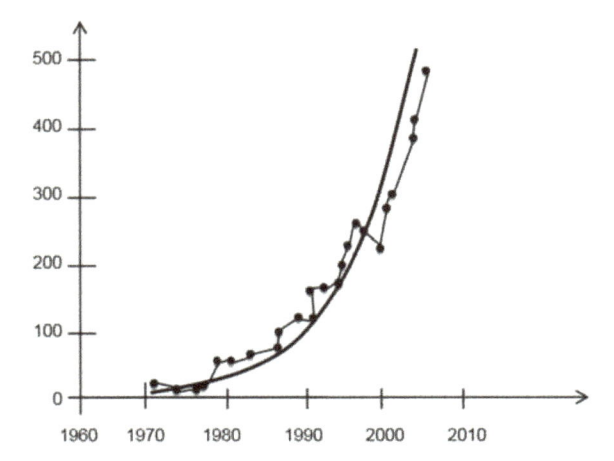

Figure 1. Exponential development of publications indexed by sociological abstracts containing the phrase "social network" in the abstract or title [29].

The rapid growth in research on networks in management results in a need for analysis and classification of what has been done in this area. It should be noted that since the 1990s, the network theory has been referred to in the literature in virtually all traditional areas of management such as: leadership, sales, satisfaction, work performance, entrepreneurship, relationships, knowledge, innovation, profit maximization, horizontal integration and many others [29]. H. Hakanson and I Snehota define a network as three interrelated categories: participants in the network, the resources that they have at their disposal and the actions taken [30]. C. Martin Rios defines inter-firm networks as voluntary agreements of independent companies that involve knowledge exchange and sharing [31]. J.C. Jarillo understands that a network is a grouping of organizations in which at least one controls the flow of tangible and intangible assets (including knowledge) between other organizations [32]. The principal value of the network is its ability to create tacit knowledge, a company-integrator and diffusion to cooperants at the first, second and nth level [33]. Network categorization by G.J. Hooley, J.A. Saunders, N. F. Piercy distinguishes the following network types: hollow networks, flexible networks, virtual networks and value-added networks [34].

R. Achrol divides networks into the internal networks markets, opportunity networks, marketing channel networks and intermarket networks [35].

On the basis of broad, multidimensional bibliographic research on networks and the network environment, the author has defined network attributes found in the relevant literature that can be used for the conceptualization and operationalization of a scalable business model operating in a networked environment (Table 1).

Table 1. Network attributes defined in the literature used for the conceptualization and operationalization of a scalable business model developed based on [7,26–32,36–60].

No.	Network Attributes	Definition
1.	Network size	The number of network members.
2.	Network diameter	The length of the longest of all the shortest paths connecting pairs of network elements.
3.	Network density	The ratio of links between network nodes to the maximum number of links between those nodes [36].
4.	Network concentration	The ratio of network nodes in the center of the network to those that are on the periphery.
5.	Number of networks	The number of network nodes.
6.	Heterogeneity	The extent of nodes heterogeneity.
7.	Network diversity	The number of various categories of entities participating in the network.
8.	Dynamics of network interaction	The number of initiatives in a year implemented by network members to the benefit of the network.
9.	Network members turnover	The number of transactions of network entries and exits.
10.	Network coordination costs	Total costs incurred by the network coordinator in a year to support the network.
11.	Potential for conflict in the network	The number of conflicts between network members related to activity in the network.
12.	Competition in the network	The number of network participants who are competitors.
13.	The average length of paths	The average number of connections of any two entities in the network.
14.	Connection measure	The proportion of the pairs of nodes interconnected by relationships with those that have no connections in the network.
15.	The proximity of centrality	Centrality can be regarded as generating expected values for certain kinds of node outcomes (such as speed and frequency of reception) of given implicit models of how traffic flows in the network, which provides a new and useful way of thinking about centrality Centrality as defined by the measure of proximity (the average distance of a unit from other nodes) or transitivity (the frequency of the occurrence on the shortest path of relationships between any two nodes in the network, assuming that information/phenomenon is transmitted on the shortest path).
16.	The proximity of centrality	The distance of a network member (a node) from the headquarters of the cluster coordinator (the main node).
17.	Coherence	Percentage share of units included in the so-called great component (interconnected with a direct or indirect relationship) in relation to all network nodes.
18.	Network complexity	The number of different entities that have to establish inter-organizational relationships so that a network organization could develop.
19.	Network potential	The number and type of entities that may be involved or participate in the network activities including resources (also competencies) that are at the disposal of these entities that may potentially be useful in performing network tasks and achieving the set objective.
20.	The formal structure of the network (the formalization of relationships)	The area of formalizing the relationship between the entities forming the network, network complexity and degree of its centralization.

Table 1. *Cont.*

No.	Network Attributes	Definition
21.	The intensity of the relationship	The number of interactions between network members at a given time.
22.	Trust in the network	The mechanism based on the assumption that the other community members are characterized by honest and cooperative behavior on the basis of shared standards, which is significant and measurable economic value.
23.	The micro-position of a network node	The micro-position reflects the potential of the node related to forming the relationships with other network nodes, compared to the nodes that cannot form such relationships or do it inefficiently [61].
24.	The macro-position of a network node	The macro-position reflects the role of a node across the network, dependent on its ability to shape the relationship between resources and activities of nodes within the network. This results partly from the activities taking place inside the node, and partly from what the node achieves from the activities of other network nodes [61].
25.	Bargaining power of a network node	The ability of a node to use and convert rare and valuable environmental resources [62].
26.	Network capability	Network capability is a set of processes and routine organizational behavior aimed at taking advantage of opportunities related to embedding the company in the inter-organizational network [63].

4. Business Models

The concept of business models is now one of the most explored subjects in the theory and practice of management. This is evidenced, for example, by the number of publications with the term "business model" in the EBSCO (Elton B. Stephens Company) database between 1975 and 2009, as shown in Figure 2.

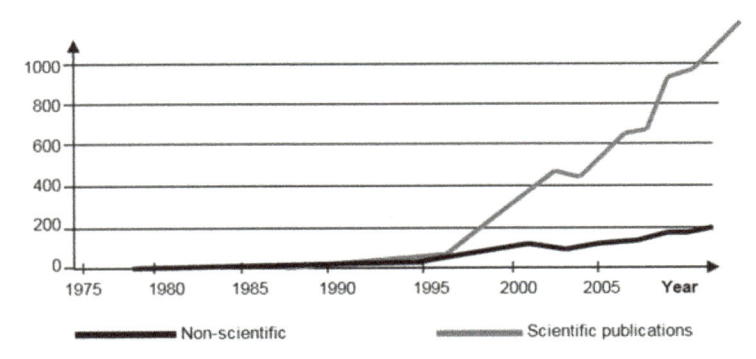

Figure 2. Number of publications with the term "business model" in the EBSCO database between 1975 and 2009 [64].

This also leads to a multitude of definitions of business models and various multidimensional approaches.

B.W. Wirtz presents the stages of the development of approaches to business models over the years 1950–2010+ (Figure 3).

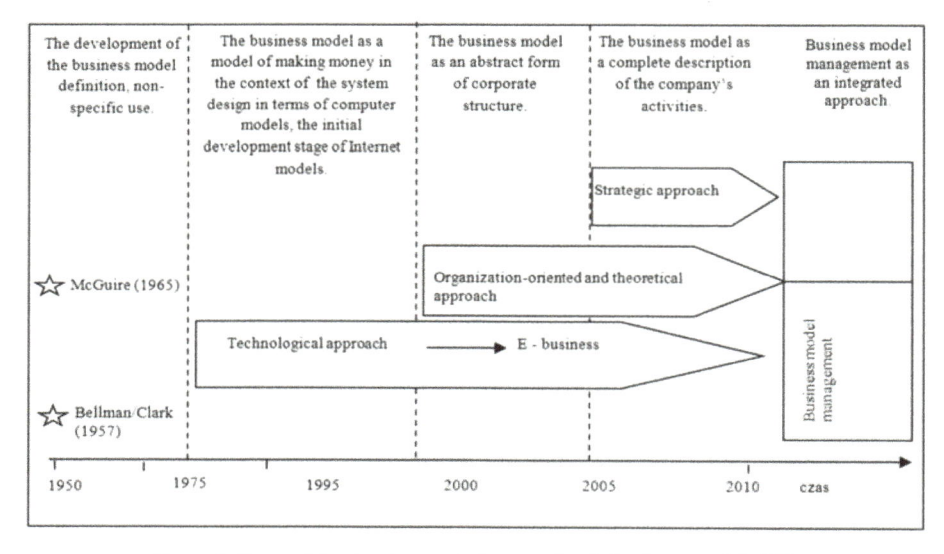

Figure 3. Stages of the development of approaches to business models [65].

The above figure shows that, currently, an integrated approach to business model management prevails. This gives rise to the need to review the business model from multiple perspectives.

In order to effectively express the concept of the business model, the author quotes the definition by D. Teece, who says that "a business model determines the way in which a company creates and delivers value to customers, and then converts the payments received into profits" [66]. In addition, based on extensive bibliographic research, a synthetic review of the literature on the concept of business models from different perspectives has been presented below.

The business model approach understood as a type of a market player in the value chain is highlighted, for example, by K. Obłój [67] (operator, integrator, conductor), T. Gołębiowski, T. M. Dudzik, M. Lewandowska and M. Witek-Hajduk [68] (traditionalist, market player, contractor-specialist, distributor, integrator). The approach to the e-business model from the perspective of the player market is presented, for example, by P. Timmers (e-shop, e-procurement, e-mall, e-auction, value chain service providers, virtual business community, cooperation platform) [69], Rappa [70] (advertising, brokerage, community, infomediary, manufacturer, merchant, subscription, utility) and Applegate [71] (focused distributor models-retailer, marketplace, aggregator, infomediary, exchange, portal models–horizontal portals, vertical portals, affinity portals, producer models-manufacturer, service provider, educator, advisor, information and news services, custom supplier and infrastructure provider models with a number of sub-models, e.g., infrastructure portals.

A business model understood through the prism of the company's profitability has been presented by, among others, by A. Slywotzky. Together with his team he described 22 profitable business models based on the experiences of American companies [72].

The link between the business model and strategy and business processes is highlighted by A. Osterwalder, Y. Pigneur [73] and L. Bossidy, R. Charan [74] and J. Niemczyk [75]. In terms of value creation, the definition of the business model is presented by, among others, P.B. Seddon, G.P. Lewis, P. Freeman, G. Shanks [76], B. de Witt, R. Meyer [77]. The following authors focus on studying the business model from the perspective of stakeholders: F. Hoque [78] and S. Voelpel, M. Leibold, E. Tekie, G. von Krogh (2005) [22] and A. Jabłoński [79]. The definitions of networked business models are presented, *inter alia*, by K. Perechuda [33] A. Jabłoński, M. Jabłoński [80]. The link between the business model and resource-based view is highlighted by K. Krzakiewicz and S. Cyfert [81]. The business model ensuring the stability and continuity of the company is presented, among others, by B. Demil, X.

Lecocq [82], K.D. Sandberg [83], A. Afuah, C. Tucci [84]. B. Nogalski [85] defines a business model from the development perspective. A hybrid business model is presented by S.J. Deodhar, K. Saxena, R.K. Gupta, M. Ruohonen [86], and A. Jabłoński [87]. The definition of a sustainable business model is presented, among others, by W. Stubbs and C. Cocklin [88] and F. Boons, F. Lüdeke-Freund [89] and A. Jabłoński [90], while A. Neely, R. Delbridge [91] focus on a geometric business model.

The above approaches describe the particular complexity of the concept of business models in management science. The bibliographic research indicates a multidimensional look at the business model and creates further implications for research.

5. Sustainable Business Models

If we assume that the company's business model is based on the principles of balancing the business from a number of perspectives, it will become a sustainable business model. This definition is also consistent with the assumptions relevant to a sustainable company. The sustainable business model can be better understood by understanding:

- the role of different sustainability drivers,
- causal relationships in relation to the various actions to be taken,
- the impact of these actions on sustainable results,
- the potential and actual impact on the financial results [92].

T. Dyllick and K. Hockerts present a model based on the concept of corporate sustainability (balancing and integrating the activities of the company) mapped in the form of a triangle. In three corners of the triangle there are: focus on business case, natural case and societal case [93]. W. McDonough and M. Braungart present the model of corporate sustainability in the form of a fractal triangle, whose corners include: ecology–ecology, equity–equity and economy–economy [94].

An interesting sustainable business model based on the original concept of SMART (sustainability modeling and reporting system) has been developed by M. Daud Ahmed and D. Sundaram [95]. In this model they define the sustainable business transformation roadmap, where its key elements include:

- design,
- transformation,
- monitoring and control,
- discovery and learning,
- strategy.

M. Yunus, B. Moingeon, L. Lehmann-Ortega [96] define the concept of a social business model, which can be a sustainable business model. They have developed five principles of building a social business model consisting of two areas:

(1) Framework common also for innovative models.
(2) Areas specific to social models.

The similarities with conventional and innovative business models include:

(1) The challenges of conventional wisdom and fundamental assumptions.
(2) The discovery of complementary business partners.
(3) Undertakings in improving process experiments.

Specific objectives for social business models include:

(1) Creating favorable conditions for social orientation in terms of profit by the shareholders.
(2) Clear, specific objectives for profit for society.

The social business model is adopted by the social company. P. Kotler, H. Kartajaya and I. Setiawan define three measures of the success of a social company that will indicate whether the company will be able to strengthen the economic foundations of society. Using these measures, it is easy to say which company is a social company and which is not. First of all, such a company attains disposable income. Secondly, it extends this income. Thirdly, it increases it [97] (p. 136). B. Nogalski notes that in order to implement a new model (and, therefore, change), harmony between organizational structures, support systems, processes, workforce skills, resources and the incentive system, and the time horizon is necessary. All these elements and supporting processes (including corporate culture that should also be adapted to the business model) should support the implementation of changes in the model and the strategy in a consistent manner [98] (p. 123). Harmony and match are the factors conducive to the application of the principles of sustainability.

An interesting approach to the business model based on sustainability has been introduced by A. Osterwalder and Y. Pigneur [99] (p. 62), who have presented the concept of innovative business models of responsible companies in the form of a coordinate system. They determine the relationship between corporations and non-profit organizations, believing that corporations in their business models should move towards the development of social potential and its impact on business (currently the undervalued area in corporation management). In contrast, non-profit organizations should develop their business models towards seeking greater profit potential (currently the undervalued area in non-profit organizations management).

F. Boons and F. Lüdeke-Freund present sustainable business models that enable social entrepreneurs to create social value and maximize social profit; of significance is the business models' ability to act as market device that helps in creating and further developing markets for innovations with a social purpose [89] (p. 20). S. Schaltegger, F. Lüdeke-Freund, and E. Hansen present that based on the understanding of a business case for sustainability, a business model for sustainability can be defined as supporting voluntary or mainly voluntary activities which solve or moderate social and/or environmental problems. By doing so, it creates positive business effects which can be measured or at least argued for. A business model for sustainability is actively managed in order to create customer and social value by integrating social, environmental, and business activities [100].

Looking at the business model from the point of view of fulfilling the needs and requirements of stakeholders as a source of competitive advantage in the market, a key factor in building an effective strategy might be:

(1) Treating the organization as a system which determines the adoption of an appropriate management philosophy, an optimal organizational structure, and an appropriate shape of intra-process relationships.
(2) Building the appropriate structure of dynamic marketing focused on the business partnership with stakeholder groups in a balance of forces between stakeholders' impact on the company and *vice versa*.
(3) Focus on internal and external communication for the collectivization of joint activities in an in-out-in system, inside the organization–outside the organization–inside the organization.
(4) The resource-based approach, taking into account all members of the organization to achieve key objectives of the company.

The adoption of such a shape of the model of the defined strategy line can make it possible to answer the following questions strategically for the company:

(1) Who is responsible for the interpretation and the formation of objectives?
(2) Which stakeholders do we have a relationship with?
(3) How do services and innovative processes proceed?
(4) What are the incentives and the structure of the incentive system to stakeholders?
(5) What rights and responsibilities do we have towards the company?

(6) What are the decision-making processes between the company and supervisory authorities?
(7) How recognizable is the company brand?
(8) How have company resources been defined qualitatively and quantitatively in the processes [101] (pp. 35–36)?

These questions also shift the focus of the business model on both internal and external factors, where trust is an important factor.

In this case, trust can be based on values, motivation and structures, which indicates how highly the values, motivation and structures that help to achieve the strategic objectives of the organization are valued. Furthermore, in this context, the following are important: clarity, fairness and stability of the procedures used [102] (p. 109). Building the model using the concept of Sustainable Enterprises requires the company to integrate the key strategic factors constituting the business model towards sustainability in the economic, environmental and social area:

- economic sustainability—it requires an increase in the profitability of the company through the efficient use of resources (human, raw materials, finance), effective projects and undertakings, good management, planning and control,
- ecological sustainability—it is essential that harmful and irreversible consequences for the environment are prevented through the efficient use of natural resources, promoting renewable resources, soil and water protection, and skillful waste management,
- social sustainability—requires the response to the needs of society including all other stakeholders [103] (p. 277).

In summary, the sustainable business model building the long-term value of a socially responsible company is a model built by the combined use of the corporate social responsibility and value-based management concepts which guarantees that the needs of shareholders and other stakeholder groups are fulfilled, by balancing the company potential skillfully to generate value allocated in a sustainable way, allowing the continuity of company management. The sustainable business model is a hybrid model, *i.e.*, a model built in a subject- object system. Components of this model are entities gathered around business-forming relationships, influencing the company value drivers and strategic factors related to the theory of corporate social responsibility, company value–based management, the stakeholder theory, and the shareholder theory, which are in a mutual relationship based on the principles of sustainability. This model is a holistic model of reduced nature, which could be applied in various sectors of the economy that are treated as a subsystem of the whole ecosystem. This means that the model and its construction are included in mid-range theory [90] (pp. 400–403).

6. Hybrid Organizations

The functioning of contemporary companies often requires them to use a dual perspective in defining their strategic goals. They should be cost-effective and, at the same time, open to social purposes. Then they can take advantage of the potential inherent in the network of company stakeholders.

A company where the ability to generate value for shareholders and the widely understood business community is ensured is called a hybrid company.

This approach determines the rules for providing the context for scientific discussion. This context providing a framework for discussion relates to presenting the picture of reality determining the conduct of business today. A company which currently performs many economic and social functions is searching for a new strategic reference.

This strategic reference becomes more complex and complicated. The market of customers that are often prosumers co-developing an offer with the company creates changes in cooperation and co-development. It all has a hybrid dimension. The hybrid dimension refers to the place and role of the company and its functions and combining objectives and activities as well as the cooperation between the ontological beings of the company such as strategy, a business model and business processes.

In general terms, a hybrid is a combination of different elements in a coherent whole. Creating hybrids involves combining two or more different approaches (methodologies) to form a new single approach (methodology).

A heterosis effect (called hybridization in the case of deliberate procedures) is a hybrid showing longer life and increased fertility. The individual elements in a hybrid can work together, and they can also compete with each other. The motivation for creating hybrid systems can be a conviction that there is a positive synergistic effect of their use. Hybridity may consist of the pragmatic and coordinated (parallel, serial, hierarchical and virtual) cooperation of many factors with each other, consequently, however, forming a coherent whole which is the combination of elements derived from other systems. As regards inorganic systems, in a hybrid-artifact (a computer program, method) showing increased usability, the quality of solutions, *etc.*, will be evaluated positively. A. Ultsch uses the term "hybrid" in the context of hermaphrodite forms created through a merger or crossing [104]. The hybrid model in physics is the model that couples two or more devices that are used for shaping physical processes in various ways, for example analog-digital devices are used here. The hybrid system is a drive system where two different energy sources or generally different power sources co-work. A hybrid scheme in electronics is used to describe the parameters of electronic circuits. A hybrid drive is a combination of two types of drives to move a single device. A hybrid vehicle is a vehicle that has at least (usually) an engine with two drives. Three basic types of hybrid can be distinguished in terms of action: parallel, serial and mixed action.

A hybrid approach in business can combine numerous divisions according to selected criteria for classification, in particular the following [105] (p. 4):

(1) By the extremes: for profit–non-profit [106,107].
(2) By the social sector of: the market–civil society–state [108–110].
(3) By the type of integration: external–integrated–built-in [111,112].
(4) By the goods produced: private–public [113–115].
(5) By the product status: goods–services [116].
(6) By the agents of value creation: manufacturers–consumers [117–119].
(7) By ownership (corporate governance): private–cooperative–public [105,107,110].

Hybrids offer alternative solutions, probably the optimal ones, when significant limitations in obtaining contractors occur [120] (p. 19).

Hybrid organizations can exist on either side of the for profit/non-profit divide, blurring this boundary by adopting social and environmental missions like nonprofits, but generating income to accomplish their mission like for-profits. Hybrids are built on the assertion that neither traditional for-profit or non-profit models adequately address the social and environmental problems we currently face. Entrepreneurs of hybrids seek to build viable organizations and markets to address specific social and environmental issues.(...) Hybrid organizations are underpinned by a new and growing demographic of individuals who place a higher value on healthy living, environmental and social justice, and ecological sustainability in the products and services they purchase, the companies in which they invest, the politicians and policies they support, the companies for which they work and, ultimately, the lifestyles they lead. This demographic is recognized with labels such as Cultural Creatives and Lifestyles of Health and Sustainability (LOHAS) [121] (p. 126).

One of the key approaches to hybrids in terms of the common implementation of social and economic goals has been proposed by F.M. Santos. He defines four important proposals related to social entrepreneurship:

Proposition 1. The distinctive domain of action of social entrepreneurship is addressing neglected problems in society involving positive externalities.
Proposition 2. Social entrepreneurs are more likely to operate in areas with localized positive externalities that benefit a powerless segment of the population.

Proposition 3. Social entrepreneurs are more likely to seek sustainable solutions than to seek sustainable advantages.

Proposition 4. Social entrepreneurs are more likely to develop a solution built on the logic of empowerment than on the logic of control [122].

A strategic hybrid, according to A. Jabłoński, is understood in strategic terms as a blend of the business model, strategy and business processes used to achieve an acceptable level of company performance in the short and long term. Due to its eclectic character, the strategic hybrid may lead to achieving the set results more quickly. The relationships between the strategy, business model and business processes may also determine the simultaneous development of a company in terms of products, market and resources. Strategic hybrid consistency is the mutual and interdependent compliance of all components of the business model, strategy and business processes with the specific criteria that ensure the company's ability to achieve high performance in the long and short term. The result of hybridization is the so-called synergistic effect (a hybrid demonstrates the features that are difficult to see in the original compositions). The hybrid creates new value based on the non-standard configuration consisting of predefined components while maintaining its proper full integrity. The adoption of such a solution is a decision made by prudent managers [87] (p. 46). A.-C. Pache and F. Santos suggest, based on their own research, that hybrid organizations combine the competing logics in which they are embedded through selective coupling [123]. In contrast to decoupling, which entails the ceremonial espousal of a prescribed practice with no actual enactment, selective coupling refers to the purposeful enactment of selected practices among a pool of competing alternatives. Selective coupling allows hybrids to satisfy symbolic concerns, just as decoupling does [123]. By plotting two dimensions in a matrix, A.C. Pache, F.M. Santos and C. Birkholz derive a typology of four social business hybrid models that we call Market Hybrids, Blending Hybrids, Bridging Hybrids, and Coupling Hybrids (Table 2) [124].

Table 2. A typology of social business hybrids [124] (p. 45).

Dimensions	Clients = Beneficiaries	Clients ≠ Beneficiaries
Automatic Value Spillovers	MARKET HYBRID Examples: BOP initiatives for access to basic services (energy, health) **Risk of Mission Drift:** Low Financial Sustainability: Easy	BRIDGING HYBRID Examples: integrated business model with job-matching for people with disabilities **Risk of Mission Drift:** Intermediate (lower risk for more integrated models) **Financial Sustainability:** Moderately Difficult
Contingent Value Spillovers	BLENDING HYBRID Examples: Microfinance, integration models that require regular support or change of behavior for value to be created **Risk of Mission Drift:** Intermediate **Financial Sustainability:** Moderately Difficult	COUPLING HYBRID **Example:** Work integration social enterprises that require a dual value chain that serves both clients and beneficiaries **Risk of Mission Drift:** High **Financial Sustainability:** Difficult

Vivek K. Velamuri, Anne-Katrin Neyer and Kathrin M. Möslein believe that a "Hybrid" in the creation of hybrid value is the presence of two distinct types of components in the offer: (1) the existence of the product (tangible component) and (2) the existence of the non-material service (intangible component). They define the creation of hybrid value as a process of generating additional value through the innovative integration of the product (tangible component) and service (intangible component). Similarly, each business model that satisfies the above criteria (the creation of value and hybridity) will be included in the process of hybrid value creation [125]. Such an approach to a hybrid creates a new dimension to the implementation of key strategic objectives of the company. Being receptive to many economic and social aspects and their interconnections generates new dynamics of the company. This is the basis for building business models that are evolutionary in their nature and based on the stability generating the continuity of business.

7. Scalability

Scalability aims to provide more work and more efficient work with an increasing number of components. It is, among other things, a feature of computer networks consisting of the ability to expand continuously. Scalability is sometimes defined as "the ease with which a system or component can be modified depending on the type of problem". A scalable system has three basic features:

- The system can adapt to its increased use.
- The system can accommodate larger amounts of data.
- The system is easy to maintain technically and works with reasonable efficiency.

Scalability is not only speed. Effectiveness and scalability of the system vary and correlate with each other. Effectiveness measures how quickly and efficiently the system can perform certain calculations, while scalability measures the trend of effectiveness with an increased load [126].

Daniel A. Menascé and Virgilio A.F. Almeida think that the system is scalable if there is a "simple" way to update the system to enable support for increased trade while maintaining proper efficiency. Simple means that no change in the system architecture or software should be required to scale the system [127]. The Universal Scalability Law (USL) in computing is a model used for forecasting the scalability of hardware and software. It uses the system performance as a function of load to forecast system scalability. The USL function is used to create a model from the formula and data frame. The USL model produces two coefficients as result: sigma models the contention and kappa the coherency delay of the system. The Universal Scalability Law was formulated by Neil J. Gunther [128,129].

Scalability is an essential element for studies in strategic management, yet is unrecognized fully and sufficiently. The concept of scalability can thus be adapted now to the important debate on the mechanisms of strategic management.

Business model scalability is the capacity of the business model to maintain similar or better effectiveness while continuously increasing or reducing the number of its components and while constantly adjusting the boundaries of its impact (e.g., in a network environment).

Scaling in the business model thus refers to, *inter alia*, adding or removing a component and/or components of the business model in order to improve its effectiveness. Scalability is a key parameter that determines the company's ability to grow, and it is based on the contention that not every unit of revenue is generated by an equal cost unit. Assessing the capability of business models to increase the company's value, investors first of all appreciate models that allow companies to have higher revenues and create higher and higher profitability. However, a common feature of e-business models especially is that they have high market value at low or even no profits in the long term. Market value is high because of attributes, which are characteristic of business models such as an innovative solution in the area of social networks, a unique technical solution forming interesting value added, *etc.* Therefore, their scalability is important then.

In the literature, for example, Amit and Zott [130], Rappa [131], and Bouwman and MacInnes [132] define scalability as a key factor of innovative business models contributing to the achievement of results by the company. Scalability, therefore, is an important feature of the business model as it is included in its configuration, whereas strategy sets a business model in motion and gives its resources the right direction, in line with the expectations of business model decision-makers, and scalable business processes are used to implement operational objectives and will be more effective when a business model is highly scalable as well.

According to Christian Nielsen and Morten Lund, scalable business models have the following characteristics:

- The business potential is characterized by exponentially increasing returns to scale
- They remove themselves from otherwise typical capacity constraints of that type of business
- Partners enrich the value proposition without hurting profits
- Stakeholders take multiple roles and create value for one another
- The business model becomes a platform that attracts new partners, including competitors [133] (pp. 16–17).

Based on the literature review and interviews with entrepreneurs and investors, Georg Stampfl, Reinhard Prügl and Vincent Osterloh identify the key factors in scaling the business model and some consequences of scalability. Their discussions are illustrated by examples of well-known Internet companies. Their findings show that the factors that affect the scalability of the business model include technology, cost and earnings structure, institutional capacity for adaptation (*i.e.*, the ability to adapt to different legal standards), and network effects and user orientation [134] (pp. 219–220).

According to R. Green, a scalable business model is a simple concept. The model is scalable when increased revenues cost less to deliver than current revenues. In other words, the operating margin increases with increasing revenues [135].

The following are 10 tips to build the most scalable company:

(1) If investors are needed, start with a scalable idea.
(2) Create a business plan and model that is attractive to investors.
(3) Use a product with a minimum necessary functionality (MVP) to authenticate a model.
(4) Build a strong team to get out of the critical path.
(5) Subcontract what is not strategic to optimize financial leverage.
(6) Focus on indirect and marketing channels to quickly convey a message.
(7) Make the most of automation.
(8) Attract and use investment funds.
(9) Take into account the possibility of buying licenses and franchising.
(10) Define a business that is flexible and constantly improving [136].

E-commerce system scalability is one of the key factors in e-business. This is so because the trade on e-commerce websites is periodic: there are high seasons, there are variations between days, and campaigns and events can attract the attention of an unexpectedly large number of customers. The most important part of scalability management is that the company is trying to avoid such technological systems that have a predetermined maximum performance (new performance requires an entirely different platform/technology/system structure). In this context, performance can be seen as:

- the number of the same users/connections that the system can handle without errors/problems;
- the number of transactions possible at the same time;
- the maximum data transfer (download, *etc.*).

Speaking of accessibility, we mean the time of the system operation from the point of view of the customer. It is a concept closely related to scalability and contracts at the service level because it is a measure of how good the access is that customers have to services in real time, *i.e.*, starting a call, receiving a response and returning to the transaction when it is possible. Technical measures to ensure availability range from session control to transaction maintenance to databases supporting the required operations [137] (p. 59).

Business model scalability can be applied to startup organizations.

According to S. Blank and B. Dorf, a startup is a temporary organization dedicated to looking for a scalable, repeatable and profitable business model [138] (p. 19). Such a definition clearly indicates startup characteristics such as:

(1) Temporality.
(2) Lack of durability.
(3) Volatility.
(4) Risk and uncertainty.

The proposed definition explicitly refers to the concept of a business model as a factor determining the success or failure of the company. In startup organizations it is not a strategy that will determine its success but a well-designed business model, based on credible premises. S. Blank highlights a new approach to the design of startup organizations, believing that the startup founders should not begin by developing a business plan, but searching for a business model [139] (p. 7).

Factors stimulating changes in the business model component arise from the implementation of open innovation, which in many cases requires business model configuration changes for their effective implementation. In this case, the level of business model scalability will also depend on the level of company innovation in the context of open innovation (arising from relationships with other entities). Business model scalability of the company embedded in the network can be conducted according to the following criteria:

(1) In terms of size—the ability to add/remove components of the business model.
(2) Geographical—the possibility of spreading (acquisition and transfer through a network) business model components in different locations of the network.
(3) Administrative—the possibility of different hierarchies of business model configuration coordination from the perspective of the company (company co-ordination) and/or a network perspective (network coordination).

Business model scalability refers, *inter alia*, to:

- adjusting the size of the company to the expectations of the market,
- adjusting the volume of engaged resources to building an efficient, networked business model,
- adjusting the structure of costs and revenues,
- adjusting the selected technologies resulting from the above elements.

Oversizing or undersizing one of the above elements may have a negative influence on achieving assumed performance by the company.

Scalability may be of vertical and/or horizontal nature.

Vertical scalability is scaling in which the components of the business model within a company are added or removed.

Horizontal scalability involves scaling which is adding or removing companies embedded in the network which creates its own network business model.

By way of analogy to information systems, business model scalability can be divided into:

- Linear—with an increase in the number of business model components, the company increases its performance linearly, so the effectiveness of scaling is 100%. It also means there is infinite scalability of the business model (Figure 4).

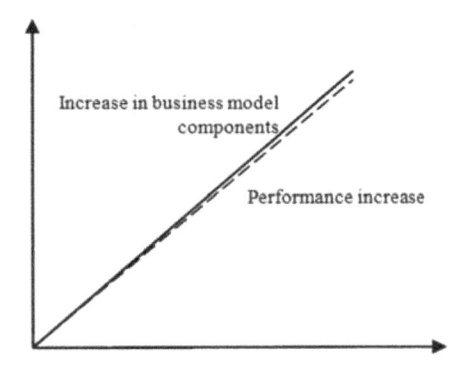

Figure 4. Linear scalability.

- Sub-linear—this means that with the expansion of the business model by other components, company performance increases more and more slowly until it reaches a certain limit. This means there is a finite business model scalability (Figure 5).

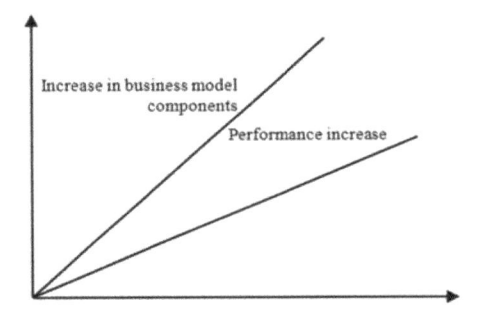

Figure 5. Sub-linear scalability.

- Negative—this means that with the expansion of the business model by other components, company performance declines. This effect can be observed for companies not adapted to scaling (Figure 6).

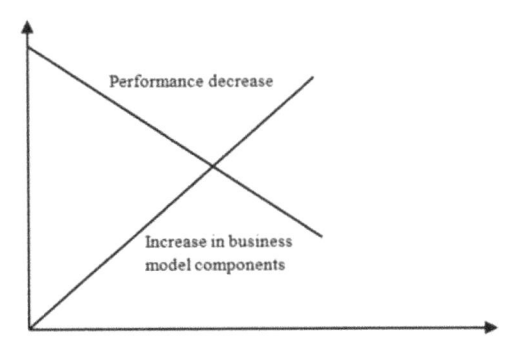

Figure 6. Negative scalability.

- Super-linear—this is a special case when company performance is growing faster than linearly with an increasing number of business model components (Figure 7).

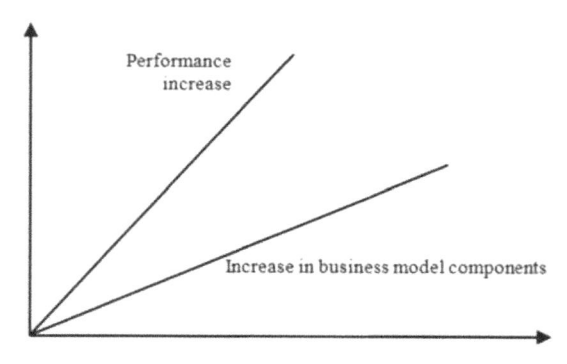

Figure 7. Super-linear scalability.

Examining the concept of business model scalability, it is essential to define the attributes that determine the design and operationalization towards its scalability.

Key features of the business model affecting its scalability, which ensure its ability to achieve high company performance and are defined based on the literature, are presented in Table 3.

Table 3. Key features of the business model affecting its scalability.

No.	Business Model Features
1.	Dynamics
2.	Adaptability
3.	Repeatability
4.	Coherence
5.	Economization
6.	Profitability
7.	Innovation and e-innovation
8.	The ability to migrate
9.	Availability
10.	The scale of impact

The measurement system used to measure business model scalability is implemented so that the business model will be vulnerable to changes with respect to the environment; thus, it constantly responds to market needs. Then measurement indicators serve to better understand the business model and market needs relationship. The network is conducive to scalability as, through the relationships in the network, it is easier to change the business and such changes may occur faster due to obtaining information faster by participating in the network. Such performance measures that will relate more to the business model rather than to the whole company should be sought within the business model, so it is necessary to answer the question of whether the rules that govern the business are correct. The appropriateness of the adopted business model should be constantly evaluated. Therefore, good measures used to describe the business model are measures used in classic "business plans" and even strategies and they are validated by clashing them with direct customers of the company. Therefore, the concept of lean startup emerged, which is the concept appropriate for companies starting their activity. It results from the assumption that it is difficult to measure a company's achievements at the beginning of the business if they have none yet. Instead, startup development in the early stages should be measured (if possible) by means of appropriate qualitative and quantitative measures. Qualitative measures will describe a business model in terms of its attributes (e.g., business model innovation), while quantitative measures include, in the case of e-business models using Internet communities, for example, the number of users that can increase or decrease and the measure may be, for example, the dynamics of growth or decline.

In view of the above reflections, it can be assumed that the issue of designing scalable business models is now a key challenge for both theoreticians and practitioners of management. The design process, or design in short, is a substantial and creative activity of man that is a conceptual and pragmatic preparation (related to methodology) for executive functions. This general expression contains the creative feature of the design, and therefore it gives it more or less originality. The sense of preparation is obvious, because the design is the structure to be verified, and then implemented [140] (p. 168).

The art of designing a model of the customer-oriented company activity begins with the single most important element—getting to know the customer and going on to develop the correct design. Managers actually focusing their attention on the customer always make other decisions related to the scope of activity. Their first question is not what the core competencies of the company are, but what their importance to the customer is. They will make the company offer products based on what a customer needs, wants and what he or she is willing to pay [72] (p. 50).

The process of designing the business model in a synthetic way can be divided into thefollowing steps:

(1) Outlining the concept of the designed business model (business idea, potential recipients of values, characteristics of produced value and method of delivering this value to customers, *etc.*).
(2) Developing strategic objectives of the business model configuration.
(3) Developing the necessary financial analyses to implement the business model in market conditions.
(4) Linking the financial aspects of the business model feasibility with the aspects related to the assumptions of its design.
(5) Identifying weaknesses of the business model when it is treated as a system and in the case of visible gaps, complementing the design of the business model.
(6) Identifying innovative features of the business model and their critical analysis.
(7) Assembling the business model in a system of features that allow for building capacity to compete.
(8) Designing the assumptions of the company management system based on business model attributes [141] (pp. 29–30).

It should be remembered that in order to design a business model effectively, the trick is not only to adopt the proper way of thinking and its attributes, but also to use them skillfully.

8. The Conceptualization of Business Model Scalability

The criteria of business model scalability can include:

- The ability to customize the technology to the customer's expectations and requirements of the product,
- The flexibility of infrastructure resources, expressed by the ability to adopt to their current needs (increase or reduction of resources),
- The ability to reduce or increase costs adequately for the needs and resources used,
- The dynamics of processes are constantly adapted to respond to impulses from the environment,
- Continuous adaptability to changing legal requirements,
- The ability to use the network effect—the occurrence of the phenomenon consisting of the fact that the more nodes a network has, the more benefits membership brings to individual nodes. Each additional node in the network increases its value, encouraging more potential nodes to join in,

- The acceptable level of adjusting the number of customers served to the capacity of the company,
- Continuous ability to improve the company's business model,
- The ability to simplify the business model (if possible),
- The ability to continuously educate company customers,
- The ability to permanently deliver new value to the customer,
- The ability to transfer and internationalize the company business model,
- The ability of the business model to adjust to the differences arising from international, cross-cultural, and legal exchange,
- The ability to create innovation through the business model,
- The ability to flexibly modify the business model depending on the internal and external conditions,
- No restrictions in the location of the company,
- The ability of the company to form partnerships with the network members.

In the logical interpretation of the application of business model scalability, the mechanisms of analogy can be used, referring to Moore's law and Wright's law, which are widely used not only in computer science [142].

In this sense, key assumptions of business model scalability can be developed using the principles of Moore's law and Wright's law.

(1) We treat the company embedded in the network as an organization capable of achieving high performance through the network.
(2) We define core resources, processes and stakeholders of the company embedded in the network that are necessary to build a scalable business model.
(3) We determine the technological and organizational boundaries of the business model of the company embedded in the network.
(4) We convert the business model of the company embedded in the network into a discrete model.
(5) Using Moore's law and Wright's law, we analyze how to expand the business model in the best possible way in terms of components and apply the principle of how much we can reduce the cost of its operation.
(6) We conduct a simulation of business model development assuming the boundary conditions for the developed measuring system, being a tool of assessing the business model of the company embedded in the network.
(7) Then we change the parameters of the business model and the structure of its components until we adjust the founded discrete model to the actual situation in business.
(8) We validate the designed scalable business model by implementing it into practice.
(9) When conducting a further analysis of the business model scalability concept, it can be assumed that the business model that is subject to scalability consists of two groups of components:

    a. Primary components.
    b. Secondary components.

Primary components constitute the core of the business model, being the basis for its building at the stage of its design.

Secondary components are added to the business model in order to improve company performance. They are an extension of primary components. Ensuring business model scalability is of special importance in adding and removing them. The increasing complexity of the business model in terms of a scalability criterion consists of incremental change in the business model components as a function of time. Figure 8 shows the concept of incremental changes in the business model components of the network company by the scalability criterion.

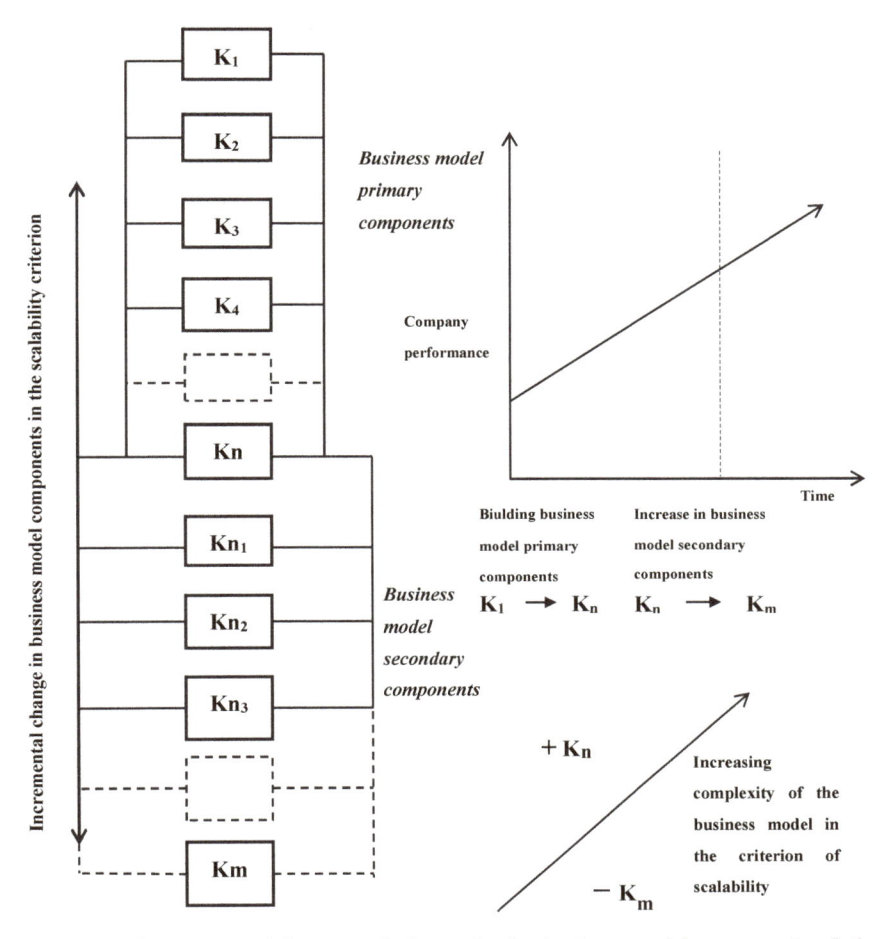

Figure 8. The concept of incremental change in the business model components of the network/company by the scalability criterion.

In order to determine business model scalability, its proper configuration has to be defined. This configuration can be determined using the QCA method. A Qualitative Comparative Analysis (QCA) was first proposed by Charles Ragin in 1987 as a method of analyzing data sets, which include binary variables [143]. By adopting this method, a list of all possible configurations of n components of the business model can be defined which affect its scalability in the context of the impact that this configuration has on the performance of the company embedded in the network.

It is worth noting that the QCA integrates qualitative and quantitative research methods [144].

Table 4 presents the matrix of possible configurations for a business model built with four components, along with defining the key configurations for this relationship.

Table 4. The model matrix of possible configurations for a business model built with four components, along with defining the key configurations for this relationship.

Configuration	Component 1	Component 2	Component 3	Component 4	High Performance
1	0	0	0	0	
2	0	0	0	1	
3	0	0	1	0	
4	0	0	1	1	
5	0	1	0	0	
6	0	1	0	1	
7	0	1	1	0	
8	0	1	1	1	1
9	1	0	0	0	
10	1	0	0	1	
11	1	0	1	0	
12	1	0	1	1	
13	1	1	0	0	
14	1	1	0	1	1
15	1	1	1	0	
16	1	1	1	1	

For example, high company performance is achieved with configurations 8 and 14 of the business model. In the case of configuration number 8: High Performance = 1 if K1 = 0 and K2 = 1 and K3 = 1 and K4 = 1

In the case of configuration number 14: High Performance = 1 if K1 = 1 and K2 = 1 and K3 = 0 and K4 = 1

High performance is, therefore, a variable dependent on the configuration of independent variables (business model component 1, component 2, component 3 and component 4) observed in such a way that all 16 possible configurations could be evaluated. The configuration assessment process can be repeated for the primary components of the business model. Then components can be added or removed and it is possible to evaluate with what configurations the company can achieve high performance. It is very important as scalability, by adding and removing components, focuses on quantitative assessment. The premise of business model scalability is a dynamic change in the number of its components, which is quantitative in nature. Additionally, achieving the configuration of components favorable to high performance is qualitative. In this context, it is reasonable to use the QCA method.

9. The Operationalization of Scalability in Sustainable Business Models of Hybrid Organizations

In order to perform the operationalization of sustainable business model scalability, the first step is to define a sustainable business model canvas composed of the so-called primary components. Primary components are also called indispensable components, without which a business model cannot exist.

In the scientific discourse on the operationalization of scalability in the sustainable business models of hybrid organizations, a nine-component business model canvas by A. Osterwalder and Y. Pigneur [73,145,146] was applied (Figure 9). The structure of this model is focused on the operationalization attributes of the business model helping the company to achieve high performance.

Based on the verification of network attributes defined in the literature and described in Section 3, key network attributes have been identified which, selected by multivariate bibliographic analysis, shape its business model, determining the network development in a given function of time. The use of multivariate analysis aimed to reduce a large amount of collected data and information to several important categories, which could be used as a subject of further analysis and to obtain groups of objects homogeneous in terms of properties describing them, which then makes it easier to determine their key properties.

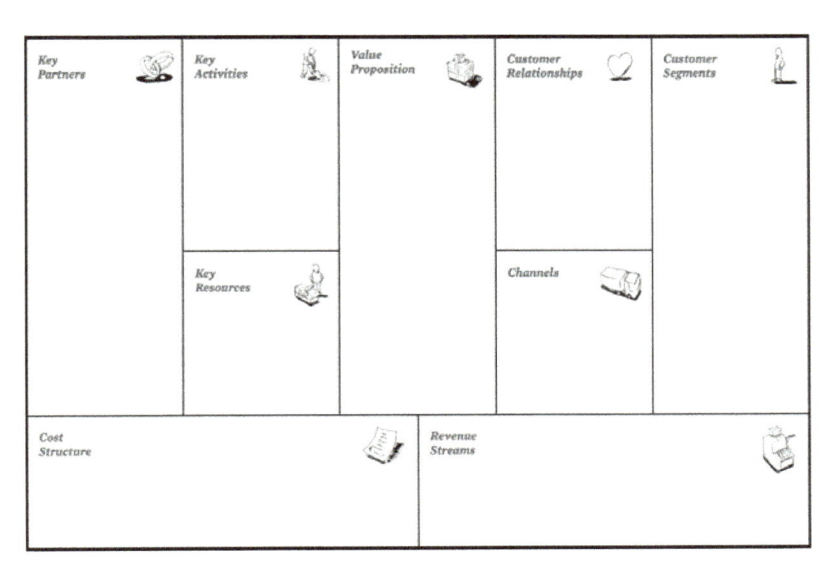

Key Partners	Key Activities	Value Proposition	Customer Relationships	Customer Segments
	Key Resources		Channels	
Cost Structure			Revenue Streams	

Figure 9. Business model canvas by A. Osterwalder, Y. Pigneur [73,145,146].

Assuming that business model scalability is associated with the functioning of the company in the network environment, the attributes of this model are focused precisely on the network. Therefore, while reviewing network attributes, the canvas of a networked, scalable business model consisting of its key attributes which determine that the company is embedded in this environment may be proposed (Figure 10).

Network size	Closeness of network centrality	Network density	Interaction Dynamics in the network	Network coordination costs
	Diversity in the network		Network members turnover	
Conflict potential in the network			Competition in the network	

Figure 10. The canvas of a networked scalable business model.

The proposed nine attributes of a networked, scalable business model make it possible to use it in the network.

While ensuring the ability of the company to survive, it is important to find mechanisms for functioning by which, by following the principles of sustainability, business continuity is ensured, its values are created, and high performance is achieved at the same time.

The proposal for a nine-component canvas of a sustainable business model based on longitudinal research and bibliographic research is shown in Figure 11.

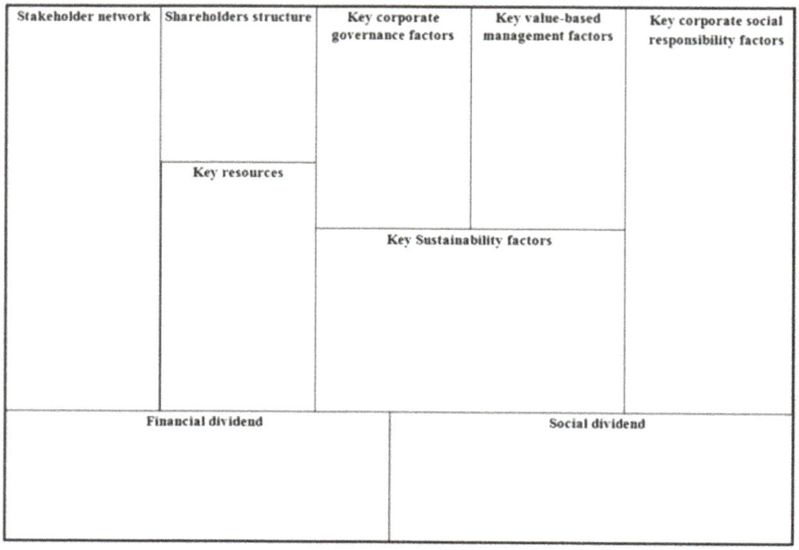

Stakeholder network	Shareholders structure	Key corporate governance factors	Key value-based management factors	Key corporate social responsibility factors
	Key resources			
		Key Sustainability factors		
	Financial dividend		Social dividend	

Figure 11. Sustainable business model canvas composed of primary components.

The next step in the operationalization of a scalable business model is to determine mechanisms for key features of the business model that affect its scalability. This is described in Table 5.

Table 5. Key features of the business model affecting its scalability.

No.	Key Features of the Business Model Affecting Its Scalability	Adopted Operationalization Mechanisms
1.	Dynamics	Shaping changes in the business model configuration dynamically.
2.	Adaptability	Continuous adaptation to permanent changes.
3.	Repeatability	Continuous repetition of behavior patterns using the business model and generating reproducible value materializing in increased profit.
4.	Coherence	Ensuring continuous business model integrity for its maximum functionality.
5.	Economization	Business model commercialization at fixed time intervals.
6.	Profitability	Ensuring continuous profit from the business model.
7.	Innovation	Creating innovative behavior while still being a leader. Avoiding imitation in building a business model.
8.	The ability to migrate	Searching, adding, removing and subsequently configuring business model components obtained from networks surrounding the company.
9.	Availability	Ensuring the possibility of using the business model at any time and place. The possibility of interfering with the business model quickly.
10.	The scale of impact	Continuous expansion of the usage of the business model. Expanding the boundaries of business.

The next step of operationalization for the defined primary components of a sustainable business model is to determine the mechanisms for their scalability, as shown in Table 6.

Table 6. Scalability mechanisms for a sustainable business model attribute.

L.P.	Primary Component of a Sustainable Business Model	Scalability Mechanisms Used for a Sustainable Business Model Attribute
1.	Stakeholder network	Seeking synergy, symbiosis and symmetry between various stakeholders in the company.
2.	Shareholders structure	Seeking the common goal and common values in the functioning shareholders structure.
3.	Key resources	Seeking optimal configuration mechanisms based on own resources.
4.	Key corporate governance factors	Seeking a coherent system for the exchange of information, data and knowledge in the process of mutual reporting and supervision.
5.	Key corporate social responsibility factors	Seeking correlations between corporate social responsibility factors.
6.	Key value-based management factors	Seeking correlations between value-based management factors.
7.	Key Sustainability factors	Seeking correlations between sustainability factors.
8.	Financial dividend	Applying the principle of sustainable dividends.
9.	Social dividend	Applying the mechanisms creating social capital in conjunction with the expectations of the various groups of stakeholders.

The primary components should be extended by the secondary components, which, for a sustainable business model, have been proposed in Table 7. It is also necessary to define scalability mechanisms for the secondary attributes of a sustainable business model, as shown in Table 8.

Table 7. The list of secondary sustainable business model components.

No.	List of Secondary Sustainable Business Model Components
1.	Quality of a product/service
2.	Innovation of a product/service
3.	Environmental performance of a product/service
4.	Product safety
5.	Technologies
6.	Trust
7.	Company image and brand awareness
8.	Competence
9.	Relationships with customers
10.	Social capital

Table 8. Scalability mechanisms for the secondary attributes of a sustainable business model.

No.	Secondary Components of a Sustainable Business Model	Scalability Mechanisms Used for the Sustainable Business Model Attributes
1.	Quality of a product/service	Seeking high quality products/services with regard to ensuring repeatability and standardization
2.	Innovation of a product/service	Seeking a high level of innovation while achieving a high quality of products/services
3.	Environmental performance of a product/service	Seeking the mutual fulfillment of environmental criteria, taking into account qualitative criteria, implementing the principles of ecological quality.
4.	Product safety	Seeking a high level of safety while maintaining procedural conduct and implementation of the standardization principles.
5.	Technologies	Seeking mechanisms for optimum configuration at the level of conceptualization and operationalization of technological solutions.
6.	Trust	Seeking standards of conduct and implementation of mutual communication principles so that trust is not destroyed.
7.	Company image and brand awareness	Seeking the principles of building brand value while implementing the standardization principles.
8.	Competence	Seeking mechanisms for the optimum configuration of staff qualifications, training, experience and skills.
9.	Relationships with customers	Seeking mechanisms for mutual communication and mutual exchange of values in order to ensure optimum value for value relationships.
10.	Social capital	Seeking mechanisms for mutual communication to develop social potential and social participation.

The next step taken in order to determine sustainable business model scalability for the defined components is applying the QCA (Qualitative Comparative Analysis) method described in the previous section.

The process of configuration assessment involves repeating actions aimed at adding or removing components from the business model's primary components and then the secondary ones and assessing in which configurations the company can achieve high performance.

10. Discussion

Scalability and sustainability of the business model seem to be an important area of scientific exploration of strategic management mechanisms. Scalability is important for constantly arising dilemmas by seeking answers about to what extent to expand or reduce business models while maintaining high company performance. Sustainability is important as a way to ensure the continuity of business using the owned business model is continuously sought. After multidimensional reflections, the following conclusions, which are the source of scientific debate, are presented below:

(1) Scalability and sustainability are key attributes of the business model of the hybrid organization.

(2) In order for a business model to be sustainable, it must first of all be scalable.
(3) A hybrid organization is an organization, which has a scalable business model that can be sustainable as long as possible, achieving high performance.
(4) An effective business model is a model of an organization that, due to the proper configuration of its attributes, is capable of scalability and sustainability.
(5) A scalable and sustainable business model should be built from primary and secondary attributes.
(6) Primary attributes are non-transferable and secondary attributes of the business model can be added or removed depending on the strategic context of the company.
(7) Scaling depends on the ability of the business model to expand or be reduced.
(8) The adopted operationalization mechanisms should create a pattern of behavior which ensures that the adopted business model is used to the full extent.
(9) Defined attributes that make up the configuration should ensure business model functionality such that the company achieves high performance.

11. Conclusions

It is essential to use scalability in the conceptualization and operationalization of a sustainable business model of hybrid organizations in the network environment to achieve their high performance. The search for the appropriate business model configuration in the system of controlling its components incrementally seems to be an important factor in determining its functioning, ensuring adequate dynamics. The adopted and described logic of using scalability as a key attribute of a sustainable business model can provide a platform for further implementation and discussions aimed at searching for mechanisms of enhancing company performance. Using the primary and secondary components of the business model, configured by using the QCA method, provides a chance to match a business model to the most effective structure.

To sum up the theses contained in the paper, the core conclusions that are the basis for further scientific discussion should be defined.

(1) The developed assumptions of the business model scalability concept indicate that the concept of scalability is a management science theory that is possible to develop further, especially because of the constant search for features describing its scalability
(2) The proposed attributes of sustainable business model scalability are important to increase the chance of survival and development in a difficult, dynamically challenging market environment.
(3) Skillful scaling of the business model in time is a core attribute of companies that are characterized by the ability to change.
(4) Business model scalability is not an easy issue in the research process. This is due to the fact that scalability is based on a set of quality features describing the company's business model at any given time. The more accurate the description of the business model configuration is, the easier it is to capture the components responsible for business model scalability.
(5) Scalability is a temporary feature, which can be easily lost, for example, when an inefficient configuration of linked business model components appears. Therefore, there is a need to continuously measure and monitor the characteristics describing business model scalability.
(6) The performance of the business model depends on its scalability which results from the dynamics of adding and removing individual components, and this can very often be the result of unconscious actions taken by managers or unplanned effects of configuration changeability.
(7) Scalability is therefore a development concept that in times of environment changeability becomes a determinant and condition of the survival of modern companies.

Theoretical and research limitations resulting from the above reflections include:

(1) A small amount of research on business model scalability.
(2) The complex nature of the interpretation of business model sustainability.

(3) Variability in the environment that gives rise to new research dilemmas related to the features and attributes of business models.

The author believes that on the basis of longitudinal and bibliographic research, it can be assumed that the hypotheses are proven.

Hypothesis 1. Scalability and sustainability are key determinants of building a business model of the hybrid organizations embedded in a network environment.

Hypothesis 2. The network environment is favorable to building sustainable business models that are highly scalable.

Hypothesis 3. In order for a business model of the hybrid organizations to be sustainable, it must first of all be scalable.

The author has proven the hypotheses based on the above research.

Conflicts of Interest: Conflicts of Interest: The author declares no conflict of interest.

References

1. Kimberly, J.R. Issues in the Design of Longitudinal Organizational Research. *Sociol. Methods Res.* **1976**, *4*, 321–348. [CrossRef]
2. Venkatesh, A.; Vitalari, N.P. Longitudinal Surveys in Information Systems Research: An Examination of Issues, Methods, and Applications. In *The Information Systems Challenge: Survey Research Methods*; Harvard University Press: Location, UK, 1991; pp. 115–144.
3. Janson, C. Some Problems of Longitudinal Research in the Social Sciences. In *Longitudinal Research: Methods and Uses in Behavioral Science*; Schulsinger, F., Mednick, S., Knop, J., Eds.; Martinus Nijhoff Publishing: Boston, MA, USA, 1981.
4. Jourdan, Z.; Rainer, K.; Marshall, T. Business Intelligence: An Analysis of the Literature. *Inform. Syst. Manag.* **2008**, *25*, 121–131. [CrossRef]
5. Massaro, M.; Dumay, J.; Guthrie, J. On the Shoulders of Giants: Undertaking a Structured Literature Review in Accounting, Accounting. *Audit. Account. J.* **2015**, *28*, 267–284.
6. World Economic Outlook: Adjusting to Lower Commodity Prices. In *World Economic Situation and Prospects 2015*; OECD Economic Outlook, Volume 2015/1 © OECD 2015–Preliminary Version; International Monetary Fund: Washington, DC, USA, 2015.
7. Porter, M.E. *Competitive Advantage, Creating and Sustaining Superior Performance*; The Free Press: New York, NY, USA, 1985.
8. Mintzberg, H.; Ahlstrand, B.; Lampel, J. Strategy safari: The complete guide through the wilds of strategic management, FT Prentice Hall, London 1998. In *Competitive Advantage: Creating and Sustaining Superior Performance*; Porter, M.E., Ed.; The Free Press: New York, NY, USA, 1985.
9. Volberda, H.W., Elfring, T., Eds.; *Rethinking Strategy*; SAGE: London, UK, 2001.
10. Farjoun, M. Towards an organic perspective on strategy. *Strateg. Manag. J.* **2002**, *23*, 561–594. [CrossRef]
11. Freeman, R.E. *Strategic Management: A Stakeholder Approach*; Pitman: Boston, MA, USA, 1984.
12. Clarkson, M. A risk Based Model of Stakeholder Theory. In Proceedings of the Second Toronto Conference of Stakeholder Theory; Centre for Corporate Social Performance and Ethics, University of Toronto: Toronto, ON, Canada, 1994.
13. Lantgry, B. Stakeholders and Moral Responsibilities of Business. *Bus. Ethics Quart.* **1994**, *4*, 431–443.
14. Harrison, J.G. *Strategic Management of Organisation and Stakeholder*; West: St. Paul, MN, USA, 1994.
15. Mitchell, R.K. Toward A Theory of Stakeholder. Identification and Salience: Defining the Principle of Who and What Really Counts. *Acad. Manag. Rev.* **1997**, *22*, Article 4.
16. Freeman, E.; Reed, D. Stockholders and Stakeholders: A New Perspective on Corporate Governance. *Calif. Manag. Rev.* **1983**, *25*, 88–106. [CrossRef]
17. Svendsen, A. The Stakeholder Strategy. In *Profiting from Collaborative Business Relationships*; Berret-Koehler Publishers, Inc.: San Francisco, CA, USA, 1998.

18. Morin, R.A.; Jarrell, S.L. *Driving Shareholder Value: Value–Building Techniques for Creating Shareholder Wealth*; McGraw-Hill: New York, NY, USA, 2001.
19. Martin, J.D.; Petty, J.W.; Wallace, J.S. *Value–Based Management with Corporate Social Responsibility*; University Press: Oxford, UK, 2009.
20. Fu, R.; Qiu, L.; Quyang, L. A Networking-based View of Business Model Innovation: Theory and Method, A Networking-based View of Business Model Innovation. *Commun. IIMA* **2006**, *6*, Article 7.
21. Calia, R.C.; Guerrini, F.M.; Moura, G.L. Innovation networks: From technological development to business model reconfiguration. *Technovation* **2007**, *27*, 426–432. [CrossRef]
22. Voelpel, S.; Leibold, M.; Tekie, E.; von Krogh, G. Escaping the Red Queen Effect in Competitive Strategy: Sense-testing Business Models. *Eur. Manag. J.* **2005**, *23*, 37–49. [CrossRef]
23. Wirtz, B.W.; Schilke, O.; Ullrich, S. Strategic Development of Business Models Implications of the Web 2.0 for Creating Value on the Internet. *Long Range Plan.* **2010**, *43*, 272–290. [CrossRef]
24. Hakanson, H. *International Marketing and Purchasing of Industrial Goods: An Interaction Approach*; Wiley: Chichester, UK, 1982.
25. Pfeffer, J.; Salancik, G. *The External Control of Organisations*; Harper and Row: New York, NY, USA, 1978.
26. Cook, K.S.; Emerson, R. *Exchange Networks and the Analysis of Complex Organisations, Research of the Sociology of Organisations*; JAI press: Greenwich, CT, USA, 1984; Volume 3.
27. Porter, M.E. *Competitive Strategy: Techniques for Analyzing Industries and Competitors*; The Free Press: New York, NY, USA, 1980.
28. Williamson, O.E. *Markets and Hierarchies, Analysis and Antitrust Implications: A Study in the Economics of Internal Organization*; Free Press: New York, NY, USA, 1975.
29. Borgatti, S.P. The Network Paradigm in Organizational Research: A Review and Typology. *J. Manag.* **2003**, *29*, 991–1013.
30. Hakanson, H.; Snehota, I. *Developing Relationships in Business Networks*; Routledge: London, UK, 2005.
31. Martin-Rios, C. Why do firms seek to share human resource management knowledge? The importance of inter-firm networks. *J. Bus. Res.* **2014**, *67*, 190–199. [CrossRef]
32. Jarillo, J.C. *Strategic Networks*; Creating the Borderless Organization, Butterworth—Heinemann: Oxford, UK, 1995.
33. Perechuda, K. *Dyfuzja Wiedzy w Przedsiębiorstwie Sieciowym. Wizualizacja i Kompozycja*; Wydawnictwo Uniwersytetu Ekonomicznego we Wrocławiu: Wrocław, Poland, 2013. (In Polish)
34. Hooley, G.J.; Saunders, J.A.; Piercy, N.F. *Marketing Strategy and Competitive Positioning*; Prentice Hall: Englewood Cliffs, NJ, USA, 1998.
35. Achrol, R. Changes in the theory of interorganizational relations in marketing: Toward network paradigm. *J. Acad. Mark. Sci.* **1997**, *25*, 56–71. [CrossRef]
36. Czakon, W. *Sieci w Zarządzaniu Strategicznym*; Oficyna a Wolters Kluwer Business: Warszawa, Poland, 2012.
37. Gorynia, M.; Jankowska, B. Teorie internacjonalizacji. *Gospodarka Narodowa.* **2007**, *10*, 21–44. (In Polish)
38. Jaki, A. Mechanizmy rozwoju paradygmatów zarządzania. *Przegląd Organizacji* **2014**, *2*, 8–13.
39. Płoszaj, A. *Sieci Instytucji Otoczenia Biznesu*; Scholar: Warszawa, Poland, 2013. (In Polish)
40. Koźmiński, A.K.; Latusek-Jurczak, D. *Rozwój Teorii Organizacji, Od Systemu do Sieci*; Oficyna a Wolters Kluwer business: Warszawa, Poland, 2011. (In Polish)
41. Nogalski, B.; Średnicka, J. Dyfuzja logiki sieci i jej znaczenie dla współpracy organizacyjnej w warunkach niepewności i nieciągłości współczesnej gospodarki. In *Nauki o Zarządzaniu Wobec Nieprzewidywalności i Złożoności Zmian, Praca Zbiorowa pod Redakcją J. Rokity, Górnośląska Wyższa Szkoła Handlowa im*; Wojciecha Korfantego: Katowice, Poland, 2011. (In Polish)
42. Brilman, J. *Nowoczesne Koncepcje i Metody Zarządzania*; Polskie Wydawnictwo Ekonomiczne: Warszawa, Poland, 2002. (In Polish)
43. Stachowicz, J. Rola i udział koryfeusza nauk zarządzania w okresie wyłaniania się nowego paradygmatu nauk o zarządzaniu. In *Irena Hejduk i Andrzej Herman*; Przyszłości, D., Ed.; Difin: Warszawa, Poland, 2014. (In Polish)
44. Noga, A. Sieci w Ujęciu Teorii Ekonomii. In *Relacje Międzyorganizacyjne w Naukach o Zarządzaniu*; Praca zbiorowa pod red. naukową; Koźmińskiego, A.K., Latusek-Jurczak, D., Eds.; Oficyna a Wolters Kluwer business: Warszawa, Poland, 2014. (In Polish)

45. Niemczyk, J. *Strategia, od Planu do Sieci*; Wydawnictwo Uniwersytetu Ekonomicznego we Wrocławiu: Wrocław, Poland, 2013. (In Polish)
46. Hakansson, H.; Snehota, I. No business is an island: The network concept of business strategy. *Scand. J. Mgmt.* **2006**, *22*, 256–270. [CrossRef]
47. Watts, D.J. Networks Dynamics and the Small-World Phenomenon. *Am. J. Soc.* **1999**, *105*, 493–527.
48. Ciesielski, M., Ed.; *Sieci w Gospodarce*; Polskie Wydawnictwo Ekonomiczne: Warszawa, Poland, 2013. (In Polish)
49. De Man, A.P. *The Network Economy. Strategy, Structure and Management*; Edward Elgar: Cheltenham, UK, 2004.
50. Niemczyk, J.; Stańczyk-Hugiet, E.; Jasiński, B. *Sieci Międzyorganizacyjne, Współczesne Wyzwanie dla Teorii i Praktyki Zarządzania*; C.H. Beck: Warszawa, Poland, 2012. (In Polish)
51. Rybicki, J.M. *Myślenie Geometryczne w Teorii Strategii Organizacji*; Wydawnictwo Uniwersytetu Gdańskiego: Gdańsk, Poland, 2013. (In Polish)
52. Hakansson, H.; Ford, D. How should companies interact in business networks? *J. Bus. Res.* **2002**, *55*, 133–139. [CrossRef]
53. Krzakiewicz, K. Zastosowanie podejścia sieciowego w zarządzaniu strategicznym. In *Organizacja i Zarządzanie*; Zeszyt pięćdziesiąty drugi, Zeszyty naukowe nr 1147; Politechnika Łódzka: Łódź, Poland, 2013. (In Polish)
54. Cyfert, S. *Granice Organizacji*; Wydawnictwo Uniwersytetu Ekonomicznego w Poznaniu: Poznań, Poland, 2012. (In Polish)
55. Cyfert, S.; Krzakiewicz, K. Granice w świecie sieciowych i wirtualnych organizacji. In *Granice Strukturalnej Złożoności Organizacji*; Redakcja Naukowa Agnieszka Sopiński, Sylwester Gregorczyk; Oficyna Wydawnicza, Szkoła Główna Handlowa: Warszawa, Poland, 2014. (In Polish)
56. Zimniewicz, S. Orkiestracja sieci według Li & Fung Ltd. In *Zarządzanie Łańcuchami Dostaw*; Ciesielski, M., Ed.; PWE: Warszawa, Poland, 2011. (In Polish)
57. Perechuda, K. Wirtualizacja procesów opartych na wiedzy podstawą nowoczesnego niewolnictwa. Nowe paradygmaty i determinanty przestrzeni przepływów w przedsiębiorstwie sieciowym. In *Wirtualizacja, Problemy, Wyzwania, Skutki*; Zacher, L.W., Ed.; Poltext: Warszawa, Poland, 2013. (In Polish)
58. Goold, M.; Campbell, A. Structured Networks towards the Well-Designed Matrix. *Long Range Plan.* **2003**, *36*, 427–439. [CrossRef]
59. Powell, W.W.; White, D.R. Network Dynamics and Field Evolution: The Growth of Interorganizational Collaboration in the Life Sciences. *Am. J. Sociol.* **2005**, *110*, 1132–1205. [CrossRef]
60. Cygler, J.; Sroka, W. Structural pathologies in inter-organizational networks and their consequences. *Procedia Soc. Behav. Sci.* **2014**, *110*, 52–63. [CrossRef]
61. Stańczyk-Hugiet, E.; Gorgól, J. Elementy sieci międzyorganizacyjnych–aspekty organizacyjno-zarządcze. In *Sieci Międzyorganizacyjne. Współczesne Wyzwanie dla Teorii i Praktyki Zarządzania*; Niemczyk, J., Stańczyk-Hugiet, E.; Jasiński, B., Eds.; C.H. Beck: Warszawa, Poland, 2012. (In Polish)
62. Yuchtman, R.F.; Seashore, S. A system resource approach to organizationaleffectiveness. *Am. Sociol. Rev.* **1967**, *32*, 891–903. [CrossRef]
63. Mitręga, M. Zdolności sieciowe małych i średnich przedsiębiorstwa a jakość relacji z klientami. *Handel Wewn.* **2010**, *2*, 27–32. (In Polish)
64. Zott, C.; Amit, R.; Massa, L. The Business Model: Theoretical Roots, Recent Developments, and Future Research. Available online: http://www.iese.edu/research/pdfs/DI-0862-E.pdf (accessed on June 2010).
65. Wirtz, B.W. *Business Model Management Design–Instrumente–Erfolgsfaktoren von Geschäftsmodellen*; Gabler Verlag/Springer Fachmedien Wiesbaden GmbH: Berlin, Germany, 2011.
66. Teece, D.J. Business Models, Business Strategy and Innovation. *Long Range Plan.* **2010**, *43*, 172–194. [CrossRef]
67. Obłój, K. *Pasja i Dyscyplina Strategii, Jak z Marzeń i Decyzji Zbudować Sukces Firmy*; Poltext: Warszawa, Poland, 2010. (In Polish)
68. Gołębiowski, T.; Dudzik, T.M.; Lewandowska, M.; Witek-Hajduk, M. *Modele Biznesu Polskich Przedsiębiorstw*; Szkoła Główna Handlowa: Warszawa, Poland, 2008. (In Polish)
69. Timmers, P. *Electronic Commerce: Strategies and Models from Business-to-Business Trading*; Wiley & Sons: Chichester, UK, 1999.

70. Rappa, M. Managing the Digital Enterprise: Business Models on the Web, 2002, Retrieved May 14. Available online: http://digitalenterprise.org/models/models.html (accessed on 14 May 2002).
71. Applegate, L.M. E-Business Models: Making Sense of the Internet Business Landscape. In *Information Technology and the New Enterprise: Future Models for Managers*; Applegate, L.M., Dickson, G.W., DeSanctis, G., Eds.; Prentice Hall: Upper Saddle River, NJ, USA, 2000.
72. Slyvotzky, A.J.; Morrison, D.J.; Andelman, B. *Strefa Zysku*; PWE: Warszawa, Poland, 2000.
73. Osterwalder, A.; Pigneur, Y. An e-Business Model Ontology for Modeling e-Business. In Proceedings of the 15th Bled Electronic Commerce Conference e-Reality: Constructing the e-Economy, Bled, Slovenia, 17–19 June 2002.
74. Bossidy, L.; Charan, R. *Szósty Zmysł w Zarządzaniu Firmą. Tworzenie Wykonalnych Planów i Modeli Biznesowych*; MT Biznes: Warszawa, Poland, 2010. (In Polish)
75. Niemczyk, J. Modele biznesowe. In *Zarządzanie. Kanony i Trendy*; Morawski, M., Niemczyk, J., Perechuda, K., Stańczyk-Hugiet, E., Eds.; Beck, C.H.: Warszawa, Poland, 2010. (In Polish)
76. Seddon, P.B.; Lewis, G.P.; Freeman, P.; Shanks, G. The Case for Viewing Business Models as Abstractions of Strategy. *Commun. Assoc. Inform. Syst.* **2004**, *13*, 426–442.
77. De Witt, B.; Meyer, R. *Synteza Strategii, Tworzenie Strategii Konkurencyjnej Przez Tworzenie Paradoksów*; Polskie Wydawnictwo Ekonomiczne: Warszawa, Poland, 2007.
78. Hoque, F. *The Alignment Effect: How to Get Real Business Value Out of Technology*; Financial Times Prentice Hall: Upper Saddle River, NJ, USA, 2002.
79. Jabłoński, A. Modele biznesu w sektorach pojawiających się i schyłkowych. In *Tworzenie Przewagi Konkurencyjnej Przedsiębiorstwa Opartej na Jakości i Kryteriach Ekologicznych*; Wydawnictwo Wyższej Szkoły Biznesu w Dąbrowie Górniczej: Dąbrowa Górnicza, Poland, 2008. (In Polish)
80. Jabłoński, A.; Jabłoński, M. Projektowanie sieciowych modeli biznesu. *Ekonomika i Organizacja Przedsiębiorstwa.* **2013**, *12*, 29–39. (In Polish)
81. Cyfert, S.; Krzakiewicz, K. Wykorzystanie koncepcji modeli biznesu w zasobowej teorii firmy. In *Rozwój Szkoły Zasobowej Zarządzania Strategicznego*; Krupskiego, R., Ed.; Prace Naukowe Wałbrzyskiej Wyższej Szkoły Zarządzania i Przedsiębiorczości: Wałbrzych, Poland, 2011. (In Polish)
82. Demil, B.; Lecocq, X. Business model evolution: In search of dynamic consistency. *Long Range Plan.* **2010**, *43*, 2–3. [CrossRef]
83. Sandberg, K.D. Is It Time to Trade In Your Business Model? *Harvard University Update* 2002.
84. Afuah, A.; Tucci, C. *Biznes Internetowy Strategie i Modele*; Oficyna ekonomiczna: Kraków, Czech Republic, 2003. (In Polish)
85. Nogalski, B. Modele biznesu jako narzędzia reorientacji strategicznej przedsiębiorstw. *MBA* **2009**, *2*, 3–14.
86. Deodhar, S.J.; Saxena, K.; Gupta, R.K.; Ruohonen, M. Strategies for software-based hybrid business models. *J. Strateg. Inform. Syst.* **2012**, *21*, 274–294. (In Polish) [CrossRef]
87. Jabłoński, A. *Spójność Hybrydy Strategicznej w Środowisku Sieciowym*; Difin: Warszawa, Poland, 2015. (In Polish)
88. Stubbs, W.; Cocklin, C. Conceptualizing a "sustainability business model". *Org. Environ.* **2008**, *21*, 103–127. [CrossRef]
89. Boons, F.; Lüdeke-Freund, F. Business models for sustainable innovation: State of the art and steps towards a research agenda. *J. Clean. Prod.* **2013**, *45*, 9–19. [CrossRef]
90. Jabłoński, A. *Modele Zrównoważonego Biznesu w Budowie Długoterminowej Wartości Przedsiębiorstw z Uwzględnieniem ich Społecznej Odpowiedzialności*; Difin: Warszawa, Poland, 2013. (In Polish)
91. Neely, A.; Delbridge, R. Effective Business Models: What Do They Mean for Whitehall. 2007. Available online: http://www.nationalschool.gov.uk/sunningdaleiinstitute.
92. Epstein, M.J.; Rejc Buhovac, A. Solving the sustainability implementation challenge. *Org. Dyn.* **2010**, *39*, 306–315. [CrossRef]
93. Dyllick, T.; Hockerts, K. Beyond the business case for corporate sustainability. *Bus. Strategy Environ.* **2002**, *11*. [CrossRef]
94. Mc Donough, W.; Braugnart, M. The next industrial revolution. The Atlantic Monthly, October 1998.

95. Daud Ahmed, M.; Sundaram, D. Sustainability modelling and reporting: From roadmap to implementation. *Decis. Support Syst.* **2012**, *53*, 611–624. [CrossRef]
96. Yunus, M.; Moingeon, B.; Lehman-Ortega, L. Biulding Social Business Models: Lessons from the Grameen Experience. *Long Range Plann.* **2010**, *43*, 308–325. [CrossRef]
97. Kotler, P.; Kartajaya, H.; Setiawan, I. *Marketing 3.0, Dobry produkt? Zadowolony klient? Spełniony Człowiek!*; MT Biznes: Warszawa, Poland, 2010. (In Polish)
98. Nogalski, B. Idea strategii "błękitnego oceanu" w rozwiązywaniu kluczowych problemów polskich przedsiębiorstw w zakresie zarządzania. In *Ku Nowym Paradygmatom Nauk o Zarządzaniu, Praca Zbiorowa pod Redakcją J. Rokity, Wydawnictwo Górnośląskiej Wyższej Szkoły Handlowej im*; Wojciecha Korfantego: Katowice, Poland, 2008. (In Polish)
99. Osterwalder, A.; Pigneur, Y. Aligning Profit and Purpose through Business Model Innovation. In *Responsible Management Practices for the 21 Century*; Palazzo, G., Wentland, M., Eds.; Pearson Education France: Paris, France, 2011.
100. Schaltegger, S.; Lüdeke-Freund, F.; Hansen, E. Business Cases for Sustainability: The Role of Business Model Innovation for Corporate Sustainability. *Int. J. Innov. Sustain. Dev.* **2012**, *6*, 95–119. [CrossRef]
101. Schwarz, P. *Organisation in Nonprofit-Organisationen, Grundlagen, Strukturen*; Haupt Verlag: Bern, Switzerland, 2005.
102. Grudzewski, W.M.; Hejduk, I.K.; Sankowska, A.; Wańtuchowicz, M. *Zarządzanie Zaufaniem w Organizacjach Wirtualnych*; Difin: Warszawa, Poland, 2007. (In Polish)
103. Abidin, N.Z.; Pasquire, C.L. Revolutionize value management: A mode towards sustainability. *Int. J. Proj. Manag.* **2007**, *25*, 275–282. [CrossRef]
104. Ultsch, A. The Integration of Connectionist Models with Knowledge-Based Systems: Hybrid Systems. In Proceedings of the IEEE SMC 98 International Conference, San Diego, CA, USA, 14 October 1998.
105. Grassl, W. Business Models of Social Enterprise: A Design Approach to Hybridity. *ACRN J. Entrep. Perspect.* **2012**, *1*, 37–60.
106. Brozek, K.O. Exploring the Continuum of Social and Financial Returns: When Does a Nonprofit Become a Social Enterprise? *Community Dev. Invest. Rev.* **2009**, *5*, 7–17.
107. Boyd, B.; Henning, N.; Reyna, E.; Wang, D.E.; Welch, M.D. *Hybrid Organizations: New Business Models for Environmental Leadership*; Greenleaf: Sheffield, UK, 2009.
108. Brandsen, T.; Van de Donk, W.; Putters, K. Griffins or Chameleons? Hybridity as a Permanent and Inevitable Characteristic of the Third Sector. *Int. J. Public Admin.* **2005**, *28*, 9–10. [CrossRef]
109. Defourny, J.; Nyssens, M. Conceptions of Social Enterprise in Europe and the United States: Convergences and Divergences. *J. Soc. Entrep.* **2010**, *1*, 32–53.
110. Billis, D. *Hybrid Organizations and the Third Sector*; Basingstoke: Palgrave, Macmillan, 2010.
111. Alter, S.K. Social Enterprise Models and Their Mission and Money Relationships. In *Social Entrepreneurship: New Models of Sustainable Social Change*; Nicholls, A., Ed.; Oxford University Press: Oxford, UK, 2006.
112. Malki, S. Social Entrepreneurship and Complexity Models: Goldstein. *Hazy Silberstang* **2009**.
113. Bruni, L.S. *Zamagni, Civil Economy: Efficiency, Equity, Public Happiness*; Peter Lang: Bern, Switzerland, 2007.
114. Becchetti, L.; Bruni, L.; Zamagni, S. *Microeconomia: Scelte, Relazioni, Economiacivile*; ilMulino: Bologna, Italy, 2011. (In Polish)
115. Bruni, L. L'ethos del mercato. In *Un'introduzioneaifondamentiantropologici e Relazio-nalidell'economia*; Mondadori: Milan Italy, 2010. (In Polish)
116. Lusch, R.F.; Vargo, S.L. Service-dominant Logic: A Necessary Step. European. *J. Mark.* **2011**, *45*, 1298–1309. [CrossRef]
117. Ramírez, R. Value Co-Production: Intellectual Origins and Implications for Practice and Research. *Strateg. Manag. J.* **1999**, *20*, 49–65.
118. Payne, A.F.; Storbacka, K.; Frow, P. Managing the Co-Creation of Value. *J. Acad. Mark. Sci.* **2008**, *36*, 83–96. [CrossRef]
119. Lessig, L. *Remix: Making Art and Commerce Thrive in the Hybrid Economy*; Penguin Press: New York, NY, USA, 2008.
120. Ménard, C.; Gibbons, R.; Roberts, J. *Hybrid Modes of Organization, Alliances, Joint Ventures, Networks, and Other "Strange" Animals*; Handbook of Organizational Economics, Princeton University Press: Princeton, NJ, USA, 2011.

121. Haigh, N.; Hoffman, A.J. Hybrid organizations: The next chapter of sustainable business. *Org. Dyn.* **2012**, *41*, 126–134. [CrossRef]
122. Santos, F. A Positive Theory of Social Entrepreneurship. *J. Bus. Ethics* **2012**, *111*, 335–351. [CrossRef]
123. Pache, A.-C.; Santos, F. Inside the hybrid organization: Selective coupling as a response to competing institutional logics. *Acad. Manag. J.* **2013**, *56*, 972–1001. [CrossRef]
124. Santos, F.M.; Pache, A.-C.; Birkholz, C. Making Hybrids Work: Aligning business models and organizational design for social entreprises. *Calif. Manag. Rev.* **2015**, *57*, 36–58. [CrossRef]
125. Velamuri, V.K.; Neyer, A.K.; Möslein, K.M. Hybrid Value Creation, Understanding the Value Creating Attributes, *MKWI 2010*–Integration von Produkt und Dienstleistung–Hybride Wertschöpfung. 2003. Available online: http://webdoc.sub.gwdg.de/univerlag/ 2010/mkwi/03_ anwendungen/ integration_ von_produkt_und_dienstleistung_-_ hybride_wertschoepfung/01_hybrid_value_creation.pdf (accessed on 19 February 2016).
126. Khare, A.; Huang, Y.; Doan, H.; Kanwal, M.S. A Fresh Graduate's Guide to Software Development Tools and Technologies. Available online: http://www.comp.nus.edu.sg/~seer/book/2e/Ch06.%20Scalability.pdf (accessed on 19 February 2016).
127. Menascé, D.A.; Virgilio Almeida, A.F. Challenges in Scaling E-Business Sites. In Proceedings of the 2000 Computer Measurement Group Conference, Orlando, FL, USA, 10–15 December 2000.
128. Gunther, N.J. A general theory of computational scalability based on rational functions. 2008; arXiv:0808.1431. Available online: http://arxiv.org/abs/0808.1431 (accessed on 25 August 2008).
129. Gunther, N.J. *Guerrilla Capacity Planning: A Tactical Approach to Planning for Highly Scalable Applications and Services*, 1st ed.; Springer: Heidelberg, Germany, 2007.
130. Amit, R.; Zott, C. Value Creation in E-Business. *Strateg. Manag. J.* **2001**, *22*, 493–520. [CrossRef]
131. Rappa, M.A. The utility business model and the future of computing services. *IBM Syst. J.* **2004**, *43*, 32–42. [CrossRef]
132. Bouwman, H.; MacInnes, I. Dynamic Business Model Framework for Value Webs. In Proceedings of the 39th Annual Hawaii International Conference on System Sciences (HICSS2006), Kauai, HI, USA, 4–7 January 2006.
133. Nielsen, C.; Morten, L. The Concept of Business Model Scalability. 2015. Available online: http://vbn.aau.dk/files/208921589/BM_Scalability_WP.pdf (accessed on 30 December 2015).
134. Björkdahl, J.; Holmén, M. Business model innovation–the challenges ahead. *Int. J. Prod. Dev.* **2013**, *18*, 213–215.
135. Green, R. Scalable Business Model. 2014. Available online: http://www.briefing.com/ investor/ learning-center/general-concepts/scalable-business-models/ (accessed on 28 October 2014).
136. Information taken from. Available online: http://www.forbes.com/sites/martinzwilling/2013/09/06/10-tips-for-building-the-most-scalable-startup/ (accessed on 19 February 2016).
137. WP3–E-Business Model Roadmap Deliverable 3.1 (Revised): "E-Factors Report Part 1: Overview, and Current Trends on E-Business Models", Task Leader: University of Jyväskylä (Finland). Available online: http://www.wi1.uni-muenster.de/wi/studies/archive/izi/ss05/E-FACTORS_D3_1.pdf (accessed on 19 February 2016).
138. Blank, S.; Dorf, B. *Podręcznik Startupu, Budowa Wielkiej Firmy krok po Kroku*; Helion: Gliwice, Poland, 2013.
139. Blank, S. Why the Lean Start-Up Changes Everything. Available online: https://hbr.org/2013/05/ why-the-lean-start-up-changes-everything (accessed on 19 February 2016). (In Polish)
140. Stabryła, A. Generalne formuły postępowania badawczego w procesie projektowania. *Zeszyty Naukowe Małopolskiej Wyższej Szkoły Ekonomicznej w Tarnowie* **2012**, *1*, 167–180. (In Polish)
141. Jabłoński, A.; Jabłoński, M. System zarządzania a atrybuty modeli biznesu. *Probl. Jakości.* **2014**, *4*, 26–30.
142. Moore, G.E. Cramming more components onto integrated circuits. *Electron. Maga.* **1965**, *38*, 82–85. (In Polish). [CrossRef]
143. Ragin, C.C. The comparative method. In *Moving Beyond Qualitative and Quantitative Strategies*; University of California Press: Berkeley, CA, USA, 1987.
144. Rohwer, G. Qualitative comparative analysis: A discussion of interpretations. *Eur. Sociol. Rev.* **2010**. [CrossRef]

145. Osterwalder, A.; Pigneur, Y.; Tucci, C.L. Clarifying business models: Origins, present, and future of the concept. *Commun. AIS* **2005**, *16*, 1–25.
146. Osterwalder, A. The Business Model Ontology a Proposition in a Design Science Approach, Licencié en Sciences Politiques de l'Université de Lausanne Diplômé postgrade en Informatique et Organisation (DPIO)de l'Ecole des HEC de l'Université de Lausanne Pour l'obtention du grade de Docteur en Informatique de Gestion. 2004. Available online: http://www.hec.unil.ch/aosterwa/PhD/Osterwalder_PhD_BM_Ontology.pdf (accessed on 19 February 2016). (In Polish)

© 2016 by the author. Licensee MDPI, Basel, Switzerland. This article is an open access article distributed under the terms and conditions of the Creative Commons Attribution (CC BY) license (http://creativecommons.org/licenses/by/4.0/).

Article

The Effect of the Internal Side of Social Responsibility on Firm Competitive Success in the Business Services Industry

M. Isabel Sánchez-Hernández [1], Dolores Gallardo-Vázquez [2], Agnieszka Barcik [3] and Piotr Dziwiński [4,*]

1. Business Administration and Sociology Department, School of Economics, University of Extremadura, Ave. Elvas s/n, Badajoz 06006, Spain; isanchez@unex.es
2. Financial Economics and Accountancy Department, School of Economics, University of Extremadura, Ave. Elvas s/n, Badajoz 06006, Spain; dgallard@unex.es
3. Department of Management and Transport, University of Bielsko-Biała, Willowa 2, Bielsko-Biala 43-309, Poland; abarcik@ath.bielsko.pl
4. Department of Law and Administration, The University of Dąbrowa Górnicza, Cieplaka 1c, Dąbrowa Górnicza 43-300, Poland
* Correspondence: pdziwinski@wsb.edu.pl; Tel.: +48-606-113-729

Academic Editor: Adam Jabłoński
Received: 27 December 2015; Accepted: 14 February 2016; Published: 18 February 2016

Abstract: This work focuses on the internal side of social responsibility of organizations in a regional context. Through a survey of 590 managers in classical business services (human-capital intensive) and representative of the productive economy of the Region of Extremadura (Spain), an empirical analysis is conducted. First, a factor analysis is conducted to explore the main dimensions of the internal face of Social Responsibility and second, a structural equations model is developed to look for a relationship with business competitiveness. Business performance and innovation are also considered in the model. The main contribution of the article is the establishment of a set of indicators that will help to build an ongoing and meaningful dialogue with employees improving their quality of life at work that will also serve as important guidance for the increasing of the firm's competitiveness through responsible human resources practices. Some suggestions for a research agenda emerge from this first attempt to approach the internal side of responsibility in business.

Keywords: human recources management (HRM); internal social responsibility (ISR); service sector; social responsibility (SR)

1. Introduction

The rise of service economy has been the predominant pattern over the last few years [1–3]. We know a great deal about the organization and management of Social Responsibility (SR) and the link with Human Resources Management (HRM), but comparatively little about how applicable this is to the service sector. In this work, we identify the components of the internal side of Social Responsibility in the services industry.

Freeman [4] gave a broad definition of stakeholders as any group or individual who can affect or is affected by the achievement of the organization's objectives. This author also highlights how *stakeholders* are simply constituents within and outside the organization, who have a stake in an organization's functioning and outcomes. The well-known *Stakeholder Theory* offers an instrumental value in providing a framework for guiding the actions of organizational members to ensure that the relationships that contribute to their financial viability are managed responsibly [5,6]. Some authors refer to the moral claim on the actions of the firms to define the stakeholders [7] such as consumers, employees, competitors, suppliers, government, as well as other actors in society. It is evident that the firm responds to multiple *stakeholders* for different reasons and in various ways [8,9].

According to the *Stakeholder Theory*, it is generally recognized that Social Responsibility (SR) has two dimensions: the external dimension and the internal one. On the one hand, the external dimension of SR is reflected in a large relationship of organizations with their communities. Companies interact with their external stakeholders when they provide business operations by guaranteeing economic activity, tax revenues, investing in the local economic system, concluding contracts with the local distributors, respecting human rights, and encouraging protection activities on environment by considering environmental concerns in business operations. On the other hand, the understudied internal side of SR has the emphasis on employees. Mason and Simmons [10] say that employees expect SR values similar to other stakeholders, arguing that employees seek functional, economic, psychological, and ethical benefits from their employing organizations. In this sense, if employers provide challenging, stimulating and fulfilling work, some functional benefits will be obtained and it will also be perceived as indicative of a socially responsible employer and a main driver of Internal Social Responsibility (ISR) practices [11,12].

In general terms, SR has been considered to be "an organization's obligation to maximize its positive impact on stakeholders and to minimize its negative impact" [13]. However, the heterogeneity of definitions has been highlighted by Matten and Moon [14], (p.405) when they said "SR is an umbrella term overlapping with some, and being synonymous with other, conceptions of business-society relation". According to the renewed definition by the European Commission, SR is the responsibility of enterprises for their impacts on society with reference to collaborate with stakeholders "to integrate social, environmental and ethical concerns, respect for human rights and consumer concerns into their business operations and their core strategy" [15] (p.7). Taking into account that classical organizational boundaries have become obsolete because "what once was 'outside' the organization is now 'inside' and *vice versa*" [16] (p.449) we found in this fact a fundamental reason for the emergence of the internal face of SR. Nowadays, the external side of SR and the internal one are more related than ever showing higher interconnectivity as have been shown by Sánchez-Hernández and Grayson [17]. According to this work, companies should discover the social and environmental potential of employees in order to integrate their interests and skills into the overall SR efforts. This will be the way to internalize a Social Responsible Strategy within the organization creating dynamic capabilities likely to lead to competitive advantages. The interaction of Strategy and HRM issues [18] explains how employees are important to a firm's success. According to the *Resource-Based Theory* (RBT) of the firm, human capital is a key factor explaining performance differences across firms [19]. In this respect, Crook [20] has pointed out the importance of "specific" employees, referring to the best and brightest human capital available in the labor market, to achieve high performance. Shoemaker [16] argued that treating HRM and SR separately is an outdated approach because organizations develop towards open systems where cooperative action is based on the willingness of employees to bring in and expand their talents as part of communities of work.

Despite the huge academic literature devoted to SR, literature about ISR is surprisingly scarce and empirical studies are inexistent as far as we know. However, the need for real improvement in organizational capability for doing well, and also for doing well in respect to stakeholders, as a basis for competitive strategy and competitive advantage, has received widespread attention in the academic and professional management literature [21]. In addition, competitive advantage is increasingly achieved through the mobilization of the accumulated know-how of individual employees to create value through processes that are not easily imitable [22]. Consequently, ISR has to be analyzed for one important reason: because employees are stakeholders able to create social value for the company mediating between the company and the consumers.

Worried about the under-studied internal side of SR, this work focuses upon regional businesses in Extremadura (Autonomous Region in the southwest of Spain) interacting with the local community by investing in the regional economic system, contracting with the local distributors, taking into account environmental concerns (external side of SR) and also recruiting employees, guaranteeing jobs, wages, training, and employees quality of life (the internal one).

The paper exposes what could be considered socially responsible management of human resources, called sustainable HRM—what actions related to human capital any organization could perform to state that employees' management is sustainable. In previous work, the authors have developed and empirically validated an SR scale in the regional context of study [23]. Now, we address internal practices considered sustainable in academic management literature by isolating the internal aspects of the general scale mentioned. For the definition of indicators that reflect these actions, we have covered several areas. All of them include some determinants of pleasant working conditions, and are oriented to the pursuit of social welfare [24–29].

There are many different areas that could be addressed. Thus, we start to refer to the actions devoted to support the employment of people at risk of social exclusion [30,31] and, at the same time, the fact that the company values the contribution of disabled people to the business world [32–34]. Moreover, the interest in the employee's quality of life [29,35], the importance of payments of wages above the industry average and the existence of pension plans [36,37], or the fact that employee compensation will be related to their skills and results [38,39], are aspects that determine a responsible management into the organization. We can add the standards of health and safety beyond the legal minimum (because every company has to fulfill the law) [40], the commitment with the job creation [41] and the training and development programs for employees [32,42]. In addition, it is important to consider the conciliation of professional and personal lives [43,44] and the equal opportunities for all employees [32,42,45–47]. In the line of social commitment, the participation of the organization in social projects [48,49] and the organization of volunteer activities in collaboration with NGOs [49,50], define new responsible actions in management.

Moreover, to be responsible, the organization must have dynamic mechanisms of dialogue with employees. In this respect, Preuss and others [51] conclude after some case study analyses that dialogue with employee representatives and trade unions could play an active role in SR and, in some cases, even a pivotal one. While the company is doing SR actions, it must raise awareness and inform employees on SR and the actions committed. Finally, the fact that the organization was an active member of any association that promotes the implementation of SR, as could be the case of the United Nations Global Compact for instance, is considered very important [52].

After this theoretical introduction, employees could be considered the center of any responsible business. European firms pursue SR for concerns of stakeholders such as government, regulatory bodies, customers or pressure groups. This is the external SR orientation. However, the aim of this paper is to study the ISR of organizations. In this sense, we say that SR behavior and values should also include internal aspects of management related to intra-organizational elements, organizational capabilities and HRM. As follows, through a survey of managers, we first carry on a factor analysis to explore the main dimensions of the ISR. Once the multidimensionality of this new construct is empirically determined, interpreted, and understood, the empirical analysis continues by looking for a relationship between ISR and business competitiveness. The work finishes with conclusions, limitations of the study, and lines of research for the near future.

2. Method

2.1. Sample and Procedure

The information for this investigation was collected from business services managers in the Autonomous Community of Extremadura, in southwestern Spain. The broad argument to choose services in this work is that the match between HRM and SR strategy should be greater in services than in manufacturing, highlighting the internal side of SR. According to Legge [53], services are competing in the knowledge-based economy. Services are used to characterize high skilled people and high cost industry. In this context, it is likely to adopt HRM policies very well linked to SR strategy that treat employees as an asset that enables the company to create added-value.

To justify the selected region, we have to say that, since 2010, a special plan for the promotion of SR exists in the Region. The main pillars for building a responsible culture in the region are: The *Law of SR* in Extremadura (15/2010 of 9 December) and the *Decree* (110/2013 of 2 July) for the establishment of the Autonomous Council for the promotion of Social Responsibility of Extremadura, the Office of Corporate Social Responsibility, and the Procedure for qualification and registration of socially responsible companies. At this point, it is important to highlight that the special plan for the promotion of SR in the Region is enhancing both the external and the internal side of SR. Table 1 presents the study's technical data sheet.

Table 1. Technical data sheet.

Data Sheet	
Geographical Scope	Region of Extremadura (Spain)
Universe	SMEs (Small and medium–sized enterprises) Business Services—Source: Spain's Central Enterprise Directory 2009
Method of information collection	Phone contact
Emitted calls	14,580
Population	5332 contacted firms
Final sample	590 SMEs
Index of participation	11.07%
Measurement error	3.3%
Trust level	95% z = 1.96 p = q = 0.5
Sampling method	Simple random
Average duration of the interview	14:35 (minutes:seconds)

Source: Own work.

The representative sample of regional business services comprised 590 SMEs (Small and medium-sized enterprises) with their corresponding predetermined substitute firms to control the non-response index. The objective universe was drawn from Spain's Central Enterprise Directory (SCED). Before beginning the study, we calibrated the representativeness of the sample of firms that were to participate in the survey. To this end, weighting coefficients were established according to the defined strata of the firms in the sample. Possible biases relative to the characteristics of the total population of the Directory were checked for using statistical tests, comparing the structure of the sample with the total population of the SCED. The results justified the validity of the sample for the purposes of the study. A pilot test was also carried out in order to check that the survey would be appropriately interpreted by the respondent. The administration of one *ad hoc* questionnaire was by telephone interviews with business services managers. They were carried out using the Computer Aided Telephone Interviewing (CATI) system. The participation index was 11.07%, corresponding to the percentage of firms in which a valid interlocutor agreed to participate in the study. A total of 590 completed surveys were collected, which resulted in a response rate of 11.07%.

2.2. The Measurement Instrument

An *ad hoc* questionnaire was provided to inquire into the manager's perceptions with responses on a 10-point Likert scale. These responses went from "0: totally in disagreement" to "10: totally in agreement" for the ISR items, and from "0: far below the competition" to "10: far above the competition" for the items corresponding to the rest of the constructs. With this instrument, we analyze the ISR as a first attempt to standardize it aligned with the "Guidance on Social Responsibility" published for the International Organization for Standardization (ISO 26000) in 2010. The aim is to assist companies to expand their responsible behavior from external actions to internal actions looking for synergies and better performance. Thus, and according to previous work [23,32,54], the selected indicators reflecting ISR actions are shown in Table 2 (from INTR1 to INTR18) selectively supported by Turker [42], Agudo-Valiente *et al.* [45], Lu *et al.* [47] and Pérez *et al.* [46]. All indicators are considered internal activities related to ISR rather than external activities because, in these actions, we can observe how employees mediate the relationship between the company and the society.

Table 2. Selected indicators about the internal dimension of social responsibility (SR).

Indicators	
INTR1	We support the employment of people at risk of social exclusion
INTR2	We value the contribution of disabled people to the business world
INTR3	We are aware of the employees' quality of life
INTR4	We pay wages above the industry average
INTR5	Employees compensation is related to their skills and their results
INTR6	We have standards of health and safety beyond the legal minimum
INTR7	We are committed to job creation (fellowships, creation of job opportunities, ...)
INTR8	We foster our employees' training and development
INTR9	We have human resource policies aimed at facilitating the conciliation of employees' professional and personal lives
INTR10	Employees' initiatives are taken seriously into account in management decisions
INTR11	Equal opportunities exist for all employees
INTR12	We participate in social projects to the community
INTR13	We encourage employees to participate in volunteer activities or in collaboration with NGOs
INTR14	We have dynamic mechanisms of dialogue with employees
INTR15	We understand the importance of pension plans for employees
INTR16	We put into practice specific actions to raise awareness, to educate, and to inform employees on the principles and actions related to SR
INTR17	The values related to SR are present in the vision and strategy of the firm
INTR18	We are active members of organizations, businesses, or professional association or discussion groups that promote the implementation of SR

Source: Own work.

2.3. Factor Analysis

We observe that the selected indicators from the formulated domain of the internal side of SR offered in Table 2 are measures or variables related to ISR. However, we wonder whether they could be correlated with each other. In this case, it means that scores on each variable share information contained in the others [55]. In general, factor analysis is a collection of methods to explain the correlations among variables in terms of more fundamental elements called factors. Specifically, and according to Jolliffe [56], the central idea of a principal component analysis is to reduce the dimensionality of a data set in which there is a large number of interrelated variables, as is the case of the first approximation to ISR shown in Table 2, while retaining as much as possible of the variation present in the data set. This reduction is achieved by transforming the factors or principal components to a new set of variables, which are uncorrelated, and which are ordered so that the first few retain most of the variation present in all of the original variables. In addition, and considering that in the factor analysis literature attention has been given to the issue of sample size, it is important to remark that our sample ($N = 590$) is good enough. Taking into account the recommendations given by Mundfrom et al. [57] even under the worst imaginable conditions of low communities and a larger number of weakly determined factors, the very large required sample is over 500.

In this research, a factor analysis is used as a method for grouping the proposed variables related to ISR according to a similar correlation pattern in order to discover the main factors for this construct. An exploratory principal components factor analysis has allowed us to check the factorial composition and validity. Thus, the initial 18-item instrument is performed to determine the structure of ISR. In our analysis, the value of the Kaiser–Meyer–Olkin measure of sampling adequacy (KMO = 0.873) and the Bartlett sphericity test showed the existence of good correlations between the variables, so that we could continue with the factorial analysis. The principal components factor analysis with varimax rotation has produced five factors (Table 3).

We can observe how the eigenvalues and explained variance decline following the extraction of the first factor. The factors extracted explained 61% of the total variance. To validate the exploratory factor analysis, we took two random sub-samples. The validity of the factor analysis was confirmed since the communities of the sub-samples were found to be similar in value to those of the initial sample, the total explained variance was also similar, and the factor loadings after varimax rotation were also close to the initial sample. While the values of Cronbach's alpha is always lie between 0 and 1, the values calculated are all well in excess of the generally accepted rule-of-thumb lower limit of 0.60 to be acceptable [58]. Cronbach's alpha are good for the first three factors ($\alpha_1 = 0.813$; $\alpha_2 = 0.735$; $\alpha_3 = 0.711$) and acceptable for the others ($\alpha_4 = 0.64$; $\alpha_5 = 0.67$). This result is good enough because Cronbach's alpha has a positive relationship with the number of items in the scale and the questionnaire contained only 18 items. The magnitude of the alpha values obtained is an evidence for the internal consistency of the items forming the scales.

Table 3. Factor analysis.

Items	Factor 1	Factor 2	Factor 3	Factor 4	Factor 5
INTR10	0.754	0.106	0.137	0.105	0.122
INTR14	0.747	−0.010	0.248	0.081	0.171
INTR11	0.737	0.031	0.145	0.206	0.103
INTR9	0.659	0.153	0.100	0.136	−0.014
INTR8	0.656	0.276	0.031	0.278	0.074
INTR7	0.433	0.315	0.014	0.244	0.113
INTR18	0.059	0.785	0.126	0.045	0.049
INTR17	0.179	0.729	0.262	0.005	0.163
INTR16	0.160	0.708	0.230	0.176	0.003
INTR13	0.115	0.144	0835	0.086	0.015
INTR12	0.107	0.199	0.775	0.111	0.101
INTR15	0.266	0.231	0.599	0.052	−0.008
INTR4	0.128	0.048	0.104	0.798	0.087
INTR5	0.288	−0.031	0.136	0.708	0.085
INTR6	0.225	0.263	0.016	0.622	0.032
INTR1	0.068	0.122	0.093	0.018	0.836
INTR2	0.158	0.044	0.103	0.103	0.835
INTR3	0.461	0.052	0.042	0.362	0.483
% of standard deviation	31.133	10.315	7.640	6.228	5.687
Accumulated %	31.133	41.448	49.088	55.316	61.003

Notes: Determinant of the correlation matrix = 0.003; Kaiser-Meyer-Olkin Index = 0.873; Barlett Test (Chi-squared; sf) = 4335 (153); Signification level = 0.000. *Source:* Own work.

Another aspect of construct validity is the ability of factors to reflect the theoretical dimensions or those argued by academic literature accurately. The individual factors contributing to the ISR model and their theoretical explanation are the following:

- Factor one—*Responsible HR (RHR)* (31.1% of explained variance): This factor can be described and interpreted as representing the responsiveness of HRM policies in respect to employees' needs and wants. This first factor is aligned with previous work in Internal Marketing [17,59] where employees are considered clients, internal clients, and a very important stakeholder to attend. Job creation, training, conciliation and equal opportunities and dynamic mechanisms of employees' participation in management decisions fostering dialogue form part of this composite factor.
- Factor two—*Responsible Organizational Culture (ROC)* (10.3% of explained variance): Internalization of SR principles and values into the vision and strategy of the business, relationship with associations promoting SR, and the effort to communicate SR aspects to employees internally form the essential elements of a culture of responsibility and form this second factor in the analysis.

In this respect, some authors have highlighted the importance of the culture of responsibility as the first step to become a responsible business [17,60].

- Factor three—*HR and Social Issues (HRSI)* (7.6% of explained variance): This factor can be best described as representing the link between internal HRM practices and the external side of SR in their relationship with the community in any effort for attending social issues. Being aware of problems in society including pension plans for retirement and fostering corporate volunteering are included in this factor and theoretically defended before in the same context [49] and previously in others [61,62].
- Factor four—*Responsible Compensation (RC)* (6.2% of explained variance): Aligned to previous studies [63,64], going beyond the legal minimum and beyond the average in the sector in human resources tools such as wages, health and safety and linking employees' compensation to their performance, form the essential elements of this factor.
- Factor five—*Employees Quality of Life (EQL)* (5.6% of explained variance): The essential element of this final factor forming ISR, also previously analyzed [29], is the aim to improve employees' quality of life including the disabled and people in risk of social exclusion.

These five factors were perceived as ISR dimensions for the purposes of our study, and their compatibility with the following step in this research is indicative of the validity of the study. In addition, the requirement of discriminant validity to demonstrate that any indicator should correlate more highly with another construct than with the construct it intends to measure [65] is also satisfactory in all factors in the analysis. Once the five dimensions have been found and described, the path analysis to test the relationship between ISR and competitive success is carried out in the following session.

2.4. Path Analysis

Structural equations modeling (SEM) has been used, considering it is very suitable for our research interests, because the construct under study, ISR, is relatively new and the theoretical model and their measures are not well formed [66]. According to literature review, when companies are involved in SR activities, the internal dimension determines relations with their internal stakeholders, especially their employees, and higher competitive success could be expected. Business performance and innovation have also been considered in the developed structural model. The relationship between performance and competitive success has been noted in business strategy fieldwork by Porter [67,68]) and other authors [69,70], and previous work has demonstrated the mediation role of innovation between SR and competitive success [32]. Innovation that is intrinsically about identifying and using opportunities to create new products, services, or work practices [71] is also identified in the model as a mediator variable when considering ISR because it is theoretically and widely accepted that improvements to HRM have a positive impact on innovation [72,73]. According to Cano and Cano [74], certain HR practices such as goal recognition or reward for achievement, have a positive effect on innovation performance in the company. In fact, these HR improvements promote the ability to innovate because they first improve the ability to deal with complexity [75]. In addition, academic literature on HRM has demonstrated how better HR practices are also linked to firm performance [76]. Finally, the link of these previous variables to competitive success is the soul of the *Resource-Based Theory* of the firm [5,6] previously exposed. The focus of management on sustainable HRM is the key to enhance employee commitment and satisfaction, which, in turn, increases the service innovation and performance, and will ultimately generate better overall competitive success [77]. The model shown in Figure 1 includes four related latent variables that make up the proposed relationships defined in the following hypotheses.

> *Hypothesis 1*—There is a direct and positive relationship between the ISR and business performance.
> *Hypothesis 2*—There is a direct and positive relationship between business performance and competitive success.
> *Hypothesis 3*—There is a direct and positive relationship between the ISR and innovation.
> *Hypothesis 4*—There is a direct and positive relationship between innovation and competitive success.

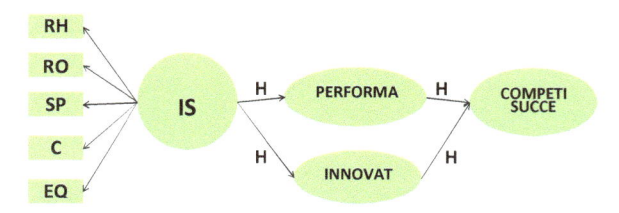

Figure 1. The structural model. Source: own work.

To measure ISR, we have considered the five dimensions found in the previous factor analysis (with the sort names RHR, ROC, HRSI, RC and EQL). Consequently, ISR has been defined as a second order construct. Indicators for each dependent variable are shown in Table 4.

Table 4. Original Indicators for performance, innovation and competitive success.

	Indicators for Performance (PER), Innovation (INV) and Competitive Success (COM)
PER1	Level of before-tax profits
PER2	Level of profitability
PER3	Increase in sales
PER4	Profit margin
PER5	Market share for our products and/or services
PER6	Level of customer satisfaction and loyalty
PER7	Satisfaction and retention of the best employees
PER8	Market positioning, image, and reputation
INV1	We try to carry out R&D projects
INV2	We have put new products or services on the market
INV3	We have introduced new practices to foster entry into new national markets
INV4	We have introduced new practices to foster entry into new international markets
INV5	We are aware of the importance of working as a network, and we have created new alliances or associations
INV6	We have put into place improvements in our production and/or distribution process or techniques
INV7	We have intensified our information and communication technologies
INV8	We have increased our presence on the Internet
INV9	We have initiated changes in the marketing area (design, packaging, prices, ...)
INV10	Our firm has introduced new methods with a view to satisfying the norms of certification
INV11	We have implemented internal or external employee training in order to improve knowledge and creativity within the firm
INV12	We have implemented new managerial practices related to the organization of work and the corporate structure
INV13	We have introduced standards of production or customer management that take social and environmental aspects into account
COM1	Quality in our human resource management
COM2	The levels of training and empowerment of our personnel
COM3	The leadership capabilities of our managers
COM4	Our capabilities in the field of marketing
COM5	Quality of our products and services
COM6	The levels of organizational and administrative management quality
COM7	Technological resources and information systems
COM8	Transparency of our financial management
COM9	The cohesion of our corporate values and culture
COM10	Market knowledge, know-how, and accumulated experience

Source: Own work.

To measure performance, innovation and competitive success, we have considered scales previously used by Gallardo-Vázquez and Sánchez-Hernández [32]. Performance is considered a reflective construct with eight indicators (from PER1 to PER8) as well as innovation with thirteen indicators (from INV1 to INV13) and competitive success with ten indicators (from COM1 to COM10). At this point, it is important to distinguish performance from competitive success in the model. Performance considers firm results going beyond short-term financial performance and pursuing sustainable development. Instead, competitive success considers aspects of competition. Firms have competitive success when they are able to attain favorable positions in the market and obtain superior results, while avoiding the need to have recourse to an extremely poor retribution of the factors of production. Consequently, competitive success implies getting better positions than your competitors because of "something more" than performance.

For the measurement of performance, this construct was taken to be multi-dimensional in accordance with the literature and basing the dimensions considered on a combination of the contribution of Wiklund and Shepherd [78] with that of Pelham and Wilson [79] to include growth in market share and sales. In addition, we consider a very broad conception of innovation. The construct is conceived as the adoption of new idea or practice capable of leading to new products or services [80] to enter new markets [81] or to the generation of new organizational or administrative processes [82].

With respect to the last dependent variable in the model, a firm was taken to have competitive success when it is able to attain a favorable position in the market and obtain superior results, while avoiding the need to have recourse to an extremely poor retribution of the factors of production. To measure competitive success, we used indicators previously considered in academic literature [83,84].

Once the model and related constructs have been described, the first statistical step was to analyze whether the theoretical concepts where properly measured by the observed indicators. This analysis was carried out for the two attributes *validity* (measuring what one really wanted to measure) and *reliability* (whether the process is stable and consistent). To this end, we calculate the individual item reliability, the internal consistency or reliability of the scales, the average variances extracted (AVE), and the discriminant validity. Results are shown in Table 5.

Table 5. Results from the measurement model.

Constructs	Reliable Indicators	Loadings (λ)	AVE	Crombach's Alpha	Composite Reliability
ISR	RHR	0.671	0.5167	0.6943	0.8097
	ROC	0.728			
	RC	0.671			
	EQL	0.675			
Performance	D6	0.892	0.7514	0.8327	0.9004
	D7	0.906			
	D8	0.798			
Innovation	INV5	0.717	0.5336	0.8747	0.9012
	INV6	0.678			
	INV7	0.768			
	INV8	0.698			
	INV9	0.721			
	INV11	0.772			
	INV12	0.785			
	INV13	0.695			

Table 5. Cont.

Constructs	Reliable Indicators	Loadings (λ)	AVE	Crombach's Alpha	Composite Reliability
Competitive Success	COM1	0.761	0.5768	0.8530	0.8909
	COM2	0.784			
	COM3	0.768			
	COM5	0.800			
	COM6	0.744			
	COM8	0.708			

Source: Own work.

The most remarkable result in this step is the confirmation of four of the five dimensions found in ISR. The dimension linking HRM and Social Issues, factor three, has been removed from the model, as we have kept only factor loadings greater than 0.67 on ISR construct, which implies more shared variance between ISR and its four items than error variance [85].

The second step of the analysis of the structural model consisted of the estimation of the assumed linear relationships among exogenous and endogenous latent constructs. The correlations among study variables are shown in Table 6. Correlations indicate that the managers' perceptions regarding the ISR of their company were positively related to competitive success, innovation and performance, providing preliminary support for hypotheses.

Table 6. Inter-correlations matrix.

Variable	1	2	3	4
1. ISR	1			
2. Innovation	0.505	1		
3. Performance	0.242	0.161	1	
4. Competitive Success	0.394	0.312	0.575	1

Source: Own work.

The hypotheses have been tested by examining the magnitude of the standardized parameters estimated between constructs with the corresponding t-values that indicate the level of significance. We employ the bootstrap routine [66], a non-parametric re-sampling technique that offers the t-statistic values. All hypotheses were verified as it is shown in Table 7.

Table 7. Hypotheses testing.

HYPOTHESIS/Structural Relation A → B	Original Path Coefficients (β)	Mean of Sub-Sample Path Coefficients	Standard Error	t-Value
H_1: ISR →Performance	0.2425	0.2453	0.0729	3.32 ***
H_2: Performance → Competitive Success	0.5394	0.5504	0.0530	10.17 ***
H_3: ISR →Innovation	0.5054	0.5133	0.0550	9.16 ***
H_4: Innovation → Competitive Success	0.2249	0.2242	0.0542	4.14 ***

Source: Own work.

Finally, to measure the relevance of the dependent construct's prediction, PLS (Partial Least Squares) uses the Q^2 index from Stone–Geisser as a criterion, which is calculated based on the redundancies that result from the product of communities (λ^2) with the AVE indicator and is also cross-validated. According to Chin [86], the Stone–Geisser criterion Q^2 values have been obtained from running a blindfolding procedure and range above the threshold level of zero (0.48 for performance; 0.40 for innovation; 0.45 for competitive success), indicating that the exogenous constructs have predictive relevance for the endogenous construct under consideration.

3. Results and Discussion

While acknowledging that the regional context of the study puts limits on the generalization of our findings, we nonetheless see a number of interesting conclusions. The main contribution of the article is the establishment of a set of indicators that define ISR as a result of a dynamic process that provides information about a firm's actions in responsible HRM. This article argues in favor of a stronger focus upon the management of ISR policies and practices in enterprises. Our results show the main factors determining the ISR structure as they have been perceived by a big sample of services business managers in the region under study. The obtained empirical evidence is a contribution to the SR research where there is a lack in studies devoted to the internal side. Therefore, this study contributes to the generation of knowledge on internal responsible behavior of companies. As demonstrated, ISR in service business, which is more influenced by human resources practices, is defined by five well-delimited dimensions such as: responsible human resources practices; organizational culture of responsibility; social projects promotion; significant compensation policies and employee quality of life. A point of interest that needs to be highlighted is the important role that HRM could play in the SR strategy of any business, an aspect that has been analyzed with the developed structural equation model.

It has been demonstrated empirically that ISR has an effect on increasing the firm's competitiveness. The conceptual model has been tested empirically confirming the four hypotheses H_1, H_2, H_3 and H_4. Consequently, the model has been validated where innovation and performance have the role of mediator variables between ISR and competitive success in accordance with previous work in general SR [23,32], where ISR was not isolated from the holistic construct of firm responsibility.

4. Conclusions

Although an abundance of research exists on the general topic of SR, little has been run toward identifying, or perhaps more importantly, measuring its internal aspects in business services. This investigation provides ample foundation for further research on this topic and contributes to a better appreciation and understanding of the role of responsible HRM practices.

To conclude, it should be noted that results from the analysis should be interpreted for SMEs, overcoming the limitations coming from the regional context of study and also from the selection of the sample limited to the service sector, and limited to a single Spanish Autonomous Community. Consequently, our results are not directly extrapolated to other environments that differed greatly in their defining variables. However, since the predominance of business services and the predominance of SMEs are characteristic for the whole Spanish territory, and even the whole European Union, we can accept the results satisfactorily. We believe that our study represents a substantial contribution to the knowledge of ISR, but, in the near future, qualitative and quantitative research should be done on the topic. Managers have to be aware that one of the most important stakeholders the company has is the employee. Employees have to be considered an internal client [59,87] and, consequently, SR should start inside the company. In fact, we question whether there is sufficient focus upon investment in employees, which could be regarded as an important driver of external SR practice [88].

Some suggestions for a research agenda emerge from this attempt to approach the internal side of responsibility in business. First, new studies in the same direction but in other sectors and regions have to be addressed, and second, and related to SR and internal management, we suggest an analysis of the theoretical and hypothetical relationship between the internal and the external side of SR in order to determine the direct effect in external SR fostered by responsible HR policies internally. In line with other authors [59,89], we remark on the importance of internal marketing as a way to sell the responsible company culture internally to employees to somehow help external SR to develop at the same time that companies improve their competitive success. The more important the concept and practice of ISR becomes, the more likely the companies will improve their competitive advantage. It should be taken as an important opportunity for the responsible reinvention of management.

In conclusion, ISR and HRM are interrelated concepts influencing the business competitive success, and their effectiveness depends on responsible practices inside the spheres of the company.

Acknowledgments: Acknowledgments: The authors are grateful to all the managers in business services who participated in the survey and contributed to the paper.

Author Contributions: Author Contributions: M. Isabel Sánchez-Hernandez designed the research, analyzed the data and wrote the manuscript, Dolores Gallardo-Vázquez collected data and performed research, Agnieszka Barcik analyzed the data and revised the research and paper, and Piotr Dziwiński analyzed the data, revised the research and corrected the final version of manuscript.

Conflicts of Interest: Conflicts of Interest: The authors declare no conflict of interest.

References

1. Peneder, M.; Kaniovski, S.; Dachs, B. What follows tertiarisation? Structural change and the role of knowledge-based services. *Serv. Ind. J.* **2003**, *23*, 47–66. [CrossRef]
2. Ehret, M.; Wirtz, J. Division of labor between firms: Business services, non-ownership-value and the rise of the service economy. *Serv. Sci.* **2010**, *2*, 136–145. [CrossRef]
3. Buera, F.J.; Kaboski, J.P. Scale and the origins of structural change. *J. Econ. Theory* **2012**, *147*, 684–712. [CrossRef]
4. Freeman, R.E. *Strategic Management: A Stakeholder Approach*, 1st ed.; Harpercollins College Div., Pitman Series: Marshfield, MA, USA, 1994.
5. Donaldson, T.; Preston, L. The Stakeholder Theory of the Corporation: Concepts, Evidence, and Implications. *Acad. Manag. Rev.* **1995**, *1*, 65–91.
6. Freeman, R.E.; Harrison, J.E.; Wicks, A.C. *Managing for Stakeholders: Survival, Reputation, and Success*; Yale University Press: New Haven, CT, USA, 2007.
7. Kaler, J. Evaluating stakeholder theory. *J. Bus. Eth.* **2006**, *69*, 249–268. [CrossRef]
8. Berrone, P.; Surroca, J.; Tribo, J.A. Corporate ethical identity as a determinant of firm performance: A test of the mediating role of stakeholder satisfaction. *J. Bus. Eth.* **2007**, *76*, 35–53. [CrossRef]
9. Verbeke, A.; Tung, V. The Future of Stakeholder Management Theory: A Temporal Perspective. *J. Bus. Eth.* **2013**, *112*, 529–543. [CrossRef]
10. Mason, C.; Simmons, J. Embedding Corporate Social Responsibility in Corporate Governance: A Stakeholder Systems Approach. *J. Bus. Eth.* **2013**, *119*, 77–86. [CrossRef]
11. Mont, O.; Leire, C. Socially responsible purchasing in supply chains: Drivers and barriers in Sweden. *Soc. Responsib. J.* **2009**, *5*, 389–407. [CrossRef]
12. Barcik, A.; Dziwiński, P. Relations with employees in CSR strategies at Polish enterprises with regard to compliance mechanism. *Responsib. Sustain.* **2015**, *3*, 13–26.
13. Ferrell, O.C.; Fraedrich, J.; Ferrell, L. *Business Ethics: Ethical Decision Making and Cases*; Houghton Mifflin: Boston, MA, USA, 2008.
14. Matten, D.; Moon, M. "Implicit" and "explicit" CSR: A conceptual framework for a comparative understanding of Corporate Social Responsibility. *Acad. Manag. Rev.* **2008**, *33*, 404–424. [CrossRef]
15. Commission of the European Communities, COM. Communication from the Commission to the European Parliament, the Council, the European Economic and Social Committee and the Committee of the Regions. Available online: http://eur-lex.europa.eu/legal-content/EN/TXT/?uri=CELEX%3A52011DC0681 (accessed on 17 February 2016).
16. Schoemaker, M.; Nijhof, A.; Jonker, J. Human value management. The influence of the contemporary developments of corporate social responsibility and social capital on HRM. *Manag. Rev.* **2006**, *17*, 448–465.
17. Sánchez-Hernández, M.I.; Grayson, D. Internal marketing for engaging employees on the corporate responsibility journey. *Intang. Cap.* **2012**, *8*, 275–307. [CrossRef]
18. Barney, J. Firm resources and sustained competitive advantage. *J. Manag.* **1991**, *17*, 99–120. [CrossRef]
19. Acedo, F.J.; Barroso, C.; Galán, J.L. The resource-based theory: Dissemination and main trends. *Strateg. Manag. J.* **2006**, *27*, 621–636. [CrossRef]
20. Crook, T.R.; Todd, S.Y.; Combs, J.G.; Woehr, D.J.; Ketchen, D.J., Jr. Does human capital matter? A meta-analysis of the relationship between human capital and firm performance. *J. Appl. Psychol.* **2011**, *96*, 443–456. [CrossRef] [PubMed]

21. Porter, M.E.; Kramer, M.R. The link between competitive advantage and corporate social responsibility. *Harv. Bus. Rev.* **2006**, *84*, 78–92. [PubMed]
22. Varey, R.J. Internal marketing: A review and some interdisciplinary research challenges. *Int. J. Serv. Ind. Manag.* **1995**, *6*, 40–63. [CrossRef]
23. Gallardo-Vázquez, D.; Sánchez-Hernández, M.I. Measuring Corporate Social Responsibility for competitive success at a regional level. *J. Clean. Prod.* **2014**, *72*, 14–22. [CrossRef]
24. Carroll, A. A three-dimensional conceptual model of corporate performance. *Acad. Manag. Rev.* **1979**, *4*, 497–505.
25. Aupperle, K.; Carroll, A.B.; Hatfield, J. An empirical examination of the relationship between corporate social responsibility and profitability. *Acad. Manag. J.* **1985**, *28*, 446–463. [CrossRef]
26. Wood, D.J.; Jones, R.E. Stakeholder mismatching: A theoretical problem in empirical research on corporate social performance. *Int. J. Organ. Anal.* **1995**, *3*, 229–267. [CrossRef]
27. Quazi, A.M.; O'Brien, D. An empirical test of a cross-national model of corporate social responsibility. *J. Bus. Eth.* **2000**, *25*, 33–51. [CrossRef]
28. Maignan, I.; Ferrell, O.C. Measuring Corporate Citizenship in Two Countries: The Case of the United States and France. *J. Bus. Eth.* **2000**, *23*, 283–297. [CrossRef]
29. Sánchez-Hernández, M.I.; García-Míguelez, M.P. Improving Employees Quality of Life. In *Best Practices in Marketing and Their Impact on Quality of Life*; Alves, H., Vázquez, J.L., Eds.; Springer Dordrecht Heidelberg: New York, NY, USA; London, UK, 2013; pp. 241–254.
30. Zinn, J.O. Introduction: Risk, social inclusion and the life course. *Soc. Policy Soc.* **2013**, *12*, 253–264. [CrossRef]
31. Hayman, L.W.; McIntyre, R.B.; Abbey, A. The bad taste of social ostracism: The effects of exclusion on the eating behaviors of African-American women. *Psychol. Health* **2014**, *3*, 1–16. [CrossRef] [PubMed]
32. Gallardo-Vázquez, D.; Sánchez-Hernández, M.I. *Corporate Social Responsibility in Extremadura*; Fundación Obra Social La Caixa: Badajoz, Spain, 2012. (In Spanish)
33. Bruyére, S.; Filiberto, D. The green economy and job creation: Inclusion of people with disabilities in the USA. *Int. J. Green Econ.* **2013**, *7*, 257–275. [CrossRef]
34. Kulkarni, M.; Rodrigues, C. Engagerment with disability: Analysis of annual reports of Indian organizations. *Int. J. Human Resour. Manag.* **2014**, *25*, 1547–1566. [CrossRef]
35. Cullinane, S.J.; Bosak, J.; Flood, P.C.; Demerouti, E. Job design under lean manufacturing and the quality of working life: A job demands and resources perspective. *Int. J. Human Resour. Manag.* **2014**, *25*, 2996–3015. [CrossRef]
36. Amstrong, M. Amstrong's Handbook of Reward Management Practice. In *Improving Performance through Reward*, 4th ed.; Kogan Page: London, UK, 2012.
37. Esping-Andersen, G. *The Three Worlds of Welfare Capitalism*; John Wiley & Sons: Chichester, UK, 2013.
38. Cohen, E. *CSR for HR: A Necessary Partnership for Advancing Responsible Business Practices*; Greenleaf Publishing Limited: Sheffield, UK, 2010.
39. Long, C.S.; Perumal, P. Examining the impact of human resource management practices on employees' turnover intention. *Int. J. Bus. Soc.* **2014**, *15*, 111–126.
40. Lozano, R.; Huisingh, D. Inter-linking issues and dimensions in sustainability reporting. *J. Clean. Prod.* **2011**, *19*, 99–107. [CrossRef]
41. Bischoff, C.; Wood, G. Micro and small enterprises and employment creation: A case study of manufacturing micro and small enterprises in South Africa. *Dev. South. Afr.* **2013**, *30*, 564–579. [CrossRef]
42. Turker, D. Measuring Corporate Social Responsibility: A Scale Development Study. *J. Bus. Eth.* **2009**, *85*, 411–427. [CrossRef]
43. Vázquez-Carrasco, R.; López-Pérez, M.E.; Centeno, E. A qualitative approach to the challengues for women in management: Are they really starting in the 21st century? *Qual. Quant.* **2012**, *46*, 1337–1357. [CrossRef]
44. Tato-Jiménez, J.L.; Bañegil-Palacios, T.M. Effects of formal and informal practices of reconciling work and life on the performance of Spanish listed companies. *Res. J. Bus. Manag.* **2015**, *9*, 391–403. [CrossRef]
45. Agudo-Valiente, J.M.; Garcés-Ayerbe, C.; Salvador-Figueras, M. Social responsibility practices and evaluation of corporate social performance. *J. Cleaner Prod.* **2012**, *35*, 25–38. [CrossRef]
46. Pérez, A.; Martínez, P. Rodríguez del Bosque, I. The development of a stakeholder-based scale for measuring corporate social responsibility in the banking industry. *Serv. Bus.* **2012**, *7*, 459–481. [CrossRef]

47. Lu, R.X.A.; Lee, P.K.C.; Cheng, T.C. Socially responsible supplier development: Construct development and measurement validation. *Int. J. Prod. Econ.* **2012**, *140*, 160–167. [CrossRef]
48. Hillman, A.J.; Keim, G.D. Shareholder value, stakeholder management, and social issues: What's the bottom line? *Strateg. Manag. J.* **2001**, *22*, 125–139. [CrossRef]
49. Sanchez-Hernandez, M.I.; Gallardo-Vázquez, D. Approaching corporate volunteering in Spain. *Corpor. Gov.* **2013**, *13*, 397–411. [CrossRef]
50. Knutsen, W.L.; Chan, Y. The Phenomenon of Staff Volunteering: How Far Can You Stretch the Psychological Contract in a Nonprofit Organization? *VOLUNTAS Int. J. Volunt. Nonprofit Organ.* **2015**, *26*, 1–22. [CrossRef]
51. Preuss, L.; Haunschild, A.; Matten, D. The rise of CSR: Implications for HRM and employee representation. *Int. J. Hum. Resour. Manag.* **2009**, *20*, 953–973. [CrossRef]
52. Cetindamar, D. Corporate social responsibility practices and environmentally responsible behavior: The case of the United Nations Global Compact. *J. Bus. Eth.* **2007**, *76*, 163–176. [CrossRef]
53. Legge, K. Human Resource Management: Rhetorics and Realities. MacMillan Press: London, UK, 1995.
54. Gallardo-Vázquez, D.; Sánchez-Hernández, M.I. Structural analysis of the strategic orientation to environmental protection in SME's. *BQR—Bus. Res. Q.* **2014**, *17*, 115–128. [CrossRef]
55. Cudeck, R. Exploratory Factor Analysis. In *Handbook of Applied Multivariate Statistics and Mathematical Modeling*; Tinsley, H., Brown, S., Eds.; Academic Press: San Diego, CA, USA, 2000; pp. 265–296.
56. Jolliffe, I. *Principal Component Analysis*; John Wiley & Sons: Chichester, UK, 2005.
57. Mundfrom, D.J.; Shaw, D.G.; Ke, T.L. Minimum sample size recommendations for conducting factor analyses. *Int. J. Test.* **2005**, *5*, 159–168. [CrossRef]
58. Nunnally, J.C.; Bernstein, I.H. *Psychometric Theory*, 3rd ed.; McGraw Hill: New York, NY, USA, 1994.
59. Sánchez-Hernández, M.I.; Miranda, F.J. Linking internal market orientation and new service performance. *Eur. J. Innov. Manag.* **2011**, *14*, 207–226. [CrossRef]
60. Pohl, M. Corporate Culture and CSR-How They Interrelate and Consequences for Successful Implementation. In *The ICCA Handbook on Corporate Social Responsibility*; Hennigfeld, J., Pohl, M., Tolhurst, N., Eds.; John Wiley & Sons: Chichester, UK, 2006.
61. Muthuri, J.N.; Matten, D.; Moon, J. Employee volunteering and social capital: Contributions to corporate social responsibility. *Br. J. Manag.* **2009**, *20*, 75–89. [CrossRef]
62. Kim, H.R.; Lee, M.; Lee, H.T.; Kim, N.M. Corporate social responsibility and employee–company identification. *J. Bus. Eth.* **2010**, *95*, 557–569. [CrossRef]
63. Mahoney, L.S.; Thorne, L. Corporate social responsibility and long-term compensation: Evidence from Canada. *J. Bus. Eth.* **2005**, *57*, 241–253. [CrossRef]
64. Collier, J.; Esteban, R. Corporate social responsibility and employee commitment. *Bus. Eth. A Eur. Rev.* **2007**, *16*, 19–33. [CrossRef]
65. Barclay, D.; Higgins, C.; Thompson, R. The partial least squares (PLS) approach to causal modeling: Personal computer adoption and use as an illustration. *Technol. Stud.* **1995**, *2*, 285–309.
66. Chin, W. Issues and Opinion on Structural Equation Modelling. *MIS Q.* **1998**, *2*, vii–xv.
67. Porter, M.E. *Competitive Strategy: Techniques for Analyzing Industries and Competitors*; The Free Press: New York, NY, USA, 1980.
68. Porter, M.E. Towards a dynamic theory of strategy. *Strateg. Manag. J.* **1991**, *12*, 95–117. [CrossRef]
69. Spanos, Y.E.; Lioukas, S. An Examination into the Causal Logic of Rent Generation: Contrasting Porter's Competitive Strategy Framework and the Resource Based Perspective. *Strateg. Manag. J.* **2001**, *22*, 907–934. [CrossRef]
70. Wagner, M.; Schaltegger, S. Introduction: How Does Sustainability Performance Relate to Business Competitiveness? *Greener Manag. Int.* **2003**, *44*, 5–16. [CrossRef]
71. Van de Ven, A.H. Central problems in the management of innovation. *Manag. Sci.* **1986**, *32*, 590–660. [CrossRef]
72. Sánchez-Hernández, M.I.; Gallardo-Vazquez, D.; Dziwiński, P.; Barcik, A. Innovation through corporate social responsibility—Insights from Spain and Poland. In *Handbook of Research on Internationalization of Entrepreneurial Innovation in the Global Economy*; IGI Global: Hershey, PA, USA, 2015; pp. 313–328.
73. Subramaniam, M.; Youndt, M.A. The influence of intellectual capital on the types of innovative capabilities. *Acad. Manag. J.* **2005**, *48*, 450–463. [CrossRef]

74. Cano, C.P.; Cano, P.Q. Human resources management and its impact on innovation performance in companies. *Int. J. Technol. Manag.* **2006**, *35*, 11–28. [CrossRef]
75. Lund Vinding, A. Absorptive capacity and innovative performance: A human capital approach. *Econ. Innov. New Technol.* **2006**, *15*, 507–517. [CrossRef]
76. Mavondo, F.T.; Chimhanzi, J.; Stewart, J. Learning orientation and market orientation: Relationship with innovation, human resource practices and performance. *Eur. J. Mark.* **2005**, *39*, 1235–1263. [CrossRef]
77. Little, M.M.; Dean, A.M. Links between service climate, employee commitment and employees' service quality capability. *Manag. Serv. Qual. Int. J.* **2006**, *16*, 460–476. [CrossRef]
78. Wiklund, J.; Shepperd, D. Knowledge-based resources, entrepreneurial orientation and the performance of small and medium-sized businesses. *Strateg. Manag. J.* **2003**, *24*, 1307–1314. [CrossRef]
79. Pelham, A.; Wilson, D. A longitudinal study of the impact of market structure, firm structure, strategy, and market orientation culture on dimensions of small-firm performance. *Am. Mark. Assoc.* **1996**, *24*, 27–43. [CrossRef]
80. Yalcinkaya, G.; Calantone, R.J.; Griffith, D.A. An examination of exploration and exploitation capabilities: Implications for product innovation and market performance. *J. Int. Mark.* **2007**, *15*, 63–93. [CrossRef]
81. Medrano-Sáez, N.; Olarte-Pascual, M.C. Marketing Innovation as an Opportunity in a Situation of Uncertainty: The Spanish Case, 327–341. In *Soft Computing in Management and Business Economics*; Springer: Berlin Heidelberg, Germany, 2012.
82. Carmona-Lavado, A.; Cuevas-Rodríguez, G.; Cabello-Medina, C. Social and organizational capital: Building the context for innovation. *Ind. Mark. Manag.* **2010**, *39*, 681–690. [CrossRef]
83. Hughes, M.; Ireland, R.D.; Morgan, R.E. Stimulating dynamic value: Social capital and business incubation as a pathway to competitive success. *Long Range Plan.* **2007**, *40*, 154–177. [CrossRef]
84. Abraham, S.C. *Strategic Planning: A Practical Guide for Competitive Success*; Emerald Group Publishing: Bingley, UK, 2012.
85. Carmines, E.G.; Richard, A.Z. *Reliability and Validity Assessment*; Sage Publications: Beverly Hills, CA, USA, 1979.
86. Chin, W.W. Issues and opinion on structural equation modeling. *MIS Q.* **1988**, *22*, vii–xvi.
87. Ahmed, P.K.; Rafiq, M. *Internal Marketing—Tools and Concepts for Customer-Focused Management*; Butterworth-Heinemann Publications: Oxford, UK, 2002.
88. Bansal, H.S.; Mendelson, M.B.; Sharma, B. The impact of internal marketing activities on external marketing outcomes. *J. Qual. Manag.* **2001**, *6*, 61–76. [CrossRef]
89. Ariza-Montes, J.A.; Muniz, R.N.M.; Leal-Rodríguez, A.L.; Leal-Millán, A.G. Workplace bullying among managers: A multifactorial perspective and understanding. *Int. J. Environ. Res. Public Health* **2014**, *11*, 2657–2682. [CrossRef] [PubMed]

© 2016 by the authors. Licensee MDPI, Basel, Switzerland. This article is an open access article distributed under the terms and conditions of the Creative Commons Attribution (CC BY) license (http://creativecommons.org/licenses/by/4.0/).

Article

Automobile Industry Strategic Alliance Partner Selection: The Application of a Hybrid DEA and Grey Theory Model

Chia-Nan Wang [1], Xuan-Tho Nguyen [1,*] and Yen-Hui Wang [2]

1. Department of Industrial Engineering and Management, National Kaohsiung University of Applied Sciences, No. 415 Chien Kung Road, Sanmin District, Kaohsiung City 80778, Taiwan; cn.wang@cc.kuas.edu.tw
2. Department of Information Management, Chihlee University of Technology, New Taipei City 22050, Taiwan; ttxyhw@mail.chihlee.edu.tw
* Correspondence: nguyenhanam188@gmail.com; Tel.: +886-970-456-070

Academic Editor: Adam Jabłoński
Received: 21 December 2015; Accepted: 6 February 2016; Published: 17 February 2016

Abstract: Finding the right strategic alliance partner is a critical success factor for many enterprises. Therefore, the purpose of this study is to propose an effective approach based on grey theory and data envelopment analysis (DEA) for selecting better partners for alliance. This study used grey forecasting to predict future business performances and used DEA for the partner selection of alliances. This research was implemented with realistic public data in four consecutive financial years (2009–2012) of the world's 20 biggest automobile enterprises. Nissan Motor Co., Ltd was set to be the target decision making unit (DMU). The empirical results showed that, among 19 candidate DMUs, Renault (DMU10) and Daimler (DMU11) were the two feasible beneficial alliance partners for Nissan. Although this research is specifically applied to the automobile industry, the proposed method could also be applied to other manufacturing industries.

Keywords: strategic alliance; data envelopment analysis; grey prediction; automobile industry

1. Introduction

The automobile industry is a pillar of the global economy and a main driver of macroeconomic growth and innovation. Its cycle intertwines with all major business cycles [1]. Since it has strong linkages with other parts of the economy, this industry has been severely affected by the economic recession starting in 2008. In spite of manufacturers trying various strategies, production is still below its pre-crisis level.

This research investigation began with the top 50 automobile enterprises, by using the World Ranking OICAs' survey of 2012 [2]. However, the study was obliged to focus on the top 20, due to a lack of public data. These enterprises played major roles and could fully represent the automobile industry. Among them, Nissan Motor Company was ranked sixth by production volume. Established in Japan in 1933, Nissan manufactures vehicles in 20 countries now. It also provides products and services in more than 160 countries. Figure 1 shows Nissan's global retail sales volume and market share. Except for 2008, the enterprise had increased its sale volume and market share year by year (3,569,000–5,650,000 units and 5.6%–6.7% from 2005 to 2014) [3].

Renault-Nissan Alliance chairman, Carlos Ghosn, said: "Renault-Nissan Alliance is deeply committed to the twin goals of zero emissions and zero fatalities. That's why we are developing autonomous driving and connectivity for mass-market, mainstream vehicles on three continents". This alliance will launch more than 10 vehicles with autonomous drive technology in the next four years in the US, Europe, Japan and China. The years 2016 and 2018 will mark the debut of vehicles with "single-lane control", and "multiple-lane control". The year 2020 will see the launch of "intersection autonomy", which can allow cars to navigate city intersections and heavy urban traffic without driver intervention. In addition, the alliance will launch a suite of new connectivity applications (APPs), including for mobile devices, and the first "alliance multimedia system" in later years. Renault-Nissan alliance is already the industry's zero-emission leader with 300,000 all-electric vehicles sold since December 2010. They have proven their ability to provide safe and efficient vehicles over time [4].

Figure 1. Global retail sales volume/market share.

However, the enterprise is faced with many difficulties, such as product recall (1.56 million vehicles from 2008 to 2015, with about 25 million vehicles recalled with Takata airbags among 10 different carmakers worldwide since 2008) [5]. Moreover, Nissan's 2013 annual report stated that they aimed to increase their global market share to 8% by the end of the fiscal year 2016, up from the current level of 6.2% [6]. The company is counting on expansion in big emerging markets such as Brazil, Russia, India and China (BRIC) to drive sales and profit growth.

The tight competition among automakers leads to the continuous improvement of science and technology, and especially their ability to meet the customer's wishes. Important questions are raised for the future of the automobile industry and Nissan. How will Nissan create value for the customers, societies and for Nissan itself in the pursuit of perfection? How will it maintain its competitiveness in fierce markets, expand its scale, produce high quality products while maintaining low-costs and protecting the environment? The purpose of this study is to propose an effective approach based on grey forecasting and data envelopment analysis (DEA) to find the best partners of alliance. The model predicts future business and measures operation efficiency by using critical input and output variables. From that, the enterprises can find their suitable candidates when setting international business strategies. For this purpose, this study sets Nissan as a target decision making unit (DMU) in order to conduct empirical research. The study's results can be referenced for worldwide automobile manufactures.

James *et al.* stated that "Alliances are fueling the success of a wide range of firms, including British Petroleum, Eli Lilly, General Electric, Corning Glass, Federal Express, IBM, Starbucks, Cisco Systems, Millennium Pharmaceuticals, and Siebel Systems" [7]. However, many enterprises have failed with alliances or have not met the conditions of their partner. In this section, the research helps to define strategic alliances and provides a literature review.

Mockler difined "Strategic alliances are agreements between companies (partners) to reach objectives of common interest" [8]. International strategic alliances (ISAs) are voluntary, long-term, contractual, cross-border relationships between two firms, designed to achieve specific objectives [9]. These definitions emphasize the importance of common business goals with the involved companies. Cravens *et al.*, distinguished strategic alliance as a horizontal collaborative relationship that does not include any kind of equity exchange or creation of a new entity as in joint ventures [10]. Chan *et al.* stated that: Strategic alliance is a cooperative agreement between different organizations. The purpose of action aims at achieving the competitive advantages and sharing resources in product design, production, marketing and/or distribution [11]. The types of alliances range from simple agreements with no equity ties to more formal arrangements involving equity ownership and shared managerial control over joint activities. The alliance activities can be supplier–buyer partnerships, outsourcing agreements, technical collaboration, joint research projects, shared new product development, shared manufacturing arrangements, common distribution agreements, and cross-selling arrangements. The type that should be applied depends on the structures or objectives of each enterprise.

Besides that, the alliance should conform to competition laws, with the world's largest and most influential anti-trust law systems existing in the United States and European Union. However, business cooperation could be seen as one kind of alliance as well. This research focuses on the selection of business partners, so anti-trust law issues are not major focus of this study.

Candace *et al.* had investigated 89 high technology alliances and suggested that direct-competitor alliances might be an inefficient means for innovating [12]. Cho *et al.* observed the trend of world telecommunication and sought to answer whether alliance strategies needed to be regulated by the government. By reviewing global alliance strategies in some countries, the research pointed towards some reasonable recommendations for regulation of telecommunication enterprises [13]. Kauser and Shaw investigated strategic alliance agreements among UK firms and their European, Japanese and US partners. The results indicated that the majority of UK firms engaged in international partnerships for marketing of relevant activities and for entering a foreign market. The findings had also indicated that the majority of UK managers were satisfied with the overall performance of their international strategic alliances [14]. Those papers had investigated alliances in various type of firms, however, the lack of focus on the automobile industry is one of the impetuses for this research.

Forecast time series have been used quite regularly by researchers. There are various forecasting models which have different mathematical backgrounds such as fuzzy predictors, neural networks, trend extrapolation, and grey prediction. Grey system theory as an interdisciplinary scientific area was first introduced in the early 1980s by Deng in 1982 [15].From then on, the theory has become a quite popular method to deal with the uncertainty problems under partially unknown parameters and poor or missing information. Superior to conventional statistical models, grey models claim only a limited amount of data to evaluate the action of unknown systems [16].

The techniques of frontier analysis had been described by Farrel in 1957 [17], but a mathematical framework to handle frontier analysis was established only after two decades. The DEA was introduced by Charnes *et al.* [18]. They proposed a "data oriented" approach for measuring the performance of multiple DMUs, by converting multiple input into multiple output. DMU could include manufacturing units, schools, universities, bank branches, hospitals, power plants, *etc*. Recently, there have been various DEA applications in private and public sectors of different countries.

Martín and Roman used DEA to analyze the technical efficiency and performance of each individual Spanish airport. They used the results to put forward some policy considerations in preparation for the process of privatization of the Spanish airport system [19]. Wang *et al.* applied data envelopment analysis and the heuristic technique approach to help department stores find the most proper partners for strategic alliances. The results indicated that candidate selection of strategic alliances could be an effective strategy for enterprises to find out the right partners for cooperation [20]. Wang *et al.* used Grey and DEA techniques to measure production and marketing efficiencies of 23 companies in the printing circuit board industry. The results showed that 15 companies require improvements in both production and marketing efficiency, while four companies had their production efficiency improved and the remaining four firms experienced both improvement in production and marketing efficiency [21]. Yuan and Tian applied the two-stage method of the DEA model to analyze the science and technology resources efficiency of industrial enterprises and its influencing factors. The results reflected the independence of the input element and the concentration of the output element [22].

For the above reasons, the integrating model of Grey and DEA in alliance decision making is a new effective approach in this research. The model predicts future business and measures operation efficiency by using critical input and output variables. From that, automobile manufacturers can find feasible candidates for alliance strategies.

2. Methodologies

2.1. Research Development

In this study, the researchers use GM(1,1) [16] and DEA models to construct a systematic forecast and assessment approach. Figure 2 provides an overview of how to combine GM and DEA through detailed steps. The study uses future data (prediction data by grey forecasting) as the inputs and outputs of DEA. Then, the DEA method is used to compare alliance combinations. The research uses GM(1,1) to develop a forecast approach through the use of time series data with four inputs and three outputs. The prediction results are continuously put in the DEA model to measure the efficiency of all DMUs before and after alliance. The steps involved in data collection and inputs-outputs selection constitute the initial work of this study. Step 3 involves forecast work by using grey model GM(1,1) to predict the data values in future years. In order to ensure that the forecasting error is reliable, MAPE is employed to measure the prediction accuracy in Step 4. The researcher has to reselect input and output factors if there is a high level of error.

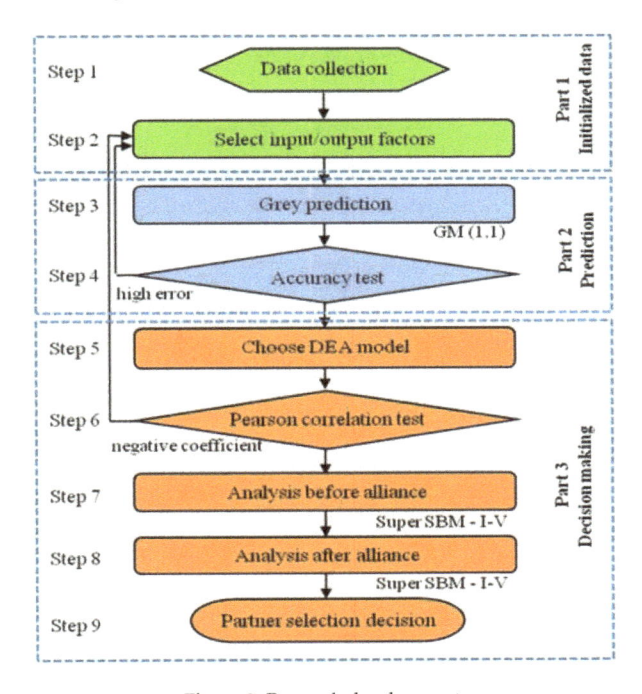

Figure 2. Research development.

DEA is a linear programming methodology. It measures the efficiency of multiple DMUs with a structure of multiple inputs and outputs. Hence, the super SBM-I-V model of DEA-Solver software is applied for the calculations in Step 5. Step 6 employs the Pearson Correlation Coefficient Test to check correlation values between inputs and outputs and whether they are positive or not. If the variables have a negative coefficient, we remove them and go back to Step 2 to rebuild a new variable until it can meet our requirements.

The aim of Step 7 is to find out the target company's position in comparison with the other 19 automobiles competitors via ranking the efficiency of each decision making unit, by applying the Super-SBM-I-V model in the realistic data. Step 8 is performed to establish new virtual alliances by combining the target DMU6 with the other 19 DMUs, respectively. After consolidation, the Super-SBM-I-V model is used to evaluate and rank new companies in comparison with existing ones. Suggestions will be provided based on the analysis results of this step, but they do not necessarily presume feasibility until further analysis in Step 9. In this step, the researcher looks more closely at the candidate firms to determine possible approaches for forming alliances.

2.2. Collecting the DMUs

This research was only conducted examining the 20 companies in the World Ranking of Manufacturing [2]. They have demonstrated a steady performance and can provide complete data for four consecutive financial years (2009–2012) as reported in Bloomberg Business Week [23]. Furthermore, these enterprises are representative of the entire auto industry in the global market (Table 1). DMU6 Nissan is set as the target company. Recently, this auto maker has faced great challenges with regards to globalization and competition. Hence, a strategic alliance could be part of an effective strategy for DMU6 to acquire resources and build business relationships.

Table 1. List of Automobile Manufacturing Companies.

Number Order	Code DMUs	Companies Name	Headquarter Address	Founded Year
1	DMU1	Toyota Motor Corporation	Japan	1937
2	DMU2	General Motors Company	U.S	1908
3	DMU3	Volkswagen Group AG	Germany	1937
4	DMU4	Hyundai Motor Company	Korea	1967
5	DMU5	Ford Motor Co.	U.S	1903
6	DMU6	Nissan Motor Co. Ltd.	Japan	1933
7	DMU7	Fiat Automobiles S.p.A	Italy	1899
8	DMU8	Honda Motor Co., Ltd.	Japan	1948
9	DMU9	Suzuki Motor Corporation	Japan	1909
10	DMU10	Renault S.A	France	1899
11	DMU11	Daimler AG	Germany	1926
12	DMU12	Bayerische Motoren Werke AG(BMW)	Germany	1916
13	DMU13	Mazda Motor Corporation	Japan	1920
14	DMU14	DongFeng Motor Corporation	China	1969
15	DMU15	Mitsubishi Motors Corporation	Japan	1970
16	DMU16	Chang An Automobile (Group) Co. Ltd.	China	1862
17	DMU17	Tata Motors Ltd. (TTMT)	India	1945
18	DMU18	Geely Automobile Holdings Ltd.	China	1986
19	DMU19	Isuzu Motors Ltd.	Japan	1916
20	DMU20	Daihatsu Motor Co. Ltd.	Japan	1907

Source: World Ranking of Manufacturers [2].

2.3. Grey Forecasting Model

GM(1,1) model of this study is built based on two basic operations. Accumulated generation operation (AGO) is applied to reduce the randomization of the raw data, and inverse accumulated generation (IAGO) is used to find the predicted values of initial data. The data series must be more than four, taking equal intervals and in consecutive order without neglecting any data [16]. The GM(1,1) model establishment process in this study is summarized as follows:

Establish the initial series $X^{(0)}$ by

$$X^{(0)} = \left(X^{(0)}(1), X^{(0)}(2), \ldots, X^{(0)}(n)\right), n \geqslant 4 \tag{1}$$

where $X^{(0)}$ is a non-negative sequence and n is the number of years observed.

Based on initial series $X^{(0)}$, a new sequence $X^{(1)}$ is set up through the AGO, which is

$$X^{(1)} = \left(X^{(1)}(1), X^{(1)}(2), \ldots, X^{(1)}(n)\right), n \geqslant 4 \tag{2}$$

where $X^{(1)}(1) = X^{(0)}(1)$ and $X^{(1)}(k) = \sum_{i=1}^{k} X^{(0)}_{(i)}, k = 1, 2, 3, \ldots, n$ (3)

Define mean value series $Z^{(1)}$ of adjacent data $X^{(1)}$ as:

$$Z^{(1)} = \left(Z^{(1)}(1), Z^{(1)}(2), \ldots, Z^{(1)}(n)\right) \tag{4}$$

where $Z^{(1)}(k)$ is calculated as follow:

$$Z^{(1)}(k) = 0.5 \times \left(X^{(1)}(k) + X^{(1)}(k-1)\right), k = 2, 3, \ldots, n \tag{5}$$

The GM(1,1) model can be built by establishing first order differential equation for $X^{(1)}(k)$.

$$\frac{dX^{(1)}(k)}{dk} + aX^{(1)}k = b \tag{6}$$

where parameter a is developing coefficient and b is grey input.

The solution to Equation (6) can be found by using the least square method to find parameters a and b:

$$\begin{bmatrix} a \\ b \end{bmatrix}^T = \left(B^T B\right)^{-1} B^T \overline{Y}_N \tag{7}$$

$$B = \begin{bmatrix} -Z^{(1)}(2) & 1 \\ \ldots\ldots\ldots & \ldots \\ -Z^{(1)}(n) & 1 \end{bmatrix} \tag{8}$$

and

$$Y_N = \begin{bmatrix} X^{(0)}(2) \\ \ldots\ldots\ldots \\ X^{(0)}(n) \end{bmatrix} \tag{9}$$

(B is called data matrix, Y is called data series, and $[a, b]^T$ is called parameter series).

According to Equation (6), the solution of $X^{(1)}(k)$ at time k:

$$\hat{X}^{(1)}(k+1) = \left[X^{(0)}(1) - \frac{b}{a}\right] e^{-ak} + \frac{b}{a} \ (k = 1, 2, 3, \ldots) \tag{10}$$

We acquired $\hat{X}^{(1)}$ from Equation (10). Let $\hat{X}^{(0)}$ be the GM(1,1) fitted and predicted series

$$\hat{X}^{(0)} = \left(\hat{X}^{(0)}(1), \hat{X}^{(0)}(2), \ldots, \hat{X}^{(0)}(n), \ldots\right), \text{ where } \hat{X}^{(0)}(1) = X^{(0)}(1) \tag{11}$$

Finally, to obtain the predicted value of the primitive data at time (k + 1), the inverse accumulated generating operation (IAGO) is used to establish the following grey model:

$$X^{(0)}(k+1) = \left[X^{(0)}(1) - \frac{b}{a}\right] e^{-ak}(1 - e^a) \quad (k = 1, 2, 3, \ldots) \tag{12}$$

In general, the grey forecasting model uses this operation to construct differential Equations.

2.4. Non-Radial Super Efficiency Model (Super-SBM)

The super SBM was developed on a non-radial model called SBM "Slacks-based measure of efficiency" introduced by Tone in 2001 [24], which directly deals with input and output slacks and return efficiency scores between 0 and 1. SBM deals with n DMUs, each DMU having input/output matrices $X = (x_{ij}) \in R^{m \times n}$ and $Y = (Y_{ij}) \in R^{s \times n}$, respectively. λ is a non-negative vector in R^n. Vectors $S^- \in R^m$ and $S^+ \in R^s$ are the input excess and output shortfalls, respectively [25]. To estimate the efficiency of (x_0, y_0), the SBM programwas formulated as follows [24]:

$$\min \rho = \frac{1 - \frac{1}{m}\sum_{i=1}^{m} S_i^-/x_{i0}}{1 + \frac{1}{s}\sum_{i=1}^{s} S_i^+/y_{i0}} \tag{13}$$

$$st. x_0 = X\lambda + S^-, \; y_0 = Y\lambda - S^+, \; \lambda \geq 0, \; S^- \geq 0, \; S^+ \geq 0 \tag{14}$$

Let an optimal solution for SBM be $(p^*, \lambda^*, S^{-*}, S^{+*})$. A DMU$(x_0, y_0)$ is SBM-efficient, if $p^* = 1$. That means $S^{-*} = 0$, and $S^{+*} = 0$ (or no input excesses and no output shortfalls). Based on this assumption, Tone has proposed a super-efficiency model for ranking DMUs and it was identified as following program [26]:

$$\min \delta = \frac{\frac{1}{m}\sum_{i=1}^{m} \overline{x}_i/x_{i0}}{\frac{1}{s}\sum_{r=1}^{s} \overline{y}_r/y_{r0}} \tag{15}$$

$$st. \overline{x} \geq \sum_{j=1, \neq 0}^{n} \lambda_j x_j, \; \overline{y} \leq \sum_{j=1, \neq 0}^{n} \lambda_j x_j, \; \overline{x} \geq x_0, \text{ and } \overline{y} \leq y_0, \; \overline{y} \geq 0, \; \lambda \geq 0 \tag{16}$$

If the denominator is equal to 1, the objective function will become the input-oriented of the super SBM model and it returns a value for the objective function which is greater or equal to one.

By the nature of things, inputs should be positive, but outputs may be negative. Nevertheless, many DEA models including SBM models cannot handle non-positive outputs, until a new scheme was introduced in DEA-Solver pro 4.1 Manual [25].

Suppose that $y_{r0} \leq 0$. It has defined $\overline{y}_r^+$ and $\overline{y}_{-r}^+$ by

$$\overline{y}_r^+ = \max_{j=1,\ldots,n} \{y_{rj}|y_{rj} > 0\}, \tag{17}$$

$$\overline{y}_r^+ = \min_{j=1,\ldots,n} \{y_{rj}|y_{rj} > 0\}, \tag{18}$$

In the objective function, if the output r has no positive elements, then it is defined as $\overline{y}_r^+ = y_{-r}^+ = 1$. The term s_r^+/y_{r0} will be replaced in the following way. (The value y_{r0} of in the constraints has never changed).

If $\bar{y}_r^+ > y_{-r}^+$, the term is replaced by:

$$s_r^+ / \frac{y_{-r}^+ (\bar{y}_r^+ - y_{-r}^+)}{\bar{y}_r^+ - y_{r0}} \quad (19)$$

If $\bar{y}_r^+ = y_{-r}^+$, the term is replaced by:

$$s_r^+ / \frac{(y_{-r}^+)^2}{B(\bar{y}_r^+ - y_{r0})} \quad (20)$$

where B is a large positive number, (in DEA-Solver B = 100).

Furthermore, the denominator is positive and strictly less than y_{-r}^+. Moreover, it is inverse to the distance $\bar{y}_r^+ - y_{r0}$. Hence, this scheme concerns the magnitude of the nonpositive output positively. The score obtained is units invariant; it is independent of the units of measurement used [25].

2.5. Establishing Input/Output Variables

In order to adequately measure the efficiency of a DEA model and simultaneously help the target DMU to find the right alliance partners, the selection of input and output elements should be carefully considered. Based on literature reviews of DEA, automobile operations, the International Accounting Standard (IAS) [27], and also the suitable correlation between input and output, in this research we decided to select four inputs factors, including fixed assets (Fix.as), cost of goods sold (Cogs), operating expenses (O.exp) and long-term investment (L.inv). Revenues (Rev), total equity (T.eq) and net incomes (Net.in) are chosen as output factors. These indicators provide a signal to measure the health of a firm and the benefit it could bring through a strategic alliance to all owners and investors. In the interest of length, the researcher only shows the data from 2012. Detailed data are shown in Table 2.

Table 2. Inputs and outputs data of all DMUs in 2012.

DMUs	Inputs (1,000,000 U.S Dollars)				Outputs (1,000,000 U.S Dollars)		
	(I) Fix.as	(I) Cogs	(I) O.exp	(I) L.inv	(O) Rev	(O) T.eq	(O) Net.in
DMU1	65,703.40	172,721.40	19,298.00	71,530.40	211,595.60	122,619.40	9227.10
DMU2	24,196.00	135,963.00	12,231.00	7062.00	152,256.00	37,000.00	6188.00
DMU3	73,415.80	193,658.50	29,135.30	18,222.00	262,873.60	111,594.60	16,412.90
DMU4	26,870.00	61,106.30	10,402.50	13,809.10	79,443.80	45,066.50	8052.40
DMU5	26,228.00	112,578.00	12,175.00	3133.00	134,252.00	16,311.00	5665.00
DMU6	41,837.50	76,937.30	10,389.50	5825.40	92,347.60	39,069.60	3284.10
DMU7	25,559.20	96,989.80	11,667.40	2693.50	114,181.50	17,919.60	473.30
DMU8	22,987.50	70,440.10	19,220.80	6370.80	94,729.50	49,794.40	3521.00
DMU9	5829.00	18,386.10	4935.10	2602.20	24,700.30	12,440.10	770.10
DMU10	15,687.20	46,373.20	8772.20	22,333.90	56,137.10	33,385.90	2410.30
DMU11	60,398.20	120,679.40	24,397.90	9401.60	155,483.90	61,910.90	8291.30
DMU12	14,607.30	63,896.00	8537.50	4367.10	104,556.30	41,360.70	6933.40
DMU13	7522.30	16,583.90	4047.30	1299.80	21,148.50	4921.80	329.00
DMU14	4264.70	16,536.50	2503.80	316.40	20,484.50	9518.10	1501.50
DMU15	3714.30	14,161.40	2616.90	929.40	17,425.10	3371.80	364.60
DMU16	2383.40	3970.00	1004.00	1292.70	4865.50	2541.50	238.90
DMU17	5970.30	21,734.80	6206.30	246.60	30,701.70	6183.90	1608.50
DMU18	1157.00	3313.40	475.70	32.80	4066.10	2180.00	336.80
DMU19	4799.80	13,420.40	1187.20	1369.50	15,860.50	5948.80	924.80
DMU20	4267.20	13,378.20	2582.20	5787.30	17,261.50	15,512.00	796.20

Sources: Bloomberg news [23].

3. Results and Discussion

3.1. Prediction Results

This research applies the GM(1,1) model to predict the input/output factors for future years. The fixed assets of DMU_6 were selected as an example to condcut the experiment (Table 3), and other variables are computed in line with the following steps:

Table 3. Inputs and outputs factors of DMU6 in the period of 2009–2012.

DMU6	Inputs (1,000,000 U.S dollars)				Outputs (1,000,000 U.S dollars)		
	(I) Fix.as	(I) Cogs	(I) O.exp	(I) L.inv	(O) Rev	(O) T.eq	(O) Net.in
2009	36,999.50	55,140.60	10,264.70	2548.20	72,090.70	28,914.90	406.50
2010	34,879.20	68,617.40	10,362.20	5113.30	84,134.00	31,395.60	3061.30
2011	35,782.60	74,541.50	10,456.50	4916.10	90,232.60	33,085.50	3274.30
2012	41,837.50	76,937.30	10,389.50	5825.40	92,347.60	39,069.60	3284.10

Sources: Bloomberg news [23].

1st: establish the original series:

$$X^{(0)} = (36,999.50; 34,879.20; 35,782.60; 41,837.50)$$

2nd: create $X^{(1)}$ series by executing the accumulated generating operation (AGO):

$$X^{(1)} = (36,999.50; 71,878.70; 107,661.30; 149,498.80)$$

3rd: calculate mean sequence $Z^{(1)}$ of $X^{(1)}$ by the mean equation:

$$Z^{(1)}(k) = (54,439.10; 89,770.00; 128,580.05), \; k = 2, 3, 4$$

4th: solve equations:
To find a and b, the original series are substituted into the Grey differential equation:

$$\begin{cases} 34,879.20 + a \times 54,439.10 = b \\ 35,782.60 + a \times 89,770.00 = b \\ 41,837.50 + a \times 128,580.05 = b \end{cases}$$

and convert the linear equations into the form of a matrix:

$$\text{Let } B = \begin{bmatrix} -54,439.10 & 1 \\ -89,770.00 & 1 \\ -128,580.05 & 1 \end{bmatrix}, \hat{\theta} = \begin{bmatrix} a \\ b \end{bmatrix}, Y_N = \begin{bmatrix} 34,879.20 \\ 35,782.60 \\ 41,837.50 \end{bmatrix}$$

Before using the least square method to find a and b

$$\hat{\theta} = \left(B^T B\right)^{-1} B^T \overline{Y}_N = \begin{bmatrix} -0.094869531 \\ 28,873.31 \end{bmatrix}$$

use the two coefficients a and b to generate the whitening equation of the differential equation:

$$\frac{dX^{(1)}}{dk} - 0.09486531 \times X^{(1)} = 28,873.31$$

Find the prediction model from equation:

$$\hat{X}^{(1)}(k+1) = \left[X^{(0)}(1) - \frac{b}{a}\right]e^{-ak} + \frac{b}{a} = 341,347.05 * e^{0.094869531\,k} - 304,347.56$$

Finding $X^{(1)}$ series by substituting different values of k into above equation:

$$K = 0 \quad X^{(1)}(1) = 36,999.50$$
$$K = 1 \quad X^{(1)}(2) = 70,968.78$$
$$K = 2 \quad X^{(1)}(3) = 108,318.53$$
$$K = 3 \quad X^{(1)}(4) = 149,385.16$$
$$K = 4 \quad X^{(1)}(5) = 194,538.55$$
$$K = 5 \quad X^{(1)}(6) = 244,185.39$$
$$K = 6 \quad X^{(1)}(7) = 298,772.86$$
$$K = 7 \quad X^{(1)}(8) = 358,792.60$$
$$K = 8 \quad X^{(1)}(9) = 424,785.30$$

Originate the predicted value of the original series according to the IAGO and obtain:

$$\hat{X}^{(0)}(1) = \hat{X}^{(1)}(1) = 36,999.50$$
$$\hat{X}^{(0)}(2) = \hat{X}^{(1)}(2) - \hat{X}^{(1)}(1) = 33,969.28$$
$$\hat{X}^{(0)}(3) = \hat{X}^{(1)}(3) - \hat{X}^{(1)}(2) = 37,349.75$$
$$\hat{X}^{(0)}(4) = \hat{X}^{(1)}(4) - \hat{X}^{(1)}(3) = 41,066.63$$
$$\hat{X}^{(0)}(5) = \hat{X}^{(1)}(5) - \hat{X}^{(1)}(4) = 45,153.39$$
$$\hat{X}^{(0)}(6) = \hat{X}^{(1)}(6) - \hat{X}^{(1)}(5) = 49,646.84$$
$$\hat{X}^{(0)}(7) = \hat{X}^{(1)}(7) - \hat{X}^{(1)}(6) = 54,587.47 \text{ (predicted value of 2015)}$$
$$\hat{X}^{(0)}(8) = \hat{X}^{(1)}(8) - \hat{X}^{(1)}(7) = 60,019.76 \text{ (predicted value of 2016)}$$
$$\hat{X}^{(0)}(9) = \hat{X}^{(1)}(9) - \hat{X}^{(1)}(8) = 65,992.65 \text{ (predicted value of 2017)}$$

Using the above computation process, this research could obtain the forecasting result of all DMUs for subsequent years; the detailed data is shown in the following Table 4:

Table 4. Predicted inputs and outputs value of all DMUs in 2016 and 2017 (calculated by GM).

DMUs	Inputs (1,000,000 U.S Dollars)									Outputs (1,000,000 U.S Dollars)					
	(I) Fixed Assets		(I) Cost of Goods Sold		(I) Operating Expenses		(I) Long-Term Investments		(O) Revenues		(O) Total Equity		(O) Net Income		
	2016	2017	2016	2017	2016	2017	2016	2017	2016	2017	2016	2017	2016	2017	
1	76,687.0	80,030.2	217,158.9	231,159.2	21,093.2	21,674.4	124,614.0	143,671.4	283,274.9	306,795.8	166,888.2	181,102.1	86,510.6	163,021.6	
2	38,145.7	42,570.8	178,534.5	190,828.1	13,791.7	14,196.5	4366.8	3925.1	193,191.1	204,363.3	37,327.8	37,250.5	7218.4	7225.4	
3	175,325.5	218,068.3	440,708.4	541,512.0	70,484.0	88,446.5	13,915.8	12,926.1	597,532.6	733,901.5	309,703.8	400,581.0	39,379.8	48,592.5	
4	48,927.6	56,836.7	97,854.3	109,970.5	13,680.6	14,598.0	30,158.2	36,413.7	125,928.4	141,029.0	94,663.7	113,980.0	18,263.2	22,307.3	
5	30,115.6	31,336.1	132,009.9	136,898.3	12,647.2	12,809.7	4785.4	5321.4	146,889.9	149,806.7	255,175.4	480,692.6	9401.7	9142.5	
6	60,019.8	65,992.7	97,057.8	102,672.3	10,471.0	10,484.7	7474.2	8014.2	111,709.3	116,949.5	60,499.7	67,763.5	3806.0	3939.1	
7	90,406.1	122,177.9	467,417.7	694,650.7	48,355.5	69,039.4	4189.9	4586.4	553,201.8	823,165.7	19,817.2	20,392.2	666.2	614.5	
8	35,211.1	39,412.1	88,989.2	95,371.2	22,491.6	23,502.5	7113.9	7335.8	112,881.3	119,350.7	63,448.4	67,790.1	840.9	634.9	
9	7800.2	8453.0	17,034.6	16,740.1	4814.0	4813.7	3,808.5	4288.3	23,871.2	23,731.1	17,023.6	18,511.6	2539.4	3452.4	
10	15,696.1	15,716.8	58,170.3	61,220.3	8950.3	8957.0	26,398.2	27,397.1	63,902.8	65,684.6	39,160.3	40,631.7	517.4	360.8	
11	93,944.0	104,884.2	168,675.6	183,521.6	30,441.0	32,120.4	11,399.9	11,929.0	212,500.5	229,667.8	88,905.4	97,380.6	15,001.0	17,320.3	
12	14,614.5	14,620.7	111,821.0	128,629.1	11,900.1	12,919.7	8890.3	10,659.5	168,383.5	189,641.2	66,600.4	75,028.9	16,066.7	19,633.6	
13	7483.8	7475.0	13,790.7	13,258.6	3682.3	3611.6	2085.2	2361.6	18,188.0	17,676.6	6989.7	7626.8	(26.9)	(15.5)	
14	8247.3	9742.0	18,320.8	18,691.4	2980.0	3107.2	584.8	677.3	21,475.1	21,612.5	18,359.5	21,633.1	1061.7	969.0	
15	3752.8	3769.3	12,944.6	12,671.4	3134.7	3283.5	195.9	139.7	17,123.7	17,060.5	6888.1	8292.9	2053.7	3194.6	
16	10,976.2	16,122.6	2782.9	2577.6	1169.5	1228.2	2212.4	2512.8	3431.6	3193.3	5032.9	5927.1	72.9	57.5	
17	12,773.6	15,467.8	48,191.7	58,533.9	18,354.1	24,129.1	315.3	336.3	70,654.4	86,707.7	20,429.5	27,357.7	2009.5	2060.9	
18	1887.2	2120.0	4968.6	5520.2	691.8	763.2	569.9	1214.5	6098.0	6776.8	4676.1	5689.8	761.0	938.4	
19	5078.6	5165.0	17,717.1	19,116.2	1424.2	1495.0	2995.5	3645.7	21,553.3	23,418.1	15,263.3	19,376.8	2746.9	3565.4	
20	4868.4	5042.3	16,840.6	17,860.6	3156.8	3324.7	10,075.6	11,595.4	22,055.2	23,479.8	40,887.8	52,126.0	1894.9	2357.8	

Source: Calculated by researcher.

3.2. Forecasting Accuracy

Forecasting method is implemented to predict future results using the present uncompleted information, so we do not introduce new errors. Hence, the MAPE (Mean absolute percent error) is employed to measure the accuracy values in statistics. The smaller values of MAPE demonstrate that the forecasting values are more reasonable [28]. The results of MAPE are shown in Table 5:

Table 5. Average MAPE of DMUs.

DMUs	Average MAPE	DMUs	Average MAPE
DMU1	5.84809%	DMU11	0.79240%
DMU2	3.52436%	DMU12	1.30784%
DMU3	1.90186%	DMU13	10.8717%
DMU4	1.71334%	DMU14	1.65806%
DMU5	45.3331%	DMU15	3.07850%
DMU6	1.51432%	DMU16	6.56818%
DMU7	11.4944%	DMU17	3.83133%
DMU8	6.64905%	DMU18	3.48085%
DMU9	3.99930%	DMU19	2.67108%
DMU10	2.22754%	DMU20	0.68057%
Average MAPE of 20 DMUs		5.95730%	

Most of the MAPE values are good and qualified, being smaller than 10%. The average of all MAPE reaches 5.95730%. This affirms that the GM(1,1) model offers a high accurate prediction. DMU5 obtains a 45% higher MAPE value because it is strongly affected by the 2008 crisis. However, based on the MAPE accuracy standards, only this value is qualified.

3.3. Pearson Correlation

The homogeneity and isotonicity are two major basic DEA data assumptions. The basic DEA assumption between input data and output data needs to be isotonic. The means the input data and output data need to have a positive correlation. Correlation test is an important step in applying the DEA technique to ensure the relationship between input and output factors is isotonic (*i.e.*, an increase in any input should not result in a decrease in any output) [29]. This study employs a simple correlation test—Pearson correlation—to measure the strength of the linear relationship of normal distributed variables [30]. If the correlation coefficient is positive, these factors are isotonically related and will be put into the DEA model; when the factor demonstrates a weak isotonic relationship, it will be reexamined [31]. The correlation coefficient is always between -1 and $+1$.

The results of correlation coefficients between input and output variables in Tables 6–9 show strong positive associations and comply with the precondition of the DEA model. Hence, these positive correlations also prove that the selection of input and output variables is appropriate. This means those data are proper for DEA assumption and can be used for the analysis for DEA calculations.

Table 6. Correlation of input and output data in 2009.

	Fix.as	Cogs	O.exp	L.inv	Rev	T.eq	Net.in
Fix.as	1	0.900516	0.902008	0.770458	0.924567	0.868580	0.010851
Cogs	0.900516	1	0.916182	0.750937	0.989125	0.788681	0.334254
O.exp	0.902008	0.916182	1	0.666827	0.938334	0.799956	0.140062
L.inv	0.770454	0.750937	0.666827	1	0.745437	0.887277	0.090390
Rev	0.924567	0.989125	0.938334	0.745437	1	0.812591	0.225816
T.eq	0.868580	0.788681	0.799956	0.887277	0.812591	1	0.078414
Net.in	0.010851	0.334254	0.140062	0.090390	0.225816	0.078414	1

Table 7. Correlation of input and output data in 2010.

	Fix.as	Cogs	O.exp	L.inv	Rev	T.eq	Net.in
Fix.as	1	0.908011	0.901304	0.760279	0.915191	0.888756	0.712517
Cogs	0.908011	1	0.884399	0.701945	0.991911	0.821255	0.810075
O.exp	0.901304	0.884399	1	0.598485	0.907604	0.826895	0.827244
L.inv	0.760279	0.701945	0.598485	1	0.680493	0.878784	0.421430
Rev	0.915191	0.991911	0.907604	0.680493	1	0.831531	0.851679
T.eq	0.888756	0.821255	0.826895	0.878784	0.831531	1	0.626496
Net.in	0.712517	0.810075	0.827244	0.421430	0.851679	0.626496	1

Table 8. Correlation of input and output data in 2011.

	Fix.as	Cogs	O.exp	L.inv	Rev	T.eq	Net.in
Fix.as	1	0.908680	0.911810	0.691419	0.915207	0.909611	0.535213
Cogs	0.908680	1	0.872887	0.627072	0.991641	0.853222	0.728935
O.exp	0.911810	0.872887	1	0.547521	0.893166	0.855927	0.586748
L.inv	0.691419	0.627072	0.547521	1	0.600729	0.846506	0.142137
Rev	0.915207	0.991641	0.893166	0.600729	1	0.867635	0.750202
T.eq	0.909612	0.853222	0.855927	0.846506	0.867635	1	0.413475
Net.in	0.535214	0.728935	0.586748	0.142137	0.750202	0.413475	1

Table 9. Correlation of input and output data in 2012.

	Fix.as	Cogs	O.exp	L.inv	Rev	T.eq	Net.in
Fix.as	1	0.916378	0.921629	0.632545	0.925523	0.913111	0.85602
Cogs	0.916377	1	0.898532	0.594043	0.992487	0.861108	0.857803
O.exp	0.921629	0.898532	1	0.481858	0.919848	0.860337	0.84896
L.inv	0.632545	0.594043	0.481858	1	0.580518	0.796618	0.50826
Rev	0.925523	0.992487	0.919848	0.580518	1	0.886316	0.897967
T.eq	0.913110	0.861108	0.860337	0.796617	0.886316	1	0.874886
Net.in	0.856015	0.857803	0.84896	0.508260	0.897967	0.874886	1

Remark: Fixed assets (Fix.as), Cost of goods sold (Cogs), Operating expenses (O.exp); Long-term investment (L.inv). Revenues (Rev), Total equity (T.eq) and Net incomes (Net.in).

3.4. Analysis before Alliance

In this research, the efficiency of 20 DMUs and their ranking before alliances was measured by the Super-SBM-I-V model, with the realistic data of 2012. The empirical results of Table 10 indicated that DMU18 has the best efficiency (the first ranking with the score = 5.8965750), followed by DMU12 and DMU14 ranking second and third place. The target DMU6 is in the 18th ranking, being part of the last group. This ranking emphasizes again that it is necessary for the target company to form strategic alliances to improve its performance.

Table 10. Efficiency and ranking before alliances.

Rank	DMU	Score
1	DMU18	5.8965750
2	DMU12	1.5655136
3	DMU14	1.3982037
4	DMU17	1.3777954
5	DMU20	1.3447020
6	DMU5	1.2097953
7	DMU2	1.1359231
8	DMU4	1.0876949

Table 10. *Cont.*

Rank	DMU	Score
9	DMU19	1.0484095
10	DMU8	1.0307413
11	DMU7	1.0133168
12	DMU1	1
12	DMU3	1
14	DMU11	0.7448770
15	DMU9	0.7176400
16	DMU15	0.7105391
17	DMU10	0.7104498
18	DMU6	0.6492883
19	DMU13	0.5816934
20	DMU16	0.5283717

3.5. Analysis after Alliance

The low inefficiency score (0.6492883 < 1) and low rank (18th/20) of target DMU6 suggests that the enterprise should enhance its operating efficiency and seek advantages from cooperative partners by building a creative alliance strategy. To implement the empirical results, this research combines DMU6 with the remaining DMUs to form 39 virtual DMUs (19 alliances and 20 original cases) in total. The software of DEA-Solver Pro 8.0–Super-SBM-I-V model built by Saitech Company was employed to compute efficiency for all new DMUs. Table 11 shows the ranking results and scores of the virtual alliances.

Table 11. Performance ranking of virtual DMUs.

Rank	DMU	Score	Rank	DMU	Score
1	DMU18	5.8965750	21	DMU6 + DMU4	0.9011136
2	DMU12	1.5655136	22	DMU6 + DMU11	0.8376827
3	DMU14	1.3982037	23	DMU6 + DMU20	0.7731485
4	DMU17	1.3777954	24	DMU6 + DMU14	0.7545630
5	DMU20	1.3447020	25	DMU6 + DMU10	0.7462483
6	DMU5	1.1714878	26	DMU11	0.7229771
7	DMU3	1.1161306	27	DMU9	0.7176400
8	DMU1	1.1140650	28	DMU6 + DMU9	0.7113479
9	DMU2	1.1058616	29	DMU15	0.7105391
10	DMU4	1.0876949	30	DMU10	0.7104498
11	DMU6 + DMU5	1.0655124	31	DMU6 + DMU17	0.7013426
12	DMU19	1.0484095	32	DMU6 + DMU19	0.6720799
13	DMU6 + DMU12	1.0443239	33	DMU6 + DMU18	0.6649845
14	DMU6 + DMU2	1.0400331	34	DMU6	0.6492883
15	DMU8	1.0282731	35	DMU6 + DMU15	0.6279972
16	DMU7	1.0133168	36	DMU6 + DMU16	0.6265420
17	DMU6 + DMU8	1.0117510	37	DMU6 + DMU13	0.6219810
18	DMU6 + DMU7	1.0002026	38	DMU13	0.5816934
19	DMU6 + DMU3	1	39	DMU16	0.5283717
19	DMU6 + DMU1	1			

The results of Table 11 indicate clearly the change from original DMUs to a virtual alliance at different rates. The target DMU6 shows the highest efficiency scores in a relationship with DMU1, DMU3, DMU7, DMU8, DMU2, DMU12 and DMU5. The researcher can compare the efficiency between them by separating them into two groups (see Table 12). The fact that the group has positive results proves these alliances are better than original DMUs. A higher difference value the increased efficiency of an alliance. In contrast, the negative value of the second group means the alliance is worse.

Table 12. The good & bad alliance partnership.

Number Order	Virtual Alliance	Target DMU6 Ranking (1)	Virtual alliance Ranking (2)	Difference (1)–(2)
1st group		Good alliance		
1	DMU6 + DMU5	34	11	23
2	DMU6 + DMU12	34	13	21
3	DMU6 + DMU2	34	14	20
4	DMU6 + DMU8	34	17	17
5	DMU6 + DMU7	34	18	16
6	DMU6 + DMU3	34	19	15
7	DMU6 + DMU1	34	19	15
8	DMU6 + DMU4	34	21	13
9	DMU6 + DMU11	34	22	12
10	DMU6 + DMU20	34	23	11
11	DMU6 + DMU14	34	24	10
12	DMU6 + DMU10	34	25	9
13	DMU6 + DMU9	34	28	6
14	DMU6 + DMU17	34	31	3
15	DMU6 + DMU19	34	32	2
16	DMU6 + DMU18	34	33	1
2nd group		Bad Alliance		
1	DMU6 + DMU15	34	35	−1
2	DMU6 + DMU16	34	36	−2
3	DMU6 + DMU13	34	37	−3

In the first group, the ranking of target DMU is improved after an alliance with another 16 enterprises (DMU1, DMU2, DMU3, DMU4, DMU5, DMU7, DMU8, DMU9, DMU10, DMU11, DMU12, DMU14, DMU17, DMU18, DMU19 and DMU20). This demonstrates that target DMU can take advantages from alliance. The alliance of DMU6 + DMU5, DMU6 + DMU12, DMU6 + DMU2, DMU6 + DMU8 and DMU6 + DMU7 gets the highest efficiency (score >1). Hence, those five candidates will be firstly priority when considering alliance partners. Especially, DMU5 is one of the best potential candidates because of its largest difference value (23). The second group has three enterprises including (DMU15, DMU16, and DMU13) of which DMU6 is worse off after strategic alliances (DMUs' ranking reduced). Thus, those firms would not be chosen by a target DMU because they do not help the enterprise in its vision.

3.6. Partner Selection

In the previous section, the best alliance partnerships are identified based on the position of the target DMU6. Nevertheless, we must further analyze the feasibility of alliance partnerships and compare situations before and after alliances. It can be seen clearly, as shown in the results in Table 12, that there are 16 good partners. However, they will not cooperate with the target DMU, because, the DMU's ranking is lower. In other words, the performance of DMU1, DMU2, DMU3, DMU4, DMU5, DMU7, DMU8, DMU9, DMU12, DMU14, DMU17, DMU18, DMU19 and DMU20 are already good; if there are no special circumstances, they currently have no incentive to form an alliance partnership with the DMU6.

Figure 3 shows more clearly the change in ranking of the above DMUs before and after alliance with target DMU6. The blue line is nearer to the center-point than the red line in most DMUs. This indicates that most of the DMUs have a high efficiency before alliance, but some of them are lower before the alliance relationship (DMU6 + DMU10, DMU6 + DMU11, DMU6 + DMU13, DMU6 + DMU16).

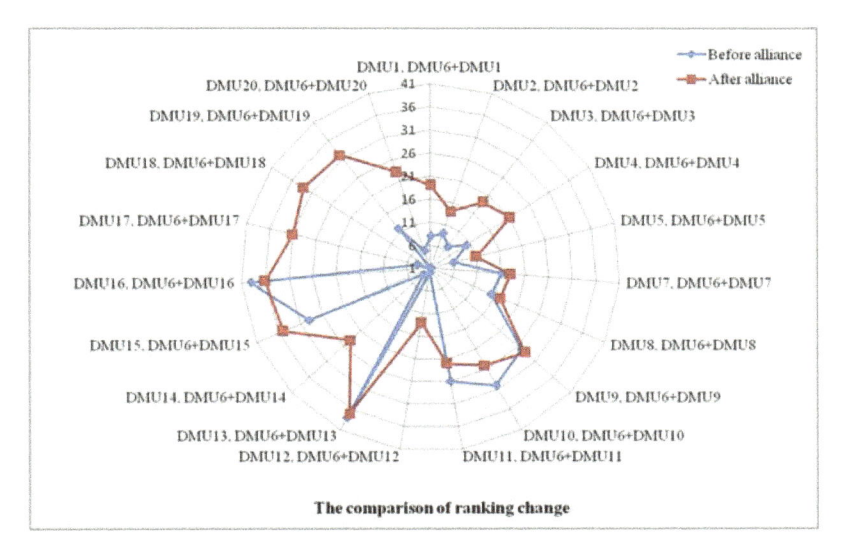

Figure 3. The comparison of changes in ranking.

Combined with Tables 10–12 the efficiency and ranking of all DMUs before and after alliance are reviewed again in Figure 3. Those points which are more close to the center are ranked higher. The points clearly point to an alliance with Renault and Daimler with the target company. Renault and Daimler are not at the level of DEA before alliance; however, their rankings improved after cooperating with Nissan. It means the alliance can bring benefits not only for Nissan but also for Renault and Daimler. In other words, through the alliance, both of Nissan–Renault and Nissan–Daimler AG, opportunities to manage their resource more effectively may arise. Hence, Renault and Daimler should have a strong desire to form an alliance.

In fact, Nissan–Renault has maintained an alliance relationship since 1999. These enterprises now are developing a three-party alliance between Renault–Nissan–Daimler AG. This once again proves the results of this paper are correct and have practical feasibility. However, Nissan should continue to cooperate to effectively utilize the resources of both parties. This will be entailing an intersection between Eastern and Western culture, in line with current globalization trends. The alliance can help to build a production system, which can reduce waste, create value for the customer and achieve perfection. Besides that, the company also needs to enhance common understanding, seeking potential cooperation opportunities from less feasible alliance partners.

In a word, the results and findings of this case study also lead to new recommendations for strategic alliances. The readers can clearly recognize the noticeable candidates for an alliance strategy are Ford Motor (DMU5, the best efficiency improvement for the target company), Renault and Daimler (the efficiency improvement for both target DMU6 and partners DMU10, DMU11).

4. Conclusions

Nowadays, the automobile industry as well as many other industries faces numerous challenges such as: How to achieve competitive advantage and enter new markets? How to obtain new technology and resources and how to reduce risk and share costs of research and development? For solving these problems, this research proposed a decision making model by using a hybrid of Grey theory and DEA. This study focused on the relationship between strategic alliances and the performance of the top 20 enterprises in the automobile industry.

Based on the realistic public data of automobile enterprises from 2009 to 2012, this study used GM(1,1) model to predict the future change in value of the specific input/output variables. The accuracy forecast value had been tested by average MAPE and a reliable percentage of 5.9573% was obtained.

Nissan was used as a case study to determine the potential benefits of strategic alliances between firms. The DEA-Super SBM model was applied to evaluate efficiency all real DMUs and virtual DMUs. The empirical results showed that 16 candidates are suitable for Nissan to form strategic alliances with, of which Ford, BMW, General Motors, Honda, and Fiat are strongly recommended. However, only two partnerships are feasible for Nissan (Nissan–Renault and Nissan–Daimler). If a firm decides to form an alliance, it is necessary to conduct extensive an assessment of performance before and after the alliance in terms of many aspects.

In conclusion, by combining Grey theory and the Super SBM model, this research proposed a new accurate and appropriate approach to forecast and evaluate automobile firms. This model provides a reference for decision making for automaker strategists when developing alliance strategies.

The DEA is one kind of sensitive method for factor selection. The selection of input/output variables could be different, and the results would be impacted. Therefore, robust checking is necessary. The different input/output variables and removing outlierd from DMUs should be re-calculated and re-discussed.

For future study, sensitive analysis for different inputs or outputs of DMUs or data of different years can be discussed further. Moreover, the methodology should be further developed by using qualitative data and should be applied in different industries.

Author Contributions: Author Contributions: In this paper, Chia-Nan Wang contributed to design the theoretical verifications. Xuan-Tho Nguyen collected and analyzed data and prepared for the manuscript. Yen-Hui Wang is involved in results discussion. All authors have both read and approved the manuscript.

Conflicts of Interest: Conflicts of Interest: The authors declare no conflict of interest.

References

1. Haugh, D.; Mourougane, A.; Chatal, O. The automobile industry in and beyond the crisis. *OECD Econ. Dep. Work. Pap.* **2010**, *2009*. [CrossRef]
2. OICA. World Ranking of Manufacturers. Available online: http://www.oica.net/wp-content/uploads/2013/03/worldpro2012-modification-ranking.pdf (accessed on 20 May 2014).
3. Global Retail Sales Volume/Market Share. Available online: http://www.nissan-global.com/EN/DOCUMENT/PDF/AR/2014/p23_e.pdf (accessed on 12 August 2015).
4. Renault-Nissan to Launch More than 10 Driverless Cars through 2020. Available online: http://www.autoevolution.com/news/renault-nissan-to-launch-more-than-10-driverless-cars-through-2020-103503.html (accessed on 25 January 2016).
5. Toyota and Nissan Recall 6.5 Million Cars Over Airbags. Available online: http://www.bbc.com/news/business-32716802 (accessed on 13 May 2015).
6. Nisan Annual Report. Available online: http://www.nissan-global.com/EN/DOCUMENT/PDF/AR/2013/AR2013_E_All.pdf (accessed on 20 May 2014).
7. James, D.B.; Benjamin, G.C.; Michael, S.R. *Mastering Alliance Strategy*; John Wiley & Sons, Inc: New York, NY, USA, 2003; pp. 1–19.
8. Mockler, R.J. Multinational strategic alliances: A manager's perspective. *Strateg. Chang.* **1997**, *6*, 391–405. [CrossRef]
9. Brouthers, K.D.; Bamossy, G.J. Post-formation processes in eastern and western European joint ventures. *J. Manag. Stud.* **2006**, *43*, 203–229. [CrossRef]
10. Cravens, D.W.; Shipp, S.H.; Cravens, K.S. Analysis of cooperative inter-organizational relationships, strategic alliance formation, and strategic alliance effectiveness. *J. Strateg. Mark.* **1993**, *1*, 55–70. [CrossRef]
11. Chan, S.H.; Kensinger, J.W.; Keown, A.J.; Martin, J.D. Do strategic alliances create value? *J. Financ. Econ.* **1997**, *46*, 199–221. [CrossRef]

12. Candace, E.Y.; Thomas, A.T. Strategic alliances with competing firms and shareholder value. *J. Manag. Mark. Res.* **2011**, *6*, 1–10.
13. Cho, B.S.; Kang, S.W.; Cha, S.M. Trends in telecommunication strategic alliance regulation. In Proceedings of the IEEE Technology Management for the Global Future, Istanbul, Turkey, 8–13 July 2006; IEEE: Piscataway, NJ, USA, 2006; Volume 4, pp. 1994–2004.
14. Kauser, S.; Shaw, V. International strategic alliances: Objectives, motives and success. *J. Glob. Mark.* **2004**, *17*, 7–43. [CrossRef]
15. Deng, J.L. Control problems of Grey systems. *Syst. Control Lett.* **1982**, *5*, 288–294.
16. Deng, J.L. Introduction to Grey system theory. *J. Grey Syst.* **1989**, *1*, 1–24.
17. Farrell, M.J. The measurement of productivity efficiency. *J. R. Stat. Soc.* **1957**, *120*, 499–513.
18. Charnes, A.; Cooper, W.W.; Rhodes, E. Measuring the efficiency of decision making units. *Eur. J. Oper. Res.* **1978**, *2*, 429–444. [CrossRef]
19. Martín, J.C.; Roman, C. An application of DEA to measure the efficiency of Spanish airports prior to privatization. *J. Air Transp. Manag.* **2001**, *7*, 149–157. [CrossRef]
20. Wang, C.N.; Li, K.Z.; Ho, C.T.; Yang, K.L.; Wang, C.H. A model for candidate selection of strategic alliances: Case on industry of department store. In Proceedings of the Second International Conference on Innovative Computing, Information and Control, Kumamoto, Japan, 5–7 September 2007; IEEE: Piscataway, NJ, USA, 2007.
21. Wang, R.T.; Ho, C.T.B.; Oh, K. Measuring production and marketing efficiency using grey relation analysis and data envelopment analysis. *Int. J. Prod. Res.* **2010**, *48*, 183–199. [CrossRef]
22. Yuan, L.N.; Tian, L.N. A new DEA model on science and technology resources of industrial enterprises. *Int. Conf. Mach. Learn. Cybern.* **2012**, *3*, 986–990.
23. Bloomberg Business Week. Available online: http://www.business-week.com/ (accessed on 5 May 2014).
24. Tone, K.A. Slacks-based measure of efficiency in data envelopment analysis. *Eur. J. Oper. Res.* **2001**, *130*, 498–509. [CrossRef]
25. Düzakın, E.; Düzakın, H. Measuring the performance of manufacturing firms with super slacks based model of data envelopment analysis: An application of 500 major industrial enterprises in Turkey. *Eur. J. Oper. Res.* **2007**, *182*, 1412–1432. [CrossRef]
26. Tone, K. A slacks-based measure of super-efficiency in data envelopment analysis. *Eur. J. Oper. Res.* **2002**, *143*, 32–41. [CrossRef]
27. IAS (International Accounting Standards). Available online: http://www.iasplus.com/en/standards/ias (accessed on 20 May 2014).
28. Stevenson, W.J.; Sum, C.C. *Operations Management: An Asian Perspective*; McGraw-Hill Education (Asia): Singapore, 2010.
29. Golany, B.; Roll, Y. An application procedure for DEA. *Omega* **1989**, *17*, 237–250. [CrossRef]
30. Pruessner, J.C.; Kirschbaum, C.; Meinlschmid, G.; Hellhammer, D.H. Two formulas for computation of the area under the curve represent measures of total hormone concentration *versus* time-dependent change. *Psychoneuroendocrinology* **2003**, *28*, 916–931. [CrossRef]
31. Lo, F.Y.; Chien, C.F.; Lin, J.T. A DEA study to evaluate the relative efficiency and investigate the district reorganization of the Taiwan power company. *IEEE Trans. Power Syst.* **2001**, *16*, 170–178. [CrossRef]

© 2016 by the authors. Licensee MDPI, Basel, Switzerland. This article is an open access article distributed under the terms and conditions of the Creative Commons Attribution (CC BY) license (http://creativecommons.org/licenses/by/4.0/).

Article

Does Business Model Affect CSR Involvement? A Survey of Polish Manufacturing and Service Companies

Marzanna Katarzyna Witek-Hajduk and Piotr Zaborek *

Institute of International Marketing and Management, Collegium of World Economy, Warsaw School of Economics, 162 Niepodległości Ave., Warsaw 02-554, Poland
* Correspondence: piotr.zaborek@sgh.waw.pl; Tel: +48-502119774

Academic Editor: Adam Jabłoński
Received: 27 November 2015; Accepted: 12 January 2016; Published: 15 February 2016

Abstract: The study explores links between types of business models used by companies and their involvement in CSR. As the main part of our conceptual framework we used a business model taxonomy developed by Dudzik and Witek-Hajduk, which identifies five types of models: traditionalists, market players, contractors, distributors, and integrators. From shared characteristics of the business model profiles, we proposed that market players and integrators will show significantly higher levels of involvement in CSR than the three other classes of companies. Among other things, both market players and integrators relied strongly on building own brand value and fostering harmonious supply channel relations, which served as a rationale for our hypothesis. The data for the study were obtained through a combined CATI and CAWI survey on a group of 385 managers of medium and large enterprises. The sample was representative for the three Polish industries of chemical manufacturing, food production, and retailing. Statistical methods included confirmatory factor analysis and one-way ANOVA with contrasts and *post hoc* tests. The findings supported our hypothesis, showing that market players and integrators were indeed more engaged in CSR than other groups of firms. This may suggest that managers in control of these companies could bolster the integrity of their business models by increasing CSR involvement. Another important contribution of the study was to propose and validate a versatile scale for assessing CSR involvement, which showed measurement invariance for all involved industries.

Keywords: business models; CSR; sustainable development; medium and large companies; Poland

1. Introduction

The concepts of Corporate Social Responsibility (CSR) and business models have been frequently addressed in academic studies in the last decades. Both of these concepts are often listed among the key concerns in contemporary management theory and practice. They are looked at from various research perspectives, including macroeconomic [1], microeconomic [2], management [3,4], and marketing [5]. There is no lack of conceptual studies trying to integrate CSR with developing strategies and business models. For example, Pyszka [6] is proposing a mechanism whereby traditional business models can be transformed into CSR-enabled ones, with the aim of enhancing a company's competitive advantage, in particular its innovativeness. When it comes to practical guidance for managers, some authors developed various sets of tools that practitioners can use to diagnose the current state of CSR and sustainability involvement and implement needed changes, bearing in mind the short- and long-term economic benefits for the company. In this vein, Bocken *et al.* [7] offer a number of value-mapping tools to support sustainable business modeling, including the interests of the four major stakeholder groups, here labeled as environment, society, customer, and network actors. The topic of the interlink between

CSR, sustainability, business models, and strategy is also ever-present in business and trade journals, where various authors often depict these management concepts as means of enhancing competitiveness and achieving other benefits [8]. What these published works, both academic and otherwise, have in common is a lack of empirical proof (as in the case of conceptual papers) or reliance on qualitative and anecdotal evidence e.g., [9,10]. In fact, there is a surprising dearth of works exploring the quantitative evidence for possible links between types of adopted business models and the level of CSR practices. As such, the aim of our paper is to address this issue and attempt to bridge the knowledge gap. Building on previous studies, we conclude that the type of business model used should affect a firm's CSR involvement, and then test this proposition with survey data collected from managers of medium and large companies in Polish manufacturing and service industries.

The paper is structured as follows. First, we summarize relevant literature sources on CSR to discuss various understandings of the concept. Next, we survey popular definitions and taxonomies of business models. The third section looks at previous studies where associations between business models and CSR were investigated. Then, we detail the business model definition and classification adopted in this paper and set out the rationale for our hypotheses. The methods section comes next, followed by findings. The paper concludes with a discussion of theoretical and practical implications of the study, limitations, and suggestions for further research.

2. Corporate Social Responsibility in Literature

Corporate Social Responsibility and related concepts (e.g., sustainable development) have been playing an increasingly prominent role in recent years, both in economic and academic research. Despite its popularity—and perhaps in part because of it—authors of numerous publications in this area have not shown a uniform understanding of these constructs, which are sometimes vague and tends to vary from publication to publication. This is reflected in how many distinct terms were used, including Corporate Sustainability and Responsibility, Corporate Citizenship, Corporate Social Rectitude, Corporate Social Performance, Corporate Social Responsiveness, Social Performance, or Sustainable Responsible Business. In fact, in a review of the CSR literature Dahlsrud [11] counted no fewer than 37 different definitions of the concept. Below we shortly outline the history of the idea of sustainable responsibility and wrap up by offering the definition that we assumed in our study.

In terms of social duties of business, for many years the dominant perspective was that of Friedman [12], who maintained that what firms should care for was generating profits, and social responsibilities were no concern of business; indeed, his strongly held conviction was that any action on the part of managers that did not amount to increased profits was tantamount to theft. However, the notion of firms supporting social goals is not new, since the first publications on this topic appeared in the 1930s, e.g., [13,14], and the first formalized definitions date back to the 1950s–60s [15–20]. Rapid growth in CSR has been particularly evident since the 70s, when accelerating globalization made the impact of companies on society and environment a more pertinent problem than ever before [21]. At that time, it was proposed that CSR could offer effective solutions for outstanding societal issues, in large part due to the strong effects of businesses, in particular multinationals, on economy, politics, environment, and local communities [22]. In the 1980s the idea of sustainable development emerged to represent such "development that meets the needs of the present without compromising the ability of the future generations to meet their own needs" [23]. Its proponents advocate sustainable development in economy, society, and the natural environment that would aim to eradicate poverty and moderate excessive consumption in both developed and developing countries [24]. As noted by Vos [25], many definitions of sustainability are similar in that they identify three aspects of the term: economic, social, and environmental.

The growing importance of CSR was recognized by the International Organization for Standardization (ISO), which set up a special task group for social responsibility. As a result of the group's work, a system of guidelines was revealed in 2010 to help businesses operate in a more "ethical and transparent way that contributes to the health and welfare of society" [26]. The ISO 2600 manual outlines specific benefits that can be derived from implementing CSR principles, including enhancing competitive advantage; attracting and retaining employees, shareholders, and clients;

improving the morale, commitment, and productivity of employees; and fostering better image and goodwill from clients, suppliers, local communities, and other stakeholders of the company.

The first definition of CSR that gained wide acceptance was that of Caroll [27]. Caroll proposed a CSR pyramid with four levels representing CSR dimensions: (1) economical (at the base of the pyramid; denoting all activities yielding profit for the company's owners), (2) legal (acting within the law regulating environmental protection, consumer and employee relations, and adhering to contractual agreements), (3) ethical (acting in an ethical and honest way towards stakeholders), and (4) philanthropic (the firm as a good citizen should undertake special programs for the benefit of the society). Later on, Schwartz and Caroll [28], building on the previous model, came up with a non-hierarchical structure with only three dimensions—economical, legal, and ethical—whereby the philanthropic element was split between economical and ethical areas, depending on the dominant underlying motivations behind specific charitable activities. Another popular conceptualization of CSR, known as the triple bottom line (TBL), calls for companies to operate in ways that are socially responsible, eco-friendly, and economically valuable [29]. The three focal points of TBL are people (involving responsible business practices towards employees, customers, society at large, and local communities), the planet (activities aimed at protecting the natural environment), and economic value, or profits earned after contributing to the other two CSR dimensions. According to the TBL perspective, its three dimensions are equal in terms of importance, which should be reflected in corporate reporting. Therefore, not only financial metrics should be reported, but also accounts of the company's social and ecological performance. Such integrative reports should merge both short-term and long-term perspectives [30]. One of the most recent outlooks on CSR and the last one reviewed in this section is that of Chen and Wongsurawat [31], whose definition we chose to adopt in our research. These authors looked to combine Caroll's [27] perspective and TBL with the ISO recommendations. In their view CSR should encompass: (1) competitiveness (*i.e.*, cooperation with stakeholders in building strong market position of the company and its products); (2) transparency (removing barriers for members of the public to accessing corporate information; the aim here is to provide means for fast and efficient communication with a wider audience on the firm's activities with potential social and environmental impacts); (3) responsibility (complying with legal regulations and contractual terms pertaining to different stakeholder groups); (4) accountability (making thoughtful and justified business decisions accommodating the interests of various groups of stakeholders).

To sum up the discussion so far on popular conceptualizations of CSR, and to present our own understanding of the concept used in this work, we distinguish the following four aspects of the CSR involvement: (1) value chain relations (entailing conscientious attitude in interactions with suppliers, customers, and other supply chain partners); (2) community relations (communication, cooperation, and support for local and wider social partners); (3) natural environment (commitment to running business operations with the smallest possible negative impacts on the environment); and (4) employee relations (all corporate socially responsible activities aimed at employees). In keeping with the above taxonomy of CSR, we developed a Likert-type scale for use in the survey questionnaire. The measurement scale was outlined in more detail in the methods section.

3. Overview of Conceptualizations of Business Models

The interest in business models has grown, particularly since the 1990s, when a number of seminal papers were published. The dominant theme for many papers was Internet business, which coincided with—and was sparked by—the dot-com boom and bust, e.g., [32–35]. Academic writing on business models, even more so than on CSR, is affected by a lack of consensus as to what constitutes a business model. So far many definitions and typologies had been proffered, some more popular than others, but no single dominant approach emerged. On the other hand, and quite similar to CSR, most views of business models have considerable overlap, which makes it easier and more meaningful to compare findings across different works. In this section we summarize the more popular ways to think about business models, and present our own approach that was used in the questionnaire design to collect responses from managers.

One way to look at business models was offered by Afuah and Tucci [33], who proposed that it is how a firm builds up and deploys its resources to provide customers with products of value superior to competitors' offerings in order to generate profits. According to Linder and Cantrell [36], a business model is a logical basis for creating a company's value, reflected in a coherent action plan aimed at developing a strategy that meets customer expectations through the optimal use of resources and relations. Here, a business model specifies such elements as: types of customers, products or services, pricing policy, customer benefits, distribution channels, unique competences, and revenue sources. Betz [37] considers a business model as a composition of three elements necessary for the firm to operate: benefits or values for customers and business partners, revenue sources, and logistics arrangements. Osterwalder *et al.* [38] give the following constituting elements of business models as part of their strategic template for crafting new or documenting existing business models: value proposition for customers, corporate infrastructure (including key activities, key resources, and partner network), targeted customers (composed of market segmentation, distribution channels, and customer relationships), cost structures, and revenue streams.

In terms of business model typologies, many authors propose divergent classifications based on different sets of criteria, with many of them mostly relevant to e-business [32,33,35,39–42]. Just a handful of authors attempted to develop a more universal typology system, suitable for classifying a wider range of business models, including traditional, "bricks-and-mortar" companies [36,37,43–46].

4. Earlier Studies on the Links between Business Models and CSR

Even though the problem of how companies with different types of business models get involved in CSR has arguably both practical and theoretical merits, it has rarely been explored as a topic of an academic study. Some authors proposed to introduce new paradigms in management to effectively counteract social and environmental degradation, e.g., [47–50], but only a few incorporated elements of business models in their analyses of CSR, e.g., [51–54]. In recent years, several new pertinent management concepts emerged, such as so-called "sustainable business models" [55–57], "sustainability business models" [58], "business models for sustainability" [51], and "sustaining supply chain management" [59–61]. All of these new constructs build on the theory of corporate sustainability management, which—at a general level—aims to integrate multiple corporate activities and impacts in societal, environmental, and economic areas. Those authors give different definitions of sustainable business models (SBM); for example, they say that it is "a model where sustainability concepts are the driving force of the firm and its decision making" [58], or "a new model of the firm where sustainability concepts play an integral role in shaping the mission or driving force of the firm and its decision making" [62]. Regarding the interplay between business models and CSR, some authors suggest the existence of a feedback loop, whereby certain types of business models can foster stronger CSR involvement [63], while implementing CSR has the potential to transform business models in the long run [53]. In the same vein, Schaltegger and Wagner [64] observe that business models of firms following CSR principles are changing both through purposeful effort and unconscious adjustments. This points to the conclusion that not only strategic management but also daily operational tasks are factors in shaping a business model setup. This view finds support in Elkington [55], who noted that business models are determinants of organizational behaviors, and as such have influence on strategic management as well as operations, including assorted CSR activities. The literature, but also more casual observations and common experience, imply that sustainable management, CSR, and business models are in constant interaction, and firms intending to improve their CSR metrics have to work towards revising their business model [65]. Indeed, deep changes to a business model can be a way of achieving radical improvement to a firm's CSR status through creating more environmental and social value in an economically viable manner [58,66,67], or—to put it another way—capturing economic value while generating social and environmental values [7]. Accordingly, the concept of business models could be a useful tool for reconciling and integrating the often divergent needs and wants of stakeholders in terms of the sustainable development of a company [68]. For that purpose, firms should make a conscious effort to plan and manage the sustainability aspects of their business models [51].

In light of the above, it seems relevant to study links between various types of business models and the CSR record of companies, since there is a good theoretical reason to believe that different business models yield different CSR attitudes and implementations. As such, we propose that:

Hypothesis 1: The intensity of CSR involvement is related to the business model followed by a company.

The second hypothesis for the study will be developed in the following sections of the paper.

5. Business Model Definition and Taxonomy Adopted in the Study

As the theoretical background for our approach to defining and classifying business models we used a framework developed by Dudzik and Witek-Hajduk [69], with further extensions and modifications by Gołębiowski et al. [46]. According to the framework, a business model represents the logic underlying a firm's business activities in a given area and encompasses a description of the value proposition offered by the firm to its customer groups, with a specification of essential resources, processes (activities), and external relationships of the firm, serving to build, offer, and deliver the value proposition, ensure the firm's competitiveness, and enhance its equity. The "area of activity" referred to in the definition, depending on the scope of operations, can concern the whole of a company or an individual strategic business unit (SBU); thus a firm can operate distinct business models in various SBUs at the same time. Gołębiowski et al. [46] point to the following constituting elements of a business model: (1) value proposition to the customer, comprising products offered, benefits delivered at different steps of the transaction process, subjective customer assessment of the acquired benefits *versus* incurred costs, and relationships with final consumers/users of the products; (2) key resources of the company, such as managerial competences, technology, brands, patents, designs, tools, equipment, infrastructure, and market knowledge; (3) the firm's role within the value chain, in particular activities within its internal value chain and their ties with external links of the integrated value chain; (4) revenue sources from selling manufactured goods and rendered services, offering rights to tangible and intangible products through leasing, renting, franchising or licensing, subscription and usage-based fees, and brokerage fees from performing the role of an intermediary for other companies.

Employing this concept of a business model, Dudzik and Witek-Hajduk [69] conducted a survey of Polish companies to arrive at a segmentation of business models that identified five distinct types of firms: (1) traditionalists, (2) market players, (3) contractors, (4) distributors, and (5) integrators.

Table 1 details the distinguishing features of each type of a business model. These descriptions were presented to managers participating in our study so they could choose the one category that was most consistent with their company.

Table 1. Characteristics of business models in the study.

Business Model	Business Model Description
Traditionalist	The main source of value for customers is functional benefits from products, and the relationship of these benefits to costs. The firm does not have unique resources (e.g., a strong brand, patents, designs, technology, and/or recipes). The internal supply chain is long (R&D, production, marketing, sales and after-sales services). Most of the revenues are sales of manufactured products.
Market player	Customers derive most of the value from functional benefits offered by products, as well as the strength of the brand and relationships with other members of the value chain. The firm deploys its unique resources, such as advanced technologies, strong brand, patents, unique designs and recipes, and managerial skills. The internal supply chain is long (R&D, production, marketing, sales and after-sales services). A market player tends to be the leader of its supply chain. Revenues are mostly obtained through the sale of self-manufactured products, supplemented by income from licensing technology, brand names and franchising.

Table 1. *Cont.*

Business Model	Business Model Description
Contractor	The value proposition for customers is mostly based on offering functional product benefits. The main asset of the company is its production facility and equipment, which it employs to manufacture products on contract for other businesses. Its internal supply chain is focused on the production function. Proceeds from manufacturing contracts account for the bulk of the revenues.
Distributor	The value proposition here relies on a favorable relation of functional and emotional benefits of products to their costs. The key distinguishing competency of the company is market knowledge (about suppliers and customers). The internal supply chain is short and focused on the sales function. Revenues are mostly earned through fulfilling the role of a trade intermediary.
Integrator	Customer benefits can come from favorable functional features of products, but also from a strong brand and cohesive partner relationships with members of a supply chain. The distinguishing attributes of an integrator are managerial competences, management information systems, recipes, designs, patents, brand names, and market knowledge. Its internal supply chain is short: as the supply chain leader, an integrator is focused on a few core competences, such as R&D, designing, marketing, sales and after-sales services, while it tends to outsource manufacturing. Income is generated through sales of its own brand-name products and offering its own unique know-how and technology by means of franchising and/or licensing.

Source: Own elaboration based on Dudzik and Witek-Hajduk [69].

From the salient features of various types of business models, as outlined in Table 1, one can reasonably expect considerable differences in the extent of CSR implementation. In seems that out of the four groups of criteria used in the segmentation procedure yielding the above classification, those that are likely to have the strongest bearing on CSR compliance are value proposition, key resources, and the role of a company within its supply chain. Arguably, no salient elements of sustainable business are conditional on a particular setup of revenue sources, so any differences in this regard should be of no consequence to the CSR standing of a company.

Value propositions of market players and integrators are set apart from those of other companies not only by unique combinations of functional features, but also an emphasis on developing strong brand names and cohesive relationships with channel partners. In the current state of the economy in Poland, similar to other developed and emerging countries, consumers in many market segments have been growing ever more sensitive to the ethical behavior of the firms they patronize. As such, these groups of consumers may derive distinctive utility from the fact that their purchasing decisions can support the good citizens among available suppliers of goods and services. On the other hand, firms that aggressively seek to increase the perceived value of their offerings, which are market players and integrators, may choose to get involved in CSR programs specifically for that reason. Consequently, these firms are apt to promote their brands more frequently through charitable programs, whereby, for example, customers can feel better knowing that a part of the paid price goes to support a socially valuable cause. In the same vein, market players and integrators may also see business rationale in establishing and financing charitable foundations, and implementing changes to their core processes (e.g., phasing in eco-friendly technologies) to make assertions of responsible behavior more credible. To further strengthen their case, they also may choose to encourage employees to get involved with local communities to assist in enhancing their capabilities to satisfy salient infrastructural, educational, cultural, and sports-related needs. If that was indeed the main motivation to get involved in CSR, companies might be inclined to follow up this initial actions by overhauling their employee relations and organizational culture—this way employees can become more involved and convinced of the true and honest nature of the managerial push towards sustainable and responsible business practices. With more involved employees it is arguably easier to make a company's CSR claims seem more genuine to its customers, which can foster higher loyalty and greater sales. Quite naturally, the other business models—traditionalists, contractors, and distributors—with their lower interest in creating strong brands will not experience the same motivation, and therefore may display weaker CSR involvement.

Another distinctive feature of market players and integrators is their reliance on unique resources to underlie their competitive advantages. Among these resources are superior managerial competences, innovative and productive organizational culture, proprietary technology, and market knowledge. Many of these capabilities have better chances of being achieved in corporate settings where employees are loyal, highly motivated, and emotionally involved with their workplace. Such conditions are among the likely benefits of implementing CSR programs aimed at improving employee relations, which is another reason to believe that these two business models will show higher CSR ratings.

In terms of a value chain position and relations, market players and integrators follow more active and "social" policies as compared to other categories of firms. Here, the goals and ways of operating create a strong incentive to develop close partnerships with other crucial supply chain members so that market players and integrators could assume the role of a dominant value chain member. This role is critical to their business strategies, which rely on the ability to shape value chains to achieve a higher level of efficiency and effectiveness than the networks controlled by competitors. One of the main prerequisites to achieving such a goal is a high level of trust and commitment among cooperating firms, which is promoted by ethical and responsible behavior from all involved parties. As such, this is another reason to expect more social responsibility (this time aimed at business partners) among market players and integrators than other firms with business models less dependent for success on the quality of everyday channel relations.

To conclude, considering the attributes of the identified types of business models and relating them to the CSR dimensions, it is possible to propose which types of companies will be most likely to operate in the manner consistent with the principles of responsible business. In particular, it can be expected that market players and integrators show higher levels of CSR implementations. On the other hand, the attributes of traditionalists, contractors, and distributors could create less of an incentive to function in a more sustainable way.

Consequently, it is possible to supplement the previous general hypothesis with a more specific proposition:

Hypothesis 2: Among the five types of business models, the highest level of CSR involvement will be found in market players and integrators.

The other possible distinctions between business models are difficult to extrapolate from an *a priori* analysis based on previous research, conceptual papers, and the authors' own observations and experiences.

The empirical part of the research was dedicated to validating the two hypotheses. The methods employed and obtained outcomes are described next.

6. Methods

The study involved a net sample of 385 mangers from medium and large enterprises, who were contacted through a combination of CATI and CAWI methods. In particular, the respondents answered via phone (the CATI part) while looking at the web-based version of the questionnaire (the CAWI component). The inclusion of the web component was essential to make respondents fully understand the rather lengthy business model characteristics presented in Table 1, and choose the model that best described their firms. The respondents were initially contacted via an e-mail outlining the research project, inviting them to participate, and offering a link to a dedicated web-page with a digital questionnaire. Within a few days of receiving the e-mail, phone calls followed during which interviews were conducted or arrangements were made to set up a later interview date. Despite several contact attempts, not all selected sample members could participate: the gross sample initially drawn from a database encompassing almost all companies in Poland was 535, which amounted to a response rate of 72%.

The final (net) sample included manufacturers of food (31.7%) and chemicals (31.2%), as well as retailers and wholesalers of these products (37.1%). In terms of the number of employees, 75.3% firms had between 50 and 249 staff, with the rest employing more than 250 people; 76.9% of the sample had solely Polish owners, while 23.1% reported various levels of foreign ownership.

The statistical analysis in this project was twofold. First, we validated our measurement model of CSR involvement with confirmatory factor analysis (CFA) using the AMOS 23 software. The second step involved employing one-way analysis of variance (ANOVA) as the means of testing the hypotheses of differences between various business models in terms of CSR involvement. Here, we used five dependent variables: one for the general level of a firm's engagement in CSR and four depicting its respective dimensions. The factor scores for each latent variable for every company were obtained through a regression method from the preciously validated CFA model.

7. Research Findings

We start this section by explaining how business models were identified. Then we specify the CSR measurement model, followed by its diagnostics and concluding with the outcomes of the ANOVA.

To determine which of the predefined business models best describes each company, managers were offered descriptions of five distinct profiles and asked to choose only one that best portrayed their main area of operation in Poland. Recognizing that this mode of collecting answers, if employed over the phone, may produce biased results (due to extensive textual descriptions) respondents were able to see the relevant parts of the questionnaire on a web page while interacting with an interviewer through the CATI method.

English translations of characteristics of business models were presented in Table 1 earlier in the paper. Table 2 below gives sample frequencies and percentages for the different types of business models.

Table 2. Frequency distribution of business models in the study sample.

Business model	Sample Frequency	Sample Percentage
Traditionalist	168	43.6
Market player	71	18.4
Contractor	30	7.8
Distributor	66	17.2
Integrator	50	13.0
Together	385	100

Source: Own elaboration.

Considering that the studied companies were part of long-established industries, it comes as no surprise that nearly half of them declared that they were operating according to a traditionalist business model. The smallest number of studied firms was identified by their managers as contractors, which is also understandable since Poland is not a very popular location for contractual manufacturing, especially compared to East Asian countries, the long-standing providers of outsourcing services. On the whole, the frequency of each of the subgroups was sufficient to perform reliable analysis of variance tests—as a rule of thumb, 20 is often given as a minimum sample size per group [70].

As discussed before, the adopted understanding of social responsibility assumed that CSR involvement is a second-order reflective construct expressed through four dimensions. The CSR dimensions, themselves being first order reflective latent variables, were measured with five-point Likert-scale items. The specific content of the items used in the survey questionnaire is given in the following table. Literature sources that were used to inform the scale building choices were also indicated in Table 3.

Table 3. Dimensionality and manifest variables in the CSR involvement model.

Item Designation in Measurement Model	Item Content	Literature Sources
\multicolumn{3}{c}{Latent variable: Value Chain Relations}		
VAL_1	We use CSR principles in selecting suppliers.	[71–78]
VAL_2	We create the image of our firm, brands, and products with reference to social values.	
VAL_3	Our customers are aware that part of our product prices supports our CSR initiatives.	
VAL_4	Payments to our suppliers are made in keeping with contractual obligations.	
VAL_5	Our firm seeks to follow international standards and certificates (e.g., ISO 26000, SA 8000, Fair Trade).	
\multicolumn{3}{c}{Latent variable: Community Relations}		
COM_1	We are involved in charitable initiatives.	[71,75,79,80]
COM_2	We have a special organizational unit (e.g., a foundation) tasked with social and/or charitable objectives.	
COM_3	Our employees are involved in voluntary charitable activities.	
COM_4	We provide financial support to local communities in terms of their infrastructural, cultural, educationalm and sports-related needs.	
\multicolumn{3}{c}{Latent variable: Natural Environment}		
ENV_1	We take care to prevent events that could have negative impacts on environment and society	[71,79–82]
ENV_2	We strive to limit our use of energy, water, and other resources.	
ENV_3	We use recycling and try to limit our waste.	
ENV_4	We aim to curb our CO_2 emissions.	
ENV_5	We use eco-friendly technologies and materials in our processes, products, and packaging.	
\multicolumn{3}{c}{Latent variable: Employee Relations}		
EMP_1	We have control and supervision mechanisms to monitor, support, and enforce ethical behavior among employees.	[80,83,84]
EMP_2	Our employees have ways to report unethical conduct without fear of retribution.	
EMP_3	We have implemented procedures to enable swift reaction against acts of breaching employee rights.	
EMP_4	In our company we respect principles of diversity management, including gender and disabilities.	
EMP_5	We have implemented a system of creating good CSR practices by employees.	
EMP_6	Employees are consulted before we implement changes in our company.	

Source: Own elaboration.

The validity of the above model was tested with confirmatory factor analysis using the maximum likelihood estimation.

Considering that the sample was composed of firms representing three distinct industries (*i.e.*, food production, chemical manufacturing, and commerce, both wholesale and retail), it was essential to test the model structure for measurement invariance. Measurement invariance is found when all relevant subgroups could be equally well represented by the same pattern of regression weights and covariances in the model. A common way to test for measurement invariance is to compare an unconstrained model (assuming that all groups have all parameters estimated independently) with a model where regression weights and covariances are set to be equal across all groups. Then chi-square statistics are computed for alternative models and the chi-square differential is obtained. Evidence for measurement invariance is found when the chi-square difference is insignificant [85] and so—consistent with the principle of parsimony—the simpler (*i.e.*, constrained) option should be retained. In the current study, the chi-square value representing discrepancies between the two models was 47.426, with 40 degrees of freedom and a p-value of 0.196. This implies that the model where all firms are pooled together as a single group is superior, as the more complex solution with different parameters across groups does not offer markedly better accuracy. From a practical perspective, our research appears to suggest that CSR involvement (at least when measured using the metrics deployed in our survey) is a universal characteristic reflected in a similar way (following the same structural patterns) in firms with various backgrounds.

The resultant CFA diagram, with its standardized regression parameters and squared multiple correlations, is depicted in Figure 1.

In order to evaluate the model fit with the sample data, we used a set of common indices as set out in Table 4.

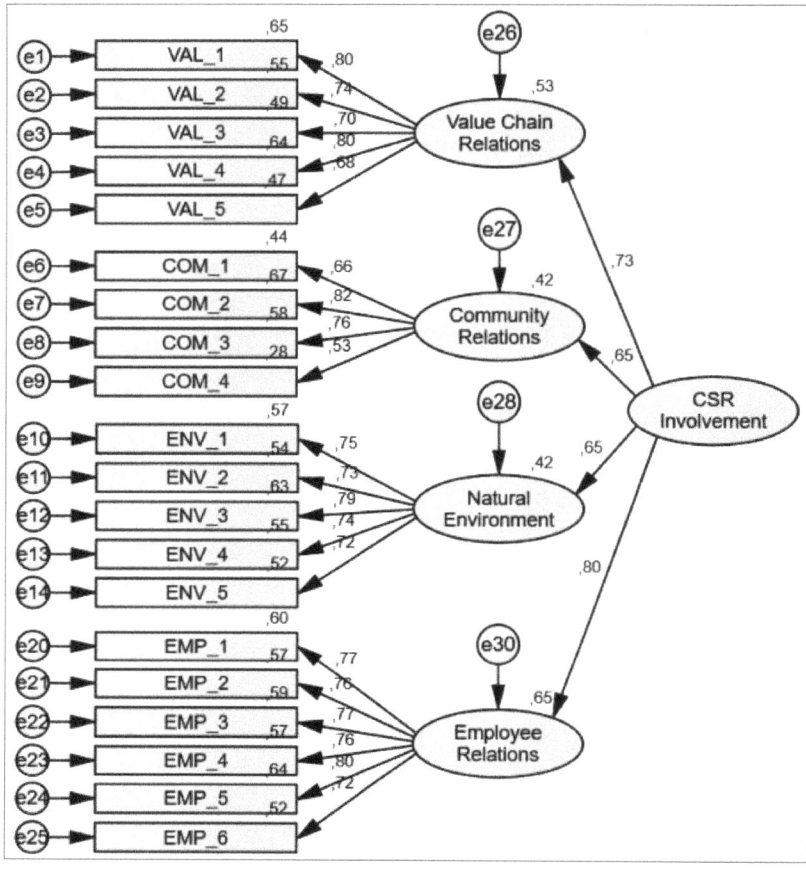

Figure 1. CFA model of the CSR involvement construct.

Table 4. Overall fit measures for the CFA model.

Metric	Value	Threshold for a Well-Fitting Model
Chi-square/df (relative chi-square)	2.326	<3 for good fit
p-value for the model	<0.001	>0.05
GFI (goodness of fit index)	0.905	⩾0.9
CFI (comparative fit index)	0.942	⩾0.9
AGFI (adjusted goodness of fit index)	0.880	⩾0.8
PCFI (parsimony comparative fit index)	0.823	⩾0.8
RMSEA (root mean square of approximation)	0.059; HI90 = 0.066	⩽0.05 for good model fit; ⩽0.08 for adequate fit; in addition, the upper 90% confidence limit (HI 90) should be no more than 0.08 for a well-fitting model

Source: Own elaboration. Cutoff points based on Garson [86].

The above metrics indicate a close match between the model and the data. The only exception is the chi-square test, which is significant and rejects the null hypothesis of the lack of differences between the observed covariance matrix and the one implied by the model. However, the chi-square statistic tends to be considerably inflated for large samples, which results in excessive sensitivity of the test. Therefore, this measure is considered unreliable and could be disregarded if other metrics point to a well-fitting solution [85,87], which is what happens in the current analysis.

Table 5 provides insights into CSR dimensions in terms of reliability (Cronbach's Alpha), convergent validity (AVE, or average variance extracted) and discriminant validity (MSV, or maximum shared variance).

Table 5. Reliability and validity measures of CSR involvement dimensions.

Construct	Cronbach's Alpha	AVE	MSV
Value Chain Relations	0.839	0.596	0.345
Community Relations	0.788	0.493	0.272
Natural Environment	0.861	0.562	0.271
Employee Relations	0.896	0.583	0.345

Source: Own elaboration.

The metrics in Table 5 are implying a solution that does not reveal any apparent issues compromising its interpretability. In particular, it seems that the manifest variables used to represent the latent constructs have high levels of internal consistency—Cronbach's alphas are all greater than 0.07, as suggested in Malhotra [88]. AVE values, which show how well hidden variables are represented by their corresponding indicators, should be at least 0.5 [89], which is true for all constructs except Community Relations; however, even there the cut-off is missed by only a small amount. As such, Community Relations appear to explain only 49% of variance in its indicators, with the rest of the variability accounted for by other factors outside of the model. This outcome is not entirely unexpected, since it could easily be argued that a firm's contributions to local communities through financial aid or the work of its employees are strongly context-sensitive and determined—for example—by the particular locale in which the firm operates. Naturally, these external influences seem to be quite independent of the company's stance on CSR.

Having concluded that the CSR involvement model is at least adequate in how it fits the collected data, we derived from it five new variables to represent the latent constructs in further analysis.

To investigate how various business models compared in terms of CSR involvement, we performed five one-way ANOVA tests. Each test had a different dependent variable; either the general CSR involvement level or one of the four of its dimensions. As an independent variable, the same factor was used in each test, which showed which of the five business models each company followed. The outcomes of the ANOVA were given in Table 6.

Table 6. One-way ANOVA outcomes for differences in CSR involvement among business models.

Business Model		N	Mean	Std. Error	ANOVA Test Results
Overall CSR Involvement	traditionalist	168	−0.141	1.007	$F(4;380) = 5.688$ $p < 0.001$
	market player	71	0.420	0.886	
	contractor	30	−0.129	0.932	
	distributor	66	−0.206	1.029	
	integrator	50	0.225	0.948	
	total	385	0.000	1.000	
Employee Relations	traditionalist	168	−0.154	1.015	$F(4;380) = 4.670$ $p = 0.001$
	market player	71	0.337	0.944	
	contractor	30	−0.011	0.930	
	distributor	66	−0.177	1.019	
	integrator	50	0.278	0.892	
	total	385	0.000	1.000	
Community Relations	traditionalist	168	−0.142	0.952	$F(4;380) = 5.542$ $p < 0.001$
	market player	71	0.431	0.921	
	contractor	30	−0.207	0.964	
	distributor	66	−0.153	1.011	
	integrator	50	0.190	1.095	
	total	385	0.000	1.000	
Natural Environment	traditionalist	168	−0.031	1.010	$F(4;380) = 3.618$ $p = 0.007$
	market player	71	0.299	0.827	
	contractor	30	−0.116	1.068	
	distributor	66	−0.303	1.087	
	integrator	50	0.150	0.924	
	total	385	0.000	1.000	
Value Chain Relations	traditionalist	168	−0.109	1.011	$F(4;380) = 3.212$ $p = 0.013$
	market player	71	0.353	0.851	
	contractor	30	−0.175	1.018	
	distributor	66	−0.084	0.994	
	integrator	50	0.081	1.066	
	total	385	0.000	1.000	

Source: Own elaboration.

As evidenced in Table 6, the ANOVA tests were all significant, implying the existence of meaningful differences among business models. This outcome supports our first hypothesis (H.1) predicting unalike involvement in CSR from firms following dissimilar business models.

Looking at the means, it is clear that market players followed by integrators consistently had the highest scores on the general metric of CSR, as well as on its particular dimensions. At the other end of the spectrum were traditionalists, contractors, and distributors, with quite similar negative averages. Considering that the basic ANOVA test only informs about the presence or lack of at least one difference between all pairs of subgroups, to formally verify our second more specific hypothesis we defined a specific comparison of two groups of firms using contrasts. As per the second hypothesis, the first group consisted of market players and integrators, while the second comprised traditionalists, contractors, and distributors. The contrast weights assigned to particular business models were as follows: market players 3, integrators 3, traditionalists −2, contractors −2, and distributors −2. It can be noted that the members of the same comparison groups have identical weights, and the sum of all weights is 0, which is required from a correctly specified test. Table 7 shows the outcomes of the contrast tests for the general CSR involvement and its respective dimensions.

Table 7. Contrast test results comparing two groups of business models in terms of CSR involvement.

CSR Metrics	Value of Contrast	Std. Error	t	df	Sig. (2-Tailed)
Overall CSR Involvement	2.887	0.707	4.082	380	0.000
Employee Relations	2.529	0.710	3.559	380	0.000
Community relations	2.865	0.708	4.048	380	0.000
Natural Environment	2.245	0.715	3.142	380	0.002
Value chain relations	2.037	0.716	2.842	380	0.005

Source: Own elaboration.

As can be seen, the values of contrasts are all positive and significant, which indicates that the first group of market players and integrators had consistently greater values on all CSR metrics then the second group. This evidence points to the second hypothesis being correct, which in substantive terms means that market players and integrators displayed stronger CSR involvement than other types of business models.

To further investigate the individual pairwise differences and similarities between various business models, it is informative to use *post hoc* tests, which compare individual ANOVA subgroups while controlling for familywise error. Hence, Table 8 sets out significant *post hoc* tests for all possible pairings of business models calculated with the Games–Howell procedure.

Table 8. Games–Howell multiple comparisons of business models on CSR involvement (only differences significant at the 0.05 and 0.1 levels were included).

Dependent Variable	Comparison Pairs of Business Models that Best Describes Respondents' Firms		Mean Difference	Std. Error	Sig.
Overall CSR Involvement	traditionalist	market player	−0.561	0.131	0.000
	market player	traditionalist	0.561	0.131	0.000
		contractor	0.549	0.200	0.061
		distributor	0.626	0.165	0.002
	contractor	market player	−0.549	0.200	0.061
	distributor	market player	−0.626	0.165	0.002
	integrator		Significant differences not found		
Employee Relations	traditionalist	market player	−0.491	0.137	0.004
		integrator	−0.432	0.149	0.036
	market player	traditionalist	0.491	0.137	0.004
		distributor	0.514	0.168	0.022
	contractor		Significant differences not found		
	integrator	market player	−0.514	0.168	0.022
		integrator	−0.456	0.178	0.085
		traditionalist	0.432	0.149	0.036
		distributor	0.456	0.178	0.085
Community Relations	traditionalist	market player	−0.572	0.132	0.000
	market player	traditionalist	0.572	0.132	0.000
		contractor	0.638	0.207	0.026
		distributor	0.583	0.166	0.005
	contractor	market player	−0.638	0.207	0.026
	distributor	market player	−0.583	0.166	0.005
	integrator		Significant differences not found		

Table 8. Cont.

Dependent Variable	Comparison Pairs of Business Models that Best Describes Respondents' Firms		Mean Difference	Std. Error	Sig.
Natural Environment	traditionalist	market player	−0.329	0.125	0.070
	market player	traditionalist	0.329	0.125	0.070
		distributor	0.602	0.166	0.004
	contractor		Significant differences not found		
	distributor	market player	−0.602	0.166	0.004
	integrator		Significant differences not found		
Value Chain Relations	traditionalist	market player	−0.462	0.128	0.004
	market player	traditionalist	0.462	0.128	0.004
		distributor	0.437	0.159	0.052
	contractor		Significant differences not found		
	distributor	market player	−0.437	0.159	0.052
	integrator		Significant differences not found		

Source: Own elaboration.

At the 0.05 significance level, the Games–Howell tests confirm the earlier observation that market players displayed the best results of all investigated business models in terms of following the CSR guidelines, in both the general and particular sense. On the other hand, traditionalists, distributors, and contractors showed significant discrepancies when compared to market players, but not to integrators. The fact that market players are significantly different from all other types of business models except integrators, coupled with the observation that there were no significant differences among traditionalists, contractors, and distributors, lends further support to our theory-based assumption that there were two general groups of business models in terms of adherence to the CSR principles. A part of that proposition was already validated with the contrast tests, but *post hoc* tests provide more evidence by implying that the two groups might be internally homogenous in their degrees of CSR implementation.

8. Theoretical and Practical Implications of the Study

This study has made several valuable contributions to the theory and practice of management.

We have shown that CSR could be a universal phenomenon in that it appears in a similar manner in manufacturing and service companies of different industries and sizes. This is not to say that all groups of companies are the same in terms of the intensity of involvement in CSR, but rather it suggests the same underlying mechanism governing relationships between the second-order CSR construct, its four dimensions, and their measurable indicators. This conclusion seems to be generally in line with many earlier works based on a case study method. Many of them are relying on the conceptual framework of CSR with four similar dimensions that appeared to show equal relevance when applied to firms from different industries, e.g., [7,9,10,57]. However, with survey research, due to its high level of standardization, developing a measurement tool adequate for many types of companies is more problematic. The previous quantitative research that we know of involved narrowly defined industries, very often manufacturing, which amounted to relatively homogeneous samples more suited for statistical analysis, e.g., [80,82,84]. In contrast, this current paper offers questionnaire scales with statistical evidence, implying that the same measurement model could be used in all three industries with similar validity and reliability. On the face of it, it would seem that firms operating in such different contexts would display considerable dissimilarities. One source of such differences could be in distinct legal frameworks regulating environmental issues in chemical industry, food manufacturing, and retailing, with the chemical industry subjected to the most stringent conditions. However, most of these differences pertain to very specific limits on emissions, use of energy and resources, and other aspects of environmental protection, while our measurement scales ask about those things only in a general way that seems to be applicable to all studied companies.

Arguably the most natural area where CSR could be applied in a similar fashion across all three industries is employee relations. This is not only because of the intrinsic versatility of human resources, which can take a similar form in many different settings, but also in large part due to the same system of legal regulations applying to each and every firm. This comes as no surprise since "it is clear that law and legal standards in various forms ... play a considerable role in relation to the substance of CSR, and for implementation and communication of CSR" [90].

Considering that the studied firms were medium and large in size, and most of those firms in said industries in Poland are operating with various implementations of ISO systems, this could also be a unifying factor. The ISO systems have many regulations that determine how firms should organize their assorted functions and processes, including guidelines that are consistent with CSR principles (e.g., environmental protection, employee relations, external stakeholder relations, value chain cooperation). The capability of ISO standards to drive similar implementations of responsible business practices was shown before in papers by other authors [91,92].

Given the discussion so far, it seems that our multiple measurement scale could be a versatile and capable tool for studying CSR in companies across various business contexts.

One practical application of our outcomes could be in the area of public policy. Even though most governments in developed countries make efforts to support responsible business standards, there are reasons to believe that these actions have only limited effectiveness [93]. As such, our findings suggest that local and national governments, as well as other policymakers interested in promoting sustainable growth and ethical standards in business, should support above all enterprises operating in line with the business models of market players and integrators. The present research indicates that these business models are most CSR-oriented, which should bring about the best effects in terms of—for example—environmental protection, employee relations, harmonious cooperation with local communities, and conscientious attitude towards other stakeholders. In other words, here public policy measures would be the most aligned with the intrinsic tendencies of these types of businesses to act in a responsible fashion.

Another possibly useful insight for mangers is our observation that CSR involvement might contribute to enhancing brand equity, leading to a higher brand value and increased value for shareholders. This corroborates some earlier research, involving quantitative surveys, demonstrating that CSR can build trust with customers, which in turn enhances corporate reputation and results in greater brand equity [94]. This stems from the fact that market players and integrators both had higher levels of CSR implementation, and one likely reason for that could be related to them building stronger brands among consumers and business partners, which is among the defining features of their business models. It should be noted, though, that this is more of a supposition than a finding based on direct evidence. Despite a degree of uncertainty, such a relationship points to an interesting topic of a follow-up study explicitly investigating the links between business models, CSR involvement, and brand value.

Our research seems to substantiate a theoretical proposition of a feedback link between CSR and business models, which can be found in many conceptual papers, e.g., [95]. According to theory and—mostly qualitative—observations, firms that adopt successful CSR programs and initiatives tend to experience changes in organizational culture, which becomes more CSR-oriented and promotes further responsible corporate behaviors, including deeper structural changes to strategies and business models [96]. This mechanism could arguably result in a self-perpetuating virtuous circle, driving sustainability commitment to become ever deeper. Based on the current study, it can be noted that the business models supporting CSR, and in turn being supported by it, are market players and integrators. Their CSR metrics, markedly better than those of other types of companies, can be interpreted as pointing to the presence of such a feedback mechanism.

The tendency of market players and integrators to act in a more socially responsible way towards their stakeholders, including value chain members, could serve other companies as a sign of good candidates for mutually beneficial partnerships. Indeed, it is more so because the business classification scheme employed in the study is easy to use by practitioners, who can readily identify market players and integrators among their potential partners.

The study findings could also provide a measure of reassurance to those consumers who are keen to support ethical companies but are uncertain about the sincerity of their CSR claims. According to a recent segmentation study of Polish households, those who are sensitive to cause-related marketing and are willing to pay more for products of firms that contribute to solving relevant social problems make up almost 30% of the adult population [97]. It seems that CSR in most active companies (market players and integrators) is not "skin deep" but tends to be implemented quite thoroughly and comprehensively. Therefore, it is believable that many of the CSR claims used as promotional devices are genuine projections of strategic orientation and organizational culture values in firms with the two most "sustainability-friendly" business models.

9. Limitations and Directions for Further Research

Similar to other projects of this kind, one rather obvious constraining feature of the study that could limit the scope of possible generalizations is the nature of the surveyed population. It could be contended that locating the survey in Poland in the context of the three industries can make it problematic to infer beyond this research setting to other countries or types of companies. However, the patterns that transpired in our data seem to be of a general nature, well grounded in theory, and explainable in terms of their underlying causal mechanism. These likely causal mechanisms, tying up the two types of business models with a more active stance in social responsibility, as explained earlier in the paper, could conceivably be found in firms using the same business models from beyond our research population. It would be, nevertheless, interesting to see if the outcomes can be replicated in different research settings.

Another idea for supplementary research is a qualitative multiple-case study where causal mechanisms, leading from types of business models to various levels of CSR involvement, could be probed in depth. Such an investigation could serve to validate our literature and experience-based suppositions about the reasons for differences between business models, and possibly identify new patterns of relevant factors. Those new factors might involve propositions of mediating or moderating variables that could be controlled for in survey research to outline a more complete picture of associations between business models and CSR.

New research, in addition to including mediating and moderating variables, could also look at financial metrics (e.g., profit margin, ROA, ROE), and how these correspond to CSR levels among firms with different business models. It is plausible that correlations from CSR involvement to financial outcomes might vary in significance and strength in different business model groups.

Author Contributions: Author Contributions: Most of the tasks involved in writing the paper were done jointly by both authors. These include: developing the concept and design, analysis and interpretation, writing the article, and its critical revision. Statistical analysis was performed by Piotr Zaborek.

Conflicts of Interest: Conflicts of Interest: The authors declare that they have no competing interests.

References

1. Ferrrero, I.; Hoffman, M.; McNulty, R. Must Milton Friedman Embrace Stakeholder Theory? *Bus.Soc. Rev.* **2014**, *119*, 37–59. [CrossRef]
2. Moczadlo, R. Creating Competitive Advantages—The European CSR-Strategy Compared with Porter's and Kramer's Shared Value Approach. *Econviews* **2015**, *28*, 243–256.
3. Nwagbara, U.; Reid, P. Corporate Social Responsibility (CSR) and Management Trends: Changing Times and Changing Strategies. *Econ. Insights Trends Chall.* **2013**, *65*, 12–19.

4. Michelini, L.; Fiorentino, D. New Business Models for Creating Shared Value. *Soc. Responsib. J.* **2012**, *8*, 561–577. [CrossRef]
5. Liu, M.T.; Wong, I.A.; Shi, G.; Chu, R.; Brock, J. The Impact of Corporate Social Responsibility (CSR) and perceived brand quality on customer-based brand preference. *J. Serv. Market.* **2014**, *28*, 181–194.
6. Pyszka, A. A CSR driven innovative business model. *Int. J. Contemp. Manag.* **2011**, *4*, 98–100.
7. Bocken, N.; Short, S.; Rana, P.; Evans, S. A value mapping tool for sustainable business modelling. *Corp. Gov.* **2013**, *13*, 482–497.
8. Creasey, D. Corporate responsibility: You can't afford to ignore it. *Gov. Dir.* **2015**, *67*, 161–163.
9. Hogevold, N. A corporate effort towards a sustainable business model: A case study from the Norwegian Furniture Industry. *Eur. Bus. Rev.* **2011**, *23*, 392–400.
10. Pelham, F. Will sustainability change the business model of event industry? *Worldw. Sustain.Tour. Themes* **2011**, *3*, 187–192.
11. Dahlsrud, A. How corporate social responsibility is defined: An analysis of 37 Definitions. *Corp. Soc. Responsib. Environ. Manag.* **2008**, *15*, 1–13. [CrossRef]
12. Friedman, M. The Social Responsibility of Business is to Increase Its Profits. Available online: http://www.colorado.edu/studentgroups/libertarians/issues/friedman-soc-resp-business.html (accessed on 15 January 2016).
13. Barnard, C.I. *The Function of the Executive*; Harvard College: Harvard, UK, 1938.
14. Clark, J.M. *Social Control of Business*, 2nd ed.; Augustus M Kelley Pubs: Westport, CT, USA, 1939.
15. Bowen, R. *Social Responsibility of the Businessman*; Harper and Borthers: New York, NY, USA, 1953.
16. Frederick, W.C. The growing concern over business responsibility. *Calif. Manag. Rev.* **1960**, *2*, 54–61. [CrossRef]
17. Eells, R.; Walton, C. *Conceptual Foundations of Business*; Richard D. Irwin, Inc., 1961.
18. Davis, K.; Blomstrom, R.L. *Business and Its Environment*; McGraw-Hill: New York, NY, USA, 1966.
19. Davis, K. Understanding the social responsibility puzzle: What does the businessman owe to society? *Bus. Horiz.* **1967**, *10*, 45–50. [CrossRef]
20. McGuire, J. *Business and Society*; McGraw-Hill: New York, NY, USA, 1963.
21. Fitch, H.G. Achieving corporate social responsibility. *Acad. Manag. Rev.* **1976**, *1*, 38–46. [CrossRef]
22. Beesley, M.E.; Evans, T. *Corporate Responsibility: A Reassessment*; Croom Helm: London, UK, 1978.
23. Brundtland, G. Report of the World Commission on Environment and Development: Our Common Future. 1987. Available online: http://www.un-documents.net/our-common-future.pdf (accessed on 10 May 2015).
24. People and the planet. The Royal Society Science Policy Centre report 01/12. April 2012 DES2470. Available online: http://www.interacademies.net/File.aspx?id=25028. 1699–1710 (accessed on 13 February 2015).
25. Vos, R.O. Defining sustainability: A conceptual orientation. *J. Chem. Technol. Biotechnol.* **2007**, *82*, 334–339. [CrossRef]
26. ISO 2600 Guidance on Social Responsibility. 2010. Available online: http://www.iso.org/iso/catalogue_detail?csnumber=42546 (accessed on 01 May 2015).
27. Carroll, A. The Pyramid of Corporate Social Responsibility: Toward the Moral Management of Organizational Stakeholders. *Bus. Horiz.* **1991**, *34*, 39–48. [CrossRef]
28. Schwarz, M.S.; Carroll, A.B. Corporate social responsibility: A three-domain approach. *Bus. Ethics Q.* **2003**, *13*, 503–530. [CrossRef]
29. Elkington, J. *Cannibals With Forks: The Triple Bottom Line of 21st Century Business*; New Society Publishers: Stony Creek, CT, USA, 1998.
30. Aras, G.; Crowther, D. *The Durable Corporation*; Gower Publishing: Farnham, England, UK, 2009.
31. Chen, C.H.; Wongsurawat, W. Core constructs of corporate social responsibility: A path analysis. *Asia Pac. J. Bus. Adm.* **2011**, *3*, 47–61. [CrossRef]
32. Rappa, M. Managing the Digital Enterprise: Business Models on the Web. North Carolina State University, 2001. Available online: http://digitalenterprise.org/models.
33. Afuah, A.N.; Tucci, C.L. *Internet Business Models and Strategies: Text and Cases*; McGraw-Hill: New York, NY, USA, 2003.
34. Applegate, L.M. E-Business Models: Making Sense of the Internet Business Landscape. In *Information Technology and the New Enterprise: Future Models for Managers*; Applegate, L.M., Dickson, G.W., DeSanctis, G., Eds.; Prentice Hall: Upper Saddle River, NJ, USA, 2000.

35. Applegate, L.M. *Emerging E-Business Models: Lessons from the Field*; Harvard Business School: Boston, MA, USA, 2001.
36. Linder, J.; Cantrell, S. Changing Business Models: Surveying the Landscape. *Accent. Inst. Strateg. Chang.* **2004**, 7–9. Available online: http://course.shufe.edu.cn/jpkc/zhanlue/upfiles/edit/201002/20100224120954.pdf (accessed on 3 December 2013).
37. Betz, F. Strategic Business Models. *Eng. Manag. J.* **2002**, *14*, 21–27. [CrossRef]
38. Osterwalder, A.; Pigneur, Y.; Tucci, C. Clarifying Business Models: Origins, Present, and Future of the Concept. *Commun. Assoc. Inf. Syst.* **2005**, *15*, 751–775.
39. Timmers, P. Business Models for Electronic Commerce. *Electron. Mark.* **1998**, *2*, 3–8. [CrossRef]
40. Weill, P.; Vitale, M.R. *Place to Space: Migrating to E-Business Models*; Harvard Business School Press: Boston, MA, USA, 2001.
41. Hartman, A.; Sifinis, J.; Kador, J. *E-Biznes: Strategie Sukcesu W Gospodarce Internetowej. Sprawdzone Metody Organizacji Przedsięwzięć E-Biznesowych*; K.E. Liber: Warszawa, Poland, 2001.
42. Doligalski, T.; Zaborek, P.; Romańczuk, S. Value Proposition and Firm Performance: Segmentation of Polish Online Companies. *Int. J. Perform. Manag.* **2015**, *16*, 133–148. [CrossRef]
43. Slywotzky, A.J.; Morrison, D.; Andelman, B. *Strefa Zysku. Strategiczne Modele Działalności*; PWE: Warszawa, Poland, 2000.
44. Chesbrough, H.; Rosenbloom, R.S. The Role of the Business Model in Capturing Value from Innovation: Evidence from Xerox Corporation's Technology Spin-off Companies. *Ind. Corp. Change* **2002**, *11*, 529–555. [CrossRef]
45. Malone, T.W.; Weill, P.; Lai, R.K.; D'Urso, V.T.; Herman, G.; Apel, T.G.; Woerner, S.L. *Do Some Business Models Perform Better than Others?*; MIT Sloan Executive Education: Cambridge, UK, 2006.
46. Gołębiowski, T.; Dudzik, T.; Lewandowska, M.; Witek-Hajduk, M.K. *Modele Biznesu Polskich Przedsiębiorstw*; Oficyna Wydawnicza SGH: Warszawa, Poland, 2008.
47. Doppelt, B. *Leading Change Toward Sustainability*; Greenleaf Publishing: Sheffield, UK, 2003.
48. Dunphy, D.; Griffiths, A.; Benn, S. *Organizational Change for Corporate Sustainability*; Routledge: London, UK, 2003.
49. Griffiths, A.; Petrick, J.A. Corporate Architecture for Sustainability. *Int. J. Oper. Prod. Manag.* **2001**, *21*, 1573–1585. [CrossRef]
50. Shrivastava, P. Ecocentric management for a risk society. *Acad. Manag. Rev.* **1995**, *20*, 118–137.
51. Lüdeke-Freund, F. Towards a conceptual framework of business models for sustainability. In Proceedings of the Knowledge Collaboration & Learning for Sustainable Innovation Conference, Delft, The Netherlands, 25–29 Octorber 2010; Wever, R., Quist, J., Tukker, A., Woudstra, J., Boons, F., Beute, N., Eds.; pp. 25–29.
52. Schaltegger, S.; Müller, M. CSR zwischen unternehmerischer Vergangenheitsbewältigung und Zukunftsgestaltung. In *Corporate Social Responsibility: Trend oder Modeerscheinung?*; Müller, M., Schaltegger, S., Eds.; Oekom Publishing: München, Germany, 2005; pp. 17–35.
53. Weber, M. The business case for corporate social responsibility: A company-level measurement approach for CSR. *Eur. Manag. J.* **2008**, *26*, 247–261. [CrossRef]
54. Seelos, C.; Mair, J. Profitable Business Models and Market Creation in the Context of Deep Poverty: A Strategic View. *Acad. Manag. Perspect.* **2007**, *21*, 49–63. [CrossRef]
55. Elkington, J. Enter the Triple Bottom Line. In *The Triple Bottom Line, Does It All Add Up?*; Henriques, A., Richardson, J., Eds.; Earthscan: London, UK, 2004.
56. Birkin, F.; Cashman, A.; Koh, S.; Liu, Z. New Sustainable Business Models in China. *Bus. Strategy Environ.* **2009**, *18*, 64–77. [CrossRef]
57. Høgevold, N.M.; Svensson, G.; Wagner, B.; Petzer, D.J.; Klopper, H.B.; Varela, J.C.S.; Padin, C.; Ferro, C. Sustainable business models. *Balt. J. Manag.* **2014**, *9*, 357–380. [CrossRef]
58. Stubbs, W.; Cocklin, C. Conceptualizing a "Sustainability Business Model". *Organ. Environ.* **2008**, *21*, 103–127. [CrossRef]
59. Seuring, B.M.; Müller, M. From a literature review to a conceptual framework for sustainable supply chain management. *J. Clean. Prod.* **2008**, *16*, 1699–1710. [CrossRef]
60. Ashby, A.; Leat, M.; Hudson-Smith, M. Making connections: A review of supply chain management and sustainability literature. *Supply Chain Manag. Int. J.* **2012**, *17*, 497–517.

61. Gimenez, C.; Tachizawa, E.M. Extending sustainability to suppliers: A systematic literature review. *Supply Chain Manag. Int. Rev.* **2012**, *17*, 531–543.
62. Wicks, A.C. Overcoming the separation thesis: The need for a reconsideration of business and society research. *Bus. Soc.* **1996**, *35*, 89–118. [CrossRef]
63. Lüdeke-Freund, F. Business Model Concepts in Corporate Sustainability Contexts. From Rhetoric to a Generic Template for Business Models for Sustainability. Centre for Sustainability Management, 2009. Available online: http://www2.leuphana.de/umanagement/csm/content/nama/downloads/download_publikationen/Business_Models_for_Sustainability.pdf (accessed on 18 January 2016).
64. Schaltegger, S.; Wagner, M. Integrative management of sustainability performance, measurement and reporting. *Int. J. Account. Audit. Perform. Eval.* **2006**, *3*, 1–19. [CrossRef]
65. Yip, G. Using Strategy to Change Your Business Model. *Bus. Strategy Rev.* **2004**, *15*, 17–24. [CrossRef]
66. Porter, M.; Kramer, M. Creating Shared Value. *Harv. Bus. Rev.* **2011**, *89*, 62–77. Available online: http://hbr.org/2011/01/the-big-ideacreating-shared-value (accessed on 18 January 2016).
67. Yunus, M.; Moingeon, B.; Lehmann-Ortega, L. Building Social Business Models: Lessons from the Grameen Experience. *Long Range Plan.* **2010**, *43*, 308–325. [CrossRef]
68. Osterwalder, A. The Business Model Ontology. In *A Proposition In A Design Science Approach. Dissertation*; Universite de Lausanne: Lausanne, Switzerland, 2004. Available online: http://www.hec.unil.ch/aosterwa/PhD/Osterwalder_PhD_BM_Ontology.pdf (accessed on 15 June 2015).
69. Dudzik, T.M.; Witek-Hajduk, M.K. Typologia modeli biznesu. *Gospod. Materiałowa i Logistyka* **2007**, *9*, 18–23.
70. Mooi, E.; Sarstedt, M. *A Concise Guide to Market Research: The Process, Data and Methods Using IBM SPSS Statistics*, 2nd ed.; Springer-Verlag: Berlin, Germany, 2014.
71. Elkington, J. Cannibals with forks: The triple bottom line of the 21st Century Business. *Environ. Qual. Manag.* **1998**, *8*, 37–51. [CrossRef]
72. Maloni, J.M.; Brown, M.E. Corporate Social Responsibility in the Supply Chain: An Application in the Food Industry. *J. Bus. Ethics* **2006**, *68*, 35–52. [CrossRef]
73. Hsueh, C.F.; Chang, M.S. Social Responsibility for Supply Chain Integration. *Eur. J. Oper. Res.* **2008**, *190*, 116–129. [CrossRef]
74. Cruz, M.; Matsypura, D. Supply chain networks with corporate social responsibility through integrated environmental decision-making. *Int. J. Prod. Res.* **2009**, *47*, 621–648. [CrossRef]
75. Mishra, S.; Suar, D. Does Corporate Social Responsibility Influence Firm Performance of Indian Companies? *J. Bus. Ethics* **2010**, *95*, 571–601. [CrossRef]
76. Maignan, I.; Ferrell, O.C.; Hult, T. Corporate Citizenship: Cultural Antecedents and Business Benefits. *J. Acad. Mark. Sci.* **1999**, *27*, 455–469. [CrossRef]
77. Baskarana, V.; Nachiappanb, S.; Rahmanc, S. Supplier assessment based on corporate social responsibility criteria in Indian automotive and textile industry sectors. *Int. J. Sustain. Eng.* **2011**, *4*, 359–369. [CrossRef]
78. Thresh Kumar, D.; Palaniappanb, M.; Kannanc, D.; Shankara, K.M. Analyzing the CSR issues behind the supplier selection process using ISM approach, Resources. *Conserv. Recycl.* **2014**, *92*, 268–278. [CrossRef]
79. Saleh, M.; Zulkifli, N.; Muhamad, R. Looking for evidence of the relationship between corporate social responsibility and corporate financial performance in an emerging market. *Asia Pac. J. Bus. Adm.* **2011**, *3*, 165–190. [CrossRef]
80. Zaborek, P. CSR and Financial Performance: The Case of Polish Small and Medium Manufacturers. *Int. J. Manag. Econ.* **2014**, *43*, 53–73.
81. Lagoarde-Segot, T. Corporate Social Responsibility as a Bolster for Economic Performance: Evidence from Emerging Markets. *Glob. Bus. Organ. Excell.* **2011**, *6*, 38–53. [CrossRef]
82. Torgusa, N.; O'Donohue, W.; Hecker, R. Capabilities, Proactive CSR and Financial Performance in SMEs: Empirical Evidence from an Australian Manufacturing Industry Sector. *J. Bus. Ethics* **2012**, *109*, 483–500. [CrossRef]
83. Buciuniene, I.; Kazlauskaite, R. The linkage between HRM, CSR and performance outcomes. *Balt. J. Manag.* **2012**, *7*, 5–24. [CrossRef]
84. Tang, Z.; Eirikur, H.; Rotenberg, S. How Corporate Social Responsibility Engagement Strategy Moderates the CSR—Financial Performance Relationship. *J. Manag. Stud.* **2012**, *49*, 1274–1303. [CrossRef]
85. Byrne, B. *Structural Equation Modeling with AMOS: Basic Concepts, Applications and Programming*, 2nd ed.; Routledge: New York, NY, USA, 2010.

86. Garson, D. *Structural Equation Modeling: Statistical Association Publishing Blue Book Series*; Statistical Association Publishing: Asheboro, NC, USA, 2012.
87. Bowen, N.; Guo, S. *Structural Equation Modeling: Pocket Guides to Social Research Methods*; Oxford University Press: New York, NY, USA, 2012.
88. Malhotra, N. *Marketing Research: An Applied Orientation*, 6th ed.; Prentice Hall: Upper Saddle River, NJ, USA, 2010.
89. Hair, J.; Black, W.; Babin, B.; Anderson, R. *Multivariate Data Analysis*, 7th ed.; Prentice-Hall: Upper Saddle River, NJ, USA, 2007.
90. Buhmann, K. Corporate Social Responsibility: What role for law? Some aspects of law and CSR. *Corp. Gov. Int. J. Bus. Soc.* **2006**, *6*, 188–202. [CrossRef]
91. Zinenko, A.; Rovira, M.R.; Montiel, I. The fit of the social responsibility standard ISO 26000 with other CSR instruments: Redundant or complementary? Sustainability Accounting. *Manag. Policy J.* **2015**, *6*, 498–526.
92. Moratis, L.; Widjaja, A.T. Determinants of CSR standards adoption: Exploring the case of ISO 26000 and the CSR performance ladder in the Netherlands. *Soc. Responsib. J.* **2015**, *10*, 516–536. [CrossRef]
93. Steuer, R. The Role of Governments in Corporate Social Responsibility: Characterising Public Policies in Europe. *Policy Sci.* **2010**, *43*, 27–49.
94. Fatma, M.; Rahman, Z.; Khan, I. Building company reputation and brand equity through CSR: The mediating role of trust. *Int. J. Bank Mark.* **2015**, *33*, 840–856. [CrossRef]
95. Maas, S.; Reniers, G. Development of a CSR model for practice: Connecting five inherent areas of sustainable business. *J. Clean. Prod.* **2014**, *64*, 104–114. [CrossRef]
96. Calabrese, A.; Costa, R.; Menchini, T.; Rosati, F.; Sanfelice, G. Turning Corporate Social Responsibility-driven Opportunities in Competitive Advantages: A Two-dimensional Model. *Knowl. Process Manag.* **2013**, *20*, 50–58. [CrossRef]
97. Zaborek, P.; Mirońska, D. Segmentation of Polish consumers based on their attitudes towards cause related marketing. Gospodarka Materiałowa i Logistyka. *PWE* **2014**, *10*, 2–10.

© 2016 by the authors. Licensee MDPI, Basel, Switzerland. This article is an open access article distributed under the terms and conditions of the Creative Commons Attribution (CC BY) license (http://creativecommons.org/licenses/by/4.0/).

Article

Analytical Business Model for Sustainable Distributed Retail Enterprises in a Competitive Market

Courage Matobobo and Isaac O. Osunmakinde *

School of Computing, College of Science, Engineering and Technology, University of South Africa, P.O. Box 392, UNISA, Pretoria 0003, South Africa; 49116762@mylife.unisa.ac.za
* Correspondence: osunmio@unisa.ac.za; Tel.: +27-11-670-9155

Academic Editors: Adam Jabłoński and Giuseppe Ioppolo
Received: 12 November 2015; Accepted: 21 January 2016; Published: 4 February 2016

Abstract: Retail enterprises are organizations that sell goods in small quantities to consumers for personal consumption. In distributed retail enterprises, data is administered per branch. It is important for retail enterprises to make use of data generated within the organization to determine consumer patterns and behaviors. Large organizations find it difficult to ascertain customer preferences by merely observing transactions. This has led to quantifiable losses, such as loss of market share to competitors and targeting the wrong market. Although some enterprises have implemented classical business models to address these challenging issues, they still lack analytics-based marketing programs to gain a competitive advantage to deal with likely catastrophic events. This research develops an analytical business (ARANN) model for distributed retail enterprises in a competitive market environment to address the current laxity through the best arrangement of shelf products per branch. The ARANN model is built on association rules, complemented by artificial neural networks to strengthen the results of both mutually. According to experimental analytics, the ARANN model outperforms the state of the art model, implying improved confidence in business information management within the dynamically changing world economy.

Keywords: sustainable business models; retail enterprises; analytical business model; analytics; distributed enterprises

1. Introduction

Business information (BI) analytics are groups of methodologies, organizational techniques and tools used collectively to gain information, analyze it and predict the outcomes of solutions to problems [1]. The field of BI analytics through the use of operational data generated from transactional systems has given business users better insight into the problems they face [2]. These insights can assist business users or managers to make better and informed decisions. BI analytics are commonly applied in sustainable retail enterprises. Retail enterprises purchase goods from manufacturers or wholesalers in large quantities. They break up the bulk and resell those goods in smaller quantities directly to consumers. Consumers can go around the shop, pick the items of their choice from the shop shelves, place them into their baskets and then the contents of each basket are captured into transactional systems. These transactional systems generate data that can be used for analysis purposes. There are two major types of retail enterprises: centralized and distributed retail enterprises. This paper concentrates on distributed retail enterprises as a way of alleviating analytics issues of enterprises in a competitive market environment.

A distributed retail enterprise issues decision rights to the branches or groups nearest to the data collection [3]. Each branch can make its own decisions, depending on the data generated. A distributed retail enterprise often maintains clustered databases for each branch for the storage of data. Data generated in a distributed retail enterprise branch usually reflects the true customer purchasing habits at that particular branch. Data analysis per branch might reveal better results than a centralized data management system. It is, therefore, important to analyze data generated in each branch to realize meaningful patterns. Analysts can apply BI analytics to branch data in order to generate meaningful patterns for each particular branch.

Retail enterprises strive for survival in view of the current challenging sales optimization models. These models affect product arrangements in retail enterprises, leading to a decline in sales levels [4], high research and marketing costs, a decline in market share, wrong product target markets and poor management decisions [5]. Figure 1 presents the quantitative impact of these challenging sales optimization models in retail enterprises. Figure 1a shows the sales decline in Hungarian retail enterprises in June 2013. The sales level of computer equipment and books declined drastically by 4.8%, while sales of non-food items had the lowest level of decline of 0.4%. Figure 1b shows the causes of the reduction in sales level. The highest scoring reason for the reduction in sales was expensiveness (48%), followed by 41% of products with features unavailable. The least common reason for a reduction in sales was lack of functionality (20%).

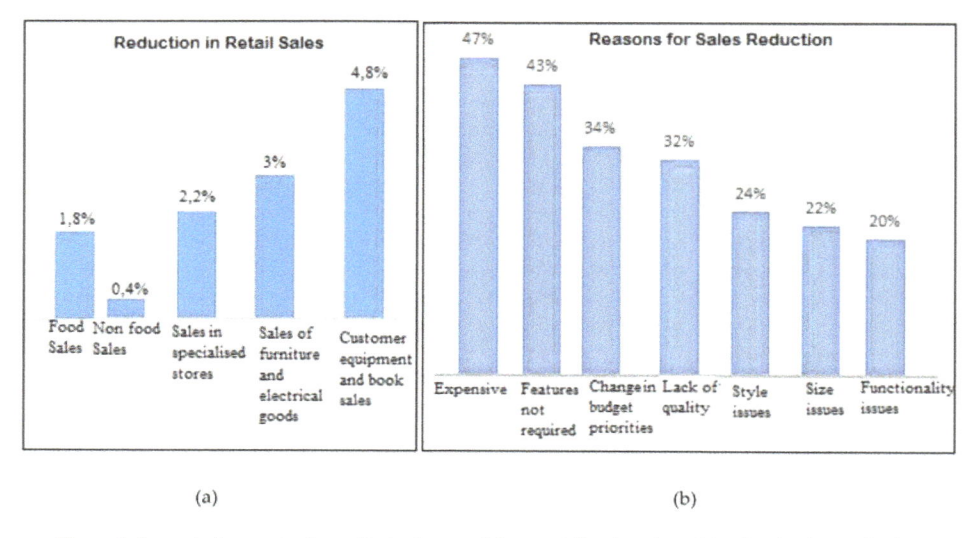

Figure 1. Impact of current sales optimization models on retail enterprises. (**a**) reduction in retail sales. Adapted from [6]; (**b**) reasons for reduction in sales. Adapted from [7].

Data quality problems also affect the quality of decisions made by managers on different levels of a retail enterprise [5]. Poor data has caused problems in both traditional and e-business companies, as shown in Figure 2. In both types of companies, extra cost to prepare reconciliations was seen as the main problem caused by inadequate data. This was seen to have an impact of 58% and 57% respectively. Inability to deliver orders or loss of sales was also a poor data quality challenge that had a higher impact in e-business (33%) than in traditional (24%) companies. The lowest-scoring problem caused by poor data was failure to meet a significant contractual requirement.

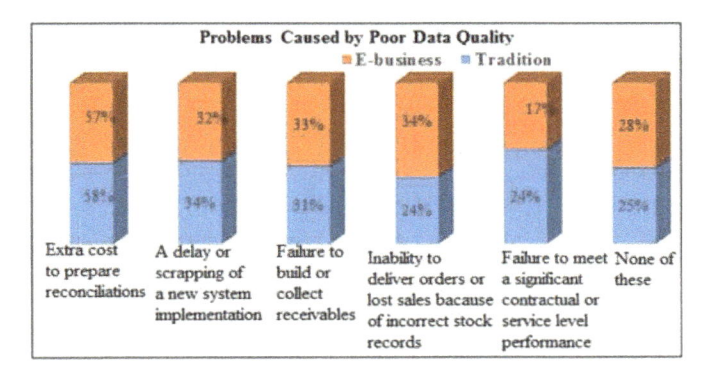

Figure 2. Problems caused by poor data quality. Adapted from [8].

An organization implemented an easy-to-use desktop and server analytics software program for the development of several business units and to improve the basis for decision-making [9]. The challenge was to test the most effective BI analytics for solving theoretical business problems. A data consolidation project was undertaken in South Africa by Altron to organize and deliver high-quality data successfully to its executives on their Apple iPads [10]. The smart phones' interfaces were too small for the style and amount of information they wanted to deliver. This approach posed the following challenges: lack of an analytics-based marketing program, failure to make BI a "matchmaker", lack of business-driven analytic strategies and failure to test the most effective BI analytics for solving theoretical business problems.

This paper develops an analytical business (ARANN) model that can be used in distributed retail enterprises within the dynamically changing world economy to implement the best arrangement of shelf products at each branch in order to improve the weaknesses highlighted in Figures 1 and 2. The ARANN model is built on a machine learning technique, association rules (AR) technique, complemented by an artificial neural network (ANN) technique to strengthen the results of the individual models. Since sustainability in this context generally requires the ability of a business to sustain itself in times of crisis, similar to competitive markets, ARANN has been specifically designed for sustainable distributed and centralized retail enterprises. The major contributions in this paper are the following:

- Development of a newly proposed analytical ARANN model that could intelligently assist distributed retail enterprise management within competitive markets to arrange products optimally on store shelves so that customers will purchase more products than planned in order to achieve an optimal profit level.
- Detailed experimental evaluations conducted on the sustainable ARANN model as measures of its performance using publicly available data and a volume of real-life retail data sets captured in ever-changing markets.
- Application of a robust business model in terms of (i) deployment scenarios, (ii) distributed and centralized analytics, (iii) time and memory scalability, and (iv) benchmark with classical methods for ease of implementation for managerial practices in IT.

To our knowledge, not enough research has presented user-friendly models and work examples to make technical information and BI available to professional managers. This paper is structured as follows: Section 2 previews work done in the area of AR and ANN, Section 3 proposes an intelligent model for distributed retail enterprises, Section 4 focuses on experimental evaluations and finally, Section 5 concludes the paper.

2. Background Studies

2.1. Related Work

Besides the analytics software programs and projects mentioned above, classical applications of AR and ANN are highlighted here. From the research conducted in [11], the authors applied AR to medical data containing combinations of categorical and numerical attributes to discover useful rules and from this experiment, useful and concise AR were discovered for prediction purposes. In [12], the authors implemented a system for the discovery of AR in web log usage data as an object-oriented application and discovered excellent associations within the data. They put forward "interestingness measures" as future work. In [13], the researchers applied an AR algorithm to a large database of customer transactions from a large retailing company to test the effectiveness of the algorithm and it exhibited excellent performance. In the study conducted in [14], it was observed that AR is effective in revealing associations though it does not take into account special interests. A comprehensive survey was conducted in [15] regarding AR on quantitative data in data mining. The authors examined it using different parameters and they concluded that the direct application of AR might produce a large number of redundant rules. This is also supported in the article in [16].

AR was applied in [4] to a sport company struggling with the arrangement of sports items in accordance with customer purchasing patterns. The retail company had no computerized mechanism for providing the best item arrangement. The study was performed to identify purchasing patterns that could be adopted by the retail enterprise. The authors analyzed historical data to identify the associated patterns from transactional data. From the study, they found relationships between sports items purchased and the best ways of arranging items, either side by side or in the same retail area, so that the items were frequently purchased together to yield high sales. In this study, AR was used for mining relationships between items purchased.

AR was applied in [11] to medical data containing combinations of categorical and numerical attributes to discover useful rules and from this experiment, useful and concise associations were discovered for prediction purposes. Ordonez [17] used AR to predict the level of contraction in four arteries and risk factors. The experiment predicted accurate profiles of patients with localized heart problems, specific risk factors and the level of disease in one artery.

ANN have been used in the past to search for patterns and predict future sales [18]. In research conducted in [19], the authors evaluated the predictive accuracy of ANNs and logistic regression (LR) in marketing campaigns of a Portuguese banking institution and their results showed that ANNs are more efficient and faster than LR. In [20], the researchers applied ANNs to a Pima Indians diabetes database and it generated rules with strong associations, thereby enhancing the decision-making process by doctors. In research conducted in [21], ANNs were applied for retail segmentation. The authors compared an ANN technique based on Hopfield networks against k-means and mixture model clustering algorithms. The results showed the usefulness of ANNs in retailing for segmenting markets. Many articles mentioned in [22] consider ANNs to be a promising machine learning technique.

In research conducted in [23], it was observed that the combination of data mining methods and a neural network model can greatly improve the efficiency of data mining methods. Craven and Shavlik [24] also supported ANN in data mining because of the ability to learn the target concept better than when using data mining methods. However, they presented two limitations that make ANNs poor data mining tools: excessive training times and incomprehensible learning. The proposed analytical model seeks to use AR complemented by ANNs to implement the best arrangement of shelf products, branch by branch, in order to use the cooperative result to make managerial decisions.

This research is undertaken to improve the following challenges of current sales optimization models: lack of analytics-based marketing programs, lack of business-driven analytic strategies and failure to leverage BI to become "matchmakers". To our knowledge, not enough research has presented working examples and considered non-expert users in proposing models that are user-friendly to professional managers. Sections 2.2 and 2.3 explain the building blocks of the analytic model where the processed data from different branches is entered.

2.2. Association Rules

AR mining is an unsupervised data mining method to find interesting associations in large sets of data items [25]. It was originally derived from point-of-sale data that describes which products are purchased simultaneously. AR discovers interesting associations that are often used by businesses such as retail enterprises for decision-making purposes; an example could be to find out which products are frequently purchased simultaneously by different customers [26]. It is one of the most common and widely used techniques in data mining, aimed at finding interesting relations [27,28] or correlations between large data items [29]. AR provides decision-makers at retail enterprises with marketing insights for cross-selling by providing information about product associations [30]. The most common AR algorithm used in market basket analysis is Apriori. However, the Apriori algorithm has an important drawback of generating numerous candidate item sets that must be repeatedly contrasted with the whole database [31]. We are going to use two measures to quantify the interestingness of a rule: support and confidence.

2.2.1. Support Value

Support determines how frequently a rule is contained in a given dataset. It is defined as the fraction of transactions that contains $A \cup B$ to the total number of transactions in the database [32] and this can be expressed as shown in Equation (1):

$$Support(A \Rightarrow B) = P(A \cup B) = \frac{n(A \cup B)}{N} \qquad (1)$$

If support (A⇒B) is greater than or equal to the minimum support threshold (min_sup) then it is a frequent item set. An item set is frequent if support (A⇒B) ⩾ min_sup().

2.2.2. Confidence Value

Confidence is the ratio of the number of transactions containing A and B to the number of transactions containing A, and can be further expressed as shown in Equation (2):

$$Confidence(A \Rightarrow B) = P(B/A) = \frac{n(A \cup B)}{n(A)} \qquad (2)$$

If confidence (A⇒B) is greater than or equal to the minimum confidence (min_con) then we are confident about the rule generated.

Furthermore, rules that satisfy both the minimum support threshold (min_sup) and the minimum confidence threshold (min_con) are called strong AR. A rule is strong if support (A⇒B) ⩾ min_sup ∧ confidence (A⇒B) ⩾ min_con. These two measures are used as inputs in the ANN technique.

2.3. Artificial Neural Networks

ANNs simulate the behavior of biological systems and are used to discover patterns and relationships. They are useful for studying complex relationships between input and output variables in a system [33]. The main advantage of an ANN is the ability to extract patterns and detect trends that are too complex to be noticed by other computer techniques or humans [34]. In [35], the research done shows that ANNs are now commonly used to solve data mining problems because of the following advantages: robustness, self-organizing adaptiveness, parallel processing, distributed storage and a high degree of fault tolerance. The ANN sums the inputs x_i against corresponding weights w_i and compares the ANN output to the threshold value, $\ominus$. The threshold is determined by the inputs used.

Let X be the net weighted input of the neuron, as shown in Equation (3). The decision of X is for discrete cases since it takes only certain values:

$$X = \sum_{i=1}^{n} xiwi \qquad (3)$$

where x_i is the input signal, w_i is the weight of input and n is the number of neurons.

If the net input is less than the threshold, the neuron output is −1; if the net input is greater than or equal to the threshold then the neuron is activated and the output attains a +1.

Let Y be the ANN output. The decision of Y is for continuous cases, since it can take any values in the range. The actual output of the neuron with the sigmoid activation function is expressed as shown in Equation (4):

$$Y = \frac{1}{1 + e^{-x}} \qquad (4)$$

3. Proposed Methodology for Sustainable Business Enterprises

3.1. Proposed System Model for Distributed Retail Enterprises

This section explores the proposed system model for BI analytics in distributed retail enterprises. The proposed model has three layers, namely data cleaning and formatting, intelligent model and distributed product shops, as shown in Figure 3. The data cleaning and formatting layer is found at the bottom of the proposed model. In this proposed model, data is collected from transactional systems branch per branch. The data is cleaned and formatted to the appropriate file type accepted by the proposed model. Processed data is input into the ARANN model branch per branch at the middle layer of the analytical model. The ARANN model cooperatively works between AR and ANN. Processed data from the bottom layer is passed into the AR model and it outputs confidence and support values. These values are passed into the ANN model as inputs in order to get the degree of belief (DoB). The DoB of sets generated is compared to the ARANN activations set. The accepted sets generated are applied on the top layer of the proposed model. This proposed model is deployed to each branch and patterns are generated independently. The choice is left for every retail enterprise branch to adopt the best results, depending on the market competitiveness and profit levels.

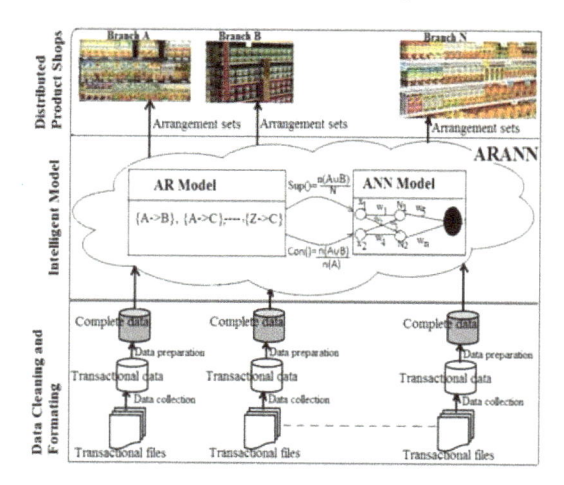

Figure 3. Proposed intelligent analytics-based framework.

The proposed intelligent analytics-based framework has the following benefits: reduction in risk of passing misleading results to all branches, no one point of failure, consumption of fewer resources, faster construction of distributed systems and no need for data integration.

This proposed analytics-based model can be implemented using the pseudo-code presented in Table 1. Table 1 shows how ARANN generates product arrangement sets that can be used by retail enterprise managers to arrange products on shop shelves so as to attract customers to purchase more products than planned. The pseudo-code is further presented mathematically, as shown in Equations (5)–(14).

Table 1. Pseudo-code for ARANN model.

		Pseudo-code
Steps	Input:	Transactional data in database (D) = {$t_1, t_2, t_3, .., t_n$} Support () Confidence () Weights (W) = {$w_1, w_2, w_3, .., w_n$}
	Output:	Products pattern

		Step 1: D = {$t_1, t_2, t_3, .., t_n$} //Transactions in the database
		 Step 2: C_k = Candidate item set of size k
		 Step 3: F_k = frequent item set of size k
		 {
		     for (k =1; F_k != ∅; k++) // F_k is not equal to empty set.
		     {
		     Scan the entire D to generate candidate sets C_k
		     {
		     Compare candidate support count from C_k with the minimum support count to generate F_k
		     }
		     }
		 Step 4: Generate Support () & Confidence ()
		 {
		 Step 5: Input Support () & Confidence () into Neuron 1 (N_1) and Neuron 2 (N_2) as inputs
		 Step 6: Generate N_1 by summing of the inputs with the corresponding weights and apply the output into sigmoid function
		 Step 7: Generate N_2 by summing of the inputs with the corresponding weights and apply the output into sigmoid function
		 Step 8: Generate the summation of N_1 & N_2 after the sigmoid function and apply the output into sigmoid function to obtain Degree of Belief (DoB)
		 Step 9: Display products pattern where **DoB ⩾ ARANN activation**
		 }
		 }

Mathematical description for the ARANN Model

$$Support\ (Sup) = \frac{n\,(A u B)}{N} \tag{5}$$

$$Confidence\ (Con) = \frac{n\,(A u B)}{n\,(A)} \tag{6}$$

The sup and con values feed the N_1 as the inputs and are multiplied with the corresponding weights.

$$N_1 = SupW_1 + ConW_3 \tag{7}$$

The output of N_1 after the sigmoid function

$$O_2 = \frac{1}{1+e^{-N_2}} \tag{8}$$

The sup and con values feed the N_2 as the inputs and are multiplied with the corresponding weights:

$$N_2 = ConW_4 + SupW_2 \tag{9}$$

The output of N_2 after the sigmoid function

$$O_2 = \frac{1}{1+e^{-N_2}} \tag{10}$$

$$F = W_5 O_1 + W_6 O_2 \tag{11}$$

$$= \frac{W_5}{1+e^{-N_2}} + \frac{W_6}{1+e^{-N_2}} \tag{12}$$

$$Degree\ of\ Belief\ (DoB) = \frac{1}{1+e^{-F}} \tag{13}$$

$$Product\ Patterns = \begin{cases} Accepted, if & DoB \geq ARANN\ activation \\ Rejected, if & otherwise \end{cases} \tag{14}$$

where N_1 and N_2 are Neuron 1 and 2 respectively; W_1, W_2, W_3, W_4, W_5 and W_6 are the corresponding weights; O_1 is Neuron 1 output after sigmoid function; O_2 is Neuron 2 output after sigmoid function, F is input to final Neuron and $ARANN\ activation$ is the threshold value set.

3.2. Evaluation Mechanism

The purpose of model evaluation is to assess the performance of the models so as to identify the best-performing model. To test the performance of the models, three sets were used. The confusion matrix shown in Table 2 was used to represent actual values and predictions.

Table 2. Confusion matrix. Adapted from [36].

		Predicted	
		True	False
Actual	True	a	b
	False	c	d

$$Error\ Rate = \frac{b+c}{a+b+c+d} \tag{15}$$

where a is the number of sets predicted true when they are true, b is the number of sets predicted false when they are true, c is the number of sets predicted true when they are false and d is the number of sets predicted false when they are false. Error rate is then defined as shown in Equation (15).

3.3. Scenario—Arrangement of Products on Shelves for Distributed Retail Branches

Figure 4 shows a scenario of how the analytical model displays placement results in distributed branches. Transactional data from each retail branch is loaded into the ARANN model to determine the arrangement sets.

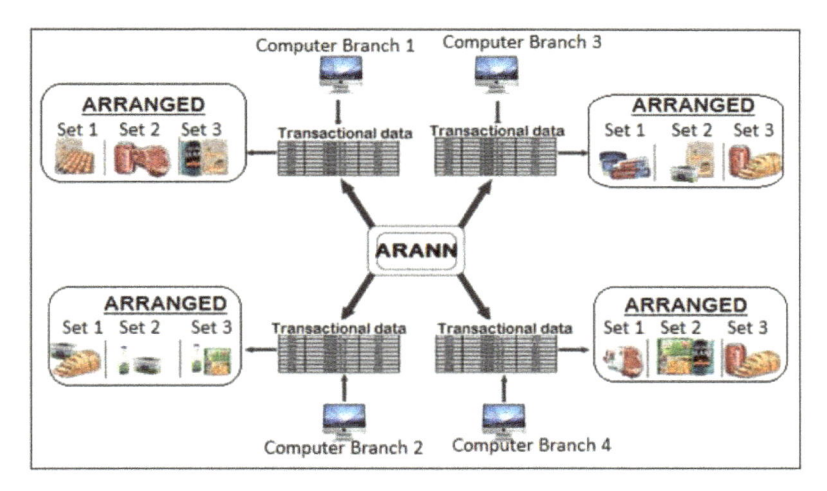

Figure 4. Intelligent Analytics-based Model for Four Branches.

Table 3. Market basket transactional data for branch 3 of a retail enterprise.

Market-basket Transaction Data—Branch 3	
TID	ITEMS
T300	Colgate, Vaseline, Geisha, Margarine, Bread
T301	Margarine, Bread, Coke, Colgate, Vaseline
T302	Coke, Colgate, Chocolate, Bread, Sweets, Margarine
T303	Geisha, Colgate, Chocolate, Towel, Vaseline, Sweets
T304	Colgate, Vaseline, Sweets, Chocolate, Bread, Margarine, Coke

Even weights were applied to each corresponding input to avoid bias on products. This was obtained by dividing the count of a_union_b over a number of records within the data set, where a, and b are different products. The following ARANN activation was used:

>= 0.75 strongly connected products (strongly accepted)
>= 0.65 moderately connected products (accepted)
< 0.65 weakly connected products (rejected)

Analysis of ARANN on tab:sustainability-08-00140-t003
{Colgate, Vaseline} => {Bread}

Support = $\dfrac{n(A \cup B)}{N} = \dfrac{3}{5} = 0.6$ Confidence = $\dfrac{n(A \cup B)}{n(A)} = \dfrac{3}{4} = 0.75$

N_1 = Supw$_1$ + Conw$_3$ N_2 = Conw$_4$ + Supw$_2$
  = (0.6 × 0.6) + (0.75 × 0.6)   = (0.75 × 0.6) + (0.6 × 0.6)
  = 0.81   = 0.81

$O_1 = \dfrac{1}{1+e^{-N1}} = \dfrac{1}{1+e^{-0.81}} = 0.69$ $O_2 = \dfrac{1}{1+e^{-N2}} = \dfrac{1}{1+e^{-0.81}} = 0.69$

F   = w5O$_1$ + w6O$_2$
    = (0.6 × 0.69) + (0.6 × 0.69) = 0.83

DoB = $\dfrac{1}{1+e^{-F}} = \dfrac{1}{1+e^{-0.83}} = 0.70$

Product pattern => 0.70 >= 0.65
Therefore it is moderately connected and is accepted.

{Coke} => {Bread}
Support = $\frac{3}{5}$ = 0.6   Confidence = $\frac{3}{3}$ = 1.0
N1 = (0.6 × 0.6) + (1.0 × 0.6)   N2 = (1.0 × 0.6) + (0.6 × 0.6)
   = 0.96   = 0.96
O1 = $\frac{1}{1+e^{-0.96}}$ = 0.72   O2 = $\frac{1}{1+e^{-0.4}}$ = 0.72
F = w5O$_1$ + w6O$_2$
  = (0.6 × 0.72) + (0.6 × 0.72) = 0.86
DoB = $\frac{1}{1+e^{-86}}$ = 0.70
Product pattern => 0.70 >= 0.65
Therefore it is moderately connected and is accepted.

Table 4. Market basket transactional data for branch 4 of a retail enterprise.

	Market-basket Transaction Data—Branch 4
TID	ITEMS
T400	Maize meal, Beef, Fish, Cooking oil, Soups, Bread, Coke
T401	Cooking oil, Beans, Beef, Soups, Maize meal
T402	Rice, Fish, Soups, Cooking oil, Bread
T403	Fruits, Coke, Bread, Milk, Chocolate, Soups
T404	Bread, Beef, Fruit, Coke, Sweets, Maize meal

Analysis of ARANN on   tab:sustainability-08-00140-t004
{Maize meal} => {Beef}
Support = $\frac{3}{5}$ = 0.6   Confidence = $\frac{3}{3}$ = 1.0
N1 = (0.6 × 0.6) + (1.0 × 0.6)   N2 = (1.0 × 0.6) + (0.6 × 0.6)
   = 0.96   = 0.96
O1 = $\frac{1}{1+e^{-0.96}}$ = 0.72   O2 = $\frac{1}{1+e^{-0.4}}$ = 0.72
F = w5O$_1$ + w6O$_2$
  = (0.6 × 0.72) + (0.6 × 0.72) = 0.86
DoB = $\frac{1}{1+e^{-86}}$ = 0.70
Product pattern => 0.70 >= 0.65
Therefore it is **moderately** connected and is **accepted**.

{Chocolate} => {Towel}
Support = $\frac{1}{5}$ = 0.20   Confidence = $\frac{1}{3}$ = 0.33
N$_1$ = (0.20 × 0.20) + (0.33 × 0.20) N$_2$ = (0.33 × 0.20) + (0.20 × 0.20)
     = 0.11   = 0.11
O$_1$ = $\frac{1}{1+e^{-0.11}}$ = 0.53   O$_2$ = $\frac{1}{1+e^{-0.11}}$ = 0.53
F = (0.2 × 0.53) + (0.2 × 0.53) = 0.212
DoB = $\frac{1}{1+e^{-0.212}}$ = 0.55
Product pattern => 0.55 < 0.65
Therefore it is **weakly** connected and is **rejected**.

4. Experimental Evaluations: Results and Discussions

4.1. Experimental Setup

Real-life data was collected from a retail enterprise situated in South Africa with several branches nationwide. The data for the experiments was collected from only eight branches within different demographics of a developing country. The retail enterprise has database servers at each branch for the storage of data. Real-life datasets consisting of 66 records were taken from each branch, to be used for running experiments. In the experiment, the 11 most frequently purchased products were considered. This data was collected for research purposes. The data was then exported to notepad application for storage. Each row in Tables 5–7 represents a transaction performed by the customer. Tables 5 and 6 show samples of real-life data from different branches.

In the public dataset 1000 transactions were used. This data set was randomly broken up into five chunks representing branches and the records for each branch contained 200 transactions. The data was saved in .txt format. The public data set in Table 7 is found in [37]. The data contains the following products: bread, beer, tea, wine, orange juice, chocolate milk and canned soup.

Table 5. Sample of real-life data for branch 1.

Body lotion	Colgate	Rice	Maize meal		
Meat	Rice	Roll on	Cooking oil	Body lotion	
-	-	-	-	-	
Drink	Roll on	Mince	Coke	Colgate	Perfume

Table 6. Sample of real-life data for branch 2.

Bread	Sugar	Rice	Meat	Salt	Cooking oil	Flour	Soup
-	-	-	-	-	-	-	-
Fruits	Sugar	Meat	Cooking oil	Salt	Soap	Bread	

Table 7. Sample of public data [37].

Fish	Orange juice	Tea	Wine	Peanuts	Canned soup	Bread	Beer
-	-	-	-	-	-	-	-
Cookies	Fish	Orange juice	Tea	Wine	Peanuts	Canned soup	Chocolate milk

Perl programming language was used to implement the ARANN model. Notepad was used as the text editor and results were displayed through the command prompt. Figures 5 and 6 show sample sets generated by the ARANN model using a real life dataset and public dataset respectively.

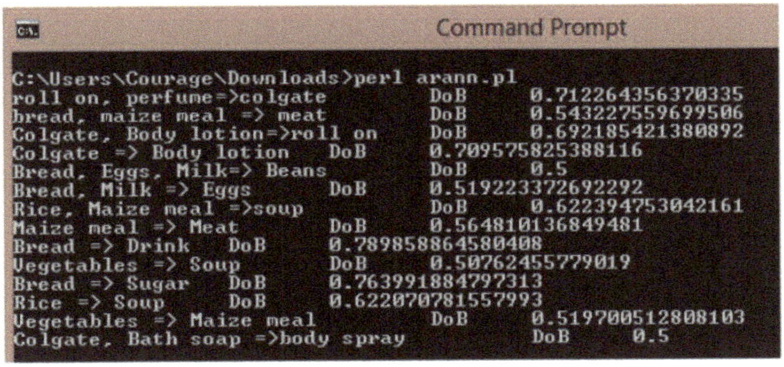

```
C:\Users\Courage\Downloads>perl arann.pl
roll on, perfume=>colgate        DoB    0.712264356370335
bread, maize meal => meat        DoB    0.543227559699506
Colgate, Body lotion=>roll on    DoB    0.692185421380892
Colgate => Body lotion   DoB    0.709575825388116
Bread, Eggs, Milk=> Beans        DoB    0.5
Bread, Milk => Eggs      DoB    0.519223372692292
Rice, Maize meal =>soup          DoB    0.622394753042161
Maize meal => Meat       DoB    0.564810136849481
Bread => Drink   DoB    0.789858864580408
Vegetables => Soup       DoB    0.50762455779019
Bread => Sugar   DoB    0.763991884797313
Rice => Soup     DoB    0.622070781557993
Vegetables => Maize meal         DoB    0.519700512808103
Colgate, Bath soap =>body spray          DoB    0.5
```

Figure 5. ARANN rules on real-life data.

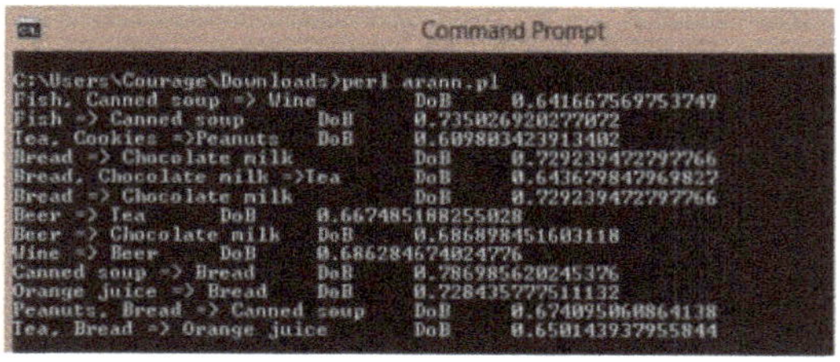

Figure 6. ARANN rules on public dataset.

4.2. Experiment 1: Observations of ARANN with Varying Activation in Distributed Analytics

In this experiment, Equation (14) was used to determine the decisions to be applied to Tables 8–11 of the analytical model. This analytical model accepts product patterns defined in Equation (14) and uses the following ARANN activations: DoB < 60%, 60% >= DoB < 70% and DoB >= 70%. The analytical model rejects arrangement sets where the DoB is less than 60% and accepts arrangement sets between 60% and 69%, while those with a DoB greater or equal to 70% are strongly accepted. To make the decision, ARANN compares the DoB value generated with the ARANN activations and a decision is made. Managers use the decision to determine how products are to be arranged in each branch.

Table 8. Real-life ARANN results for branch 1.

Dataset Branch 1	Patterns Generated	DoB	ARANN Cooperative Decision with	
			60 >= DoB < 70	DoB >= 70
	Roll on, perfume => Colgate	0.71	N/A	Strongly accepted
	Colgate, Body lotion => roll-on	0.69	Accepted	N/A
	Colgate => Body lotion	0.71	N/A	Strongly accepted
	Bread, Milk => Eggs	0.70	N/A	Strongly accepted
	Rice, Maize meal => soup	0.62	Accepted	N/A
	Bread => Drink	0.79	N/A	Strongly accepted
	Bread => Sugar	0.76	N/A	Strongly accepted

Using ARANN activation of DoB >= 70, the following sets from Table 8 are strongly accepted: {Roll-on, Perfume => Colgate}, {Colgate => Body lotion}, {Bread => Drink} and {Bread => Sugar}; these are strongly connected products. Using ARANN activation of 60 >= DoB < 70, the following examples of sets from Table 8 are accepted: {Colgate, Body lotion => Roll on}, {Rice, Maize meal => Soup} and {Rice => Soup}; these are moderately connected products. The choice is left to every retail enterprise to adopt either moderately or strongly connected products, depending on the market competitiveness and profit levels. Note that the analytical model rejects the sets with DoB < 60 (*i.e.*, weakly connected products), which are not included. One can see in Table 8 of branch 1 that the "strongly accepted" products at higher activation implies that some specific toiletry products are strongly connected, while bakery products and refreshments are strongly connected at this branch.

Table 9. Real-life ARANN results for branch 2.

Dataset Branch 1	Patterns Generated	DoB	ARANN Cooperative Decision with	
			60 >= DoB < 70	DoB >= 70
	Meat, Salt => Cooking_oil	0.64	Accepted	N/A
	Meat => Salt	0.71	N/A	Strongly Accepted
	Bread, rice => Eggs	0.66	Accepted	N/A
	Bread => Lotion	0.65	Accepted	N/A
	Bread => Eggs	0.65	Accepted	N/A

Applying ARANN activation of DoB >= 70, the following "strongly accepted" set is generated; {Meat => Salt}; these are strongly connected products. When ARANN activation of 60 >= DoB < 70 is used, the following examples of sets are accepted in Table 9: {Meat, Salt => Cooking oil}, {Bread, Rice => Eggs} and {Bread => Eggs}; these are moderately connected products. It is up to the retail enterprise's decision-makers to adopt either moderately or strongly connected products, depending on the market competitiveness and profit levels. On the other side, the analytical model rejects the sets with DoB < 60 (*i.e.*, weakly connected products), which are not included. It can be seen in Table 9 of branch 2 that the "strongly accepted" products at higher activation implies that some specific meat products are strongly connected with salt products at this branch.

Table 10. Public DATA ARANN results for branch 3.

Dataset Branch 1	Patterns Generated	DoB	ARANN Cooperative Decision with	
			60 >= DoB < 70	DoB >= 70
	Fish, Canned soup => Wine	0.64	Accepted	N/A
	Fish => Canned soup	0.74	N/A	Strongly Accepted
	Tea, Cookies => Peanuts	0.61	Accepted	N/A
	Bread => Chocolate milk	0.73	N/A	Strongly accepted
	Bread, Chocolate milk => Tea	0.64	Accepted	N/A
	Beer => Tea	0.67	Accepted	N/A
	Beer => Chocolate milk	0.69	Accepted	N/A
	Wine => Beer	0.69	Accepted	N/A
	Canned soup => Bread	0.79	N/A	Strongly Accepted
	Orange juice => Bread	0.73	N/A	Strongly Accepted
	Peanuts, Bread => Canned soup	0.67	Accepted	N/A
	Tea, Bread => Orange juice	0.65	Accepted	N/A

When ARANN activation of DoB >= 70 is applied, the following "strongly accepted" sets from Table 10 are generated: {Fish => Canned soup}, {Bread => Chocolate milk} and {Canned soup => Bread}; these products are strongly connected. Using ARANN activation of 60 >= DoB < 70, the following are examples of "accepted" sets that are generated in Table 10: {Fish, Canned soup => Wine}, {Tea, Cookies => Peanuts} and {Wine => Beer}; these are moderately connected products. Every retail enterprise is left with the choice to adopt either moderately or strongly connected products, depending on the market competitiveness and profit levels. Note that the analytical model rejects the sets with DoB < 60 (*i.e.*, weakly connected products), which are not included. In Table 10 of branch 3, one can see that the "accepted" product sets at moderate activation implies that some specific beverages are moderately connected at this branch.

Table 11. Public data ARANN results for branch 4.

Dataset Branch 1	Patterns Generated	DoB	ARANN Cooperative Decision with	
			60 >= DoB < 70	DoB >= 70
	Fish, Canned soup => Wine	0.64	Accepted	N/A
	Fish => Canned soup	0.74	N/A	Strongly Accepted
	Tea, Cookies => Peanuts	0.61	Accepted	N/A
	Bread => Chocolate milk	0.72	N/A	Strongly Accepted
	Bread, Chocolate milk => Tea	0.66	Accepted	N/A
	Beer => Tea	0.67	Accepted	N/A
	Beer => Chocolate milk	0.67	Accepted	N/A
	Wine => Beer	0.70	N/A	Strongly accepted
	Canned soup => Bread	0.80	N/A	Strongly accepted
	Orange juice => Bread	0.73	N/A	Strongly accepted
	Peanuts, Bread => Canned soup	0.68	Accepted	N/A
	Tea, Bread => Orange juice	0.67	Accepted	N/A

In Table 11 the following "strongly accepted" sets were generated using ARANN activation of DoB >= 70: {Bread => Chocolate milk} and {Fish => Canned soup}, which are strongly connected products. Using ARANN activation of 60 >= DoB < 70, the following example of sets from Table 11 were accepted: {Fish, Canned soup => Wine}, {Orange juice => Bread} and {Tea, Bread => Orange juice}, which are moderately connected products. The decision-makers of every retail enterprise are left with the choice to adopt either moderately or strongly connected products, depending on the market competitiveness and profit levels. Note that the analytical model rejects the sets with DoB < 60 (*i.e.*, weakly connected products), which are not included. In Table 11 of branch 4 one can see that the "strongly accepted" product sets at higher activation implies that some specific bakery products are strongly connected with dairy products at this branch.

4.3. Experiment 2: Performance Evaluations of ARANN in Comparison with Classical Methods

Table 12 shows the error rate of the individual AR and ANN techniques against the analytical model. Equation (15) is used to determine the error rate of each technique. The column "No. of patterns" indicates the number of sets evaluated. The column "Correctly classified sets" is composed of sets the analytical model predicted as true when they were actually true (a) and sets predicted as false when they were actually false (d), as shown in Table 2. The column "Incorrectly classified sets" is composed of sets the analytical model predicted as false when they were actually true (b) and sets predicted as true when they were false (c). Randomly generated sets were used to evaluate the performance of the three models. For example, in Branch 1 (real life), 10 rules where used in AR: five rules were predicted as true when they were actually true (a); two were predicted as false when actually false (d); three were predicted as true when actually false (c) and 0 were predicted as false when actually true (b). From the results displayed in Table 12, it is clear that the analytical model (ARANN) has a lower error rate compared to the individual classical methods.

Table 12. Quantitative evaluations of the cooperative model in distributed branches.

Dataset	Algorithms	No. of Patterns	Correctly Classifies sets (a, d)	Incorrectly Classified sets (b, c)	Error Rate
Real life Branch 1 (66 Records)	AR	10	7	3	30%
	ANN	10	6	4	40%
	ARANN	6	5	1	17%
Branch 2 (66 Records)	AR	10	8	2	20%
	ANN	10	8	2	20%
	ARANN	7	6	1	14%
Public Branch 3 (200 Records)	AR	10	8	2	20%
	ANN	10	6	4	40%
	ARANN	6	5	1	17%
Branch 4 (200 Records)	AR	10	8	2	20%
	ANN	10	7	3	30%
	ARANN	8	6	2	25%

4.4. Experiment 3: Comparing Performance of Distributed and Centralized Retail Analytics

This research compares the performance of the analytical model in a distributed retail enterprise with a centralized retail enterprise. In the distributed retail enterprise, a computer was used to represent a branch and the time taken by the analytical model to generate arrangement patterns was observed. Figure 7a shows raw integration time. Figure 7b shows the time of response (ToR) taken by the analytical model to integrate a number of records from various workstations. Figure 7c shows the ToR taken by the analytical model to generate patterns in distributed and centralized retail enterprises.

Figure 7d shows the ToR taken by the analytical model to generate product arrangement patterns across different data sizes.

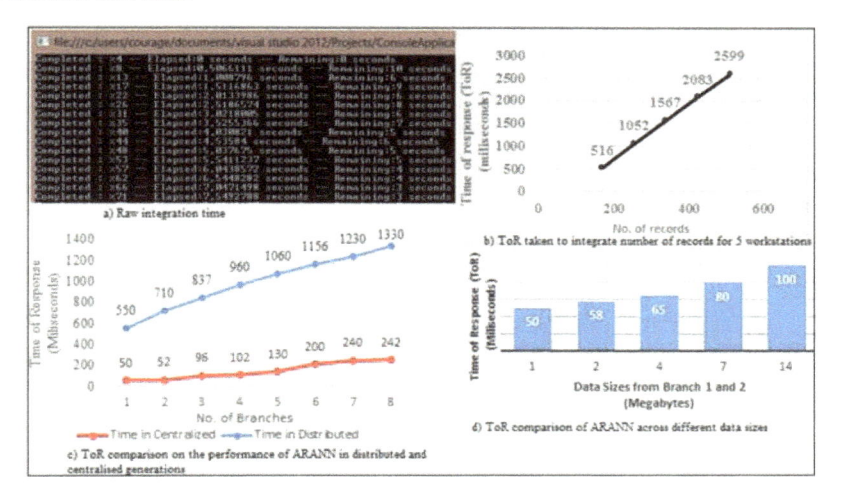

Figure 7. Comparison of the performance of ARANN in distributed and centralized retail enterprises.

From the experiment conducted, it was observed that the analytical model performs faster in distributed retail enterprises than in centralized retail enterprises, as shown in Figure 7c. The analytical model takes more time to generate patterns in a centralized retail enterprise than in a distributed retail enterprise. The ToR to integrate data depends on the number of records being integrated. The more records, the more time is needed to integrate those records. This was observed in Figure 7b. In addition, the performance time taken by the analytical model depends on the size of the data set being used. The analytical model's performance is affected by the size of the data set, as shown in Figure 7d.

5. Conclusions

In this paper, a sustainable model was proposed that can be used in distributed retail enterprises in an ever-changing economic environment to address the current laxity through the best arrangement of shelf products branch by branch. It can intelligently assist distributed retail enterprise management to arrange products optimally on shelves of shops so that customers will purchase more products than planned, in order to achieve an optimal profit level. The analytical model takes branch data and processes the data to determine the best ways of arranging items on the shelves of a retail enterprise branch by branch. It is built on AR, complemented by ANN.

The proposed analytical model for sustainable business in distributed retail enterprises was developed. A logical demonstration of working scenarios and experiments of the proposed analytical model for management practices in distributed retail enterprises was presented. This was done by inputting support and confidence values from the AR technique into the ANN technique in order to get DoB values of the analytical model. The analytical model accepts product patterns with a DoB greater than or equal to ARANN activation.

In the proposed analytical model performance evaluation experiment, ARANN proved to be better than the classical methods because of its lower error rate, implying improved confidence in the decision-making process in a competitive environment. To get the best results, the weights of the neurons need to be determined appropriately and the quality of data needs to be improved. The DoB values of the analytical model can sometimes be affected by the weights used.

It was observed that sets generated in a distributed retail enterprise portray the real purchasing habits of customers per branch better than in a centralized retail enterprise. In this research, real life datasets from eight branches of a retail enterprise and public datasets were used to conduct the experiments.

Observations of our distributed BI analytics model are: the proposed model retains complete control of product pattern generation, arrangement sets generated by the analytical model show a lower error rate (Table 12), they reveal the real buying habits of each branch, the model reduces the risk of passing misleading results to all branches (Tables 8–11) and the software runs a single process; there is no need for data integration (Figure 3). In addition, the ARANN incorporates the strengths of the AR and ANN models, improves generation of product arrangement sets, has the ability to discover complex nonlinear associations discreetly among different products, effects a reduction in poor data quality problems and losses, as well as an improvement in the effectiveness of current product sales optimization models. Since sustainability in this context generally requires the ability of a business to sustain itself in times of crisis, similar to competitive markets, ARANN has been specifically designed for sustainable distributed and centralized retail enterprises.

In future, we wish to; (i) improve on ARANN performance by considering nature-inspired algorithms; (ii) investigate a standard method of selecting the threshold; and (iii) integrate a sophisticated learning algorithm into ARANN. The strategy and observations in this research are therefore good for addressing challenges in an ever-changing economic environment.

Acknowledgments: Acknowledgments: The authors gratefully acknowledge the financial support and resources made available by the University of South Africa, South Africa.

Author Contributions: Author Contributions: All authors contributed equally to this article. They have read and approved the final manuscript.

Conflicts of Interest: Conflicts of Interest: The authors declare no conflict of interest.

References

1. Trkman, P.; McCormack, K.; de Oliveira, M.P.V.; Ladeira, M.B. The Impact of Business Analytics on Supply Chain Performance. *Decis. Support Syst.* **2010**, *49*, 318–327. [CrossRef]
2. Kohavi, R.; Rothleder, N.; Simoudis, E. Emerging Trends in Business Analytics. *Commun. ACM* **2002**, *45*, 45–48. [CrossRef]
3. Velu, C.; Madnick, S.; van Alstyne, M. Centralizing Data Management with Considerations of Uncertainty and Information-Based Flexibility. *J. Manag. Inf. Syst.* **2013**, *30*, 179–212. [CrossRef]
4. Abbas, W.; Ahmad, N.; Zaini, N. Discovering Purchasing Pattern of Sport Items Using Market Basket Analysis. In Proceedings of the 2013 International Conference on Advanced Computer Science Applications and Technologies (ACSAT), Kuching, Malaysia, 23–24 December 2013; pp. 120–125.
5. Haug, A.; Zachariassen, F.; van Liempd, D. The Costs of Poor Data Quality. *J. Ind. Eng. Manag.* **2011**, *4*, 168–193. [CrossRef]
6. Halford, Q.; Staff, S. Gap Cost Key Categories Billions. Furniture/Today, 3 September 2001, 14.
7. Hungary retail sales down in June. Regional Today, 26 August 2013, 1.
8. Data Quality. *Controller's Report*; EBSCOhost: Ipswich, MA, United States, 2001; Volume 7, p. 7.
9. Stoodley, N. Democratic Analytics: A Campaign to Bring Business Intelligence to the People. *Bus. Intell. J.* **2012**, *17*, 7–12.
10. Briggs, L. Case Study. *Bus. Intell. J.* **2011**, *16*, 39–41.
11. Aldosari, B.; Almodaifer, G.; Hafez, A.; Mathkour, H. Constrained Association Rules for Medical Data. *J. Appl. Sci.* **2012**, *12*, 1792–1800.
12. Dimitrijević, M.; Bošnjak, Z.; Cohen, E. Web Usage Association Rule Mining System. *Interdiscip. J. Inf. Knowl. Manag.* **2011**, *6*, 137–150.
13. Agrawal, R.; Imieliński, T.; Swami, A. Mining Association Rules between Sets of Items in Large Databases. In Proceedings of the 1993 ACM SIGMOD International Conference on Management of Data, Washington, DC, USA, 25–28 May 1993; pp. 207–216.

14. Klemettinen, M.; Mannila, H.; Ronkainen, P.; Toivonen, H.; Verkamo, A.I. Finding Interesting Rules from Large Sets of Discovered Association Rules. In Proceedings of the Third International Conference on Information and Knowledge Management, Gaithersburg, MD, USA, 29 November–2 December 1994; pp. 401–407.
15. Gosain, A.; Bhugra, M. A Comprehensive Survey of Association Rules on Quantitative Data in Data Mining. In Proceedings of the 2013 IEEE Conference on Information & Communication Technologies (ICT), JeJu Island, Korea, 11–12 April 2013; pp. 1003–1008.
16. Xu, Y.; Li, Y. Generating Concise Association Rules. In Proceedings the Sixteenth ACM Conference on Information and Knowledge Management, Lisbon, Portugal, 6–10 November 2007; pp. 781–790.
17. Ordonez, C. Association Rule Discovery with the Train and Test Approach for Heart Disease Prediction. *Inf. Technol. Biomed.* **2006**, *10*, 334–343. [CrossRef]
18. Vornberger, O.; Thiesing, F.; Middleberg, U. Short Term Prediction of Sales in Supermarkets. In Neural Networks, Proceedings of the IEEE International Conference, Perth, WA, USA, 27 November–1 December 1995; pp. 1028–1031.
19. Koç, A.; Yeniay, Ö. A Comparative Study of Artificial Neural Networks and Logistic Regression for Classification of Marketing Campaign Results. *Math. Comput. Appl.* **2013**, *18*, 392–398.
20. Anbananthen, S.; Sainarayanan, G.; Chekima, A.; Teo, J. Data Mining using Artificial Neural Network Tree. In proceedings of the 1st International Conference on Computers, Communications and Signal Processing with Special Track on Biomedical Engineering (CCSP), Kuala Lumpur, Malaysia, 14–16 November 2005; pp. 160–164.
21. Boone, D.; Roehm, M. Retail Segmentation using Artificial Neural Networks. *Int. J. Res. Mark.* **2002**, *19*, 287–301. [CrossRef]
22. Cerny, P. Data Mining and Neural Networks from a Commercial Perspective. In Proceedings of the ORSNZ Conference Twenty Naught One, University of Canterbury, Christchurch, New Zealand, 30 November–1 December 2001.
23. Arockiaraj, C. Applications of Neural Networks in Data Mining. *Int. J. Eng. Sci.* **2013**, *3*, 8–11.
24. Craven, M.W.; Shavlik, J.W. Using Neural Networks for Data Mining. *Future Gener. Comput. Syst.* **1997**, *13*, 211–229. [CrossRef]
25. Cios, K.; Pedrycz, W.; Swiniarski, R.; Kurgan, L. *Data Mining a Knowledge Discovery*; Springer: New York, NY, USA, 2007.
26. Berry, M.; Linoff, G. *Data Mining Techniques for Marketing, Sales, and Customer Relationship Management*; Wiley: Indianapolis, IN, USA, 2004.
27. Liu, H.; Su, B.; Zhang, B. The Application of Association Rules in Retail Marketing Mix. In Proceedings of the 2007 IEEE International Conference on Automation and Logistics, Jinan, China, 18–21 August 2007; pp. 2514–2517.
28. Chen, M.; Chiu, A.; Chang, H. Mining Changes in Customer Behavior in Retail Marketing. *Expert Syst. Appl.* **2005**, *28*, 773–781. [CrossRef]
29. Zhao, Y. *R and Data Mining: Examples and Case Studies*; Academic Press: New York, NY, USA, 2012.
30. Ahn, K. Effective Product Assignment Based on Association Rule Mining in Retail. *Expert Syst. Appl.* **2012**, *39*, 12551–12556. [CrossRef]
31. Dhanabhakyam, M.; Punithavalli, M. An Efficient Market Basket Analysis based on Adaptive Association Rule Mining with Faster Rule Generation Algorithm. *SIJ Trans. Comput. Sci. Eng. Its Appl.* **2013**, *1*, 105–110.
32. Kotsiantis, S.; Kanellopoulos, D. Association Rules Mining: A Recent Overview. *GESTS Int. Trans. Comput. Sci. Eng.* **2006**, *32*, 71–82.
33. Poh, H.; Jasic, T. Forecasting and Analysis of Marketing Data Using Neural Networks: A Case of Advertising and Promotion Impact. In Proceedings of the the 11th Conference on Artificial Intelligence for Applications, Los Angeles, CA, USA, 20–23 February 1995; pp. 224–230.
34. Mistry, J.; Nelwamondo, F.; Marwala, T. Estimating Missing Data and Determining the Confidence of the Estimate Data. In Proceedings of the Seventh International Conference on Machine Learning and Applications ICMLA '08, San Diego, CA, USA, 11–13 December 2008; pp. 752–755.
35. Nirkhi, S. Potential Use of Artificial Neural Network in Data Mining. In Proceedings of the the 2nd International Conference on Computer and Automation Engineering (ICCAE), Singapore, 26–28 February 2010; pp. 339–343.

36. Witten, I.; Frank, E.; Hall, M. *Data Mining: Practical Machine Learning Tools and Techniques*, 3rd ed.; Morgan Kaufmann: Amsterdam, The Netherlands, 2011; pp. 403–440.
37. Informatics. Available online: http://www.informatics.buu.ac.th/~ureerat/321641/Weka/Data%20Sets/supermarket/supermarket_basket_transactions_2005.arff (accessed on 21 January 2014).

© 2016 by the authors. Licensee MDPI, Basel, Switzerland. This article is an open access article distributed under the terms and conditions of the Creative Commons Attribution (CC BY) license (http://creativecommons.org/licenses/by/4.0/).

CSR Reporting Practices of Polish Energy and Mining Companies

Elżbieta Izabela Szczepankiewicz [1,*] and Przemysław Mućko [2,*]

1. Department of Accounting, Poznań University of Economics and Business, Al. Niepodległości 10, 61-875 Poznań, Poland
2. Faculty of Economics and Management, University of Szczecin, ul. A. Mickiewcza 64, 71-101 Szczecin, Poland
* Corespondence: elzbieta.szczepankiewicz@ue.poznan.pl (E.I.S.); mucko@wneiz.pl (P.M.); Tel.: +48-91-444-1944 (P.M.)

Academic Editor: Adam Jabłoński
Received: 31 December 2015; Accepted: 22 January 2016; Published: 29 January 2016

Abstract: Corporate Social Responsibility (CSR) reporting receives much attention nowadays. Communication with stakeholders is a part of assumed social responsibility, thus the quality of information disclosed in CSR reports has a significant impact on fulfilment of the responsibility. The authors use content analysis of selected CSR reports to describe and assess patterns and structure of information disclosed in them. CSR reports of Polish companies have similar structures at a very high level of analysis, but a more detailed study reveals much diversity in approaches to the report's content. Even fairly similar companies may devote significantly different amounts of space to the same issue. The number of similar stakeholders varies irrespectively of the company's size. Considerable diversity of reporting patterns results from the nature of CSR reporting, because it concerns highly entity-specific issues. Thus, such considerable diversity is not surprising. However, many initiatives and efforts are devoted to greater comparability of reporting, so a greater degree of uniformity can be expected. Similar conclusions may be drawn from integrated reports' analysis, though a small sample reflects the relative novelty of this trend.

Keywords: corporate social responsibility; sustainability reports; corporate financial statement; integrated reporting

1. Introduction

The basis of Corporate Social Responsibility (CSR) is the idea of sustainable development. Initially, CSR was interpreted in terms of economic development that respects environmental preservation and protection. Sustainable development is understood as overall socio-economic development integrating economic, political, social and environmental objectives. There are many different approaches to interpreting sustainable development. According to Garriga and Melé [1], most of the current CSR theories are focused on one of the four main aspects:

(1) meeting economic objectives that secure long-term profits (instrumental theories)
(2) using business power in a responsible way (political theories)
(3) integrating social demands (social integration theories)
(4) contributing to a good society by doing what is ethically correct (ethical theories)

Although these four approaches do not form a convenient framework for empirical research, an immediate question arises as to which of these forms prevails in practice: whether CSR is necessary to generate long-term profits, or to achieve other aims, or perhaps it reflects a natural tendency for social integration. The answer depends on the quality of CSR reports, as they are part of the social dialog between a company and its stakeholders. The scope of CSR reports consists of three main elements, *i.e.*, economic, social and environmental disclosures. As such, CSR reporting is very broad and may be viewed as very ambitious. The question arises as to whether such broad objectives are being fulfilled. The aim of the article is to provide an input into the wide strand of research on evaluation of CSR and similar reporting, which in the paper is limited to Polish companies.

2. CSR Reporting

Initially elusive, eclectic and without strict boundaries [2], CSR became more concrete after incorporation into the political and legislative activities of the EU. The EU Commission's approach to CSR has changed from rather conceptual to more prescriptive. Once defined as a concept of voluntary integration of social and environmental concerns into companies' business operations and their interaction with their stakeholders, in the new strategy for CSR it was defined simply as "the responsibility of enterprises for their impacts on society" [3]. According to the EU Commission, socially responsible companies have to implement processes that ensure integration of social, environmental, ethical, human rights and consumer concerns into their business operations and strategy, which depends on close collaboration with their stakeholders.

Adaptation to CSR models is mainly driven by a new type of consumer that is sensitive to non-financial outcomes of business activities and, if properly informed, forces companies to integrate non-financial stakeholder interests into core strategy and operations [4,5]. The necessity for proper consumer information lies at the top of EU priorities [3].

Communication is an essential part of corporate social responsibility. In the case of socially responsible companies, reporting is not just a faithful representation of business activities to inform interested parties that the organization's behaviour is in accordance with stakeholder interests. CSR reporting is *per se* part of fulfilment of social responsibility obligations. It is part of a social dialogue that in itself is an indispensable part of social responsibility. Moreover, since not all stakeholders take part in governance processes, their engagement and satisfaction is maintained through appropriate communication channels.

Thus, the shift toward CSR approaches to business is accompanied by a similar move in reporting. CSR or sustainability reports serve the purpose of disseminating information to stakeholders and the public (see Figure 1).

| Business model | Economic model | ⟹ | Corporate social responsibility model |
| Reporting model | Financial reporting | ⟹ | CSR reporting / Integrated reporting |

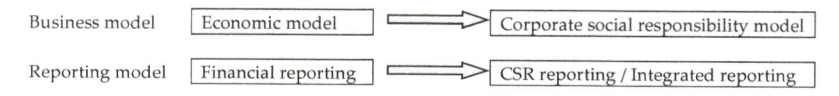

Figure 1. The parallel shift in business and reporting models.

Through these reports, organizations fulfil the dual purpose of communicating CSR and being accountable [6]. In the traditional model of business, corporations' goals are measured with financial performance indicators, such as profits, market value, and dividends. Socially responsible organizations need new measures with a broader scope of outcomes and impact on the environment. A triple bottom line is a popular proposition that assumes the necessity of measuring also social and environmental outcomes.

The triple bottom line is a handy catch phrase, also referring to another simple abbreviation "3P", *i.e.*, profits, people, planet. Although the necessity of assessing outcomes according groups represented by the three Ps is not controversial, the term TBL has been criticised. A critical point is aimed at the presumed similarity of the triple bottom line to the first bottom line, although such a similarity seems impossible. Financial measures are calculated with a degree of precision that is not possible in the social and environmental area. Besides, there are many trade-offs among various stakeholders within the "people" and "planet" bottom line that are even more difficult to assess and reflect in a single indicator. Thus, the TBL is useful rather as a rhetorical phrase to form and maintain a broader perspective in decision making processes [7,8].

Due to varied informational needs and behaviours of stakeholders, CSR communication may be performed through many channels. However, written reports are preferred by stakeholders over other possible means [9]. The advantage of written reports comes from formal tools and mechanisms that ensure reliability. Various regulations, guidelines, and standards help stakeholders obtain access to reliable information. The best known initiatives aimed at improving CSR reporting or integrated reporting include [10]:

- IFAC Sustainability Framework 2.0 (2012)
- ESG Framework (2011) and KPIs for ESG (2009)
- Prince of Wales' Accounting for Sustainability's Connected Reporting Guidance (2009)
- SustainAbility Global Reporters Program (2010)
- AccountAbility's AA1000 Standards (2008)
- ISO 26000—Guidance on social responsibility (2010, 2012)
- IRCSA—Framework for Integrated Reporting (2011)
- Guidelines of Global Reporting Initiative (GRI): G 3-1 (2011) and G 4 (2012)
- The International Framework Integrated Reporting of International Integrated Reporting Council (IIRC) (2013)

The list gives an impression of a plethora of initiatives with a common (or at least similar) aim. However, nowadays, the most prominent and widely used framework is the Global Reporting Initiative [11,12]. GRI is an international independent, non-governmental organization that aims at assisting other organizations, both businesses and governments, in understanding and communicating these organizations' impact on critical sustainability issues. The best known GRI product is the Sustainability Reporting Standards, used by thousands of companies around the world.

In spite of many advantages, GRI reporting receives also some criticism. According to some research, companies that prepare reports in accordance with GRI do not necessarily behave in a responsible way [13]. Boiral [14] reports that 90% of significant negative events were not disclosed in sustainability reports, which is a serious violation of the balance principle of GRI guidelines. Moreover, the concept of GRI reporting framework is not consistent with the essence of sustainability development, as the former is aimed at an organizational level, and the latter is relevant to the planet [15].

Nevertheless, GRI reporting is useful for research purposes, since it improves comparability of information which is otherwise difficult to compare. Since efficient communication of organizational behaviour is dependent upon comparability of reports, the GRI framework is used in the empirical part of this research.

3. Demand for Research on CSR Reporting of Polish Mining and Energy Companies

Mining and energy sectors are generally known for environmental and social issues. The case of Polish industries seems even more complicated. Poland is the world's 17th biggest emitter of CO_2 from fuels, and the fifth in the EU [16]. The environmental issues in Poland are reinforced by the country's strong reliance on coal energy [17]. About 86% of total gross power generation comes from coal and coal products [18]. The coal energy industry is under strong pressure resulting from EU climate targets. The pressure has further influence on mining and energy companies and their social and environmental impacts. Moreover, these two Polish industries are still characterized by inefficient human resource strategies and out-dated operating practices [19], which means that these industries may face additional tensions in their relations with societal stakeholders in the future.

Corporate social responsibility, and particularly CSR reporting and communication, is a method to mitigate social and environmental problems in these industries [20,21]. Although Poland may rather be seen as a regular case in this regard, authors believe that there is a particular demand to study and improve CSR reporting in mining and energy industries in this country.

4. Literature Review of Empirical Research

Corporate social responsibility and sustainability reporting draw much attention from the academic community, which results in a broad strand of literature on theoretical aspects of the issue and empirical findings. However, for the purposes of this paper, there are several studies which are relevant.

Roca and Searcy's [12] study focused on the use of indicators in CSR and similar reports. On the basis of 94 reports, they demonstrated a wide usage of various CSR indicators; they found nearly 600 indicators in these reports. Generally, a great variety of indicators were disclosed, although few were used more commonly, *i.e.*, in nearly half of all reports (indicators relating to funding, donations, sponsorship and community investments, greenhouse gas/CO_2 equivalent emissions and the total number of employees). The indicators evenly represented three bottom line elements (*i.e.*, economic, social, and environment). The study also proved the importance of the GRI reporting framework.

Gamerschlag, Möller and Verbeeten [22] sought for determinants of social and environmental disclosures of the biggest German public companies (80 companies). They used a number of keywords to assess the level of CSR reporting and found that it was correlated with the company's visibility, shareholder structure, and relationships with US shareholders.

Boiral's [14] study shows that contrary to the principles of GRI standards, 90% of negative information was not disclosed or was reported only partially (104 of 116 negative events identified in their study and affecting the reporting entities). Most of the 23 companies presented an exaggerated image of their positive achievements, virtuous commitments and external awards. Given the sensitive nature of engagement from stakeholders, such an overoptimistic and overemphasized image of a company in CSR reports may in fact undermine the credibility of stakeholder dialogue.

There are few empirical analyses of annual reports of Polish companies focusing strictly on CSR reporting. Mućko [23] carried out a content analysis of narrative reporting of public food processing companies. Although this research had broader aims, it demonstrated very limited presence of CSR issues. About 1% of information in narrative reports related to the environment, employees or customers, or suppliers (grammatical sentences were the unit of analysis). Szadziewska [24] analysed a wide spectrum of communication channels (websites, annual reports, environmental reports, and CSR and sustainability reports), but focused strictly on environmental disclosures. She revealed that companies generally disclosed information about the environment, although most of them did not measure their environmental performance. She concluded that companies would rather use this information to create a positive image of themselves than to provide relevant, credible and comprehensible information to its stakeholders. In more recent research on CSR relevant disclosures of selected Polish public companies, she divided companies disclosing CSR information into three groups, *i.e.*, companies that: (1) disclose only regulation compliance issues, (2) provide information also on social problems and their solutions, and (3) publish much information relevant to CSR [25]. Many articles provide a basic description that enables assessing the popularity of CSR reporting in Poland [26–29].

5. Concept of the Structure of Integrated Reports of Socially Responsible Companies in Poland

The specific nature of CSR reporting in Poland includes independently developed models presented in research literature. J. Samelak [30] proposed a model-based approach to the structure of integrated reports of socially responsible companies that makes up for the imperfections of financial reporting. The structure of the integrated report is divided into two parts: financial and non-financial. The first part includes traditional annual financial statements with the opinion of an auditor. The other part of the integrated report includes an activity report and a report on intangible resources and social responsibility activities omitted from the financial part. The integrated report should integrate financial information with non-financial information from both parts of the report.

Table 1 presents elements of integrated reports of socially responsible companies in Poland.

Table 1. Structure of integrated reports of socially responsible companies in Poland.

Structure of the Integrated Report	Non-Listed Polish Companies Reporting in Accordance with Domestic Regulations	Listed Polish Companies Preparing Integrated Reports in Accordance with IFRS
Financial part	(1) Introduction to the financial statements (2) Balance sheet (3) Profit and loss statement (4) Statement of changes in equity (5) Cash flow statement (6) Additional notes, excluding information on employment and managing and supervisory bodies (7) Opinion and report of an auditor	(1) Introduction to the report (2) Statement of financial position (3) Comprehensive income statement (4) Statement of changes in equity (5) Cash flow statement (6) Additional notes to the financial statements excluding information on employment and managing and supervisory bodies (7) Opinion and report of an auditor
Non-financial part	(1) Activity report according to the National Accounting Standard (NAS) No. 9, including business risk information and other information required by: • Accounting Act • Listed Companies Code • Stock exchange regulations for listed companies (2) Clear explanation of the connection between presented non-financial information with financial information disclosed in the financial part, including presentation of financial results (3) Company's social responsibility strategy (4) Information on the effect of the company's activity on the natural environment (5) Information on the company's social involvement (6) Information on intellectual capital, including data on organization capital, relational capital and human capital, as well as data excluded from additional notes on employment (7) Information on managing and supervisory bodies (including standing committees) (8) Information on independent, third-party audit of the second part of the integrated report together with an audit report.	(1) Management Commentary, including information required by other legal regulations (Accounting Act, Listed Companies Code, stock exchange regulations for listed companies)

Source: own work based on [30–36].

The IFRS conceptual framework stipulates that the basic features of financial statements include relevant and faithful representations of information. The basic features are supplemented by additional features: comparability, verifiability, timeliness, comprehensibility. Many authors treat the above classification of features as a basis for formulating a conceptual framework for integrated reports. Sometimes, they also point out additional features. Szczepankiewicz [10] considers timeliness to be a basic feature (next to relevance and faithful representation), because information should reach the stakeholder in order to factor into decision making. Integrated reports are useful to stakeholders if they are delivered on time and prepared in a reliable manner, *i.e.*, if they faithfully represent the reality. An integrated statement should contain relevant and complete information and should take into account stakeholders' expectations regarding the scope of delivered information. On the basis of the basic elements of the annual financial statements, a stakeholder (a professional analyst) can recognize a number of risks related to the organization's assets, financial condition and financial results.

Nowadays, mining and energy companies are faced with the challenge of responding to the growing demand for energy, while simultaneously improving air quality, reducing emissions and tackling climate change and shrinking resources. Therefore, introducing non-financial information and environmental indicators into integrated reports is seen as a positive move and denotes a growing interest in environmental issues (including in particular negative environmental impacts of the organization) among stakeholders. In accordance with the CSR concept, the non-financial part of the integrated report presents performance indicators in the following categories: economic, environmental and social aspects of activity (Table 2).

Table 2. Areas of presentation of performance indicators in Polish companies in the following categories: economic, environmental and social aspects of activity.

Performance Indicators by Category	Presentation of Results by Area:
(1) Economic aspects of activity	Corporate financial results: • market presence • profit • sales volume • rate of return from dividend investment • equity, liabilities and their interest rates • market share; brand strength • expenditures on research and development • taxes paid, tax reliefs enjoyed • wages • cash flows • local supplies • market practices; corruption • economic policy • court cases • corporate governance • other issues disclosed by economic or ratio analysis
(2) Environmental aspects of activity	Results in the following areas: • raw materials • products and services • natural resource consumption • energy consumption • water consumption • compliance with regulations • transportation • adherence to environmental regulations • air and water pollution • biodiversity • greenhouse gas emissions • solid and liquid waste • noise • vibrations • waste management • reduction of packaging • radioactivity • recycling • use of renewable materials and resources • soil contamination and erosion • chemical spillage • ozone-depleting substances • genetic modifications • animal rights • protection of endangered species

Table 2. Cont.

Performance Indicators by Category	Presentation of Results by Area:
(3) Social aspects of activity	Results in the following areas: • employment • wage policy • employee education and training • personnel relations in the organization • health and safety • employee programs • additional benefits • diversity of employees, diverse and equal opportunities, combating discrimination • equal pay for equal work • human rights • discrimination on race, gender, age • anti-mobbing policy • freedom to join unions and associations • right to collective bargaining • relationships with trade unions • severance policy • forced labor • child labor • public procurement and investments • free competition infringement • corruption • compliance with regulations • customers' health and safety • fair promotion and labeling of products • product quality and safety • product availability for the disabled and the poor • socially responsible sales and marketing • customer privacy protection • marketing communication • participation in public life • diversity of suppliers • support for social initiatives and local communities • donations to charity • other issues reflecting the specific nature of the organization

Source: own work based on [26,29].

An integrated report should constitute a comprehensive and coherent document divided into a number of parts (chapters), linking non-financial data (including data from the activity report, ESG reports and intellectual capital reports) with financial data (from the financial statements). The integrated report should integrate the content and GRI indicators with the content of the activity report—particularly as regards content required by applicable Polish laws. Both the financial and the non-financial part of the report should include references and relationships between financial and non-financial information. A concept of the integrated report elements is presented in Figure 2.

INTEGRATION ↑↓

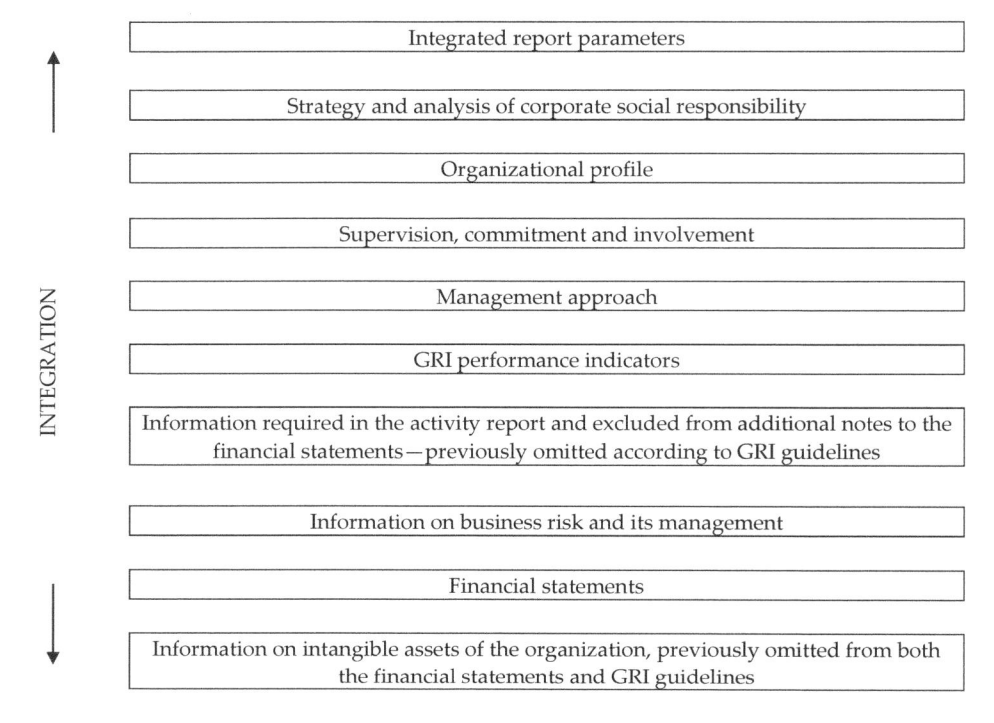

- Integrated report parameters
- Strategy and analysis of corporate social responsibility
- Organizational profile
- Supervision, commitment and involvement
- Management approach
- GRI performance indicators
- Information required in the activity report and excluded from additional notes to the financial statements—previously omitted according to GRI guidelines
- Information on business risk and its management
- Financial statements
- Information on intangible assets of the organization, previously omitted from both the financial statements and GRI guidelines

Figure 2. Concept of integrated report parts.

6. Methodology and Data

6.1. Content Analysis

This paper presents a case study of CSR reporting of selected Polish companies using a content analysis method. Content analysis is the most common research method in the field of CSR reporting. It may be performed on the basis of words, sentences or other parts of text as units of analysis that are subsequently assigned to codes. Words do not require a subjective judgment from the coder. Furthermore, searching for specific terms in the text is regarded as the most reliable form of content analysis: it always yields the same results in repeated trials, as it can be easily replicated [22]. However, an analysis of reports containing both narrative and quantitative information should be performed with caution, since content analysis is designed for narratives. Volume of information (measured by means of the chosen unit of analysis: words, sentences, paragraphs, pages or codes) is usually a proxy for the quality of information. Although such an approach may obviously lead to mistakes, it is subsequently refined by means of information structure analysis. Moreover, the extent of disclosure may be interpreted as a proxy of the relative importance of disclosed information. We used a mixed approach in the analysis: word counts were used, although the assessment was mostly based on the topic structure analysis.

In the first stage of research, CSR reports were gathered. We chose energy and mining industry companies. In the next stage, reports were coded according to the GRI indicators (version 4), but only the general standard disclosure part, in order to measure the quantity and variety of certain information. Moreover, the simple existence of certain disclosures was also checked.

6.2. Data Description

For the purposes of the research, CSR and similar reports were gathered (Table 3). We used reports submitted for the best CSR report competition, available on the organizer's website [37]. For the purpose of assessing best practices in CSR reporting, reports submitted for the competition seemed to be the best choice. In the 2015 competition, 37 reports were submitted, including nine from companies in the energy industry. The energy industry is often analysed in CSR research because of its significant sustainability problems and the usually high level of interest from its stakeholders [14]. However, out of the nine energy sector companies, two did not use any CSR reporting standards (EDF Polska and RWE Polska), and another one used GRI Guidelines version 3.1. Since most reports were prepared in accordance with GRI version 4, the other reports were excluded from the analysis. However, to ensure a better comparison and understanding of CSR reporting practices, two companies were added, both representing the mining industry. Some of the analysed energy companies own mining facilities, so comparability of the analysis was maintained. The inclusion of KGHM was additionally justified due to this company's strong reporting history: it has been repeatedly awarded for the best annual report (for both financial and non-financial parts).

Table 3. Overview of analysed reports of companies operating in the energy and mining sector in 2014.

Company Name	Sector	Turn-Over (PLN Million)	No of Employees	Covered Period (Years)	Volume (Pages)	Word Count	Type of Report	External Verification
ENEA S.A.	Energy	9855	10,063	1	60	13,736	CSR only	No
Energa S.A.	Energy	10,590	11,494	1	140	25,868	CSR only	Full
PGE	Energy	28,137	39,977	2	114	29,586	CSR only	Partial
Polskie LNG S.A.	Energy	0	118	2	112	25,246	CSR only	Full
Tauron S.A.	Energy	18,440	26,108	1	169	45,915	CSR only	Full
GK PGNiG	Mining/Energy	34,304	29,285	1	88	24,014	CSR only	Full
KGHM Polska Miedź S.A.	Mining	20,492	34,097	1	158	47,013	Integrated	No
Lubelski Węgiel "Bogdanka" S.A. (LWB)	Mining	2013	5,795	1	144	74,469	Integrated	No

All reports were prepared "in accordance" with the core version of GRI 4. Total volume of analysed reports amounts to almost 1000 pages and almost 300,000 words (though the report of LWB is bilingual, so the volume presented in the table is approximately doubled).

7. Results and Discussion

7.1. Report Type and Length

Integrated reporting is still a rather new approach. Thus, it not surprising that only two companies published integrated reports, whereas others published separate CSR reports. As expected, the amount of information in integrated reports is generally greater than in separate CSR reports, though a CSR report by Tauron was also long. A report of Enea was the shortest only because of the extensive use of external references made in the document. It seems a good strategy for reports presented on the webpages, but for further analysis only PDF files were used. It is noteworthy that none of the integrated reports were verified by external parties.

7.2. Importance of Disclosures

CSR information is highly entity-specific (Table 4). Companies and their management may differently assess the importance of separate aspects of business, and devote more or less space of reports to them, to better convey a significant message about a company, to get stronger involvement of stakeholders, or for opportunistic reasons. In order to assess the diversity of topics, the percentage share of volume of disclosure is used.

Firstly, the share of volume of information classified according to sections of GRI's general standard disclosures is presented in Table 4. At this very general level of analysis, the structure of reports seems quite similar. The majority of information was relevant to the description of the organization.

Table 4. Share of volume of information classified according to sections of general standard disclosures (GRI).

Companies Sections	ENEA	Energa	PGE	Polskie LNG	Tauron	GK PGNiG	KGHM Polska Miedź	LWB
Strategy & analysis	8.84%	14.56%	7.5%	5.2%	11.03%	11.16%	16.97%	5.95%
Organisational profile	34.89%	36.82%	38.02%	34.64%	58.86%	29.77%	33.92%	22.38%
Identified material aspects and boundaries	14.66%	10.27%	11.9%	7.24%	11.96%	14.68%	8.16%	7.09%
Stakeholder engagement	14.72%	6.89%	10.97%	7.09%	9.74%	22.34%	2.19%	6.19%
Report profile	17.98%	25.18%	24.81%	33.39%	2.55%	14.69%	24.02%	43%
Governance	3.01%	3.28%	2.95%	8.48%	1.83%	3.84%	12.55%	7.99%
Ethics and integrity	5.91%	2.99%	3.84%	3.96%	4.02%	3.51%	2.19%	7.39%

Differences with regard to the choice and importance of content (measured by the number of words) were observed even in the section describing such a relatively simple and non-controversial issue as the organizational profile. In the "Organizational profile" section, in Energa's report, the lengthiest disclosures were devoted to markets (G4-08), in PGE and LWB reports—number of employees and their structure (G4-10), in Polskie LNG and Tauron reports—information on supply value chain (G4-12), and in KGHM's report—information on the commitment to external initiatives (charters, principles, or other initiatives—G4-15, and memberships of associations—G4-16). Details are presented in Table 5.

Table 5. Percentages of words related to selected disclosures in the organizational profile section.

Company GRI Disclosure Code	ENEA	Energa	PGE	Polskie LNG	Tauron	GK PGNiG	KGHM Polska Miedź	LWB
G4-04 Primary brands, products and services	15%	0%	18%	3%	14%	15%	7%	15%
G4-06 Number and names of countries where the organisation operates	1%	0%	3%	2%	2%	0%	13%	12%
G4-08 Markets	24%	35%	11%	10%	8%	14%	7%	6%
G4-09 Scale of the organisation.	6%	0%	1%	11%	0%	23%	4%	5%
G4-10 Number of employees	7%	13%	27%	8%	20%	8%	3%	27%
G4-11 collective bargaining agreements	7%	0%	5%	3%	3%	2%	1%	4%
G4-12 supply-value chain	20%	16%	7%	26%	27%	6%	2%	11%
G4-14 precautionary approach	4%	8%	8%	3%	6%	6%	11%	1%
G4-15 charters, principles, or initiatives	2%	13%	4%	17%	9%	7%	23%	3%
G4-16 Memberships	2%	11%	11%	9%	8%	7%	23%	5%

The percentage may proxy for the relative importance of a topic in the description of a company to stakeholders. Although differences in weights are not surprising, their ranges are worth commenting on. Even quite similar companies seem to place different emphases on fundamental issues. Energa report contained hardly any narrative about primary brands, products and services (though this information was conveyed otherwise, in market disclosure), whereas Tauron's report devoted a significant part of the company profile to this topic.

7.3. Disclosures on Precautionary Approach

According to the GRI Guidelines G4 "The Precautionary Principle refers to the approach taken to address potential environmental impacts" [26]. Although Implementation Guidance allows companies to report only their approach to risk management, it is rather clearly designed for assessing one of the three bottom lines. Only two reports contained direct reference to environmental issues in this disclosure, and the other reports were limited to a general description of risk management structures, procedures or models. A general risk management description may possibly serve well the purpose of assessing risks for the environment, but it may also be seen as a tool for achieving current goals. As such, these disclosures are more closely linked to instrumental theories than to other ones. Moreover, when environmental issues were mentioned (Polskie LNG and LWB), the disclosures were very limited (up to 69 words), because they referred readers to some other sources. General risk management information was much more elaborate (up to 737 words) (Figure 3).

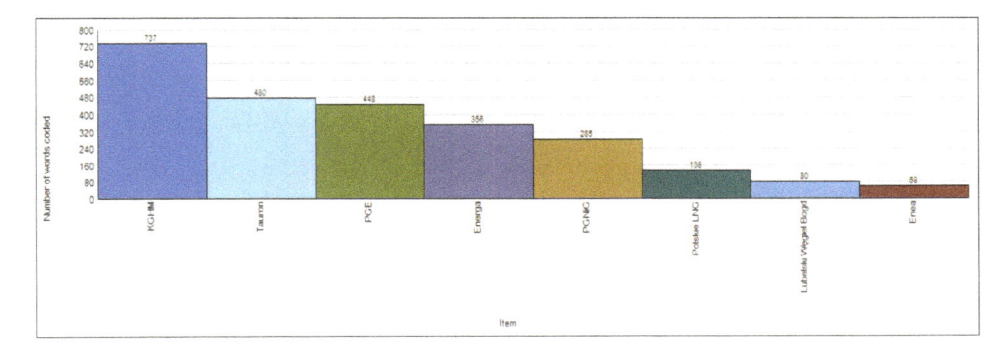

Figure 3. Amount of information on precautionary approach in CSR reports.

7.4. Closer Look at Stakeholder Approach

The idea of CSR reporting is closely related to dialogue with stakeholders [6]. Stakeholders' role is not limited to that of information recipients. CSR reporting is part of this dialogue. Thus, disclosures about stakeholders and dialogue with them may be crucial in assessing the quality of CSR reports. Data about stakeholder approach is presented in Table 6.

Table 6. Volume of disclosures on stakeholder approach.

Company	ENEA	Energa	PGE	Polskie LNG	Tauron	GK PGNiG	KGHM Polska Miedź	LWB
Number of stakeholders	11	11	15	34	21	10	15	7
Volume of information (no of words) about stakeholder engagement, including:	528	435	677	413	649	2284	172	869
• G4-25 identification and selection of stakeholders	301	229	575	95	223	240	34	202
• G4-26 stakeholder engagement	301	229	286	135	226	533	69	500
• G4-27 stakeholders' topics and organization's response	195	206	80	183	378	1510	59	31

It seems that the number of stakeholders is not correlated with the volume of information about them. However, some of the companies define their stockholders quite broadly. Polskie LNG specified 34 groups interested and engaged with the business, where the much larger company PGNiG specified only 10.

The volume of disclosure is significantly varied (when measured with words). Generally, the volume is not huge, but graphs and schemes were also used, so a general estimate may be appropriate. The three disclosures presented in the table (*i.e.*, G4-25, G4-26, and G4-27) were made in the same paragraph in the text of reports. Companies disclosed information about stakeholders' identification, selection and engagement in one narrative, though, in fact, distinct GRI indicators suggest the importance of separating information.

7.5. Quality of Integrated Reports of Analysed Companies

The authors reviewed integrated reports for 2014 prepared by Polish companies from the mining sector. Table 7 presents the scope of data included in the integrated reports of the analysed companies.

Table 7. Comparison of the scope of integrated reports of Polish companies from the mining sector.

Report Part	KGHM Polska Miedź S.A.	Lubelski Węgiel "Bogdanka" S.A. (LWB)
Integrated report parameters	About the Report	About the Report
Strategy and analysis of corporate social responsibility	<ul><li>KGHM today and tomorrow</li><li>Our Strategy and perspectives (Strategy for the years 2015–2020 with an outlook to 2040)</li><li>Support Strategies</li><li>Our results in the area of improving productivity</li><li>The most crucial modernisation and new technology projects</li><li>Environmental protection</li></ul>	<ul><li>Business Strategy</li><li>Priorities and key objectives of the CSR Strategy for 2014–2017</li><li>CSR strategy in the context of the business strategy</li><li>major development investments</li></ul>
Organizational profile	<ul><li>About us (Company profile)</li><li>Description of the Company activities</li><li>Structure of the Group</li><li>The model of value creation at the Company</li><li>The context of the Company operations</li><li>KGHM in 2014</li><li>Extraction and production</li><li>Sales</li><li>Key financial data</li><li>We are proud of our employees</li></ul>	<ul><li>About the company</li><li>Suppliers and supply chain</li><li>The situation in the coal market</li></ul>
Supervision, commitment and involvement	<ul><li>Letter from the President of the Management Board</li><li>Letter from the Chairman of the Supervisory Board</li><li>Internal control, corporate risk management and internal audit</li><li>Supervision over the process of financial reporting and external audit</li></ul>	<ul><li>Letter from the President</li><li>The Management Board and the Supervisory Board</li><li>Corporate governance and shareholding structure</li></ul>

Table 7. Cont.

Report Part	KGHM Polska Miedź S.A.	Lubelski Węgiel "Bogdanka" S.A. (LWB)
Management approach	<ul><li>Integrated management system</li><li>Research and development and innovations</li><li>Purposes, direction, and Visio</li><li>Initiatives supporting knowledge and innovation development</li><li>Financing research by external funds and international cooperation</li></ul>	<ul><li>Integrated Management System</li><li>Innovation aspects in the management culture</li><li>Ethics as component of the organisational culture</li><li>Management approach in the context of sustainable development</li><li>Management and corporate social responsibility</li><li>Social dialogue as component of the management culture</li></ul>
GRI performance indicators	<ul><li>Our results in the area of improving productivity</li><li>Our results in the area of development of the resource base</li><li>Our results in the area of income diversification and gaining independence from energy prices</li><li>Our results in the area of regional support</li><li>Our results in the area of development of organizational abilities and skills</li><li>GRI Index</li></ul>	<ul><li>Effectiveness of safety management at the workplace</li><li>Effectiveness in environmental protection</li><li>Effectiveness in building relations with the local community</li><li>GRI Indicators in table's</li></ul>
Information required in the activity report and excluded from additional notes to the financial statements—previously omitted according to GRI guidelines	<ul><li>The currency market in 2014</li><li>Investment outlays</li><li>Our results in the area of income diversification and gaining independence from energy prices</li></ul>	No
Information on business risk and its management	<ul><li>Financial risk</li><li>Risk Management System</li><li>Reporting methodology</li></ul>	<ul><li>Responsible management vs. integrated system of enterprise risk management</li></ul>
Financial statements	<ul><li>Selected items from the standalone and consolidated financial statements</li></ul>	<ul><li>Full</li></ul>
Management Commentary	<ul><li>The management board's report on the activities of the company</li></ul>	<ul><li>Only other financial and nonfinancial data tables</li></ul>
Auditor's opinion and report on its audit of the financial statement	Yes	Yes
Financial indicators	<ul><li>Revenues from sales</li><li>Review of financial performance</li><li>Basic ratios describing financial liquidity, the profitability of assets and equity and financing:</li><li>Liquidity ratios,</li><li>Profitability ratios,</li><li>Financing ratios,</li><li>Capital market ratios</li></ul>	<ul><li>Basic financial result</li><li>Business scale, production and sale</li><li>Selected financial results</li><li>Group's revenue, costs, profit and loss</li></ul>

Table 7. *Cont.*

Report Part	KGHM Polska Miedź S.A.	Lubelski Węgiel "Bogdanka" S.A. (LWB)
Information on intangible assets of the organization, previously omitted from both the financial statements and GRI guidelines	• Medical Care Package • Employees insurance • Social Fund assets and liabilities • Pillars of Corporate Governance • Shareholder Structure and Role of Shareholders (Dialogue with stakeholders in capital markets (investors, analysts, regulators) • Ethics in the Company • RESPECT Index • KGHM Organisational Membership • Dividend Policy	No

Integrated reports should address information needs of various groups of stakeholders. To that end, an adequate amount and the usefulness of disclosed information must be ensured, and the form and scope of integrated reports should be unified in order to promote comparability. Integrated reports should present factors used by the organization to ensure long-term success in pursuing its sustainable development strategy and CSR activities. To be useful, integrated reports need to be transparent, uncomplicated and understandable to stakeholders. They should be logical, cohesive, complete and compliant with a generally accepted standard.

Undoubtedly, the amount of content in integrated reports should be reasonably moderate, so as to ensure transparent, logical and cohesive presentation of information directed to stakeholders. However, too succinct and superfluous annual reports aimed at providing a positive representation of economic and social value will not always be useful to stakeholders. Management boards of companies consider using models proposed by researchers. However, Polish entities that have reported on CSR activities and sustainable development for several years have faced a number of practical problems before researchers proposed theoretical models and practical solutions for their accounting systems.

The content of the analysed integrated reports implies that stakeholders will find it difficult to benchmark the companies on that basis. Differences in the scope and form of presenting financial and non-financial information make it difficult for stakeholders to compare situations, management quality or to assess prospective results of the analysed entities. It is difficult to note any links between financial and non-financial information in the reports. Financial and non-financial information continues to be presented in two separate parts. One of the underlying reasons may be the lack of a uniform standard and detailed guidelines prescribing how to achieve such data integration in the report.

The provisions of the Directive 2014/95/EU [31] will take effect in 2017, which will also result in a number of practical problems [38]. Reporting on environmental information according to the Directive is a complex issue and gives rise to multiple dilemmas and questions:

(1) Will information presented in compliance with the Directive satisfy the needs of all report users?
(2) Will the cost associated with preparing environmental reports be proportionate to benefits enjoyed by the entity?
(3) Who will prepare this kind of report in entities that do not have a CSR department?
(4) Who will be the right person to verify environmental information?
(5) Will traditional auditing of the activity report be sufficient for confirming the authenticity of presented information?

8. Conclusions

The conclusions of the research are still preliminary but, placed within the context of other analyses of CSR reporting of Polish companies [7,18,20–22], they provide some insight into its patterns and structures. CSR reports of Polish companies have similar structures at a very high level of analysis, but a more detailed study reveals much diversity in the approaches to the report's content. Even fairly similar companies may devote significantly different amounts of space to the same issue. The number of similar stakeholders varies, irrespectively of the company's size. Considerable diversity of reporting patterns results from the nature of CSR reporting, because it concerns highly entity-specific issues. Moreover, the publication of information related to CSR is completely voluntary. Thus, such considerable diversity is not surprising. However, the guidelines and standards described in the first part of the paper are aimed at promoting *inter alia* harmonized and comparable information. The reports analysed in the research were prepared in accordance with GRI Gudelines version 4, so a greater degree of uniformity could be expected. However, research on this matter should be continued in order to explain the limitations to achieving standardization of CSR reporting.

General conclusions regarding the analysis of Polish companies in the energy and mining sectors can be formulated as follows:

(1) companies internally analyse their environmental impacts
(2) companies use environmental-economic accounting
(3) companies have implemented and operate quality management systems
(4) companies have developed and implemented sustainable development concepts in management
(5) companies have developed and implemented comprehensive environmental management concepts
(6) companies have implemented and operate environmental management systems compliant with GRI 3.1, GRI 4
(7) companies have implemented and operate risk management systems as well as systems for managing the impact of risk on sustainable company management

In Poland, the discussion of how to ensure adequate quality and comparability of CSR reports and the integration of reports should be continued. It is also necessary to consider the problem of third-party attestation of such reports. In Poland, the financial part is reviewed by auditors, and only a few auditing companies attest non-financial matters in reports.

Acknowledgments: Acknowledgments: This paper has been written as part of the project No. 51109-XX2 entitled "Business Concept of Annual Statements as a Tool for Communication with Stakeholders and for Building Economic and Social Value of the Company in its Environment". The project is carried out by the University of Economics in Poznań.

Author Contributions: Author Contributions: E.I. Szczepankiewicz was responsible and wrote Sections 2, 5 and 7.5. P. Mućko wrote Section 3, performed literature review in Section 4, and did content analysis described in Sections 6 and 7.1–7.4, (and wrote them). The rest of the paper is a result of joint cooperation.

Conflicts of Interest: Conflicts of Interest: The authors declare no conflict of interest.

References

1. Garriga, E.; Melé, D. Corporate Social Responsibility Theories: Mapping the Territory. *J. Bus. Ethics* **2004**, *53*, 51–71. [CrossRef]
2. Carroll, A.B. The pyramid of corporate social responsibility: Toward the moral management of organizational stakeholders. *Bus. Horiz.* **1991**, *34*, 39–48. [CrossRef]
3. European Commission. *Communication from the Commission to the European Parliament, the Council, the European Economic and Social Committee and the Committee of the Regions. A Renewed EU Strategy 2011–2014 for Corporate Social Responsibility*; European Commission: Brussels, Belgium, 2011.
4. Bilan, Y. Sustainable Development of a Company: Building of New Level Relationship with the Consumers of XXI Century. *Amfiteatru Econ.* **2013**, *15*, 687–701.

5. Vázquez, J.L.; Lanero, A.; García, M.P.; García, J. Altruism or strategy? A study of attributions of responsibility in business and its impact on the consumer decision making process. *Econ. Sociol.* **2013**, *6*, 108–122. [CrossRef] [PubMed]
6. Baviera-Puig, A.; Gómez-Navarro, T.; García-Melón, M.; García-Martínez, G. Assessing the communication quality of CSR reports. A case study on four spanish food companies. *Sustain. Switz.* **2015**, *7*, 11010–11031. [CrossRef]
7. Shnayder, L.; Van, R.; Hekkert, M.P. Putting your money where your mouth is: Why sustainability reporting based on the triple bottom line can be misleading. *PLoS ONE* **2015**, *10*, e0119036.
8. Norman, W.; MacDonald, C. Getting to the Bottom of "Triple Bottom Line". *Bus. Ethics Q.* **2004**, *14*, 243–262. [CrossRef]
9. Kim, H.; Hur, W.-M.; Yeo, J. Corporate Brand Trust as a Mediator in the Relationship between Consumer Perception of CSR, Corporate Hypocrisy, and Corporate Reputation. *Sustainability* **2015**, *7*, 3683–3694. [CrossRef]
10. Szczepankiewicz, E.-I. Definiowanie zakresu, zasięgu i jakości zintegrowanego sprawozdania. *Pr. Nauk. Uniw. Ekon. We Wrocławiu* **2013**, 174–186. (In Polish)
11. Brown, H.S.; de Jong, M.; Levy, D.L. Building institutions based on information disclosure: Lessons from GRI's sustainability reporting. *J. Clean. Prod.* **2009**, *17*, 571–580. [CrossRef]
12. Roca, L.C.; Searcy, C. An analysis of indicators disclosed in corporate sustainability reports. *J. Clean. Prod.* **2012**, *20*, 103–118. [CrossRef]
13. Moneva, J.M.; Archel, P.; Correa, C. GRI and the camouflaging of corporate unsustainability. *Account. Forum* **2006**, *30*, 121–137. [CrossRef]
14. Boiral, O. Sustainability reports as simulacra? A counter-account of A and A+ GRI reports. *Account. Audit. Account. J.* **2013**, *26*, 1036–1071. [CrossRef]
15. Gray, R. Is accounting for sustainability actually accounting for sustainability ... and how would we know? An exploration of narratives of organisations and the planet. *Account. Organ. Soc.* **2010**, *35*, 47–62. [CrossRef]
16. The Organisation for Economic Co-operation and Development (OECD). *CO_2 Emissions from Fuel Combustion 2015*; IAE Statistics; OECD Publishing: Paris, France, 2015.
17. Pietrzyk-Sokulska, E.; Uberman, R.; Kulczycka, J. The impact of mining on the environment in Poland—myths and reality. *Gospod. Surowcami Miner.* **2015**, *31*, 45–64. [CrossRef]
18. European Association for Coal and Lignite (EURACOAL). *Coal Industry Aross Europe*; European Association for Coal and Lignite (EURACOAL) AISBL: Bruxelles, Belgium, 2013.
19. Bogdan, W.; Boniecki, D.; Labaye, E.; Marciniak, T.; Nowacki, M. *Poland 2025: Europe's New Growth Engine*; McKinsey & Company: Boston, MA, USA, 2015.
20. Badera, J. Problems of the social non-acceptance of mining projects with particular emphasis on the European Union—A literature review. *Environ. Socio-Econ. Stud.* **2014**, *2*, 27–34. [CrossRef]
21. Badera, J.; Kocoń, P. Local community opinions regarding the socio-environmental aspects of lignite surface mining: Experiences from central Poland. *Energy Policy* **2014**, *66*, 507–516. [CrossRef]
22. Gamerschlag, R.; Möller, K.; Verbeeten, F. Determinants of voluntary CSR disclosure: Empirical evidence from Germany. *Rev. Manag. Sci.* **2010**, *5*, 233–262. [CrossRef]
23. Mućko, P. *Koncepcja zmian w Sprawozdawczości Finansowej Spółek Publicznych*; Wydawnictwo Naukowe Uniwersytetu Szczecińskiego: Szczecin, Poland, 2008. (In Polish)
24. Szadziewska, A. Environmental reporting by large companies in Poland. *Zesz. Teoretyczne Rachun.* **2012**, *68*, 97–119.
25. Szadziewska, A. Rachunkowość jako źródło informacji na temat realizacji strategii społecznej odpowiedzialności biznesu. *Zesz. Teoretyczne Rachun.* **2014**, *75*, 95–123. (In Polish) [CrossRef]
26. Szczepankiewicz, E.I. Ewolucja sprawozdawczości przedsiębiorstw—Problemy zapewnienia porównywalności zintegrowanych raportów z zakresu zrównoważonego rozwoju i CSR. *Finanse Rynki Finans. Ubezpieczenia* **2014**, *71*, 135–148. (In Polish)
27. Krasodomska, J. Informacje niefinansowe jako element rocznego raportu spółki. *Zesz. Nauk. Uniw. Ekon. W Krakowie* **2010**, *816*, 45–57. (In Polish)
28. Szczepankiewicz, E.I. Informacje tworzące wartość rynkową w raportowaniu biznesowym. *Kwart. Nauk O Przedsiębiorstwie* **2013**, *3*, 33–42. (In Polish)

29. Ferens, A. Społeczna odpowiedzialność przedsiębiorstwa w zarządczych raportach biznesowych. *Finanse Rynki Finans. Ubezpieczenia* **2014**, *71*, 31–41. (In Polish)
30. Samelak, J. *Zintegrowane Sprawozdanie Przedsiębiorstwa Społecznie Odpowiedzialnego*; Wydawnictwo Uniwersytetu Ekonomicznego: Poznań, Poland, 2013. (In Polish)
31. Szczepankiewicz, E. Ryzyka ujawniane w zintegrowanym sprawozdaniu przedsiębiorstwa społecznie odpowiedzialnego. *Ekon. Organ. Przedsiębiorstwa* **2013**, *5*, 71–82.
32. Accounting Standards Committee. *National Accounting Standard (NAS) No. 9. Management Commentary*; Accounting Standards Committee: Warsaw, Poland, 2014.
33. Republic of Polish. The Accounting Act. Available online: http://dokumenty.rcl.gov.pl/D2013000033001.pdf (accessed on 27 January 2016). (In Polish)
34. International Accounting Standards Board (IASB). *IFRS Practice Statement: Management Commentary*; International Accounting Standards Board: London, UK, 2010.
35. Szczepankiewicz, E.-I. Management Commentary jako nowe źródło informacji o działalności jednostki gospodarczej. *Zesz. Teoretyczne Rachun.* **2012**, *66*, 191–203. (In Polish)
36. Mućko, P. Atrybuty sprawozdania z działalności na tle sprawozdania finansowego. *Zesz. Teoretyczne Rachun.* **2012**, *66*, 143–152. (In Polish)
37. Biblioteka Raportów. Konkurs Raporty Społeczne. Available online: http://raportyspoleczne.pl/biblioteka-raportow (accessed on 26 January 2016). (In Polish)
38. The European Parliament; The Council of the European Union. Directive 2014/95/EU of the European Parlament and of the Council of 22 October 2014 amending Directive 2013/34/EU as Regards Disclosure of Non-financial and Diversity Information by Certain Large Undertakings and Groups. Available online: http://eur-lex.europa.eu/legal-content/EN/TXT/PDF/?uri=OJ:JOL_2014_330_R_0001&from=EN (accessed on 25 January 2016).

© 2016 by the authors. Licensee MDPI, Basel, Switzerland. This article is an open access article distributed under the terms and conditions of the Creative Commons Attribution (CC BY) license (http://creativecommons.org/licenses/by/4.0/).

Article

Inter-Organisational Coordination for Sustainable Local Governance: Public Safety Management in Poland

Barbara Kożuch [1,†] and Katarzyna Sienkiewicz-Małyjurek [2,*,†]

1   Institute of Public Affairs, Jagiellonian University, Łojasiewicza 4 Str., Kraków 30-348, Poland; barbara.kozuch@uj.edu.pl
2   Faculty of Organisation and Management, Silesian University of Technology, Roosevelta 26 Str., Zabrze 41-800, Poland
*   Correspondence: katarzyna.sienkiewicz-malyjurek@polsl.pl; Tel.: +48-32-277-7314
†   These authors contributed equally to this work.

Academic Editor: Adam Jabłoński
Received: 23 November 2015; Accepted: 25 January 2016; Published: 28 January 2016

Abstract: The goal of this article is to examine the basic characteristics and factors that impact inter-organisational coordination in sustainable local governance to address: 1. What are the factors that effective inter-organisational coordination between independent units creating public safety system on local level in sustainable local governance depends on? 2. What are the principal features of inter-organisational coordination in the public safety management system studied in the context of sustainable local governance? The article's goal was reached using desk research analysis and empirical research. The desk research covers an analysis of international scientific publications. In turn, the empirical research was based on the example of public safety management. It covered interviews with practitioners dealing with public safety and a hermeneutic process within a focus group of scholars. As a result of the conducted research, interdependencies between coordination and other factors of inter-organisational collaboration were identified and the process of inter-organisational coordination during the emergency situations was characterised.

Keywords: inter-organisational coordination; sustainable local governance; sustainability; inter-organisational collaboration; public safety management; emergency; business model

1. Introduction

Civilisational development created goods that facilitate life and raise its standards. At the same time, an increase of hazards has taken place and side effects of technical advancement and space development have come into being [1,2]. Simultaneously the hazard of industrial calamities is growing, degradation of resources and natural resources is occurring, while biological and chemical pollution impacts public life. Moreover, polarisation of society, poverty and privation, terrorism, crime, and violence are expanding [3,4]. Spatial development is gaining significance in the perspective of social development, which to a large extent is characterised by lack of organisation and harmony [5].

The consequences of unlimited civilisational growth, globalisation, urbanisation, and an economic crisis have resulted in paying attention to durability and sustainable use of the possessed potential. Consequently, in the contemporary functioning of an organisation what gains more and more significance is the concept of sustainability, which consists in the realisation of rules of sustainable development and constructive confrontation of resources, goals, and strategic factors in order for the organisation to exist and develop [6].

In our times, the basic significance in assuring safety and sustainability in the public sector is attributed to regional and local development factors [7]. This is due to the fact that in the valid legislative solutions self-governments were given independence and freedom of decision making in the scope of realised tasks. Thanks to that, they have direct possibilities of creating safety and sustainability in the managed area. However, self-governments are able to realise the rules of safety and sustainability only by collaborating with other public and private entities and with the society [8]. This interaction is characterized by inter-organisational collaboration defined as "any joint activity by two or more agencies working together that is intended to increase public value by their working together rather than separately" [9] (p. 508). According to Arthur T. Himmelman, this collaboration includes exchange of information that is favourable to all parties (networking), with altering of activities (coordinating) and sharing of resources (cooperating) [10]. A similar perspective is presented by Richard C. Feiock, In Won Lee, and Hyung Jun Park who claim that coordination is a vital instrument of managing networks [11]. On the other hand Ranjay Gulati, Franz Wohlgezogen, and Pavel Zhelyazkov treat coordination as one of two indispensable facets of inter-organisational collaboration [12]. In our article we both agree with the allegation of the above-mentioned authors and in our analyses we assume a perspective that coordination is one of the principal elements of inter-organisational collaboration. This approach is based on the broadly known five Fayol's functions: planning, organising, command, coordination, and control. By treating coordination as one of the functions of management we present it in a broad scope, considering that it includes "the activities responsible to ensure the effectiveness of the collaborative work" [13] (p. 88). Consequently, in our approach coordination is a factor of collaboration, which refers to a decentralised approach to problem solving [14].

Despite a great deal of research in the public sector, inter-organisational collaboration is still a challenge. This results above all from decentralisation and narrowing of specialisation of each public organisation [15]. In public safety management problems without inter-organisational coordination may cause serious consequences and generate additional hazards, which was observed for example during Hurricane Katrina and the World Trade Center attacks [16–19]. Moreover, contemporary development trends focused on internationalisation and at the same time regionalisation combined with a strong and stable local governance are also a challenge for coordination. Problems in this scope may result from the overlapping nature of department jurisdictions [20]. There is also a research gap in the scope of the contextual variables in shaping collaborative efforts [21]. Moreover, despite the evident importance of coordinating actions during the time of threat, relatively little attention has been paid to it [22,23]. This means that there are theoretical and empirical gaps in the literature of the field. The necessity of theoretical justification of the sustainable approach to local governance and the lack of exhaustive analyses related to coordination generate the need to conduct research studies in this scope. Thus the goal of this publication is to examine the basic characteristics and factors that impact inter-organisational coordination in the public safety management system as a part of a sustainable local governance to address: 1. What are the factors that effective inter-organisational coordination between independent units creating public safety system on local level in sustainable local governance depends on? 2. What are the principal features of inter-organisational coordination in the public safety management system studied in the context of sustainable local governance?

The article's goal was reached using desk research analysis and empirical research. The desk research covers an analysis of international scientific publications. In turn, the empirical research was based on the example of public safety management in Poland.

In our article we refer our research to organisational coordination, since we have been studying the actions taken in order to harmonise and synchronise the enterprises of various organisations, which assumption is achieving of common goals and appropriate results [24]. Although we carry out our analyses in the public sector, we do not make any reference to the model of coordinating public policies. Our approach is close to the model of relational coordination [25,26] and decentralized intelligent adaptation [14].

The paper is organised as follows: First, we review sustainability in public safety management. Then, we discuss the general theory of coordination and explain the role of inter-organisational coordination in public safety management. In the part containing the research results we identified factors influencing and influenced by inter-organisational coordination. Next, we analyse the process and the features of inter-organisational coordination during emergency situations using the example of Polish circumstances. We emphasise that inter-organisational coordination is a central attribute of sustainable public safety management. Our results contribute to better understanding of coordination complexity in dynamic circumstances.

2. Methodology Research Method and Context

To achieve the purpose of the article, the desk research method and empirical investigations were carried out.

The desk research was based on the analysis of international scientific literature and it covered issues related to inter-organisational coordination and public safety management. Publications connected with the general coordination theory, inter-organisational coordination in the public sector and in dynamic context played a key role in this scope. We focused on foreign literature, indexed in generally acclaimed databases (Web of Science, Scopus) and works in English, in order to obtain a picture of inter-organisational coordination that would be as objective as possible. We have not covered academic achievements in the scope of coordinating in specific conditions of the private sector and within one organisation. We have focused on those publications dealing with inter-organisational coordination, which concern the problems of collaboration.

Moreover, based upon the research conducted so far [27], the relations occurring between coordination and other factors of effective inter-organisational collaboration were examined. These analyses were carried out within a hermeneutic process within a focus group of scholarsconducted in December 2014 within a four-person group of researchers actively involved into investigating inter-organisational collaboration. Two of them have been involved in research in this domain for over 10 years, and the remaining two—for over 5 years. Discussions within two sessions were held in 2014 on the grounds of practical instances and analyses of typical collaborative situations.

Empirical investigation was based on free-form interviews, which were conducted with 15 medium and lower level employees employed at police and fire brigade units and medical emergency stations in the area of the Silesian Province. They concerned the course of collaborative processes in public safety management. These interviews were conducted in September and October 2013. In the scope of coordination, this research covered the following issues:

(1) coordinating actions taken within collaboration with other units prior to, during, and after the threat
(2) enterprises in each unit within common action coordination
(3) the course of the common action coordination process using a random example

In this article we presented the results and interpretation of the conducted analyses.

The research was conducted in Poland, where—in an organisational aspect—the authorities operate on two levels: government (central) and local government. The central level is responsible for the continuity of actions aiming at ensuring safety, it monitors and prevents hazards and their consequences. In turn the task of local governments is to identify hazards at the source, preventing them and eliminating their consequences. However, the decentralization of public authority ceded responsibility in the field of public safety onto each local government level *i.e.*, commune (Polish: gmina), district and also province. Local governments fulfil their tasks independently, while the government administration has only a possibility to supervise their actions, which however, is limited and briefly specified by regulations.

The obligation to take action in case of the occurrence of a hazard is borne by the authority, which was first to receive information about it. This authority promptly informs about the event that has occurred the authorities of a higher and lower level respectively, presenting at the same time their assessment of the situation and information on the intended actions [28]. If the event's nature is supralocal, management of the action is taken over by the regional level. Similarly, in case of a supraregional hazard—management is taken over by the central authorities of state power.

Information on the necessity of taking action may be transferred directly from the hazard's location or by the 112 system, which operates in Poland on the local and provincial level. On the local level it is responsible for operating emergency numbers and organisation of emergency endeavours in a given action area by means of emergency call centres. In turn, the provincial level facilitates coordination of actions of a supralocal nature. All reports are registered in an ICT (Information and Communication Technologies) system and their transfer to an appropriate intervention and rescue unit depends on verification and justification of the report and disposing of the means of rescue entities [29].

An important issue in the operations of the public safety management system in Poland is the autonomy of the units participating in the actions. In a situation of hazard, these units operate autonomously, focusing on realising their statutory tasks and the scope of their cooperation results from the valid regulations. It is worth mentioning that a similar situation occurs in many places around the world, including in the scope of coordinating foreign aid during calamities. In other countries there are solutions that enable creation of inter-organisational teams [30–32]. That is why actions realised in the examined area in Poland are mainly based on the complementary roles and competences of many units, properly coordinated work, and effective communication. Taking the above into account, the basis of managing public safety is inter-organisational collaboration and the units taking part in it realise their tasks simultaneously, complementing each other.

Our research covers the context of conducting actions in public safety management, which is dependent on the type, nature, place, and range of the hazard's occurrence and course. During stabilisation, when routine action are carried out, the realisation of actions in the examined scope, including coordinating, is similar to other areas of local governance. General methods of coordination apply here. Situation changes during extreme events. Each hazard is an individual event, which is characterised by peculiar specifics of development and duration. The principal challenges are the following: high uncertainty, sudden and unexpected events; risk and possible mass casualty; increased time pressure and urgency, severe resource shortage, large-scale impact and damage, disruption of infrastructure support, multi-authority and massive people involvement, conflict of interest, and high demand for timely information [23]. Even the same type of hazard concerns a different location, which generates the need to take different actions. The differences in the duration of the hazard's occurrence are also significant. For example, a fire in the summer time, during the occurrence of drought, will carry a greater risk of occurrence of additional hazards compared with the winter time. Moreover, the victims of each hazard are different, which also generates the need to adapt actions to the needs. During extreme events the enterprises conducted in public safety management require proper preparation, and above all coordination of actions. Moreover, the operation of rescue units may seem similar, but in practice they differ by the level of organisation, they operate based on other standards and they are also characterised by a different organisational culture [19]. It is in line with the assumption of Arjen Boin and Paul 't Hart [33], according to which there is no unique and best form of organisation and in addition each emergency situation requires an individual approach that consists of (1) applying the general principles of organisational coordination; (2) lessons learned from experience coming from collaboration in similar situations; and (3) the specifics of a given event.

3. Theoretical Background

3.1. Sustainable Public Safety Management

Public safety is one of the principal foundations of a rich and well functioning society [34]. It constitutes an organised activity realised using personnel, financial, technical, information resources of many organisations, taken in order to minimise potential hazards, ensuring an undisturbed course of social life as well as protecting people's health, life, property, and the environment, which includes law observation and protection of order with focus on realizing the public interest [35]. Public safety management covers a large scope of research, which extends from social policy, through local and criminal policy, up to crisis management [36,37]. Its aim is to ensure the most favourable level of safety using the existing capabilities and limitations and taking into account the dynamics of the environment. The principal entities participating in public safety management include the following [38,39]:

- Local government
- Response and rescue units, including: a core unit where taking actions in response to a specific type of hazard fall into its competences; basic units which mostly respond collectively and mutually collaborate in public safety management; ancillary units which supplement actions taken by a core unit and basic units, and their knowledge and competences are critical in a specific situation
- Society: local communities and enterprises operating in a given territory
- Media: radio, television, press, Internet
- Non-governmental organisations
- Research and development units

The listed groups of entities constitute mutually complementary units, which include not only lawyers and experts on administrative sciences, but also specialists in the scope of management, sociology, economics, political sciences, technical sciences, environmentalists, *etc.* They form a public safety management system that constitutes a dynamic system of units, the aim of which is ensuring safe and sustainable conditions of operating to all entities in a given administrative area by using the possessed resources and within the valid formal rules and informal relations, characterised by the uniqueness and changeability of actions and constant adaptation to current conditions and arising needs [40].

In the stabilisation phase the local government plays the leading role in the public safety management system in a given administrative area, ensuring conditions of sustainable local development. In this scope, preventing hazards achieved by education and building of resilience is of priority importance. These functions are realised above all by education, media, non-governmental organisations, and local governments within the formation of culture and national identity. Also the Police and State Fire Service prepare professional prevention programs aiming at excluding the occurrence of hazards. Local government fosters growth of the idea of inter-organisational collaboration.

However, the core of the system covers actions taken by the response and rescue units [41]. These units are appropriately prepared operation wise, they are trained and have appropriate skills and knowledge and they have at their disposal means and tools adequate to a given situation. Taking the above into account, during realisation the leading role is taken over by intervention and rescue units, while the local governments supervise their actions. Moreover, the principal function in realising intervention and rescue actions is fulfilled by: the Police, the State Fire Service, and medical rescuers. Most often these units participate in the actions in the first place. Depending on the type of hazard and the situation, other entities are engaged as well. The principal actions may be assisted by among other the Municipal Guard, Boarder Guard, Railway Guards, Road Transport Inspection, the army, or non-governmental organisations. In turn, the Environmental Protection Inspectorate, Sanitary Inspection, Construction Supervision Inspectorate, or social assistance workers may act as advisers and assist in decision making with their specialist knowledge. The type and degree of engagement of each unit depends on the level of complexity of a given situation [40].

In that context sustainability is the organisation's ability to continuously learn, adapt, and develop, and also revitalize, reconstruct, and reorientate in order to offer high value to recipients in a long period of time [42]. In the public sector it constitutes a tool which enables partner participation in making use of public goods taking into account limitations of resources.

From the analysed perspective sustainable local governance is defined as a process run by local governmental bodies aimed to socially and economically boost a specific region or locality, while respecting environmental protection and land development, being committed to sustainable management of the resources pool and tapping into cutting-edge public management tools, *i.e.*, coordination of inter-organisational collaboration [8] (p. 325). Its basis is a diagnosis of social needs, possessed resources, and condition of the environment, in which public services are offered. Based upon it, local development programs are created that serve sustaining of social life processes. Improvement of public institution actions, owing to collaboration, increases entrepreneurship and effectiveness of sustainable activities of local governments. As a result of this, the competitiveness of a given area grows, while the requiredenvironment quality standards are maintained.

Consequently, sustainability in public safety refers to efficient realisation of enterprises by taking actions that are appropriate to an existing need, without harm to society, economically justified and with the highest degree of care for the natural environment. Sustainable public safety management aims at well-balanced management of resources including local and natural ones as well as those possessed by each unit of the system being analysed. It constitutes a process realised by local response and rescue units within inter-organisational collaboration using modern public management tools, which aims at minimising potential hazards and ensuring most favourable level of public safety simultaneously respecting and ensuring of principal and integrated order. Taking into account the fact that it covers all orders of integrated development, it constitutes an interesting research area that is adequate to the issues being raised.

The characteristic features of public safety management make it an area of public governance, in which the need for coordination is especially visible. For that matter, it constitutes an interesting research area that is adequate to the issues being raised.

3.2. Coordination as a Factor of Inter-Organisational Collaboration

In local governance collaboration, which is one of the most important tasks of self-governmental sub-sector organisation, combining activities in favour of local development, is of key significance in this scope [43,44]. Local government units constitute collaborating institutions, which require appropriate coordination within co-governance. Based on the surveys and theoretical considerations, the literature state that collaboration between public sector organisations is one of several tools of local development management since it contributes to the growth of public services [45,46]. It is characterised by interdependence with simultaneous autonomy of functioning as well as settlement of collaboration rules by means of negotiation and based on organizational and legal factors. As it is emphasized by R. Lozano, collaboration constitutes a key element in running of the strategy of sustainability [47].

Inter-organisational collaboration includes sustainable relations, which join each organisation in realising their common goals. It is defined as a union of two or more organisations that is favourable to all parties and well-defined, which serves achieving of common goals [48] (p. 4). Among the causes of establishing inter-organisational collaboration one may distinguish the following: high levels of interdependence, need for resources and risk sharing, resource scarcity, previous history of efforts to collaborate, situation in which each partner has resources that other partners need, and complex issues [49]. Identified on the base of empirical evidence, the principal benefits in the scope of inter-organisational collaboration include among other [50–53]: consolidation of the resources of collaborating organisations, knowledge sharing, organisational learning, making use of the experience of other organisations, transfer of best practices, and creating innovative solutions. This is not a new concept, however it has enjoyed great interest only for about two decades [54]. Recently, more importance is given to the relational aspects.

The growing significance of inter-organisational collaboration in the activity of enterprises and public institutions results to a large extent from the dynamics of changes in the organisations' environment, seeking competitive advantage and the fact that at present it is not possible to act alone. Although the practice of collaboration between organisations is broadly applied, the presumptions of its implementation are generally known and it does not constitute a new phenomenon, it is a very difficult process [55]. The results of empirical and theoretical studies, presented in the literature, indicate that this is mainly due to its complexity, different approaches to realisation of mutual actions, potential disturbance in the course of collaboration processes, *etc.* [56,57]. Moreover, legal requirements or collaboration agreements do not constitute conditions sufficient enough to ensure sustainable inter-organisational collaboration. This is because its course is impacted by multiple factors with features that refer to both external and internal conditions, relational factors, and instruments of inter-organisational collaboration. They have a prerequisite nature. The most important one is coordination [27].

Coordination is defined as " ... the act of managing interdependencies between activities performed to achieve a goal" [58] (p. 6). It is a relational process based on task interdependencies [59]. It originates from the need for simultaneous execution of activities falling under the powers of various organisations, and results from the specifics of their operations. From the traditional perspective, it refers to hierarchical control, whereas the organisational perspective pertains to centralised, dispersed coordination or a combination of two types at the organisational level [60]. Coordination is a continual process and a component of the organisation. It depends on the specifics of the entities involved, the circumstances as well as dynamics of change in the external environment in which the entities operate. It is assumed that good coordination is nearly invisible, only being noticed most clearly when it is lacking [61].

In the subject literature there are two levels of coordination: intra- and inter-organisational [62]. The former is related to coordination within an organisation, whereas the latter to coordination between organisations. In the subject literature one may also find many types of coordination between collaborating units, for example interim coordination, cross-agency coordination, relational coordination, network coordination, or network governance [63–66]. In all of the above-mentioned cases, the aim is to ensure sustainable inter-organisational collaboration by enhancing relations and task integration. This process is based on shared goals, shared knowledge, and mutual respect [26]. For the needs of this article, the term inter-organisational coordination was assumed.

Inter-organisational coordination is related to harmonising the actions of each unit in order to common and systematic rendering of specific services [63] (p. 118). It is defined as "the deliberate and orderly alignment or adjustment of partners' actions to achieve jointly determined goals" [12] (p. 12). It is based on such mechanisms as: partner-specific communication, rules and procedures, routines, liaison, and integration roles, interim authorities, *etc.* [59] (pp. 909–910). However, in order to realise common actions, it uses above all informal interactions and pays less attention to the valid procedures and organisational structures. These mechanisms, in particular, enable sustainable local governance through building durable relations between collaborating organisations. Key characteristics and differences of collaboration and coordination were presented in Table 1.

As it results from table 1 collaboration is a broader term than coordination. The subject literature emphasises that the priority significance of coordination in inter-organisational collaboration results from its role in the continuous synchronization of tasks and the contribution of collaborating organisations. It is because it constitutes a relational process, which covers managing correlation between tasks and between the entities that perform these tasks [63]. It manifests itself through systematic and reliable communication, which strengthens social relations in order for better integration of mutual enterprises. It emphasises the significance of the organisational structure, communication, and process management [12]. According to such concept, coordination enables going beyond rigid administrative structures and task centralisation towards greater freedom of action based on goodwill, trust, and commitment. It enables a more balanced management of resources and actions. Therefore, inter-organisational coordination indicates specific ways of implementing and conducting joint actions, owing to which it complements collaboration [12]. The notion of coordination is therefore related to operational activity, while collaboration concerns strategic decisions to a greater extent.

Table 1. Characteristics of collaboration and coordination.

Characteristics	Antecedents	Features	Modes
Collaboration	Interdependence; need for resources and risk sharing; resource scarcity; previous history of efforts to collaborate; situation in which each partner has resources that other partners need [49]; trust, trustworthiness [11]	Managing resource dependencies, sharing risk [12]; Conflict management [67]	Environment (history of collaboration, collaborative group seen as a legitimate leader in the community, favourable political and social climate); membership characteristics (mutual respect, understanding, trust, ability to compromise); process and structure (members share a stake in both process and outcome, multiple layers of participation, flexibility, development of clear roles and policy guideness, adaptability, appropriate pace of development); communication (open and frequent, established informal relationships and communication links); purpose (concrete, attainable goals and objectives, shared vision; resources (sufficient funds, staff, materials, and time, skilled leadership) [48]
Coordination	Information [11]; perception of common objects, communication, group decision-making [58]	Regulating and managing interdependencies [68]; managing uncertainties [12]; Goal decomposition [58]	Impersonal (plans, schedules, rules, procedures); personal (face-to-face communication); group (meetings) [69]; communication and decision procedures; mutual monitoring or supervisory hierarchy; group decision making; Mutual monitoring or property-rights sharing; programming; Hierarchical decision making; Integration and liaison roles; authority by expectation and residual arbitration [68]; formal (departmentalization or grouping of organizational units; centralization or decentralization of decision making; formalization and standardization; planning; output and behaviour control) and informal (lateral relations; informal communication; socialization) [70]

Source: own elaboration based on quoted literature.

A great number of research studies, information, and models in the scope of coordination causes that this area has been developing in various directions, depending on the conducted analyses. In some works its cognitive nature is emphasised, while in other the behavioural one, moreover it may be understood as a form of organizational control or team-based concertive control [67]. Attempts to model the interdependencies and level of coordination in specific fields are not consistent in the scope of coordination characteristics, but they point out which specific challenges are related to coordination [71]. For example, Henry Mintzberg's coordination model relates the coordination mechanisms to the organizational structure [72]. On the other hand, the model of Thomas W. Malone and Kevin Crowston is based on a concept of coordination as management of dependency between actions [61]. Moreover, on the one hand it is assumed that the problems of coordination may be solved by implementing appropriate mechanisms, of a general nature, which means that they may be applied in various organisational systems. On the other hand, there are opinions stating that one should identify in detail the nature of the environment in which an organisation operates in case of specific events and next develop appropriate procedures in relation to them [14]. We agree with the second approach and also the assumption that the higher the degrees of interdependency and the levels of tasks and environment uncertainty are, the more developed forms of coordination are required [12]. These dependencies are especially visible in public safety management.

3.3. Basics of Inter-Organisational Coordination in Public Safety Management

According to Thomas E. Drabek [73], coordination is at the core of the practice of actions for safety. It is the philosopher's stone of public administration, and a central factor in poor performance during an response activities [74,75]. In actions for safety, coordination proceeds at diverse organisational levels [76]. It occurs in an intra-organisational dimension as coordination within specific organisations as well as an inter-organisation aspect as a regulator of external relations in an organisation. In this context, it is possible to talk about capabilities for effective resources administration in the form of inter-organisational teams, partnerships, alliances, *etc.* [77]. This capability is determined by the ability of specific organisations to adapt to dynamic conditions under which they operate, and to effective communication aimed at hammering out common agreements and a common stance regarding manners for conducting operations. At the core are both legal regulations as well as formal and informal relations emerging within collaborated organisations. Vertical coordination puts into place rigid principles as to the division of responsibility, the execution of activities and the control of outcomes. However, a new approach incorporating organisational connections gives priority to the mutual adaptation of entities and the integration of resources, authority and knowledge over formal mechanisms of authority [75,78].

Effective coordination is a necessary element of conducting action in public safety management. It is difficult to conduct in this area because it is connected with uncertainty, unexpected events, risk of hazards' accumulation, urgency, and infrastructure interdependency [23]. Apart from that, the situational complexity creates conditions, in which participation of various agencies is required and collaboration between them is necessary for realisation of actions. What is more, the higher the number of various organisations trying to achieve a common goal, the less probable that they will act in a coordinated way in order to achieve this goal [79]. In this connection, inter-organisational coordination in public safety management is a big challenge. The differences between the general theory of coordination and coordination between organisations in public safety management were presented in Table 2.

The principal difference between inter-organisational coordination in general and in public safety management lies in the nature of joint action. This influences all characteristics of coordination. It also causes that failures have more serious consequences and the intrinsic and extrinsic motivation, concerns, and results depend on the creativity and skills in making decisions in changeable and uncertain conditions, with limited pieces of information.

In the deliberations concerning inter-organisational coordination, we assume that its significance results from counterbalancing in the scope of actions and the level of participation of many independent organisations, taking into account social needs, natural environmental and spatial values as well as economic conditions. It facilitates achieving of the assumed goal avoiding excessive costs and damage. Consequently, inter-organisational coordination enables realisation of actions in changing, unsure, and dynamic conditions in accord with the philosophy of sustainability.

Table 2. General and specific approach to coordination.

Specification	General Theory of Coordination	Coordination in Public Safety Management
Substance of inter-organisational agreement	Ways of shaping interactions	Ways of shaping interactions between autonomous organizations
Motivation	More effectively managing task interdependencies and uncertainties	More effectively managing task interdependencies in order to identify and remove the sources and consequences of hazards
Concern/risks	Operational risk: inability to coordinate across organizational boundaries	Operational and situational risks: inability to coordinate joint actions of autonomous organisations in dynamic and uncertain circumstances
Typical positive results	Efficiency, effectiveness, flexibility/adaptiveness of joint action	Effectiveness, flexibility, adaptiveness of joint action in unique and rapidly changing situations
Typical failures	Omission, incompatibilities, misallocation	Inadvertent omissions leading to chaos, incompatibilities in rescue procedures, inadequate response, insufficient prevention of accumulation of hazards, increasing number of victims, additional damages
Remedies against failures	Hierarchies, authority, and formalisation; institutions and conventions; inter-personal linkages and liaisons	Changing hierarchical positions, integrated authority structures, improvement of rescue procedures, shared organising of training and simulations of events during the stabilisation phase, progressive adapting of regulations, advancing communication systems, creating good formal and informal relationships based on trust and organisational concern

Source: own elaboration based on [12] (p. 66).

4. Research Results

4.1. Relations between Coordination and other Instruments of Inter-Organisational Collaboration

Our previous research indicated that coordination is one of the key factors of inter-organisational collaboration [27]. These factors have a mutual impact on each other, which in effect influences both their role and the efficiency of collaboration itself. Taking this into consideration, we have decided to present our own reasoning based on chosen publications, which include the relations that characterise coordination and other factors of efficient inter-organisational collaboration. In our investigation a 3-level grade scale was applied to evaluate the impact of each factor, *i.e.*: 1—weak influence, 2—medium influence, and 3—strong influence. Whereas the relations between the factors were analysed in reference to the following grade scale: 0—lack of impact or minor impact, 1—significant impact, and 2—key impact.

Inter-organisational coordination was evaluated as a factor which has strong influence on the course of actions. This mainly results from specific and complementary competences of each organisation, task distribution, and responsibilities. These factors create the foundations of efficient realisation of actions. Taking this into account, inter-organisational coordination is of key importance to the course of collaboration.

Studying the relations occurring between inter-organisational coordination and other factors of efficient inter-organisational collaboration, our focus was directed to those factors that have a significant and key impact on the processes of action coordination between organisations. The relations, which were identified, are illustrated in Figure 1. It depicts those factors, which:

- only impact the course of inter-organizational coordination
- both impact and are a result of inter-organizational coordination
- are only a result of inter-organizational coordination

In figure 1 factors having a significant impact were indicated by a thinner arrow, while the key factors were indicated by a thicker one.

As it results from the verified connections, the key factors of inter-organizational collaboration, which influence inter-organisational coordination processes are:

- communication in inter-organisational working teams,
- constraints in inter-organisational collaboration,
- leadership with organisational and communication skills,
- organisation of collaborative work (e.g., time pressured, competitive, rapidly changing, stability),
- management of inter-organisational collaboration (e.g., styles, transparency of decisions and guidance),
- inter-organisational trust,
- professional communication between personnel from individual organisations.

These factors show that inter-organisational coordination depends mainly on organisational and relational conditions, which exist between collaborating units. Whereas, the key factors influenced by inter-organisational coordination include:

- organisation of collaborative work,
- support within collaborating organisations,
- adaptability to changing work requirements,
- flexibility and openness to changing circumstances of collaboration,
- performance of inter-organisational collaboration,
- self interest of individual organisations from collaboration.

These factors impact, above all, situation conditions in sustainable public safety management and the will to collaborate. The other analysed factors are also of significance, but they are not that important in inter-organisational coordination. Each of the said factors impacts the level of coordination sustainability. However, the significance of each one individually depends on the existence of other factors, which may mutually strengthen or weaken its influence. Moreover, the nature of relations taking place between inter-organisational coordination and other factors influencing and influenced by this process, is complex. This mainly results from the existing interdependency between all factors of effective collaboration and their mutual stimulating.

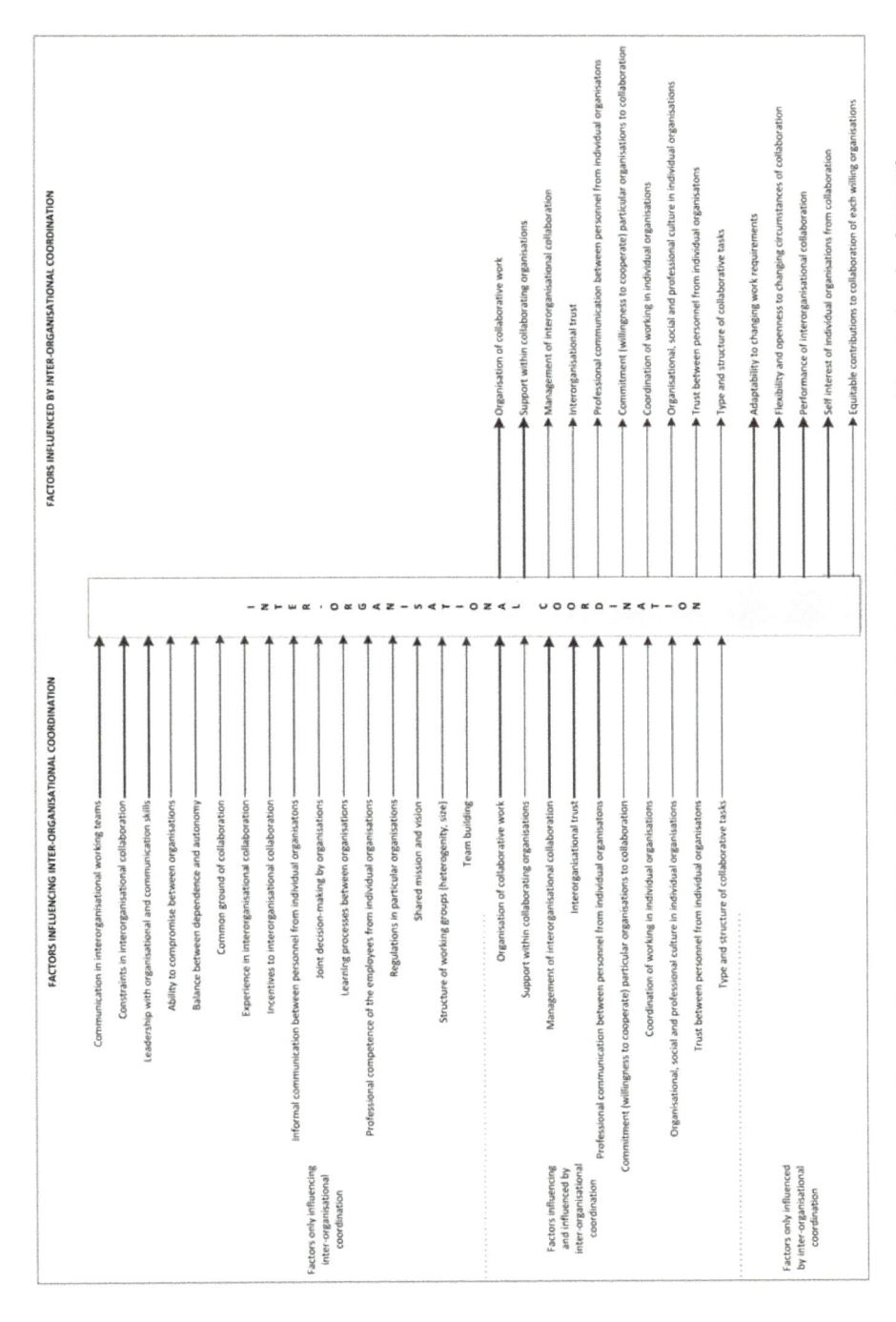

Figure 1. Factors influencing and influenced by inter-organizational coordination. Source: own elaboration based on [48,80–91].

4.2. Inter-Organisational Coordination during Emergency Situations

The process of managing public safety in terms of phases may be presented in the following cycle: actions taken prior to the hazard occurrence, during the hazard, after the hazard has been obviated [29]. Inter-organisational coordination takes place in all of the said phases, however its significance can be seen to the biggest degree in the phases in time and once the hazard has been obviated. Prior to the occurrence of the hazard, coordination is necessary in such action as preparing mutual enterprises, common training, and team building. However, these actions are conducted in stable conditions, in which considered modifications and changes are possible. The effect of turbulence and uncertainty of conditions in emergency situations is that inter-organisational coordination plays a key role in the phases prior to the occurrence and during the hazard.

The inter-organisational coordination of operations in emergency situations is executed by a single commander-in-chief. Our own empirical research showed that in Poland, responsibility for that is devolved on the Rescue Action Supervisor who is, in most cases, a fireman. Only in the event of a terrorist attack or demonstration command is taken over by a policeman with sufficient powers. Such inter-organisational coordination involves collecting, analysing, and verifying information, as well as assigning a sequence of operations performed and entities engaged. A classic example illustrating the coordination of operations in emergency management, is the flooding that took place in May and June of 2010 which engulfed the Czech Republic, Slovakia, Poland, Hungary, Ukraine, Austria, Germany, and Serbia. It was one of the largest floods in Poland in that during the period from 14 May to 30 June 2010, around 76,800 interventions related to relief and recovery actions were reported [92]. At that time, there was an increased demand for pumps with higher capacity than those the services already possessed. Efforts at the national level were launched, and firemen from other EU states took part in the operations. Persons charged with rescue actions in this event accomplished the following tasks based on communication processes:

(1) prepare scenarios for potential situations, analyses, weather forecasts, collect information, anticipate demand;
(2) calculate forces and resources, assess potential, analyse situations, prepare proposals for disposing forces depending on the demand, examine potential for requesting external forces;
(3) contribute to the formulation of solutions intended to accomplish operations, raise forces, dislocate forces, put forces into operation, continue monitoring the situation and its reporting;
(4) monitor the efficacy of the formulated solutions, participate in the work of military staff and teams, monitor the situation's progress, collaborate with commanders with regard to specific actions;
(5) control efficacy of operations conducted by operational groups, verify information handed over, e.g., by phone, with the actual situation.

Another example of operations coordination and emergency management in Poland was the head-on collision of two high-speed passenger trains on 3 March 2012 near the town of Szczekociny. As a result, 16 people were killed and 57 passengers were injured. In the first train, an electric locomotive was destroyed and the first two carriages were derailed, while in the other train the locomotive and one carriage were derailed. Services from the national emergency management level and fire brigades from four provinces were used in the rescue action, including 450 rescuers and 400 policemen. The coordination process covered such operations as evacuation of the people affected, rendering first aid, searching destroyed carriages and the surrounding crash site, enabling access to trapped passengers, designating a temporary landing strip for helicopters of the Air Rescue Service, and securing the incident site. Coordination of basic operations did not pose a problem. However, contentious issues were exposed, and they referred to extra activities and details, e.g., places for tents. These examples confirm that both formal as well as posteriori relationships provide a basis for the coordination of operations during emergency situations. Moreover, they allow us to ascertain that organisational factors and organisational behaviours constitute the key determinants for improving communication and coordination in sustainable public safety management.

The quantity of information is essential for coordination and execution of effective operations in dynamically changing circumstances requires application of cutting-edge organisational and technical solutions. In addition, "some of the major challenges (...) include information mismanagement, resource allocation issues, and ineffective communication" [93] (p. 260). These challenges can lead to communication and consequently coordination breakdowns. To ensure efficacy of rescue actions and to streamline communication as well as coordination processes, there are emergency coordination centres established and they make up complex organisational and technical structures in line with administrative division at the local, regional, and national levels. Such centres also operate at the international level, e.g., Emergency Response Coordination Centre functions in the EU. It is a one-stop-shop providing an overview of the available civil protection assets and acts as a communication hub between the participating states, the affected country and dispatched field experts. The main purpose of its existence is to facilitate collaboration in civil protection interventions in the event of major emergencies, e.g., through pool resources that can be made available to help disaster-hit countries and share best practices in disaster management [94].

Emergency coordination centres are a support centre for those in charge of rescue actions. They handle information transfer as well as vertical and horizontal communication outside the incident site. They also oversee the course of action and if needed they bring and send extra resources to action. Thus, emergency coordination centres run the so-called "external coordination". The centres operate in line with a mutual substitution principle. It means that a report which cannot be received for any reason in a centre relevant for the caller's domicile will be automatically redirected to another Centre. For receiving the reports operators are employed, there may be also officers delegated, assigned from the police or fire brigade, employees in emergency management departments as well as municipal policemen. In Poland the tasks conferred on the centres include [95]:

(1) handle alarm reports, excluding fire signalisation systems,
(2) register and store data regarding alarm reports, including phone recordings with the complete alarm report, personal data of the reporting person and other persons indicated when receiving the report, information on the incident site and its type and shortened description of the event for the period of 3 years;
(3) conduct analyses related to functioning of the system in the area handled by the centre and producing statistics with regard to numbers, types, and response time for alarm reports;
(4) collaborate and exchange information with emergency coordination centres;
(5) exchange information and data, excluding personal data, for the purposes of analyses with the Police, National Fire Service, administrators of medical rescue teams, and entities which phone numbers are handled within the system.

In other countries, tasks accomplished by centres are essentially similar. For instance, in Sri Lanka they are as follows [96]:

(1) Maintaining and operating early warning towers and other early warning dissemination equipments
(2) Dissemination of early warning messages and ensuring reception at remote vulnerable villagers
(3) Coordination of donor assistance to strengthen capacity of technical agencies for early warning
(4) Initiating awareness on activities related to early warning among various agencies and the public
(5) Guiding district disaster management units in coordinating and implementing warning dissemination-related activities in the province, district, and local authority levels.

Emergency coordination centres collaborate with services statutorily appointed for security protection as well as social rescue organisations. Their operations enable to reduce the waiting time for assistance as well as time for rescue actions themselves, properly match forces and resources to the operations, bolster information transfer as well as create a consistent database for events [97].

Receipt of alarm reports in the centre by alarm number operators and dispatchers is carried out by means of information and communication technology systems. These systems ensure automatisation of receipt and registration of reports. They allow for identification of the phone number, location, and visualisation of the place from which the emergency call comes. Besides, it also enables overseeing the actual state of calls handled, elimination of hoax calls, and their selection [98–100].

An interesting example of the emergency coordination centre is the Integrated Security Centre operating in Ostrava in the Czech Republic since 2011. Its initial concept originated in the 1990s when the urgency for collaboration among rescue services was identified. It is currently a part of the Czech Integrated Rescue System which covers a connections system as well as principles guiding collaboration and emergency coordination of local and central authorities, as well as individuals and authorised persons when the necessity arises to undertake rescue or humanitarian actions and to prepare and conduct emergency operations. The Integrated Security Centre houses such units as: fire brigade, police, medical emergency, and municipal authorities. They form the mainstay of the system. An auxiliary role is played by: municipal police, military forces, ministry of health, ministry of interior, remaining rescue units, security companies, and non-governmental organisations. The unit responsible for response activities is the fire brigade across all levels of the state organisation depending on the scale of the event. However, the conditions for conducting the operations are determined by the public administration. The functioning of the Centre has helped to eliminate problems related to communication and operations coordination and to boost inter-organisational collaboration which through direct contacts and joint resolution of problems enables to continually improve collaboration principles within the system.

The analysis of the course of inter-organisational coordination during emergency situations enables stating that coordination constitutes a liaison which bonds actions taken in the scope of public safety management. Its significance results from the span of tasks that are realised, in which performance many entities are engaged, in each case in a different quantity and configuration. The conducted actions are based on collaboration between each of the partners, which separate and autonomous units and whose competences complement each other. This leads to a conclusion that inter-organisational coordination is a key factor of public safety management, which principal features are as follows:

- integrity of actions: the enterprises of each organisation are coherent and mutually complementary, while efficiency may be achieved only within mutual realisation of tasks;
- interdependence: each organisation is mutually dependent both in the scope of conducting actions, transferring information, as well as managing resources;
- mutuality: mutual enterprises are based on relations between each organisation;
- multiplicity: there are many possibilities of coordinating actions within one enterprise;
- adaptability: methods of coordination are adapted to existing conditions.

Moreover, inter-organisational coordination is a result of legal and organisational, social, and situational conditions. The first above-mentioned conditions are related to the existing legal regulations, procedures, and by-laws. They specify the rules of coordinating commonly conducted actions. In turn, the social conditions cover inter-organisational relations, which through shaping of appropriate behaviours, influence the enterprises' efficiency. Whereas, situational conditions specify the current context of actions' realisation. They cause that flexibility and agility is required of organisations participating in the actions. Both the factors and conditions of inter-organisational coordination impact the level of sustainable local governance. In principle, local governance is characterised by accountability, transparency, openness, and publicness. These features are favourable to improving sustainable local governance.

The analyses confirm the complexity of inter-organisational coordination and significance of relational aspects in the theory and practice of managing public safety.

5. Discussion and Conclusions

In this article we analyse inter-organisational coordination in the public safety management system. In our opinion the notion of collaboration is broader than coordination, which is consistent with the analyses conducted by Arthur T. Himmelman [10]. We also adapted the opinion of Richard C. Feiock, In Won Lee, and Hyung Jun Park [11] and we believe that coordination and collaboration are not points on a simple scale of service integration, but differ in their forms and structure. Starting from Fayol's understanding of coordination, we reinforce this notion as one of the key factors of collaboration. In our deliberations we also claim that in our research the context of realisation of actions is of significant importance, since the mechanism of coordination, which regulate the ways of effective collaboration, result from it [101]. According to Elodie Gardet and Caroline Mothe groups of representative mechanisms of coordination include the following [102]: exchange formalisation, trust, result division, guarantees against opportunistic behaviour, and conflict resolution. In turn, Jody Hoffer Gittell and Leigh Weiss on the base of a nine-hospital quantitative study of patient care coordination analysed such coordination mechanisms as [103]: routines, information systems, meetings, and boundary spanners. In our research we have demonstrated that in the Polish context of public safety management the formal mechanisms of coordination play the main role, which results from institutional arrangements. In the conditions of uncertainty and risk the formal decision-making structures constitute the foundation of conducting actions, although other mechanisms—such as trust, meetings, and routines—are also significant. To a greater extent these mechanisms are applied in the period of stabilisation, during action preparation. This proves that the priority significance of each coordination mechanism results from the situational context.

The analyses presented in this article are not free from limitations. These limitations result above all from the fact that the research is of a preliminary nature and it concerns a diagnosis of the level of inter-organisational coordination in public safety management in relation to factors of effective inter-organisational collaboration. In the future, we plan to expand these research studies in relation to enhanced inter-organisational coordination endeavours. Moreover, the research is located in the Polish context. Taking that into account, it is necessary to study the course of inter-organisational coordination in other social and political conditions. It is also recommended to comprehensively analyse the internal and external conditions of effective inter-organisational coordination, for which purpose the research on business models of public safety organisations may prove useful.

Despite these limitations we have been able to achieve the assumed goal of this publication. We argue that inter-organisational coordination as an instrument of collaboration between autonomous units is the key factor in sustainable public safety management. It binds the actions taken by each organisation, enables flexible adaptation of enterprises and possessed resources to the existing conditions, it configures the networks of public services' delivery and it maximises the usage of the possessed abilities. As a result of this, it increases the efficiency of public safety management.

In conclusion we claim that:

(1) Inter-organisational coordination depends to a large extent on organisational and relational conditions, which occur between collaborating units. They include among other such factors as: communication in inter-organisational working teams, constraints in inter-organisational collaboration, leadership with organisational and communication skills, organisation of collaborative work (e.g., time pressured, competitive, rapidly changing, stability), management of inter-organisational collaboration (e.g., styles, transparency of decisions, and guidance), inter-organisational trust, and professional communication between personnel from individual organisations.

(2) Coordination in public safety management is protean. During stabilization it is carried out by public administration and it involves determination of preventive operations. Some ways of that coordination can be applied in other areas of sustainable local government. However during the realisation phase the person in charge of rescue actions coordinates activities within

the incident site. Outside the incident site the coordination function is fulfilled by emergency coordination centres. This solution is the result of complexity embedded in the unique situation and efforts to be undertaken in face of hazard. Such coordination, particularly creation of formal and informal relationships based on trust and organisational concern, can be used in sheer inter-organisational collaboration.

(3) The principal features of inter-organisational coordination considered with regard to collaborated management are: integrity of actions, interdependence, mutuality, complexity, and adaptiveness to unique and rapidly changing situations. At the same time, inter-organisational coordination is a result of legal, organisational, social, and situational conditions. Features of inter-organisational coordination have a considerable impact on the level of sustainable public safety management.

Acknowledgments: Acknowledgments: The authors would like to thank an anonymous reviewers for constructive comments and suggestions. Empirical data were collected within the authors' own investigations carried out in 2013–2015 in the project entitled "Coordination, communication and trust as factors driving effective inter-organisational collaboration in the system of public safety management", financed by the Polish funds of the National Science Centre allocated on the basis of the decision No. DEC-2012/07/D/HS4/00537. Whereas, preparing of the publication was partly developed within the Statutory Research 2013–2016 of the Institute of Public Affairs of the Jagiellonian University in Cracow entitled "Managing Public Sector".

Author Contributions: Author Contributions: Barbara Kożuch and Katarzyna Sienkiewicz-Małyjurek worked together to conceived, designed and performed the research, analyzed the data and wrote the paper.

Conflicts of Interest: Conflicts of Interest: The authors declare no conflict of interest.

References

1. Van Wassenhove, L.N. Humanitarian aid logistics: Supply chain management in high gear. *J. Oper. Res. Soc.* **2006**, *57*, 475–489. [CrossRef]
2. Szymczak, M.; Sienkiewicz-Małyjurek, K. Information in the city traffic management system. The analysis of the use of information sources and the assessment in terms of their usefulness for city routes users. *LogForum* **2011**, *7*, 37–50.
3. Slabbert, A.D.; Ukpere, W.I. Poverty as a transient reality in a globalised world: An economic choice. *Int. J. Soc. Econ.* **2011**, *38*, 858–868. [CrossRef]
4. Smith, N. Economic inequality and poverty: Where do we go from here? *Int. J. Sociol. Soc. Policy* **2010**, *30*, 127–139. [CrossRef]
5. Sienkiewicz-Małyjurek, K. Spatial and organisational conditions of public safety in cities. In *Current Problems of Regional Development*, Proceedings of the International Scientific Conference on Hradec Economical Days 2008: A Strategy for Development of the Region and the State Location, University Hradec Kralove, Czech Republic, 5–6 February 2008; Jedlicka, P., Ed.; pp. 95–99.
6. Jabłoński, A. Wieloparadygmatyczność w zarządzaniu a trwałość modelu biznesu przedsiębiorstwa. *Studia i Prace Kolegium Zarządzania i Finansów Szkoły Głównej Handlowej w Warszawie* **2014**, *139*, 51–72. (In Polish)
7. Kozłowski, S. Polska droga do zrównoważonego rozwoju. In *Rozwój zrównoważony na szczeblu krajowym, regionalnym i lokalnym—doświadczenia polskie i możliwości ich zastosowania na Ukrainie*; Kozłowski, S., Haładyj, A., Eds.; KUL: Lublin, Poland, 2006; pp. 159–166. (In Polish)
8. Kożuch, B.; Sienkiewicz-Małyjurek, K. Collaborative networks as a basis for internal economic security in sustainable local governance. The case of Poland. In *The Economic Security of Business Transactions. Management in Business*; Raczkowski, K., Schneider, F., Eds.; Chartridge Books Oxford: Oxford, UK, 2013; pp. 313–328.
9. O'Leary, R.; Vij, N. Collaborative Public Management: Where Have We Been and Where Are We Going? *Am. Rev. Public Adm.* **2012**, *42*, 507–522. [CrossRef]
10. Himmelman, A.T. On coalitions and the transformation of power relations: Collaborative betterment and collaborative empowerment. *Am. J. Community Psychol.* **2001**, *29*, 277–284. [CrossRef] [PubMed]
11. Feiock, R.C.; Lee, I.W.; Park, H.J. Administrators' and Elected Officials' Collaboration Networks: Selecting Partners to Reduce Risk in Economic Development. *Public Adm. Rev.* **2012**, *72*, S58–S68. [CrossRef]
12. Gulati, R.; Wohlgezogen, F.; Zhelyazkov, P. The Two Facets of Collaboration: Cooperation and Coordination in Strategic Alliances. *Acad. Manag. Ann.* **2012**, *6*, 531–583. [CrossRef]

13. Raposo, A.B.; Fuks, H. Defining Task Interdependencies and Coordination Mechanisms for Collaborative Systems. In *Cooperative Systems Design*; Blay-Fornarino, M., Pinna-Dery, A.M., Schmidt, K., Zaraté, P., Eds.; IOS Press: Amsterdam, The Netherlands, 2002; pp. 88–103.
14. Leonard, H.B.; Howitt, A.M. Organising Response to Extreme Emergencies: The Victorian Bushfires of 2009. *Aust. J. Public Adm.* **2010**, *69*, 372–386. [CrossRef]
15. Gregory, R. All the King's horses and all the King's men: Putting New Zealand's public sector back together again. *Int. Public Manag. Rev.* **2003**, *4*, 41–58.
16. Comfort, L.K. Crisis Management in Hindsight: Cognition, Communication, Coordination, and Control. *Public Adm. Rev.* **2007**, *67*, 189–197. [CrossRef]
17. Leonard, H.B.; Howitt, A.M. Katrina as prelude: Preparing for and responding to Katrina-Class Disturbances in the United States—Testimony to U.S. Senate Committee, 8 March 2006. *J. Homel. Secur. Emerg. Manag.* **2006**, *3*, 1547–7355. [CrossRef]
18. Comfort, L.K.; Kapucu, N. Inter-organizational coordination in extreme events: The World Trade Center attacks, 11 September 2001. *Nat. Hazards* **2006**, *39*, 309–327. [CrossRef]
19. Bharosa, N.; Lee, J.; Janssen, M. Challenges and obstacles in sharing and coordinating information during multi-agency disaster response: Propositions from field exercises. *Inf. Syst. Front.* **2010**, *12*, 49–65. [CrossRef]
20. Panday, P.K. Policy implementation in urban Bangladesh: Role of intra-organizational coordination. *Public Organ. Rev.* **2007**, *7*, 237–259. [CrossRef]
21. Meek, J.W. Nuances of Metropolitan Cooperative Networks. *Public Adm. Rev.* **2012**, *72*, S68–S69. [CrossRef]
22. Chen, R.; Sharman, R.; Chakravarti, N.; Rao, H.R.; Upadhyaya, S.J. Emergency response information system interoperability: Development of chemical incident response data model. *J. Assoc. Inf. Syst.* **2008**, *9*, 1–54.
23. Chen, R.; Sharman, R.; Rao, H.R.; Upadhyaya, S.J. Coordination In Emergency Response Management, Developing a framework to analyze coordination patterns occurring in the emergency response life cycle. *Commun. ACM* **2008**, *51*, 66–73. [CrossRef]
24. Melin, U.; Axelsson, K. Understanding Organizational Coordination and Information Systems—Mintzberg's Coordination Mechanisms Revisited and Evaluated. Available online: http://aisel.aisnet.org/ecis2005/115/ (accessed on 18 December 2015).
25. Gittell, J.H. Relationships between service providers and their impact on customers. *J. Sci. Res.* **2002**, *4*, 299–311. [CrossRef]
26. Gittell, J.H. Relational coordination: coordinating work through relationships of shared goals, shared knowledge and mutual respect. In *Relational Perspectives in Organisational Studies: A Research Companion*; Kyriakidou, O., Özbilgin, M.F., Eds.; Edward Elgar Publishers: Cheltenham, UK, 2006; pp. 74–94.
27. Kożuch, B.; Sienkiewcz-Małyjurek, K. Factors of effective inter-organisational collaboration: A framework for public management. Transylvanian Review of Administrative Sciences, forthcoming.
28. Government Centre for Security. Act of 26 April 2007 on the Crisis Management. Available online: http://rcb.gov.pl/eng/wp-content/uploads/2011/03/ACT-on-Crisis-Management-final-version-31-12-2010.pdf (accessed on 25 January 2016).
29. Kożuch, B.; Sienkiewcz-Małyjurek, K. Information sharing in complex systems: A case study on public safety management. *Procedia Soc. Behav. Sci.* **2015**, *213*, 722–727. [CrossRef]
30. Waugh, W.L.; Streib, G. Collaboration and Leadership for Effective Emergency Management. *Public Adm. Rev.* **2006**, *66*, 131–140. [CrossRef]
31. Kapucu, N.; Arslan, T.; Demiroz, F. Collaborative emergency management and national emergency management network. *Disaster Prev. Manag.* **2010**, *19*, 452–468. [CrossRef]
32. Kapucu, N. Disaster and emergency management systems in urban areas. *Cities* **2012**, *29*, S41–S49. [CrossRef]
33. Boin, A.; Hart, P. Organising for Effective Emergency Management: Lessons from Research. *Austr. J. Public Adm.* **2010**, *69*, 357–371. [CrossRef]
34. Choenni, S.; Leertouwer, E. Public Safety Mashups to Support Policy Makers. In *Electronic Government and the Information Systems Perspective*, Proceedings of the First International Conference EGOVIS 2010, Bilbao, Spain, 31 August–2 September 2010; Andersen, K.M., Francesconi, E., van Engers, A.G.T.M., Eds.; Springer-Verlag: Berlin Heidelberg, Germany, 2010; pp. 234–248.
35. Sienkiewicz-Małyjurek, K. Rola samorządów lokalnych w kształtowaniu bezpieczeństwa publicznego. *Samorz. Teryt.* **2010**, *7–8*, 123–139. (In Polish)

36. Tomasino, A.P. Public Safety Networks as a Type of Complex Adaptive System. In Unifying Themes in Complex Systems, Proceedings of the Eighth International Conference on Complex Systems, Volume VIII, Boston, MA, 26 June–1 July 2011; Sayama, H., Minai, A., Braha, D., Bar-Yam, Y., Eds.; New England Complex Systems Institute Series on Complexity, NECSI Knowledge Press: Cambridge, MA, USA, 2011; pp. 1350–1364.
37. Williams, C.B.; Dias, M.; Fedorowicz, J.; Jacobson, D.; Vilvovsky, S.; Sawyer, S.; Tyworth, M. The formation of inter-organizational information sharing networks in public safety: Cartographic insights on rational choice and institutional explanations. *Inf. Polity* **2009**, *14*, 13–29.
38. Kożuch, B.; Sienkiewicz-Małyjurek, K. Collaborative Performance In Public Safety Management Process. In *Transdisciplinary and Communicative Action*, Proceedings of the 5th International Conference Lumen 2014, Targoviste, Romania, 21–22 November 2014; Frunza, A., Ciulei, T., Sandu, A., Eds.; Medimond S.r.l.: Bologna, Italy, 2015; pp. 401–409.
39. Kożuch, B.; Sienkiewicz-Małyjurek, K. Mapowanie procesów współpracy międzyorganizacyjnej na przykładzie działań realizowanych w bezpieczeństwie publicznym. Zarządzanie Publiczne, 2015. forthcoming. (In Polish)
40. Sienkiewicz-Małyjurek, K.; Kożuch, B. System zarządzania bezpieczeństwem publicznym w ujęciu teorii złożoności. Opracowanie modelowe. *Bezpieczeństwo i Technika Pożarnicza* **2015**, *37*, 33–43. (In Polish)
41. Kożuch, B.; Sienkiewicz-Małyjurek, K. New Requirements for Managers of Public Safety Systems. *Procedia Soc. Behav. Sci.* **2014**, *149*, 472–478. [CrossRef]
42. Grudzewski, W.M.; Hejduk, I.K.; Sankowska, A.; Wańtuchowicz, M. *Sustainability w biznesie, czyli przedsiębiorstwo przyszłości, zmiany paradygmatów i koncepcji zarządzania*; Wydawnictwo Poltext: Warszawa, Poland, 2010. (In Polish)
43. Mah, D.N.; Hills, P. Collaborative governance for sustainable development: Wind resource assessment in Xinjiang and Guangdong Provinces, China. *Sustain. Dev.* **2012**, *20*, 85–97. [CrossRef]
44. Røiseland, A. Understanding local governance: Institutional forms of collaboration. *Public Adm.* **2011**, *89*, 879–893. [CrossRef]
45. Considine, M. Governance networks and the question of transformation. *Public Adm.* **2013**, *91*, 438–447. [CrossRef]
46. Lee, I.W.; Feiock, R.C.; Lee, Y. Competitors and Cooperators: A Micro-Level Analysis of Regional Economic Development Collaboration Networks. *Public Adm. Rev.* **2012**, *72*, 253–262. [CrossRef]
47. Lozano, R. Collaboration as a Pathway for Sustainability. *Sustain. Dev.* **2007**, *15*, 370–381. [CrossRef]
48. Mattessich, P.W.; Murray-Close, M.; Monsey, B.R. *Collaboration: What Makes It Work*; Amherst H. Wilder Foundation: Saint Paul, MN, USA, 2001.
49. Thomson, A.M.; Perry, J.L. Collaboration process: Inside the black box. *Public Adm. Rev.* **2006**, *66*, 20–32. [CrossRef]
50. Arya, B.; Lin, Z. Understanding collaboration outcomes from an extended resource-based view perspective: The roles of organizational characteristics, partner attributes, and network structures. *J. Manag.* **2007**, *33*, 697–723. [CrossRef]
51. Hansen, M.T.; Nohria, N. How to build collaborative advantage. *MIT Sloan Manag. Rev.* **2004**, *46*, 4–12.
52. Hardy, C.; Phillips, N.; Lawrence, T.B. Resources, Knowledge and Influence: The Organizational Effects of Interorganizational Collaboration. *J. Manag. Stud.* **2003**, *40*, 321–347. [CrossRef]
53. Powell, W.W.; Koput, K.W.; Smith-Doerr, L. Interorganizational collaboration and the locus of innovation: Networks of learning in biotechnology. *Adm. Sci. Q.* **1996**, *41*, 116–146. [CrossRef]
54. Berlin, J.M.; Carlström, E.D. Why is collaboration minimised at the accident scene? A critical study of a hidden phenomenon. *Disaster Prev. Manag.* **2011**, *20*, 159–171. [CrossRef]
55. Kaiser, F.M. *Interagency Collaborative Arrangements and Activities: Types, Rationales, Considerations*; Congressional Research Service: Washington, DC, USA, 2011.
56. McGuire, M. Collaborative Public Management: Assessing What We Know and How We Know It. *Public Adm. Rev.* **2006**, *66*, 33–43. [CrossRef]
57. Perrault, E.; McClelland, R.; Austin, C.; Sieppert, J. Working Together in Collaborations: Successful Process Factors for Community Collaboration. *Adm. Soc. Work* **2011**, *5*, 282–298. [CrossRef]
58. Malone, T.W.; Crowston, K. What is coordination theory and how can it help design cooperative work systems. In Proceedings of the Conference on Computer Supported Cooperative Work, Los Angeles, CA, USA, 7–10 October 1990.

59. Hartgerink, J.M.; Cramm, J.M.; Bakker, T.J.E.M.; van Eijsden, R.A.M.; Mackenbach, J.P.; Nieboer, A.P. The importance of relational coordination for integrated care delivery to older patients in the hospital. *J. Nurs. Manag.* **2014**, *22*, 248–256. [CrossRef] [PubMed]
60. Hossain, L.; Uddin, S. Design patterns: Coordination in complex and dynamic environments. *Disaster Prev. Manag.* **2012**, *21*, 336–350. [CrossRef]
61. Malone, T.W.; Crowston, K. The interdisciplinary study of coordination. *ACM Comput. Surv. (CSUR)* **1994**, *26*, 87–119. [CrossRef]
62. Lie, A. Coordination processes and outcomes in the public service: The challenge of inter-organizational food safety coordination in Norway. *Public Adm.* **2011**, *89*, 401–417. [CrossRef] [PubMed]
63. Bond, J.B.; Gittell, J.H. Cross-agency coordination of offender reentry: Testing collaboration outcomes. *J. Crim. Justice* **2010**, *38*, 118–129. [CrossRef]
64. Jones, C.; Hesterly, W.S.; Borgatti, S.P. A General Theory of Network Governance: Exchange Conditions and Social Mechanisms. *Acad. Manag. Rev.* **1997**, *22*, 911–945.
65. De Pablos Heredero, C.; Haider, S.; García Martínez, A. Relational coordination as an indicator of teamwork quality: Potential application to the success of e-learning at universities. *Int. J. Emerg. Technol. Learn.* **2015**, *10*, 4–8. [CrossRef]
66. Provan, K.G.; Kenis, P. Modes of Network Governance: Structure, Management, and Effectiveness. *J. Public Adm. Res. Theory* **2008**, *18*, 229–252. [CrossRef]
67. Carlson, E.J. Collaboration and Confrontation in Interorganizational Coordination: Preparing to Respond to Disasters. Available online: https://docs.google.com/viewer?url=https%3A%2F%2Fwww.ideals.illinois.edu%2Fbitstream%2Fhandle%2F2142%2F50617%2FElizabeth_Carlson.pdf%3Fsequence%3D1 (accessed on 11 January 2016).
68. Grandori, A. An Organizational Assessment of Interfirm Coordination Modes. *Organ. Stud.* **1997**, *18*, 897–925. [CrossRef]
69. Van De Ven, A.H.; Delbecq, A.L.; Koenig, R.J. Determinants of coordination modes within organizations. *Am. Sociol. Rev.* **1976**, *41*, 322–338.
70. Martinez, J.I.; Jarillo, J.C. The Evolution of Research on Coordination Mechanisms in Multinational Corporations. *J. Int. Bus. Stud.* **1989**, *20*, 489–514. [CrossRef]
71. Hossain, L.; Kuti, M. Disaster response preparedness coordination through social networks. *Disasters* **2010**, *34*, 755–786. [CrossRef] [PubMed]
72. Mintzberg, H. *The Structuring of Organizations*; Prentice-Hall: Englewood Cliffs, NJ, USA, 1979.
73. Drabek, T.E. Community Processes: Coordination. In *Handbook of Disaster Research*; Rodríguez, H., Quarantelli, E.L., Dynes, R.R., Eds.; Springer Science + Business Media: New York, NY, USA, 2007; pp. 217–233.
74. Abbasi, A.; Owen, C.; Hossain, L.; Hamra, J. Social connectedness and adaptive team coordination during fire events. *Fire Saf. J.* **2013**, *59*, 30–36. [CrossRef]
75. Morris, J.C.; Morris, E.D.; Jones, D.M. Reaching for the Philosopher's Stone: Contingent Coordination and the Military's Response to Hurricane Katrina. *Public Adm. Rev.* **2007**, *67*, 94–106. [CrossRef]
76. Comfort, L.; Dunn, M.; Johnson, D.; Skertich, R.; Zagorecki, A. Coordination in complex systems: Increasing efficiency in disaster mitigation and response. *Int. J. Emerg. Manag.* **2004**, *2*, 63–80. [CrossRef]
77. Kapucu, N. Interorganizational Coordination in Dynamic Context: Networks in Emergency Response Management. *Connections* **2005**, *26*, 33–48.
78. Wise, C.R. Organizing for Homeland Security after Katrina: Is Adaptive Management What's Missing? *Public Adm. Rev.* **2006**, *66*, 302–318. [CrossRef]
79. Bolland, J.M.; Wilson, J.V. Three Faces of Integrative Coordination: A Model of Interorganizational Relations in Community-Based Health and Human Services. *HSR Health Services Res.* **1994**, *29*, 341–366.
80. Leung, Z.C.S. Boundary Spanning in Interorganizational Collaboration. *Adm. Soc. Work* **2013**, *37*, 447–457. [CrossRef]
81. Patel, H.; Pettitt, M.; Wilson, J.R. Factors of collaborative working: A framework for a collaboration model. *Appl. Ergon.* **2012**, *43*, 1–26. [CrossRef] [PubMed]
82. Ales, M.W.; Rodrigues, S.B.; Snyder, R.; Conklin, M. Developing and Implementing an Effective Framework for Collaboration: The Experience of the CS2day Collaborative. *J. Contin. Educ. Health Prof.* **2011**, *31*, 13–20. [CrossRef] [PubMed]

83. Ansell, C.; Gash, A. Collaborative Governance in Theory and Practice. *J. Public Adm. Res. Theory* **2007**, *18*, 543–571. [CrossRef]
84. Chen, B. Antecedents or Processes? Determinants of Perceived Effectiveness of Interorganizational Collaborations for Public Service Delivery. *Int. Public Manag. J.* **2010**, *13*, 381–407. [CrossRef]
85. Daley, D.M. Interdisciplinary Problems and Agency Boundaries: Exploring Effective Cross-Agency Collaboration. *J. Public Adm. Res. Theory* **2009**, *19*, 477–493. [CrossRef]
86. Emerson, K.; Nabatchi, T.; Balogh, S. An integrative framework for collaborative governance. *J. Public Adm. Res. Theory* **2011**, *22*, 1–30. [CrossRef]
87. Fedorowicz, J.; Gogan, J.L.; Williams, C.B. A collaborative network for first responders: Lessons from the CapWIN case. *Gov. Inf. Q.* **2007**, *24*, 785–807. [CrossRef]
88. Franco, M. Determining factors in the success of strategic alliances: An empirical study performed in Portuguese firms. *Eur. J. Int. Manag.* **2011**, *5*, 608–632. [CrossRef]
89. Olson, C.A.; Balmer, J.T.; Mejicano, G.C. Factors Contributing to Successful Interorganizational Collaboration: The Case of CS2day. *J. Contin. Educ. Health Prof.* **2011**, *31*, 3–12. [CrossRef] [PubMed]
90. Raišienė, A.G. Sustainable Development of Inter-Organizational Relationships and Social Innovations. *J. Secur. Sustain. Issues* **2012**, *2*, 65–76. [CrossRef]
91. Ranade, W.; Hudson, B. Conceptual issues in inter-agency collaboration. *Local Gov. Stud.* **2003**, *29*, 32–50. [CrossRef]
92. The National Headquarters of the State Fire Service of Poland. Biuletyn Informacyjny Państwowej Straży Pożarnej za Rok 2010. Available online: http://www.straz.gov.pl/aktualnosci/biuletyn_roczny_psp_za_rok_2010 (accessed on 26 January 2016). (In Polish).
93. Reddy, M.C.; Paul, S.A.; Abraham, J.; McNeese, M.; DeFlitch, C.; Yen, J. Challenges to effective crisis management: Using information and communication technologies to coordinate emergency medical services and emergency department teams. *Int. J. Med. Inf.* **2009**, *78*, 259–269. [CrossRef] [PubMed]
94. European Commission; Humanitarian Aid and Civil Protection. Emergency Response Coordination Centre, ECHO Factsheet. Available online: http://ec.europa.eu/echo/files/aid/countries/factsheets/thematic/ERC_en.pdf (accessed on 20 September 2015).
95. Internetowy System Aktów Prawnych. *Ustawa z Dnia 22 Listopada 2013 r. o Systemie Powiadamiania Ratunkowego (Dz.U. 2013 poz. 1635)*; Available online: http://isap.sejm.gov.pl/DetailsServlet?id=WDU20130001635 (accessed on 27 January 2016). (In Polish).
96. Asees, M.S. Tsunami Disaster Prevention in Sri Lanka. Available online: http://www.jamco.or.jp/en/symposium/21/3/ (accessed on 28 September 2015).
97. Sienkiewicz-Małyjurek, K. The Flow of Information About the Actions Required in Emergency Situations: Issues in Urban Areas in Poland. *Int. J. Soc. Sustain. Econ. Soc. Cult. Context* **2013**, *8*, 61–71.
98. Aedo, I.; Díaz, P.; Carroll, J.M.; Convertino, G.; Rosson, M.B. End-user oriented strategies to facilitate multi-organizational adoption of emergency management information systems. *Inf. Process. Manag.* **2010**, *46*, 11–21. [CrossRef]
99. Lee, W.B.; Wang, Y.; Wang, W.M.; Cheung, C.F. An unstructured information management system (UIMS) for emergency management. *Expert Syst. Appl.* **2012**, *39*, 12743–12758. [CrossRef]
100. Juan, L.J.; Li, Q.; Liua, C.; Khana, S.U.; Ghani, N. Community-based collaborative information system for emergency management. *Comput. Oper. Res.* **2014**, *42*, 116–124.
101. Grandori, A.; Soda, G. Inter-firm networks: Antecedents, mechanisms and forms. *Organ. Stud.* **1995**, *16*, 183–214. [CrossRef]
102. Gardet, E.; Mothe, C. The dynamics of coordination in innovation networks. *Eur. Manag. Rev.* **2011**, *8*, 213–229. [CrossRef]
103. Gittell, J.H.; Weiss, L. Coordination Networks Within and Across Organizations: A Multi-level Framework. *J. Manag. Stud.* **2004**, *41*, 127–153. [CrossRef]

© 2016 by the authors. Licensee MDPI, Basel, Switzerland. This article is an open access article distributed under the terms and conditions of the Creative Commons Attribution (CC BY) license (http://creativecommons.org/licenses/by/4.0/).

Environmental Aspects of Social Responsibility of Public Sector Organizations

Liliana Hawrysz * and Joachim Foltys

Department of Organization and Management, Faculty of Economy and Management,
Opole University of Technology, Opole 45-758, Poland; joachimfol@onet.pl
* Correspondence: l.hawrysz@po.opole.pl

Academic Editor: Adam Jabłoński
Received: 2 October 2015; Accepted: 9 December 2015; Published: 25 December 2015

Abstract: In addition to determining social responsibility policies that affect the market and social actors, certain governments also set objectives related to their internal activity. For example, one of the activities of the German government is to implement the concept of social responsibility into public institutions. In the Netherlands, one of the government tasks is to set an example for responsible practices (government as a role model). The aim of this paper is to examine firstly whether public sector entities set an example for responsible practices, especially with regard to respect for the environment, and secondly, whether public sector organizations in Poland significantly differ from organizations abroad in terms of their practices in the field of environmental protection. A questionnaire was a basis for data collection. The questionnaires were distributed to representatives of deliberately selected public sector organizations located primarily in Europe. The study was conducted in 2012–2013 on a group of 220 public sector organizations (102 Polish and 118 other European). The paper presents only the selected part of research. Public sector organizations in Poland do not have internal mechanisms of environmental responsibility. There is a significant discrepancy between the state of the environmental responsibility of organizations located in Poland and abroad. Obtained results show that public sector organizations, those in Poland in particular, are making their first steps in developing internal environmental responsibility.

Keywords: CSR; government as a role model; public sector organizations; environment

1. Introduction

Corporate social responsibility derives from three dimensions: human, environmental and economic (Triple P: People, Planet, Profit) [1]. Business organizations intend to take responsibility for their development processes, which take place both inside and outside their organization. However, public sector organizations are mostly expected to support business entities in this respect [2]. The issue discussed less often concerns public sector organizations as socially responsible entities, that is those seeking to increase the transparency and verifiability of actions taken, creating friendly conditions for reforms. However, besides determining CSR policies that affect the market and social actors, particular governments set objectives related to their own social activity. In the German government program (National Strategy for Sustainable Development), one of the government's actions is to implement the CSR concept in public institutions. In the Netherlands, one of the government tasks is to set an example for responsible practices (government as a role model). In countries such as France, the United Kingdom and Belgium, the governments have set goals for sustainable/green procurement [3]. This way of perceiving public sector organizations shows a duality of their role in relation to social responsibility. The dual role of public sector organizations is reduced to two dimensions, external and internal. The external dimension, far more recognizable in the literature [4–9], concerns promotion of the corporate social responsibility concept in the business environment. The internal dimension applies to public sector organizations as socially responsible entities, not only because of the implementation of the tasks assigned to these units and undertaken in close correlation with the objectives that an entity should pursue, but primarily as a result of efforts to build mutual trust and transparency in relationships with both the external and internal environment of the organization. These activities are designed to create a well-established, solid belief that the funds allocated to the administration are spent efficiently, while providing maximum benefits for a society. The external and internal dimensions should remain in balance. If any of these dimensions is ailing, the credibility of the organization is undermined. The external dimension is far more recognizable in the literature, which is why this paper focuses on the internal dimension. Environmental responsibility is one of the main aspects of social responsibility. Corporate Environmental Responsibility (CER) simply means the incorporation of responsibility assumptions towards the environment in the strategic policy of the organization [10]. As research findings indicate, four elements affect the effectiveness of actions concerning environmental responsibility (the internal dimension): implementing the environmental policy into the organization strategic documents and everyday activities, stimulating employees' awareness, increasing the amount and scope of responsibility for the environment, concerns the introduction of environmental responsibility into the core values of the organization [7]. The survey questions used in the paper are based on these key activities. Due to historical heritage, public sector organizations in Poland have never been the leader of implementing modern methods of management. While leading European countries were improving their management tools, organizations in Poland had just started to implement them. This time difference is the reason for comparing environmental protection practices in organizations located in and outside Poland to find out if they are as different as expected.

There are empirical studies examining environmental sustainability in public sector organizations, but the majority of them have a single-country focus [11–15]. There are only a few studies that have a multi-country environmental focus [16,17], but none of them include Polish organizations.

The aim of this paper is to examine firstly whether public sector organizations set an example for responsible practices, especially with regard to respect for the environment, and secondly, whether public sector organizations in Poland significantly differ from organizations abroad in terms of their practices in the field of environmental protection. Therefore, two hypotheses were formulated for the purpose of research.

Hypothesis 1. Public sector organizations set an example for responsible practices in respect for the environmental protection.

Hypothesis 2. Public sector organizations in Poland differ significantly from organizations located abroad in terms of their practices concerning the environmental protection.

The basis for collecting information for research was a questionnaire sent to representative of deliberately selected public sector organizations located primarily in Europe. The study was conducted in 2012–2013 on a group of 220 public sector organizations.

2. Literature Review

The first model for social responsibility that focused on decision making was shaped by Carroll [18]. Hawken identified sustainability problems and discussed business-related solutions, which, in his opinion, could transform both companies and the economy, and possibly improve profitability [19]. However, the financial aspect of the activity is not the main one in public sector organization [20]. In the public sector, compared to the corporate sector, accountability expectations and obligations have always been higher. New public management reforms put pressure on public sector organizations to demonstrate their financial and non-financial performance. The demand is particularly relevant for public sector organizations considering that they create public value while acting in an entrepreneurial way [17,21]. Public sector organizations are expected to be more environmentally responsible than private companies as they are legitimated by public contracts. Government and public sector organizations have a special role to play as guarantors of public values. Moore believes that citizens want from their governments some combination of the following that together encompass public value: (1) high-performing service-oriented public bureaucracies, (2) public organizations that are efficient and effective in achieving desired social outcomes, and (3) public organizations that operate justly and fairly, and lead to just and fair conditions in the society at large [22]. That is why public sector organizations are obligated to citizens to operate in a sustainable way.

As previously mentioned, the role of public sector organizations in relation to social responsibility is reduced to two dimensions: external and internal. As far as the external dimension of social responsibility of public sector organizations is concerned, four institutional models are identified in the literature: observer, patron, promoter, and partner [3]. These models differ mainly in the degree to which the state takes responsibility for coordinating activities related to the implementation of the CSR concept. In the first model (the observer), there is no leader responsible for coordinating activities related to corporate social responsibility and the burden of promoting this concepts rests on socio-economic partners. In the second model (the patron), there is no leader either, but the burden of promoting the concept of corporate social responsibility rests on the government administration. The third model (the promoter) is characterized by government coordination of activities promoting the CRS concept by the institution acting as the leader. In addition, government is responsible for publishing guidelines, standards and other forms of support for development of social responsibility idea. The fourth model (the partner) is characterized by the presence of leading governmental institution coordinating the activities of other ministries, as well as advisory bodies or centers for promotion of social responsibility. Simultaneously, government actions create the framework for bottom-up initiatives of involved socio-economic partners, leading to a greater coherence of activities and effect of synergy [3]. A slightly different typology has been proposed in the document prepared by the Ministry of Foreign Affairs of the Kingdom of the Netherlands and the World Bank [23,24]. In this typology, the model of the observer has not been included and a forcing attitude appears instead, which consists in imposing the implementation of corporate social responsibility, for example by appropriate legislation, regulations, guidelines, audits, legal or fiscal penalties, *etc.* [23–25]. In the literature, a great deal of attention is devoted to describing and diagnosing the institutional models of social responsibility promotion. The analysis shows that patron and partner and forcing attitude models [24] are the least favorable. In the case of successful models, we deal with active presence of government administration authorities in intensifying efforts to promote social responsibility.

The internal dimension applies to public sector organizations as socially responsible entities, because of the efforts to build mutual trust and transparency both in relationships with the external and internal environment of the organization. These activities are designed to create a well-established, solid belief that the funds allocated to the administration are spent efficiently, while providing maximum benefits for a society.

Hypothesis 1. Public sector organizations set an example for responsible practices in respect for the environmental protection.

Hypothesis 2. Public sector organizations in Poland differ significantly from organizations located abroad in terms of their practices concerning the environmental protection.

According to Elkington, environmental responsibility is one of the dimensions of social responsibility, in addition to economic and social ones [26]. Corporate Environmental Responsibility (CER) simply means incorporation of responsibility assumptions towards the environment in the strategic policy of the organization [10]. Among the organizations operating on the market, two orientations that are not mutually exclusive in the movement for environmental responsibility can be distinguished: obligatory and optional. Obligatory (external) orientation takes the form of three types of isomorphism: coercive, mimetic and normative. Coercive isomorphism arises when organizations include in their activities the need to respect the environment in response to legal regulations; mimetic isomorphism is the result of a reference of one organization to the other, more effective one, and normative isomorphism is dictated by the requirement to improve organization's collective image.

Optional (internal) orientation involves organization's commitment to build competitive advantage based on the value and uniqueness [27].

Many authors agree that the absence of an institutional framework in promoting respect for the environment contributes to the fact that companies undertake activities of a limited nature, which do not always meet the expectations of local communities. The macroeconomic nature of the majority of policies and guidelines does not have an operationalized character and therefore requires actions at the microeconomic level [27]. Since an economic activity may result in a negative impact on the environment, there is a commitment to take responsibility for this condition. The commitment translates into developing such activities that are socially responsible, that aim at creating a society responsible for the environment on a voluntary basis and beyond the legal expectations [28]. This means that obligatory orientation is a starting point for actions, but only optional orientation makes these actions more meaningful. Optional orientation leads to the situation where responsibility for the environment is a fundamental need and commitment towards the next generations, and not the consequence of strict respect for the law. Obligatory orientation in Poland in the movement for environmental responsibility stems from, inter alia, the environmental policy for 2009–2012 with the perspective to 2016 [29]. The following are recognized as the most important directions of systemic actions:

- consideration of environmental principles in sector strategies
- activation of the market to protect the environment
- environmental management
- participation of society in the environmental protection
- development of research and technical progress
- liability for environmental damage
- ecological aspect in spatial planning

As research findings indicate, four elements affect the effectiveness of actions concerning environmental responsibility (the internal dimension). The first element is implementing the environmental policy into the organization strategic documents and everyday activities undertaken by the organization. The second one is stimulating employees' awareness and their responsibility for the environment. The third one is increasing the amount and scope of responsibility for the environment (e.g., to modify existing processes so that they will be more beneficial to the environment). The fourth element concerns the introduction of environmental responsibility into the core values of the organization [7].

An environmental policy is a publicly accessible document defining the organization's intentions toward the environment. Its content is the foundation for the entire system [30]. This policy determines an overall direction for the organization's environmental activities and establishes principles, which will guide the organization in environmental matters. An environmental policy becomes a point of reference against which organizational activities will be assessed. Moreover, an environmental policy is crucial for the process of communication with employees, and local communities, depicting the priorities of the organization for the environment protection [31]. Through the policy, the organization demonstrates that it is aware of its impact on the environment and surroundings and voluntarily commits to minimize the negative impact on the environment. An environmental policy serves as a landmark—the benchmark for taken actions. Strategic initiatives that are crucial for developing the environmental policy are formulated [32,33].

An environmental policy itself is not sufficient as it outlines only a general direction for activities. Without developing programs to measure and analyze the impact of the organization on the environment, it is impossible to give the policy a lasting nature [34]. Without operationalization, the policy is merely declarative. Measurement and analysis programs provide access to information so that decisions can be better, and above all, they take into account the welfare of local communities. In addition, these programs allow for identifying areas that need improvement, as well as setting priorities for undertaken activities [35]. They also allow effective risk management. Measurement and analysis programs identifying organization's impact on the environment allow for creating a reference point for the organization's activities [34]. Without measuring the scope of this impact, it is impossible to manage the area in accordance with the principle "you cannot manage what you do not measure".

Programs and actions for the most efficient use of natural resources are the recent trend in activities undertaken on a broad international level [36]. Nations around the world recognize the value of natural resources and they focus on their bigger protection and sustainable development. In 2012, the United Kingdom founded the Natural Capital Committee, whose role is to identify priorities for actions supporting and improving the use of natural resources. It has also begun preparations to integrate the value of natural resources into the calculation of GDP by 2020 [37]. Therefore, it can be assumed that programs and actions for the most efficient use of natural resources will be growing in significance in the next few years [36,38–40].

Because public sector organizations in Poland started to implement modern methods of management later than more developed countries, they are expected to be different.

Hypothesis 2. Public sector organizations in Poland differ significantly from organizations located abroad in terms of their practices concerning the environmental protection.

All these elements have internal character and consist of building individual environmental responsibility of employees in organizations and implementing responsibility in the organizational culture. The paper attempts to answer the question as to whether public sector organizations, in addition to taking responsibility for coordinating activities related to implementing the concept of corporate social responsibility, have also developed internal mechanisms concerning CSR. Moreover, we will consider whether this has an impact on the economic environment, and if, at the same time they can be seen as setting an example, this gives the organization credibility.

3. Methodology

The basis for collecting information for research was a questionnaire sent to representatives of deliberately selected public sector organizations located primarily in Europe. The study was conducted in 2012–2013 on a group of 220 public sector organizations. Three questions of a general nature were chosen from the questionnaire and subjected to statistical analysis. Questions were chosen in order to place the actions taken by public organizations in an appropriate time context. Since the works on the environmental policy began in the international arena roughly in the 1970s, the actions undertaken by organizations aimed at formulating their environmental policy served to keep up with international trends and are characterized by focus on the past. Interest in data analysis software and programs for reducing negative impact on the environment are relatively new as they cover the past 10–15 years [35], but not everything has been refined in this area [34]. Therefore, it can be considered as a focus on the present. Orientation on activities and programs aimed at the most efficient use of natural resources is the most current trend in the international arena, so far widely discussed [36,38–40], which is why the actions taken in this field are focused on the future.

4. Participants and Procedure

Research included public sector organizations, among others ministries and central offices, province offices, marshal offices, district offices, municipal offices, tax offices and chambers, and customs chambers. All public sector organizations registered in the EIPA database (European Institution of Public Administration) were invited to participate in the study. In this way, 1739 (according to EIPA data as of 30 November 2011) public sector organizations located outside Poland and 269 (according to EIPA data as of 30 November 2011) organizations located in Poland were identified. An invitation to participate in the study was sent via post to all organizations registered in the EIPA database. Research was conducted from November 2012 to May 2013. A total number of 2008 questionnaires were distributed to organizations' representatives, 220 completed questionnaires were returned, giving a rate of return of 11%. Not all of the questionnaires were suitable for further analysis. A total of 269 entities were located in Poland (according to EIPA data as of 30 November 2011). All of these organizations were invited to participate in research. Only 102 organizations agreed to participate in research, which gave a return rate of 38%. However, outside Poland, the largest group of organizations was represented by Belgium (12), Portugal (11), the Czech Republic (10), Italy (10), Finland (9), Germany (8), and Norway (6). The research was a trial project.

5. Instrument/Survey and Data Analysis

The questionnaire contained 46 questions with answers: yes, no, I do not know. The questions were arranged in the following way: the first questions concerned general issues, and the following questions expanded them. Generally, the questionnaire related to three dimensions of the public sector organizations' functioning: human, environmental and economic. The aim of the study was to investigate the state and prospects of development of the Corporate Social Responsibility concept in public sector organizations in Poland and abroad. The paper presents only a part of the research on the environmental aspects of corporate social responsibility. Other parts of the research are presented in the papers [41,42].

The analysis of relationships between variables was conducted using a chi-square independence test together with strength measures (Cramer's V and C contingency coefficient). The significance level α = 0.05 was assumed. The results were considered statistically significant when the calculated test probability p satisfies the inequality $p < 0.05$.

Detailed results of the analysis of three most important environmental responsibility actions are summarized in Table 1.

Table 1. Organizations' environmental responsibility.

Environmental Responsibility Actions	Poland	Abroad	χ^2	df	p	C	V
have clearly defined environmental policy based on the principles of sustainable development	54%	57%	3.30	2	0.19	0.13	0.13
have developed programs of analysis and reduction of organization's negative influence on environment	22%	58%	2.27	2	0.00	0.36	0.34
actions or programs aimed to make the most efficient use of natural resources are considered as priority	24%	56%	24.15	2	0.00	0.34	0.32

Source: own elaboration on the basis of survey results.

6. Results

6.1. Clearly Defined Environmental Policy Based on the Principles of Sustainable Development

In the research group, 54% of public sector organizations located in Poland and 57% of organizations abroad declare that they have the defined environmental policy. The analysis result of a chi-square test does not show the statistically significant relationship between a clearly defined environmental policy and location of the organization.

6.2. Developed Programs of Analysis and Reduction of Organization's Negative Influence on Environment

In the studied group, 22% of organizations located in Poland and 58% abroad declare that they have developed a program for analyzing and reducing the negative impact of their activities on the environment. The analysis result of a chi-square test shows significant correlation between location of the organization and their programs for analyzing and reducing the negative impact of the organization on the environment (χ^2 = 26.27, df = 2, p = 0.00000). Organizations located outside Poland often declare that they have these kinds of programs. The strength of this correlation is average (C = 0.36, V = 0.34).

6.3. Actions or Programs Aimed to Make the Most Efficient Use of Natural Resources are Considered as Priority

In the surveyed group, 24% of organizations located in Poland and 56% located abroad declare that they treat projects or programs aimed at the most effective use of natural resources as a priority in their actions. The analysis result of a chi-square test shows significant correlation between location of the organization, and their declaration to treat projects and programs aimed at the most effective use of natural resources as a priority ($\chi^2 = 24.15$, df = 2, $p = 0{,}00000$). Organizations located outside Poland more often declare that they treat projects or programs aimed at the most efficient use of natural resources as a priority in their activities. The strength of this correlation is average (C = 0.34, V = 0.32).

7. Discussion

Research shows that more than half of public sector organizations located in Poland declare that they have clearly defined environmental policies concerning organization's intentions towards the environment. The content of these policies is the foundation for the entire system; it is the starting point for undertaking environmental actions and establishing principles that will guide the organization in issues concerning the environment. Detailed analysis of environmental policies of organizations located in Poland shows that a large part of formulated policies concerns operation of external actors, primarily companies (e.g., introduction of rational and modern solutions for efficient water and wastewater management, improvement and rationalization of waste management system, systematic reduction of air pollution, water and soil pollution, reduction of traffic nuisance, monitoring of harmful factors in the city and their supervision and control, *etc.*). Only a small number of organizations formulated environmental policies with regard to their own activities, e.g., reducing water and energy use, reducing the amount of chemicals used, systematic training of office employees on the procedures concerning the implementation of pro-environmental actions, support of projects related to the environmental education and sustainable development based on three-sector cooperation, promoting pro-environmental behaviors among employees, customers, suppliers and subcontractors by bringing responsibility for the environment to their attention and promoting specific measures for environment protection, in particular promoting the principles of sustainable development, *etc.* [19]. Formulating the environmental policy, public sector organizations focus largely on supporting the concept of environmental responsibility in the business environment rather than on setting goals for their business activity. This way of formulating policies without taking into account the declarations towards the environment issues has contributed to a lack of programs aiming at reducing the negative impact of the organization's activity [21,22].

In these organizations, there was not simply a reference point for their formulation, but also for the optimal use of natural resources treated as a priority in the undertaken activities. The way of formulating environmental policies in Polish public sector organizations is general in its nature and mostly does not directly concern the activities of that particular organization, making it difficult to develop programs of analysis and reduction of the negative impact of their operations on the environment. It also makes it difficult to treat projects and programs aimed at the most efficient use of natural resources as a priority in business activities. Polish and foreign organizations vary in terms of having data analyzing programs and optimal use of natural resources. The obtained results allow for rejecting the first hypothesis. Public sector organizations do not set an example of responsible practices in respect for the environment. Hypothesis 2 was verified. The results show that public sector organizations in Poland differ significantly from organizations located outside Poland in terms of their practices for the environmental protection. Activities undertaken in Polish organizations allow for classifying the dominant, in their view, orientation to focus on the past trends, while more than half of organizations located outside Poland are actively involved in the implementation of current trends.

Others studies show a higher degree of environmental responsibility of public sector organizations [16]. However, it is really hard to compare the results of the studies because there are only a few studies which have a multi-country environmental focus [16,17].

8. Limitation of the Study

The research was a trial project. Its aim was to examine the state and prospects for development of the Corporate Social Responsibility concept in public sector organizations in Poland and abroad.

The issue of environmental responsibility accounted only for a small part of the study. Conducted analyzes allowed for identifying a general trend in public sector organizations, which, however, requires clarification. Completed studies are in some way a snapshot of organizations and temporary reflection of the situation. It is necessary to construct reliable indicators of environmental responsibility and employ them in a given time interval, e.g., two years. This would make it possible to capture certain trends, as well as a full picture of the examined phenomena. The presented results should be considered as a starting point for further, more extensive analyzes.

9. Conclusions

Public sector organizations in Poland do not have internal mechanisms of environmental responsibility. Some organizations declare that they have their environmental policy, but it is of a general nature and does not include the declaration of particular organizations. This situation leads to the conclusion that first steps in creating environmental responsibility have been taken, and now further steps are awaited. In particular, it concerns public sector organizations located in Poland. The study has identified a significant discrepancy between the state of the environmental responsibility of companies located in Poland and abroad.

Author Contributions: Author Contributions: This work is a result of collaboration between all authors. Author Liliana Hawrysz designed the study and wrote the report. Author Joachim Foltys wrote the first draft of the manuscript. Authors Liliana Hawrysz and Joachim Foltys reviewed the draft manuscript. All the authors managed the literature searches, read and approved the final manuscript.

Conflicts of Interest: Conflicts of Interest: The authors declare no conflict of interest.

References and Notes

1. Grigore, G. Corporate Social Responsibility-strategies in European style. *Ann. Univ. Oradea, Econ. Sci. Ser.* **2008**, *17*, 662–665.
2. Letter of 4 November 2011 from the Minister for European Affairs and International Cooperation to the House of Representatives on *Development through Sustainable Enterprise*, Parliamentary Papers, House of Representatives, 2011–2012 session, 32 605, No. 56.
3. Analiza Instytucjonalnych Modeli Promocji CSR w Wybranych Krajach, Analiza przygotowana dla Ministerstwa Gospodarki przez CSRinfo. Available online: http://odpowiedzialnybiznes.pl/public/files/analiza_instytucjonalna_promocji_csr_CSRinfo_2011.pdf (accessed on 2 September 2015). (In Polish)
4. Janković Milić, V.; Stanković, J.; Marinković, S. The capacity of local governments to improve business environment: Evidence from Serbia. Available online: http://papers.ssrn.com/sol3/papers.cfm?abstract_id=2554337 (accessed on 8 December 2015).
5. Pesmatzoglou, D.; Nikolaou, I.E.; Evangelinos, K.I.; Allan, S. Extractive multinationals and corporate social responsibility: A commitment towards achieving the goals of sustainable development or only a management strategy? *J. Int. Develop.* **2014**, *26*, 187–206.
6. Min, B.S. The effect of outside board members on energy efficiency in Korea. *J. Asia-Pacific Bus.* **2014**, *15*, 54–72.
7. Shah, K.U. Strategic organizational drivers of corporate environmental responsibility in the Caribbean hotel industry. *Pol. Sci.* **2011**, *44*, 321–344.
8. Comănescu, M. Increasing responsibility towards environment. *Theor. Appl. Econ.* **2010**, *17*, 59–72.
9. Butcher, B.; Xu, Y. Chinese cooperatives and environmental social responsibility. *Chin. Econ.* **2014**, *47*, 63–80. [CrossRef]
10. Banerjee, S. Corporate environmentalism: The construct and its measurement. *J. Bus. Resear.* **2002**, *55*, 177–191. [CrossRef]
11. Burritt, R.L.; Welch, S. Australian commonwealth entities: An analysis of their environmental disclosures. *Abacus* **1997**, *33*, 69–87. [CrossRef]
12. Fortes, H. The need for environmental reporting by companies: an examination of the use of environmental reports by Swedish public companies. *Green Manag. Int.* **2002**, *40*, 77–92.

13. Frost, G.R.; Seamer, M. Adoption of environmental reporting and management practices: An analysis of New South Wales public sector entities. *Financ. Account. Manag.* **2002**, *18*, 103–127. [CrossRef]
14. Lodhia, S.; Jacobs, K.; Park, Y.J. Driving public sector environmental reporting. The disclosure practices of Australian commonwealth departments. *Pub. Manag. Rev.* **2012**, *14*, 631–647. [CrossRef]
15. Goswami, K.; Lodhia, S. Sustainability disclosure patterns of South Australian local Councils: A case study. *Publ. Money Manag.* **2014**, *34*, 273–280. [CrossRef]
16. Lopatta, K.; Jaeschke, R. Sustainability reporting at German and Austrian universities. *Int. J. Educ. Econ. Dev.* **2014**, *5*, 66–90. [CrossRef]
17. Greiling, D.; Traxler, A.A.; Stötzer, S. Sustainability reporting in the Austrian, German and Swiss public sector. *Int. J. Public Sect. Manag.* **2015**, *28*, 404–428.
18. Carroll, A.B. A three-dimensional conceptual model of corporate social performance. *Acad. Manag. Rev.* **1979**, *4*, 497–505.
19. Hashmi, M.A.; Al-Habib, M. Sustainability and carbon management practices in the Kingdom of Saudi Arabia. *J. Environ. Plann. Manag.* **2013**, *56*, 140–157.
20. Moore, M.H. *Creating Public Value. Strategic Management in Government*; Harvard University Press: Cambridge, MA, USA, 1995; p. 31.
21. Moore, M.H. Public value as the focus of strategy. *Aust. J. Pub. Admin.* **1994**, *53*, 296–303.
22. Bryson, J.M.; Crosby, B.C.; Bloomberg, L. Public value governance: Moving beyond traditional public administration and the new public management. *Pub. Admin. Rev.* **2014**, *74*, 445–456. [CrossRef]
23. Ingram, V.; de Grip, K.; de Wildt, M.R.; Ton, G.; Douma, M.; Boone, K.; van Hoeven, H. *Corporate Social Responsibility: the Role of Public Policy: A Systematic Literature Review of the Effects of Government Supported Interventions on the Corporate Social Responsibility (CSR) Behaviour of Enterprises in Developing Countries*; The Hague: Policy and Operations Evaluation Department (IOB), Ministry of Foreign Affairs of the Netherlands: Amsterdam, The Netherlands, 2013; p. 110.
24. Ward, H. Public Sector Roles in Strengthening Corporate Social Responsibility: Taking Stock. Available online: http://siteresources.worldbank.org/INTPSD/Resources/CSR/Taking_Stock.pdf (accessed on 9 December 2015).
25. Fox, T.; Ward, H.; Howard, B. Public Sector Roles in Strengthening Corporate Social Responsibility: A Baseline Study. Available online: http://www-wds.worldbank.org/external/default/WDSContentServer/WDSP/IB/2005/12/19/000090341_20051219091246/Rendered/PDF/346550CSR1CSR1interior.pdf (accessed on 9 December 2015).
26. Elkington, J. *Cannibals With Forks: The Triple Bottom Line of the 21st Century Business*; Capstone Publishing Ltd.: Oxford, UK, 1997.
27. Pesmatzoglou, D.; Nikolaou, I.E.; Evangelinos, K.I.; Allan, S. Extractive multinationals and corporate social responsibility: a commitment towards achieving the goals of sustainable development or only a management strategy? *J. Int. Dev.* **2014**, *26*, 187–206. [CrossRef]
28. Nowakowska, A. The reverse logistics management with RFID application. *Adv. Logist. Syst.* **2008**, *2*, 41–46.
29. Warszawa. Polityka Ekologiczna Państwa W Latach 2009-2012, Z Perspektywą Do Roku 2016. Available online: https://www.mos.gov.pl/g2/big/2009_11/8183a2c86f4d7e2cdf8c3572bdba0bc6.pdf (accessed on 2 September 2015).
30. Sulaiman, M.; Mokhtar, N. Ensuring sustainability: A preliminary study of environmental management accounting in Malaysia. *Int. J. Bus. Manag. Sci.* **2012**, *5*, 85–102.
31. Sands, J.; Lee, K.H. Environmental and sustainability management accounting (EMA) for the development of sustainability management and accountability. *Issues Soc. Environ. Account.* **2015**, *9*, 1–4.
32. Quental, N.; Lourenço, J.M.; da Silva, F.N. Sustainable development policy: Goals, targets and political cycles. *Sus. Dev.* **2011**, *19*, 15–29. [CrossRef]
33. Herea, W. Policy and strategy for improving sustainable social development programmes. *Environ. Eng. Manag. J.* **2010**, *9*, 861–868.
34. Burghelea, C. Analysis of sustainable tourism (ST) in Romania. *Int. Audit. Risk Manag.* **2015**, *1*, 31–42.
35. Bass, S. A New Era in Sustainable Development, An IIED Briefing. Available online: http://pubs.iied.org/pdfs/11071IIED.pdf (accessed on 4 September 2015).

36. Schaefer, M.; Goldman, E.; Bartuska, A.M.; Sutton-Grier, A.; Lubchenco, J. Nature as capital: Advancing and incorporating ecosystem services in United States federal policies and programs. *Proc. Natl. Acad. Sci. USA* **2015**, *112*, 7383–7389. [CrossRef] [PubMed]
37. Sullivan, S. *The Natural Capital Myth; or will Accounting Save the World?*; The Leverhulme Centre for the Study of Value School of Environment, Education and Development, The University of Manchester: Oxford, UK, 2014.
38. Zhu, X.; van Ierland, E.C. Economic modelling for water quantity and quality management: A welfare program approach. *Water Resour. Manag.* **2012**, *26*, 2491–2511. [CrossRef]
39. Meena, M.S.; Singh, K.M. Information and communications technologies for natural resources management. *J. Environ. Manag. Tour.* **2013**, *2*, 77–92.
40. Calil, J.; Beck, M.W.; Gleason, M.; Merrifield, M.; Klausmeyer, K.; Newkirk, S. Aligning natural resource conservation and flood hazard mitigation in California. *PLoS ONE* **2015**, *10*, 1–14. [CrossRef] [PubMed]
41. Hawrysz, L. Patronage vs. Implementation of the Corporate Social Responsibility (CSR) Concept in the Public Sector. In Proceedings of Advanced Research in Scientific Areas, Zilina, The Slovak Republic, 2–6 December 2013; EDIS—Publishing Institution of the University of ZilinaL: Zilina, The Slovak Republic, 2013; Volume 2, pp. 184–187.
42. Hawrysz, L. Rola organizacji sektora publicznego w kształtowaniu społecznej odpowiedzialności. *Zrównoważony rozwój organizacji-aspekty społeczne* **2015**. (In Polish) [CrossRef]

© 2016 by the authors. Licensee MDPI, Basel, Switzerland. This article is an open access article distributed under the terms and conditions of the Creative Commons Attribution (CC BY) license (http://creativecommons.org/licenses/by/4.0/).

Article
A New Systematic Approach to Vulnerability Assessment of Innovation Capability of Construction Enterprises

Jingxiao Zhang [1,*], **Haiyan Xie** [2], **Klaus Schmidt** [2] **and Hui Li** [1,*]

1 Institution of Construction Economics, Chang'an University; NO.161, Chang'an Road, Xi'an 710061, China
2 Department of Technology, Illinois State University; Normal, IL 61790, USA; hxie@ilstu.edu (H.X.); kschmid@ilstu.edu (K.S.)
* Correspondence: zhangjingxiao@chd.edu.cn (J.Z.); lihui9922@chd.edu.cn (H.L.);
Tel.: +86-159-2973-9877 (J.Z.); +86-159-9138-5822 (H.L.)

Academic Editor: Adam Jabłoński
Received: 5 October 2015; Accepted: 18 December 2015; Published: 25 December 2015

Abstract: The purpose of this research is to study the vulnerability of construction enterprises' innovation capabilities (CEIC) and their respective primary influencing factors. This paper proposed a vulnerability system framework of CEIC, designed two comprehensive assessments for analysis, namely the entropy and set pair analysis method (E-SPA) and the principle cluster analysis and SPA method (P-SPA), and compared grades to verify the vulnerability assessments. Further, the paper quantitatively assessed the major influencing factors in facilitating management, reducing vulnerability, and improving the ability of construction enterprises to respond to changes in the construction industry. The results showed that vulnerability could be effectively and systematically evaluated using E-SPA. However, managing or reducing entrepreneurial sensitivity and improving the ability to respond was critical to supporting sustainable CEIC. The case studies included in this paper suggested that in ensuring sustainable CEIC, companies should concentrate on highly educated human resources, R&D investments, intellectual property related innovations, and government support. This research provided a practical framework and established a sustainable strategy for companies to manage their vulnerability in developing innovation capability. In addition, this research presented an innovative and effective way to quantitatively analyze vulnerability which offered a foundation to signify a new paradigm shift in construction sustainable development.

Keywords: construction enterprise; innovation capability; vulnerability assessment; innovation uncertainty; sustainable development

1. Introduction

As a critical driver of the sustainable development of a nation, a region, an industry, or an enterprise, innovation can provide a continual basis for sustainable socio-economic development and growth. Construction innovation, as a sustainable driver and a crucial condition, represents the pulse of construction economic development of any nation [1–3]. The innovative capabilities of construction enterprises thus hold a key position in advancing industrial and national development [4,5]. The current innovation status of the construction industry reflects the complex features of the industry [6]. As any nation or region will have demand for continued construction, statistics related to this construction make up a major portion of an economy's well-being. The innovation accomplishments of construction enterprises are affected by the innovation efforts of other firms, and are achieved through the continuing cooperation among industries for breakthroughs in products, processes, and designs. These breakthroughs reflect the strength and innovative desires and interests of construction companies. However, compared to other industries, there is a lack of focus on the diffusion rates of innovation in different sectors of construction, such as building and civil infrastructure. Depending on the developmental level of an economy, the need for civil infrastructure may vary. However, innovation is needed at all levels of economic development [7]. Civil infrastructure companies are large in size and have potential for radical innovations, while residential construction companies are usually small and give limited consideration as to how to effectively convert new research and development into innovation. Often, large companies do not invest sufficiently in innovation as they already dominate a major portion of the existing market. Smaller companies on the other hand need to demonstrate higher degrees of innovation in order to enter or even stay in the market [8]. A similar observation was made by Hultgren and Tantawi [9] in the study of potential radical innovation in large firms.

However, researchers recently noticed that sustainable economic development has its vulnerability, which was considered as a new paradigm shift in the analysis of uncertainty in economic studies of system sensitivity and response capability. Vulnerability research has a wide range of applications, including climate change prediction, natural disaster prevention, food security, and public health improvement [10–21]. Generally, innovation vulnerability relates to the risk or uncertainty of a company's innovation capability. Therefore, eliminating risks or identifying weaknesses is perhaps a preferred method of overcoming vulnerability. Elimination should, however, not simply lead to the avoidance of uncertainty when studying innovation capability, because uncertainty can sense or trace new directions or paths of economic development and thereby represents an innovative strength [18,19]. This new cognitive reasoning requires firms to treat uncertainty as part of innovation capability and develop a strategy to overcome it, or manage uncertainty instead of eliminating it. Construction entrepreneurs should consider the opportunities stemming from uncertainties as well. With this understanding, it is a crucial prerequisite for successful promotion of construction enterprise's innovation capability (CEIC) to develop and implement a strategy when managing the uncertainty that is part of CEIC. However, there is still a lack of quantitative research to assess the uncertainty involved in innovation, particularly in relation to estimating innovation capability at a firm, industrial, or national level [22,23]. A similar discussion can be found in Costanza et al. [24] "to say that we should not do valuation of ecosystems is to deny the reality that we already do, always have and cannot avoid doing so in the future". The research by Costanza et al. [24] emphasized the importance of quantifying ecosystem values for the support of policy decisions or influencing public opinions. This research stressed the necessity for quantitative research in innovation uncertainty. This research was based on an inverse perspective of the relationship between uncertainty and innovation capability. Furthermore, it studied the vulnerability of CEIC and worked to build a system approach to assess the vulnerability of CEIC [11,13,15–17,20,21,25–27]. This new approach aimed to manage and reduce the vulnerability of CEIC and to support the sustainable improvement of CEIC.

In order to assess the vulnerability of CEIC, this research quantitatively analyzed the individual vulnerabilities of the major influence factors of CEIC with the objective to manage and improve their responsive abilities. In order to achieve this goal, this research constructed a framework of vulnerability of CEIC, using two comprehensive methods of vulnerability assessment in socio-economic research. The two methods were the entropy and set pair analysis method (E-SPA) and the principle cluster analysis and SPA method (P-SPA). This research also implemented these methods in eight construction enterprises to analyze their CEIC, and compared the respective results. The results demonstrated the functions of the vulnerability framework in the uncertainty analysis of construction innovation. The results are applicable to other industries too.

This research expands the field of innovation functions of a company to enhance its competitiveness and sustainable development from an inverse perspective when managing innovation risks. It identified new areas of economic growth with potential broad impact on multiple industries. At an industrial level, the research may help governments, industrial associations, and other organizations implement targeted incentives for innovation planning, to reduce uncertainty and risk, to respond to an innovation-driven service economy, and to promote regional and national innovation. In the long run, the research can help to enhance the positions of industries and facilitate national innovation strategies for economic development and restructuring.

The rest of the paper is structured as follows. Section 2 focuses on the review of literature, links of analysis levels, and the research agenda. Section 3 provides the research methods. Section 4 builds the vulnerability framework based on the selected theories and methods and implements the research procedure and measurements to analyze the vulnerability of CEIC. Section 5 presents the research results, summarizes the conclusions, and highlights the implications of vulnerability assessment for innovation capability in enterprises, and at industrial and national levels.

2. Literature Review

2.1. Innovation and Uncertainty

Enterprises are becoming more specialized than ever before. Based on the technological know-how of a company, competition may lead to additional challenges with respect to innovation and handling uncertainty. Adaptability paired with innovation therefore becomes a key factor to advance technological diversity and the willingness to experiment with new products and services. According to Bell and Pavitt [27], firms rarely fail because of an inability to master a new field of technology, but because of the lack of adaptability and responsiveness to new industry demands and the inability to proactively embrace and discover new technological opportunities [28].

Companies are vulnerable to external factors if they are not well prepared or not strategically aligned with the new innovative technologies. Companies need to be willing to take risks in order to succeed in the competitive construction industries. Finding the right approach to balancing risk *versus* a company's vulnerability and its innovative capability is key to success. Facing constant competition in the advancement of any industry for new technology separates company strategies that are sustainable from those that are not. Major differences in this approach seem to exist between larger and smaller companies in the same industries since key challenges for the strategic management of technology depend on a company's size and its core business: small firms must focus on defining and defending their product niche while large firms focus on building and exploiting competences based on R&D or on complex production or information systems. Companies require continuous learning, the capacity to integrate specialists, and a willingness both to break down established functional and divisional boundaries and to take a view to the long term [29].

Among a multitude of research, Schumpeter's concept of long waves, a theory of technical innovation and structural change, shows that the successful diffusion of this technology depends on a wide variety of institutional changes. Freeman *et al.* points to a number of policies including flexible working hours, training and less restrictive macroeconomic demand policies which would help to generate higher levels of innovation [30]. This concept could certainly be extended to the sustainability of an innovation friendly company environment. Innovation does not lead to success just by itself if it is not supported by progressive and flexible federal, regional, and company specific policies. Otherwise, potential risk factors or the perception of uncertainty will hinder the advancement and sustainability of a progressive innovative environment.

Nevertheless, innovation processes are often criticized because they do not accurately portray the process of industry movement, in which there were uncertain and dynamic interactions among knowledge, resources, and environments [31]. Therefore, striving to remove uncertainty might lead to the risk of hindering or even completely impeding innovation rather than promoting it. Despite much success in overcoming uncertainty, it has become clear that uncertainties can never be completely removed. Instead, uncertainty keeps emerging in new forms accompanying complex scientific processes, organization structures, and technical systems. Strategies should be prepared at different levels of acceptance of uncertainty and be utilized to benefit social-economic developments [18]. Uncertainty is not a deficiency, but a structural feature embedded in any entrepreneurial entity.

Likewise, uncertainty is not strictly a shortcoming, rather an important factor that can lead to growth. The endeavor to eliminate uncertainty holds the risk of jeopardizing rather than promoting innovation.

Dealing with uncertainty is a continuous process for construction innovation. The concept of coping with uncertainty, as opposed to removing it through planning and control, was presented and substantiated by Bohle [32]. This new cognitive approach to manage uncertainty in innovation processes is not just wishful thinking. For example, Bohle [32] proposed approaches such as experience-led and subject-based actions in project management. They provided new ways of dealing with uncertainty in project management. However, these methods have barely been further developed into quantitative instruments for systematic promotion of innovation processes [32]. This paper developed a new system with quantitative methods to manage the uncertainty in construction innovation. Meanwhile, the system has the ability to react and overcome uncertainty with countermeasures, instead of eliminating uncertainty which might weaken the power of innovation.

2.2. Vulnerability

As an emerging area, systematic studies of vulnerability began with research on natural disasters, with the purpose to achieve sustainable development of the environment through reducing uncertainty, sensitivity, and vulnerability [10]. At present, scholars widely use the methodologies of vulnerability research to explore economic domains, such as financial vulnerability and household vulnerability [10,21,33–35]. For example, Dominitz and Manski [17] first discussed the vulnerability of a country's economic system. United Nations Development Programme (UNDP) [35] defined the concept of economic vulnerability as the capability to suffer the damage due to the impact of unanticipated events in the process of economic development. Vulnerability relates to the sensitivity to disturbance inside and outside of a system and the lack of capability to respond to make necessary changes to the system's structure and functions. In addition, sensitivity and adaptability are key components of the evaluation of the vulnerability of a system [14,16,21,33,34,36–39].

Vulnerability management includes the assessment of a system's sensitivity and adaptability by managing or restricting the potential hazards to realize the systematic promotion in the political, social, economic, or environmental fields. In recent years, examples of systems for which vulnerability assessments were performed include, but are not limited to, climate changes, natural disasters, ecological crises, food security, and public health. The research methods used include composite index method, fuzzy method, scenario analysis, and input-output method [14,16,21,25,33,34,36–39]. Such assessments were conducted on behalf of a range of different organizations, from small businesses to large enterprises. For example, Gnangnon [25] endowed different weights to various economic growth-indicators to calculate economic vulnerability indices in developing countries. Turner *et al.* [21] proposed a framework of factors and linkages to study the potential effects of the vulnerability of a couple of human–environment systems which was also related to the sensitivity and resilience of the system.

However, innovation capability is an important driver of any economic system, and the assessment of the vulnerability of innovation capability has not drawn enough attention, especially in regards to CEIC. Therefore, it is urgent to study how to measure the level of vulnerability, select indices, and manage index information to conduct a vulnerability assessment of CEIC. In this research, the authors first selected indices of vulnerability by using the entropy method. The entropy method is a common method to generate the objective weight of index system [40,41]. The next method used in this research is Set Pair Analysis (SPA), which is a novel method to target the uncertainty in a system [42,43]. The core thought of set pair analysis was to treat the confirmed uncertainty of the object to be studied as a confirmed uncertainty system, and to analyze and study the connection and conversion of the research objects for the similarities and differences. The core concept of set pair analysis was the set pair and the connection degree [42]. Another comparison method of principle cluster analysis (PCA) was also used to assess vulnerability. PCA assessment is usually used for the vulnerability assessment of tourism economic systems or city economic systems [38,44–47]. Using Entropy SPA (E-SPA) and PCA-SPA (P-SPA), the authors analyzed cases of large construction companies to reveal their vulnerability levels.

2.3. Construction Enterprise's Innovation Capability (CEIC)

From a system point of view, construction innovation capabilities at firm, regional, and national levels are three closely related categories, which support and influence each other, characterized by general factors to realize the overall achievement of sustainable innovation. In innovation systems, the national, regional or industrial technical changes and economic growth are the outcomes of the innovation activities that take place among all firms. However, the changes are not simply the summation of firm-level innovation capabilities, but the result of their interactions at national, regional or industrial levels instead. At national or regional levels, innovation measurements are calculated by agencies such as European Innovation Scoreboard [48], OECD STI Outlook [49], Nordic Innovation Monitor [50], UNCTAD indicators [51] and World Bank indicators [52]. The measured innovation efficiencies refer to innovation input and output, innovation activity, innovation environment, *etc.* with relevant indicators.

CEIC can be used as an important carrier for national and regional innovation strategies. It is usually implemented at a micro level to foster, form, and upgrade innovation capabilities [3,23,53–58], such as innovation environments, innovation investment capabilities, cooperative innovation capabilities, intellectual property capabilities, and change-innovation capabilities [1]. Innovation capabilities enable construction enterprises to create, deploy, and maintain advantageous business performance in the long run. The representations of innovation capabilities, such as distinct skills, processes, procedures, organizational structures, decision rules, and disciplines, undergird enterprise-level sensing, seizing, and reconfiguring capacities.

At the enterprise-level, there are three main types of studies that focused on construction innovation capability. The first type of studies concentrated on analyzing and evaluating the major changes in overall innovation capability and specified the current status and history of innovation capability, e.g., international comparative study [59–61]. The second type of studies focused on the evaluations of enterprise innovation capabilities in key sectors (or areas), a.k.a. primary businesses' innovation. For example, equipment manufacturing, strategic approaches for emerging markets, and process plant construction are considered as business innovation [1,2,4,62–65]. The third type focused on evaluating and comparing the different types and sizes of CEIC [53,66–71], such as domestic and foreign-funded enterprises, large, small-and-medium and micro enterprises, or state-owned and private enterprises.

In terms of types of constitution, CEIC refers to industrial innovation, technological innovation, system innovation, organizational innovation, and collaborative innovation [1,3,72,73]. The participants of CEIC involve government, business, universities, individuals, and community groups. The input factors of CEIC include capital investment, intellectual property, training, human resources (HR), *etc.* Researchers noticed that CEIC contributed to the enhancement of national competitive advantage, optimization of industrial resource allocation and the employment market, reduction of energy dissipation and pollution, and improvement of social welfare [3]. The systematic framework of CEIC gradually transited from individual and closed-end efforts into open-ended and multilateral cooperative processes. The multilateral interactions help to form the cooperative effects to improve the efficiency of labor, information, knowledge, technology, management and capital to implement CEIC strategies [4,74,75]. Even though the above studies focused on product capability, technology patents, knowledge transfer, university–industry–government cooperation, or output efficiency, there is still deficiency in holistic understanding of the social and organizational aspects of innovations. For example, as an important innovation resource, HR and the associated working conditions become key enablers and central factors of innovations. So, instead of studying the individual parameters of production, technology, and organization *etc.*, this research studied CEICs systematically in a framework. Additionally, the generic innovation models [71,76] put forward that the frameworks with successful innovation outcomes were built by considering the focus of innovation, contextual factors, organizational capabilities and innovation processes. The links between the key concepts used in this research are shown in Figure 1. With the adoption of the extensions of generic innovation models, the framework of CEIC included the following items:

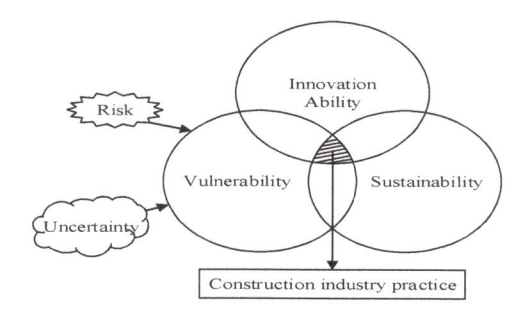

Figure 1. Links between key concepts.

(A) An ideal environment for innovation capability. The environment of CEIC should be at a high level of economic development, enterprise information management, and human resource access, and with the support from government and social sectors to create an accessible and sustainable environment [77,78].

(B) Adequate resources for innovation capability. Without an innovation resource pool, it is difficult for CEIC to carry out innovation activities, such as management innovation, technology innovation, and product innovation [79,80]. CEIC is the carrier of a national and regional innovation strategy. The cooperation among university, industry, and society, together with the alliance of capital, market demands and human resource (HR) pools for business innovation, are key to complying with CEIC [81–84].

(C) Progressive innovation activities. CEIC is important to the foundation of the entire innovation in an economic society. It also contributes to product innovation, process innovation, marketing innovation and organizational innovation. Resources, technology, and knowledge (tangible and intangible) are bundled, linked and incorporated for innovation activities, which then would be converted and organized into routines and systems to formalize innovation capabilities and lead to production competencies and performance [85,86]. In order to strengthen innovation activities, construction enterprises should actively and continuously promote the innovation investments in human and financial resources, pay good attention to integration and absorption of external technologies, and sustain the creation and ownership of intellectual properties.

(D) Emerging innovation output. As a measurement of the CEIC levels, innovation output includes the number of patents registered, technical trading expansion, and brand building promotion efforts [2,66,87]. Innovation in the area of high-tech and knowledge-intensive service helps the optimization of production and service structure at the industrial level; meanwhile, the new production or service methods enable enterprises to further optimize the product structure. This reciprocal process is an important aspect of innovation outputs [88–91].

(E) Improved economic efficiency. The economic efficiency of CEIC includes the efficiencies of labor input, capital investment, and energy investment, which contribute to sustainable development of business environments [92–95]. The construction enterprises with strong dynamic capabilities are highly entrepreneurial, with innovation-capability uncertainty, and are highly vulnerable to innovation environments. From a system uncertainty perspective, this uncertainty or dynamic feature is mainly due to the sensitivity of CEIC to internal and external system disturbances. In addition, the lack of responsiveness of CEIC hinders the sustainable development of those companies. The theoretical framework in this research quantitatively evaluated the vulnerability of CEIC to improve innovation capability. The analysis of the vulnerability or uncertainty of CEIC helps to promote the sustainability of innovation capability.

2.4. Analysis Level and Framework

Items A to E in the aforementioned framework of CEIC can be summarized in the following Table 1. Table 1 shows that there are three implications for CEIC. The implications are reflected in the following aspects. (a) Innovation capability is inherently unstable. (b) Innovation capability is sensitive to the interferences and changes from the outside world. (c) CEIC is vulnerable to risk. Thus, the vulnerability of CEIC is a comprehensive system affected by sensitivity and adaptability. Sensitivity is the degree of susceptibility to external shocks, or ability to deal with innovation uncertainty and risk [77,83–86]. If a system has weak sensitivity, it would be less susceptible and demonstrate stronger resistance than one with strong sensitivity. Adaptability is the ability to quickly adjust from a risky or uncertain situation to a stable or sustainable situation. It also demonstrates the ability of a system to maintain itself. Adaptability has a direct relationship with the innovation self-maintenance capability of a system.

Table 1. Analysis level.

Topic	Innovation and uncertainty	Innovation capability	Vulnerability
Literature summary	Managing uncertainty is absolutely necessary from the perspective of construction innovation. There will always be something unforeseeable. Flexibility and creativity are important features of a successful innovation strategy.	System dynamics and uncertainty are likely affected by product, technology, organization, and people. The current influence factors and measurement methods are not industry specific.	Uncertainty threats are studied using system sensitivity and adaptability to analysis the vulnerability in political, social, economic fields. Comprehensive methods or mixed method such as E-SPA, PCA, and SPA were used to assess economic vulnerability.
Major trends in research	Systematical description or linkage to deal with uncertainty with quantitative methods to promote innovation process.	Uncertainty measurement of CEIC with generic influence factors	Exploratory implementation of the measurements and verification of innovation vulnerability.
Research Focus	This research constructed the vulnerability-assessment framework, implemented the corresponding indices, and verified CEIC using common comprehensive methods from economic vulnerability areas.		

In summary, the vulnerability indicator (X) of CEIC could be expressed in Equation (1).

$$X = f(S, A) \quad (1)$$

Letter S represents sensitivity. Letter A represents adaptability. Large value of X indicates the tendency towards exposure to risk and uncertainty. It also means that CEIC will be slowed down to return to a sustainable state. Thus, the framework of Equation (1) is used to analyze vulnerability from two aspects, namely system sensitivity and adaptability. This research extracted data from 2013 National Innovation Index Reprot [96] to build the vulnerability indices in Table 2. In Table 2, the target layers include Innovation Input Capability (IIC), Cooperative Innovation Capability of Enterprise (CICE), Intellectual Property Capability (IPC), Change Innovation Capability (CIC), and Innovation Environment (IE). Each target layer is further divided into sensitivity indices and adaptability indices. The explanations of both sensitivity and adaptability indices in Table 2 include their indicators, measurement units, descriptions, and tropisms. For sensitive and adaptive indicators, a positive tropism (+) indicates a direct relationship between the index and the sensitivity or adaptability; a negative tropism (−) indicates an inverse relationship between the index and the sensitivity or adaptability.

Table 2. Vulnerability-assessment framework and indices of construction enterprise's innovation capability (CEIC).

Target layer	Sensitivity (S)	Indicators	Sensitive indicator description and its tropism	Adaptability (A)	Indicators	Adaptive indicator description and its tropism
Innovation Input Capability (IIC)	$IICS_1$	Innovative funding accounted for the main business revenue/%	It reflects the strength of innovation funding (−)	$IICA_1$	R&D expenditure accounts for the main business revenue	It reflects R & D expenditure intensity (+)
	$IICS_2$	The proportion of R & D types of HR employed/%	It reflects the intensity of R & D personnel investment (−)	$IICA_2$	The proportion of PhD graduates in HR of a corporate	It reflects the structure of highly educated personnel in an enterprise (+)
	$IICS_3$	The funding of R & D specific sector accounted for corporate R & D expenditure/%	It reflects the state of the R & D funding of a specific sector (−)	$IICA_3$	The personnel R & D investment of a specific sector accounted for that of corporate R & D /%	It reflects the manpower situation of R & D institutions (+)
Cooperative Innovation Capability of Enterprise (CICE)	$CICES_1$	Cooperation Project accounted for the whole research project/%	It reflects the cooperative scope of the enterprise (+)	$CICEA_1$	The R & D expenditure proportion of universities and research institutions in whole corporate R&D expenditures/%	It reflect R & D cooperation with universities and research institutions (+)
	$CICES_2$	The ratio of technology import expenditure accounted for the whole R & D funding	It reflects the introduction status of technology with respect to independent research (+)	$CICEA_2$	The ratio of digestion and absorption funds accounted for technology import funds	It reflects the absorption and re-innovation status for the introduction technology (−)
	$CICES_3$	The proportion of cooperation innovative project accounted for the whole enterprise project/%	It reflects the innovation state of the business cooperation with external institutions (−)	$CICEA_3$	The proportion of cooperation patent accounted the total patent application/%	It reflects the cooperation scale of technological inventions (+)
Intellectual Property Capability (IPC)	$IPCS_1$	The percent of enterprise invention patent applications accounted for the whole patent applications/%	It reflects patent application levels. (−)	$IPCA_1$	100,000 RMB R & D funding per invention patent applications/(No./100,000 RMB)	It reflects the patents output efficiency (+)
	$IPCS_2$	The patent-owned project accounted for the whole enterprises' projects/%	It reflects the patent protection awareness of enterprises (−)	$IPCA_2$	10,000 patents-owned of enterprise employees/(piece /10,000 employees)	It reflects the size of enterprise patent pool (+)
	$IPCS_3$	# of implementations of invention patents accounted for overall implemented patents/%	It reflects the transformation and application status of invention patents (−)	$IPCA_3$	The ratio of patent licensing and transfer income accounted for new product sales revenue	It reflects the ratio of patent assets income and new product sales revenue (+)
Change Innovation Capability (CIC)	$CICS_1$	New product marketing expenses accounted for all marketing costs/%	It reflects the marketing strength of new-investment products (−)	$CICA_1$	New product sales revenue accounted for the main business revenue/%	Reflects the impact of business activities on the entire production of innovative activities(+)
	$CICS_2$	PCT applications accounted for the whole patent applications/%	It reflects the potential technology inventions an enterprise in the international market (−)	$CICA_2$	Income from patented project accounted for the entire project income of an enterprise/%	It reflects the corporate innovation competitiveness (+)
	$CICS_3$	Labor productivity/(RMB/person)	It reflects the innovation impact on labor productivity (−)	$CICA_3$	Comprehensive energy output/%	It reflects social performance of corporate energy consuming (−)
Innovation Environment (IE)	$IEGS_1$	Direct government support (GS)extent/%	The ratio of direct government support accounted for the whole R & D expenses (+)	$IEGS_2$	Indirect government support(GS) extent/%	The ratio of indirect government support accounted for the whole R & D expenses (−)
	$IESS_1$	The extent of Social capital to support (SS) R&D/%	The ratio of financial institutions support R&D accounted for the whole R & D expenses (+)	$IESS_2$	The extent Social capital to support (SS) project development/%	The ratio of social-capital development projects accounted for the total capital of enterprises (−)

Note 1: Indices from 2013 National Innovation Index Report [96]; Note 2: For sensitive and adaptive indicators, a positive tropism (+) indicates a direct relationship between the index and the sensitivity or adaptability; a negative tropism (−) indicates an inverse relationship between the index and the sensitivity or adaptability.

The authors designed the research steps and framework as per Figure 2. This research used the common mixed methods of E-SPA and P-SPA to analyze the vulnerability of CEIC. Particularly, Zhao's grade standards [97] were used as SPA method of the inventor to grade the vulnerabilities of selected cases. In addition, the major influencing factors of response capability were ranked to manage the vulnerability of CEIC.

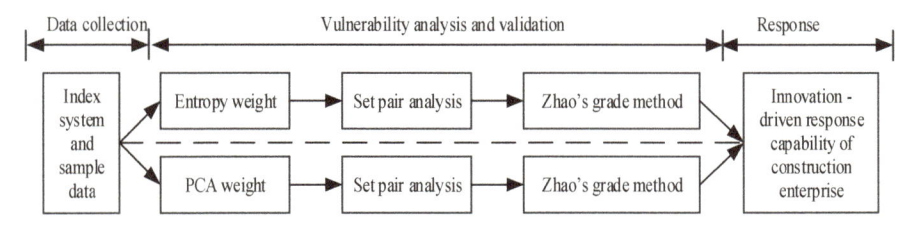

Figure 2. Research steps and framework.

3. Research Method

3.1. Entropy and SPA (E-SPA) Method

3.1.1. Entropy Weight

Many generic evaluation models rely on subjective weighting methods to determine the weights of indices in their evaluations. Entropy method [41] is an objective empowerment approach used to reflect the disorder degree of information in information theories, which now has been expanded to social and economic areas [40,41,47,98,99]. The weights of individual indicators are determined by calculating the entropy and entropy weight of each of them. The greater the entropy is, the smaller the corresponding entropy weight will be for any indicator. If an entropy weight is zero, the indicator provides no useful information to decision-makers. That indicator may be removed in the evaluation process. The amount of useful information that an indicator provides to a decision-maker is objective. So, using the entropy method to determine index weights could provide realistic and objective insight into the CEIC vulnerability system. The four main steps [41,44] taken are as follows.

Step 1: The formation of the evaluation matrix (Table S1).

Suppose there are m units and n indicators to be evaluated to establish the original data matrix in Equation (2).

$$R = (r_{st})_{m \times n} (s = 1, 2, ..., m; t = 1, 2, ..., n) \tag{2}$$

where r_{st} represents the actual value of the tth index of sth unit.

Step 2: The standardization of the evaluation matrix.

The following equation is used to normalize the matrix B,

$$B = (b_{st})_{m \times n} (s = 1, 2, ..., m; t = 1, 2, ..., n) \text{ with } b_{st} = \frac{r_{st} - r_{min}}{r_{max} - r_{min}} \tag{3}$$

where r_{max} and r_{min} represent the maximum and minimum values, respectively, for the evaluation unit.

If indicator is the positive tropism (+)

$$b_{st} = \frac{r_{st} - r_{min}}{r_{max} - r_{min}} \tag{3a}$$

If indicator is the negative tropism (−)

$$b_{st} = \frac{r_{max} - r_{st}}{r_{max} - r_{min}} \tag{3b}$$

Step 3: The calculation of the entropy

The entropy of the system can be defined by using the following calculations:

$$H_t = -\left(\sum_{s=1}^{m} f_{st}\ln f_{st}\right)/\ln m \quad (s = 1, 2, ..., m; t = 1, 2, ..., n) \tag{4}$$

where $f_{st} = b_{st}/\sum_{s=1}^{m} b_{st}$; if $f_{st} = 0$, redefine the f_{st} as

$$f_{st} = (1 + b_{st})/\sum_{s=1}^{m}(1 + b_{st}) \tag{5}$$

Step 4: The calculation of the entropy weight

$$w = (\omega_t)_{1\times n}, \quad \omega_t = (1 - H_t)/\left(n - \sum_{t=1}^{n} H_t\right) \text{ with } \sum_{t=1}^{n}\omega_t = 1 \tag{6}$$

3.1.2. Set Pair Analysis (SPA)

Given two sets v and u, the set pair is expressed as $H = (v, u)$. Equation (7) calculates the connection degree of the two sets:

$$\mu = \frac{S}{N} + \frac{F}{N}i + \frac{P}{N}j = a + bi + cj, \text{ where } a + b + c = 1 \tag{7}$$

In Equation (7), N is the total number of characteristics of a set pair; S is the number of characteristics of two sets; P is the number of opposite characteristics of two sets; F is the number of characteristics of two sets, which are independent to each other. The ratio $\frac{S}{N}$ is the similarity degree of two sets; $\frac{F}{N}$ is the difference degree of two sets; $\frac{P}{N}$ is the opposite degree of two sets.

In summary, a in Equation (7) is the coefficient of similarity degree; c is the coefficient of opposite degree. i and j are the coefficients of the difference and the opposite degrees. i takes the uncertain value in the section $[-1, 1]$ according to different situations; j takes the value of -1 in general situations to indicate that $\frac{P}{N}$ is the opposite to the similarity degree $\frac{S}{N}$.

3.1.3. E-SPA Vulnerability Method

(1) The formation of vulnerability evaluation matrix of CEIC

Given that vulnerability system of CEIC is $Q = \{E, G, W, D\}$, the m evaluation unit is $E = \{e_1, e_2 \cdots e_m\}$, the n indices of each unit is $G = \{g_1, g_2 \cdots g_n\}$, the index weight is $W = \{w_1, w_2 \cdots w_n\}$ (see also Equation (6)), the index evaluation is d_{kp} ($k = 1, 2, \cdots, m; p = 1, 2, \cdots, n$), then the evaluation matrix D of vulnerability system of CEIC is shown in Equation (8).

$$D = \begin{bmatrix} d_{11} & d_{12} & \cdots & d_{1n} \\ d_{21} & d_{22} & \cdots & d_{2n} \\ \cdots & \cdots & \cdots & \cdots \\ d_{m1} & d_{m2} & \cdots & d_{mn} \end{bmatrix} \tag{8}$$

(2) Identification of similarity and opposite degree

Identify the maximum index set $U = \{u_1, u_2, \cdots u_n\}$ and the minimum index set $V = \{v_1, v_2, \cdots v_n\}$ in the evaluation unit to generate the similarity degree a_{kp} and opposite degree c_{kp} of d_{kp} in the evaluation matrix D on basis of the set $\{v_p, u_p\}$.

If d_{kp} is a positive tropism (+),

$$\begin{cases} a_{kp} = \dfrac{d_{kp}}{u_p + v_p} \\ c_{kp} = \dfrac{u_p v_p}{d_{kp}(u_p + v_p)} \end{cases} \quad (9a)$$

If d_{kp} is a negative tropism (−),

$$\begin{cases} a_{kp} = \dfrac{u_p v_p}{d_{kp}(u_p + v_p)} \\ c_{kp} = \dfrac{d_{kp}}{u_p + v_p} \end{cases} \quad (9b)$$

(3) The connection degree of vulnerability

The connection degree μ of set pairs $\{E_k, U\}$ in $[V, U]$ is shown in Equation (10).

$$\begin{cases} \mu_{(E_k, U)} = a_k + b_{ki} + c_{kj} \\ a_k = \sum \omega_p a_{kp} \\ c_k = \sum \omega_p c_{kp} \end{cases} \quad (10)$$

(4) The vulnerability indicator X of CEIC

Given x_k represents the connection degree between evaluation unit E_k and the max index set $U = \{u_1, u_2, \cdots u_n\}$ for the Kth construction enterprise, which is shown in Equation (10), the larger x_k is or the closer vulnerability to the max value, the more vulnerable and uncertain the CEIC, and vice versa.

$$x_k = \dfrac{a_k}{a_k + c_k} \quad (11)$$

3.2. PCA and SPA (P-SPA) Method

The PCA Score process is shown in the following seven steps [100,101].

Step 1: Using SPSS 22 software to implement the factor analysis to extract the principal component $F_1, F_2, \ldots, F_n$.

Step 2: Calculating the loading of F_1 score. Factor scores were generated and standardized through loadings. The F_1 loading was divided by the square root of the corresponding eigenvalues of F_1, to generate its orthogonal eigenvectors. N indicators were given as $a_1, a_2, \ldots, a_N$.

Step 3: Calculating F_1 score (f_1) with Equation (12). In Equation (12), $x_1, x_2, \ldots, x_N$ were the standardized data of N items with the first sample.

$$f_1 = a_1 \times x_1 + a_2 \times x_2 \cdots \cdots a_N \times x_N \quad (12)$$

Step 4: Repeating the steps to calculate F_2, F_3 and F_n scores ($f_2, f_3, \cdots, f_N$) in the first sample.

Step 5: According to the variance % ($v_1, v_2, v_3, \cdots v_n\%$) and cumulative variance % ($cv\%$) of Initial eigenvalues, the weighted sum score Fs was calculated by Equation (13) in the first sample.

$$Fs = (v_1 f_1 + v_2 f_2 + v_3 f_3 + \cdots + v_n f_n)/cv \quad (13)$$

Step 6: Repeating the process on other samples. Then, N indicators were normalized score to calculate the weight, and the weight set WP,

$$WP = [wp_1, wp_2, \cdots, wp_n] \quad (14)$$

Step 7: Constructing the P-SPA Vulnerability method. After using Equations (8) and (14) to alternate the entropy weight, the authors followed the analogy steps of E-SPA method to analysis the vulnerability of CEIC.

4. Empirical Analysis

4.1. Data Collection

In order to verify the vulnerability method of CEIC, comprehensive, accurate, and representative data were retrieved from the "E01Civil Construction Industry Classification Guideline of the Chinese Securities Regulatory Commission (CSRC)", which included a total of 51 public construction companies (E01 and E05 Building Decoration Classification Guideline) in the Shanghai stock exchange and the Shenzhen stock exchange, P.R. China in 2014. A set of these enterprises was identified and used to test the vulnerability framework. Enterprises from the CSRC list are usually large-scale, global competitors and ideal for CEIC analysis. The annual reports of the CSRC provide the enterprise specific information. The authors carefully cleansed the data using the following criteria. (1) The company is listed in the CSRC list for at least eight consecutive years; and (2) there must be an accurate business description. After data cleansing, there were eight enterprises that fit the criteria and were used in the model construction.

On average, researchers used between five and 25 companies with time durations of one to four consecutive years for validation or verification in research projects [92–98]. Additional data were collected from internal sources such as HR, intellectual property, government support, enterprise, innovation investment, management reports, secretarial files, and electronic records. All of the selected companies produced and maintained such information for their day-to-day managerial and operational use. In other words, these data were secondary in nature and were readily available within the business organizations.

The selected companies are listed in Table 3, and the corresponding data are listed in Table 4a,b. The eight companies included in Table 3 are large construction enterprises. The following framework does not contain any parameters that would be affected by the company size of a sample. In addition, the assessment method and framework are applicable to small and medium enterprises (SMEs).

Table 3. Selected samples of the eight construction enterprises.

ID	The Listed Time	Domain Business Area	Research Time Span	The Code
A	2007	Construction of structural steel, Industrial construction	2007–2014	1
B	2001	Railway Engineering and other engineering construction, real estate projects, sales	2007–2014	2
C	1994	Industrial construction, commercial construction, real estate, food service, design and consulting, and facility rental (since 2008)	2007–2014	3
D	2004	Road and bridge construction, asphalt concrete sales, environmental protection business	2005–2014	4
E	1997	Project contracting, cement production and sales, civil explosive, hydroelectric power construction, management of expressways, real estate	2004–2014	5
F	2006	Construction, real estate development	2006–2014	6
G	2005	Installation of cement production lines, manufacturing of machinery and equipment, design and technology transfer, supervision	2007–2014	7
H	2005	Civil construction, Industrial construction, public facilities construction, building decoration, sales of building materials	2005–2014	8

Table 4. Sensitivity data of vulnerability of CEIC.

	Innovation Input capability			Cooperation Innovation Capability			Intellectual Property Capability			Innovation Change Capability			Innovation Environment	
	$IICS_1$	$IICS_2$	$IICS_3$	$CICES_1$	$CICES_2$	$CICES_3$	$IPCS_1$	$IPCS_2$	$IPCS_3$	$CICS_1$	$CICS_2$	$CICS_3$	$IEGS_1$	$IESS_1$
A	9.15%	30.8%	40.98%	0.9%	1.692	24.2%	12.37%	9.89%	40.0%	4.0%	12.95%	267879	21.57%	3.41%
B	8.78%	30.5%	37.29%	1.17%	1.12	24.4%	12.49%	10.59%	38.7%	5.8%	10.54%	254396	26.62%	4.05%
C	9.17%	28.9%	44.22%	0.97%	1.43	25.7%	11.92%	13.66%	42.9%	3.9%	12.62%	266902	19.89%	3.92%
D	7.98%	30.9%	39.89%	1.50%	0.99	22.8%	12.51%	10.79%	32.6%	3.3%	14.55%	267983	23.09%	2.97%
E	8.46%	27.3%	42.25%	1.32%	1.01	23.9%	13.05%	14.82%	45.5%	4.9%	13.21%	259987	20.99%	3.38%
F	9.22%	28.4%	43.77%	0.73%	1.73	23.1%	13.58%	13.37%	36.1%	3.1%	12.74%	269808	19.72%	3.02%
G	9.01%	29.1%	39.83%	0.68%	1.66	25.5%	11.47%	9.52%	39.9%	2.9%	13.09%	270002	21.03%	3.96%
H	8.69%	31.0%	40.17%	1.01%	1.59	24.9%	12.06%	12.22%	40.8%	3.7%	13.11%	268147	20.76%	3.55%

4.2. E-SPA Result

4.2.1. Entropy Weight of Indices

The authors constructed the evaluation matrix and matrix standardization with Equations (2) and (3). They then used Equations (4)–(6) to deal with the standardization data in Tables 4 and 5. The results of entropy weights of indices are shown in Table 6. The corresponding calculation process in this research could be seen in the Supplementary Materials.

Table 5. Adaptability data of vulnerability of CEIC.

	Innovation Input capability			Cooperation Innovation Capability			Intellectual Property Capability			Innovation Change Capability			Innovation Environment	
	$IICA_1$	$IICA_2$	$IICA_3$	$CICEA_1$	$CICEA_2$	$CICEA_3$	$IPCA_1$	$IPCA_2$	$IPCA_3$	$CICA_1$	$CICA_2$	$CICA_3$	$IEGS_2$	$IESS_2$
A	9.15%	3.31%	11.35%	44.19%	0.139	21.84%	0.231	993	13.9%	52.99%	10%	27.0%	36.9%	6.8%
B	10.27%	1.49%	10.98%	42.97%	0.152	21.55%	0.301	899	15.3%	53.73%	9.77%	26.3%	40.3%	10.7%
C	8.96%	2.99%	11.77%	43.58%	0.144	24.31%	0.240	967	15.1%	52.92%	9.31%	27.9%	39.6%	8.9%
D	9.39%	4.01%	11.09%	45.76%	0.098	17.67%	0.229	952	14.7%	53.88%	10.34%	25.4%	43.3%	9.7%
E	7.29%	4.21%	12.03%	44.62%	0.101	18.23%	0.206	1007	13.6%	51.64%	9.69%	25.9%	39.8%	9.5%
F	8.98%	3.13%	10.84%	40.88%	0.127	19.71%	0.200	981	14.2%	53.01%	10.51%	27.3%	38.1%	8.4%
G	9.37%	3.47%	9.96%	41.47%	0.130	16.89%	0.236	1017	13.7%	52.68%	9.98%	28.5%	39.9%	10.6%
H	9.59%	3.00%	10.38%	43.51%	0.136	19.01%	0.219	977	15.0%	53.03%	10.01%	27.2%	40.4%	10.9%

4.2.2. Identification of Vulnerability

The author constructed the assessment matrix using Equation (8) with indices data to generate the similarity and opposition degrees. In step 1, the authors identified the maximum data set U and minimum data set V as shown in Table 7.

In step 2, the authors used the Equations (9a) and (9b) to generate the similarity a_{kp} and opposition degree c_{kp} in the d_{kp} of Equation (8).

In step 3, the authors used Equation (10) to deal with index weight, the similarity a_{kp}, and opposition degree c_{kp}. The calculations generated the similarity a and opposition degree c of vulnerability of enterprise innovation capability in Table 8. The authors used Equation (11), the similarity a, and opposition degree c to calculate the vulnerability indicator X in Table 8.

In step 4, the authors used the analogy process to deal with sensitivity and adaptability data respectively, the similarity a, opposition degree c, and vulnerability indicator X of enterprise' sensitivity. The data of adaptability of innovation capability were also generated as shown in Table 8.

Table 6. Entropy weight and PCA weight of indices.

Index	IICS₁	IICS₂	IICS₃	CICES₁	CICES₂	CICES₃	IPCS₁	IPCS₂	IPCS₃	CICS₁	CICS₂	CICS₃	IEGS₁	IESS₁
Entropy Weig	0.0432038	0.049067048	0.035248156	0.03877084	0.053206164	0.040532366	0.028819682	0.038867465	0.029726585	0.030631336	0.024660397	0.047492491	0.039519158	0.04478313
PCA Weig	0.106823571	0.01461821	0.027886806	0.047262562	0.003170126	0.265283625	0.185939536	0.185937161	0.163610376	0.125805123	0.185006011	0.108780112	0.048122622	0.278513069

Index	IICA₁	IICA₂	IICA₃	CICEA₁	CICEA₂	CICEA₃	IPCA₁	IPCA₂	IPCA₃	CICA₁	CICA₂	CICA₃	IEGS₂	IESS₂
Entropy Weig	0.02301168	0.025365134	0.032359383	0.033075712	0.041265951	0.037907817	0.033785378	0.026661727	0.048286338	0.026045051	0.028806943	0.033478911	0.024799668	0.04062169
PCA Weig	0.090782332	0.185267733	0.014451584	0.036046266	0.219449805	0.185363984	0.185020389	0.099616493	0.174176412	0.005760201	0.261574165	0.136289993	0.005362125	0.110553235

Table 7. The max data set U and min data set V.

V	0.0922	0.31	0.4422	0.0068	0.99	0.257	0.1358	0.1482	0.455	0.058	0.1455	270002	0.1972	0.0297
U	0.0798	0.273	0.3729	0.015	1.73	0.228	0.1147	0.0952	0.326	0.029	0.1054	254396	0.2662	0.0405
Sign.	−1	−1	−1	1	1	1	−1	−1	−1	−1	−1	−1	1	1
V	0.0729	0.0149	0.0996	0.4088	0.152	0.1689	0.2	899	0.136	0.5164	0.0931	0.285	0.433	0.109
U	0.1027	0.0421	0.1203	0.4576	0.098	0.2431	0.301	1017	0.153	0.5388	0.1051	0.254	0.369	0.068
Sign.	1	1	1	1	−1	1	1	1	1	1	1	−1	−1	−1

Table 8. a, c and X of vulnerability framework of CEIC.

		Sensitivity			Adaptability			Vulnerability		
		a_s	c_s	X_s	a_a	c_a	X_a	a_v	c_v	X_V
A	E-SPA	0.498155954	0.89206403	0.50453205	0.512365605	0.477439407	0.517642969	0.504628	0.4838469	0.5105117
	P-SPA	0.491235713	0.492601156	0.499306062	0.45408915	0.556627269	0.449274536	0.471400152	0.526789897	0.47225491
B	E-SPA	0.503231366	0.487123778	0.508132228	0.482450401	0.515158926	0.483606546	0.4937662	0.499893	0.4969171
	P-SPA	0.459289356	0.541436498	0.458956221	0.595191645	0.39944844	0.598399013	0.531858619	0.465617555	0.533204334
C	E-SPA	0.481693552	0.503798343	0.488784894	0.499736677	0.488092023	0.505894066	0.4899117	0.4966446	0.4965877
	P-SPA	0.487313981	0.504576976	0.491297937	0.49295145	0.525135707	0.484193761	0.490324286	0.515554954	0.487458401
D	E-SPA	0.503713135	0.491682509	0.506043138	0.512686689	0.481130567	0.51587622	0.5078003	0.4868764	0.510518
	P-SPA	0.546644712	0.443842588	0.551894721	0.424835683	0.568083583	0.427865284	0.48160099	0.51018494	0.485589657
E	E-SPA	0.471534032	0.520072564	0.475525308	0.503390354	0.492286234	0.505576168	0.4860437	0.5074167	0.4892431
	P-SPA	0.441540415	0.547433388	0.446463207	0.372700497	0.615243849	0.377248474	0.404781199	0.5836429	0.409521783
F	E-SPA	0.487024256	0.507239244	0.48983419	0.491055936	0.496107288	0.497441481	0.4888606	0.502169	0.4932856
	P-SPA	0.544361307	0.451137158	0.546822849	0.409052674	0.601814228	0.404655324	0.47210905	0.531595876	0.470366378
G	E-SPA	0.511031793	0.485367578	0.512874879	0.477164652	0.513768697	0.481530521	0.4956063	0.4983035	0.4986431
	P-SPA	0.572003164	0.424703054	0.573893444	0.364723594	0.642851229	0.361981647	0.461319784	0.54119007	0.460164838
H	E-SPA	0.493845236	0.491114037	0.501386452	0.480387508	0.508383974	0.485842803	0.4877156	0.49898	0.4942919
	P-SPA	0.493941132	0.491211171	0.501385553	0.413605743	0.605142191	0.405994191	0.451043552	0.552048191	0.449653339

Note: (a) a_s, c_s and X_s refer to the similarity, opposition and vulnerability in the single sensitivity system of CEIC. (b) a_a, c_a and X_a refer to the similarity, opposition and vulnerability in the single adaptability system of CEIC. (c) a_v, c_v and X_V refer to the similarity, opposition and vulnerability in the whole vulnerability system of CEIC.

According to Table 9, the comparison of X_v indicates that companies A and D had the most vulnerability and company F had the least vulnerability of CEIC. At the same time, the ranking of vulnerabilities of CEIC in the eight companies was E, F, H, C, B, G, A and D, in an ascending order. By comparing the X_s of sensitivity, it was found that G, B, D are the three most sensitive companies. E is the least sensitive. By comparing the X_a of adaptability, it was found that A, D and C are the three most adaptable companies. E is the least adaptable.

Therefore, the less sensitive a company is, the better the vulnerability of their CEIC is managed. The more sensitive and adaptable they are, the more likely it is that vulnerability of their CEIC is increased. For the sustainable development of CEIC, it is a pertinent practical solution to manage and reduce sensitivity and promote adaptability. Not only should attention be given to adaptability, sensitivity is important to address in examining the linkage between innovation capability and vulnerability factors.

4.3. P-SPA Result and Validation

Using Equation (14), the weights of indices of the PCA method were generated as shown in Table 6. Further, the authors used the weight indices of PCA method to alternate the entropy weight in Equation (8) in order to calculate the vulnerability of CEIC. The results are shown in Table 8.

Following the steps in Section 3.2, the authors extracted the six principal components from F1 to F6 and their variances (%) in Table 9 to build Equation (15). The weighted sum scores of Fs are shown in Equation (15).

$$Fs = (0.30251 f_1 + 0.25894 f_2 + 0.18625 f_3 + 0.10871 f_4 + 0.07236 f_5 + 0.05256 f_6)/0.98133 \quad (15)$$

Table 9. Total variance explained of original questionnaire.

Component	Initial Eigenvalues			Extraction Sums of Squared Loadings		
	Total	% of Variance	Cumulative %	Total	% of Variance	total %
1	8.470	30.251	30.251	8.470	30.251	30.251
2	7.250	25.894	56.145	7.250	25.894	56.145
3	5.215	18.625	74.770	5.215	18.625	74.770
4	3.044	10.871	85.641	3.044	10.871	85.641
5	2.026	7.236	92.877	2.026	7.236	92.877
6	1.472	5.256	98.133	1.472	5.256	98.133
7	0.523	1.867	100.000			

Extraction Method: Principal Component Analysis.

Using PCA and SPA (P-SPA) methods, the authors found that company B had the greatest vulnerability X_v and company E had the least vulnerability X_v of CEIC. At the same time, the companies with the ascending vulnerability X_v of CEIC were E, H, G, F, A, D, C and B.

With the results of P-SPA method in Tables 7 and 8 through comparing the X_s and X_a of sensitivity and adaptability, the authors found that companies E and F both had lower vulnerability X_v, lower sensitivity, and higher adaptability correspondingly. The calculation results of P-SPA validate the vulnerability system discussed in Section 4.2. While companies A and D both had higher vulnerability X_v, the higher sensitivity X_s and lower adaptability X_a correspondingly. The findings help to develop CEIC by promoting adaptability and managing sensitivity simultaneously.

4.4. Vulnerability Grade

The authors used Zhao's grade standard [97] to calculate indicators for the SPA method. The calculation of the SPA classic grade method is shown in the following three evaluation conditions.

If $\max[a, b, c] = b$, it is grade 2; If $\max[a, b, c] = a$, and $a + b \geqslant 0.7$, it is grade 1, otherwise it is grade 2; If $\max[a, b, c] = c$, and $b + c \geqslant 0.7$, it is grade 3, otherwise it is grade 2.

Grade 1 indicates that the vulnerability of innovation capability is high. A company needs to reduce risk in the system and manage its CEIC. Grade 2 indicates that the vulnerability is satisfactory. A company needs to be more active in managing the uncertainty of its innovation capability. Grade 3 indicates that the vulnerability is low. It is recommended to continue current operations to maintain innovation capability.

The calculations of the vulnerability grades of both the E-SPA and P-SPA methods are based on Equation (7) and Table 8, with further comparison shown in Table 10. The samples are at level 2 from the calculations of both the E-SPA method and P-SPA method. These companies were in a good position to manage risk or uncertainty of innovation capability. The results show that the P-SPA method effectively validates the E-SPA method to assess the vulnerability and its grade of CEIC.

Table 10. The vulnerability grade of innovation capability.

Code	A	B	C	D	E	F	G	H
E-SPA method	2	2	2	2	2	2	2	2
P-SPA validation	2	2	2	2	2	2	2	2

4.5. Response with Major Influencing Factors

The vulnerability X_v of CEIC comes from the combined effects of sensitivity and adaptability. The authors constructed a vulnerability matrix of CEIC using the horizontal axis with low and high sensitivity and the vertical axis with low and high adaptability. The high sensitivity and low adaptability interval is an ideal area for CEIC. It shows an effective path to improve the adaptability and management or to reduce sensitivity. With low sensitivity and high adaptability, it helps to reduce the vulnerability of CEIC. Thus, an innovation strategy might look for the major influencing factors and compose a targeted solution to improve the adaptability of CEIC to maintain this sustainable path. This research used the major impact index formula [14,20,102] to generate and compare the impact extent of the adaptable indices, which are shown in Equation (16) and Table 11.

$$A_i = \omega_i d_i / \sum_{i=1}^{n} \omega_i d_i \times 100\% \quad (16)$$

A_i represents the impact extents of indices. ω_i represents the entropy weight of an index. d_i represents the standardization value of an index. n represents the index number in the adaptability system of CEIC. This research used $Ai \geqslant 5\%$ [14,20,102] to evaluate the extent of impacts of indices and compared their frequencies. The indices were then placed in descending order of their frequencies. The top frequencies were the major influencing factors of the adaptability system in the vulnerability of CEIC.

Table 11. Major influence factors in the adaptability system.

	$IICA_1$	$IICA_2$	$IICA_3$	$CICEA_1$	$CICEA_2$	$CICEA_3$	$IPCA_1$	$IPCA_2$	$IPCA_3$	$CICA_1$	$CICA_2$	$CICA_3$	$IEGS_2$	$IESS_2$
A	5.4254	6.4111	8.208	8.4744	3.7526	9.5526	3.9171	8.0228	3.2187	5.9293	6.2568	6.1192	9.3678	15.344
B	9.9312	0	6.8815	6.1135	0	10.274	14.580	0	20.8391	10.487	4.7657	10.253	5.017	0.8552
C	5.2773	5.7243	11.578	7.4888	2.5018	15.512	5.4755	6.2874	17.435	6.0904	0	2.6517	5.8671	8.1089
D	5.6946	8.2524	6.2032	11.615	14.491	1.3994	3.4066	4.2053	10.971	9.1461	8.6829	11.756	0	4.1751
E	0	11.532	14.713	11.525	17.720	3.1127	0.9126	11.095	0	0	4.1477	12.766	6.1665	6.3067
F	6.104	7.1534	6.4344	0	8.9359	6.7386	0	8.666	7.9712	7.4507	13.474	6.0616	9.4247	11.585
G	11.374	13.076	0	2.832	11.906	0	8.5283	18.881	2.0115	8.5637	11.390	0	9.3303	2.105
H	8.8239	6.996	3.262	8.8562	6.0746	5.381	3.1576	8.7559	19.756	8.0296	8.3486	6.9752	5.583	0
Freq.	7	7	6	6	5	5	3	6	5	7	5	6	7	4
Freq.%	0.875	0.875	0.75	0.75	0.625	0.625	0.375	0.75	0.625	0.875	0.625	0.75	0.875	0.5

The largest frequency (0.875%) indices in the adaptability system of CEIC were $IICA_1$, $IICA_2$, $CICA_1$ and $IEGS_2$. Table 11 also shows that the major influencing factors (0.875%) for CEIC mainly focus on (a) investment, especially R&D expenditure and the proportion of highly educated employees [103]; (b) innovation and change, especially the impact of new service or innovation activities on the market [78]; (c) government support, for example, large program support and taxation exemptions for application of certain innovation technologies [3,56,60,104–106].

The second-tier factors (0.75%) are IICA$_3$, CICEA$_1$, IPCA$_2$ and CICA$_3$. They emphasize the key roles of HR investment and innovation in change, referring to the amount of HR of R&D institutions and the management of corporate energy consumption. In addition, cooperative innovation of enterprise and IP capability played major roles in sustainable CEIC, such as the enterprise investment in university–industry cooperative innovation and the size of enterprise patent pools [69,84,107].

However, much attention should be given to output performance of IP capability (IPCA$_1$, 0.375%) to promote IP marketing and to solve IP transformation problems [108,109]. The lack of social capital [3,110] support given to corporate total capital (IESS$_2$, 0.5%) also leads to inadequate investment in CEIC.

4.6. Discussion

As discussed in this paper, CEIC is vulnerable, and this vulnerability can be measured. The researchers applied and confirmed a quantitative system approach to address the vulnerability of an enterprise's innovation efforts. Vulnerability research, as a new paradigm of sustainable development, uncertainty and risk, sheds light on how to best analyze the uncertainty of innovation capability. As an innovative method, SPA focuses on uncertainty and is widely applied in the economic and social fields [11,12,18,26,111–114], and is combined with some common comprehensive methods, such as E-SPA and P-SPA [44,100–102]. Innovation capability is an important driver of economic development and is closely linked to uncertainty and risk. However, within the new paradigm of reducing uncertainty, very little research exists to develop a systematic approach to assessing the vulnerability of innovation capability [22,23].

In order to extend a generic model of construction innovation [71,76], this new vulnerability framework of CEIC focuses on the extent of innovation investment, IP capability, cooperative innovation, change innovation and the overall environment to foster companies' innovation. Further, this research used the corresponding index in the 2013 National Innovation Survey System of MOST, China to match and test the proposed framework (see also Section 2.4) of the vulnerability system of CEIC, which contained two subsystems referred to as the sensitivity and adaptability of a systematic approach and includes the above five criteria and 28 indicators.

Meanwhile, this paper applied the E-SPA as the main method to analyze the case data to evaluate levels of vulnerability, comparing the results of P-SPA to confirm the empirical results. The authors used the E-SPA and P-SPA measurements regarding the vulnerability and uncertainty of innovation capability and quantitatively bridged the gap in system assessments of vulnerability of CEIC. More importantly, this research justified the necessity for a new approach to examining construction innovation uncertainty and built a foundation for overcoming construction innovation uncertainty, with a view to provide a basis for further research on this topic.

For two subsystems of CEIC, sensitivity referred to the ability of the system to withstand external or internal interferences or pressures. The less the sensitivity, the greater a system's resilience, and vice versa. Adaptability refers to the ability to respond to change which embodies an uncertain state or crisis situations. In other words, the greater the adaptability of a company, the stronger will be the ability of a company to respond to those challenges, and vice versa.

In this research, case studies showed that the sustainable CEIC needed to increase the innovation investment capability such as to enhance HR funding for highly skilled or talented individuals and R&D expenditure for individuals that show the greatest potential for innovation. Much attention seems to be given to the collaboration innovation between universities and research institutions, with the objective to impact business and marketing strategies that already demonstrate a high level performance of intellectual property, which could increase social recognition and capital support, in order to obtain more government assistance [104,115–118]. Thus, at the policy planning or strategic levels, positive industrial and corporate environments may lead to an optimization of an enterprise's innovation efforts and may attract sustainable government support. Furthermore, well established policy and strategic planning may encourage investment in corporate innovation. Topics for further research may include how to implement a practical strategy and operation of a market-oriented university–industry cooperative innovation approach, and how to strengthen and improve the innovation performance of intellectual property capabilities.

5. Conclusions

This study discussed the vulnerability framework of CEIC, and attempts to quantify an evaluation system for CEIC. It opened doors to future research in the theory and application areas in this field. This study proposed a new systematic approach to supplement the quantitative framework and methods in examining the uncertainty regarding a company's ability to innovate applied to the case of construction enterprises. Uncertainty regarding CEIC should not simply be ignored. Rather, it should be managed intelligently and, in an ideal world, help to develop an environment conducive to ongoing innovation. Vulnerability, and the management thereof, is a new domain in the large field of socioeconomic research. This research built a vulnerability framework for CEIC, which examines the subsystems of sensitivity and adaptability and a number of factors including innovation investment capability, cooperation innovation capability, intellectual property capability, change innovation capability, and innovation environment. Further, this research assessed the vulnerability of CEIC, using the comparative results of E-SPA and P-SPA methods for confirmation. It analyzed the major influencing factors in promoting sustainable CEIC.

Case studies showed that the two comparative methods confirm the same grade level of vulnerability of CEIC. We identified a stronger practical approach to reduce the vulnerability of CEIC by managing or reducing sensitivity and strengthening adaptability to respond to new economic environments. The major influencing factors of CEIC are focused on (a) the highly educated HR innovation team, (b) R&D investment intensity, (c) substantial market-led corporate–university–industry cooperation on intellectual property performance, (d) government support and social capital support, and (e) change innovation in construction energy consumption.

In summary, this research provided a theoretical framework and an application method to assess and evaluate both the vulnerability and uncertainty involved in innovation. This research can be implemented to evaluate and grade the vulnerability of CEIC at national, industrial or enterprise levels with the corresponding sequential data and indices. A limitation of this research may result due to the sequential data boundary, *i.e.*, at industrial or national levels, in conducting a systematic analysis to conceptualize innovation capability. A possible future research project may be to expand the dynamic data collection to analyze the vulnerability of construction innovation at both the macro and industrial levels.

Supplementary Materials: Supplementary Materials: Supplementary can be found at www.mdpi.com/2071-1050/8/1/17/s1.

Acknowledgments: Acknowledgments: This research is supported by the National Nature Science Foundation of China (NO.71301013), Humanity and Social Science Program Foundation of Ministry of Education of China (NO.13YJA790150), China ASC Fund (NO. asc-kt2014022 and asc-kt2014023), China scholarship council, Shaanxi Nature Science Fund (NO.2014JM2-7140), Shaanxi Social Science Fund (NO.2014HQ10, NO. 2015Z071 and NO. 2015Z075), Xi'an Science Technology Burea Fund(NO.CXY1512(2)), and Special Fund for Basic Scientific Research of Central College (Humanities and Social Sciences), Chang'an University (NO.0009-2014 G 6285048 and NO. 310828155031).

Author Contributions: Author Contributions: Prof. Zhang and Prof. Li analyzed the data and contributed to drafting the paper. Prof. Zhang and Prof. Li contributed to the concept and design of the paper. Prof. Xie and Prof. Schmidt contributed useful advice and modified the paper. Prof. Zhang is in charge of the final version of the paper.

Conflicts of Interest: Conflicts of Interest: The authors declare no conflict of interest.

Abbreviations

The following abbreviations are used in this manuscript:

CEIC: Construction enterprises' innovation capabilities
E-SPA: The entropy and set pair analysis method
P-SPA: The principle cluster analysis and SPA method
R&D: Research and development
UNCTAD: United Nations Conference on Trade and Development
UNDP: United Nations Development Programme
OECD: Organization for Economic Co-operation and Development
OECD STI: OECD Science, Technology and Innovation
MOST, China: Ministry of Science and Technology of the People´s Republic of China

References

1. Akintoye, A.; Goulding, J.; Zawdie, G. *Construction Innovation and Process Improvement*; Wiley-Blackwell: Hoboken, NJ, USA, 2012.
2. Brochner, J. Construction contractors as service innovators. *Build. Res. Inf.* **2010**, *38*, 235–246. [CrossRef]
3. Castro-Lacouture, D.; Irizarry, J.; Ashuri, B.; American Society of Civil Engineers; Construction Institute. Construction research congress 2014 construction in a global network. In Proceedings of the 2014 Construction Research Congress, Atlanta, GA, USA, 19–21 May 2014; American Society of Civil Engineers: Reston, VA, USA, 2014.
4. Forbes, L.H.; Ahmed, S.M.; Ebooks Corporation. Modern construction lean project delivery and integrated practices. In *Industrial Innovation Series*; CRC Press: Boca Raton, FL, USA, 2011.
5. Goh, B.; Tjoa, A.; Xu, L.; Chaudhry, S. Intelligent enterprises for construction: Bridging the technology and knowledge gaps through innovation and education. *Res. Pract. Issues Enterp. Inf. Syst.* **2006**, *205*, 119–131.
6. Blayse, A.M.; Manley, K. Key influences on construction innovation. *Constr. Innov.* **2004**, *4*, 143–154. [CrossRef]
7. Suprun, E.V.; Stewart, R.A. Construction innovation diffusion in the Russian Federation. *Constr. Innov.* **2015**, *3*, 278–312. [CrossRef]
8. Kulatunga, U.; Amaratunga, R.; Haigh, R. Construction Innovation: A Literature Review on Current Research. 2006. Available online: http://usir.salford.ac.uk/9886/1/205_Kulatunga_KJ_et_al_CONSTRUCTION_INNOVATION_A_LITERATURE_REVIEW_ON_CURRENT_RESEARCH_2006.pdf (accessed on 21 December 2015).
9. Hultgren, A.; Tantawi, A. *Front-End Idea Screening of Potential Radical Innovation in Large Firms: A Holistic Framework for the Volvo Group*; Chalmers University of Technology: Göteborg, Sweden, 2014.
10. Baker, S.M. Vulnerability and resilience in natural disasters: A marketing and public policy perspective. *J. Public Policy Mark.* **2009**, *28*, 114–123. [CrossRef]
11. Le Breton-Miller, I.; Miller, D. The paradox of resource vulnerability: Considerations for organizational curatorship. *Strat. Manag. J.* **2015**, *36*, 397–415. [CrossRef]
12. Dabla-Norris, E.; Gündüz, B.Y. Exogenous shocks and growth crises in low-income countries: A vulnerability index. *World Dev.* **2014**, *59*, 360–378. [CrossRef]
13. Dass, M.; Kumar, P.; Peev, P.P. Brand vulnerability to product assortments and prices. *J. Mark. Manag.* **2013**, *29*, 735–754. [CrossRef]
14. Li, F.; Wan, N.Q.; Shi, B.L.; Liu, X.M.; Guo, Z.J. The vulnerability measure of tourism industry based on the perspective of "environment-structure" integration a case study of 31 provinces in mainland China. *Geogr. Res.* **2014**, *33*, 569–581.
15. Herceg, I.; Nesti, D. A new cluster-based financial vulnerability indicator and its application to household stress testing in Croatia. *Emerg. Markets Finance Trade* **2014**, *50*, 60–77.
16. Holand, I.S.; Lujala, P.; Rød, J.K. Social vulnerability assessment for Norway: A quantitative approach. *Nor. J. Geogr.* **2011**, *65*, 1–17. [CrossRef]
17. Rodríguez-Núñez, E.; García-Palomares, J.C. Measuring the vulnerability of public transport networks. *J. Transp. Geogr.* **2014**, *35*, 50–63. [CrossRef]

18. Rossignol, N.; Delvenne, P.; Turcanu, C. Rethinking vulnerability analysis and governance with emphasis on a participatory approach. *Risk Anal. Int. J.* **2015**, *35*, 129–141. [CrossRef] [PubMed]
19. Springer, N.P.; Garbach, K.; Guillozet, K.; Haden, V.R.; Hedao, P.; Hollander, A.D.; Huber, P.R.; Ingersoll, C.; Langner, M.; Lipari, G.; et al. Sustainable sourcing of global agricultural raw materials: Assessing gaps in key impact and vulnerability issues and indicators. *PLoS ONE* **2015**, *10*, 1–22. [CrossRef] [PubMed]
20. Hong, T.; Jian, Z. Regional vulnerability evaluation index system of environmental emergencies in petrochemical industry. *Adv. Mater. Res.* **2014**, *1073–1076*, 400–404.
21. Turner, B.L.; Kasperson, R.E.; Matson, P.A.; McCarthy, J.J.; Corell, R.W.; Christensen, L.; Eckley, N.; Kasperson, J.X.; Luers, A.; Martello, M.L.; et al. A framework for vulnerability analysis in sustainability science. *PNAS* **2003**, *100*, 8074–8079. [CrossRef] [PubMed]
22. Dassen-Housen, P. Management of uncertainty—A contradiction in itself? In *Enabling Innovation: Innovative Capability—German and International Views*; Jeschke, S., Isenhardt, I., Hees, F., Trantow, S., Eds.; Springer-Verlag: Berlin, Germany, 2011; pp. 30–33.
23. Trantow, S.; Hees, F.; Jeschke, S. Innovative capability. In *Enabling Innovation: Innovative Capability —German and International Views*; Jeschke, S., Isenhardt, I., Hees, F., Trantow, S., Eds.; Springer-Verlag: Berlin, Germany, 2011; pp. 1–13.
24. Costanza, R.; d'Arge, R.; Groot, R.D.; Farber, S.; Grasso, M.; Hannon, B.; Limburg, K.; Naeem, S.; O'Neill, R.V.; Paruelo, J.; et al. The value of ecosystem services: putting the issues in perspective. *Ecol. Econ.* **1998**, *25*, 67–72. [CrossRef]
25. Gnangnon, S.K. Does structural economic vulnerability matter for public indebtedness in developing countries? *J. Econ. Stud.* **2014**, *41*, 644–671. [CrossRef]
26. Pérez Agúndez, J.A.; Yimam, E.; Raux, P.; Rey-Valette, H.; Girard, S. Modeling economic vulnerability: As applied to microbiological contamination on the Thau Lagoon shellfish farming industry. *Mar. Policy* **2014**, *46*, 143–151. [CrossRef]
27. Ransbotham, S.; Mitra, S.; Ramsey, J. Are markets for vulnerabilities effective? *MIS Q.* **2012**, *36*, 43–64.
28. Bell, M.; Pavitt, K. Technological accumulation and industrial growth: Contrasts between developed and developing countries. *Ind. Corp. Change* **1993**, *2*, 157. [CrossRef]
29. Pavitt, K. What we know about the strategic management of technology. *Calif. Manag. Rev.* **1990**, *32*, 17–26. [CrossRef]
30. Freeman, C. The 'national system of innovation' in historical perspective. *Camb. J. Econ.* **1995**, *19*, 5–24.
31. OECD. *Proposed Guidelines for Collecting and Interpreting Technological Innovation Data: Oslo Manual*; OECD Publication Services: Paris, France, 1997.
32. Böhle, F. Management of uncertainty–A blind spot in the promotion of innovations. In *Enabling Innovation–German and International Views*, 1st ed.; Al, S.J.E., Ed.; Springer-Verlag: Berlin, Germany, 2011; pp. 17–29.
33. Dominitz, J.; Manski, C.F. *Perceptions of Economic Vulnerability: First Evidence from the Survey of Economic Expectations/Jeff Dominitz and Charles f. Manski*; Institute for Research on Poverty, University of Wisconsin-Madison: Madison, WI, USA, 1995.
34. Berry, P.M.; Rounsevell, M.D.A.; Harrison, P.A.; Audsley, E. Assessing the vulnerability of agricultural land use and species to climate change and the role of policy in facilitating adaptation. *Environ. Sci. Policy* **2006**, *9*, 189–204. [CrossRef]
35. UNDP. *Human Development Report 1999*; Oxford University Press: Oxford, UK, 1999.
36. Erol, O.; Sauser, B.; Mansouri, M. A framework for investigation into extended enterprise resilience. *Enterp. Inf. Syst.* **2010**, *4*, 111–136. [CrossRef]
37. Prewitt, K. The federal statistical system: Its vulnerability matters more than you think—Section four: Strengthening the statistical system: Future of innovation in the federal statistical system. 2010. Available online: https://us.sagepub.com/en-us/nam/the-federal-statistical-system-its-vulnerability-matters-more-than-you-think/book235999 (accessed on 22 December 2015).
38. Han, R.; Tong, L.; Tong, W.; Yu, J. Research on vulnerability assessment of human-land system of Anshan city based on set pair analysis. *Progr. Geogr.* **2012**, *31*, 344–351.
39. Reed, M.S.; Podesta, G.; Fazey, I.; Geeson, N.; Hessel, R.; Hubacek, K.; Letson, D.; Nainggolan, D.; Prell, C.; Rickenbach, M.G.; et al. Surveys: Combining analytical frameworks to assess livelihood vulnerability to climate change and analyse adaptation options. *Ecol. Econ.* **2013**, *94*, 66–77. [CrossRef] [PubMed]

40. Aldana-Bobadilla, E.; Kuri-Morales, A. A clustering method based on the maximum entropy principle. *Entropy* **2015**, *17*, 151–180. [CrossRef]
41. Benedetto, F.; Giunta, G.; Mastroeni, L. A maximum entropy method to assess the predictability of financial and commodity prices. *Dig. Signal Process.* **2015**, *46*, 19–31. [CrossRef]
42. Zou, Q.; Zhou, J.Z.; Zhou, C.; Song, L.X.; Guo, J. Comprehensive flood risk assessment based on set pair analysis-variable fuzzy sets model and fuzzy AHP. *Stochast. Environ. Res. Risk Assess.* **2013**, *27*, 525–546. [CrossRef]
43. Xia, C.; Yi, M.; Wei, W.; Yu, Z. Discussion of annual runoff dry-wet classification based on set pair analysis. *Yangze River* **2015**, *46*, 21–24.
44. Su, M.R.; Yang, Z.F.; Chen, B. Set pair analysis for urban ecosystem health assessment based on emergy-vitality index. *China Environ. Sci.* **2009**, *29*, 892–896.
45. Meng, X.M.; Hu, H.P. Application of set pair analysis model based on entropy weight to comprehensive evaluation of water quality. *J. Hydraul. Eng.* **2009**, *40*, 257–262.
46. Sun, B.; Wang, H. Inventory Evaluation Model and Application of Shipbuilding Enterprise Based on the Method of Optimal Combination. *Int. J. U- E-Serv. Sci. Technol.* **2015**, *8*, 175–184. [CrossRef]
47. Li, B.; Yang, Z.; Su, F. Measurement of vulnerability in human-sea economic system based on set pair analysis: A case study of Dalian city. *Geogr. Res.* **2015**, *34*, 967–976.
48. Gobble, M.M. The 2009 European innovation scoreboard: EU lags us & Japan while China closing gap with EU. *Res. Technol. Manag.* **2010**, *53*, 2–4.
49. OECD. OECD Science, Technology and Industry Outlook 2014. Available online: http://dx.doi.org.libproxy.lib.ilstu.edu/10.1787/sti_outlook-2014-en (accessed on 21 December 2015).
50. Gupta, P.; Trusko, B.E. *The Innovation Radar and enterprise Business System: Innovation in Five Nordic Countries and Beyond*; McGraw-Hill Professional: New York, NY, USA, 2014.
51. UNCTAD. UNCTAD at 50: A short History. 2014. Available online: http://unctad.org/en/PublicationsLibrary/osg2014d1_en.pdf (accessed on 23 December 2015).
52. Bank, W. *World Development Indicators 2010*; World Bank: Washington, DC, USA, 2010; p. xxiii.
53. Azubuike, V.M.U. Technological innovation capability and firm's performance in new product development. *Commun. IIMA* **2013**, *13*, 43–55.
54. Carcary, M.; Doherty, E.; Thornley, C. Business innovation and differentiation: Maturing the IT capability. *IT Prof.* **2015**, *17*, 46–53. [CrossRef]
55. Daqi, X.U. Research on improving the technological innovation capability of SMEs by university-industry collaboration. *J. Eng. Sci. Technol. Rev.* **2013**, *6*, 100–104.
56. Fagerberg, J.; Feldmany, M.P.; Srholec, M. Technological dynamics and social capability: US states and European Nations. *J. Econ. Geogr.* **2014**, *14*, 313–337. [CrossRef]
57. Hansen, U.E.; Ockwell, D. Learning and technological capability building in emerging economies: The case of the biomass power equipment industry in Malaysia. *Technovation* **2014**, *34*, 617–630. [CrossRef]
58. Tseng, C.-Y. Technological innovation capability, knowledge sourcing and collaborative innovation in Gulf Cooperation Council countries. *Innov. Manag. Policy Pract.* **2014**, *16*, 212–223.
59. Raymond, L.; St-Pierre, J.; Uwizeyemungu, S.; Dinh, T. Internationalization capabilities of SMEs: A comparative study of the manufacturing and industrial service sectors. *J. Int. Entrep.* **2014**, *12*, 230–253. [CrossRef]
60. Manseau, A.; Seaden, G. *Innovation in Construction: An International Review of Public Policies*; Spon Press: London, UK; New York, NY, USA, 2001.
61. Brooker, P.; Wilkinson, S. *Mediation in the Construction Industry: An International Review*; Routledge: London, UK, 2010.
62. Altenburger, R. Green product innovation: Values and networks in open innovation processes. In Proceedings of ISPIM Conferences, Dublin, Ireland, 8–11 June 2014.
63. Bindroo, V.; Mariadoss, B.J.; Pillai, R.G. Customer clusters as sources of innovation-based competitive advantage. *J. Int. Mark.* **2012**, *20*, 17–33. [CrossRef]
64. Chan, I.; Liu, A.; Fellows, R. Role of leadership in fostering an innovation climate in construction firms. *J. Manag. Eng.* **2014**. [CrossRef]
65. Elmualim, A.; Gilder, J. Bim: Innovation in design management, influence and challenges of implementation. *Archit. Eng. Design Manag.* **2014**, *10*, 183–199. [CrossRef]

66. Blindenbach-Driessen, F.; van den Ende, J. Innovation in project-based firms: The context dependency of success factors. *Res. Policy* **2006**, *35*, 545–561. [CrossRef]
67. Chen, L.; Marsden, J.R.; Zhang, Z. Theory and analysis of company-sponsored value co-creation. *J. Manag. Inf. Syst.* **2012**, *29*, 141–172. [CrossRef]
68. Gann, D.; Salter, A. Innovation in project-based, service-enhanced firms: The construction of complex products and systems. *Res. Policy* **2000**, *29*, 955–972. [CrossRef]
69. Iammarino, S.; Piva, M.; Vivarelli, M.; von Tunzelmann, N. Technological capabilities and patterns of innovative cooperation of firms in the UK regions. *Reg. Stud.* **2012**, *46*, 1283–1301. [CrossRef]
70. Leiringer, R.; Schweber, L. Managing multiple markets: Big firms and PFI. *Build. Res. Inf.* **2010**, *38*, 131–143. [CrossRef]
71. Sexton, M.; Barrett, P. Appropriate innovation in small construction firms. *Constr. Manag. Econ.* **2003**, *21*, 623–633. [CrossRef]
72. Kuo, Y. Technology readiness as moderator for construction company performance. *Ind. Manag. Data Syst.* **2013**, *113*, 558–572. [CrossRef]
73. Ruwanpura, J.; Mohamed, Y.; Lee, S. Construction research congress 2010: Innovation for reshaping construction practice. In Proceedings of the 2010 Construction Research Congress, Banff, AL, Canada, 8–10 May 2010.
74. Pellicer, E.; Correa, C.L.; Yepes, V.; Alarcón, L.F. Organizational improvement through standardization of the innovation process in construction firms. *Eng. Manag. J.* **2012**, *24*, 40–53. [CrossRef]
75. Pryke, S.; Ebooks Corporation. Construction supply chain management concepts and case studies. In *Innovation in the Built Environment*; Wiley-Blackwell: Chichester, UK; Malden, MA, USA, 2009.
76. Barrett, P.; Sexton, M.; Lee, A. *Innovation in small Construction Firms*; Taylor & Francis: London, UK; New York, NY, USA, 2008; p. 107.
77. Patanakul, P.; Pinto, J.K. Examining the roles of government policy on innovation. *High Technol. Manag. Res.* **2014**, *25*, 97–107. [CrossRef]
78. Chesbrough, H.W.; Appleyard, M.M. Open innovation and strategy. *Calif. Manag. Rev.* **2007**, *50*, 57–76. [CrossRef]
79. Wu, I.-L.; Chiu, M.-L. Organizational applications of it innovation and firm's competitive performance: A resource-based view and the innovation diffusion approach. *J. Eng. Technol. Manag.* **2015**, *35*, 25–44. [CrossRef]
80. Kamasak, R. Determinants of innovation performance: A resource-based study. *Procedia-Soc. Behav. Sci.* **2015**, *195*, 1330–1337. [CrossRef]
81. Han, J.-W.; Lim, H.-S. Strategic analysis and success factors of the enterprises through the convergence. *Int. J. Appl. Eng. Res.* **2014**, *9*, 15715–15726.
82. Lusch, R.F.; Nambisan, S. Service innovation: A service-dominant logic perspective. *MIS Q.* **2015**, *39*, 155–176.
83. Palm, K. Understanding innovation as an approach to increasing customer value in the context of the public sector. 2014. Available online: https://www.diva-portal.org/smash/get/diva2:773180/FULLTEXT01.pdf (accessed on 21 December 2015).
84. Wu, J. Cooperation with competitors and product innovation: Moderating effects of technological capability and alliances with universities. *Ind. Mark. Manag.* **2014**, *43*, 199–209. [CrossRef]
85. Aalbers, R.; Dolfsma, W. *Innovation Networks: Managing the Networked Organization/Rick Aalbers and Wilfred Dolfsma*; Routledge: London, UK, 2015.
86. Cabanelas, P.; Omil, J.C.; Vázquez, X.H. A methodology for the construction of dynamic capabilities in industrial networks: The role of border agents. *Ind. Mark. Manag.* **2013**, *42*, 992–1003. [CrossRef]
87. Macaulay, L.A.; Miles, I.; Wilby, J.; Tan, Y.L.; Zhao, L.; Theodoulidis, B. *Case Studies in Service Innovation*; Springer: Berlin, Germany, 2012.
88. Anumba, C.J.; Egbu, C.O.; Carrillo, P.M. *Knowledge Management in Construction*; Blackwell Pub.: Oxford UK; Malden, MA, USA, 2005; xiv; p. 226.
89. Connaughton, J.; Meikle, J. The changing nature of UK construction professional service firms. *Build. Res. Inf.* **2013**, *41*, 95–109. [CrossRef]
90. Gabbott, M.; Hogg, G. Consumer involvement in services: A replication and extension. *J. Bus. Res.* **1999**, *46*, 159–166. [CrossRef]
91. Halpin, D.W.; Senior, B.A. *Construction Management*, 4th ed.; Wiley: Hoboken, NJ, USA, 2011; p. 448.

92. Giang, D.T.H.; Pheng, L.S. Role of construction in economic development: Review of key concepts in the past 40 years. *Habitat Int.* **2011**, *35*, 118–125. [CrossRef]
93. Kazi, A.S. *Knowledge Management in the Construction Industry: A Socio-Technical Perspective*; Idea Group Pub.: Hershey, PA, USA, 2005; p. 384.
94. Korman, T.M.; Huey-King, L. Industry input for construction engineering and management courses: Development of a building systems coordination exercise for construction engineering and management students. *Pract. Period. Struct. Design Constr.* **2014**, *19*, 68–72. [CrossRef]
95. McCarthy, J.F. *Construction Project Management*; Pareto–Building Improvement: Westchester, IL, USA, 2010; p. 432.
96. Chinese Academy of Science and Technology for Development. China National Innovation Index Report 2013. Available online: http://www.most.gov.cn/kjtj/201511/P020151117383919061369.pdf (accessed on 21 December 2015).
97. Zhao, K.; Xuan, A. Set pair theory-a new theory method of non-define and its applications. *Syst. Eng.* **1996**, *14*, 14–26.
98. Xing, W.; Ye, X.; Kui, L. Measuring convergence of China's ICT industry: An input–output analysis. *Telecommun. Policy* **2011**, *35*, 301–313. [CrossRef]
99. Bereziński, P.; Jasiul, B.; Szpyrka, M. An entropy-based network anomaly detection method. *Entropy* **2015**, *17*, 2367–2408. [CrossRef]
100. Faed, A.; Chang, E.; Saberi, M.; Hussain, O.K.; Azadeh, A. Intelligent customer complaint handling utilising principal component and data envelopment analysis (PDA). *Appl. Soft Comput. J.* **2015**. [CrossRef]
101. Dong, X.; Guo, J.; Höök, M.; Pi, G. Sustainability assessment of the natural gas industry in China using principal component analysis. *Sustainability* **2015**, *7*, 6102–6118. [CrossRef]
102. Chen, J.; Yang, X.; Wang, Z.; Zhang, L. Vulnerability and influence mechanisms of rural tourism socio-ecological systems: A household survey in China's Qinling mountain area. *Tour. Trib.* **2015**, *30*, 64–75.
103. Likar, B.; Kopa, J.; Fatur, P. Innovation investment and economic performance in transition economies: Evidence from Slovenia. *Innov. Manag. Policy Pract.* **2014**, *16*, 53–66. [CrossRef]
104. Hemphill, T.A. Policy debate: The US advanced manufacturing initiative: Will it be implemented as an innovation—Or industrial—Policy? *Innov. Manag. Policy Pract.* **2014**, *16*, 67–70. [CrossRef]
105. Cabrilo, S.; Grubic-Nesic, L. Ic-Based Innovation Gap Assessment: A Support Tool for the Creation of Effective Innovation Strategies in the Knowledge Era. In Proceedings of the 4th European Conference on Intellectual Capital, Helsinki, Finland, 23–24 April 2012.
106. Martinez, M.G. Co-creation of value by open innovation: Unlocking new sources of competitive advantage. *Agribusiness* **2014**, *30*, 132–147. [CrossRef]
107. Hsieh, M.; Wu, C.; Ting, P.; Lin, T. A study on project partner's alignment process and value innovation. *Mark. Rev.* **2013**, *10*, 345–370.
108. Reitzig, M.; Puranam, P. Value appropriation as an organizational capability: The case of IP protection through patents. *Strat. Manag. J.* **2009**, *30*, 765–789. [CrossRef]
109. Giannopoulou, E.; YstrÖM, A.; Ollila, S. Turning open innovation into practice: Open innovation research through the lens of managers. *Int. J. Innov. Manag.* **2011**, *15*, 505–524. [CrossRef]
110. Roy, M.; Donaldson, C.; Baker, R.; Kerr, S. The potential of social enterprise to enhance health and well-being: A model and systematic review. *Soc. Sci. Med.* **2014**, *123*, 182–193. [CrossRef] [PubMed]
111. Bolanos, A.B. External Vulnerabilities and Economic Integration: Is the Union of South American Nations a Promising Project? *J. Econ. Dev.* **2014**, *39*, 97–131.
112. Culpepper, P.D.; Reinke, R. Structural power and bank bailouts in the United Kingdom and the United States. *Polit. Soc.* **2014**, *42*, 427–454. [CrossRef]
113. Murphy, E.; Scott, M. Household vulnerability in rural areas: Results of an index applied during a housing crash, economic crisis and under austerity conditions. *Geoforum* **2014**, *51*, 75–86. [CrossRef]
114. Ala, M.U. A firm-level analysis of the vulnerability of the Bangladeshi pharmaceutical industry to the trips agreement: Implications for R&D capability and technology transfer. *Proced. Econ. Finance* **2013**, *5*, 30–39.
115. Tomes, A. UK government science policy: The 'enterprise deficit' fallacy. *Technovation* **2003**, *23*, 785–792. [CrossRef]

116. Al-Sudairi, M.; Bakry, S.H. Knowledge issues in the global innovation index: Assessment of the State of Saudi Arabia versus countries with distinct development. *Innov. Manag. Policy Pract.* **2014**, *16*, 176–183. [CrossRef]
117. Kiskiene, A. Scientific knowledge and technology transfer policy in the EU. *Econ. Bus.* **2014**, *26*, 36–43. [CrossRef]
118. Ljungquist, U. Unbalanced dynamic capabilities as obstacles of organizational efficiency: Implementation issues in innovative technology adoption. *Innov. Manag. Policy Pract.* **2014**, *16*, 82–95. [CrossRef]

© 2015 by the authors. Licensee MDPI, Basel, Switzerland. This article is an open access article distributed under the terms and conditions of the Creative Commons Attribution (CC BY) license (http://creativecommons.org/licenses/by/4.0/).

Article

Research on Consumers' Use Willingness and Opinions of Electric Vehicle Sharing: An Empirical Study in Shanghai

Ning Wang * and Runlin Yan

School of Automotive Studies, Tongji University, Shanghai 201804, China; woaiwojia13147@163.com
* Correspondence: wangning@tongji.edu.cn; Tel.: +86-21-6958-3874

Academic Editor: Adam Jabłoński
Received: 19 October 2015; Accepted: 17 December 2015; Published: 23 December 2015

Abstract: An empirical study in Shanghai was performed to explore consumers' use willingness and opinions on electric vehicle sharing (EVS) to help operators effectively operate and expand the new business model. Through the multinomial logistic regression developed for different groups, the results show that the factors of the main trip mode in daily use, monthly transportation expenditure, driving range of electric vehicles, gender, age, marital status and occupation have significant influences on consumers' use willingness. In short, the population characteristics of people choosing to use EVS are male, aged between 18 and 30 and usually taking the subway and bus as the daily transportation modes. Otherwise, the factors of the acceptable highest price of EVS, occupation and personal monthly income have significant impacts on the use willingness of people who keep a neutral stance. These people pay more attention to convenience and the economy of EVS. These results reveal that a reasonable price, accurate positioning of target groups, convenient site layout and usage are required for operators to successfully launch a new transportation mode of EVS.

Keywords: electric vehicle sharing; multinomial logistic regression; survey; use willingness

1. Introduction

Research indicates that electric vehicles are not only able to decrease vehicle emissions [1] and slow global warming [2], but also are able to enhance the sustainability of road traffic in the future [3]. With energy, environment and other issues becoming increasingly prominent, many countries began to realize the importance of environmentally-friendly electric vehicles. Most manufacturers also have started to develop and commercialize environmentally-friendly electric vehicles [4]. However, electric vehicles are currently limited by insufficient charging infrastructures and driving mileage (the longest driving range per battery charge). Considering that car sharing is more suitable for people's short-term travel demands, the combination of electric vehicles and car sharing is a good way to avoid these weaknesses and to provide a cleaner transport mode.

Certain cities in the world, such as Barcelona, Paris, Berlin, Hamburg, Rotterdam and Stockholm, are implementing electric vehicle sharing (EVS) [5]. In China, EVS is still in the initial development phase. China Car Club in Hangzhou and Eduoauto in Beijing are the pioneers for developing EVS. China Car Club was invested in by Intunecapital in early 2013, and it is based on the model of self-purchasing cars. Eduoauto is based on the model of light assets, and the operational vehicles are mainly provided by enterprises qualified for car rental, not bought by the company itself. eHi Car Services launched a pilot EVS program in Jading district of Shanghai in June 2013, but the progress is very slow. At present, there are several EVS services, such as EVCARD hosted by Shanghai International Automobile City, YiKaZuChe in Beijing, Weigongjiao in Hangzhou, *etc.*

In recent years, governments have begun to attach more importance to EVS, which contributed to the rapid development of EVS. In July 2014, the General Office of the State Council in China released the No. 35 document of "Instructions on accelerating the promotion and application of new energy vehicles" [6], which emphasized the needs of "exploring innovative business models, such as the time-sharing leasing, car sharing, vehicle leasing, mortgage purchase for new energy vehicles, *etc.*". The EVS program also has received support from the local governments. The Beijing Municipal Science and Technology Commission has listed EVS as a key supported project and set up many operational indicators. Other cities, such as Shanghai, Hangzhou, Shaoxing, Ningbo, Wuhan, Shenzhen, Yancheng, Chongqing, and so on, have launched or are actively ready to launch an EVS program.

From the analysis above, it can be known that the number of EVS enterprises operating is few, and most of them lack experience. With the support from the government, there will be more and more domestic companies involved in EVS in the next few foreseeable years. Nevertheless, how consumers think about EVS, whether they will use the service and their related preference are still unclear. Therefore, in order to promote all-round development of EVS and to help the enterprises achieve better operation, a questionnaire was designed to collect information about the acceptance of consumers and influencing factors for using EVS. Some suggestions are provided for EVS operators to promote its rapid development in China.

2. Literature Review

In the late 1980s, a preliminary model of car sharing appeared abroad. However, scholars started to research car sharing in the 1990s. At the beginning of the research, most studies were at the qualitative level, and scholars paid more attention to the feasibility of the car sharing model and consumer usage. Based on a large number of empirical studies, Meijkamp [7] in The Netherlands pointed out that car sharing as an alternative to private cars, because it had higher economic and ecological efficiency. Barth and Shaheen [8] had an opinion that car sharing could improve the traffic efficiency by reducing the number of private cars and improve the efficiency of energy and emissions. They also introduced a variety of car sharing systems and described the development prospect of car sharing in China. Prettenthaler and Steininger [9] researched how driving mileage influenced the car sharing users to make decisions. Results showed that using car sharing was better than using private cars when user's travel range was less than 18,000 km per year. However, if insurance and the vehicle depreciation rate are taken into account, the balanced driving distance of users decreased to 15,000 km. Seik [10] studied car sharing in Singapore and found that members still mainly used public transport for travelling to work after attaining membership, but turned more often to shared cars rather than public transport for marginal uses, such as leisure and social trips. Most of them chose car sharing for its marginal use and cost savings.

Entering the 21st century, foreign scholars gradually began to study the operation system of car sharing, the optimization of staff, site layout, vehicle allocation, *etc.*, from the quantitative perspective. Barth and Todd [11] used a computer to simulate the distribution of available vehicles and energy consumption in car sharing sites. Results showed that the influencing factors of the car sharing system were the proportion of demand, the charging strategy for the electric vehicles and the vehicle allocation algorithm. The main problems of the car sharing service that should be considered at the beginning of the establishment were service pricing, target customer selection, vehicle type selection, site location, *etc.* [12]. Xu and Lim [13] established a mathematical model for the vehicles sharing site layout in Singapore and used the improved neural network model to predict the car sharing net flows. Kek *et al.* [14] provided a three-stage decision optimization model for the car sharing operator. They analyzed the optimal distribution of staff and vehicles and used operational data from the Singapore sharing company to verify the model. Correia and Antunes [15] had studied the problem of car sharing site planning. Under the goal of maximizing the profit for the car sharing operating company, they established a mixed integer programming model to solve the unbalanced number of sharing cars between different sites.

At present, there are few research works on EVS abroad, and most of them focus on operating status analysis and consumer surveys. Quantitative studies on EVS are rare. Alessandro et al. [16] introduced the EVS project of Green Move and studied the shared service strategies and objectives. By investigating the feasibility of EVS as a private car for elderly, Shaheen et al. [17] found that 30% of respondents were interested in participating, but all participants would make a plan before they would use the car, indicating that EVS still has the range anxiety problem. This problem is caused by the limited driving range of electric vehicles. Using data from 533 members of the EVS program in Seoul, Kim et al. [18] found that the participants were rather reluctant to change their car ownership, but had intensions to continue participating in the program. Social and economic perspectives were the most important factors affecting the participants' attitudes. In addition, the attitudes varied depending on personal characteristics, such as gender, age and income.

Domestic research progress on the car sharing model is relatively late. In 2000, Huang and Yang [19] were the first to research car sharing and introduced its development history abroad. They summarized the benefits of this new public transport pattern, the impact on travel behavior and its possible target market (people who have no private cars or have a high cost of ownership). Market demand, quality of service and advanced public transportation are important factors for successful car sharing. Ye and Yang [20] summarized and introduced the concept, development status and influence of car sharing. They also explained its characteristics (low-cost, flexible) and target group (replacement selection for people who wanted to buy a second car). Gao [21] explained the concept of "shared car" in detail and presented the concept of "Auto Club". Its development prospect in China was also studied. Qiu [22] analyzed the key influencing factors for car sharing development in China. Results showed that educational level of respondents, number of owned private cars and convenience of EVS had impacts on consumers' use willingness. Xue et al. [23] combed the classification of car sharing and analyzed the impact of this service on car ownership, travel cost, usage cost, energy savings and emission reduction. Through an empirical study, they found that the target group of car sharing was people who are 25–40 years old and have an above average educational level. The model of Zipcar in the United States was studied by Wu [24]. He investigated the potential market of car sharing service in Guangzhou and demonstrated the significance of promoting car sharing. He pointed out that car sharing is very promising in China and will be an alternative to other means of transportation. By introducing the development of car sharing in Hanover, He [25] pointed out that a shared car could replace 6–10 private cars and radically reduce automobile usage. Xia et al. [26] had carried out empirical research on an informal car sharing service in Beijing from the perspective of economic and ecological efficiency. They suggested that the government should regulate such an industry and formulate relevant policies to support the development of shared services.

From the analysis above, it is obvious that domestic research on EVS is very small in quantity. More studies are focused on the operating model description, case analysis and the prospect forecast of traditional vehicle sharing. From the perspective of operators, a questionnaire was implemented in Shanghai to find factors affecting consumers' use willingness of electric vehicle sharing, including travel characteristics, expectation of EVS and socio-demographics and then proposed corresponding suggestions for station location, driving range choice and model selection for EVS. At the same time, the target group and potential market in Shanghai for using EVS were pointed out. This will help the operations of enterprises effectively.

3. Research Method

3.1. Questionnaire Design

The paper questionnaire was implemented and disseminated offline. Through this, we have learned comprehensive knowledge about EVS acceptance. Finally, the target population of EVS was pointed out by analysis.

The questionnaire was divided into three parts. The first part has three questions about travel characteristics, including main trip mode in daily use, factors considered when choosing the trip mode and monthly transportation expenditure. Based on a simple explanation of EVS, the second part was questions about the expectations of EVS, including the use willingness, the attractive point for the respondent, the suitable usage scenario, *etc*. The last part was personal information, including gender, age, occupation, educational level, marital status, personal monthly income, *etc*. The whole questionnaire was designed as shown in Table 1.

Table 1. The designed questionnaire for investigation. EVS, electric vehicle sharing.

	Variable	Description
Travel characteristics	Main trip mode in daily use	Subway, bus, private car, taxi, walking, bicycle, **motorcycle/scooter riders**
	Factors considered when choosing the trip mode	Time, expenditure, weather condition, degree of comfort, travel distance, travel purpose, body condition, others
	Monthly transportation expenditure	⩽100 yuan, 101–200 yuan, 201–300 yuan, 301–400 yuan, **⩾401 yuan**
Expectation of EVS	Whether to choose EVS	Will choose, keep neutral stance, **will not choose**
	Attractive points of using EVS	Convenient appointment, cost-effective, shorter distance, parking space saving, no overhead cost, others
	Suitable usage scenario of EVS	Work, school, shopping, entertainment, seeing a doctor, visiting relatives or friends, individual business, work business, others
	Suitable vehicle type for EVS	Mini car, small car, compact car, midsize car, medium and large size car, luxury car, SUV, MPV (multi-purpose vehicles), microvan
	Acceptable minimum driving range of EV	Not less than 50 km, not less than 80 km, not less than 120 km, not less than 150 km, not less than 200 km, not less than 250 km, not less than 300 km, **not less than 350 km**
	Acceptable maximum duration for going to stations	Time for walking is 5 min, time for walking is 10 min, **time for walking is 15 min**
	Acceptable maximum duration for waiting and handling procedure	5 min, 10 min, **15 min**
	Acceptable highest price of EVS	30 yuan/month + 60 yuan/h, 30 yuan/month + 40 yuan/h, **30 yuan/month + 20 yuan/h**
Socio-demographics	Gender	Male, female
	Age	Under 18, 18–25, 26–30, 31–40, 41–50, **above 50**
	Number of owned private cars	None, one, **not less than two**
	Marital status	Single, married, but have no child, **married and have kids**
	Educational level	Junior high school and the following: senior high school, junior college, Bachelor's, **Master's and above**
	Occupation	Party and government cadre/teacher/police, clerk, business owner/shareholder, *etc.*, technicist, worker/server, company management personnel, freelancer, **retired staff/student**
	Personal monthly income	Under 1000 yuan, 1000–3000 yuan, 3001–6000 yuan, 6001–10,000 yuan, 10,001–15,000 yuan, above 15,001 yuan, **no fixed income**

* The black bold items are reference categories used in the multinomial logistic regression model.

3.2. Data Collection

From May 2014–November 2014, 410 respondents participated in the survey. As is known to all, EVS is more convenient than bus, more predictable and accurate than taxi and more economical than private cars. For the above reasons, EVS will replace part of the public and private transportation in the future. Therefore, the investigation object should be universal to balance people with different characteristics. Choosing residents in Shanghai as the main investigation object, questionnaires were distributed randomly at railway stations, commercial shopping centers, bus stop waiting areas, public squares, university areas, and so on. According to the standard that the number of answers for one questionnaire should be not less than half, 394 effective questionnaires were received.

3.3. Model Formulation

In this paper, choice willingness for EVS ("will not choose" is coded as 1, "keeping neutral" as 2, "will choose" as 3) is the dependent variable, which is ordinal. Ordinal regression was used, and a test of the parallel lines was done to check whether the method was appropriate. According to the research of Zhang [27] and Li *et al.*, [28], when the value of P for the test of parallel lines is far less than 0.05, this indicates that the ordinal regression is not appropriate, and multinomial logistic regression should be used. As shown in Table 2, the value of significance (Sig.) is 0.001, which is far less than 0.05. Therefore, multinomial logistic regression is used in this paper, finally.

Table 2. Test of parallel lines.

Model	−2 Log Likelihood	Chi-Square	df	Sig.
Null Hypothesis	667.011			
General	579.259	87.751	51	0.001

The multinomial logistic regression model is often used to handle the case where the dependent variable has several classified categories (N > 2). During the process, the model will choose one category of dependent variable as the reference category to establish the general logits models. Furthermore, if the dependent variable Y is coded 0, 1 or 2 and using Y = 0 as the baseline, the probabilities of each dependent variable category [29] are:

$$P(Y=0) = \frac{1}{1 + e^{g_1(x)} + e^{g_2(x)}} \quad (1)$$

$$P(Y=1) = \frac{e^{g_1(x)}}{1 + e^{g_1(x)} + e^{g_2(x)}} \quad (2)$$

$$P(Y=2) = \frac{e^{g_2(x)}}{1 + e^{g_1(x)} + e^{g_2(x)}} \quad (3)$$

where:

$$g_1(x) = \text{logit} \frac{P(Y=1)}{P(Y=0)} = \beta_{10} + \beta_{11}x_1 + \ldots + \beta_{1p}x_p \quad (4)$$

$$g_2(x) = \text{logit} \frac{P(Y=2)}{P(Y=0)} = \beta_{20} + \beta_{21}x_1 + \ldots + \beta_{2p}x_p \quad (5)$$

where $\beta_{10}, \beta_{11}, \beta_{1p}, \ldots, \beta_{2p}$ are coefficients for the logistic regression model, which can be obtained by using SPSS software.

4. Analysis Results

4.1. Descriptive Statistics

4.1.1. Demographic Variable

Table 3 illustrates the demographic characteristics of respondents. As shown in Table 3, most respondents are male (61.6%), which is higher than the proportion of women. The main age groups are 20s and 30s, which should be the major groups for using EVS. Forty one-point-seven percent of respondents are single, and the percentage of married having kids is 37.6%. Fifty eight-point-six percent of people have private cars, and 7.9% of them even have two or more cars. Most respondents (68.3%) had a Bachelor's degree or above. The monthly income is mainly concentrated in 3001–10,000 yuan (49.1%), and more than 15,000 yuan or below 1000 yuan are the least, which accords with the research. The distribution of the occupation is relatively balanced overall. Ordinary staff and technical staff account for 20.2%, respectively.

Table 3. Descriptive statistics for the demographic characteristics of respondents.

Variable	Description	Percentage
Gender	Male	61.6%
	Female	38.4%
Age	Under 18	1.5%
	18–25	28.1%
	26–30	30%
	31–40	24.6%
	41–50	8.4%
	Above 50	5.4%
Number of owned private cars	None	41.4%
	One	50.7%
	Not less than two	7.9%
Marital status	Single	41.7%
	Married, but have no child	20.7%
	Married and have kids	37.6%
Educational level	Junior high school and the following:	3.6%
	Senior high school	10.2%
	Junior college	17.9%
	Bachelor's	49.1%
	Master's and above	19.2%
Occupation	Party and government cadre/teacher/police	7.2%
	Clerk	20.2%
	Business owner/shareholder, *etc.*	4.3%
	Technicist	20.2%
	Worker/server	5.4%
	Company management personnel	7.9%
	Freelancer	5.4%
	Retired staff/student	29.4%
Personal monthly income	Under 1000 yuan	5.3%
	1000–3000 yuan	18.5%
	3001–6000 yuan	26.6%
	6001–10,000 yuan	24.0%
	10,001–15,000 yuan	10.6%
	Above 15,001 yuan	6.6%
	No fixed income	8.4%

4.1.2. Travel Characteristics

As shown in Figure 1, 83.5% of percipients have a monthly transportation expenditure within 300 yuan. The percentage spending more than 400 yuan monthly is only 10.4%. In the aspect of factors considered when choosing the trip mode, most respondents consider time primarily. The secondary is travel purpose, and cost is the least considerable factor (Figure 2). The above result conforms to the normal situation that residents in big cities consider travel time, cost, convenience, safety and comfort when they choose the trip mode [30].

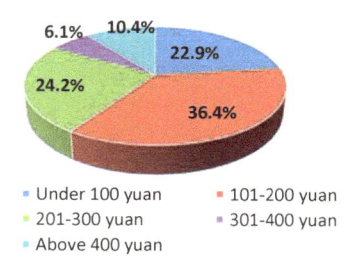

Figure 1. Distribution of monthly transportation expenditure.

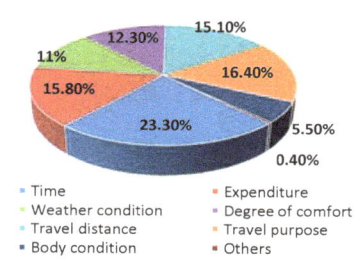

Figure 2. Factors considered when choosing the trip mode.

4.1.3. Expectations for EVS

With assistance from the investigators, respondents had preliminarily knowledge of EVS. The percentage of people who chose to use EVS is 42.4%. About 27% of people kept a neutral stance, which means quite a few people still maintain a wait-and-see attitude towards new things. This will be a customer resource to pursue during the development of EVS in the near future. The distribution of use willingness is shown as Figure 3.

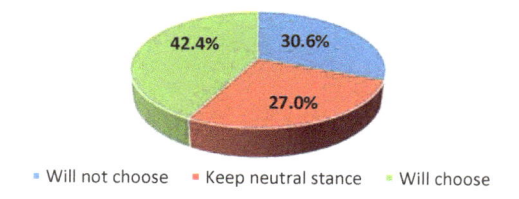

Figure 3. Whether to choose EVS.

When the respondents were asked about the attractiveness of EVS, their opinions were rather dispersed. More respondents selected the options of "the appointment and self-help picking cars are convenient and efficient", "it charges by hour and that is more cost-effective than renting for one day" and "it is more flexible than leasing and has no overhead costs" (as shown in Figure 4). It can be concluded that most consumers pay more attention to the convenience and economic benefits of the EVS service. Therefore, the service price should be as low as possible to offer consumers a chance to experience its economy and convenience, thus enlarging customer population.

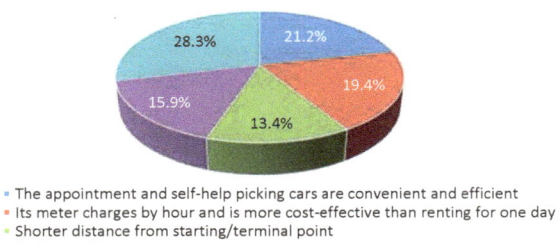

- The appointment and self-help picking cars are convenient and efficient
- Its meter charges by hour and is more cost-effective than renting for one day
- Shorter distance from starting/terminal point
- Saving parking space
- It is more flexible than leasing and has no overhead costs

Figure 4. Attractive points of using EVS.

When the respondents were asked about the suitable usage scenario of EVS, the two options that had the largest proportions are shopping and entertainment, with percentages of 22.1% and 23.8%, respectively (Figure 5). As a result, stations for EVS can be deployed around shopping malls, entertainment and leisure centers, so it can be convenient for users to rent and return vehicles.

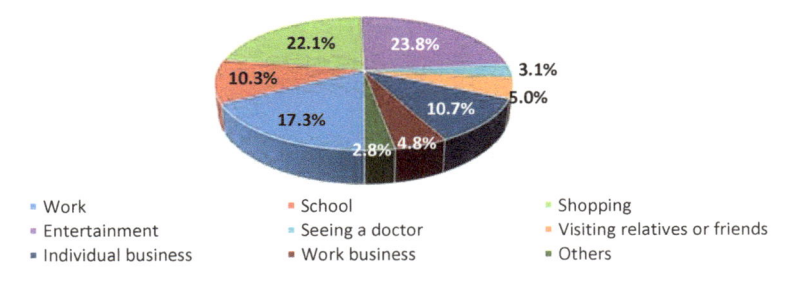

- Work
- Entertainment
- Individual business
- School
- Seeing a doctor
- Work business
- Shopping
- Visiting relatives or friends
- Others

Figure 5. Suitable usage scenario of EVS.

For the question of suitable vehicle type for EVS, respondents said that compact, small or mini cars would be more suitable. Cars of the A0 segment (small cars) accounted for the highest percentage of 27.2%. Respondents also preferred compact cars and mini cars (Figure 6). This also suggests that EVS is mainly used to meet people's needs for daily short-distance flexible transportation, and their demand for space is small.

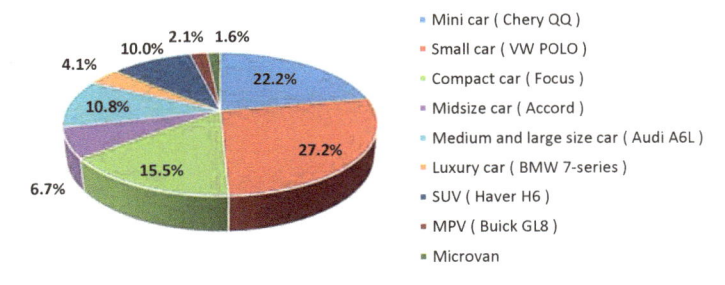

- Mini car (Chery QQ)
- Small car (VW POLO)
- Compact car (Focus)
- Midsize car (Accord)
- Medium and large size car (Audi A6L)
- Luxury car (BMW 7-series)
- SUV (Haver H6)
- MPV (Buick GL8)
- Microvan

Figure 6. Suitable vehicle types for EVS.

When asked about the acceptable minimum driving range of electric vehicles, 26.8% of respondents held the opinion that it should not be less than 150 km, as shown in Figure 7. The sum of percentages for "not less than 50 km", "not less than 80 km", "not less than 120 km" and "not less than 150 km" is 79.2%. A deep travel behavior investigation was done in 2014 with 67 residents in Shanghai. All travel behaviors were recorded for 14 days, including trip mode, time, distance, *etc.* The results show that the average travel distance for a single trip is 15.8 km, and the average daily travel range is 33.8 km, which is far lower than what the mainstream models on the market can offer. Another research work showed that when consumers were asked about the driving range for private electric vehicles, 35.8% of them responded that it should be between 120 km and 160 km [31]. Thus, it can be seen that most participants have higher tolerance towards the driving range of shared electric vehicles than private ones.

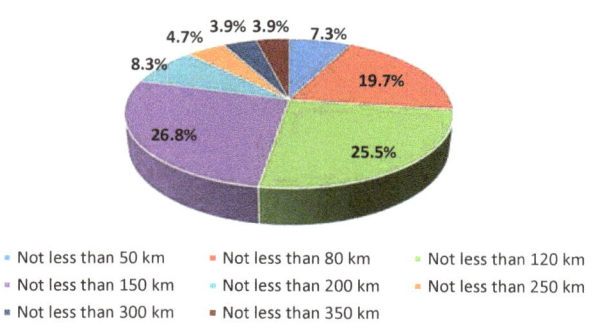

Figure 7. Acceptable minimum driving range of EV.

4.2. Statistics in Cross Tabulation Table

Figure 8 indicates that the number of owned private cars has an impact on the willingness to use EVS.

(1) With an increase in the number of owned private cars, the ratio of people who are willing to use the service shows a declining trend soon after rising. That is to say, the EVS acceptance of people in possession of only one private car is higher than that of people who do not have or have more than one private car. The reasons for this phenomenon may be that: (i) people in possession of private cars have more driving experience, and it is easier for them to accept a new transportation pattern; (ii) the EVS is a new type of transportation, and even the people who have a private car want to experience this new transportation system; (iii) because of severe traffic jams during rush hour, parking difficulty and high parking fees, a car owner is more willing to choose EVS as a method for short trips; (iv) the economic environment of people who have two or more private cars is better, and they tend not to consider whether the means of travel is economical. Compared to people who only have one car, reducing their usage willingness is also reasonable. At the same time, it also indicates that the target group of EVS is not only the people who have no private cars.

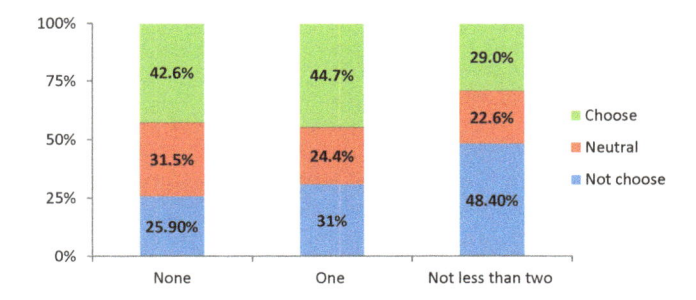

Figure 8. The relationship between willingness and the number of owned private cars.

(2) Along with the increase of owned private cars, people's attitude towards whether to adopt EVS becomes clearer. The ratio of keeping neutral decreases.

4.3. Multinomial Logistic Regression for the Target Group

In this paper, the dependent variable is the choice willingness for EVS ("will not choose" is coded as one, "keeping neutral" as two, "will choose" as three). In order to define the target group of EVS, multinomial logistic regression was used. Independent variables were selected from three aspects: (1) travel characteristics (including main trip mode in daily use and monthly transportation expenditure), (2) expectations for EVS (including acceptable minimum driving range of the EV, acceptable maximum duration for going to stations, acceptable maximum duration for the waiting and handling procedure and acceptable highest price of EVS) and (3) demographic characteristics (including gender, age, number of owned private cars, marital status, educational level, occupation and personal monthly income).

4.3.1. Model Fitting Test

SPSS20.0 was used to analyze the questionnaires, and Table 4 shows the likelihood ratio test for the final model and the intercept-only model. Here, the value of chi-squared is equal to the difference value between the −2 log likelihood in the intercept-only model and the final model. The significance level of the chi-squared test was 0.001, which is far less than 0.05. Therefore, the final model is superior to the intercept-only model, which means that the final model is established, and the fitting effect is significantly good. The indexes of Cox and Snell R-squares, Nagelkerke R-squared and McFadden R-squared were used to test the explainable degree of the equations on the variation of the explained variables. The bigger the R-squared is, the better the goodness of fit is. The value of these three indexes are 0.353, 0.400 and 0.204, and they indicate that independent variables can explain 35.3%, 40% and 20.4% of the variation of the explained variables. Although the three R-squared values are not very high, the result is acceptable.

Table 4. Model fitting information.

Model	Model Fitting Criteria	Likelihood Ratio Tests		R^2		
	−2 log likelihood	Chi-square	Sig.	Cox and Snell	Nagelkerke	McFadden
Intercept-only	762.673	-	-	-	-	-
Final	607.323	155.350	0.001	0.353	0.400	0.204

4.3.2. Coefficient Test of Variables

Table 5 shows the likelihood-ratio test in the final model for each independent variable. Through the statistical results, it can be seen that main trip mode in daily use, monthly transportation expenditure, acceptable minimum driving range of the EV, acceptable highest price of EVS, age and marital status have significant influences on the willingness to use EVS when the significance level is 0.1 [18]. People who usually take the subway or bus for daily transportation have a strong willingness to use EVS. People with a high monthly transportation expenditure are more likely to pursue the economical mode of EVS. Marital status often decides whether the respondents need to buy private cars, and this has a great impact on the decision to use the EVS service. The driving range of EV affects respondents' decisions of whether to choose the shared service instead of other modes of transportation. Respondents aged between 20 and 40 years old show a stronger receptivity to new things and the concept that they must have private cars is weaker. This makes them more willing to use the EVS service.

Table 5. Likelihood ratio test.

Effect	Model Fitting Criteria	Likelihood Ratio Tests	
	−2 log likelihood of reduced model	Chi-square	Sig.
Intercept	607.323 [a]	0.000	0.000
Main trip mode in daily use	632.206	24.883	0.015
Monthly transportation expenditure	631.696	24.373	0.002
Acceptable minimum driving range of EV	638.755	31.432	0.005
Acceptable maximum duration for going to stations	611.525	4.202	0.379
Acceptable maximum duration for waiting and handling procedure	612.404	5.081	0.279
Acceptable highest price of EVS	615.445	8.122	0.087
Gender	611.914	4.591	0.101
Age	633.589	26.266	0.003
Number of owned private cars	610.889	3.566	0.468
Marital status	624.302	16.979	0.002
Educational level	620.193	12.870	0.116
Occupation	624.859	17.536	0.229
Personal monthly income	621.654	14.331	0.280

[a] The ellipsis effect does not increase the degree of freedom. As a result, the simplified model is equal to the final model.

4.3.3. Parameter Estimation Results

Tables 5 and 6 show the parameter estimation results of different groups. The reference category for the dependent variable is choose not to use. The reference categories for the independent variables are in black bold, as shown in Table 1.

If the estimated coefficient of a factor (B) is significantly positive, then the probability of this factor belonging to the current category level is higher than the probability of it belonging to the reference category, with all of the other factors being fixed [32].

Estimated Model Results of the Choose to Use Group

As shown in Table 6, the factors of main trip mode in daily use, monthly transportation expenditure, driving range of electric vehicles, gender, age, marital status and occupation are statistically significant. The following is a detailed analysis of these results. (1) People who usually take the subway, bus or bike are more willing to use EVS. (2) With the increase of monthly transportation expenditure, its regression coefficient changes from negative to positive, which indicates that the higher the monthly transportation expenditure is, the more consumers prefer to choose EVS. (3) The driving range of electric vehicles has a significant influence on consumers' willingness to use EVS, with a negative coefficient. The absolute value of the coefficient increases as the driving range of electric vehicles increases, indicating that when the driving range of electric vehicles is higher, more consumers tend not to use EVS services. This result conflicts with previous expectations. The reasons may be that EVS is designed to provide a short commute for people, and the driving range of general electric vehicles has been able to meet that demand. The total cost of the operator increases as the driving range of electric vehicles increases, and then, the single use price for EVS may increase. For reasons of travel economy, consumers are more reluctant to use this business. It should be pointed out that the front reason is just guesswork; further research is required to give more information and to find out the cause. (4) Gender is significant to consumers' use willingness, with the probability ratio of male being 2.081-times higher than that of female. This means that males are more willing to use EVS than females. (5) Age has a significant influence on consumers' choices, and the coefficient is positive. The absolute value of the coefficient decreases as the age increases, which indicates that consumers' use willingness of EVS will be reduced as the age increases. People who are aged between 18 and 30 have the strongest use willingness. The reasons may be that this group is at the beginning of economic independence and usually pursue economic and effective ways to travel, and their receptivity to new modes of transportation is better. (6) Marital status is significant with a negative coefficient, indicating that the use willingness of unmarred people is lower than that of married people. This may controvert the former expectations. However, through the former analysis, the results can be obtained that people who own private cars have a stronger use willingness than people having no cars (that can be found in Figure 8). In this investigation, 73.2% of participants having private cars are married. Therefore, the use willingness of married people being higher than that of unmarried people is understandable. From the analysis above, the population characteristics of people choosing to use EVS are male, aged between 18 and 30, and usually taking the subway and bus as the daily transportation modes.

Table 6. Parameter estimation results: choose to use.

Independent Variables	B	Wald	Sig.	Exp(B)
Intercept	−2.283	1.437	0.231	
[Main trip mode in daily use = 1]: subway	1.705	2.870	0.090	5.499
[Main trip mode in daily use = 2]: bus	2.016	3.750	0.053	7.508
[Main trip mode in daily use = 6]: bicycle	3.226	7.190	0.007	25.173
[Monthly transportation expenditure = 1]: 0–100 yuan	−1.260	3.092	0.079	0.284
[Monthly transportation expenditure = 4]: 301–400 yuan	1.606	3.593	0.058	4.981
[Minimum driving range of EV = 4]: not less than 150 km	−1.882	3.523	0.061	0.152
[Minimum driving range of EV = 6]: not less than 250 km	−2.564	4.403	0.036	0.077
[Minimum driving range of EV = 7]: not less than 300 km	−4.939	12.600	0.000	0.007
[Gender = 1]: male	0.733	4.517	0.034	2.081
[Age = 2]: 18–25 years old	3.571	10.951	0.001	35.556
[Age = 3]: 26–30 years old	2.194	4.545	0.033	8.969
[Marital status = 1]: single	−2.289	11.271	0.001	0.101
[Occupation = 3]: business owner/shareholder, etc.	2.154	4.159	0.041	8.619

Estimated Model Results of the Choose to Remain Neutral Group

As shown in Table 7, the factors of acceptable highest price of EVS, occupation and personal monthly income have significant impacts on the use willingness of people who keep a neutral stance. The detailed analysis is as follows. (1) The acceptable highest price of EVS is significant to consumers' use willingness with a negative coefficient, indicating that the increasing service price could reduce consumers' willingness to use it. (2) Business owners/shareholders hold a neutral opinion about the EVS service. This may relate to their existing economic and social status, *etc.* These people have better living conditions, and they may not need this service to save money or improve travel conditions. (3) The probability of keeping neutral is higher than that of not choosing, which indicates that the exclusion effect of people with lower average monthly income for EVS is reduced. From the analysis above, people who keep a neutral stance have lower personal monthly income. If we want to encourage these people to change their existing attitude to use the EVS, a reasonable price should be offered to attract them to join in on the premise of guaranteeing profits.

Table 7. Parameter estimation results: choose to remain neutral.

Independent Variables	B	Wald	Sig.	Exp(B)
Intercept	−2.888	1.743	0.187	
[Acceptable highest price of EVS = 1]: 30 yuan/month + 60 yuan/h	−0.829	2.864	0.091	0.436
[Occupation = 3]: business owner/shareholder, *etc.*	1.887	2.924	0.087	6.598
[Personal monthly income = 1]: below 1000 yuan	2.348	4.402	0.036	10.463
[Personal monthly income = 2]: 1000–3000 yuan	1.767	4.051	0.044	5.854

Prediction for Use Proportion

As shown in Table 2, most respondents are male clerks aged 26–30 years old and have an average monthly income of 3001–6000 yuan. For a respondent having these features, the probability that he will choose, not choose and keep a neutral stance can be calculated by Equations (1)–(5) according to the multinomial logistic regression results.

$$g_1 = -2.283 + 0.733 + 2.194 + 1.169 = 1.758 \tag{6}$$

$$g_2 = -2.888 + 0.363 + 0.817 + 0.768 = 0.215 \tag{7}$$

$$P(Y = \text{will choose}) = \frac{e^{g_1}}{1 + e^{g_1} + e^{g_2}} = 0.721 \tag{8}$$

$$P(Y = \text{wil keep a neutral stance}) = \frac{e^{g_2}}{1 + e^{g_1} + e^{g_2}} = 0.154 \tag{9}$$

$$P(Y = \text{will not choose}) = \frac{1}{1 + e^{g_1} + e^{g_2}} = 0.125 \tag{10}$$

Therefore, the probability for a 26–30-year-old male clerk who has a personal monthly income of 3001–6000 yuan to use EVS is 72.1%.

According to the calculation method above, when other factors remain unchanged, the relationship between age and the use probability ratio of male clerks who have a 3001–6000 yuan monthly income can be obtained and is shown in Figure 9. It is possible to see that age has a great influence on personal decisions to use the EVS, which is consistent with the former analysis. People aged 18–30 are more likely to use EVS. When people's age is more than 30 years old, the probability of not choosing is bigger than that of choosing. Additionally, as the age increases, the probability of a neutral stance increases, and consumers are more reluctant to use EVS. Furthermore, the post-1990s generation in China is growing up, and their receptivity is better than other groups. They will be the major customers of EVS in the near future. Therefore, the market space for EVS business is huge. The suggestion is that the EVS service could aim at young people aged between 18 and 30 as their customers.

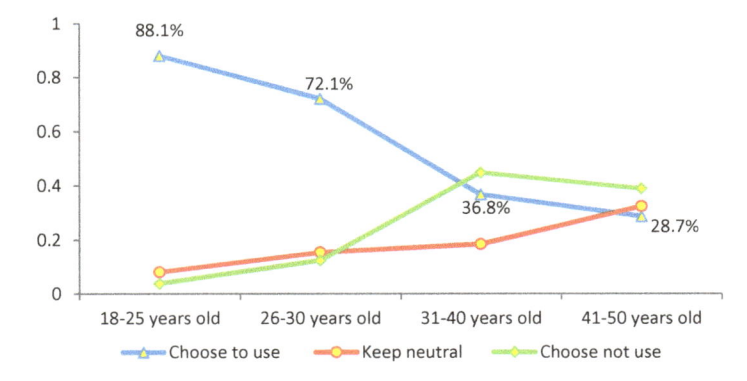

Figure 9. The relationship between age and the willingness to using EVS.

In a similar way, when other factors keep constant, the relationship between personal monthly income and the willingness to use EVS is shown as Figure 10. The following is the results. (1) Overall, with the increase of personal monthly income, the choice probability of individuals to use EVS decreases after rising first. When the personal monthly income is 3001–6000 yuan, the probability of choosing reaches the maximum of 72.1%. (2) When the personal monthly income is low, the probability of not choosing is high. The reason may be the relatively weak economic capacity of the low income group. When the monthly income is higher (more than 15,001 yuan), the probability of choosing is higher than that of not choosing. However, the value of the former is still below 50%, which indicates that the probability of not choosing for consumers with high monthly income (more than 15,001 yuan) is very big. This may be related to their social status, economic condition, *etc.* Therefore, EVS should be geared toward the needs of the main group at middle-income level.

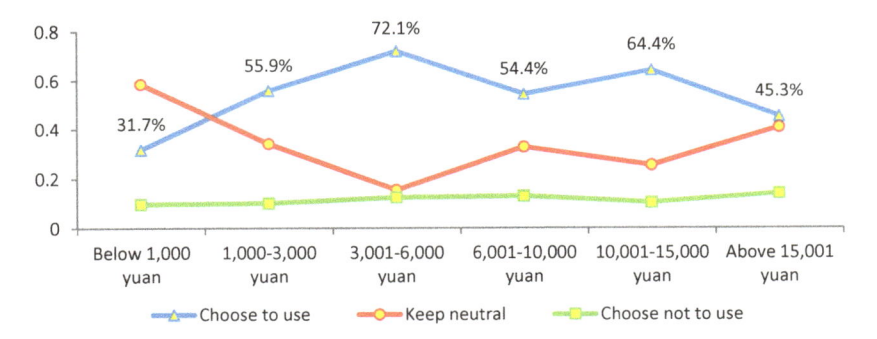

Figure 10. The relationship between monthly income and the willingness to use EVS.

5. Suggestions

In the operational aspect, the following suggestions are offered for the development of EVS.

(1) According to the regression analysis results (Tables 6 and 7), people who are male, aged between 18 and 30 and usually taking the subway and bus as the daily transportation mode are the target group for using EVS. Combined with the probability calculation (Figures 9 and 10), the suggestion is that operators should pay more attention to young people who are 18–30 years old and have a middle-level income.

(2) In the early development of EVS, the type of shared electric vehicles should give priority to compact, small or mini cars.

Car sharing is designed to satisfy people's short, temporary and flexible transportation demand. Most people will use it for shopping and entertainment (Figure 5), and they expect that the EVS would be economical (Figure 4). Most people who would like to use EVS are young, and their income is not very high (Figure 10). In order to decrease consumers' use-cost to show the economy of sharing and satisfy the need to carry certain items at the same time, the type of shared EV should focus on compact, small or mini cars. This can reduce the cost of operators and indirectly reduce the use-cost of shared cars. On the other hand, governments can offer certain subsidies to reduce the enterprises' pressure on operating funds in the early stage. This can promote the industrialization of electric vehicles and also improve the operational enterprises' enthusiasm.

(3) In the early developmental stage, the driving range of shared electric vehicles should reach 120 km.

More than half of the respondents (Figure 7) said the driving range of shared electric vehicles should reach 120 km at least, which indicates that most people hold tolerant attitudes towards the problem of driving range. However, there were more than a quarter of people who hoped that the driving range could reach 150 km. From regression the result in Table 6, it is indicated that the increasing driving range will decrease consumers' use willingness (the reason is stated in Section 4.3.3). Therefore, in the early stage of development, for reasons of cost, capital, *etc.*, it is recommended that the driving range of shared electric vehicles should reach 120 km.

(4) When laying out the sites, the walking time for consumers to stations should be controlled to be within 10 min.

Theoretically, the walking time for consumers to the stations should be as short as possible, which means more sites are needed. However, more sites mean large amounts of money for investment, and it is also likely to cause high operational and maintenance cost, a low utilization rate, *etc*. Therefore, a reasonable number and layout of sites are needed to improve vehicle utilization, reduce operating costs, and at the same time, meet consumers' need for the convenient usage of cars. According to Figures 11 and 12 92.5% of participants accept the walking time within 10 min. When the walking time increases from five to 10 min, the percentage of people who are willing to use EVS decreases by 4.7%, which is acceptable. Considering the cost and utilization rate, the suggestion is that the walking time for consumers to the station should be controlled to be within 10 min.

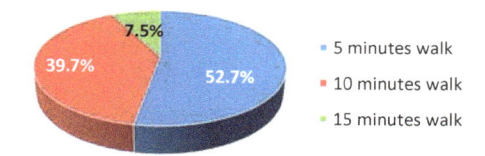

Figure 11. Acceptable maximum duration for going to stations (N = 385).

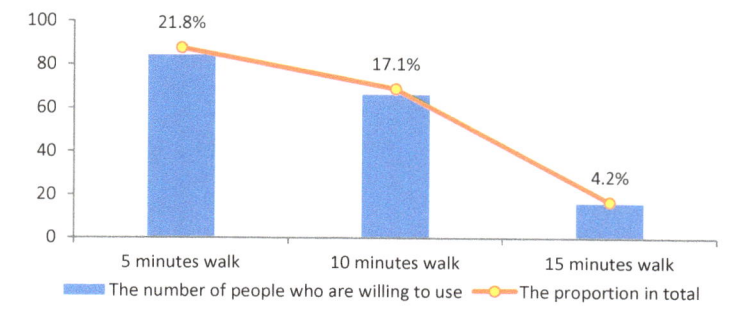

Figure 12. The relationship between time for going to stations and use willingness (N = 385).

(5) The waiting time for consumers to go through the formalities and pick up cars should be controlled within five minutes.

Convenient appointments and self-help picking up cars are some of the most attractive points that consumers think the EVS service should have. As shown in Figures 13 and 14 89.4% of participants can accept that the longest waiting time is within 10 min. However, when waiting time increases from five to 10 min, the percentage of people who are willing to use EVS decreases from 24% to 14%, which is a big decline. Therefore, services, such as picking up the cars or returning the cars, should be automatic and self-supported. The suggestion is that operators should open a variety of channels for customers to complete the procedures of booking, picking up cars, returning cars and paying the bill conveniently and effectively. These can help control the total waiting time to be within five minutes.

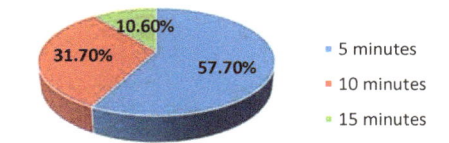

Figure 13. Acceptable maximum duration for the waiting and handling procedure (N = 385).

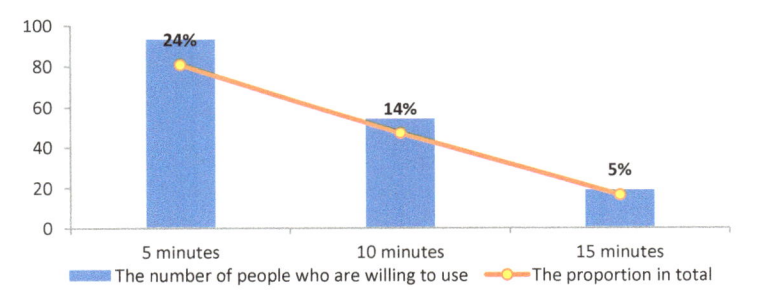

Figure 14. The relationship between waiting time and use willingness (N = 385).

6. Conclusions

In the early development of EVS, in order to achieve a good commercial operation, it is necessary to investigate with respect to the consumers the important influencing factors for the acceptance of EVS. Therefore, to solve these problems, a questionnaire was conducted in Shanghai. According to the results, relevant suggestions are offered to achieve a wide range promotion of EVS.

Through the multiple logistic regression analysis, the factors of the main trip mode in daily use, monthly transportation expenditure, acceptable minimum driving range of electric vehicles, gender, age, marital status and occupation have significant influences on the willingness to choose EVS. Males are more willing to use EVS than females. Younger people have a stronger receptivity to new things than the old. As age increases, the use willingness of consumers decreases. In short, the population characteristics of people choosing to use EVS are male, aged between 18 and 30 and usually taking the subway and bus as the daily transportation modes. Otherwise, the factors of acceptable highest price of EVS, occupation and personal monthly income have a significant impact on the use willingness of people who keep a neutral stance. The increase of service price will reduce the use willingness, and the exclusion effect of people with a low average monthly income is lower. As a result, if we want to encourage these people to change their existing attitude to use EVS, a reasonable price should be made to attract them to join on the premise of incurring no deficit. The probability for a 26–30 year-old male clerk who has a personal monthly income of 3001–6000 yuan in Shanghai to use EVS is as high as 72.1%, which indicates that the development prospect for EVS in Shanghai is good.

In the operational aspects, suggestions are provided for operators as follows. (1) The operators should pay more attention to people who are 18–30 years old and have a middle-level income. (2) In the early development of EVS, the electric vehicles used for sharing should be concentrated on compact, small or mini cars to achieve the aim of low-cost operation and good sharing economy. (3) The driving range of shared electric vehicles should not be less than 120 km to reduce consumers' range anxiety. (4) During the laying out of sites, a reasonable number of sites are necessary to guarantee that the walking time to stations is within 10 min for consumers. (5) Operators need to optimize the leasing system and implement automation and self-support as far as possible. This can help control the total waiting time to within five minutes.

Acknowledgments: Acknowledgments: The research has been funded under the China MOST project of Electric Car Sharing Technology Integration and Demonstration Operation (2015BAG11B00).

Author Contributions: Author Contributions: Ning Wang designed and performed this research. Runlin Yan analyzed the data and wrote this paper. All authors have read and approved the final manuscript.

Conflicts of Interest: Conflicts of Interest: The authors declare no conflict of interest.

References

1. Brady, J.; O'Mahony, M. Travel to work in Dublin. The potential impacts of electric vehicles on climate change and urban air quality. *Transp. Res. Part D* **2011**, *16*, 188–193. [CrossRef]
2. Hawkins, T.R.; Singh, B.; Majeau-Bettez, G.; Stromman, A.H. Comparative environmental life cycle assessment of conventional and electric vehicles. *J. Ind. Ecol.* **2013**, *17*, 53–64. [CrossRef]
3. Hanschke, C.B.; Uyterlinde, M.A.; Kroon, P.; Jeeninga, H.; Londo, H.M. Duurzame Innovatie in Het Wegverkeer. Available online: https://www.ecn.nl/docs/library/report/2008/e08076.pdf (accessed on 2 December 2015). (In Dutch)
4. Sierzchula, W.; Bakker, S.; Maat, K.; Van Wee, B. The competitive environment of electric vehicles: An analysis of prototype and production models. *Environ. Innov. Soc. Transit.* **2012**, *2*, 49–65. [CrossRef]
5. IEA (International Energy Agency). EV City Casebook. 2012. Available online: http://www.iea.org/publications/freepublications/publication/EVCityCasebook.pdf (accessed on 2 December 2015).
6. Instructions of the General Office of the State Council in China on Accelerating the Promotion and Application of New Energy Vehicles. Available online: http://www.gov.cn/zhengce/content/2014-07/21/content_8936.htm (accessed on 21 July 2014).
7. Meijkamp, R. Changing consumer behaviour through eco-efficient services: An empirical study of car sharing in the Netherlands. *Bus. Strateg. Environ.* **1998**, *7*, 234–244. [CrossRef]
8. Barth, M.; Shaheen, S.A. The Potential for Shared-Use Vehicle Systems in China. Available online: http://76.12.4.249/artman2/uploads/1/UCD-ITS-RR-03-11.pdf (accessed on 2 December 2015).
9. Prettenthaler, F.E.; Steininger, K.W. From ownership to service use lifestyle: The potential of car sharing. *Ecol. Econ.* **1999**, *28*, 443–453. [CrossRef]
10. Seik, T.F. Vehicle ownership restraints and car sharing in Singapore. *Habitat Int.* **2000**, *24*, 75–90. [CrossRef]
11. Barth, M.; Todd, M. Simulation model performance analysis of a multiple station shared vehicle system. *Transp. Res. Part C* **1999**, *7*, 237–259. [CrossRef]
12. Brook, D. Carsharing–Start Up Issues and New Operational Models. In Poceedings of the Transportation Research Board Annual Meeting, Chicago, IL, USA, 18–20 November 2004.
13. Xu, J.X.; Lim, J.S. A new evolutionary neural network for forecasting net flow of a car sharing system. In Proceedings of the Evolutionary Computation, Singapore, 25–28 September 2007.
14. Kek, A.G.; Cheu, R.L.; Meng, Q.; Fung, C.H. A decision support system for vehicle relocation operations in carsharing systems. *Transp. Res. Part E* **2009**, *45*, 149–158. [CrossRef]
15. Correia, G.H.; Antunes, A.P. Optimization approach to depot location and trip selection in one-way carsharing systems. *Transp. Res. Part E* **2012**, *48*, 233–247. [CrossRef]
16. Luè, A.; Colorni, A.; Nocerino, R.; Paruscio, V. Green move: An innovative electric vehicle-sharing system. *Procedia Soc. Behav. Sci.* **2012**, *48*, 2978–2987. [CrossRef]

17. Shaheen, S.; Cano, L.; Camel, M. Exploring Electric Vehicle Carsharing as a Mobility Option for Older Adults: A Case Study of a Senior Adult Community in the San Francisco Bay Area. *Int. J. Sustain. Transp.* **2015**. [CrossRef]
18. Kim, D.; Ko, J.; Park, Y. Factors affecting electric vehicle sharing program participants' attitudes about car ownership and program participation. *Transp. Res. Part D* **2015**, *36*, 96–106. [CrossRef]
19. Huang, Z.Y.; Yang, D.Y. The development of car sharing abroad. *Urban Plan. Forum* **2000**, *6*, 50–55.
20. Ye, L.; Yang, D.Y. The development and applied research on car sharing and mobile management in China. In Proceedings of the China's Sustainable Development Forum, Shandong, China, 2010; Available online: http://cpfd.cnki.com.cn/Article/CPFDTOTAL-ZKZC201010001051.htm (accessed on 2 December 2015).
21. Gao, Y.M. Car Sharing—A new model of automobile consumption. *Traffic Trans.* **2005**, *4*, 39–40.
22. Qiu, L. Market prospects and marketing research on car sharing service in China's. Master's Thesis, Fudan University, Shanghai, China, 2009.
23. Xue, Y.; Yang, T.Y.; Wen, S.B. Social Characteristics and Development Models of Car Sharing. *Techno-econ. Manag. Res.* **2008**, *1*, 54–58.
24. Wu, W.D. Research on car sharing pattern and analysis on its development in Chinese market. Master's Thesis, Zhongshan University, Guangzhou, China, 2010.
25. Jing, H. The green traffic of car sharing in Hanover. *Traffic Trans.* **2005**, *6*, 13.
26. Kaixuan, X.; Mingsheng, H.; Hua, Z. The economic and ecological efficiency of car sharing service and the feasibility to implement the service in Beijing. *China Soft Sc.* **2006**, *12*, 64–70.
27. Zhang, W.T. *Advanced Courses for SPSS Statistical Analysis*; Higher Education Press: Beijing, China, 2004; pp. 189–203. (In Chinese)
28. Li, K.; Guo, Z.; Hu, L.; Xu, Y. Analysis method for ordered categorical data of cumulative score model. *Chin. J. Health Stat.* **1993**, *4*, 35–38.
29. Hosmer, D.W.; Lemeshow, S. *Applied Logistic Regression, Second ed*; Wiley: New York, NY, USA, 2000.
30. Wen, X.X.; Tan, G.X.; Yao, S.S.; Huang, Z. Traffic flow characteristics and short-term prediction model of urban intersection. *J. Traffic Transp. Eng.* **2006**, *1*, 103–107.
31. Zhou, M.J. An empirical study of factors affecting electric car purchase decision. *Shanghai Auto* **2013**, *4*, 39–44.
32. Sun, Y.; Shang, J. Factors affecting the health of residents in China: a perspective based on the living environment. *Ecol. Indic.* **2015**, *51*, 228–236. [CrossRef]

© 2015 by the authors. Licensee MDPI, Basel, Switzerland. This article is an open access article distributed under the terms and conditions of the Creative Commons Attribution (CC BY) license (http://creativecommons.org/licenses/by/4.0/).

Article

Effects of Employees' Work Values and Organizational Management on Corporate Performance for Chinese and Taiwanese Construction Enterprises

Jeng-Wen Lin [1,*], Pu Fun Shen [2] and Yin-Sung Hsu [3]

1. Department of Civil Engineering, Feng Chia University, Taichung 407, Taiwan
2. Ph.D. Program in Civil and Hydraulic Engineering, Feng Chia University, Taichung 407, Taiwan; p0043264@fcu.edu.tw
3. Department of Water Resources Engineering and Conservation, Feng Chia University, Taichung 407, Taiwan; yshsu@fcu.edu.tw
* Correspondence: jwlin@fcu.edu.tw; Tel.: +886-4-2451-7250 (ext. 3150); Fax: +886-4-2451-6982

Academic Editors: Adam Jabłoński and Giuseppe Ioppolo
Received: 20 July 2015; Accepted: 16 December 2015; Published: 21 December 2015

Abstract: Through questionnaire surveys, this study explored the discrepancies in work values and organizational management between employees and cadre members of construction enterprises on the two sides of the Taiwan Strait. Statistical methods including data reliability, regression analysis, and tests of significance were utilized for modelling a case study. The findings of this study included: (1) in terms of work values, employees from China focused on their lives "at present", while those from Taiwan focused on their lives "in the future", expecting to improve the quality of their lives later on through advanced studies and promotion; (2) according to the data obtained from the questionnaires, the answers regarding income and welfare in terms of work values and satisfaction were contradictory on the two sides of the Strait, which could be interpreted in terms of influence from society; and (3) there was a significant influence of organizational management on employees' intentions to resign. If enterprises could improve current organizational management systems, their employees' work attitudes would be improved and the tendency to resign would be reduced.

Keywords: corporate performance; organizational management; questionnaire survey; test of significance; work value

1. Introduction

Employees' work values change from generation to generation. Understanding employees' work values has become a key issue for organizations aiming to achieve higher performances. Choi and Kim recognized the individual human resource (HR) as a core asset of corporate value creation and devoted significant effort to developing and managing competency-based HR in order to strengthen corporate competitiveness [1]. Jia *et al.* addressed the concern that generational changes could be reflected in various management aspects such as organizational structure, HR, and enterprise culture [2]. Chau *et al.* indicated how to provide construction managers with information about and insight into the existing data, so they could make decisions more effectively [3]. Park showed that the effect of resource coverage on project performance was quantified and the policy implications were determined for dynamic resource management by simulating the model with heuristic and industry data [4]. Scholars in China have started to study work values of employees on either side of the Taiwan Strait. Chen pointed out that with increasingly frequent economic and trade exchanges across the Taiwan Strait, interdependency between Taiwan and mainland China was increasingly higher [5]. Through studies on cross-cultural exchange and on differences between the cultures of the two sides, it was revealed that, although there were some empirical research achievements made on the national culture and consumer culture of the two sides of the Taiwan Strait, reliable research about corporate culture is lacking and needs to be conducted [5]. For example, Phua examined three things regarding whether (1) national cultural differences influence individuals' preferences for types of remuneration and levels of job autonomy; (2) actual organizational human resource management (HRM) practices reflect such preferences; and (3) gaps between individuals' preferences and actual organizational HRM practices affect job satisfaction [6].

1.1. Organizational Management and Corporate Performance

Many factors may influence an organization's interests. Among them, two important ones are the organizational management and performance of HR. Kamath's empirical analysis found that HR was the one factor which had a major impact on the profitability and productivity of the firms studied [7]. Though there was growing importance and efficiency in the utilization of intellectual resources in the Indian pharmaceutical industry, its potential to impact the industry's financial performance was missing in the empirical analysis [7]. Kim *et al.* claimed that HRM had been identified as very important for site management compared with such management at other locations [8]. Cheng *et al.* applied business process reengineering and organization planning philosophy to HRM and focused on HR planning in construction management process reengineering (CMPR) to develop a team-based HR planning (THRP) method for deploying labor [9]. Druker *et al.* examined HRM practices in relation to the role of personnel departments, line management responsibility, performance management, and values and beliefs of personnel managers [10]. Fatimah claimed that HR improvement in an organization played an important role in determining the success of an organization [11].

Corporate organizational management is ultimately important to corporate performance. Rob *et al.* analyzed whether Japanese firms with many governance provisions had better corporate performance than firms with few governance provisions and discovered that well-governed firms significantly outperformed poorly governed firms by up to 15% per year [12]. Saito performed a comparative study according to two surveys conducted in Japan and the United States to understand how facility managers recognized and practiced universal design in their workplaces and to identify what factors were likely to facilitate or obstruct their practice [13]. Wong *et al.* claimed that workplace environment affected employees' well-being and comfort, which in turn influenced their productivity and morale [14]. Teizer *et al.* indicated that better safety and productivity could be achieved when construction resources, including people and equipment, could be monitored [15]. The work of Li *et al.* showed that the abilities of management and technology were two common factors that could transcend different institutions and systems [16].

On the other hand, an incentive system is also essential in an organization. Pattarin *et al.* proposed that employee perks were positively associated with current and future returns on assets, which supported the view that some types of perks might increase firm profitability and/or that perks were paid as a bonus to reward performance [17]. Findings from stratified samples suggested that perks might incentivize managers, even after controlling for firm size, growth opportunity, and leverage [17].

Pfeffer claimed that ignoring the influences of working environments on employees' performances might cause organizations to lose their competitiveness [18]. Hence, more emphases have been placed on studies of "person–organization fit" or "person–job fit", For example, Schein indicated that environment was an important factor for person–organization fit [19]. Schneider believed that person–organization fit might influence one's performance in an organization [20]. In short, HRM and its performance practice change due to the role of values and identity change and have also become the conceptual framework of this study.

1.2. Issues Regarding Work Values

In recent years, many scholars have studied issues related to work values. Ralston *et al.* assessed the impact of economic ideology and national culture on the individual work values of managers in the United States, Russia, Japan, and China [21]. Reichel *et al.* presented evidence that work values could be a good indicator for the selection and career development of personnel [22]. Lee and Yen explored the connection between work values and career orientation for employees in high-tech production [23].

All organizations are unique and, thus, practice different cultural values within the organization. In a university setting, it was discovered that leadership values have a significant impact on university-wide cultural values, employee values, and stakeholder values [24,25]. Cultural values considerably affect productivity values and employee values. Further, employee values have significant influence on productivity and stakeholder values [24,25]. Scholars believed there were many aspects of work values. For example, Wu and Chiang explored how Chinese values impacted employees' satisfaction (ES). Taiwanese employees viewed "career planning" as the most important, while Chinese employees thought "organizational management" was most important. For Taiwanese employees, "salary and benefits", "workload", and "organizational management" had effects on ES, while age and education were important to Chinese employees [26]. Leung *et al.* indicated that the construction industry had been recognized as a stressful industry, and a great deal of stress was placed on various construction professionals (CPs). However, due to the different "values" among CPs in Hong Kong, susceptibility to stressors varied a great range among workers. People who grew up and lived in different cultural environments had different values and this led to different perceptions of stressors [27]. Ochieng *et al.* examined challenges faced by senior construction managers in managing cross-cultural complexity and uncertainty [28]. Francis and Lingard claimed that societal attitudes and work values were changing and that these changes had been reflected in the employment practices of many construction companies [29]. Morrison and Thurnell addressed that, in order to attract and retain valuable employees, the New Zealand construction industry must provide useful work-life benefits, reasonable working hours, and supportive workplace cultures in line with such initiatives [30].

1.3. Prime Novelty Statements

Based on the arguments above regarding the effects of employees' work values and organizational management on corporate performance and based on the extension of the work by Lin *et al.* [31], Lin and Shen [32], Shen [33], we proposed three novelty statements.

(1) This paper is a "case study". It was conducted with a questionnaire survey to offer organizations some references, in which the reliability of the data was determined based on Cronbach's alpha values. According to the results of this study, all the Cronbach's alpha values from the reliability analyses were higher than 0.7, implying that all the organizational data were highly trustworthy.

(2) This study examined the results of questionnaires regarding issues of work values and organizational management, and compared the issues. The results clearly showed the needs and viewpoints of employees from the two sides of the Strait, and therefore the relevant organizational management skills that could be utilized as references.

(3) Three regression models were used to verify this study regarding the issues of work values and organizational management. Interpretations were provided of unpredictable outcomes, so that management could understand and compare the extent to which the employees from the two sides of the Strait devoted themselves to their jobs, whether the employees would like to stay or leave the enterprise, and what they thought about the welfare systems of the enterprise.

2. Analysis Methods for Questionnaires

The subjects of this study were Taiwanese and Chinese employees of branches of Taiwanese companies in China. The differences in work values and organizational management models were reviewed. The influences of the differences in work values and work satisfaction on organizations were also explored. The questionnaires were designed according to the job diagnostic survey by Hackman and Oldham [34], proposing to (1) diagnose existing jobs so to determine whether (and how) they might be redesigned to improve employee motivation and productivity and (2) assess the effects of job changes on employees. The tool is based on a theory of how job design affects work motivation and provides means of (a) individual psychological states because of these dimensions and (b) affective reactions of employees to the working environment. The survey questionnaire focused on the "work characteristics questionnaire", including questions for (1) work values and (2) organizational management. Participants used a five-point Likert Scale to answer the questionnaire.

This study analyzed the data using the software SPSS (Statistical Package for the Social Sciences). The statistical methods adopted in this study were listed below for quantitative measures.

(1) Reliability analysis for questionnaires: Reliability indicated stability and consistency. This study utilized Cronbach's alpha values, whose set of criteria were proposed by Guieford [35] to verify the reliability of the collected data. The standard value of Cronbach's alpha was 0.5. High alpha values (>0.7) represented high reliability and low alpha values (<0.35) meant low reliability.

(2) Descriptive statistics: They were used to describe the properties of the samples and the averages, standard deviations, and distributions of variables for the samples.

(3) Regression analysis: By adopting multiple regression analysis, the effects of the independent variables (work values and organizational management) on the dependent variables should be examined with moderating variables being controlled. In addition, work values and work satisfaction for employees from both sides of the Strait were modeled to determine their differences.

Using regression analysis, three models were established based on three most important indicators of managing an organization, as selected from the perspectives of business managers according to the interviews and to the works by Huang, Huang, and Tang [36–38]. The three indicators included (1) employees' devotion to their jobs; (2) their commitment to the organization and whether to resign; and (3) their salaries and welfare provided by enterprises. The capabilities of the independent variables to predict and explain the dependent variables were discussed. For employees' devotion to their jobs, the selected dependent variable Y was that "My boss thinks I am doing a great job at work". Huang believed that the more devoted employees are to their jobs, the more praises they are going to get from their bosses [36]. For whether employees will resign, the selected dependent variable Y was the "In order to stay employed by the company, I am willing to accept any assignment". Huang believed that only employees who can accept companies' arrangements are loyal to the companies [36]. For employees' salaries and welfare, the selected dependent variable Y was that "I am very satisfied with the welfare provided by the company I work for". On the other hand, the independent variables X for the three models were questions in the work values and organizational management questionnaires corresponding to the selected dependent variables.

(4) Test of significance: statistical significance is a kind of evaluation metric. For example: A and B are two sets of data with statistical significance at the 0.05 level, which indicates the possibility of the two data sets having significant difference of 5%, or 95% probability that the two sample sets have no difference. This 5% difference is caused by simple random sampling error. Typically, the statistical significance achieved at the .05 or .01 level can refer to significant differences between the data sets. If $P(X = x) < p = 0.05$ is significant, SPSS statistical analysis software uses * mark, while $P(X = x) < p = 0.01$ is considered extremely significant and is usually marked by **.

3. Results of Data Reliability, Data Validity, and Descriptive Statistics

A total amount of 250 questionnaires was handed out to Taiwanese and Chinese employees of different ranks in the company. After precluding 30 invalid questionnaires (non-response samples) and 69 unreturned ones, a total amount of 181 questionnaires were found to be valid. The response rate was 72.4% as illustrated in Table 1 (adapted from Lin *et al.* [31]). With the data obtained from the questionnaires, the reliability analysis was first conducted, followed by a series of statistical analyses.

Table 1. Information regarding returned questionnaires.

Sample	No. of Questionnaires Distributed	No. of Valid Questionnaires	Response Rate
All employees	250	181	72.4%
Taiwanese employees	90	58	64%
Chinese employees	90	73	81%
Taiwanese cadre members	50	36	72%
Chinese cadre members	20	14	70%

3.1. Reliability Analysis for Questionnaires

Reliability is the degree of consistency of results from repeated measurements of the same population or similar populations. It represents the correctness or precision of the tools used for measurement. In order to avoid the correctness of the collected and classified questionnaires being influenced by the low reliabilities for the measured categories, reliability analysis was applied for each of the categories as listed in Table 2. It shows that, in this study, all the reliabilities were greater than 0.7, implying that the collected samples were stable and satisfactorily consistent.

Table 2. Reliability analyses.

Cronbach's Alpha	Chinese	Taiwanese
Work values	0.736	0.703
Organizational management	0.716	0.743

3.2. Validity Analysis for Questionnaires

Validity means "exploratory factor analysis" [31], characteristics of main features being the following assessment, with the corresponding results listed in Table 3.

(1) Kaiser-Meyer-Olkin (KMO) measure of sampling adequacy assesses whether the partial correlations among variables are small (KMO > 0.6);

(2) Bartlett's Test of Sphericity assesses whether the correlation matrix is an identity matrix, indicating that the factor model is inappropriate (Sig < 0.05);

Table 3. Validity analyses.

Exploratory Factor	Chinese	Taiwanese
Work values	KMO = 0.817 Sig = 0.000	KMO = 0.809 Sig = 0.000
Organizational management	KMO = 0.738 Sig = 0.000	KMO = 0.743 Sig = 0.000

3.3. Descriptive Statistics

The research subjects of this study were employees of a company from Taiwan invested in China. After the questionnaires were retrieved, the number of samples was obtained and the frequencies and weighted averages of the questions were computed. From this information, how important work values were for the employees from both sides of the Strait and their differences could be determined. The ranking of work values for the employees from both sides of the Strait and the ranking of the organizational management of cadre members from both sides of the Strait were summarized in Tables 4 and 5 respectively (questionnaires adopted from [31–33]).

Table 4. Ranking of work values of employees from both sides of the Strait.

Chinese		Taiwanese	
The insurance system of the company is good.	4.79	The insurance system of the company is good.	4.93
When I am sick, the company takes good care of me.	4.44	When I am sick, the company takes good care of me.	4.89
The quality of my life can be improved through my work.	4.38	I never feel confused or scared while working.	4.69
My own dream can be realized at work.	4.28	There are chances for advanced studies at work.	4.67
My life becomes richer due to my work.	4.23	There are many chances of promotion.	4.59
There are chances for advanced studies at work.	4.05	I can arrange my own schedule properly because of the flexibility of my work.	4.37
I am proud of my work.	4.05	The quality of my life can be improved through my work.	3.82
I devote myself to my work.	3.95	My own dream can be realized at work.	3.67
I can arrange my own schedule properly because of the flexibility of my work.	3.92	My life becomes richer due to my work.	3.55
I want to be perfect when it comes to my work.	3.92	I want to be perfect when it comes to my work.	3.44
There are many chances of promotion.	3.69	I am proud of my work.	3.38
My income is higher than that of others with the same conditions as me.	3.49	I devote myself to my work.	3.31
Even if there is no extra pay for working overtime, I would still work overtime to finish my work at night.	3.47	I can get a raise or bonus of a proper amount.	3.07
I usually go to work earlier to prepare the tasks I have to handle.	3.33	The welfare system of the company is good.	3.07
I never feel confused or scared while working.	3.22	My income is higher than that of others with the same conditions as me.	3.07
I can get a raise or bonus of a proper amount.	3.22	I usually go to work earlier to prepare the tasks I have to handle.	2.93
The welfare system of the company is good.	3.22	Even if there is no extra pay for working overtime, I would still work overtime to finish my work at night.	2.66

Table 5. Ranking of the organizational management of cadre members from both sides of the Strait.

Chinese		Taiwanese	
I think the training provided by the company I work for can meet the demands of the employees.	4.21	Compared with other companies in the same field, I think the salary and welfare offered by the company I work for are better.	4.81
If there is a training opportunity, the management of the company I work for usually encourages the employees to participate.	4.14	I think the employees' salaries offered by the company are closely related to the employees' performances at work.	4.55
The company I work for would communicate with its employees regarding their achievements and offer them suggestions.	3.86	I think the training provided by the company I work for can meet the demands of the employees.	4.16
I think the employees' salaries offered by the company are closely related to the employees' performances at work.	3	If there is a training opportunity, the management of the company I work for usually encourages the employees to participate.	4.13
Compared with other companies in the same field, I think the salary and welfare offered by the company I work for are better.	2.93	The company I work for would communicate with its employees regarding their achievements and offer them suggestions.	3.83
I think the employees of the company I work for are highly involved in decision making at work.	2.5	I think the employees of the company I work for are highly involved in decision making at work.	3.36

According to the obtained statistical values, the Chinese cadre members believed that the most important thing was the demands of the employees, followed by the training opportunities and the communication between the company and its employees, and the least important ones were decision making at work, the salaries, and welfare offered by the company. On the other hand, the Taiwanese cadre members believed that the most important thing was the salaries and welfare offered by the company, followed by the employees' performances at work and the demands of the employees, and the least important ones were decision making at work and the communication between the company and its employees.

4. Correlation and Regression Analyses

4.1. Employees' Devotion to Their Jobs

The six variables from work values as listed in Table 6 (questions selected from [31–33]), including (1) "I devote myself to my work"; (2) "Even if there is no extra pay for working overtime, I would still work overtime to finish my work at night"; (3) "I usually go to work earlier to prepare the tasks I have to handle"; (4) "I am proud of my work"; (5) "I want to be perfect when it comes to my work"; and (6) "I never feel confused or scared while working", were selected as the independent variables X to explain the dependent variable Y: "My boss thinks I am doing a great job at work". The R value was 0.709 with the Taiwanese employees and 0.791 with the Chinese employees, indicating that there was a relationship between superintendents' praise for the employees and the employees' devotion to their jobs. One explanation is that the more devoted the employees were to their jobs, the more praise they could get from their superintendents. Hence, one of the six important indicators from work values for selecting employees was their devotion to their jobs.

Table 6. Employees' devotion to their jobs from both sides of the Strait.

Independent variables (X)	1. I devote myself to my work. 2. Even if there is no extra pay for working overtime, I would still work overtime to finish my work at night. 3. I usually go to work earlier to prepare the tasks I have to handle. 4. I am proud of my work. 5. I want to be perfect when it comes to my work. 6. I never feel confused or scared while working.
Dependent variable (Y)	My boss thinks I am doing a great job at work.
R value with the Taiwanese employees	0.709
R value with the Chinese employees	0.791

4.2. Influence of Organizational Management on Employees' Decisions to Resign

The five variables from organizational management as listed in Table 7 (questions selected from [31–33]), including (1) "I think the employees of the company I work for are highly involved in decision making at work"; (2) "If there is a training opportunity, the management of the company I work for usually encourages the employees to participate"; (3) "I think the training provided by the company I work for can meet the demands of the employees"; (4) "The company I work for would communicate with its employees regarding their achievements and offer them suggestions"; and (5) "Compared with other companies in the same field, I think the salary and welfare offered by the company I work for are better", were selected as the independent variables X to explain the dependent variable Y: "In order to stay employed by the company, I am willing to accept any assignment". The results show that the cadre members from both sides of the Strait believed that identification with the company and decisions to stay were highly related to the company's organizational management. Of course, the organizational management system could not fully interpret its employees' decisions to stay or whether they associated themselves with the company. However, it was a reasonable indicator as to why some employees decided to resign.

Table 7. Influence of the organizational management on employees' decision to resign from both sides of the Strait.

Independent variables (X)	1. I think the employees of the company I work for are highly involved in decision making at work. 2. If there is a training opportunity, the management of the company I work for usually encourages the employees to participate. 3. I think the training provided by the company I work for can meet the demands of the employees. 4. The company I work for would communicate with its employees regarding their achievements and offer them suggestions. 5. Compared with other companies in the same field, I think the salary and welfare offered by the company I work for are better.
Dependent variable (Y)	In order to stay employed by the company, I am willing to accept any assignment.
R value with the Taiwanese employees	0.759
R value with the Chinese employees	0.736

4.3. Employees' Salaries and Welfare

The five variables among work values as listed in Table 8 (questions selected from [31–33]), including (1) "When I am sick, the company takes good care of me"; (2) "The insurance system of the company is good"; (3) The welfare system of the company is good"; (4) My income is higher than that of others with the same conditions as me"; and (5) "I can get a raise or bonus of a proper amount", were selected as the independent variables X to explain the dependent variable Y: "I am very satisfied with the welfare provided by the company I work for". The R values with both the Taiwanese and Chinese employees were relatively low, implying that it was not adequate to explain the employees' satisfaction with the company's welfare using their work values. Such results of both sides of the Strait are similar to the work of Huang [36]. This means that the employees were not satisfied when their superintendents used one of their work values as standards to offer welfare, due to the fact that the welfare satisfaction may be relevant to "the influence of social desirability" [36]. Excluded variables in Table 8 further show that the factor "I can get a raise or bonus of a proper amount" showed a very significant difference (p-value = 0.00) than other factors. Thus, the factor was removed and the regression analysis was rerun once again. The consequent R values were drastically increased for the Taiwanese and Chinese employees from 0.435–0.764 and from 0.308–0.687, respectively, as listed in Table 9 (questions selected from [31–33]). This verifies the assumption that the welfare satisfaction may be relevant to "the influence of social desirability".

Table 8. Employees' salaries and welfare on both sides of the Strait.

Independent variables (X)	1. When I am sick, the company takes good care of me. 2. The insurance system of the company is good. 3. The welfare system of the company is good. 4. My income is higher than that of others with the same conditions as me. 5. I can get a raise or bonus of a proper amount.					
Dependent variable (Y)	I am very satisfied with the welfare provided by the company I work for.					
R value with the Taiwanese employees	0.435					
R value with the Chinese employees	0.308					
Excluded Variables						
Model	Beta	t	Sig.	Partial Correlation	Collinearity Statistics Tolerance	p-value
I can get a raise or bonus of a proper amount.	.	.	.	.	0.000	0.000

Table 9. Employees' salaries and welfare on both sides of the Strait with a variable excluded.

Independent variables (X)	1. When I am sick, the company takes good care of me. 2. The insurance system of the company is good. 3. The welfare system of the company is good. 4. My income is higher than that of others with the same conditions as me.
Dependent variable (Y)	I am very satisfied with the welfare provided by the company I work for.
R value with the Taiwanese employees	0.764
R value with the Chinese employees	0.687

5. Evaluation by Test of Significance

Analyses via the statistical significance assists in comprehending the differences in work values and organizational management of the employees and cadres between the two sides of the Strait, as listed in Tables 10 and 11 (questionnaires adopted from [31–33]). Table 10, regarding the work values of employees of both sides of the Strait, shows significant differences for the three questions: (1) "There are many chances of promotion"; (2) "Even if there is no extra pay for working overtime, I would still work overtime to finish my work at night"; and (3) "I never feel confused or scared while working". Table 11, regarding the organizational management of cadre members of both sides of the Strait, shows significant differences for the three questions: (1) "I think the employees' salaries offered by the company are closely related to the employees' performances at work"; (2) "Compared with other companies in the same field, I think the salary and welfare offered by the company I work for are better"; and (3) "I think the employees of the company I work for are highly involved in decision making at work".

Table 10. Test of significance of work values of employees of both sides of the Strait.

Work Values	Chinese	Taiwanese	p-Value
The insurance system of the company is good.	4.79	4.93	0.082
When I am sick, the company takes good care of me.	4.44	4.89	0.057
The quality of my life can be improved through my work.	4.38	3.82	0.044 *
My own dream can be realized at work.	4.28	3.67	0.037 *
My life becomes richer due to my work.	4.23	3.55	0.034 *
There are chances for advanced studies at work.	4.05	4.67	0.039 *
I am proud of my work.	4.05	3.38	0.032 *
I devote myself to my work.	3.95	3.31	0.036 *
I can arrange my own schedule properly because of the flexibility of my work.	3.92	4.37	0.056
I want to be perfect when it comes to my work.	3.92	3.44	0.054
There are many chances of promotion.	3.69	4.59	0.005 **
My income is higher than that of others with the same conditions as me.	3.49	3.07	0.058
Even if there is no extra pay for working overtime, I would still work overtime to finish my work at night.	3.47	2.66	0.009**
I usually go to work earlier to prepare the tasks I have to handle.	3.33	2.93	0.061
I never feel confused or scared while working.	3.22	4.69	0.000 **
I can get a raise or bonus of a proper amount.	3.22	3.07	0.081
The welfare system of the company is good.	3.22	3.07	0.082

Table 11. Test of significance of the organizational management of cadre members of both sides of the Strait.

Organizational Management	Chinese	Taiwanese	p-value
I think the training provided by the company I work for can meet the demands of the employees.	4.21	4.16	0.093
If there is a training opportunity, the management of the company I work for usually encourages the employees to participate.	4.14	4.13	0.098

Table 11. Cont.

Organizational Management	Chinese	Taiwanese	p-value
The company I work for would communicate with its employees regarding their achievements and offer them suggestions.	3.86	3.83	0.096
I think the employees' salaries offered by the company are closely related to the employees' performances at work.	3	4.55	0.000 **
Compared with other companies in the same field, I think the salary and welfare offered by the company I work for are better.	2.93	4.81	0.000 **
I think the employees of the company I work for are highly involved in decision making at work.	2.5	3.36	0.007 **

Statistical significance is a kind of evaluation metric; significant is indicated by an * and extremely significant is usually marked by **. Thus, it is clear to see the differences in work values and organizational management of the employees and cadres between the two sides of the Strait from Tables 10 and 11.

6. Conclusions

The conclusions of the analyses in this study are summarized, anticipating that they will offer domestic enterprises some references when developing and implementing organizational management strategies on both sides of the Strait.

(1) Comparative results of Chinese and Taiwanese employees:

(a) Work values: The Chinese employees valued "The quality of my life can be improved through my work", "My own dream can be realized at work", and "My life becomes richer due to my work", which all focused on their lives "at present". On the other hand, the Taiwanese employees valued "I never feel confused or scared while working", "There are chances for advanced studies at work", and "There are many chances of promotion", which all focused on "the future". From this perspective, the Chinese employees focus on their current situation and how it can improve the quality of their lives, while the Taiwanese employees tend toward a stable job that reflects the opportunity for promotion.

(b) Organizational management: The Chinese cadre members were satisfied with the employee training provided by the company, while the Taiwanese cadre members thought that the salaries and welfare offered by the company were better than other companies. In general, the Taiwanese cadre members thought more highly of their organization's management than their Chinese counterparts did. It appeared that the management model used in China was similar to the one used in Taiwan, showing that the Chinese cadre members were unable to integrate in the company completely. The Taiwanese cadre members thought better welfare could improve employees' performances, while the Chinese cadre members focused on encouragement and communication.

(2) An organization should know how devoted its employees are to their jobs:

Another important indicator influencing the company's performance was the employees' devotion to their jobs. When recruiting new staff, applicants' devotion and enthusiasm for their jobs should be tested so that the organization's performance could be improved.

(3) An organization should pay attention to defects in its organizational management and reduce employees' tendency to resign:

In this study, we discovered that the influences of organizational management on employees' tendency to resign were significant. If an enterprise could improve its current organizational management, its employees' work attitudes could be improved as well, and their tendency to resign should be reduced. The interviews revealed that many enterprises in Taiwan that were invested in China did not have well-established systems for employees' repatriation. Those assigned to work in

China felt uncertain about their future, and this was reflected in their performance. Besides increasing employees' salaries, a repatriation system should be established: this ought to entail not only allowing staff to return to their jobs in Taiwan, but also proper in-service training for Taiwanese employees in China so that they may remain in China for long-term development. Otherwise, it is very likely that further salary raises would be futile in increasing employees' commitment to an organization.

Acknowledgments: Acknowledgments: The work described in this paper comprises part of the research project sponsored by Ministry of Science and Technology, Taiwan (Contract No. MOST 102-2221-E-035-049), whose support is greatly appreciated.

Author Contributions: Author Contributions: Jeng-Wen Lin designed the research and wrote the paper; Pu Fun Shen performed research and analyzed the data; and Yin-Sung Hsu revised the paper.

Conflicts of Interest: Conflicts of Interest: The authors declare no conflict of interest.

References

1. Choi, J.H.; Kim, Y.S. An analysis of core competency of construction field engineer for cost management. *J. Constr. Eng. Manag.* **2013**, *14*, 26–34. [CrossRef]
2. Jia, G.; Ni, X.; Chen, Z.; Hong, B.; Chen, Y.; Yang, F.; Lin, C. Measuring the maturity of risk management in large-scale construction projects. *Autom. Constr.* **2013**, *34*, 56–66. [CrossRef]
3. Chau, K.W.; Cao, Y.; Anson, M.; Zhang, J. Application of data warehouse and decision support system in construction management. *Autom. Constr.* **2003**, *12*, 213–224. [CrossRef]
4. Park, M. Model-based dynamic resource management for construction projects. *Autom. Constr.* **2005**, *14*, 585–598. [CrossRef]
5. Chen, C.-C. Comments on relevant study on corporate culture across the Taiwan Straits. *Asian Soc. Sci.* **2011**, *7*, 59–63. [CrossRef]
6. Phua, F.T. Do national cultural differences affect the nature and characteristics of HRM practices? Evidence from Australian and Hong Kong construction firms on remuneration and job autonomy. *Constr. Manag. Econ.* **2012**, *30*, 545–556. [CrossRef]
7. Kamath, G.B. Intellectual capital and corporate performance in Indian pharmaceutical industry. *J. Intellect. Cap.* **2008**, *9*, 684–704. [CrossRef]
8. Kim, J.H.; Cho, H.H.; Lee, U.K.; Kang, K.I. Development of a hybrid device based on infrared and ultrasonic sensors for human resource management. In Proceedings of the 24th International Symposium on Automation & Robotics in Construction, Kochi, India, 19–21 September 2007; pp. 111–115.
9. Cheng, M.Y.; Tsai, M.H.; Xiao, Z.W. Construction management process reengineering: Organizational human resource planning for multiple projects. *Autom. Constr.* **2006**, *15*, 785–799. [CrossRef]
10. Druker, J.; White, G.; Hegewisch, A.; Mayne, L. Between hard and soft HRM: human resource management in the construction industry. *J. Constr. Eng. Manag.* **1996**, *14*, 405–416. [CrossRef]
11. Fatimah, P.R. The development of FFMD pyramid: Fuzzy Family Marriage Deployment as decision support method to improve human resources performance. *Qual. Quant.* **2014**, *48*, 659–672. [CrossRef]
12. Rob, B.; Bart, F.; Rogér, O.; Alireza, T.-R. The impact of corporate governance on corporate performance: Evidence from Japan. *Pac. Basin Financ. J.* **2008**, *16*, 236–251.
13. Saito, Y. Awareness of universal design among facility managers in Japan and the United States. *Autom. Constr.* **2006**, *15*, 462–478. [CrossRef]
14. Wong, J.K.W.; Li, H.; Wang, S.W. Intelligent building research: A review. *Autom. Constr.* **2005**, *14*, 143–159. [CrossRef]
15. Teizer, J.; Cheng, T.; Fang, Y. Location tracking and data visualization technology to advance construction ironworkers' education and training in safety and productivity. *Autom. Constr.* **2013**, *35*, 53–68. [CrossRef]
16. Li, J.; Chiang, Y.H.; Choi, T.N.; Man, K.F. Determinants of Efficiency of Contractors in Hong Kong and China: Panel Data Model Analysis. *J. Constr. Eng. Manag.* **2013**, *9*, 1211–1223. [CrossRef]
17. Pattarin, A.; Ilan, A.; Tianyu, Z. Executive perks: Compensation and corporate performance in China. *Asia Pac. J. Manag.* **2009**, *28*, 401–425.
18. Pfeffer, J. Fighting the War for Talent is Hazardous to Your Organization's Health. *Organ. Dyn.* **2001**, *29*, 248–259. [CrossRef]

19. Schein, E. *Organization Culture and Leadership*; Jossey-Bass: San Francisco, CA, USA, 1985.
20. Schneider, B. The People Make The Place. *Pers. Psychol.* **1987**, *40*, 437–453. [CrossRef]
21. Ralston, D.A.; Holt, D.H.; Terpstra, R.H.; Yu, K.-C. The impact of national culture and economic ideology on managerial work values: A study of the United States, Russia, Japan, and China. *J. Int. Bus. Stud.* **1997**, *28*, 177–207. [CrossRef]
22. Reichel, A.; Neumann, Y.; Pizam, A. The Work Values and Motivational Profiles of Vocational, Collegiate, Nonconformist, and Academic Students. *Res. High. Educ.* **1981**, *14*, 187–199. [CrossRef]
23. Lee, H.W.; Yen, K.W. A study of the relationship between work values and career orientation of employed in the high technology industry. *Qual. Quant.* **2013**, *47*, 803–810. [CrossRef]
24. Ab Hamid, M.R.; Mustafa, Z.; Idris, F.; Abdullah, M.; Suradi, N.M.; Ismail, W.R. Multi-factor of cultural values: a confirmatory factor analytic approach. *Qual. Quant.* **2013**, *47*, 499–513. [CrossRef]
25. Ab Hamid, M.R.B. Value-based performance excellence model for higher education institutions. *Qual. Quant.* **2015**, *49*, 1919–1944. [CrossRef]
26. Wu, C.-C.; Chiang, Y.-C. The impact on the cultural diversity to employees' job satisfaction between mainland China and Taiwan: A comparison of Taiwanese invested companies. *Int. J. Hum. Resour. Manag.* **2007**, *18*, 623–641. [CrossRef]
27. Leung, M.Y.; Chan, Y.S.; Chong, A.M.L. Chinese values and stressors of construction professionals in Hong Kong. *J. Constr. Eng. Manag.* **2010**, *136*, 1289–1298. [CrossRef]
28. Ochieng, E.G.; Price, A.D.F.; Ruan, X.; Egbu, C.O.; Moore, D. The effect of cross-cultural uncertainty and complexity within multicultural construction teams. *Eng. Constr. Archit. Manag.* **2013**, *20*, 307–324. [CrossRef]
29. Francis, V.; Lingard, H. The case for family-friendly work practices in the Australian construction industry. *Aust. J. Constr. Econ. Build.* **2012**, *2*, 28–36. [CrossRef]
30. Morrison, E.; Thurnell, D. Employee preferences for work-life benefits in a large New Zealand construction company. *Aust. J. Constr. Econ. Build.* **2012**, *12*, 12–25. [CrossRef]
31. Lin, J.-W.; Shen, P.F.; Lee, B.-J. Repetitive model refinement for questionnaire design improvement in the evaluation of working characteristics in construction enterprises. *Sustainability* **2015**, *7*, 15179–15193. [CrossRef]
32. Lin, J.-W.; Shen, P.F. Factor-analysis based questionnaire categorization method for reliability improvement of evaluation of working conditions in construction enterprises. *Struct. Eng. Mech.* **2014**, *51*, 973–988. [CrossRef]
33. Shen, P.F. Impact of Employees' Work Values at Two Sides of Taiwan Straits on Corporate Performance. Master's Thesis, Feng Chia University, Taichung, Taiwan, July 2011.
34. Hackman, J.R.; Oldham, G.R. Development of the Job Diagnostic Survey. *J. Appl. Psychol.* **1975**, *60*, 159–170. [CrossRef]
35. Guieford, J.P. *Fundamental Statistics in Psychology and Education*, 4th ed.; McGraw Hill: New York, NY, USA, 1965.
36. Huang, G.-L. The Differences in Work Values between Enterprise Employees on both Sides of the Strait. Paper Collection for the Differences in Work Values between Enterprise Employees on both Sides of the Strait Seminar, Taiwan, 1994. Available online: http://readopac2.ncl.edu.tw/nclserialFront/search/ref_book.jsp?la=ch&id=A00039972 (accessed on 18 December 2015).
37. Huang, T.C. *Human Resource Management of Taiwanese Businessmen in Mainland China*; Fongheh Publishing Co.: Taipei, Taiwan, 1995.
38. Tang, S.C. Discussions of corporate culture between different business strategies—A case study of Taiwan's home appliance industry. Master's Thesis, National Chung Hsing University, Taichung, Taiwan, July 1995.

© 2015 by the authors. Licensee MDPI, Basel, Switzerland. This article is an open access article distributed under the terms and conditions of the Creative Commons Attribution (CC BY) license (http://creativecommons.org/licenses/by/4.0/).

Article

How Firms Can Get Ideas from Users for Sustainable Business Innovation

Chanwoo Cho and Sungjoo Lee *

Department of Industrial Engineering, Ajou University, 206 Worldcup-ro, Yeongtong-gu, Suwon 16499, Korea; cchanw@ajou.ac.kr

* Correspondence: sungjoo@ajou.ac.kr; Tel.: +82-31-219-2419

Academic Editors: Adam Jabłoński and Marc A. Rosen
Received: 3 October 2015; Accepted: 27 November 2015; Published: 3 December 2015

Abstract: The importance of user information and user participation for seeking business opportunities has been widely acknowledged in a variety of industries. Therefore, this study aims to suggest a typology for user innovation models as a strategy for sustainable development and to investigate the characteristics of different types user innovation to encourage and support improved utilization of user innovation in firms. For this purpose, we began by collecting 435 relevant papers from the most-cited academic journals. Then, we developed a typology of user innovation models, which consist of four types including workshop-based, consortium-based, crowdsourcing-based and platform-based, and we investigated the characteristics of the suggested types in terms of applications and research trends. The analysis results reveal that each type has different characteristics and that there exist some research gaps in the user innovation field. Our results are expected to foster understanding of user innovation for guiding sustainable business development and provide useful information for both researchers and innovation mangers.

Keywords: user innovation; typology; sustainable business; business innovation; innovation model; research trends

1. Introduction

The technological environment has changed rapidly in the past decade, and technological convergence has occurred across a diverse range of technologies. These changes have prompted companies to seek out and cooperate with external partners, such as government officials, research organizations and other firms in order to strengthen their capabilities and have increased the necessity for firms to engage in strategic planning in order to survive in the market. Paying attention to customers' diverse requirements for new products and services has become one of the essential factors for firms' survival, highlighting the user as a firm's principal external partner for developing sustainable business models. Corporate sustainability can be defined as meeting the needs of a firm's stakeholders such as employees, customers and communities [1], by transposing the idea of sustainable development to the firm level [2]. Considering that users are one of the most significant stakeholders, firms need to understand users' needs accurately and reflect these needs within their innovation processes for developing sustainable business models. Thus, it has been critical for a firm to incorporate users' needs, ideas and feedbacks in innovation for its sustainable growth.

For decades, firms have investigated user behaviors [3,4], and users have been recognized as a source of innovation [5–7], suggesting innovative ideas or creating prototypes of innovative products that organizations can utilize in their new product development (NPD) processes and develop new business models [8,9]. A great deal of relevant research has been conducted on diverse cases of user innovation in practice. Earlier studies focused on the analysis of users' role in innovation [9–13], a comparison of user innovation with supplier-driven innovation [14], and an exploration of a suitable form of governance for user innovation [15]. Similarly, recent studies have dealt with topics such as the analysis of users' roles as innovators in specific industries [16,17] and interactions between users and manufacturers [18]. At the same time, changes in user innovation have been significantly discussed in previous studies by analyzing interactions among users [19–21] and providing suggestions for the ways in which firms can utilize user communities and crowd sourcing [22–24] for innovation.

Although these studies have examined aspects of user innovation and helped to establish relevant theories, there is a need for further studies. First, most of the empirical research has focused on one or a few cases of user innovation in specific industries. There exist many different types of user innovation in the various industries. Thus, it is essential to investigate the characteristics of each type in order to fully understand user innovation as an approach to designing sustainable business models.

Second, although much research has suggested types of user innovation, most of them were user-initiated cases. As reported by existing studies, there exist a lot of user innovation cases that were initiated by firms. Moreover, business model innovation is more closely related to firm-initiated cases rather than user-initiate cases. In diverse industries, firms have tried to collect user information, knowledge and ideas to seek solutions to problems or to create innovation and business opportunities. Thus, it is time to suggest types of user innovation from the firm perspective to support and foster user innovation in firms.

Third, there is a lack of studies on the overall research trends in user innovation. User innovation has spread widely to industries, and various types of user innovation have been suggested over time. A clear understanding of its evolution is a prerequisite for the better utilization of user innovation in practice. Although past research can enhance our understanding of user innovation, it is not easy to understand the changes in user innovation. To address this issue, it would be meaningful to investigate past and emerging user innovation models by analyzing patterns in user innovation research.

Therefore, this study aims to suggest a typology of user innovation models and investigate them to encourage and support the better utilization of user innovation in firms as a method to find sustainable business opportunities. For this purpose, first, we collected publications on user innovation from the top 25 most-cited journals in the technology and innovation management area. Second, we identified the user innovation context by developing an analysis strategy and a typology of user innovation models. Third, we derived four types of user innovation models according to a typology, and investigated the characteristics of each type in terms of the context of applications, research trends and sustainable business models. Finally, we tried to find implications and research gaps in the user innovation field in order to propose future research directions, especially for the purpose of business model innovation for sustainability. The research findings are expected to enhance the understanding of user innovation and help in the utilization of user innovation in firms for their sustainable growth.

The rest of the paper is organized as follows: In Section 2, we review existing studies of user innovation and sustainable business models. In Section 3, we explain the overall research process and the detailed processes of this study. We describe the data collection process in Section 4 and discuss the typology of user innovation models in Section 5. In Section 6, we investigate the characteristics of each type of user innovation model based on the data. In Section 7, the implications, research gaps and future research directions are explained. Finally, in Section 6, we present the contributions and limitations of the current study.

2. Background

This study proposes a typology of user innovation models and investigates the characteristics of the various types. To this end, we must first define the concept of user innovation models and the criteria of a typology. Therefore, this section reviews the literature on innovation models, which can provide a basis for defining user innovation models.

2.1. User Innovation Models

An innovation model is a framework for understanding the relationship between technology, science, and economics [25]. Based on the relationship, types of innovation models are defined. For example, Rothwell [26] suggested five generations of innovation process models. Chesbrough [27] suggested the concept of an open innovation model. In this model, internal R & D using external resources that were acquired through cooperation with external partners is crucial. User innovation is similar to the open innovation model in that the sharing of knowledge and information by interactions and co-operation between actors plays an important role in innovation. Meanwhile, it is different from the open innovation model in that its main actors consist of *users, firms*, or *facilitating organizations (intermediary firms, NGOs, universities, research funding agencies and governmental agencies)*. Further, interactions and co-operation between users or user and firm are the principal sources of innovative ideas. To better use open innovation, firms should not only adopt information and knowledge from external partners, but also freely reveal their own information and knowledge to the public. However, openness generally conflicts with firms' need to protect their intellectual property [28]. User innovation overcomes these limitations of open innovation and, therefore, has received much interest from both industry and academia. However, it is not easy to define a "single" general user innovation model because the characteristics of user innovation differ in each case of user innovation. Therefore, this research examines cases of user innovation from past studies and suggests a typology of user innovation models.

Most relevant research in user innovation has been conducted on actual cases, and such research has yielded insights into several aspects of user innovation. Among them, how innovation outputs are used and for whom are one of the most significant factors to define types of user innovations, considering that the ultimate goal of innovation is to create value for the company, the users, and the deliverable itself. In this vein, user innovation types can be grouped into three categories by innovation initiators—user-initiated innovation, firm-initiated innovation, and intermediary-initiated innovation.

The existing literature tended to focus on user-initiated innovation. A representative case is that of the user-innovator [29,30]. Though innovation outputs acquired through user innovation are objects of commercialization, they can be a means to satisfy users' needs. User-innovators develop their ideas to fulfill their own needs [31–34], and share and diffuse their resulting innovations freely to other users [29]. In several industries, such as rodeo kayaks [35,36], kite surfing equipment [30], motorcycles [37], computer games [38] and sports-related consumer products [29], user-innovators developed a novel product and launched it to the market. In these cases, user-innovators became user manufacturers who led the overall innovation processes from idea generation to commercialization.

However, as new types of user innovation tools such as crowdsourcing, open-source software, and a user toolkit have been suggested to assist firms in idea gathering from users, firm-initiated user innovation has started to prevail in diverse industries. A lot of firms in software industries prefer to use open source software as a platform to grab users' ideas [39–41]. User toolkits have been used to make users self-design their own product, and firms adopt users' ideas to develop new products or services in computer game [42], ski [43], and watch industries [44].

Recently, cases of user innovation led by facilitating organizations such as intermediary firms, NGOs, universities, research funding agencies, and governmental agencies have been reported. In these cases, intermediary firms facilitate the bringing together of users and firms to make innovative products. InnoCentive [45], TopCoder [46], and direct firm solicitation of innovation by Procter and Gamble [47] are good examples.

Since the concept of user innovation has come to prominence, diverse types of user innovation initiated by different actors have been reported. Thus, these types should be considered in the process of developing a typology of user innovation models. Among the three types, we restrict our focus to the second type, which is worth investigating because more firms are required to innovate their product and service offerings in collaboration with potential users in the era of open innovation.

2.2. User Innovation for Designing Sustainable Business Models

With global development and as associated resource use has been accelerated, it seems apparent that business as usual is not an option for a sustainable future [48]. Firms have to create value by seizing business opportunities, deliver an economic value to customers, and provide ecological and/or social value to the public for their continuous growth. Emphasizing the importance of business as a driver of innovation, previous studies suggested that a business model is a useful framework for corporate innovation [49–51], and business model innovation is a key to success of firms [52,53]. However, long-run sustainability needs clear understanding about economic, environmental and social factors of sustainability [54] and may require radical, fundamental and difficult changes in corporate business models [55].

The business model is the rationale of how an organization creates, delivers, and captures value and can be described through nine building blocks: (1) customer segments; (2) value proposition; (3) channels; (4) customer relationships; (5) revenue streams; (6) key resources; (7) key activities; (8) partner network; and (9) cost structure [56]. In particular, a "sustainable" business model is defined as a business model that creates competitive advantage through superior customer value as well as contributes to sustainable development of the company and society [52]. To build a sustainable business model, firms have to transform their business models towards creating positive impacts or reduce negative impacts for the environment and society. This business model innovation for sustainability is realized by changing the way of firms' value network creation, value capture and delivery, and value proposition [48]. Hence, firms have to generate new sources of profit by finding novel value proposition and value constellation combinations for developing sustainable business models [57].

Users, as major customers, can be valuable sources in developing sustainable business models. Stubbs and Cocklin [50] asserted that sustainable business models must develop internal structural and cultural capabilities to achieve firm-level sustainability and collaborate with key stakeholders to achieve sustainability for the system that a firm is part of. Here, one of the major stakeholders is users. They reveal who the key customers are and what values they want to have. In addition, they are willing to develop and even offer their own innovation ideas to firms. In a similar vein, Osterwalder and Pigneur [56] also emphasized the significance of users for business model development by arguing that customer segments, customer relationships and channels should be aligned, considering potential trade-offs, to conceptualize an effective business model. By adopting user innovation that consists of user-own information and knowledge, therefore, firms can generate a novel value proposition, leading to sustainable business model innovation. Here, it should be noted that business model innovation is not just changing the product and service offerings for the customer. It involves changing "the way of business", rather than "what firms do" and must go beyond process and products [58].

Accordingly, business model innovation for sustainability should be pursued from the perspective of sociotechnical systems, not in terms of the technical system. Quite naturally, the role of users as sources of innovative ideas for sustainable business models should also be analyzed within the framework of sociotechnical systems. For example, in the case of living labs, users shape the innovation in their own real-life environments, unlike the traditional approaches to users where the insights of users were captured and interpreted by experts [59]. Innovation occurs in value network constellations and users play a significant role. This notion indicates that it is worth investigating the role of users in the process of business model innovation, which is expected to help facilitate the adoption of user innovation models by firms for designing sustainable business models.

3. Overall Research Processes

The overall research process of this study is shown in Figure 1. First, we collected relevant papers on user innovation from online academic journals. Second, we identified a user innovation context based on collected papers. Here, we adopted the 5W1H (*i.e.*, who, when, where, what, why, how) method to develop an analysis strategy and a typology of user innovation models. Third, we investigated user innovation types. The context of applications and the research trends of each type were analyzed. At last, we derived implications and future research trends based on the analysis results.

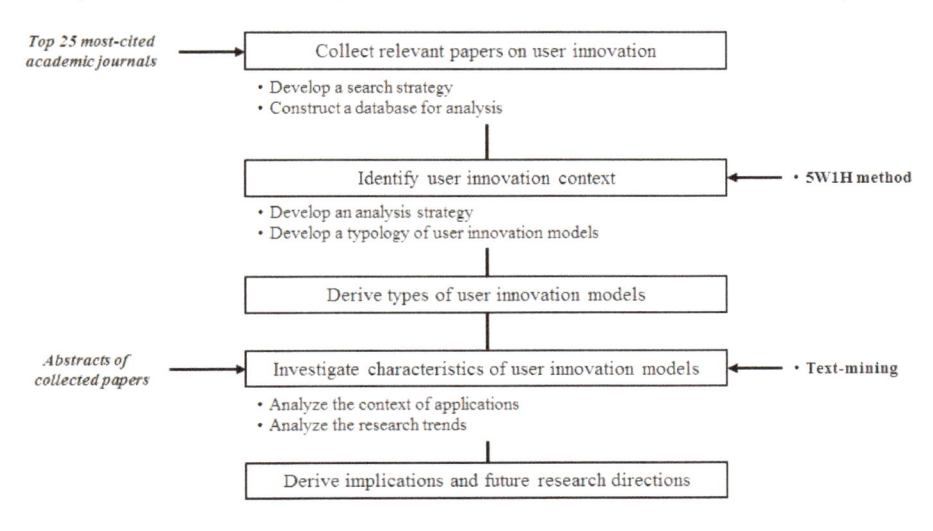

Figure 1. Overall research process.

3.1. Step 1: Collect Data for Analysis

3.1.1. Develop a Search Strategy

We collected papers published between 1976 and 2015 from the top 25 most-cited technology and innovation management journals that were mentioned in past studies [60,61]. We used "user innovation" and "user-innovation" as the initial search keywords. All of the publications that include the term "user innovation" or "user-innovation" in the title, abstract, or keywords were collected. The initial keywords were too simple in order to search for sufficient amounts of relevant publications, so we tried to analyze the author keywords of collected publications to extend the search terms. Keywords which have been used more frequently than others were selected; then, among them, meaningful keywords in the user innovation context were chosen to extend the search keywords set (see Table 1). The extended keyword set includes "open source software", "user community", "co-creation", "crowdsourcing", "user design", "self design", "user toolkit" and "lead user". These are the top eight keywords most frequently appearing as keywords in the papers obtained by our initial search.

Table 1. Extended keywords set.

Keywords	Number of Publications	Search Term
Open source software	4	"open source software", "open-source software"
User community	8	"user community", "user-community"
User toolkit	6	"user toolkit", "user-toolkit"
Lead user	3	"lead user", "lead-user"
Co-creation	2	"cocreation", "co-creation"
Crowdsourcing	2	"crowdsourcing", "crowd-sourcing"
User design	2	"user design", "user-design"
Self design	2	"self design", "self-design"

3.1.2. Construct a Database for Analysis

The collected publications were screened to construct a database for analysis. In order to identify the user innovation context, publications that described a theoretical approach without a concrete mention of user innovation cases or processes were excluded.

3.2. Step 2: Identify User Innovation Context

3.2.1. Develop an Analysis Strategy

To identify the user innovation context, we first developed an analysis strategy by adopting the 5W1H method, and the results of using this method to find out how firms get ideas from users are presented in Table 2.

Table 2. 5W1H: how firms get ideas from users.

5W1H	How Firms Get Ideas from Users
Who	Types of users
Where	Types of industries
What	Innovation ideas—types of problems
When	Firms' innovation processes
Why	Firms' purposes of getting information
How	Types of tools firms utilize to get information from users

3.2.2. Develop a Typology of User Innovation Models

According to the types of initiators—user, firm, and facilitating organizations—user innovation models can be distinguished. Hence, a typology of user innovation models has to cover those diverse types. However, because the current study investigates user innovation from the firm perspective, the suggested typology just covers firm-initiated user innovation models. We regarded the motivation of firms initiating innovation as the most important aspect of firm-initiated user innovation. They correspond to "what" and "why" in Table 1. Thus, we defined the "purpose of getting ideas" ("why" firms start to get ideas) and the "types of problems" ("what" problems are they dealing with) as the criteria of a typology. Accordingly four type of innovation models can be identified from a two-by-two matrix. We also attempted to assign types of tools ("how" firms get ideas from users) to each type of user innovation model, which is also significant for firms in order to implement user-driven innovation.

3.3. Step 3: Investigate Types of User Innovation Models

The four types of suggested user innovation models were analyzed in terms of the context of applications and the research trends. The analysis results provide information about "who," "where," and "how" in the user innovation context. The criteria "when" was removed from our analysis because relatively little information about when user ideas were utilized during the innovation process was provided in the papers. In addition, innovation processes are so diverse across firms that it is infeasible to define a standard innovation process, which is a preliminary procedure for our analysis.

3.3.1. Analyze the Context of Applications

To investigate "who," "where," and "how" in the user innovation context, the kinds of users, industry, and tools in each type were analyzed. Particularly, the industry is worth investigating because user innovation may not be appropriate for all industries. Many researchers regarded users as product developers who contribute to innovation [9] in the semiconductor [12], scientific instrument [7], and machine tool industries [11]. However, different industries many need different types of user innovation models. For the analysis, we adopted the International Standard Industrial Classification

(ISIC) to clearly distinguish the types of industry and we standardized the types of users based on the existing studies (see Table 3).

Table 3. Types of users.

Types of Users	Definitions
General users	Individuals or groups who use or may use a product/service from a target firm
Expert users	Users who own technical skills and knowledge
Lead users	Users who experienced needs still unknown to general users
Innovative users	Users who self-developed an innovation for their own needs
User community	A group of users

3.3.2. Analyze the Research Trends

To investigate the research trends for each type of user innovation model, the annual number of publications was analyzed and the keywords that were frequently used in pairs were extracted from abstracts of publications. To extract keywords, a text-mining tool, TextAnalyst, was used.

4. Data Collection

As a result of the initial search, 140 publications were collected. By investigating the author keywords of 140 collected publications, an extended keywords set that consists of eight terms was defined as shown in Table 3. Using the extended keywords set, an additional 295 publications were collected.

Consequently, a total of 435 publications were collected from 25 journals. The annual number of publications from 1976–2015 was stable at one to two before 2000, but it has rapidly increased since then (See Figure 2). We screened 435 collected papers to construct a database for analysis. After the screening, 149 publications on user innovation were chosen for our analysis (see Appendix 1).

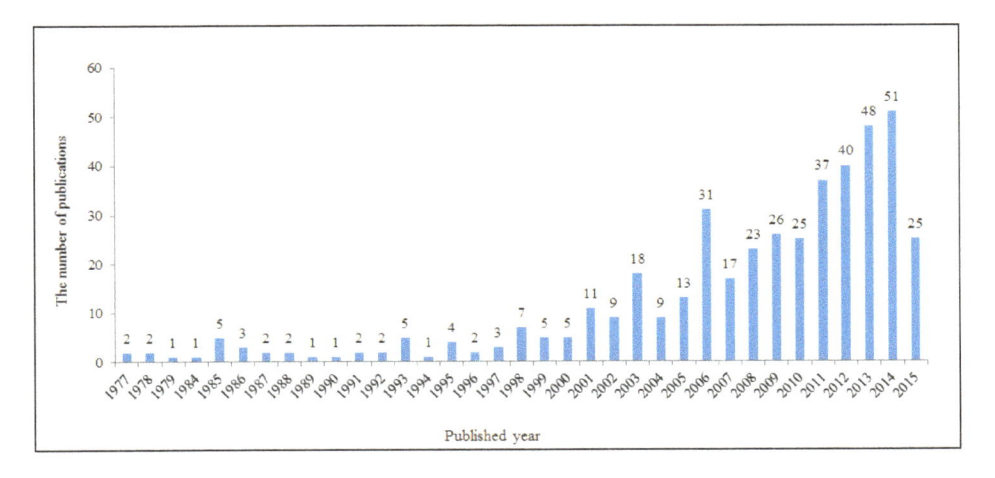

Figure 2. The annual number of collected publications (1976–July 2015).

5. Types of User Innovation Models

To derive the types of user innovation models, we first define the levels of the criteria. Firms may utilize users' innovation ideas to seek solutions for problems or to co-create innovation with users based on user-own information or knowledge.

Hence, the first criterion, "purpose of getting ideas," consists of two levels: idea adoption and idea co-creation. In the former case, interactions between firms and users are likely to be one-directional; users transfer their innovation ideas to a firm while firms try to capture ideas from users. Whereas, in the latter case, relationships between firms and users are interactional; discussions and feedback may be developed between firms and users to co-create innovation ideas. User–firm interactions and user–user interactions have been recognized as factors affecting innovation performance [6]. Particularly, it was discovered that user–firm interactions reduce the uncertainty of innovation, and this is linked to the successful commercialization of new products or services [18]. As was mentioned above, there are two types of user–firm interactions: one-directional, such as innovation contests [62,63], and interactional, such as direct user involvement in a firm's innovation process [64–66]. The interaction can also happen between users. User–user interactions enable the diffusion of knowledge, information, and experience that individual users own, and encourage user innovation [67]. However, as the focus of this study is firm-initiated user innovation, only the user–firm interactions are considered for further analysis.

The second criterion, "types of problems," consists of two levels: a given problem and an open problem. Firms may adopt user ideas to solve a pre-defined problem, for example, finding a way to improve a particular function of their products/services, which is the former case. Actually, lead users own much of the solution knowledge about specific problems, and thus, they frequently play a key role in the creation of knowledge [68]. On the other hand, firms may utilize user ideas to handle an open-ended problem, for example, exploring all possible ways to improve their existing product/services. These are the two most critical factors that will affect the way firms adopt user innovation.

According to the criteria of a typology, four types of firm-initiated user innovation models are derived (see Figure 3). We named the four types that were derived by considering the available types of tools for getting ideas, information, and knowledge for each type, focusing on the most frequently used ones.

Innovation initiators	Firm		Facilitating organizations	User-innovator
	(Firm-initiated user innovation)			
Purposes of getting ideas — Idea co-creation	Workshop-based	Consortium-based	(Intermediated user innovation)	(User-driven innovation)
Purposes of getting ideas — Idea adoption	Crowdsourcing-based	Platform-based		
	Given problem	Open problem		
	Types of problems			

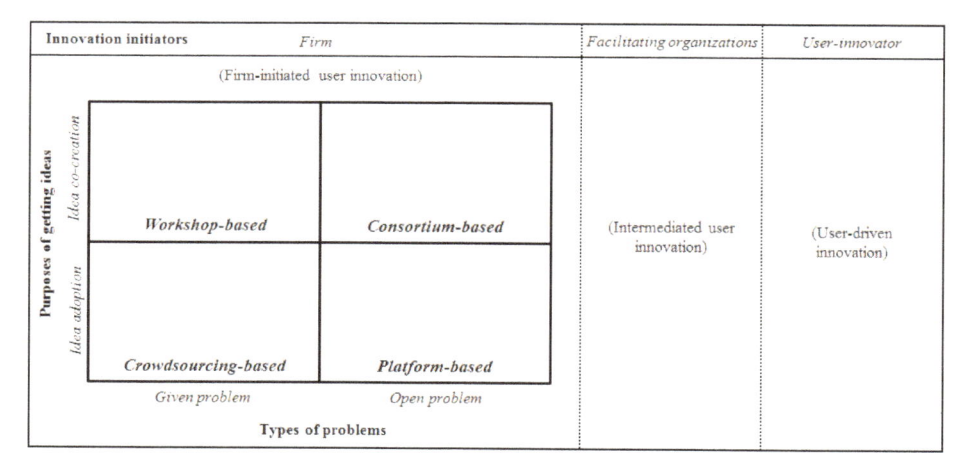

Figure 3. Four types of user innovation models.

At first, in the case of type 1, firms can organize user-involved workshops to seek solutions for problems by cooperating with users. Thus, the name "*workshop-based*" was given to this type. Second, in the case of type 2, firms generally co-work with users who possess technical knowledge, such as experts, technicians and professional users to determine some problems and to co-create novel innovation. Hence, the name "*consortium-based*" was assigned to this type. Third, when firms want to seek solutions for given problems, they tend to crowdsource innovation ideas by using idea competition or contest. Thus, this type was named *"crowdsourcing-based"*. At last, in the case of type 4, firms are likely to develop online or offline platforms that are open to users for the purpose of problem-seeking. This case was called *"platform-based"*.

After the designation, we assigned 149 publications to each type. The result is shown in Table 4. Among 149 publications, 57 were assigned to the *"platform-based"* category, 36 to the *"workshop-based"* type, 21 to the *"crowdsourcing-based"* format, and seven to the *"consortium-based"* type. The other 28 publications were not assigned to any of the four types because they addressed user innovation cases in which the innovation initiators were not firms.

Table 4. The number of assigned publications to each type of user innovation models.

Types of User Innovation Models	The Number of Publications
Workshop-based	36
Consortium-based	7
Crowdsourcing-based	21
Platform-based	57
Others	28
Total	149

6. Characteristics of User Innovation Models

6.1. The Context of Applications

The analysis results of the context of applications for each type of user innovation model are as follows.

Firstly, the results for the *"workshop-based"* type are shown in Table 5. In this type, firms generally got ideas from general or lead users; the workshop, lead user method, user research interviews, surveys, and group research are the main types of tools. This type has occurred in diverse sectors such as the manufacturing, information and communication, and many service industries. The results mean that because this type utilizes relatively basic and traditional tools, it has widely spread to a diverse range of industries. The firms in this type must determine solutions based on user-owned information and knowledge; thus, they seem to prefer selected users to large groups of people, such as the user community, for their purposes. Figure 4 depicts the model for this type.

Next, the results for the *"consortium-based"* type are shown in Table 6. In this type, firms generally got ideas from expert users via collaboration. Firms in professional, scientific, and technical activities industries prefer this type. The purpose of a consortium is to explore ideas to find out potential problems and solutions for them. Thus, expert users who possess technical knowledge and skills seem to be preferred. Figure 5 depicts the model of this type.

The results for the *"crowdsourcing-based"* type are shown in Table 7. In this type, general users and the user community are the main types of users and crowdsourcing and idea competition are primarily used as tools for getting ideas. Firms in manufacturing, such as the computer, automotive, and information and communication industries, prefer this type. In this type, crowdsourcing or idea competition for the design of products (e.g., the design of sporting goods, jewellery, and baby products) are frequently used as the main tools. Thus, general users or the user community are preferred. However, some cases of idea competition which focused on a lead or expert users also appeared. Figure 6 depicts the model of this type.

Table 5. Characteristics of types of user innovation models: workshop-based.

	The Number of Cases
Types of users	
General users	18 (45.0%)
Lead users	16 (40.0%)
Expert users	2 (5.0%)
Innovative users	-
User community	-
Types of industry	
Manufacturing	21 (52.5%)
Information and communication	7 (17.5%)
Professional, scientific, and technical activities	4 (10.0%)
Financial and insurance activities	2 (5.0%)
Wholesale and retail trade	1 (2.5%)
Administrative and support service activities	1 (2.5%)
Types of tools	
Workshop (customer participation, user involvement)	11 (27.5%)
Others (repertory grid, skepticism-identification, casemap)	11 (27.5%)
Lead user method	9 (17.5%)
User research (interview, survey, group research)	4 (10.0%)

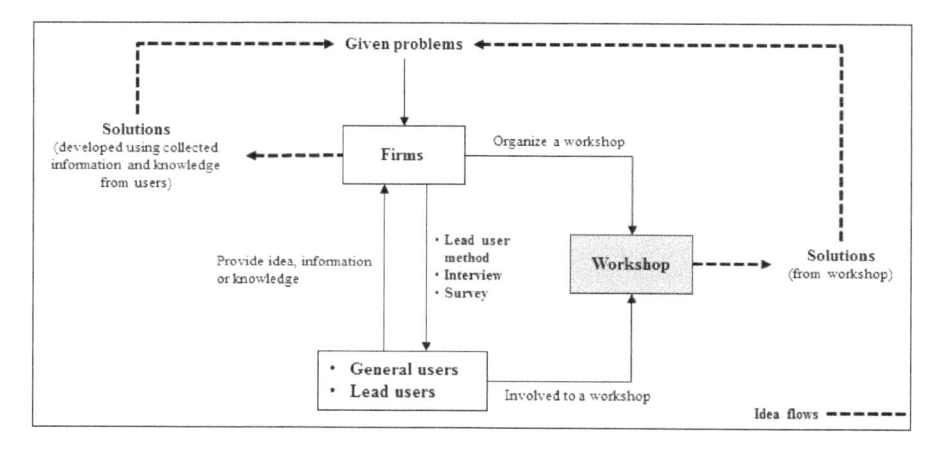

Figure 4. Innovation model: "workshop-based" type.

Table 6. Characteristics of types of user innovation models: consortium-based.

	The Number of Cases
Types of users	
Expert users	5 (75.4%)
Lead users	1 (14.3%)
General users	1 (14.3%)
Innovative users	-
User community	-
Types of industry	
Professional, scientific, and technical activities	4 (57.1%)
Information and communication	2 (28.6%)
Manufacturing	1 (14.3%)
Types of tools	
Collaboration (co-development, co-invention)	5 (83.3%)
Living lab	1 (16.7%)

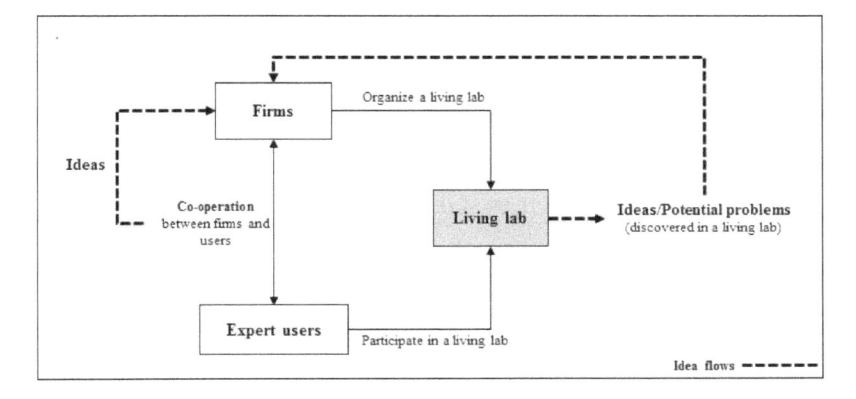

Figure 5. Innovation model: "consortium-based" type.

Table 7. Characteristics of types of user innovation models: crowdsourcing-based.

	The Number of Cases
Types of users	
General users	11 (50.0%)
User community	6 (27.3%)
Innovative users	2 (9.1%)
Lead users	1 (4.5%)
Expert users	1 (4.5%)
Types of industry	
Manufacturing	13 (59.1%)
Information and communication	6 (27.3%)
Financial and insurance activities	1 (4.5%)
Construction	1 (4.5%)
Types of tools	
Crowdsourcing	9 (83.3%)
Competitions (idea contest, idea competition)	8 (16.7%)
Open platform	1 (4.5%)
Lead user method	1 (4.5%)

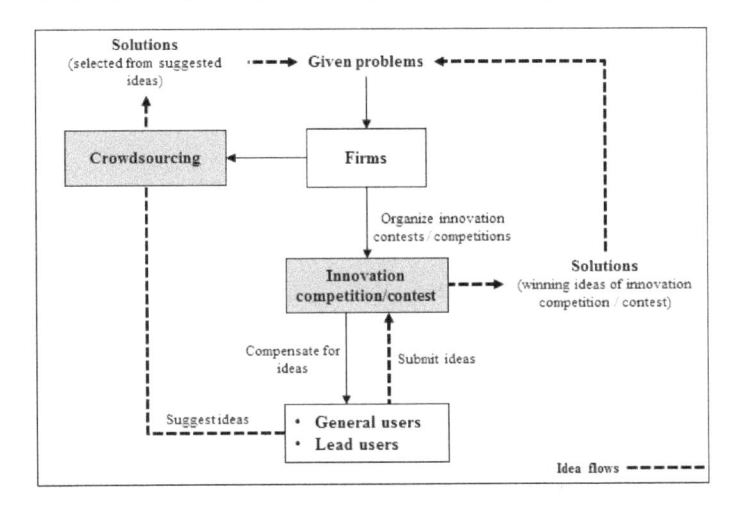

Figure 6. Innovation model: "crowdsourcing-based" type.

At last, the results for the *"platform-based"* type are shown in Table 8. In this type, firms generally acquire ideas from general users and the user community by using an open platform, such as an open-source software and online community or user toolkits. Thus, firms in the software industry that use open-source software and manufacturing firms that provide users with toolkits both prefer this type. Figure 7 depicts the model of this type.

Table 8. Characteristics of types of user innovation models: platform-based.

	The Number of Cases
Types of users	
User community	21 (37.5%)
General users	20 (35.7%)
Expert users	7 (12.5%)
Innovative users	5 (8.9%)
lead users	4 (7.1%)
Types of industry	
Information and communication	30 (53.6%)
Manufacturing	24 (42.9%)
Professional, scientific, and technical activities	3 (5.4%)
Human health and social work activities	1 (1.8%)
Types of tools	
Open platform (open source software)	24 (42.9%)
User toolkit	13 (23.2%)
Online community	10 (17.9%)
Virtual worlds	3 (5.4%)
Crowdsourcing	2 (3.6%)

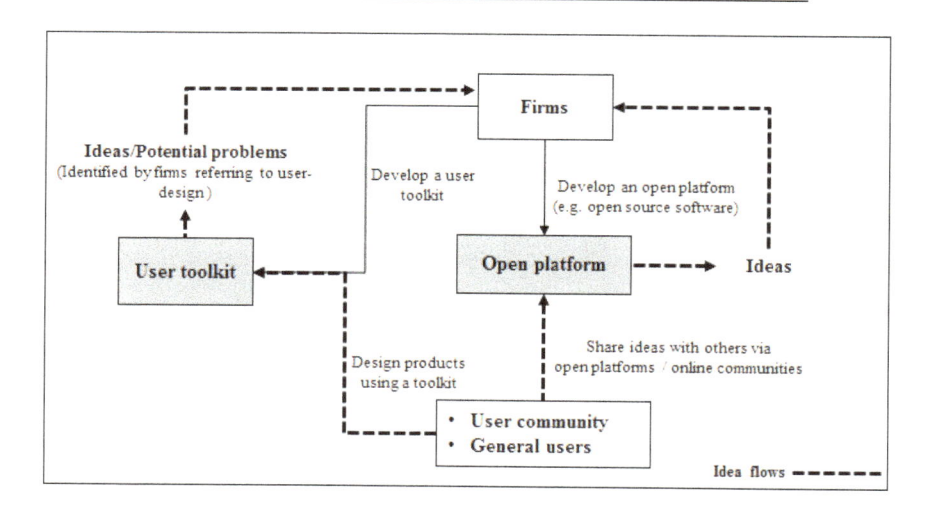

Figure 7. Innovation model: "platform-based" type.

6.2. The Research Trends

The research trends for the types of user innovation models are as follows: First, the trends of publications for the four types are shown in Table 9. The number of publications in the *"workshop-based"* type has consistently increased since 1986. Since this type is relatively traditional, relevant research seems to be published earlier than other types. The number of publications in the "platform-based" type has rapidly increased since 2003. This may be affected by the special issue on open-source software that was published in 2003 (*Research Policy*) and 2006 (*Management Science*). The number of publications in the "*crowdsourcing-based*" type shows increasing trends since 2010, which means that crowdsourcing is one of the recent hot topics within the user innovation field. The top five papers with the largest number of citations in each type are listed in Appendix 2.

Table 9. The research trends: the number of publications.

Year	Workshop-Based	Consortium-Based	Crowdsourcing-Based	Platform-Based
1977				
1985		1		
1986	1			
1988	1			
1993			1	
1999	1			
2000				
2001	1			1
2002	1		1	1
2003	2			7
2004	3			1
2005				4
2006		1	1	7
2007	1			1
2008	3		1	4
2009	4	1		4
2010	1		1	2
2011	1		4	3
2012	6		4	3
2013	6	1	3	6
2014	6	2	4	9
2015	2	1	2	3

Next, the keywords for the four types that we extracted are shown in Table 10. In the "*workshop-based*" type, judging from pairs of keywords such as "product-user," "user-idea," and "user-knowledge," we can infer that firms in this type usually get ideas or knowledge from people who use their products. In the "*consortium-based*" type, pairs of keywords such as "collaborative-prototyping," "problem-prototyping," and "user-collaboration" show that the main characteristics of this type is a collaboration of firms and users to derive some prototypes. In the "*crowdsourcing-based*" type, pairs of keywords such as "user-crowdsourcing," "idea-crowdsourcing," and "user-competition" show the main types of tools in this type. In the "*platform-based*" type, "user-community," "user-toolkit," "software-community," and "source-software" indicate the frequently used tools and the main kinds of users of this type. A time-series analysis was also conducted but it offered few meaningful implications, indicating that the research focus has remained largely the same in each category when judged by keywords.

Table 10. The research trends: a pair of keywords in abstracts.

Workshop-Based	Consortium-Based	Crowdsourcing-Based	Platform-Based
Product-development	Product-innovation	Idea-competition	User-community
Product-user	Collaborative-prototyping	Idea-generation	(Open)Source-software
(lead) user-method	Product-user	User-idea	User-product
User-idea	Problem-prototyping	Product-idea	User-toolkit
User-development	User-collaboration	User-crowdsourcing	Product-community
Product-idea		Idea-crowdsourcing	Innovation-community
Product-concept		User-competition	Software-community
User-knowledge			User-development
Professional-user			
Expert-user			
Product-development			

6.3. Consortium-Based User Innovation for Sustainable Business Models

For designing sustainable business models, one of the key challenges is to enable a firm to gain economic value for itself through delivering social and environmental benefits [69]. In addition, many researchers argue that considering social practices is of importance for making changes to existing routines and lifestyles to more appropriate ones for sustainability purposes [70–72]. A consortium-based innovation can be one of the ways to tackle these challenges by taking a sociotechnical approach to developing sustainable business models.

Living labs are an emerging and representative approach to consortium-based user innovation. Being characterized by openness and user involvement, this approach requires firms to consider ideas stemming from external sources in the innovation processes, particularly those from users [73]. It stresses the central role of the user and users are active participants. Thus, the living labs approach is regarded as a method of innovation, a collection of open innovation tools and networks, experimentation platforms, and a tool for user involvement from the sociotechnical perspective. For example, Liedtke *et al.* [74] introduce the sustainable living lab research infrastructure as an example of a setting for socio-technical experiments in product-service-systems. Other researchers have focused on living labs as a tool for research and governance [75,76], for solving social problems [77], or for social innovation [78].

In our analysis, the living lab was used as a tool for user innovation in a *"consortium-based"* type (see Table 6). However, there are few papers having both keywords "user innovation" and "Living lab(s)" in the top 25 most-cited innovation journals, possibly because the living lab research is building its own research streams. Actually, we could find more living lab papers published in other journals than our target innovation journals. About 303 publications are retrieved by searching on GoogleScholar using "living lab" and "user innovation" as searching keywords. These studies were conducted to suggest a framework to fertilize user innovation by using a living lab [79,80], explore user innovation in living labs [81], seek out affecting factors of user participation in living lab field trials [82], and explore differences between several test methods for user involvement in a living lab context [83]. User innovation studies, adopting a living lab approach, have been conducted sporadically. Investigating these studies in detail will provide meaningful implications for developing sustainable business models.

7. Implications and Future Research Directions

Several implications that can be derived from the analysis and future research possibilities are discussed here. First, the number of studies about the *"consortium-based"* type is relatively small. Recently, research about living lab, a representative approach for a *"consortium-based"* type, has been actively conducted in practice and academia. Seeking new innovation ideas in a consortium enables to change a firm's business models from the perspective of industrial eco-systems and not within the firm. Therefore, it may be valuable to study the *"consortium-based"* type in the future; for instance, how a living lab approach can be utilized to facilitate user innovation in the context of innovation studies. Among 149 publications on user innovation (see Appendix 1), we could find only one relevant paper, which uses the keyword "living lab" in its abstract. Though most of the living lab research is expected to be published in other journals, more discussions would be needed in the innovation journals.

Second, the user community has hardly been utilized for idea co-creation; however, it has widely been utilized for idea adoption. It is possible that the user community possesses plenty of useful information and knowledge for the development of products, technology and service if it is comprised of lead or expert users. Thus, if firms establish a workshop or a consortium with a user community, then there exists a possibility that firms can get useful ideas for new business development. Therefore, it is worthwhile to study a potentiality of the user community as a cooperation partner for idea adoption in firms.

Third, service firms have seldom utilized crowdsourcing or an open platform. In a *"workshop-based"* type, firms in service industries (*e.g.*, the financial, insurance, and mobile telephone sectors) have held workshops to obtain ideas from users. In contrast to the *"workshop-based"* type, in the *"crowdsourcing-based"* and *"platform-based"* types, just a few firms in service industries have adopted ideas from users. Service quality is influenced by firm–user interactions, meaning that user innovation is significant for sustainable business development not only in manufacturing fields but also service fields. Hence, the way in which firms adopted users' ideas to seek out solutions or problems can be a valuable research subject in future studies.

Finally, there exists a lack of studies on the intermediated user innovation, though we restricted our focus to firm-initiated user innovation. Most of the existing studies tended to link user innovator roles mainly to organizational tasks by restricting their focus to innovation processes taking place inside the firm. However, the recent trend towards openness brings about new inter actor tasks between the organizations and individuals participating in open innovation, where the role of the intermediary to facilitate or manage these emerging tasks would emphasized. Of course, we could find a few user innovation cases led by intermediaries that support cooperation between firms and users but relevant research has hardly been conducted. Intermediated user innovation led by intermediaries can be a good alternative for firm-initiated or user-led innovation, and the characteristics of this type of user innovation may be valuable to analyze. That is, using an intermediary can be another option for seeking new business ideas. Therefore, in future studies, research on the intermediaries of user innovation must be conducted.

8. Conclusions

Users can be a valuable source for new business development. This study aims to suggest a typology of user innovation models that can encourage and support utilization of user innovation for seeking new business opportunities and further designing sustainable business models based on the opportunities. We retrieved relevant papers from the 25 most-cited journals in the technology and innovation management field and adopted a 5W1H method to develop an analysis strategy and a typology of user innovation models. Four types of user innovation models were derived according to a suggested typology, and the characteristics of each type of user innovation model were investigated in terms of applications and research trends. As a result of the study, we found that each type of user innovation model prevailed in different industries, and firms of each type utilized different tools to adopt ideas, information and knowledge from various kinds of users. We determined that there are some research gaps and suggest future research directions to achieve user innovation for sustainable business growth.

This study contributes to future research in two ways: First, our results on a typology of user innovation model and analysis results for each type can provide useful information to the decision makers of firms that want to get ideas from users for their new business development. For example, firms that want to get ideas from users in specific industries can acquire information about which types of users and tools are suitable for their purposes. Second, we identified gaps on user innovation research and suggest directions for future study. Although there exist many studies on user innovation, research on trends of user innovation has not been conducted. The results of research trends enhance our understanding of user innovation studies and future research directions can encourage further studies on user innovation as a meaningful approach to business innovation.

Although this study has made meaningful contributions, it also has some limitations. First, it only focuses on firm-initiated user innovation. Since a proposed typology covers only firm-initiated user innovation, it is not a complete one. In addition, our typology for user innovation models was developed completely according to literature on the assumption that frequently used innovation models are often studied in academia and, thus, may not coincide with the reality of user innovation in the field. Second, more in-depth trends analysis needs to be carried out because this study investigated only the number of papers in each type of user innovation model. However, more meaningful implications can be derived from time-series analysis on types of users, industries, or tools in each type. Finally, there is still room for further improvements in data collection. The data source for analysis was restricted to the 25 most-cited journals in the technology and innovation management field. However, user innovation is a multi-disciplinary research field, and there may exist relevant papers in other fields. Hence, future research will address these issues.

Acknowledgments: Acknowledgments: This work was partially supported by the National Research Foundation of Korea (NRF) grant founded by the Korea government (NRF-2013R1A2A2A03016904, 2014S1A5A2A03065010).

Author Contributions: Author Contributions: Cho, C. and Lee, S. conceived and designed the research; Cho, C. performed the research and analyzed the data; Lee, S. supervised the research; Cho, C. wrote the paper.

Conflicts of Interest: Conflicts of Interest: The authors declare no conflict of interest.

Appendix

Appendix 1. The List of the Top 25 Most-Cited Journals and the Number of Collected Publications from Each Journal

Journals	The Number of Publications	
	Collected	Analyzed
Academy of Management Journal	5	1
Academy of Management Review	4	1
Administrative Science Quarterly	2	2
American Economic Review	-	-
California Management Review	13	5
Economic Journal	1	-
Harvard Business Review	16	4
IEEE Transactions on Engineering Management	7	1
Industrial and Corporate Change	7	3
International Journal of Technology Management	16	4
Journal of Marketing	12	7
Journal of Marketing Research	1	-
Journal of Political Economy	-	-
Journal of Product Innovation Management	92	29
Long Range Planning	6	3
Management Science	26	11
MIS Quarterly	24	3
MIT Sloan Management Review	12	4
Organization Science	11	4
R & D Management	52	17
Research Policy	54	28
Research-Technology Management	21	8
Strategic Management Journal	21	1
Technological Forecasting and Social Change	19	6
Technovation	13	7
Total	435	149

Appendix 2. Key Papers in Each Type of User Innovation

Appendix 2.1. Workshop-Based

No	Title	Journals	Citations *
1	Lead users: a source of novel product concepts	Management science	3943
2	Lead user analyses for the development of new industrial products	Management science	1077
3	From experience: Developing new product concepts via the lead user method: a case study in a "low tech" field	Journal of product innovation management	730
4	Creating breakthroughs at 3M	Harvard business review	729
5	Characteristics of innovating users in a consumer goods field: an empirical study of sport-related product consumers	Technovation	464

* The number of citations is based on Google Scholar data.

Appendix 2.2. Consortium-Based

No	Title	Journals	Citations *
1	Users' contributions to radical innovation: evidence from four cases in the field of medical equipment technology	R&D Management	334
2	The role of the interaction between the user and manufacturer in medical equipment innovation	R&D Management	261
3	Community engineering for innovations: the ideas competition as a method to nurture a virtual community for innovations	R&D Management	242
4	Using users: when does external knowledge enhance corporate product innovation?	Strategic Management Journal	26
5	Collaborative prototyping: cross-fertilization of knowledge in prototype-driven problem solving	Journal of product innovation management	9

* The number of citations is based on Google Scholar data.

Appendix 2.3. Crowdsourcing-Based

No	Title	Journals	Citations *
1	Performance assessment of the lead-user idea-generation process for new product development	Management science	788
2	Toolkits for idea competitions: a novel method to integrate users in new product development	R & D Management	545
3	The value of crowdsourcing: can users really compete with professionals in generating new product ideas?	Journal of product innovation management	290
4	Crowdsourcing as solution to distant search	American management review	258
5	Users as service innovators: the case of banking services	Research policy	195

* The number of citations is based on Google Scholar data.

Appendix 2.4. Platform-Based

No	Title	Journals	Citations *
1	Open source software and the "private-collective" innovation model: issues for organization science	Organization science	1756
2	Motivation of software developers in open source projects: an internet-based survey of contributors to the Linux kernel	Research policy	1202
3	Shifting innovation to users via toolkits	Management science	1014
4	Community, joining, and specialization in open source software innovation: a case study	Research policy	844
5	Satisfying heterogeneous user needs via innovation toolkits: the case of Apache security software	Research policy	716

* The number of citations is based on Google Scholar data.

References

1. Dyllick, T.; Hockerts, K. Beyond the business case for corporate sustainability. *Bus. Strategy Environ.* **2002**, *11*, 130–141. [CrossRef]
2. Brundtland, G.; Khalid, M.; Agnelli, S.; Al-Athel, S.; Chidzero, B.; Fadika, L.; Hauff, V.; Lang, I.; Shijun, M.; de Botero, M.M.; et al. *Our Common Future*; World Commission on Environment and Development: Brussels, Switzerland, 1987.

3. Park, E.; Lee, S.; Kwon, S.J.; del Pobil, A.P. Determinants of behavioral intention to use South Korean airline services: Effects of service quality and corporate social responsibility. *Sustainability* **2015**, *7*, 12106–12121. [CrossRef]
4. Lee, S.; Park, E.; Kwon, S.J.; del Pobil, A.P. Antecedents of behavioral intention to use mobile telecommunication services: Effects of corporate social responsibility and technology acceptance. *Sustainability* **2015**, *78*, 11345–11359. [CrossRef]
5. Bogers, M.; Afuah, A.; Bastian, B. Users as innovators: A review, critique, and future research directions. *J. Manag.* **2010**, *36*, 857–875. [CrossRef]
6. Gales, L.; Mansour-Cole, D. User involvement in innovation projects: Toward an information processing model. *J. Eng. Technol. Manag.* **1995**, *12*, 77–109. [CrossRef]
7. Von Hippel, E. The dominant role of users in the scientific instrument innovation process. *Res. Policy* **1976**, *5*, 212–239. [CrossRef]
8. Baker, N.R.; Green, S.G.; Bean, A.S. Why R & D project succeed or fail. *Res. Manag.* **1986**, *29*, 29–34.
9. Voss, C.A. The role of users in the development of applications software. *J. Prod. Innov. Manag.* **1985**, *2*, 113–121. [CrossRef]
10. Holt, K. The role of the user in product innovation. *Technovation* **1988**, *7*, 249–258. [CrossRef]
11. Lee, K.R. The role of user firms in the innovation of machine tools: The Japanese case. *Res. Policy* **1996**, *25*, 491–507. [CrossRef]
12. Von Hippel, E. The dominant role of the user in semiconductor and electronic subassembly process innovation. *IEEE Trans. Eng. Manag.* **1977**, *24*, 60–71. [CrossRef]
13. Von Hippel, E. A customer-active paradigm for industrial product idea generation. *Res. Policy* **1978**, *7*, 240–266. [CrossRef]
14. Slaughter, S. Innovation and learning during implementation: A comparison of user and manufacturer innovations. *Res. Policy* **1991**, *22*, 81–95. [CrossRef]
15. Foxall, G. Marketing new technology: Markets, hierarchies, and user-initiated innovation. *Manag. Decis. Econ.* **1988**, *9*, 237–250. [CrossRef]
16. Chen, J.S.; Tsou, H.T.; Ching, R.K.H. Co-production and its effects on service innovation. *Ind. Mark. Manag.* **2011**, *40*, 1331–1346. [CrossRef]
17. Oliveira, P.; von Hippel, E. Users as service innovators: The case of banking services. *Res. Policy* **2011**, *40*, 806–818. [CrossRef]
18. Heiskanen, E.; Lovio, R. User-producer interaction in housing energy innovations. *J. Ind. Ecol.* **2010**, *14*, 91–102. [CrossRef]
19. Lakhani, K.R.; von Hippel, E. How open source software works: "Free" user-to-user assistance. *Res. Policy* **2003**, *32*, 923–943. [CrossRef]
20. De Jong, P.J.P.; von Hippel, E.; Gault, F.; Kuusisto, J.; Raasch, C. Market failure in the diffusion of consumer-developed innovations: Patterns in Finland. *Res. Policy* **2015**, *44*, 1856–1865. [CrossRef]
21. Hyysalo, S.; Usenyuk, S. The user dominated technology era: Dynamics of dispersed peer-innovation. *Res. Policy* **2015**, *44*, 560–576. [CrossRef]
22. Bayus, B.L. Crowdsourcing new product ideas over time: An analysis of the Dell IdeaStorm community. *Manag. Sci.* **2013**, *59*, 226–244. [CrossRef]
23. Gangi, P.M.; Wasko, M. Steal my idea! organizational adoption of user innovations from a user innovation community: A case study of Dell IdeaStorm. *Decis. Support. Syst.* **2009**, *48*, 303–312. [CrossRef]
24. Mladenow, A.; Bauer, C.; Strauss, C. Social crowd integration in new product development: Crowdsourcing communities nourish the open innovation paradigm. *Glob. J. Flex. Syst. Manag.* **2014**, *15*, 77–86. [CrossRef]
25. Godin, B. The linear model of innovation: The historical construction of an analytical framework. *Sci. Technol. Hum. Val.* **2006**, *31*, 639–667. [CrossRef]
26. Chesbrough, H.W. *Open Innovation: The New Imperative for Creating and Profiting from Technology*; Harvard Business School Publishing: Boston, USA, 2003.
27. Rothwell, R. Towards the fifth-generation innovation process. *Int. Market. Rev.* **1994**, *11*, 7–31. [CrossRef]
28. Henkel, J. Selective revealing in open innovation processes: The case of embedded Linux. *Res. Policy* **2006**, *35*, 953–969. [CrossRef]
29. Franke, N.; Shah, S. How communities support innovative activities: An exploration of assistance and sharing among end-users. *Res. Policy* **2003**, *32*, 157–178. [CrossRef]

30. Franke, N.; von Hippel, E.; Schreier, M. Finding commercially attractive user innovations: A test of lead-user theory. *J. Prod. Innov. Manag.* **2006**, *23*, 301–315. [CrossRef]
31. Franke, N.; von Hippel, E. Satisfying heterogeneous user needs via innovation toolkits: The case of apache security software. *Res. Policy* **2003**, *32*, 1199–1215. [CrossRef]
32. Lüthje, C.; Herstatt, C. The lead user method: An outline of empirical findings and issues for future research. *R D Manag.* **2003**, *34*, 553–568. [CrossRef]
33. Morrison, P.D.; Roberts, J.H.; von Hippel, E. Determinants of user innovation and innovation sharing in a local market. *Manag. Sci.* **2000**, *46*, 1513–1527. [CrossRef]
34. Urban, G.L.; von Hippel, E. Lead user analyses for the development of new industrial products. *Manag. Sci.* **1988**, *34*, 569–582. [CrossRef]
35. Baldwin, C.; Hienerth, C.; von Hippel, E. How user innovations become commercial products: A theoretical investigation and case study. *Res. Policy* **2006**, *35*, 1291–1313. [CrossRef]
36. Hienerth, C. The commercialization of user innovations: The development of the Rodeo Kayak industry. *R D Manag.* **2006**, *36*, 273–294. [CrossRef]
37. Marchi, G.; Giachetti, C.; de Gennaro, P. Extending lead-user theory to online brand communities: The case of the community Ducati. *Technovation* **2011**, *31*, 350–361. [CrossRef]
38. Jeppesen, L.B.; Molin, M.J. Consumers as co-developers: Learning and innovation outside the firm. *Technol. Anal. Strateg. Manag.* **2003**, *15*, 363–383. [CrossRef]
39. Von Hippel, E.; von Krogh, G. Open source software and the "private-collective" innovation model: Issues for organization science. *Organ. Sci.* **2003**, *14*, 209–223. [CrossRef]
40. Von Krogh, G.; Spaeth, S.; Lakhani, K.R. Community, joining, and specialization in open source software innovation: A case study. *Res. Policy* **2003**, *32*, 1217–1241. [CrossRef]
41. Shah, S.K. Motivation, governance, and the viability of hybrid forms in open source software development. *Manag. Sci.* **2006**, *52*, 1000–1014. [CrossRef]
42. Jeppesen, L.B. User toolkits for innovation: Consumers support each other. *J. Prod. Innov. Manag.* **2005**, *22*, 347–362. [CrossRef]
43. Franke, N.; Keinz, P.; Schreier, M. Complementing mass customization toolkits with user communities: How peer input improves customer self-design. *J. Prod. Innov. Manag.* **2008**, *25*, 546–559. [CrossRef]
44. Franke, N.; Piller, F. Value creation by toolkits for user innovation and design: The case of the watch market. *J. Prod. Innov. Manag.* **2004**, *21*, 401–415. [CrossRef]
45. Jeppesen, L.B.; Lakhani, K.M. Marginality and problem solving effectiveness in broadcast search. *Organ. Sci.* **2010**, *21*, 1016–1033. [CrossRef]
46. Archak, N. Money, Glory and Cheap Talk: Analyzing Strategic Behavior of Contestants in Simultaneous Crowdsourcing Contests on TopCoder.com. In Proceedings of the 19th International Conference on World Wide Web, Raleigh, NC, USA, 26–30 April 2010.
47. Orgawa, S.; Piller, F.T. Reducing the risks of new product development. *MIT Sloan Manag. Rev.* **2006**, *47*, 65–71.
48. Bocken, N.; Short, S.; Rana, P.; Evans, S. A literature and practice review to develop Sustainable Business Model Archetypes. *J. Clean. Prod.* **2014**, *65*, 42–56. [CrossRef]
49. Boons, F.; Lüdeke-Freund, F. Business models for sustainable innovation: State-of-the-art and steps towards a research agenda. *J. Clean. Prod.* **2013**, *45*, 9–19. [CrossRef]
50. Stubbs, W.; Cocklin, C. Conceptualizing a "Sustainability Business Model". *Organ. Environ.* **2008**, *21*, 103–127. [CrossRef]
51. Teece, D. Business Models, Business Strategy and Innovation. *Long Range Plan.* **2010**, *43*, 172–194. [CrossRef]
52. Lüdeke-Freund, F. *Towards a Conceptual Framework of Business Models for Sustainability*; ERSCP-EMU Conference: Delft, The Netherlands, 2010.
53. Zott, C.; Amit, R.; Massa, L. The business model: Recent developments and future research. *J. Manag.* **2011**, *37*, 1019–1042.
54. Elkington, J. *Cannibals with Forks: The Triple Bottom Line of 21st Century Business*; Capstone: Oxford, UK, 1997.
55. Ehrenfeld, J.R. The Roots of Sustainability. *MIT Sloan Manag. Rev.* **2005**, *46*, 23–26.
56. Osterwalder, A.; Pigneur, Y. *Business Model Generation: A Handbook for Visionaries, Game Changers, and Challengers*; John Wiley & Sons: Hoboken, NJ, USA, 2010.

57. Yunus, M.; Moingeon, B.; Lehmann-Ortega, L. Building social business models: Lessons from the Grameen experience. *Long Range Plann.* **2010**, *43*, 308–325. [CrossRef]
58. Amit, R.; Zott, C. Creating value through business model innovation. *MIT Sloan Manag. Rev.* **2012**, *53*, 41–49.
59. Almirall, E.; Wareham, J. Innovation: A question of fit – the Living labs approach. In Proceedings of Symposium on Transversal Topics, Barcelona, Spain, 2–3 April 2009.
60. Linton, J.D.; Thongpapanl, N.T. Ranking the technology innovation management journals. *J. Prod. Innov. Manag.* **2004**, *21*, 123–139. [CrossRef]
61. West, J.; Bogers, M. Leveraging external sources of innovation: A review of research on open innovation. *J. Prod. Innov. Manag.* **2014**, *31*, 814–831. [CrossRef]
62. Boudreau, K.J.; Lakhani, K.R. Using the crowd as an innovation partner. *Harv. Bus. Rev.* **2013**, *91*, 60–69. [PubMed]
63. Bullinger, A.C.; Neyer, A.K.; Rass, M.; Moeslein, K.M. Community-based innovation contests: Where competition meets cooperation. *Creativity Innov. Manag.* **2010**, *19*, 290–303. [CrossRef]
64. Lehoux, P.; Miller, F.A.; Hivon, M.; Demers-Payette, O.; Urbach, D.R. Clinicians as health technology designers: Two contrasting tales about user involvement in innovation development. *Health Policy Technol.* **2013**, *2*, 122–130. [CrossRef]
65. Magnusson, P.R. Exploring the contributions of involving ordinary users in ideation of technology-based services. *J. Prod. Innov. Manag.* **2009**, *26*, 578–593. [CrossRef]
66. Still, K.; Huhtamäki, J.; Isomursu, M.; Lahti, J.; Koskela-Huotari, K. Analytics of the Impact of User Involvement in the Innovation Process and its Outcomes. Case Study: Media-Enhanced Learning (MEL) Service. In Proceedings of the Paper Presented at the 4th World Conference on Educational Sciences, Barcelona, Spain, 2–5 February 2012.
67. Harrison, D.; Waluszewski, A. The development of a user network as a way to re-launch an unwanted product. *Res. Policy* **2008**, *37*, 115–130. [CrossRef]
68. Jeppesen, L.B.; Laursen, K. The role of lead users in knowledge sharing. *Res. Policy* **2009**, *38*, 1582–1589. [CrossRef]
69. Schaltegger, S.; Lüdeke-Freund, F.; Hansen, E.G. Business cases for sustainability: The role of business model innovation for corporate sustainability. *Int. J. Innov. Sustain. Dev.* **2012**, *6*, 95–119. [CrossRef]
70. Reckwitz, A. Toward a Theory of Social Practices—A Development in Culturalist Theorizing. *Eur. J. Soc. Theory* **2002**, *5*, 243–263. [CrossRef]
71. Shove, E. Social theory and climate change questions often, sometimes and not yet asked. *Theory Cult. Soc.* **2010**, *27*, 277–288. [CrossRef]
72. Spaargaren, G. Theories of practices: Agency, technology, and culture Exploring the relevance of practice theories for the governance of sustainable consumption practices in the new world-order. *Glob. Environ. Chang.* **2011**, *21*, 813–822. [CrossRef]
73. Bergvall-Kåreborn, B.; Eriksson, C.L.; Ståhlbröst, A.; Svensson, J. A Milieu for Innovation—Defining Living Labs. In Proceedings of the 2nd ISPIM Innovation Symposium, New York, NY, USA, 6–9 December 2009.
74. Liedtke, C.; Baedeker, C.; Hasselkuβ, M.; Rohn, H. User-integrated innovation in Sustainable LivingLabs: An experimental infrastructure for researching and developing sustainable product service systems. *J. Clean. Prod.* **2015**, *97*, 106–116. [CrossRef]
75. McCormick, K.; Kiss, B. Learning through renovations for urban sustainability: The case of the Malmö Innovation Platform. *Curr. Opin. Environ. Sustain.* **2015**, *16*, 44–50. [CrossRef]
76. Voytenko, Y.; McCormick, K.; Evans, J.; Schliwa, G. Urban living labs for sustainability and low carbon cities in Europe: Towards a research agenda. *J. Clean. Prod.* **2015**, in press.
77. Franz, Y. Designing social living labs in urban research. *Info* **2015**, *17*, 53–66.
78. Liedtke, C.; Welfens, M.J.; Rohn, H.; Nordmann, J. LIVING LAB: User-driven innovation for sustainability. *Int. J. Sustain. High. Educ.* **2012**, *13*, 106–118. [CrossRef]
79. Guzmán, G.; del Carpio, A.F.; Colomo-Palacios, R.; de Diego, M.V. Living labs for user-driven innovation—A process reference model. *Res. Technol. Manag.* **2013**, *56*, 29–39. [CrossRef]
80. Ståhlbröst, A.; Bertoni, M.; Følstad, A.; Ebbesson, E.; Lund, J. Social media for user innovation in Living Labs: A framework to support user recruitment and commitment. In Proceedings of the 26th ISPIM Conference, Helsinki, Finland, 16–19 June 2013.

81. Leminen, S.; Nyström, A.G.; Westerlund, M. A typology of creative consumers in living labs. *J. Eng. Technol. Manag.* **2015**, in press. [CrossRef]
82. Georges, A.; Schuurman, D.; Baccarne, B.; Coorevits, L. User engagement in living lab field trials. *Info* **2015**, *17*, 26–39.
83. Karin, W.; Annika, Å.; Ståhlbröst, A. Exploring differences between central located test and home use test in a living lab context. *Int. J. Consum. Stud.* **2015**, *39*, 230–238. [CrossRef]

© 2015 by the authors. Licensee MDPI, Basel, Switzerland. This article is an open access article distributed under the terms and conditions of the Creative Commons Attribution (CC BY) license (http://creativecommons.org/licenses/by/4.0/).

Article

Weak and Strong Compensation for the Prioritization of Public Investments: Multidimensional Analysis for Pools

Gianluigi De Mare [1,*], Maria Fiorella Granata [2,†] and Antonio Nesticò [1,†]

1. Department of Civil Engineering, University of Salerno, Via Giovanni Paolo II, 132, Fisciano (SA) 84084, Italy; anestico@unisa.it
2. Department of Architecture, University of Palermo, Viale delle Scienze, ed, 14, Palermo 90128, Italy; maria.granata@unipa.it
* Correspondence: gdemare@unisa.it; Tel.: +39-089-964118
† These authors contributed equally to this work.

Academic Editor: Adam Jabłoński
Received: 9 September 2015; Accepted: 24 November 2015; Published: 2 December 2015

Abstract: Despite the economic crisis still heavily affecting most of Europe, a possible resumption can be found in the revitalization of public and private investments. These investments should be directed not only towards the strategic areas of infrastructures and production, but also to those which allow for a higher level of the quality of life (sports facilities, parks, *etc.*). In such cases, the need to balance the reasons of financial sustainability with environmental and social profiles is even more evident. Thus, multicriteria techniques, supporting complex assessments, should be implemented together with a monetary feasibility study (cost-benefit analysis). Multidimensional methods allow for the aggregation of different profiles into overall indicators. This study gives an account of how the application and comparison of multi-criteria approaches based on tools characterized by a higher or lower level of compensation between criteria can broaden the spectrum of analysis of the problems and lead to a more subtle logic of funding for public works and works of public utility, with a more current and mature sharing of profitability between private investors and users of community infrastructures.

Keywords: multicriteria evaluation; economic assessment; sports facilities; strong and weak sustainability; SMART; PROMETHEE II

1. Introduction

The formation of metropolitan cities, with geographic extensions much greater than the past, and the integration of original cultures from different countries raise the level of complexity of infrastructures in urban systems (transport, education, health, sports, *etc.*). At the same time, the recent economic crisis has placed the institutions that have historically been producers of the investment needed for such public works in front of the problem of having to find sufficient financial resources. In Europe, the financing channels have been primarily identified as the resources made available by the European Community, as well as the most advanced forms of public-private partnership. Private partners base the decision about their adhesion to projects of public interest on the fundamental criterion of the economic and financial convenience, which must be verified by using the appropriate financial evaluation techniques. Although the verification of the economic and financial feasibility is a necessary requirement for the realization of the project by private parties, the interest of the local community can be measured through a purely monetary analysis [1–4]. Therefore, the point of view of the public authority is broader. Based on the adopted strategic policies, it is interesting to know the level of satisfaction on social, cultural and environmental requests [5].

Public authorities should therefore be able to expertly mediate between the monetary feasibility of investments and its social and political coherence compared to the demands of growth and development from the population. In this perspective, it is important to be capable of "measuring" the suitability of either a public project or a project of public interest, in meeting the needs expressed by the local community. The measure of this capacity can be applied to a dual purpose: (1) identification of local priority projects to be considered within the definition of tools for territorial government; and (2) preparation of appropriate measures supporting the projects of public interest, which, although possibly characterized by a smaller economic attractiveness for private investors, can make a more significant contribution to the welfare of the community.

The assessment of the ability of a project of public interest in meeting the needs of the local community has a multidimensional nature and must be able to integrate the local political preferences delegated to land management.

To this end, the definition of composite indices, capable of integrating the quality of the urban projects from the point of view of the community into an overall assessment, is useful. These synthetic indexes can be used as evaluation instruments of the quality of urban projects from the perspective of the community and can pose parameters of judgment to identify reliefs, for example of a financial or tax nature, that can direct the membership of private partners to projects that are more favorable to the community. They can also be used to identify priority actions in the field of local strategic and financial planning.

The main functions of a composite index of sustainability related to a public work or a work of public interest can be identified in the ability to synthetically express the quality of the project in terms of the objectives of sustainability, to encourage communication with all of the involved parties and to legitimize choices derived from a rational and transparent analysis of the available alternatives [6].

The purpose of this paper is the construction of socio-environmental convenience indexes and integrated sustainability indexes for the provision of sports facilities. The index must summarize the main needs expressed by the stakeholders. Composite indicators of this type can also be defined for different types of projects.

This objective is pursued using different multi-criteria evaluation techniques, in view of the distinction between "weak sustainability" and "strong sustainability", opposing the idea of the almost complete against the idea of only the limited substitutability of natural capital with physical capital, respectively [7]. In particular, two different decision-making models, suitable for evaluating the contribution of public investments and private investments of public interest from the two-fold point of view of sustainability understood in a weak and strong sense, are proposed.

The model described in this paper is useful for the construction of a multi-dimensional index of "restricted social convenience" and "overall social convenience" or "overall sustainability" for investments targeted at the creation or adaptation of municipal swimming pools in the province of Salerno (Italy). The paper is organized in some introductory Section 2, Section 3, Section 4, Section 5, Section 6 and Section 7 on multicriteria tools for the construction of convenience indicators, in sections on the processing of models (8 and 9) and sections summarizing and discussing the results in Section 10 and Section 11.

2. The Formulation of a Social Convenience Index for Investments of a Public Nature

Synthetic indexes or composite indicators are evaluation tools widely used in decision-making on economy, environment, globalization, society, innovation and technology [8], public policies [9], sustainability about single civil engineering works [10] and at a local level [11], as well as in ranking countries [12].

Several aggregation procedures have been proposed to build a composite indicator integrating manifold issues [13,14]; however, from an operational point of view, they are the result of an aggregation rule applied to values representing the performance of a given alternative on a set of criteria.

The construction of a social synthetic index includes the following fundamental steps:

1. the carrying out of a detailed analysis of the basic needs of the local community as an instrument guiding the identification of the relevant points of view in the analysis of alternatives [15];
2. the choice of a suitable aggregation procedure, considering the use of the composite indicator in the sustainable management of the territory and the necessity of being easily understandable for local administrators, even if they do not have specific technical competences in decision analysis;
3. the weighting of considered indicators;
4. the implementation of the aggregative model for each alternative, in order to obtain the value of the indexes.

In general, either weights are directly attributed by experts or special techniques used in order to achieve more objective values. The assignment of weights to single indicators for their aggregation is considered a crucial step in social multicriteria evaluation, and a good solution could be the renunciation of their same assignment, considering, therefore, equal weights for all of the indicators. In this case, the number of the considered indicators will represent the importance of the criterion that they express [8].

The choice of aggregation procedure is also an important step for the essential implications of each procedure. Furthermore, it is known that the application of different decision models can lead to different results for the same decision problem [6,16].

The main aggregation approaches belong to Multiple Attribute Utility Theory (MAUT) [17,18], outranking methods, introduced by Bernard Roy [19], and other "non-classical" approaches [20].

Procedures belonging to classical approaches are all suitable for handling the aggregation of single one-dimensional indicators in a comprehensive index, since they can deal with both quantitative and qualitative information, as well as give as an outcome a measure of the performance of the considered alternatives.

The procedures belonging to the outranking approach, like the PROMETHEE (Preference Ranking Organization METHod for Enrichment Evaluations) [21] and ELECTRE (ELimination Et ChoixTraduisant la REalité) methods [19], which are based on a pair-wise comparison of the alternatives, use weights representing the coefficient of importance and are not, in general, totally compensatory methods [22]. This is the reason why they are able to support a strong sustainability concept in which a bad performance on an indicator is not fully compensated by a good performance on another one [8]. The outranking approach assumes the hypothesis of the preferential independence of any sub-family of indicators [22].

Approaches based on multi-attribute utility theory require the consideration of an n-dimensional utility function that assigns a value to each alternative, representing its preferability. In general, the n-dimensional utility function is constructed by aggregating one-dimensional utility functions on a single criterion, to which a weight may be associated [18]. Using this kind of procedure, the preferential independence of the family of indicators is also assumed, so that the marginal utilities can be assessed; the different indicators have to be expressed on the same scale; and the weights represent substitution rates [22].

The additive and multiplicative techniques are the most widely used form of aggregation function [23]. Other aggregation techniques, such as the class of Ordered Weighted Averaging (OWA) operators [24] and the Choquet integral [25,26], belong to the MAUT framework and are extensions of weighted means. OWA operators are able to express vague quantifications, and the Choquet integral can model interactions among criteria [27].

3. Social Convenience Indexes for Investments in Swimming Pools

In the present paper, a synthetic index of "restricted social convenience" related to projects for supplying sports facilities to a local community is defined. The proposed composite indicator comprehends both environmental aspects, as well as appropriate social aspects. Furthermore, a composite index of "overall social convenience", also called "overall sustainability", for the same projects is defined. It synthesizes the environmental, social and financial aspects.

Various reasons can explain the preference commonly given to the use of procedures based on additive value functions in the construction of synthetic indexes of sustainability:

- the modeling of preferences is rather intuitive and therefore easily understandable by non-experts;
- the value functions assign a comprehensive value to each alternative and not a measure of the degree of preference of an alternative over another;
- unlike the outranking methods, the comparability of alternatives is always possible [22];
- the outcomes are robust due to the independent evaluation of each alternative [28].

The above-mentioned reasons also justify the decision to use the MAUT approach, in the weighted linear form, for the formulation of an index of social convenience relating to investments for the creation or adaptation of sports facilities [29]. Furthermore, MAUT approaches allow for compensation among the different points of view integrated in the assessment procedure [22], with the result being agreeable to the assumption of a weak conception of sustainability [8], that is suitable for local contexts with several social needs to be satisfied.

With the aim of testing the results obtained with different aggregation techniques, in relation to the conception of sustainability in the strong or weak sense, in the present study, a comparison is made between the results achieved with the use of a compensatory aggregation procedure and of one that tends to partly compensate for the poor performance on some criteria with the favorable performance on other criteria. Therefore, the outcomes of the available alternatives' evaluation through the weighted linear sum aggregation model, in the simplified version SMART (simple multi-attribute rating technique), will be compared to those obtained by using a less compensatory aggregation technique. In particular, the PROMETHEE II procedure will be used. The choice of the two aggregation procedures is justified in the following section.

4. Reasons for the Choice of Aggregation Procedures

Using multi-criteria assessments for real decision-making problems in the public sector, the easiness of understanding the method and the minimum request for preference information from the decision-makers have been highlighted as key features of a suitable decision-making model [6]. Since in the evaluation process for the formulation of the aggregate index of the investments' social convenience, the role of the decision-maker is held by political institutions, in general not equipped with specific skills in the field of mathematical techniques for multi-criteria evaluation; the simplicity of the method is considered essential for the contribution of the decision-makers in eliciting their preferences, with it being more conscious and less prone to errors of interpretation.

As stated, the use of the MAUT approach is a widespread choice in the elaboration of sustainability indexes. In view of the difficulties detected in practice for defining the trade-off between the criteria [28] and due to the lack of information on the marginal utility functions, it was decided to resort to the simplified formulation of the linear model MAUT, known as SMART. In contrast to the SMART method, which like the other additive models is fully compensatory, an outranking method is used. Procedures belonging to this class may have more or less a degree of compensation between the criteria [22].

Endowed with a greater comprehensibility for the decision-makers than ELECTRE methods [30], the PROMETHEE II procedure is implemented here. It provides a single complete preorder, although the non-compensatory level is more limited compared to other ELECTRE methods, in particular in the absence of thresholds of preference, indifference and veto [31]. Applying the PROMETHEE II, we opt for the functional form of the "usual criterion", which avoids the definition of indifference and/or preference thresholds, which is typically a complex [28,31,32] and time-consuming [33] exercise for decision-makers. Neglecting the use of thresholds implies that any difference between two evaluations produces a strict preference for the alternative having a better, even if small, evaluation with respect the considered criterion.

SMART and PROMETHEE II are relatively simple multi-criteria evaluation procedures and therefore easily comprehensible by non-expert actors involved in the assessment. In particular, as previously mentioned, among the possible forms adoptable for the preference function of the outranking procedure, the "usual criterion" is chosen, since it does not require the definition of additional parameters and whose understanding is intuitive. The application domains of both procedures fit our decision problem [34], since they can treat discrete cardinal and ordinal information; they can also solve choice and ranking decision problems; they use the same type of inter-information between criteria, since weights reflect the relative importance between criteria [21,35]; they can be implemented using a simple spreadsheet. In addition, weights do not depend on the measurement scale of the criteria, both in the PROMETHEE II procedure [30] and in SMART, since in the latter, the measurement scales are normalized [35]. These circumstances make their task easier for decision-makers [33] and allow for the comparison of the results obtained by the two procedures.

5. Insertion of the Present Work in Literature Reviews

SMART and PROMETHEE methods are among the most used aggregation tools and have been applied to a wide variety of decision problems.

A literature review up to the year 2010 is given by Behzadian *et al.* [30], revealing an abundant production of the applications of PROMETHEE methods concerning logistic and transportation problems; energy, water, environment and business management; chemistry, manufacturing and social topics. In more recent years, there has been a great deal of interest in applying the various PROMETHEE methods, and a large number of applications about the management of natural resources is available; see Kuang *et al.* [36]. Only a recent interest has been shown for the specific field of assessment for the sustainability of cities and territories. The surveyed applications are on decisions at a building scale [37], urban scale [32,38] and on an overall assessment of global cities [39].

The main application of SMART is on environmental management decisions [40–42], but it is also proposed for a public assessment application for mitigation and adaptation policy [43], as well as transport [44]. On an urban scale, it is used in assessing the sustainability of built heritage [45], local energy systems [46] and urban ecosystems [47–50].

The main aspects central to the present work are the comparison between different aggregation procedures in multicriteria assessment and the issue of weak and strong sustainability. Previous works have made comparisons between different assessment methods, according to the technical characteristics of algorithms, as in [16,51], in order to make choices coherent with sustainability assessment problems [23] or to compare the results with aided decisions [52]. Compared to previous works, we aim to compare the outcomes from different assessment methods with regard to the compensatory effect, and confronting SMART and PROMETHEE II, we exclude the use of thresholds, as in [51], in order to investigate the differences between the considered methods under maximum similarity conditions. Regarding sustainability assessment, there is a very large amount of literature on every sector and, in particular, urban areas, as in [53], while the issue of weak and strong sustainability has been mainly addressed from a methodological point of view [8,13,54–56]. Although there have been some specific applicatory works on regions [57], countries [58,59], fisheries [60] and urban heritage [61], the need to address the issue of assessment application on weak and strong sustainability [62] has been recognized. In this work, the SMART and PROMETHEE II methods are used to assess the sustainability of single public projects in an urban context. In particular, they are applied to a swimming pool ranking problem.

6. Aggregation by the SMART Procedure

The weighted linear aggregation is the usual procedure used in the computation of composite indicators. Using SMART, a simplified form of MAUT [35,63] given a set of alternatives $\{A_1, A_2, \ldots A_m\}$, a set of indicators $\{c_1, c_2, \ldots c_n\}$ and their respective weights $\{w_1, w_2, \ldots w_n\}$, a synthetic index (V)

related to the alternative j is obtained by applying a weighted additive aggregation model, according to the following mathematical rule:

$$V(A_i) = \sum_i v_{ij} \cdot w_i \quad i = 1, 2, ..., n \tag{1}$$

with:

$$\sum_i w_i = 1 \text{ and } 0 \leq w_i \leq 1 \tag{2}$$

where $v_{i,j}$ is the normalized performance value on the indicator ci and w_i is the normalized weight [8].

The assessment $v_{i,j}$ is standardized to a 0–1 scale, where zero and one represent the worst and best performances, respectively [36]. The weights can be assigned by the direct rating method, according to which raw weights are assigned to criteria ranked according to their importance, attributing a score of 10 to the least important criterion, then assigning increasing scores to the other criteria in relation to the first score and, finally, normalizing the sum of the assigned weights to one [35].

While in MAUT models, weights reflect both scale and importance, in SMART, weights reflect only importance, since the scales are transformed to a common basis [64].

7. Aggregation by the PROMETHEE II Procedure

PROMETHEE procedures are based on the outranking relation, according to which an alternative outranks another alternative if, given the preferences of the decision-makers, there are sufficient arguments for recognizing that the first alternative is not less preferable than the second one [22]. The construction of the outranking relation in the PROMETHEE II method is characterized by the use of variables and parameters that are easily understandable by unexperienced decision-makers [22].

Introduced by Brans and Vincke [21], the PROMETHEE methods have been used in applications related to multiple fields [32], but their use is not widespread in the construction of composite indicators.

Given a set of alternatives $\{A_1, A_2, ... A_m\}$ and a system of indicators $\{c_1, c_2, ... c_n\}$ with their respective weights $\{w_1, w_2, ... w_n\}$ and knowing the performances of alternatives on single criteria, the outranking degree corresponding to an ordered couple of alternatives (A_r, A_s) is defined by the aggregated preference index, expressing the preference of A_r over A_s according to all of the criteria [65]:

$$\pi(A_r, A_s) = \sum_{i=1}^{n} P_i(A_r, A_s) w_i \text{ with } i = 1, 2, ..., n \tag{3}$$

in which $P_i(A_r, A_s)$ is a preference function related to the criteria i. Preference functions are defined by suitable functional forms and associated parameters, assigning to the differences between the performance of two alternatives on a criterion, $d_i(A_r, A_s) = c_i(A_r) - c_i(A_s)$, a preference degree ranging from 0–1. Among the available forms of the preference function [65], the one able to better express the preferences of the decision-makers will be chosen for each criterion. In the proposed assessment model, the usual criterion has been adopted for all of the considered criteria. In case of a criterion i to be maximized, comparing the alternatives A_r and A_s, the usual criterion expresses a strict preference of A_r in comparison with A_s only if the difference di (A_r, A_s) is positive. The choice is founded on the need to use a very simple assessment model that can be easily understood by decision-makers and on the advisability of not requiring the use of a threshold of indifference and/or of strict preference. Thus, the generalized usual criterion does not require additional information in comparison to the simple formulation of MAUT considered here. The preference function related to the usual criterion is expressed as follows [65]:

$$P_i(A_r, A_s) = \begin{cases} 0 \text{ if } d_i(A_r, A_s) \leq 0 \\ 1 \text{ if } d_i(A_r, A_s) > 0 \end{cases} \tag{4}$$

This form of the generalized criterion corresponds to the "true criterion" [66], expressing a strict preference for any difference between two evaluations [67].

Finally, the PROMETHEE II procedure leads to a unique complete preorder ranking the alternatives according to a decreasing order of values of the net outranking flow $\varphi(A_r)$ for each alternative that is given by:

$$\varphi(A_r) = \varphi^+(A_r) - \varphi^-(A_r) \qquad (5)$$

where $\varphi^+(A_r)$ is the positive flow and $\varphi^-(A_r)$ is the negative flow, representing how the alternative A_r outranks the other ones and how A_r is outranked by the other alternatives. Positive and negative flows are expressed as follows [65]:

$$\varphi^+(A_r) = \frac{1}{m-1} \sum_{k \neq i} \pi(A_r, A_s) \text{ with } r = 1, 2, ..., m \qquad (6)$$

$$\varphi^-(A_r) = \frac{1}{m-1} \sum_{k \neq i} \pi(A_s, A_r) \text{ with } r = 1, 2, ..., m \qquad (7)$$

8. Three Projects for Municipal Pools in the Province of Salerno (Italy)

8.1. The swimming pool in Nocera Inferiore

The project involves the construction of an indoor swimming center to be built in the town of Nocera Inferiore (Salerno). The plant will be able to be approved by the Italian Swimming Federation, based on the safety standards of the Italian Olympic National Committee (CONI) and the Ministry of Interior, which set the size of the tanks according to the activities that must take place. The plant is designed to emit into the atmosphere the least possible amount of pollutants and adopts alternative methods of energy production, in the present case thermo-photovoltaic hybrid panels.

The project involves the construction of a semi-Olympic indoor pool with a size of 25 per 16.66 m and of two smaller swimming pools of 16.66 per 8 m, one dedicated to children and the other for rehabilitation activities and water aerobics. Some services dedicated to users are also planned. They include a bar, a solarium, a sauna and a gym. The structure is articulated on a single level consisting of a space for the swimming pools and a service block. The structure of external cladding of the service block will be made of panels with improved thermal performances, while the coverage of the swimming pool area will be in curved laminated wood.

8.2. The swimming pool in Sapri

This swimming pool will be realized in the city of Sapri, more precisely in the south, in Brizzi, close to the town center. Currently, the area is a sports ground, and with the realization of the structure, it will become a real sports center. This project involves the construction of a concrete structure cast *in situ* to be used as a reception and dressing room for athletes. The construction of the roof of the swimming pool is planned in precast prestressed concrete.

The pool for sports (swimming, water polo) has dimensions of 12.60 m for 25.00 m and a constant depth of 2.00 m, with an area of 315 m^2 and a volume of 630 m^3. The flat roof around the pool will have a width of 2.50 m along the long side and of 4.00 m along the other side, according to the norms of the Italian Olympic National Committee (CONI).

The pool cover, entirely prefabricated, will consist of prestressed elements and pillars, with a total area of 747 m^2 (40.60 m for 18.40 m) and a practicable deck.

8.3. The swimming pool in Salerno

The plant is located in the center of Salerno. The project will cover the top of the adult pool, the reconstruction of the same pool, the construction of adjacent changing rooms, the renovation of the existing building and the installation of parking areas equipped with photovoltaic shelters. The projected plant includes an outdoor swimming pool of 28 m × 20 m × 1.60 m, an outdoor swimming pool for children of 11 m × 6 m × 0.50 m, a solarium around the swimming pools, two changing rooms with toilets and showers, a waiting room with reception, an infirmary, a bar room, an engine room, a boiler room, an outdoor parking area for about fifty cars and a green area adjacent to the swimming plant.

9. Calculation of the Composite Indicators for the Three Municipal Pools

Relevant indicators have been selected on the basis of an in-depth analysis of the local context conducted by the provincial public authority [68], as well as data taken from ISTAT (Istituto Nazionale di Statistica—National Institute of Statistics) on the local social, environmental and economic characteristics. According to ISTAT, young people are the main users of sports facilities; some student associations as the potential user basin of each swimming pool were involved in a discussion aimed at understanding their opinions about what features they expected a sustainable swimming pool should have. Table 1 presents the final value tree, including the goal, criteria and indicators, while Table 2 describes the single indicators, and Table 3 shows their direction and the measurement scales. The set of selected criteria represents all of the key sustainability aspects in relation to the specific context, avoiding redundancy [66].

While the environmental and social aspects define the "restricted social convenience" of the investments in question, the addition of the pre-taxation internal rate of return allows for the assessment of the "overall sustainability", which integrates the financial feasibility.

The aesthetic quality of the projects has not been included in the set of criteria, because the alternatives can be considered as having the same level of architectonic quality.

While indicators I1, I4, I6 and I7 are measured in their natural scales, indicators I2, I3 and I5 express qualitative judgments. Their levels of performance are measured according to the values shown in Table 4.

Table 1. Value tree.

Goal	Criteria	Codes-Indicators
Overall sustainability	Environmental issues	I1—Spared emissions from plants I2—Preservation of natural land I3—Accessibility
	Social issues	I4—Level of supply of swimming services I5—Synergistic effect I6—Employment effect
	Financial issue	I7—Pre-taxation internal rate of return

Table 2. Description of indicators.

Codes-Indicators	Description
I1—Spared emissions from plants	It measures the spared emission of CO_2 per user due to the reduction of energy consumption from traditional energy sources
I2—Preservation of natural land	It expresses the quality of a project regarding the shift of natural land to artificial areas
I3—Accessibility	It regards the presence of dedicated parking for users and the quality of a suitable public transport service
I4—Level of supply of swimming services	It concerns the level of the supply of swimming services against the local level of demand.
I5—Synergistic effect	It is achieved if the swimming plant is localized near other sports facilities, creating an integrated system of sports facilities useful also as a center for social gathering
I6—Employment effect	It expresses the contribution to the development of new employment
I7—Pre-taxation internal rate of return	It expresses the financial feasibility of the investment

Table 3. Information on indicators.

Codes-Indicators	Direction	Measurement Scale
I1—Spared emissions from plants	To be maximized	kg CO_2/year
I2—Preservation of natural land	To be maximized	Judgment measured on an ordinal scale
I3—Accessibility	To be maximized	Judgment measured on an ordinal scale
I4—Level of supply of swimming services	To be maximized	Supply of swimming services/relative demand
I5—Synergistic effect	To be maximized	Judgment measured on an ordinal scale
I6—Employment effect	To be maximized	Number of employees
I7—Pre-taxation internal rate of return	To be maximized	Value on 0–1 scale

Table 4. Levels of performance for indicators I2, I3 and I5.

I2		I3		I5	
Performance-Score		Performance-Score		Performance-Score	
Reuse of already built land	10	Presence of dedicated parking and of a suitable public transport service	10	Nearness to more than one sports facility	10
		Presence of dedicated parking and of an insufficient public transport service	5	Nearness to one sports facility	5
Shifting of natural land to artificial area	0	Absence of dedicated parking and of a suitable public transport service	0	Nearness to no sports facility	0

Table 5 summarizes the performance of the considered projects for swimming facilities on the set of indicators. The projects cover three geographical areas of the province of Salerno, which are the city of Salerno, the city of Nocera and the city of Sapri.

Table 5. Performance table.

Indicators		Projects		
		Salerno	Nocera	Sapri
Environmental issues	I1 (kg CO_2/year)	81,620	80,465	106,000
	I2 (ordinal judgment)	10	0	0
	I3 (ordinal judgment)	10	5	5
Social issues	I4 (supply/demand)	0.96	1	1
	I5 (ordinal judgment)	5	10	5
	I6 (number of employees)	25	40	15
Fin. issue	I7 (Pre-taxation internal rate of return)	0.129	0.117	0.140

For the purposes of the aggregation of the performances of the alternatives using the SMART method, we consider the standardized marginal utility functions assigning the value one to the best performance according to the considered indicator and the value zero to the worst one with the linear form of marginal utilities for indicators.

The aggregation of performances by the PROMETHEE II method does not require the transformation into a common scale, thanks to a pairwise comparison between the alternatives.

Initially, we calculated the synthetic index of the "restricted" social convenience relative to the alternatives under consideration. Regarding the weights, in the first assessment, we attached the same value to all of the indicators (0.166), by giving the same importance to the social and environmental criteria. This choice is justified by the consideration that the social and environmental issues are the main topics of sustainability in the considered local context.

Using the "distance from the best and worst performers" technique [6], the normalized performance table is obtained (Table 6).

Finally, according to Equations (1) and (5), the composite indicators of the restricted social convenience (RSC) related to the considered projects are calculated (Table 7). They express the environmental and social quality of each project.

The local administrations involved can choose the system of weights that best suit their policies. The composite indicators shown in Table 7 refer to a situation in which the same importance is attached to individual indicators and then to the two social and environmental criteria. However, if the social aspects are considered doubly more important than the environmental ones, the composite indicators will become the RSC' ones of Table 8.

Table 6. Normalized performance table.

Criteria	Projects		
	Salerno	Nocera	Sapri
I1	0.05	0	1
I2	1	0	0
I3	1	0	0
I4	0	1	1
I5	0	1	0
I6	0.40	1	0

Table 7. Composite indicators of social convenience obtained by assuming equal importance of the social and environmental aspects. RSC, restricted social convenience; SMART, simple multi-attribute rating technique.

Projects	Composite Indicators	
	RSC (SMART)	RSC (PROM.)
Salerno	0.41	0.083
Nocera	0.50	0.082
Sapri	0.33	−0.167

On the contrary, if the environmental issues are twice preferred in comparison to the social issues, the requested synthetic indexes are those in the columns RSC" of Table 8. The different preferences related to the relative importance among the indicators could still be considered to better represent the preferences of the decision-maker.

Table 8. Composite indicators of social convenience obtained taking a double preference for the social aspects with respect to the environmental ones (RSC') and *vice versa* (RSC").

Projects	RSC' (SMART)	RSC' (PROM.)	RSC" (SMART)	RSC" (PROM.)
Salerno	0.316	−0.111	0.499	0.278
Nocera	0.667	0.333	0.333	−0.167
Sapri	0.333	−0.222	0.333	−0.111

We then calculated the composite indicators of the overall sustainability (SC) obtained by integrating in the evaluation the contribution of the financial feasibility to the aspects of social convenience.

Table 9 shows the composite indexes of integrated sustainability obtained with the SMART and PROMETHEE II procedures assuming equal importance to the three categories (the social, environmental and financial one) of the indicators.

Table 9. Composite indicators of integrated sustainability obtained by assuming equal importance for the social, environmental and financial aspects.

Projects	Composite Indicators	
	SC (SMART)	SC (PROM.)
Salerno	0.449	0.055
Nocera	0.333	−0.278
Sapri	0.555	0.222

Finally, Table 10 presents the aggregate indices obtained by attributing to the social aspects a double importance compared to the environmental ones, while the environmental and financial aspects are considered of equal importance (SC′) and the aggregate indices obtained by giving to the environmental aspects a double importance in comparison to the social ones, while the financial and social aspects are considered of equal importance (SC″).

Table 10. Composite indicators of integrated sustainability obtained by assuming a double preference for the social aspects over the environmental and financial ones (SC′) and *vice versa* (SC″).

Projects	SC′ (SMART)	SC′ (PROM.)	SC″ (SMART)	SC″ (PROM.)
Salerno	0.371	−0.083	0.509	0.208
Nocera	0.501	0.000	0.250	−0.375
Sapri	0.500	0.083	0.500	0.167

10. Summary and Discussion of the Results

In this paper, the simplified linear aggregative model SMART and the PROMETHEE II model have been tested with the aim of verifying their utility in the elaboration of synthetic indexes for the choice or ranking of investments in urban development. Table 11 presents the rankings obtained through the use of the two procedures for the aggregation of the partial evaluation of the alternatives on the criteria.

As expected, the outcomes of the evaluation carried out by the considered methods lead to different scenarios. The comparison between the evaluation table (Table 3) and the ranking table (Table 11) induces the following considerations.

Assuming the same importance attributed to the classes of indicators, the exclusion of the financial parameter in the valuation of the synthetic index penalizes the investment in the territory of Sapri, which is the most disadvantaged for two out of three indicators for both the social category and the environmental aspects. Using SMART, the best performances of the alternative A2 (Nocera) on the social indicators offset the very bad performances on the environmental aspects. On the contrary, PROMETHEE II rewards the more balanced performances of the alternative A1 (Salerno).

If an equal importance is recognized for the various classes of indicators, the inclusion of the financial parameter in the evaluation of the synthetic index reverses the ranking of the investment in Sapri, which is the most disadvantaged for two out of three indicators for both the social and environmental categories. The drawback is re-balanced by the best financial performance.

Assuming a greater importance is attributed to the class of indicators on the social aspects compared to all of the remaining considered classes, the exclusion of the financial parameter in the evaluation of the synthetic index rewards, using both aggregation procedures, the investment in the territory of Nocera, which has the best performance on the social category. For the successive positions of the ranking, while PROMETHEE II awards the most balanced performances for the environmental aspects of the alternative A1-Salerno, SMART gives the highest-ranking to the alternative A3-Sapri, for which the best performance on the indicator I1 is able to balance the bad performances on the remaining environmental indicators. Analogous considerations can be made about the remaining rankings.

Nevertheless, the analysis of the results outlines some clearly legible trends.

Table 11. The obtained rankings.

RSC (SMART)	RSC (PROM.)
Nocera	Salerno
Salerno	Nocera
Sapri	Sapri
SC (SMART)	**SC (PROM.)**
Sapri	Sapri
Salerno	Salerno
Nocera	Nocera
RSC' (SMART)	**RSC' (PROM.)**
Nocera	Nocera
Sapri	Salerno
Salerno	Sapri
SC' (SMART)	**SC' (PROM.)**
Nocera	Sapri
Sapri	Nocera
Salerno	Salerno
RSC'' (SMART)	**RSC'' (PROM.)**
Salerno	Salerno
Nocera-Sapri	Sapri
Nocera-Sapri	Nocera
SC'' (SMART)	**SC'' (PROM.)**
Salerno	Salerno
Sapri	Sapri
Nocera	Nocera

In the aggregation carried out neglecting the financial criterion, both aggregative models indicate that the project in Sapri is the poorer. In fact, four times it is the last in the ranking, and two times it is penultimate. On the contrary, the projects in Nocera and Salerno share the leadership, with three first positions and two second places in the rankings.

Moreover, the compensatory effect of the procedure SMART seems to show itself. In fact, the procedure favors the project in Nocera (two first places and one second place in the rankings), whose profile of performances consists of three maximum values and three minimum values (see Table 4). Instead, the PROMETHEE method favors the project with a more balanced profile (Salerno; two times in the first position in the rankings and one time in the second position).

The outlined framework dismantles itself with the introduction of the financial criterion. First, the project in Sapri becomes by far the dominant one (three times it is in the first position of the rankings and three times first in the second one). It is followed by the project in Salerno (two times in the first position of the rankings and two times in the second one) and then by the project in Nocera (one time in the first position of the rankings and one time in the second one).

However, what is most striking is the substantial stabilization of the rankings obtained using the two methods. In developing the indices SC and SC'', the rankings obtained by the two methods do not change. Sapri-Salerno-Nocera is the ranking outlined applying both SMART and PROMETHEE in the calculus of the index SC. Salerno-Sapri-Nocera is the ranking obtained using both SMART and PROMETHEE for the index SC''. In the calculation of SC', the project in Salerno always occupies the third position in the rankings, regardless of the used aggregation procedure, while the projects in Nocera and Sapri are reversed in the leadership.

This last evidence has strategic implications that deserve attention. The substantial stabilization of the results achieved using a more compensatory aggregation procedure (SMART) or a less compensatory one (PROMETHEE) leads to distrust of easy propaganda proclamations. In fact, it would be easy for decision-makers to convey the use of a non-compensatory aggregation procedure as a political choice of strong sustainability, when the same results are reached using a compensatory method. Therefore, in such cases, the prevalence of a project over another one does not arise from the application of stricter selective rules, but from the same nature of the projects that shows a very stable relative placement (obviously with respect to the introduced criteria).

11. Conclusions

As previously stated, the reconciliation of social, environmental and financial requirements places decision-makers in front of scenarios that are often complex, articulated or even conflicting. Multicriteria analysis techniques can support decision-makers in making aware and rational choices.

In comparison with the analysis carried out by the same authors in a previous work [29] where the rankings of the considered investments for supplying swimming pools in the south of Italy were completely opposite when a sustainable approach from an exclusively socio-environmental point of view or a merely financial approach were alternatively considered, the analysis presented in this paper characterizes the use of a multicriteria technique and a more articulated pattern of evaluation with regards to the considered set of weights.

Unlike the previously mentioned experiences, the new pattern of valuation combines the financial profile with the socio-environmental one in the versions SC' and SC", and this integration destabilizes the previously obtained rankings.

In fact, if the overall effects are considered, the investment in Sapri, which according to the first analysis conducted neglecting the financial criterion ranks four times out of six in the bottom position, rises to a top position three times out of six when the financial criterion is taken into consideration. The investment in Nocera, which was the best one three times out of six, ranks in the bottom position four times out of six.

However, the main difference is recorded for the investment in Salerno. If only the criteria belonging to the social and environmental class are considered when calculating the synthetic index [29], it ranks in an intermediate position, both attributing a greater importance to the socio-environmental aspects. In the new implementation, it has a better position in the rankings, whether the financial criterion is neglected or is taken into consideration.

Figure 1 shows the prevailing projects according to the considered assessment procedures. Using SMART, the project in Nocera prevails three times over the others, while using PROMETHEE, the more balanced project in Salerno is preferred three times. This result confirms the less compensative effect of the used outranking method.

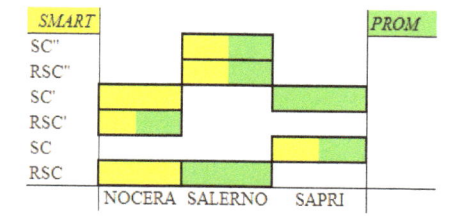

Figure 1. Prevailing projects according to the considered aggregation methods

The present analysis, which deserves further investigation from the point of view of the stability of outcomes on the basis of statistical techniques, highlights the huge responsibility of decision-makers when choices are also based on social and environmental principles and not merely on monetary criteria, even if a multidimensional assessment is carried out. This consideration is confirmed by the strictness imposed by the European Commission on the management of public funds, but also poses limits that must be revised when funds are of a private nature, considering the levels of profitability that can be shared with the community.

Another interesting development of this work could be a comparison of the outcomes of the assessment methods used with those coming from the use of specific aggregation procedures able to include interaction effects among the criteria, such as the Choquet integral or the ELECTRE III method with interactions between the criteria [69], in order to consider the different levels of strong and weak compensability.

Finally, it should be noted that the results of the implemented calculations seem to indicate that certain investment projects have performances on the criteria that make the rankings obtained robust through more or less compensatory aggregation procedures. This condition, where conveniently checked on a larger sample of study, leads to repudiation of the necessity of the adoption of a non-compensatory aggregation procedure in order to obtain a decision of strong sustainability. The adoption could instead simply hide manipulative intentions in the choices on the allocation of public resources.

Acknowledgments: The authors are grateful to the anonymous reviewers for the valuable comments that contributed to the improvement of the manuscript.

Author Contributions: The authors contributed equally to this work.

Conflicts of Interest: The authors declare no conflict of interest.

References

1. Fusco Girard, L., Ed.; *Le Valutazioni per lo Sviluppo Sostenibile Della Città e del Territorio*; FrancoAngeli: Milano, Italy, 1997.
2. Nijkamp, P., (Ed.) *Sustainability of Urban System*; Aldershot: Avebury, UK, 1990.
3. Rizzo, F. *Il Capitale Sociale Della Città. Valutazione, Pianificazione e Gestione*; Franco Angeli: Milano, Italy, 2003.
4. De Mare, G.; Nesticò, A.; Tajani, F. Building Investments for the Revitalization of the Territory: A Multisectoral Model of Economic Analysis. In Proceedings of the 3th International Conference, ICCSA 2013, Ho Chi Minh City, Vietnam, 24–27 June 2013; Murgante, B., Misra, S., Carlini, M., Torre, C., Nguyen, H.-Q., Taniar, D., Apduhan, B.O., Gervasi, O., Eds.; Springer Verlag: Berlin, Germany; Heidelberg, Germany, 2013; Volume 7973, pp. 493–508.
5. European Ministers Responsible for Urban Development. *Leipzig Charter on Sustainable European Cities. Final Draft*; European Ministers Responsible for Urban Development: Leipzig, Germany, 2007.
6. Lahdelma, R.; Salminen, P.; Hokkanen, J. Using Multicriteria Methods in Environmental Planning and Management. *Environ. Manag.* **2000**, *26*, 595–605. [CrossRef] [PubMed]
7. Daly, H.E.; Cobb, J.B., Jr. *For the Common Good*; Beacon Press: Boston, MA, USA, 1989.
8. Munda, G. Multiple Criteria Decision analysis and Sustainable Development. In *Multiple Criteria Decision Analysis: State of the Art Surveys*; Figueira, J., Greco, S., Ehrgott, M., Eds.; Springer: New York, NY, USA, 2005; pp. 953–986.
9. Munda, G. *Social Multi-Criteria Evaluation*; Springer-Verlag: Heidelberg, Germany; New York, NY, USA, 2007.
10. Bob, C.; Dencsak, T.; Bob, L. A Sustainability Model for the Assessment of Civil Engineer Works. In *Recent Advances in Energy, Environment, Biology and Ecology*, Proceedings of the 10th WSEAS International Conference on Energy, Environment, Ecosystems and Sustainable Development (EEESD '14), Tenerife, Spain, 10–12 January 2014; WSEAS Press: Sofia, Bulgaria, 2014; pp. 161–168.
11. Lazăr, C.; Lazăr, M. Proposal of a sustainable development synthetic indicator at local level. In Proceedings of the 9th WSEAS International Conference on Mathematics & Computers in Business and Economics (MCBE '08), Bucharest, Romania, 24–26 June 2008; WSEAS Press: Sofia, Bulgaria, 2008; pp. 74–78.
12. OECD. *JRC European Commission, Handbook on Constructing Composite Indicators. Methodology and User Guide*; OECD Publishing: Paris, France, 2008.

13. Munda, G. Choosing aggregation rules for composite indicators. *Soc. Indic. Res.* **2012**, *109*, 337–354. [CrossRef]
14. Granata, M.F. The city management: Methodological Considerations on the Multiple Criteria Techniques. In *The Right to the City. Human Rights and the City Crisis*; Beguinot, C., Ed.; Giannini Editore: Naples, Italy, 2012; pp. 295–319.
15. Sustainable Cities International—Canadian International Development Agency. *Indicators for Sustainability. How Cities Are Monitoring and Evaluating Their Success*; Sustainable Cities International—Canadian International Development Agency: Vancouver, BC, Canada, 2012.
16. Olson, D.L. Comparison of three multicriteria methods to predict known outcomes. *Eur. J. Oper. Res.* **2001**, *130*, 576–587. [CrossRef]
17. Von Neumann, J.; Morgenstern, O. *Theory of Games and Economic Behaviour*, 2nd ed.; Princeton University Press: Princeton, NJ, USA, 1947.
18. Keeney, R.L.; Raiffa, H. *Decisions with Multiple Objectives Preferences and Value Tradeoffs*; John Wiley&Sons: New York, NY, USA, 1976.
19. Roy, B. Classement et choix en presence de points de vue multiples (la méthode ELECTRE). *RAIRO* **1968**, *8*, 57–75.
20. Figueira, J.; Greco, S.; Ehrgott, M. Introduction. In *Multiple Criteria Decision Analysis: State of the Art Surveys*; Figueira, J., Greco, S., Ehrgott, M., Eds.; Springer: New York, NY, USA, 2005; pp. xxi–xxxvi.
21. Vincke, P.; Brans, J.P. A preference ranking organization method. The PROMETHEE method for MCDM. *Manag. Sci.* **1985**, *31*, 641–656.
22. Vincke, P. *Multicriteria Decision-Aid*; John Wiley & Sons: Chichester, UK, 1992.
23. De Montis, A.; de Toro, P.; Droste-Franke, B.; Omann, I.; Stagl, S. Assessing the quality of different MCDA methods. In *Alternatives for Environmental Valuation*; Getzner, M., Spash, C., Stagl, S., Eds.; Routledge: London, UK, 2005; pp. 99–133.
24. Yager, R.R. On ordered weighted averaging aggregation operators in multi-criteria decision making. *IEEE Trans. Syst. Man Cybernet. Part B* **1988**, *18*, 183–190. [CrossRef]
25. Choquet, G. Theory of capacities. *Ann. de l'Inst. Fourier* **1953**, *5*, 131–295. [CrossRef]
26. Sugeno, M. Theory of Fuzzy Integrals and Its Applications. Ph.D. Thesis, Tokyo Institute of Technology, Tokyo, Japan, 1974.
27. Grabisch, M. The application of fuzzy integrals in multicriteria decision making. *Eur. J. Oper. Res.* **1996**, *89*, 445–456. [CrossRef]
28. Munda, G. The issue of consistency: Basic discrete multi-criteria "Methods". In *Social Multi-Criteria Evaluation for a Sustainable Economy*; Munda, G., Ed.; Springer-Verlag: Berlin, Germany; Heidelberg, Germany, 2008; pp. 85–109.
29. De Mare, G.; Granata, M.F.; Nesticò, A. Complex efficiency of sports facilities. Multicriteria and financial analysis for swimming pools. In *Advances in Environmental and Geological Science and Engineering*, Proceedings of the 8th International Conference on Environmental and Geological Science and Engineering (EG '15), Salerno, Italy, 27–29 June 2015; WSEAS Press: Sofia, Bulgaria, 2015; pp. 96–103.
30. Behzadian, M.; Kazemzadeh, R.B.; Albadvi, A.; Aghdasi, M. PROMETHEE: A comprehensive literature review on methodologies and applications. *Eur. J. Oper. Res.* **2010**, *200*, 198–215. [CrossRef]
31. Polatidis, H.; Haralambopoulos, D.A.; Munda, G.; Vreeker, R. Selecting an appropriate multi-criteria decision analysis technique for renewable energy planning. *Energy Sources Part B* **2006**, *1*, 181–193. [CrossRef]
32. Cilona, T.; Granata, M.F. Multicriteria Prioritization for Multistage Implementation of Complex Urban Renewal Projects. In Proceedings of the 15th International Conference Computational Science and Its Applications—ICCSA 2015, Banff, BC, Canada, 22–25 June 2015; Gervasi, O., Murgante, B., Misra, S., Gavrilova, M.L., Rocha, A.M.A.C., Torre, C., Taniar, D., Apduhan, B.O., Eds.; Part III, LNCS 9157. Springer Verlag: Berlin, Germany; Heidelberg, Germany, 2015; pp. 3–19.
33. Cinelli, M.; Coles, S.R.; Kirwan, K. Analysis of the potentials of multi criteria decision analysis methods to conduct sustainability assessment. *Ecol. Indic.* **2014**, *46*, 138–148. [CrossRef]
34. Guitouni, A.; Martel, J.M. Tentative guidelines to help choosing an appropriate MCDA Method. *Eur. J. Oper. Res.* **1998**, *109*, 501–521. [CrossRef]
35. Von Winterfeldt, D.; Edwards, W. *Decision Analysis and Behavioral Research*; Cambridge University Press: Cambridge, UK, 1986.

36. Kuang, H.; Kilgour, D.M.; Hipel, K.W. Grey-based PROMETHEE II with application to evaluation of source water protection strategies. *Inf. Sci.* **2015**, *294*, 376–389. [CrossRef]
37. Le Téno, J.F.; Mareschal, B. An interval version of PROMETHEE for the comparison of building products' design with ill-defined data on environmental quality. *Eur. J. Oper. Res.* **1998**, *109*, 522–529. [CrossRef]
38. Juan, Y.-K.; Roper, K.O.; Castro-Lacouture, D.; Kim, J.H. Optimal decision making on urban renewal projects. *Manag. Decis.* **2010**, *48*, 207–224. [CrossRef]
39. Kourtit, K.; Macharis, C.; Nijkamp, P. A multi-actor multi-criteria analysis of the performance of global cities. *Appl. Geogr.* **2014**, *49*, 24–36. [CrossRef]
40. Ulvila, J.W.; Snider, W.D. Negotiation of international oil tanker standards: An application of multiattribute value theory. *Oper. Res.* **1980**, *28*, 81–96. [CrossRef]
41. Comer, J.L.; Kirkwood, C.W. Decision analysis applications in the operations research literature 1970–1989. *Oper. Res.* **1991**, *39*, 206–219.
42. Taylor, J.M., Jr.; Love, B.N. Simple multi-attribute rating technique for renewable energy deployment decisions (SMART REDD). *J. Def. Model. Simulat. Appl. Methodol. Technol.* **2014**, *11*, 227–232. [CrossRef]
43. Papadopoulos, A.M., Konidari, P., Eds.; *Overview and Selection of Multi-Criteria Evaluation Methods for Mitigation/Adaptation Policy Instruments*; PROMITHEAS—4: Athens, Greece, 2011.
44. Barfod, M.B., Leleur, M., Eds.; *Multi-Criteria Decision Analysis for Use in Transport Decision Making*, 2nd ed.; Technical University of Denmark: Copenhagen, Denmark, 2014.
45. Dutta, M.; Husain, Z. An application of Multicriteria Decision Making to Built Heritage. The case of Calcutta. *J. Cult. Herit.* **2009**, *10*, 237–243. [CrossRef]
46. Kılkış, Ş. Composite index for benchmarking local energy systems of Mediterranean port cities. *Energy* **2015**. [CrossRef]
47. Kılkış, Ş. Sustainable development of energy, water and environment systems index for Southeast European cities. *J. Clean. Product.* **2015**. [CrossRef]
48. Dizdaroglu, D.; Yigitcanlar, T. A parcel-scale assessment tool to measure sustainability through urban ecosystem components: The MUSIX model. *Ecol. Indic.* **2014**, *41*, 115–130. [CrossRef]
49. Dizdaroglu, D.; Yigitcanlar, T.; Dawes, L. A micro-level indexing model for assessing urban ecosystem sustainability. *Smart Sustain. Built Environ.* **2012**, *1*, 291–315. [CrossRef]
50. Yigitcanlar, T.; Dur, F.; Dizdaroglu, D. Towards prosperous sustainable cities: A multiscalar urban sustainability assessment approach. *Habitat Int.* **2015**, *45*, 36–46. [CrossRef]
51. Salminen, P.; Hokkanen, J.; Lahdelma, R. Comparing multicriteria methods in the context of environmental problems. *Eur. J. Oper. Res.* **1998**, *104*, 485–496. [CrossRef]
52. Hajkowicz, S. A comparison of multiple criteria analysis and unaided approaches to environmental decision making. *Environ. Sci. Policy* **2007**, *10*, 177–184. [CrossRef]
53. Kostevšek, A.; Klemeš, J.J.; Varbanov, P.S.; Čuček, L.; Petek, J. Sustainability assessment of the locally integrated energy sectors for a Slovenian municipality. *J. Clean. Product.* **2015**, *88*, 83–89. [CrossRef]
54. Roy, B. Decision aid and decision making. In *Readings in Multiple Criteria Decision Aid*; Bana e Costa, C.A., Ed.; Springer-Verlag: Berlin, Germany; Heidelberg, Germany, 1990; pp. 17–35.
55. Munda, G. Intensity of preference and related uncertainty in non-compensatory aggregation rules. *Theory Decis.* **2012**, *73*, 649–669. [CrossRef]
56. Pollesch, N.; Dale, V.H. Applications of aggregation theory to sustainability assessment. *Ecol. Econ.* **2015**, *114*, 117–127. [CrossRef]
57. Floridi, M.; Pagni, S.; Falorni, S.; Luzzati, T. An exercise in composite indicators construction: Assessing the sustainability of Italian regions. *Ecol. Econ.* **2011**, *70*, 1440–1447. [CrossRef]
58. Ostasiewicz, K. Ordering EU countries according to indicators of sustainable development. *Statistika* **2012**, *49*, 30–51.
59. Dietz, S.; Neumayer, E. Weak and strong sustainability in the SEEA: Concepts and measurement. *Ecol. Econ.* **2007**, *61*, 617–626. [CrossRef]
60. Garmendia, E.; Prellezo, R.; Murillas, A.; Escapa, M.; Gallastegui, M. Weak and strong sustainability assessment in fisheries. *Ecol. Econ.* **2010**, *70*, 96–106. [CrossRef]
61. Dalmas, L.; Geronimi, V.; Noël, J.-F.; Sang, J.T.K. Economic evaluation of urban heritage: An inclusive approach under a sustainability perspective. *J. Cult. Herit.* **2015**, *16*, 681–687. [CrossRef]

62. Janeiro, L.; Patel, M.K. Choosing sustainable technologies. Implications of the underlying sustainability paradigm in the decision-making process. *J. Clean. Product.* **2015**, *105*, 438–446. [CrossRef]
63. Edwards, W. How to use multiattribute utility measurement for social decision making. *IEEE Trans. Syst. Man Cybernet.* **1977**, *7*, 326–340. [CrossRef]
64. Edwards, W.; Barron, F.H. Smarts and Smarter: Improved Simple Methods for Multi Attribute Utility Measurement. *Organ. Behav. Hum. Decis. Process.* **1994**, *60*, 306–325. [CrossRef]
65. Brans, J.P.; Mareschal, B. Promethee methods. In *Multiple Criteria Decision Analysis: State of the Art Surveys*; Figueira, J., Greco, S., Ehrgott, M., Eds.; Springer: New York, NY, USA, 2005; pp. 163–195.
66. Roy, B. *Méthodologie Multicritère d'Aide à la Décison*; Economica: Paris, France, 1985.
67. Bouyssou, D. Building criteria: A prerequisite for MCDA. In *Readings in Multiple Criteria Decision Aid*; Bana e Costa, C.A., Ed.; Springer-Verlag: Berlin, Germany; Heidelberg, Germany, 1990; pp. 58–80.
68. Relazione Previsionale e Programmatica 2012–2014. Available online: http://googo.pw/url?sa=t&rct=j&q=&esrc=s&source=web&cd=1&ved=0ahUKEwiFwNDpxa3JAhXBF5QKHedtB08QFggcMAA&url=http%3A%2F%2Fwww.comune.rozzano.mi.it%2Findex.php%2Fmodulistica%2Fdoc_download%2F697-relazione-previsionale-e-programmatica-2012-2014.html&usg=AFQjCNHewDYQAw5x7gsCoUT-9znqiRisOQ&cad=rja (accessed on 18 November 2015).
69. Figueira, J.R.; Greco, S.; Roy, B. ELECTRE methods with interaction between criteria: An extension of the concordance index. *Eur. J. Oper. Res.* **2009**, *199*, 478–495. [CrossRef]

© 2015 by the authors. Licensee MDPI, Basel, Switzerland. This article is an open access article distributed under the terms and conditions of the Creative Commons Attribution (CC BY) license (http://creativecommons.org/licenses/by/4.0/).

Article

The Concept of Sustainable Strategy Implementation

Joanna Radomska

Strategic Management Department, Wrocław University of Economics, ul. Komandorska 118/120, 53-345 Wrocław, Poland; joanna.radomska@ue.wroc.pl; Tel.: +48-71-36-80-195

Academic Editor: Adam Jabłoński
Received: 21 October 2015; Accepted: 19 November 2015; Published: 27 November 2015

Abstract: The idea of sustainable development has been present in the field of management for many years, yet the challenges and rules of contemporary business mean that it remains topical. At the same time, the results of much research indicates an unsatisfactory level of execution of development concepts. Due to this, the subject of the study encompasses the implementation of the idea of sustainability in the strategy execution process, lending it a holistic and balanced nature. The purpose of the paper is an examination of the relationship between strategy implementation and the effectiveness of the strategy execution process. The relationships between the perspectives defined and results obtained by organizations were investigated. The research demonstrated the existence of a positive correlation of varied intensity. It is thus possible to identify a positive influence of the integration of the idea of sustainability with strategy execution, which is reflected in the effectiveness of activities undertaken.

Keywords: strategy execution; sustainability; strategic management process

1. Introduction

An increasing pressure to ensure productivity and effectiveness forces companies to improve their management systems, making them ever more complex. Confirmation of this trend is visible in the implementation of holistic management models which emphasize the need to concentrate on the high quality of the functionality of their components [1]. It is thus possible to find recommendations referring to the sustainable design of the strategic management process in the literature. Sustainability is defined as a concept of the holistic perspective of development integrated with organizational goals, internal incentives and evaluation systems, and organizational decision support systems [2]. Sustainable strategic management is an effect of the natural evolution of strategic thinking towards meeting expectations placed by the environment [3]. An ever greater number of organizations have therefore begun to notice that the idea of sustainability is becoming a natural element of their actions and not an issue separated from a strategy being executed [4]. Additionally, as some of the research results prove, it is a factor leading to a reduction in risk accompanying the strategy realization [5]. It results not only in a change in perspective and perception of organizing the strategy implementation process, but also indicates the need for an integration of its aspect [6]. It is described in Figure 1.

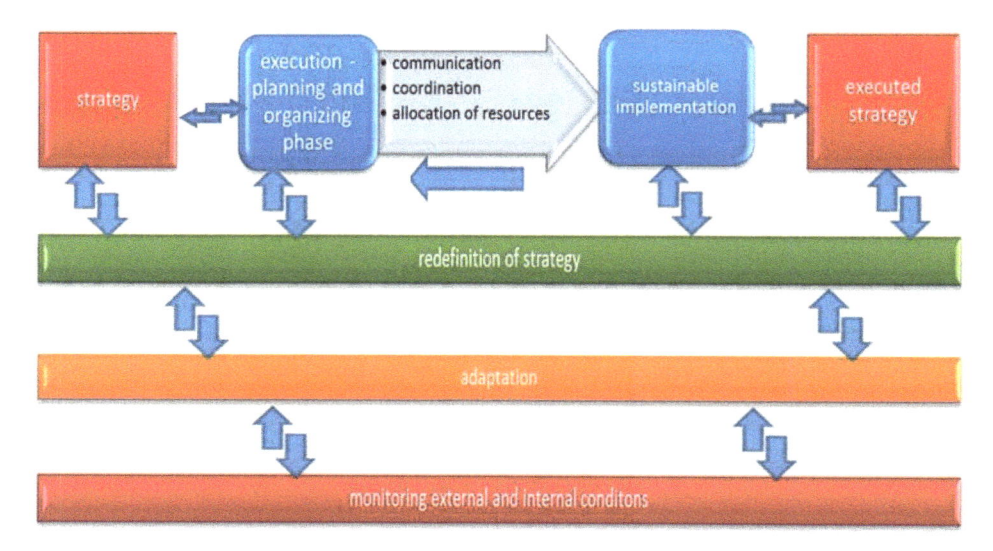

Figure 1. Strategy implementation process (including the sustainability concept). Source: own work based on [7].

Despite application advantages, sustainability is still rarely combined with strategic management [8]. The objective of this work is an examination of the relationships between sustainable strategy implementation and the effectiveness of the strategy execution process. On the basis of the literature, sustainable strategy implementation has been defined using seven perspectives: leadership, strategy, employees, corporate values, resources, tools and processes. The effectiveness of strategy execution, however, comprises both the level to which the strategic aims established are achieved and income dynamics.

As some of the authors indicate, the discipline of strategic management evolves in the direction of a comprehensive and systematic approach, while openness to differentiation and complexity is becoming the domain of those organizations that demonstrate efficacy and consistency in the realization of development concepts devised [9]. It is worth mentioning that the decisions connected with the aspect of sustainability are treated as strategic decisions reflected in the strategy itself as well as in the corporate culture and values [10,11]. In this context, the idea of sustainability, based on continuity, flexibility and comprehensiveness, is becoming of key importance [12]. This comprehensiveness and balance should characterize the perspectives forming a strategy implementation process. Various approaches to their definition may be adopted, beginning with standard elements of the concept of sustainability [6], through an approach derived from the concept of the Balanced Scorecard [13] or Total Quality Management [14], to the use of models depicting key aspects of the strategy execution process [15] or approaches based on them, for instance distinguishing systems, people and programs [16]. For this article, we chose those which combine the approaches mentioned above and form a comprehensive set of elements of a varied nature, which is considered to be a condition for efficacy in the realization of the idea of sustainability [17]. In order to speak of sustainable strategy implementation, it is necessary to accept a strategic approach [18] guaranteeing that the concept of sustainability is an integrated part of a strategic management process [19]. This means that it is essential to incorporate it at three levels—the normative (corporate values, employees, leadership) [20], the strategic (strategy, goals) [21] and the operational (processes, resources, tools) [22].

The first of the perspectives described contains the element naturally associated with sustainability: corporate values. Taking actions which serve the promotion of basic rules and ensuring their cohesion with the vision is a complement to a sustainable strategy execution process. It is an integral element combining operational activities with expected results [23]. The literature indicates the existence of a phenomenon described as a "value gap" based on the maladjustment of strategy and the process of its execution to higher values. It becomes crucial then to introduce changes to the process necessary to ensure that activities and expected results remain cohesive [24]. One of the tools assisting with this, and included in this area, is the system of informal communication supporting the comprehension of the vision and strategic goals [25], and at the same time, the integration of the entire strategy execution process [26].

The second perspective is the area of employees, significant because of the necessity, emphasised by many researchers, of paying attention to the nature of the objectives being accomplished by a company and the way in which the results achieved are measured. Aside from financial outcomes, organizational outcomes are mentioned ever more often [27]. These are inseparably linked with the issue of employee engagement in strategies being executed and competitive advantage achieved as a result [28]. Some research indicates that this perspective should be treated as a leading element in strategy implementation as it has a substantial influence on the improvement of company results [29]. It is linked not only with involving employees in work on strategy formulation, but also with the supporting role which they play in achieving long-term goals [30]. Those organizations which obtain good implementation results are able to focus employee attention effectively on tasks connected with strategic goal achievement, which involves assigning decision-making powers as well as establishing clear measures for the appraisal of their effects [31].

The third of the perspectives described is emphasized by a great many authors: leadership as an element linking a strategy, on the one hand, with resources and employees, on the other [32]. The attitudes of managers toward sustainable strategy execution and the perception of particular perspectives of this process directly affect not only its course [33], but also the attitudes of other employees (especially mid-level management) [34]. In order to implement the concept successfully, a change in thinking and attitude is crucial, as these are inseparably linked with leadership [35]. This is also pointed out by [36], who emphasises that the duties of leaders should encompass such tasks as the creation of an aligned mental model, the promotion of individual ownership of the whole, and the cultivation of aligned behaviors.

The fourth perspective, associated with the strategic level, encompasses both strategy and strategic goals. Results of some research indicate that, in many cases, it is not poor execution, but the strategy itself which results in unsatisfactory outcomes [37]. This relates especially to ambiguous definition, a lack of priorities indicated, or a concept of development not adjusted to internal and external determiners [38]. Cocks [39] mentions a vague and blurred strategy among the reasons for failures in implementation, with this often directly linked to a lack of clarity in basic development rules and their coherence with the set of objectives specified [40]. It is indicated in the literature on the subject that the perspective of strategy is closely associated with resources and people and should not be separated from them, but treated holistically as an integral part of a larger whole [41].

Moving on to the operational level, it is worth beginning with the perspective of resources, mainly due to the fact that ensuring sustainability means efficient as well as effective use of available resources with a simultaneous orientation toward strategic objective accomplishment [42]. Moreover, the results of research conducted indicate that resource constraints are a significant and frequently occurring obstacle to strategy execution [43]. Additionally, the question of problems relating to allocation and effective use must be considered [44]. Effectiveness, in this case, does not refer only to an economic aspect, but should also encompass the idea of sustainability, and therefore an allocation of resources which ensures the coherence and integrity of all processes, including the process of strategy realization.

In considering the perspective of strategy execution, it is worth mentioning that the most important role is played by the controlling and implementation of progress measurement systems, which are, at the same time, an element supporting the integration process for all of the perspectives described [45]. It is related to the greatest extent to resources and especially to the issue of changes in organizational structure allowing the efficient use of resources possessed [46]. On the other hand, it is necessary to analyze not only the process by which the results of a strategy are measured, since aligning processes and systems to reinforce the desired behaviors and outcomes of equal importance [47]. This therefore relates also to the motivation system, which should be associated with the strategy execution stage [48]. This makes necessary actions aimed at indicating connections between a strategy introduced and other processes within the organization and their design such that they comply with the idea of sustainability.

The last of the perspectives described covers implementation tools. Within the set utilized in the process of strategy execution, Balanced Scorecard displays the greatest integration with the concept of sustainability [49], particularly the non-financial measures [50]. The authors also indicate the use of scheduling and budgeting as well as formal implementation programs, this serving the appropriate allocation of resources and identification of key performance indicators [51]. Measurement may, on the other hand, be supported by strategic controlling [52]. The catalogue of tools is complemented by the strategy map, which may also be considered an element of sustainability due to the fact that it serves the presentation of the manner in which the organization creates value [53] and is able to support other perspectives thanks to its flexibility, operating character, and indication of certain decision-making powers [54].

2. Experimental Section

2.1. Sample and Data Collection, Research Tools

The group of respondents included managers of 200 corporate headquarters that have been operating for at least five years and are listed among the 500 largest Polish companies in the ranking of *Polityka* magazine (101 entities) and in the "Forbes Diamonds 2013" ranking (99 companies). The first ranking takes account of sales revenues, the total revenues of the companies, the gross and net profits, as well as the number of employees. The "Diamonds" list included the companies showing the fastest increase in value. The research sample was selected based on the participation in the rankings and thereby achieving market success in the implementation of developed strategies. The obtained results thus could be perceived as an example of good practices, and proposals formulated on this basis could have a universal character. The grounds for undertaking research in the field of strategy implementation were based on the importance of implementation actions and the necessity to ensure consistency between the effects of implementation projects or programs and their operating results. It was especially crucial to identify barriers that hinder the combination of ongoing actions with their strategic implications. The results of the conducted research could be applied, in practice, as a base of knowledge used by the management staff to increase the flexibility and effectiveness of the strategic management process.

The study was conducted using the PAPI (Paper and Pencil Interview) technique; the quantitative survey was carried out with the use of a method based on collecting the data the standardized way. In order to ensure the highest possible representativeness, the sample was selected using the stratified random sampling method. The primary goal of the research was to diagnose the factors that support and hinder the implementation of the strategy. The research tool focused on:

(1) identification of instruments and tools used during the strategy implementation process
(2) defining the procedures and systems supporting strategy execution
(3) analyzing the system for monitoring the effects of strategy implementation

The questions in the questionnaire were of nominal value (the respondents declared the existence of specific issues) and ordinal variable nature (the respondents indicated the strength of their impact on a five-point scale). In order to test the hypotheses, Pearson's correlation coefficient was calculated.

2.2. Hypotheses

As described above, it was assumed that sustainable strategy implementation consists of seven perspectives:

- Leadership (1): the activities of leaders motivating employees effectively; their possession of sufficient knowledge and skills; a clear division of competences, decision-making powers, and responsibility
- Strategy (2): clearly formulated assumptions, internal coherence in development concept (cohesion of vision, objectives, schedule, and budget) and its flexibility (a lack of single-variant solutions adopted in the strategy)
- Employees (3): employee identification with the strategy being executed and acceptance, elimination of internal interest groups hindering strategy execution, employee participation at the strategy formulation phase
- Corporate Values (4): organization of the work of multi-tasking teams, establishment of an efficient informal communication process, provision of coherence between the vision and corporate values
- Resources (5): possession of appropriate financial resources, deployment of the knowledge of employees at various levels, changes in organizational structure allowing effective use of resources possessed
- Tools (6): the use of Balanced Scorecard, strategy maps, strategic controlling and implementation programs as well as budgeting and task scheduling
- Processes (7): a regular measurement of progress in implementation, an incentive system relating employee salary level to the degree to which strategic goals are achieved, a system monitoring the company environment

Effectiveness of strategy execution has been defined by:

- the level of achievement of strategic goals assumed (A): as an indicator of the efficacy of activities performed
- income dynamics (B): as an indicator of the effects of activities performed

In order to accomplish the research objectives assumed, the following hypothesis was formulated:

H: There is a positive interdependency between a sustainable strategy implementation and the effectiveness of its execution.

Auxiliary hypotheses were formulated to verify which of the sustainable strategy implementation areas has the greatest influence on the effectiveness of strategy execution.

H1: Competent leadership affects growth in effectiveness of strategy execution.

H2: Smooth functioning of processes affects growth in effectiveness of strategy execution.

H3: Proper formulation of a strategy affects growth in effectiveness of its execution.

3. Results and Discussion

The first stage of the research was the calculation of the average responses to the perspectives of sustainable strategy implementation described above and the degree of effectiveness of strategy execution for each entity surveyed. Table 1 presents the results of the research.

Table 1. Averages for the sustainability perspectives and degree of effectiveness of strategy execution.

Perspective	Mean	SD
Leadership	3.84	0.872
Strategy	3.41	0.932
Employees	3.94	0.836
Corporate Values	2.98	0.854
Resources	3.05	0.902
Tools	3.95	0.934
Processes	3.89	0.875
Strategy Execution Effectiveness	3.75	0.869

As the research results show, received values are quite similar. The lowest level was obtained in the case of corporate values, which may indicate that this aspect is emphasized less than the others or the extent of the activities within the organizations surveyed is relatively low. It is certainly connected with their intangible nature and difficult transposition to particular activities of defined measurability (this relating in particular to informal communication along with the coherence of the vision and corporate values).

Further interdependencies between specified perspectives and results obtained (presented in Table 2) were investigated.

Table 2. Correlations between perspectives of sustainable strategy execution.

Perspective	Leadership	Strategy	Employees	Corporate Values	Resources	Tools	Processes
Leadership	1.00	0.763	0.854	0.553	0.638	0.558	0.785
Strategy	0.763	1.00	0.706	0.606	0.714	0.842	0.869
Employees	0.854	0.706	1.00	0.536	0.521	0.684	0.637
Corporate Values	0.553	0.606	0.536	1.00	0.516	0.498	0.502
Resources	0.638	0.714	0.521	0.516	1.00	0.873	0.742
Tools	0.558	0.842	0.684	0.498	0.873	1.00	0.863
Processes	0.785	0.869	0.637	0.502	0.742	0.863	1.00

The analysis of results obtained once more indicates the lowest level of correlation between corporate values and other perspectives. This is quite a surprising result, as most publications emphasize the role of this area in effective organization management, while the research conducted indicates that this is a rather marginal role compared with other perspectives. The highest results were received in the case of the perspective related to strategy, which demonstrates the importance of the development concept itself and its connection with other areas. This confirms results of research conducted by other authors, indicating that precision, coherence and flexibility of strategy are of great significance in the process of its execution. This interdependency should therefore be highlighted, being a basis for an effective strategy execution process for managers. Relatively high results were also obtained in the case of processes. This also confirms assumptions of other researchers concerning the procedure of the measurement process, motivation and analysis of information flowing from the environment as the elements which contribute to the proper functioning of other areas connected to strategy execution.

The interdependency between a sustainable strategy implementation and the effectiveness of the execution of this process was also examined.

The result obtained (correlation 0.693) allows for the claim that the interdependency between the issues examined is high. This means that the higher the coherence and comprehensiveness of activities, and thus the fuller the provision of a sustainable perspective of the strategy implementation process for the organization, the higher its degree of effectiveness. Those organizations which are aware of the mutual interrelations of particular perspectives obtain better results in activities undertaken and are therefore more effective at achieving strategic goals, which may also translate into a growth in income dynamics. The main hypothesis can therefore be accepted. Further analysis of the results, however, indicated certain differences in the interdependencies between particular perspectives, as the results below show (Table 3).

Table 3. Correlation between particular perspectives of sustainable strategy implementation and the effectiveness of strategy execution.

Perspectives	Strategy Execution Effectiveness
Leadership	0.686
Strategy	0.523
Employees	0.574
Corporate Values	0.358
Resources	0.632
Tools	0.741
Processes	0.753

Analyzing the results, it is worth paying attention first to the lowest correlation level in the case of corporate values (0.358), which confirms the earlier observations that this element does not constitute a factor substantially affecting results obtained. Other correlations show at least an average positive level of interdependency, with the highest results received for tools (0.741), processes (0.753) and leadership (0.686). This proves that these perspectives are the most powerful elements improving the results of implementation operations and should be treated as priorities. It is worth mentioning, however, that positive correlations were obtained for all of the perspectives, which may be considered a basis for the indication of certain implications: ensuring a holistic, coherent and sustainable attitude to the strategy execution process has a positive influence on the effectiveness of the results achieved. The sustainable nature of the process may be reached through a concentration not only on issues related to human capital and values, but also on operational matters (organization of processes or tools). Although some of these appear to be of greater importance, all have an impact on the success of the process. All of the hypotheses may therefore be accepted.

4. Conclusions

There is no doubt that there is no one universal model of sustainable strategy implementation that can be applied successfully to different types of organizations, as this is closely related not only to the specifics of the company, but also the types or nature of the strategies being executed [55]. This means that it is possible to identify various levels of advancement of activities ensuring a sustainable strategy execution process [56] of a varied level of effectiveness [57]. However, as indicated by a great many results of studies, some of which were mentioned in this article, it is possible to identify the positive influence of the integration of the idea of sustainability with strategy implementation, which is reflected in the effectiveness of activities undertaken.

On the basis of the research, practical implications for executives may also be indicated. The strategy execution process is a complex question which consists of interdependent elements. Accepting a sustainable approach allows for the adoption of a holistic perspective and comprehension of the reciprocal influence of particular aspects and enables a balanced implementation procedure. This paper allows us to understand better what factors should be considered while analyzing the process of strategy execution in order to ensure complex development integrated with organizational goals. Moreover, the findings of the study provide interesting insights for implementing the sustainable approach which might help to improve organizational decision support systems. Those are the reasons identified in this paper that could be mentioned as practical implications connected with the concept of a sustainable strategy execution process.

The main limitation of this study is connected with the subjectivity of the answers provided. Although the group of respondents was chosen among the managers and executives, there is a risk that the answers could have been incomplete or did not fully represent the processes and examined issues in a particular organization. The chosen perspectives of sustainability could also be further examined and their number or description could be investigated. Moreover, it is necessary to verify with further study the extent to which the idea of sustainable strategy implementation differs depending on the size of the organization and the branch in which it operates.

Acknowledgments: Acknowledgments: The project was financed with the funds of The National Science Centre, the project number 2014/13/D/HS4/01425 and DEC-2011/03/B/HS4/04247.

Conflicts of Interest: Conflicts of Interest: The author declares no conflict of interest.

References

1. Cierna, H.; Sujova, E. Parallels between corporate social responsibility and the EFQM excellence model. *MM Sci. J.* **2015**, *10*, 670–676. [CrossRef]
2. Hallstedt, S.; Ny, H.; Robert, K.; Broman, G. An approach to assessing sustainability integration in strategic decision systems for product development. *J. Clean. Prod.* **2010**, *18*, 703–712. [CrossRef]
3. Stead, J.; Stead, W. The coevolution of sustainable strategic management in the global marketplace. *Organ. Environ.* **2013**, *26*, 162–183. [CrossRef]
4. Vencato, C.; Gomes, C.; Scherer, F.; Kneipp, J.; Bichueti, R. Strategic sustainability management and export performance. *Manag. Environ. Qual. Int. J.* **2014**, *25*, 431–455. [CrossRef]
5. Yilmaz, A.K.; Flouris, T. Managing corporate sustainability: Risk management process based perspective. *Afri. J. Bus. Manag.* **2010**, *4*, 162–171.
6. Talwar, B. Business excellence models and the path ahead. *TQM J.* **2011**, *23*, 91–109. [CrossRef]
7. Ignacy, J. Strategy execution model based on research results. In *Strategy Implementation in Polish Enterprises*; Moszkowicz, K., Ed.; PWN Warsaw: Warsaw, Poland, 2015; p. 193.
8. Kiron, D.; Kruschwitz, N.; Rubel, H.; Reeves, M.; Fuisz-Kehrbach, S.-K. Sustainability's next frontier: Walking the talk on the sustainability issues that matter most. *MIT Sloan Manag. Rev.* **2013**, *12*, 3–26.
9. Doz, Y.; Thanheiser, H. Regaining competitiveness: A process of organizational renewal. In *Strategic Thinking. Leadership and the Management of Change*; Hendry, J., Johnson, G., Newton, J., Wiley, J., Eds.; Wiley: New York, NY, USA, 1993.
10. Stead, J.; Stead, W. Eco-enterprise strategy: Standing for sustainability. *J. Bus. Ethics* **2000**, *24*, 313–329. [CrossRef]
11. Jin, B.Z.; Bai, Y. Sustainable development and long-term strategic management. Embedding a long-term strategic management system into medium and long-term planning. *World Future Rev.* **2011**, *3*, 49–69. [CrossRef]
12. Szulanski, G.; Kruti, A. Learning to make strategy: Balancing discipline and imagination. *Long Range Plan.* **2001**, *34*, 537–556. [CrossRef]
13. Goswami, P.; Banwet, D.; Goswami, K. Sustainable operation management using the balanced score card as a strategic Tool–A research summary. *Procedia Soc. Behav. Sci.* **2015**, *189*, 133–143.
14. Gómez Gómez, J.; Martínez Costa, M.; Martínez Lorente, Á. A critical evaluation of the EFQM model. *Int. J. Qual. Reliab. Manag.* **2011**, *28*, 484–502. [CrossRef]
15. Higgins, J. The eight 'S's of successful strategy execution. *J. Change Manag.* **2005**, *5*, 3–13. [CrossRef]
16. Branzei, O.; Nadkarni, A. The Tata way: Evolving and executing sustainable business strategies. *Ivey Bus. J.* **2008**, *72*, 1–5.
17. Lozano, R. A holistic perspective on corporate sustainability drivers. *Corp. Soc. Responsib. Environ. Manag.* **2015**, *22*, 32–44. [CrossRef]
18. Galbreath, J. Building corporate social responsibility into strategy. *Eur. Bus. Rev.* **2009**, *21*, 109–127. [CrossRef]
19. Engert, S.; Rauter, R.; Baumgartner, R. Exploring the integration of corporate sustainability into strategic management: A literature review. *J. Clean. Prod.* **2015**, in press. [CrossRef]

20. Baumgartner, R. Managing corporate sustainability and CSR: A conceptual framework combining values, strategies and instruments contributing to sustainable development. *Corp. Soc. Responsib. Environ. Manag.* **2014**, *21*, 258–271. [CrossRef]
21. David, F. *Strategic Management*; Merrill Publishing Company: Columbus, OH, USA, 1989; p. 34.
22. Bonn, I.; Fisher, J. Sustainability: The missing ingredient in strategy. *J. Bus. Strat.* **2011**, *32*, 5–14. [CrossRef]
23. Van Marrewijk, M. A value based approach to organization types: Toward a coherent set of stakeholder-oriented management tools. *J. Bus. Ethics* **2004**, *55*, 147–158. [CrossRef]
24. Pateman, A. Linking strategy to operations: Six stages to execution. *Bus. Perform. Manag.* **2008**, *12*, 10–13.
25. Epstein, M.; Burchard, B. *Counting What Counts: Turning Corporate Accountability to Competitive Advantage*; Perseus Books: Cambridge, MA, USA, 2000; p. 52.
26. De Sousa Filho, J.M.; Wanderley, L.; Gómez, C.; Farache, F. Strategic corporate social responsibility management for competitive advantage. *Braz. Adm. Rev.* **2010**, *7*, 294–309. [CrossRef]
27. Kramar, R. Beyond strategic human resource management: Is sustainable human resource management the next approach? *Int. J. Hum. Resour. Manag.* **2014**, *25*, 1069–1089. [CrossRef]
28. Buller, P.; McEvoy, G. Strategy, human resource management and performance: Sharpening line of sight. *Hum. Resour. Manag. Rev.* **2012**, *22*, 43–56. [CrossRef]
29. Para-González, L.; Jiménez-Jiménez, D.; Martínez-Lorente, Á. The importance of intellectual capital in the EFQM model of excellence. In Proceedings of the European Conference on Intellectual Capital, Cartagena, Spain, 9–10 April 2015; pp. 253–261.
30. Paraschiv, D.; Nemoianu, E.; Langă, C.; Szabó, T. Eco-innovation, responsible leadership and organizational change for corporate sustainability. *Amfiteatru Econ.* **2012**, *14*, 404–419.
31. Henman, L. Turn great strategy into great execution. *MWorld Winter* **2010**, *9*, 29.
32. Heras-Saizarbitoria, I.; Marimon, F.; Casadesús, M. An empirical study of the relationships within the categories of the EFQM model. *Total Qual. Manag. Bus. Excel.* **2012**, *6*, 1–18. [CrossRef]
33. Baumgartner, R.; Ebner, D. Corporate sustainability strategies: Sustainability profiles and maturity levels. *Sustain. Dev.* **2010**, *18*, 76–89. [CrossRef]
34. Harmon, J.; Fairfield, K.; Behson, S. A comparative analysis of organizational sustainability strategy: Antecedents and performance outcomes perceived by U.S. and Non-U.S. based managers. In Proceedings of the International Eastern Academy of Management Conference, Rio de Janeiro, Brazil, 21–25 June 2009.
35. Millar, C.; Hind, P.; Magala, S. Sustainability and the need for change: Organizational change and transformational vision. *J. Organ. Chang. Manag.* **2012**, *25*, 489–497. [CrossRef]
36. Haudan, J. Successful strategy execution takes people—Not paper. *Employ. Relat. Today* **2007**, *33*, 38–39. [CrossRef]
37. Martin, R. The execution trap. Drawing a line between strategy and execution almost guarantees failure. *Harv. Bus. Rev.* **2010**, *88*, 64–71, 168.
38. Sterling, J. Translating strategy into effective implementation: Dispelling the myths and highlighting what works. *Strat. Leadersh.* **2003**, *31*, 32–33. [CrossRef]
39. Cocks, G. Emerging concepts for implementing strategy. *TQM J.* **2010**, *22*, 262. [CrossRef]
40. Sabourin, V. Through the lenses of strategy execution: Obstacles in engineering management. *Leadersh. Manag. Eng.* **2012**, *12*, 54. [CrossRef]
41. Araújo, M.; Sampaio, P. The path to excellence of the Portuguese organisations recognised by the EFQM model. *Total Qual. Manag. Bus. Excel.* **2014**, *25*, 427–438. [CrossRef]
42. Siebenhüner, B.; Arnold, M. Organizational learning to manage sustainable development. *Bus. Strat. Environ.* **2007**, *16*, 339–353. [CrossRef]
43. How hierarchy can hurt strategy execution. *Harv. Bus. Rev.* **2010**, *7–8*, 74–75.
44. Morgan, J. Strategy execution a four-step process. *MWorld Winter* **2010**, *9*, 14.
45. Arjaliès, D.-L.; Mundy, J. The use of management control systems to manage CSR strategy: A levers of control perspective. *J. Manag. Account. Res.* **2013**, *24*, 284–300. [CrossRef]
46. Hülsmann, M.; Grapp, J. Recursivity and dilemmas of a sustainable strategy management—New visions for a corporate balancing efficiency and sustainability by autonomous co-operation in decision making processes. In Foresight Management in Corporations and Public Organisations—New Visions for Sustainability, Proceedings of the 7th Annual International Conference Foresight Management in Corporations and Public Organisations, Helsinki, Finland, 9–10 June 2005; pp. 1–15.

47. Coon, B.; Wolf, S. The alchemy of strategy execution. *Employ. Relat. Today* **2005**, *32*, 29–30. [CrossRef]
48. Hrebiniak, L. *Making Strategy Work: Leading Effective Execution and Change*; Pearson Education: Upper Saddle River, NJ, USA, 2005.
49. Figge, F.; Hahn, T.; Schaltegger, S.; Wagner, M. The sustainability balanced scorecard—Linking sustainability management to business strategy. *Bus. Strat. Env.* **2002**, *11*, 268–284. [CrossRef]
50. Nathan, M. 'Lighting tomorrow with today': Towards a (strategic) sustainability revolution. *Int. J. Sustain. Strat. Manag.* **2010**, *2*, 29–40. [CrossRef]
51. Saunders, M.; Mann, R. Implementing strategic initiatives: A framework of leading practices. *Int. J. Oper. Prod. Manag.* **2008**, *28*, 1104–1106. [CrossRef]
52. Ramsey, R. Strategic management: Formulation, implementation, and control in a dynamic environment. *Int. J. Commer. Manag.* **2010**, *20*, 188–189. [CrossRef]
53. Kaplan, R.; Norton, D. The strategy map: Guide to aligning intangible assets. *Strat. Leadersh.* **2004**, *32*, 10–17. [CrossRef]
54. Free, C.; Qu, S. The use of graphics in promoting management ideas: An analysis of the balanced scorecard, 1992–2010. *J. Account. Organ. Chang.* **2011**, *7*, 158–189. [CrossRef]
55. Lee, M.-D. Configuration of external influences: The combined effects of institutions and stakeholders on corporate social responsibility strategies. *J. Bus. Ethics* **2011**, *102*, 281–298. [CrossRef]
56. Van Marrewijk, M.; Werre, M. Multiple levels of corporate sustainability. *J. Bus. Ethics* **2003**, *44*, 107–119. [CrossRef]
57. White, P. Building a sustainability strategy into the business. *Corp. Gov. Int. J. Bus. Soc.* **2009**, *9*, 386–394.

© 2015 by the author. Licensee MDPI, Basel, Switzerland. This article is an open access article distributed under the terms and conditions of the Creative Commons Attribution (CC BY) license (http://creativecommons.org/licenses/by/4.0/).

sustainability

Article

Repetitive Model Refinement for Questionnaire Design Improvement in the Evaluation of Working Characteristics in Construction Enterprises

Jeng-Wen Lin [1,*], Pu Fun Shen [2] and Bing-Jean Lee [1]

1 Department of Civil Engineering, Feng Chia University, Taichung 407, Taiwan; bjlee@fcu.edu.tw
2 Ph.D. Program in Civil and Hydraulic Engineering, Feng Chia University, Taichung 407, Taiwan; p0043264@fcu.edu.tw

* Author to whom correspondence should be addressed; jwlin@fcu.edu.tw; Tel: +886-4-2451-7250 (ext. 3150); Fax: +886-4-2451-6982.

Academic Editors: Adam Jabłoński and Marc A. Rosen

Received: 15 July 2015; Accepted: 11 November 2015; Published: 17 November 2015

Abstract: This paper presents an iterative confidence interval based parametric refinement approach for questionnaire design improvement in the evaluation of working characteristics in construction enterprises. This refinement approach utilizes the 95% confidence interval of the estimated parameters of the model to determine their statistical significance in a least-squares regression setting. If this confidence interval of particular parameters covers the zero value, it is statistically valid to remove such parameters from the model and their corresponding questions from the designed questionnaire. The remaining parameters repetitively undergo this sifting process until their statistical significance cannot be improved. This repetitive model refinement approach is implemented in efficient questionnaire design by using both linear series and Taylor series models to remove non-contributing questions while keeping significant questions that are contributive to the issues studied, *i.e.*, employees' work performance being explained by their work values and cadres' organizational commitment being explained by their organizational management. Reducing the number of questions alleviates the respondent burden and reduces costs. The results show that the statistical significance of the sifted contributing questions is decreased with a total mean relative change of 49%, while the Taylor series model increases the *R*-squared value by 17% compared with the linear series model.

Keywords: confidence interval; construction enterprises; questionnaire design; repetitive model refinement; statistical significance; working characteristics evaluation

1. Introduction

The questionnaire approach is widely used for surveying and collecting sample data with regard to an issue, with a list of questions to be answered and the results aggregated for statistical analysis. However, the main factors or questions influencing the findings of the models used need to be validated and simplified for efficient questionnaire design. In order to acquire accurate evaluations of working characteristics in construction enterprises and to alleviate problems of relatively large-dimensional and nonlinear models, this study develops a confidence interval based repetitive parametric model refinement approach for questionnaire design improvement.

1.1. General Information about the Questionnaires

A total of 250 questionnaires were distributed to Taiwanese and Chinese employees of two ranks in the company being studied. After excluding 30 invalid questionnaires (being incomplete or with missing values, or regarded as "outliers" through a set a mathematical analysis) and 39 unreturned ones, a total of 181 questionnaires were valid. The response rate was 72.4%.

1.2. Questionnaire Design Improvement

Questionnaire surveys are a widely used method to collect opinions and views. A customized questionnaire is developed based on the parameters revealed by context immersion in a given field (Kim [1]). However, many factors such as tedious design formats (Saris [2], Saris and Gallhofer [3]), redundant content, and excessive length (Weimiao and Zheng [4]) may lead to an inconsistent comparison matrix for the decision problem. Invalid or bad results from a questionnaire survey may cause decision makers to make faulty inferences (Ergu and Kou [5]). Suzuki et al. [6] introduced procedures to design reasonable questionnaires using statistical analysis to obtain high accuracy. Reducing the length of a survey by using a more streamlined set of questions can lead to more reasonable data being acquired and to better explanations of the issues in question. Other examples of this approach include Edwards *et al.* [7], who reduced the effective sample size and introduced bias. Finding ways to increase response rates to postal questionnaires would improve the quality of health research. Landsheer and Boeije [8] used qualitative facet analysis, an application of Guttmann's facet theory, to investigate whether item content sufficiently covered the intended subject area. This form of content analysis constitutes a systematic, effective, and critical tool for improving the content of questionnaires. Jacqui *et al.* [9] improved questionnaire design by enabling iterations of qualitative and quantitative testing, evaluation, and redevelopment. Results from such tests enable evidence-based decisions to be made regarding trade-offs between measurement error, processing error, non-response error, respondent burden, and costs. By enabling targeted improvements at the questionnaire design level according to specific needs, we can create valuable reference resources (Xu *et al.* [10]).

1.3. Model Refinement and Repetitive Computation

To alleviate problems of respondent burden and costs as well as relatively large-dimensional and nonlinear models, the issue of model refinement has increasingly drawn much attention in many fields. Smith [11] addressed the study of algorithms and system designs. Adrian [12] presented a refinement process with respect to data list building using model generators. Kapova and Goldschmidt [13] proposed model-driven application engineering based on the concept of analytical transformations. Liu [14] established two optimization models for a wireless optical communication system based on a four-level pulse amplitude modulation scheme. Ragnhild *et al.* [15] explored the behavior inheritance consistency of both refined and re-factored models with respect to the original model. Steven *et al.* [16] addressed model refinement as an iterative process. Zhuquan *et al.* [17] proposed that measurements permitted the repeated application of a system identification procedure operating on closed-loop data, together with successive refinements of the designed controller.

1.4. Nonlinear Models and Statistical Confidence Intervals

A nonlinear model is often adopted in system applications. Khorshid and Alfares [18] developed a parameter identification technique in creating a mathematical model of vehicle components by solving an inverse problem using a non-linear optimization method. Lin and Chen [19] proposed a statistical confidence interval based nonlinear parameter refinement approach and applied it to the standard power series model (Lin [20], Lin and Betti [21]) for the identification of structural systems. Other statistical confidence interval based studies include Tryon [22], who employed a graphical inference confidence interval approach in analyzing independent and dependent approaches for statistical difference, equivalence, replication, indeterminacy, and trivial difference. Yang *et al.* [23] proposed control limits based on the narrowest confidence interval to analyze problems, if the traditional three-sigma control limits or probability limits were adopted and some points with relatively high probability of occurrence were excluded; yet, some points with relatively small probability of occurrence may still be accepted in asymmetrical or multimodal distributions. Bonett and Price [24] proposed an adjusted Wald interval for paired binomial proportions that was shown to perform as well as the best available methods. In construction management, it has been shown to be feasible to use nonlinear models to deal with construction cost overruns (Ahiaga-Dagbui and Smith [25], Anastasopoulos *et al*. [26]) and schedule forecasting patterns (Kim and Kim [27], Patel and Jha [28]).

1.5. Prime Novelty Statement

In contrast with the conventional tests of reliability and validity, the designed questionnaires in this study were analyzed to identify the main factors and associated questions influencing the model studied using the proposed repetitive model refinement approach so as to streamline the number of questions in surveys of working characteristics in construction enterprises. Problems of respondent burden and costs as well as relatively large-dimensional and nonlinear models were thus alleviated. To reduce the number of questions with a more streamlined set, it was feasible to refine the model by repetitively removing non-contributing questions. Each time non-contributing questions were removed, the questionnaire model would be updated and rerun once again in a multiple regression setting. This model refinement approach for the content validity of the questionnaire was implemented using both linear and Taylor series models by conserving significant questions that were contributive to the issue being studied, *i.e.*, employees' work performance explained by their work values and cadres' organizational commitment explained by their organizational management. The results have been verified by calculating the statistical significance values of the sifted contributing questions and the R-squared values of established models.

2. Questionnaires Evaluating Working Characteristics in Construction Enterprises

In this study, the research subjects of the questionnaires were the Taiwanese employees and cadres of Taiwan-based construction enterprises in China. Questionnaire findings of similarities and differences in work values, work satisfaction, organizational management, and organizational commitment were preliminarily reviewed. The effects of work values and organizational management on work satisfaction and organizational commitment, respectively, were analyzed using questionnaires based on the job diagnostic survey by Hackman and Oldham [29]. The "working characteristics questionnaires" included questionnaires for (1) work values; (2) work performance and satisfaction; (3) organizational management; and (4) organizational commitment and identification (Lin and Shen [30], Shen [31]).

3. Repetitive Model Refinement Approach and Analyses

Questionnaire data were used in multiple regression analyses using four models, comprising the linear series, the refined linear series, the Taylor series, and the refined Taylor series model, where for the employees' part the independent variables are X = work values, which are used to explain the dependent variables Y = work performance and satisfaction; and for the cadres' part, X = organizational management, used to explain Y = organizational commitment and identification.

Two linear regression models were generated to identify the causal links between work values and work performance on the one hand, and organizational management and organizational commitment on the other. The original linear series model was refined through an iterative approach. This refined model was developed to streamline the questionnaire by removing non-contributing questions. The Taylor series model expanded the original linear series model up to the third moments. As a consequence, the R-squared value in the regression setting was increased. The refined Taylor series model was obtained from the original Taylor series model by the repetitive refinement approach in a regression setting. It was thus feasible to obtain the R-squared values of the regression between X and Y defined above and the mean relative change of the statistical significance as two indicators of result verification, so as to prove the accuracy of the refined model and to validate the sifted questions as genuinely significant contributors to the refined model.

The iterative refinement approach provides for the sifting of model components and related questions by repetitively using the 95% confidence interval in a regression setting. The 95% confidence interval is selected by convention and because the higher confidence interval enables more stringent selection of the components and thus a lower possibility of incorporating nonlinear elements, which is generally problematic for systems with a degree of nonlinear behavior; such nonlinearity will be verified in the results, showing the nonlinear Taylor series model significantly increases the R-squared value when compared with the linear series model. If the estimated confidence interval of a parameter contains the "null" (zero) value, it is statistically valid to remove such a parameter and its corresponding component, while maintaining those parameters whose confidence intervals do not cover the zero value. This component/question sifting process is repeated by rerunning the regression and refining the model until none of the estimated 95% confidence intervals of the remaining parameters cover the zero value (Lin and Chen [19]). In addition, the interval method proposed in this article has proved more reasonable than the mean value method. Using the interval method considers an interval which covers zero or not. However, using the mean value method to remove those close to zero values has a problem; *i.e.*, what values are "close" to zero (e.g., 10^{-10}, 10^{-20}, or 10^{-30}, *etc.*)?

The employees' section of the questionnaire data is used in this study to demonstrate the model refinement approach using 95% confidence intervals in a regression. Using question Ey1 ("I think my work ability is excellent") as an example to show the model refinement approach, we assign Y = Ey1 in the questionnaire for employees' work performance and satisfaction, while X = Ex1–24, being all 24 questions in the questionnaire for employees' work values. In other words, the question Ey1 is explained by the questions Ex1–24. The consequent repetitive sifting process to select the real contributing components/questions out of the 24 questions (Ex1–24) to Ey1 is listed in Tables 1–4 (adapted from Lin and Shen [30], Shen [31]). Each table presents the outcome of a new regression after the component sifting process. Each of the highlighted upper and lower bounds for a given component indicates that the 95% confidence interval covers the zero value in the regression analysis.

Removing those components/questions with 95% confidence intervals covering the zero value in the regression setting of Table 1 and rerunning a new regression of the remaining components leads to Table 2. Continuing this repetitive sifting process by rerunning the regression analysis for the remaining components in Table 2 we obtain Table 3. By the same component sifting process, Table 4 is derived from Table 3. The 95% confidence interval for each remaining component in Table 4 does not cover the zero value, implying that the remaining components are genuine contributing factors in explaining the component Ey1. Hence, it is statistically valid to stop the component sifting process at this point. It is noteworthy that the significance value of each remaining component from Table 2 to Table 4 decreases in average a new regression is conducted in the repetitive refinement approach. The removed components correspond to relatively high significance values while the remaining components correspond to successively declining significance values in each round of regression.

Table 1. Multiple regression of original questionnaire model.

		R-square = 0.410	[95% Conf. Interval]		
			Lower Bound	Upper Bound	Significance
Ey1	I think my work ability is excellent.				
Ex1	New knowledge and technologies can be learned at work.		−0.54	0.732	0.761
Ex2	There are chances for advanced studies at work.		−0.657	0.458	0.719
Ex3	My own dream can be realized at work.		−0.394	0.36	0.929
Ex4	The quality of my life can be improved through my work.		−0.502	−0.244	0.486
Ex5	My life becomes richer due to my work.		−0.476	−0.204	0.421
Ex6	I can have the sense of achievement at work.		0.126	0.612	0.19
Ex7	My boss at work is very understanding.		0.69	0.284	0.402
Ex8	My colleagues always take care of each other.		0.285	0.802	0.34
Ex9	My colleagues never attack each other for their own benefits.		−0.472	0.502	0.95
Ex10	My colleagues get along with each other well.		−0.45	0.36	0.821

Table 1. Cont.

	R-square = 0.410		[95% Conf. Interval]	
Ex11	I can work in an environment which is not harmful to my body and mind.	0.152	0.499	0.683
Ex12	I can arrange my own schedule properly because of the flexibility of my work.	0.203	1.025	0.183
Ex13	When I am sick, the company takes good care of me.	0.845	2.044	0.404
Ex14	The insurance system of the company is good.	−1.654	2.033	0.836
Ex15	I can get a raise or bonus of a proper amount.	−2.445	−1.391	0.58
Ex16	The welfare system of the company is good.	0.145	2.375	0.605
Ex17	My income is higher than that of others with the same conditions as me.	−3.329	−1.822	0.556
Ex18	I never feel confused or scared while working.	0.371	1.672	0.204
Ex19	There are many chances of promotion.	−1.107	−0.416	0.362
Ex20	I devote myself to my work.	−0.841	0.757	0.916
Ex21	Even if there is no extra pay for working overtime, I would still work overtime to finish my work at night.	−0.529	0.69	0.79
Ex22	I usually go to work earlier to prepare the tasks I have to handle.	−0.474	0.642	0.762
Ex23	I am proud of my work.	0.189	1.407	0.13
Ex24	I want to be perfect when it comes to my work.	−2.01	−0.193	0.019

Table 2. Multiple regression of the refined questionnaire model in the first round.

	R-square = 0.399		[95% Conf. Interval]	
		Lower bound	Upper bound	Significance
Ey1	I think my work ability is excellent.			
Ex4	The quality of my life can be improved through my work	−0.43	−0.174	0.398
Ex5	My life becomes richer due to my work.	−0.384	−0.177	0.461
Ex6	I can have the sense of achievement at work.	0.109	0.431	0.235
Ex7	My boss at work is very understanding.	0.499	0.176	0.339
Ex8	My colleagues always take care of each other.	0.156	0.591	0.247
Ex11	I can work in an environment which is not harmful to my body and mind.	−0.651	0.356	0.558
Ex12	I can arrange my own schedule properly because of the flexibility of my work.	0.131	0.814	0.152
Ex13	When I am sick, the company takes good care of me.	0.566	1.852	0.289
Ex15	I can get a raise or bonus of a proper amount.	−1.991	−1.038	0.529
Ex16	The welfare system of the company is good.	−0.888	2.231	0.39
Ex17	My income is higher than that of others with the same conditions as me.	−3.244	−0.951	0.276
Ex18	I never feel confused or scared while working.	0.117	1.647	0.087
Ex19	There are many chances of promotion.	−1.105	−0.174	0.149
Ex23	I am proud of my work.	0.107	1.113	0.104
Ex24	I want to be perfect when it comes to my work.	−1.674	−0.362	0.003

Table 3. Multiple regression of the refined questionnaire model in the second round.

		R-square = 0.395	[95% Conf. Interval]		
			Lower bound	Upper bound	Significance
Ey1	I think my work ability is excellent.				
Ex4	The quality of my life can be improved through my work.		−0.44	−0.15	0.327
Ex5	My life becomes richer due to my work.		−0.386	−0.153	0.387
Ex6	I can have the sense of achievement at work.		0.084	0.446	0.176
Ex7	My boss at work is very understanding.		0.463	0.197	0.42
Ex8	My colleagues always take care of each other.		0.189	0.529	0.345
Ex12	I can arrange my own schedule properly because of the flexibility of my work.		0.076	0.645	0.119
Ex13	When I am sick, the company takes good care of me.		0.499	1.874	0.249
Ex15	I can get a raise or bonus of a proper amount.		−2.109	−0.823	0.381
Ex17	My income is higher than that of others with the same conditions as me.		−2.258	0.771	0.426
Ex18	I never feel confused or scared while working.		0.03	1.694	0.058
Ex19	There are many chances of promotion.		−1.12	−0.141	0.125
Ex23	I am proud of my work.		0.103	1.05	0.105
Ex24	I want to be perfect when it comes to my work.		−1.633	−0.39	0.002

Table 4. Multiple regression of the refined questionnaire model in the third round.

		R-square = 0.392	[95% Conf. Interval]		
			Lower bound	Upper bound	Significance
Ey1	I think my work ability is excellent.				
Ex4	The quality of my life can be improved through my work.		−0.452	−0.128	0.267
Ex5	My life becomes richer due to my work.		−0.394	−0.139	0.341
Ex6	I can have the sense of achievement at work.		0.088	0.439	0.186
Ex7	My boss at work is very understanding.		0.473	0.18	0.372
Ex8	My colleagues always take care of each other.		0.206	0.5	0.405
Ex12	I can arrange my own schedule properly because of the flexibility of my work.		0.074	0.645	0.117
Ex13	When I am sick, the company takes good care of me.		0.582	1.55	0.065
Ex15	I can get a raise or bonus of a proper amount.		−2.21	−0.409	0.173
Ex18	I never feel confused or scared while working.		0.089	1.453	0.082
Ex19	There are many chances of promotion.		−1.015	−0.134	0.17
Ex23	I am proud of my work.		0.058	1.076	0.077
Ex24	I want to be perfect when it comes to my work.		−1.629	−0.392	0.002

4. Results and Verifications

4.1. Statistical Significance of Question

The relative change of the statistical significance value before and after each round of the repetitive refinement approach in the regression setting is defined as:

$$\frac{x_j^f - x_j^i}{x_j^i} \quad (1)$$

where x_j^f denotes the final statistical significance value for the jth component of the model, while x_j^i denotes the initial statistical significance value for the jth component of the model. The statistical significance is defined as follows: If the p-value is less than or equal to alpha, we say that the data are statistically significant at level alpha. In statistics (where "significant" means "corresponds to a real difference in fact") the term is used to indicate only that the evidence against the null hypothesis reaches the standard set by alpha (Moore and McCabe [32]). Since the lower the significance value of a component the higher will be its contribution to the model, a negative value for the relative change of the statistical significance in Equation (1) signifies that the effect of the corresponding component/question on the model is increased, while the opposite is true for the case of a positive value. Tables 5 and 6 list the relative change of the statistical significance as a percentage (%) for each question of Ey explained by Ex1–24 and for each question of Cy explained by Cx1–8, respectively.

Table 5. Employees' part: relative change of the statistical significance for each question of Ey explained by Ex1–24.

Work Values \ Work Satisfaction	Ey1	Ey2	Ey3	Ey4	Ey5	Ey6	Ey7	Ey8	Ey9	Ey10
Ex1		−34%		−50%		−38%	−97%		−19%	−90%
Ex2		42%				−50%			−59%	−17%
Ex3		−13%				−28%		−20%	−37%	
Ex4	−45%				20%	−77%	−74%	−77%	−28%	−32%
Ex5	−19%			−1%		−47%			−55%	0.3%
Ex6	−2%				−45%		−64%	−21%		
Ex7	−7%				−59%	−56%		−42%	−46%	
Ex8	19%			−80%	−26%	−90%	−0.3%	−72%		
Ex9				−31%	−20%		−66%		−44%	−50%
Ex10				−17%			−13%		−8%	
Ex11		−74%		−48%			−67%	−27%	−58%	−100%
Ex12	−36%			−71%			−58%	−43%	−61%	−38%
Ex13	−84%	−70%		−15%		−69%		−7%		−14%
Ex14					−31%	−70%	−32%	−24%	−51%	−23%
Ex15	−70%	−85%			−48%		−8%	−2%		−12%
Ex16		−79%			−59%					
Ex17				−94%		−100%	−21%	−97%		−81%
Ex18		−78%		−27%		−71%		−25%		
Ex19	−53%			−4%		−70%		−42%		
Ex20		−13%		−6%		−34%		−30%		
Ex21				−44%	−37%	−17%				−55%
Ex22		−91%		−28%	−50%		−20%	−77%	−97%	−74%
Ex23	−41%			−15%	−56%		−61%	−46%		−60%
Ex24	−89%	−31%		−40%		−38%	−84%	−58%		−49%
Mean change	−41%	−48%		−37%	−37%	−57%	−48%	−42%	−47%	−46%
Total Mean Change							−45%			

Table 6. Cadres' part: relative change of the statistical significance for each question of Cy explained by Cx1–8.

Organizational management \ Organizational commitment	Cy1	Cy2	Cy3	Cy4	Cy5	Cy6	Cy7	Cy8	Cy9	Cy10
Cx1	−68%		−56%	−40%	−74%	−57%	0%	−5%		−72%
Cx2	−85%	−7%	−64%		−25%	−83%	0%	−33%	−91%	−27%
Cx3		−91%		−83%		−53%	0%	−33%	−92%	−11%
Cx4	−96%		−98%	−74%	−60%		0%	−35%	−93%	−11%
Cx5	−88%	−48%				−53%	0%	12%		−37%
Cx6			−45%		−42%		0%	−19%		−2%
Cx7		−48%		−74%	−69%	−40%	0%	−35%	−93%	
Cx8		1%		−85%	−39%	−36%	0%		−92%	−95%
Mean change	−84%	−39%	−66%	−71%	−52%	−54%	0%	−21%	−92%	−36%
Total mean change							−52%			

In Table 5, a blank indicates that the question used to explain the corresponding question Ey in a model has been removed. All the questions used to explain the question Ey3 have been removed, implying that Ey3 ("My boss thinks I am doing a great job at work") has nothing to do with any of the questions relating Ex1–24. Such a question should be removed to improve questionnaire design for accurate evaluations of working characteristics. It is clear that all the significance values of the remaining questions are decreased except for the four marked values. Such a decrease in the significance value refers to the increase of the effect of the question on a model, verifying that the remaining questions are the real contributing questions/factors for the refined model. The total mean relative change of the statistical significance of the remaining variables is −45%.

Similarly in Table 6, a blank indicates that the question used to explain the corresponding question Cy in a model has been removed. Again, the significance values of the remaining questions are clearly decreased except for the two marked values. Such a decrease in the significance value verifies that the remaining questions are the real contributing questions/factors to the refined model. The total mean relative change of the statistical significance of the remaining variables is −52%. In particular, the question Cy7 "Staying and working for this company doesn't do me any good" needs to be explained by all eight questions Cx1–8 relating to organizational management. In other words, choosing whether to stay and work for the company depends on the entire range of the company's management strategies.

4.2. R-Squared Value of Regression Analysis

In the regression setting, the final R-squared value of each Ey for the employees' part through the repetitive refinement approach implemented in the linear series, refined linear series, Taylor series, and refined Taylor series models is listed in Table 7 (adapted from Lin and Shen [30], Shen [31]). The total mean R-squared value is decreased by 0.02 for the refined linear series model from the linear series model, signifying that the model refinement approach developed here cannot truly affect the R-squared value when searching for the genuinely contributory questions for survey improvement. On the other hand, the Taylor series model increases the mean R-squared value by 0.19 from the linear series model, which greatly improves the modeling process in the multiple regression setting.

Table 7. Employees' part: Final R-squared values for linear series, refined linear series, Taylor series, and refined Taylor series models.

	X = Work Values Y = Work Performance and Satisfaction	Linear Series	Refined Linear Series	Taylor Series	Refined Taylor Series
Ey1	I think my work ability is excellent.	0.41	0.392	0.593	0.533
Ey2	I can always finish my work rapidly on time.	0.407	0.366	0.624	0.562
Ey3	My boss thinks I am doing a great job at work.	0.285	0.208	0.389	0.26
Ey4	My professional knowledge is enough to do my job.	0.46	0.449	0.684	0.638
Ey5	I am highly cooperative with my team.	0.314	0.302	0.521	0.479
Ey6	I am very satisfied with the welfare provided by the company I work for.	0.555	0.53	0.692	0.632
Ey7	I am very satisfied with what this job has to offer to help improving my future development.	0.521	0.499	0.743	0.694
Ey8	I am very satisfied with my salary.	0.493	0.487	0.699	0.656
Ey9	I am very satisfied with my relationships with my colleagues.	0.495	0.481	0.708	0.661
Ey10	I am very satisfied with the opportunities and the system of promotion.	0.531	0.524	0.713	0.663
	Overall mean per model	0.44	0.42	0.63	0.57

Similarly, the final R-squared value of each Cy for the cadres' part obtained by the repetitive refinement approach in the linear series, refined linear series, Taylor series, and refined Taylor series models is listed in Table 8 (adapted from Lin and Shen [30], Shen [31]). The total mean R-squared value is again decreased by 0.02 for the refined linear series model. The Taylor series model on average increases the R-squared value by 0.17 from the linear series model, greatly improving the modeling process. In Table 8, all the questions implemented in the Taylor series model achieve high R-squared values of greater than 0.85, implying a satisfactory result in modeling the causal explanations for questionnaire design.

Table 8. Cadres' part: Final R-squared values for linear series, refined linear series, Taylor series, and refined Taylor series models.

X = Organizational Management Y = Organizational Commitment and Identification		Linear Series	Refined Linear Series	Taylor Series	Refined Taylor Series
Cy1	I care about the future development of the company.	0.785	0.757	0.942	0.879
Cy2	In order to stay employed by the company, I am willing to accept any assignment.	0.723	0.681	0.911	0.793
Cy3	In order to help the company to be successful, I am willing to pay extra efforts.	0.757	0.753	0.934	0.848
Cy4	It doesn't matter to work for another company as long as job content and conditions are similar.	0.724	0.692	0.894	0.817
Cy5	I think the company I work for is a good company, and it's worthy to work hard for it.	0.769	0.765	0.938	0.842
Cy6	The style of this company is close to my values.	0.797	0.772	0.956	0.844
Cy7	Staying and working for this company doesn't do me any good.	0.97	0.97	0.999	0.999
Cy8	I would leave this company as long as my job status is slightly changed.	0.647	0.613	0.854	0.768
Cy9	I can identify myself with the company's policy for its employees.	0.781	0.771	0.939	0.897
Cy10	I am glad that I decided to take this job instead of others.	0.656	0.653	0.859	0.753
	Overall mean per model	0.76	0.74	0.93	0.84

4.3. Reliability and Validity

Verifications and error analyses were also conducted to compare the above results using the repetitive model refinement approach with those using methods of reliability and validity.

This study adopted Cronbach's alpha to represent the reliability in data analysis. Guieford [33] proposed a set of criteria for Cronbach's alpha. The standard value of Cronbach's alpha is 0.5. High alpha values (>0.7) mean high reliability while low ones (<0.35) mean low reliability. Table 9 shows that through the repetitive model refinement approach the number of questions was reduced and all the reliabilities were over 0.7, indicating that the sample was adequately stable and consistent.

Table 9. Reliability analyses.

	Before deleting questions	After deleting questions
Employees' work values	Cronbach's alpha = 0.623	Cronbach's alpha = 0.720
Employees' work performance and satisfaction	Cronbach's alpha = 0.577	Cronbach's alpha = 0.742
Cadres' organizational management	Cronbach's alpha = 0.565	Cronbach's alpha = 0.740
Cadres' organizational commitment and identification	Cronbach's alpha = 0.590	Cronbach's alpha = 0.780

Validity in SPSS on the other hand means "exploratory factor analysis" (according to SPSS online help), whose main features are the following tests:

(1) Kaiser–Meyer–Olkin (KMO) measure of sampling adequacy tests whether the partial correlations among variables are small (KMO > 0.6);
(2) Bartlett's Test of Sphericity tests the null hypothesis that the correlation matrix is an identity matrix, indicating that the factor model is inappropriate (Sig < 0.05);
(3) SPSS analysis defines communality as the proportion of a parameter's variance that is explained by the factor structure.

This repetitive model refinement approach thus reduces the number of questions and can be shown to promote communality significantly; this also indicates that validity was not reduced after questions had been deleted, as illustrated in Table 10.

Table 10. Exploratory factor analysis.

	Before Deleting Questions	After Deleting Questions
Employees' work values	KMO = 0.816 Bartlett Test Sig = 0.03 Communality = 0.768	KMO = 0.772 Bartlett Test Sig = 0.01 Communality = 0.811
Employees' work performance and satisfaction	KMO = 0.763 Bartlett Test Sig = 0.01 Communality = 0.798	KMO = 0.733 Bartlett Test Sig = 0.00 Communality = 0.828
Cadres' organizational management	KMO = 0.741 Bartlett Test Sig = 0.00 Communality = 0.739	KMO = 0.709 Bartlett Test Sig = 0.00 Communality = 0.801
Cadres' organizational commitment and identification	KMO = 0.712 Bartlett Test Sig = 0.01 Communality = 0.754	KMO = 0.700 Bartlett Test Sig = 0.01 Communality = 0.799

5. Conclusions

This study is consistent with sustainable development issues, dealing with four areas: employees' work values; employees' work performance and satisfaction; cadres' organizational management; and cadres' organizational commitment and identification. The questionnaire data are available for reference and for enterprises' development. In addition, the questionnaire design improvement can assist researchers to design more precise and effective questionnaires. In this study, an effective repetitive model refinement approach using 95% confidence intervals in a multiple regression setting has been applied to the analysis of questionnaire design improvement for evaluating working characteristics in construction enterprises. Such an approach sifts components/questions by removing non-contributing questions of the model, inducing only a 2% decrease in the model's corresponding R-squared value, while keeping the genuinely contributory questions of the model for questionnaire design improvement. This not only reduces the time to complete the questionnaire in surveys, but also reduces the cost of production of the questionnaire. The results prove that the developed Taylor series model significantly increases the R-squared value by 17% when compared with the linear series model. After repeatedly running the screening process of the estimated parameters, almost all the remaining questions of the model for both the employees' and cadres' sections show decreased significance values with a total mean relative change of 49%, verifying that the remaining questions are indeed the real contributing ones to the models studied. In particular, the question "My boss thinks I am doing a great job at work" in evaluating employees' work performance cannot be successfully explained by the contents of the questionnaire relating to employee work values. Such a question should instead be evaluated by a manager within the repetitive model refinement approach. However, the question "Staying and working for this company doesn't do me any good" can be evaluated through the full content of the questionnaire relating to organizational management. In other words, an employee's decision to stay in the company is substantially dependent on the company's management strategies. Further, limitations of the study indicate that the developed questionnaire design improvement should be applied to data with high reliability.

Acknowledgments: The work described in this paper comprises part of the research project sponsored by Feng Chia University (Contract No. 14I42315), whose support is greatly appreciated.

Author Contributions: Jeng-Wen Lin designed the research and wrote the paper; Pu Fun Shen performed research and analyzed the data; and Bing-Jean Lee revised the paper.

Conflicts of Interest: The authors declare no conflict of interest.

References

1. Kim, M.J. A framework for context immersion in mobile augmented reality. *Autom. Constr.* **2013**, *33*, 79–85. [CrossRef]
2. Saris, W.E. Questionnaire Design. 2014. Available online: http://link.springer.com/referenceworkentry/10.1007%2F978-94-007-0753-5_2392#page-1 (accessed on 12 November 2015).

3. Saris, W.E.; Gallhofer, I.N. Design, Evaluation, and Analysis of Questionnaires for Survey Research. 2014. Available online: https://books.google.com.tw/books?hl=zh-TW&lr=&id=NTKpAgAAQBAJ&oi=fnd&pg=PT12&ots=xHVXLPqMua&sig=Vfoid8qPqQZ2we861FwFBaI3Ccs&redir_esc=y#v=onepage&q&f=false (accessed on 12 November 2015).
4. Weimiao, F.; Zheng, Y. Factors Affecting Response Rates of the Web Survey: A Systematic Review. *Comput. Hum. Behav.* **2009**, *26*, 132–139.
5. Ergu, D.; Kou, G. Questionnaire Design Improvement and Missing Item Scores Estimation for Rapid and Efficient Decision Making. *Ann. Oper. Res.* **2012**, *197*, 5–23. [CrossRef]
6. Suzuki, S.; Ando, M.; Hashimoto, H.; Asama, H. Design Procedure and Improvement of a Mathematical Modeling to Estimate Customer Satisfaction. 2014. Available online: http://link.springer.com/chapter/10.1007/978-4-431-54816-4_2#page-1 (accessed on 12 November 2015).
7. Edwards, P.J.; Roberts, I.; Clarke, M.J.; DiGuiseppi, C.; Wentz, R.; Kwan, I.; Cooper, R.; Felix, L.M.; Pratap, S. Methods to Increase Response to Postal and Electronic Questionnaires. *Cochrane Database Syst. Rev.* **2009**. [CrossRef]
8. Landsheer, J.A.; Boeije, H.R. In Search of Content Validity: Facet Analysis as a Qualitative Method to Improve Questionnaire Design An Application in Health Research. *Qual. Quant.* **2008**, *44*, 59–69. [CrossRef]
9. Jacqui, J.; Pete, B.; Sarah, W.; Jane, C. Improved Questionnaire Design Yields Better Data: Experiences from the UK's Annual Survey of Hours and Earnings. In Proceedings of the International Conference on Establishment Survey (ICES–III), Montréal, QC, Canada, 18–21 June 2007.
10. Xu, S.; Zhou, S.; Cao, Q.; Lei, J.; Li, X.; He, Y. Questionnaire Design and Analysis of Online Teaching and Learning: A Case Study of the Questionnaire of "Education Online" Platform of Beijing University of Technology. 2014. Available online: http://link.springer.com/chapter/10.1007/978-94-007-7618-0_419 (accessed on 12 November 2015).
11. Smith, D.R. Model Refinement: Calculating Refinements in Algorithm and System Design. 2009. Available online: ftp://kestrel.edu/pub/papers/smith/mr.pdf (accessed on 12 November 2015).
12. Adrian, V. Performance Criteria for Software Metrics Model Refinement. *J. Appl. Quant. Methods* **2007**, *2*, 118–128.
13. Kapova, L.; Goldschmidt, T. Automated Feature Model-Based Generation of Refinement Transformations. In Proceedings of the 2009 SEAA '09, 35th Euromicro Conference on Software Engineering and Advanced Applications, Patras, Greece, 27–29 August 2009; pp. 141–148.
14. Liu, X. Solution Refinement of Wireless Optical System Model with Multi-level Modulation. *Electron. Lett.* **2009**, *45*, 475–476. [CrossRef]
15. Ragnhild, V.D.S.; Viviane, J.; Tom, M. A Formal Approach to Model Refactoring and Model Refinement. *Softw. Syst. Model.* **2005**, *6*, 139–162.
16. Steven, J.L.; Philip, R.B.; Chiu, W. EMAN: Semiautomated Software for High-Resolution Single-Particle Reconstructions. *J. Struct. Biol.* **1999**, *128*, 82–97.
17. Zhuquan, Z.; Bitmead, R.R.; Gevers, M. H2 Iterative Model Refinement and Control Robustness Enhancement. In Proceedings of the 30th IEEE Conference on Decision and Control, Brighton, UK, 11–13 December 1991; Volume 1, pp. 279–284.
18. Khorshid, E.; Alfares, M. Model Refinement and Experimental Evaluation for Optimal Design of Speed Humps. *Int. J. Veh. Syst. Model. Test.* **2006**, *2*, 80–99. [CrossRef]
19. Lin, J.W.; Chen, H.J. Repetitive Identification of Structural Systems using a Nonlinear Model Parameter Refinement Approach. *Shock Vib.* **2009**, *16*, 229–240. [CrossRef]
20. Lin, J.W. Adaptive Algorithms for the Identification of Nonlinear Structural Systems. Ph.D. Thesis, Columbia University, New York, NY, USA, 2001.
21. Lin, J.W.; Betti, R. On-line Identification and Damage Detection in Non-linear Structural Systems using a Variable Forgetting Factor Approach. *Earthq. Eng. Struct. Dyn.* **2004**, *33*, 419–444. [CrossRef]
22. Tryon, W.W. Evaluating Independent Proportions for Statistical Difference, Equivalence, Indeterminacy, and Trivial Difference Using Inferential Confidence Intervals. *J. Educ. Behav. Stat.* **2009**, *34*, 171–189. [CrossRef]
23. Yang, J.; Xie, M.; Goh, T.N. Control Limits Based on the Narrowest Confidence Interval. *Commun. Stat. Theory Methods* **2011**, *40*, 2172–2181. [CrossRef]
24. Bonett, D.G.; Price, R.M. Adjusted Wald Confidence Interval for a Difference of Binomial Proportions Based on Paired Data. *J. Educ. Behav. Stat.* **2012**, *37*, 479–488. [CrossRef]

25. Ahiaga-Dagbui, D.D.; Smith, S.D. Dealing with Construction Cost Overruns Using Data Mining. *Constr. Manag. Econ.* **2014**, *32*, 682–694. [CrossRef]
26. Anastasopoulos, P.C.; Haddock, J.E.; Peeta, S. Cost Overrun in Public-Private Partnerships: Toward Sustainable Highway Maintenance and Rehabilitation. 2014. Available online: http://ascelibrary.org/doi/abs/10.1061/%28ASCE%29CO.1943-7862.0000854 (accessed on 12 November 2015).
27. Kim, B.C.; Kim, H.J. Sensitivity of Earned Value Schedule Forecasting to S-Curve Patterns. *J. Constr. Eng. Manag.* **2014**, *140*, 04014023. Available online: http://ascelibrary.org/doi/10.1061/%28ASCE%29CO.1943-7862.0000856 (accessed on 12 November 2015). [CrossRef]
28. Patel, D.A.; Jha, K.N. Neural Network Model for the Prediction of Safe Work Behavior in Construction Projects. 2015. Available online: http://ascelibrary.org/doi/10.1061/%28ASCE%29CO.1943-7862.0000922 (accessed on 12 November 2015).
29. Hackman, J.R.; Oldham, G.R. Development of the Job Diagnostic Survey. *J. Appl. Psychol.* **1975**, *60*, 159–170. [CrossRef]
30. Lin, J.W.; Shen, P.F. Factor-analysis Based Questionnaire Categorization Method for Reliability Improvement of Evaluation of Working Conditions in Construction Enterprises. *Struct. Eng. Mech.* **2014**, *51*, 973–988. [CrossRef]
31. Shen, P.F. Impact of Employees' Work Values at Two Sides of Taiwan Straits on Corporate Performance. Master's Thesis, Feng Chia University, Taichung, Taiwan, 2011.
32. Moore, D.S.; McCabe, G.P. *Introduction to the Practice of Statistics*, 3rd ed.; W.H. Freeman and Company: New York, NY, USA, 2000.
33. Guieford, J.P. *Fundamental Statistics in Psychology and Education*, 4th ed.; McGraw Hill: New York, NY, USA, 1965.

© 2015 by the authors. Licensee MDPI, Basel, Switzerland. This article is an open access article distributed under the terms and conditions of the Creative Commons Attribution (CC BY) license (http://creativecommons.org/licenses/by/4.0/).

Article

Development of an Innovation Model Based on a Service-Oriented Product Service System (PSS)

Seungkyum Kim [1], Changho Son [2], Byungun Yoon [3] and Yongtae Park [1],*

[1] Department of Industrial Engineering, Seoul National University, 1 Gwanak-ro, Gwanak-gu, Seoul 151-742, Korea; hdglace8@snu.ac.kr
[2] Department of Weapon System Engineering, Korea Army Academy at Yeong-Cheon, 135-1 Changhari, Young-Cheon, Gyeongbuk 770-849, Korea; c13981@snu.ac.kr
[3] Department of Industrial & Systems Engineering, Dongguk University, Seoul 04620, Korea; postman3@dongguk.edu

* Author to whom correspondence should be addressed; parkyt1@snu.ac.kr; Tel./Fax: +82-2-878-3511

Academic Editor: Adam Jabłoński

Received: 1 August 2015; Accepted: 20 October 2015; Published: 28 October 2015

Abstract: Recently, there have been many attempts to cope with increasingly-diversified and ever-changing customer needs by combining products and services that are critical components of innovation models. Although not only manufacturers, but also service providers, try to integrate products and services, most of the previous studies on Product Service System (PSS) development deal with how to effectively integrate services into products from the product-centric point of view. Services provided by manufacturers' PSSes, such as delivery services, training services, disposal services, and so on, offer customers ancillary value, whereas products of service providers' PSSes enrich core value by enhancing the functionality and quality of the service. Thus, designing an effective PSS development process from the service-centric point of view is an important research topic. Accordingly, the purpose of this paper is to propose a service-oriented PSS development process, which consists of four stages: (1) strategic planning; (2) idea generation and selection; (3) service design; and (4) product development. In the proposed approach, the PSS development project is initiated and led by a service provider from a service-centric point of view. From the perspective of methodology, customer needs are converted into product functions according to Quality Function Deployment (QFD), while Analytic Hierarchy Process (AHP) is employed to prioritize the functions. Additionally, this paper illustrates a service-oriented PSS development that demonstrates the application of the proposed process. The proposed process and illustration are expected to serve as a foundation for research on service-oriented PSS development and as a useful guideline for service providers who are considering the development of a service-oriented PSS.

Keywords: Product Service System (PSS); service-oriented PSS development process; English education; Analytic Hierarchy Process (AHP); Quality Function Deployment (QFD)

1. Introduction

Recently, customer needs have become increasingly diversified and ever-changing. Under this circumstance, because it is very difficult to fulfill sophisticated customer needs by product innovation alone, many attempts to overcome this problem have involved combining products and services. In practice, companies, such as General Electric, Xerox, Canon, and Parkersell, have shown a considerable increase in sales and profits from services since the mid-1990s [1]. Although such companies had originally made profits by only selling products, they have maintained growth by integrating services into their products. These attempts can be regarded as Product Service Systems

(PSS), which are firstly defined as a set of products and services that fulfills customer needs and has lower environmental impact [2]. Most of the early studies on PSS focused on the environmental aspect. However, the scope and concept of PSS have been expanded, as various studies on PSS have been actively conducted. Nowadays, PSS is regarded as an integrated system of products and services to provide customers with functions and value that they need [3]. Thus, it is one of the critical components of innovation models that can create value on existing and new businesses.

Most of the previous studies on PSS are based on the viewpoint of manufacturers [4–11]. Particularly, studies on PSS development deal with how to effectively integrate services into products from the product-centric point of view, and they focus on a specific phase, not the whole development process. Low *et al.* [4] suggested an idea generation method using theory of solving inventive problem (TRIZ) methodology, while Uchihira *et al.* [8] proposed a method that identifies PSS opportunities along with product usage. Aurich *et al.* [6] and Yang *et al.* [11] utilized product life-cycle data for idea generation and design of PSSes. In summary, there is a lack of research on PSS development covering the whole development process, and it is rare to find PSS research conducted from the service-centric point of view. However, service providers are also making attempts to integrate products into their services for effective service deliveries and differentiated customer value. Amazon's Kindle is an example of this case. PSSes developed by manufacturers and service providers have different characteristics in terms of customer value. Services of manufacturers' PSSes, such as delivery services, training services, disposal services, and so on, offer customers ancillary value instead of core value that customers recognize when consuming the product, whereas products of service providers' PSSes ensure that core value is enriched by enhancing functionality and quality of the service. In the case of Kindle, e-book contents are instantly delivered with lower cost, easier access, and easier payment; therefore, Kindle enriches the core value that Amazon has offered customers as an online bookstore. Thus, a different approach for developing a service-centric PSS is required. Therefore, designing an effective PSS development process from the service-centric point of view is an important research topic.

Accordingly, this paper proposes a service-oriented PSS development process in which the PSS development project is initiated and led by a service provider from a service-centric viewpoint to generate a new innovation model. In contrast to a single product or service development, PSS development is carried out by multiple actors, including manufacturers and service providers; hence, the role of each actor should be defined clearly. In the proposed process, which consists of four stages, the actor and its role are specified for each stage. Additionally, this paper introduces a real PSS development case from the education industry sector, which demonstrates the application of the proposed process and discusses the practical issues that can occur during the PSS development project. The fact that the proposed process was applied to real business practices has practical significance and, furthermore, this research could serve as a useful guideline for service providers to develop a service-oriented PSS.

The remainder of this paper is organized as follows. In the next section, the previous studies on PSS development are reviewed, which build a foundation for the proposed approach. In Section 3, a service-oriented PSS development process is proposed including the concept, framework, and detailed processes. Section 4 introduces the case of service-oriented PSS development in detail. Finally, this research ends with conclusions that include contributions, limitations and directions for future research.

2. Literature Review

2.1. Definition of PSS

Recently, PSS has received much attention from both industry and academia. Accordingly, active research regarding PSS is underway. Goedkoop *et al.* [2] initially suggested the PSS concept, which is defined as "a system of products, services, networks of players, and supporting infrastructure that continuously strives to be competitive, satisfy customer needs and have a lower environmental impact than traditional innovation models" [2]. On the other hand, Wong [12] defined PSS as follows; "Product Service-Systems (PSS) may be defined as a solution offered for sale that involves both a product and a service element, to deliver the required functionality", which was not limited to the environmental impact. Although many researchers have since proposed different definitions of PSS, it has generally been considered as "product(s) and service(s) combined in a system to enable new innovation models aiming to fulfill customer needs" [2,3,13,14].

2.2. Characteristics of PSS

The main characteristics of PSS, in comparison with pure products or services, are threefold. First, firms can improve the level of interaction with their customers through PSS. In terms of customer relationships, the products, and services offered through PSS play a complementary role in satisfying the customers' requirements. For instance, if a company that sells washing machines also provides laundry service to its customers, the interaction with customers will be increased because of the characteristics of this add-on service. Second, there are a variety of types of payment and ownership of PSS [15]. This is because PSS is an integrated model of ownable and tangible products and non-owned and intangible services. Accordingly, most PSS providers have ownership of their PSS and sell the usage rights or results. Tukker [15] suggested three main categories of PSS, including product-oriented services, use-oriented services, and result-oriented services. In case of use-oriented services and result-oriented services, the payment reference is not for the product, but a payment per unit time or unit use, and so on. The product stays in ownership with the provider in the above cases, whereas products are mainly sold and some extra services are added in product-oriented services. Here, there is no pre-determined product involved for result-oriented services.

Lastly, stakeholders creating PSS value are very diverse [16,17], including PSS providers and customers. A representative example where integrated products and services are provided through collaboration among several firms is Apple's AppStore.

2.3. Types of PSS

The most widely accepted of the proposed PSS types is the work by Tukker [15]. The three main categories are as follows: product-oriented PSS, use-oriented PSS, and result-oriented PSS. First, the product-oriented PSS is the most similar to the concept of the traditional product, since the value is achieved by selling the product. However, this is accompanied by additional services such as after-sales services to guarantee the functionality of the product. Second, use-oriented PSS basically sells the "use" of a product, not the product itself. What is delivered to the customer is a function that the customer wants, for example, leasing or sharing services. Finally, result-oriented PSS sells a result or capability instead of a product. The customer pays only for the provision of agreed results. Selling laundered clothes instead of a washing machine is a good example of result-oriented PSS [3,15].

2.4. Research on PSS Development Process

Most studies of the PSS development process have been based on the development process of products or services and consist of three main phases: analysis, idea generation, and selection, and implementation [17]. The first phase, analysis, includes environmental analysis, SWOT analysis, and so on, which has been treated as a small part of PSS development research. Nevertheless, some methodologies have been developed and employed in the analysis phase. The "Innovation Scan" was developed for analyzing and forecasting the relationship between customer needs and product functions [18], while the product-service integrated roadmap was proposed for the strategic planning of product-service integrated offerings [19]. The next phase, idea generation and selection, has been the most actively studied. Lee and Kim [20] classified PSS by function and developed PSS ideas using a combination of products and services. Low *et al*. [4], Chen and Huang [21], and Chen and Li [22] utilized TRIZ for idea generation. The TRIZ method stands for "Teoriya Resheniya Izobretatelskikh

Zadatch" in Russian which means theory of inventive problem solving [23,24]. This method solves technical problems and offers innovative product structures by employing a knowledge base built from the analyses of approximately 2.5 million patents, primarily on mechanical design [25]. TRIZ consists of three basic tools: (1) 40 principles to resolve conflicts effectively; (2) a knowledge database system that consists of physical, chemical, and geometrical effects and rules for problem solving; and (3) modeling a technological problem.

Uhlmann and Stelzer [26] suggested seven dimensions to determine PSS ideas through a case study. The seven dimensions are composed of customer skills, customer will to build up skills, property rights, human resources, outsourcing of product, existing network of suppliers, and process monitoring to determine PSS ideas through a case study.

Meiner and Kroll [27] proposed an approach to creating a new PSS model based on service processes. In addition, many tools, such as extended service blueprint [10], system map, interaction storyboard, stakeholder motivation matrix [28], modified IDEF0 [29], and many others to design PSSes using generated and selected new ideas have been developed. Finally, in the implementation phase, Schuh and Gudergan [30] suggested a framework using QFD (Quality Function Deployment) and Yang *et al.* [11] provided a methodology for the realization of PSSes through the utilization of product life-cycle data. The QFD has been widely used since Akao suggested it in 1990. The tool that has been used most frequently in QFD is a matrix called the House Of Quality (HOQ), which is utilized for the aim of converting market information into product strategies for business [31].

As we have explained, most previous research on PSS development has focused on a specific phase, not the whole development process. In particular, these studies have been mainly conducted from the product-centric point of view. In other words, previous studies of PSS development dealt with products and relevant supporting services, but the converse was not the case. While the term, "service-oriented product" was utilized in some studies [32,33], it represented use-oriented PSS rather than service-supporting products. Therefore, research on the entire development process for service-oriented PSS is still the domain of a few pioneers.

3. Service-Oriented PSS Development

3.1. Concept

This research proposes the service-oriented PSS development process for developing a new innovation model. The term, "service-oriented PSS" stands for a PSS in which a product is integrated into a service as a supporting tool to make the existing service more competitive. The distinctive characteristics of the service-oriented PSS are twofold. First, customer needs for the existing service are the starting point of service-oriented PSS development, whereas product-centric PSS development begins with the needs for the product itself or the context of product usage. After customer needs for the service are investigated, the product functions to fulfill these needs are derived from the investigation result. Subsequently, new services are developed by combining the existing service with the new product. Where a single service cannot meet customer needs without a product, it can be complemented by the integration of the service and product. That is to say, functions required for the product are derived from customer needs for the service, and the product makes the service more competitive. The integration of the service and product constitutes the service-oriented PSS, which can provide greater competitiveness and value than a stand-alone service.

Second, in service-oriented PSS development, the role of the product manufacturer should receive greater emphasis than that of the service provider in product-centric PSS development. Most previous studies on PSS development considered services as the means to offer customers ancillary value in order to raise lock-in effects and sales from the manufacturers' viewpoint, and manufacturers introduce and operate their own services in many cases [7]. On the other hand, it is hard for service providers to develop and produce products. In a relative sense, products are dependent on technologies, equipment, and facilities, whereas services are dependent on humans. Thus, service providers should establish strong partnerships with manufacturers to develop service-oriented PSSes and closely collaborate with partners on product and service developments. In these regards, service-oriented PSS development differs from product-centric PSS development.

3.2. Framework

The service-oriented PSS development process proposed in this research is derived from the product development process of Cooper *et al.* [34,35], the service development process of Brügemann [36], and several cases of PSS development projects summarized by Tukker and Tischner [17]. The product development process of Cooper *et al.* [34,35] is represented by the stage-gate process which comprises a five-stage (scoping, build business case, development, testing and validation, and launch), five gate (idea screen, second screen, go to development, go to testing, and go to launch) process incorporating a discovery stage and a post-launch review, whereas the service development process of Brügemann [36] is composed of eight stages: "situation analysis", "objectives", "strategy", "idea finding", "generation of requirements", "development", "implementation", and "delivery of service". Tukker and Tischner [17] investigated PSS development methods used in PSS development projects and grouped them into three phases, "analysis", "idea generation and selection", and "implementation". Based on these references, we made the service-oriented PSS development process by grouping similar stages and excluding stages related to marketing, distribution, and use in order to focus on development. The result consists of four stages, "strategic planning", "idea generation and selection", "service design", and "product development". Between every stage, an intermediate evaluation and back-loop scheme using the results of intermediate evaluation is applied like Cooper *et al.*'s five gates. Contrary to the previous sequential processes, the proposed process is a hybrid of sequential and parallel processes, because PSS development includes product development as well as service development. The planning and idea generation for PSS development are carried out sequentially and service design proceeds in parallel with product development.

As shown in Figure 1, the service-oriented PSS development process has two layers, a service provider layer and product partner (manufacturer) layer, which show the participants for each stage. Service-oriented PSS development is initiated by the service provider, hence the first stage, "strategic planning" is carried out by the service provider alone. The next stage, "idea generation and selection" is performed by the service provider and the product partner selected in the previous stage. Together they generate detailed ideas for planned PSS development. Subsequently, the third and fourth stages, "service design" and "product development", are conducted concurrently by the service provider and the product partner, respectively. At this time, the key aspect to successful PSS development is to achieve consensus on the service and product through effective communication and interaction between the two actors. To this end, the results of service design should be delivered to the product partner in order to verify the technical feasibility of the required service functions, and the pilot product should also be delivered to the service provider in order to judge the suitability of the design and functions. These collaborations are expressed as arrows between "service design" and "product development" in Figure 1. Here, a service-oriented PSS can be developed from the open innovation concept of Chesbrough [37]. From a service-centered point of view, product partners can be considered as external; *i.e.*, the use of purposive inflows and outflows of knowledge is to accelerate internal innovation and expand the markets for external use of innovation. Actors and key features for each stage of the service-oriented PSS development process are summarized in Table 1.

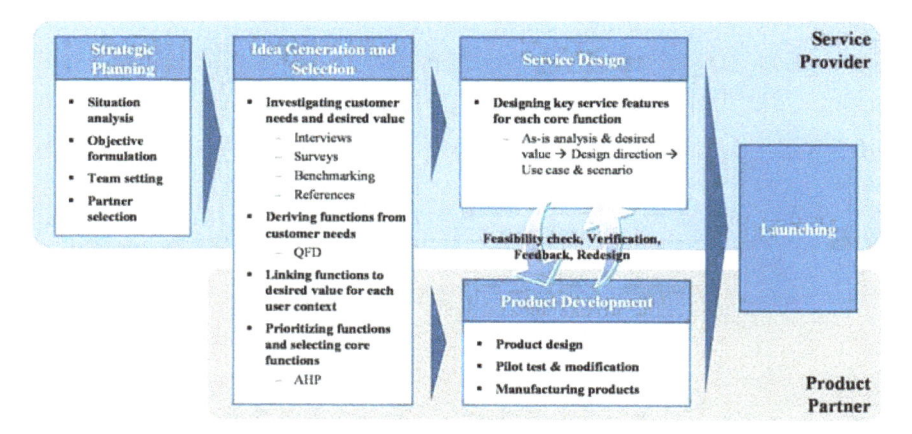

Figure 1. Service-oriented PSS development process.

Table 1. Actors and key features for each stage of the service-oriented PSS development process.

Stage		Actor	Key Feature
Strategic Planning		Service Provider	The service-oriented PSS development is initiated by the service provider, and a product partner is selected.
Idea Generation and Selection		Service Provider & Product Partner	During this stage, there is a preliminary check of the feasibility of the ideas and consensus on the detailed PSS concept is achieved through collaboration between the two actors.
PSS Development	Service Design	Service Provider	Detailed service features and product functions are verified and redesigned based on feedback. Finally, the final service-oriented PSS is developed.
	Product Development	Product Partner	
Launching		Service Provider & Product Partner	The service-oriented PSS is launched in the market.

3.3. Detailed Process

3.3.1. Strategic Planning

A service-oriented PSS development project is initiated by the service provider and the first stage is strategic planning. First, the service provider determines what to develop. In the case that services, alone, are provided, the service provider builds a general concept of PSS development that combines the existing services and product in order to increase competitiveness and customer satisfaction as well as add new value for customers. Thereafter, the service provider conducts situation analyses, including market analysis, competence analysis, competitor analysis, and so on. Subsequently, the concrete objectives of the PSS development project and the team that will lead it are formulated. Lastly, the product partner that will cover the product development is selected. The selection of a product partner to develop the service-oriented PSS can be accomplished through a variety of methods. Among them, an emergent theory of partner selection through collaboration, similar to that produced by Emden et al. [38], is utilized. The model is composed of three broad phases: (1) technological alignment; (2) strategic alignment; and (3) relational alignment. Technological capability, resource complementarity, and overlapping knowledge bases are considered in the first phase. Then, motivation and goal correspondence are checked in the second phase. Finally, compatible cultures, propensity to change, and long-term orientation are screened in the third phase.

3.3.2. Idea Generation and Selection

The second stage is idea generation and selection, which are conducted by the service provider and the product partner selected in the previous stage. In this stage, it is essential to investigate customer needs for the existing service and derive product functions from these needs. To this end, expected user groups are firstly selected, and each group's needs for the existing service are investigated thoroughly. At this point, not only customer needs but also their desired requirements i.e., what they ultimately want from the service, should be identified. Interviews and surveys are the most useful and representative methods for this purpose. Particularly, in-depth interviews with customers and related experts are an effective means to figure out the ideal service scenarios and product functions required when the service is combined with the product. In addition, reviews in relevant professional publications and reports, and benchmarking of existing relevant services and products can provide the implications of success and failure factors that help derive product functions.

The next step is to derive product functions based on prior investigations of customer needs. At this point, customer needs are converted into product functions in a similar manner to QFD, which transforms customer needs into engineering/process requirements. Subsequently, additional functions can be added from the benchmarking results. Eventually, the customer needs generated from the service are analyzed and converted into product functions.

The following step is to match up functions with desired requirements using QFD. The desired requirements can be varied according to the purpose and situation of each user group. Thus, the functions that will be provided should differ in accordance with user groups. To deal with this problem, the actors in this stage should analyze the user context and derive desired requirements according to each user group's context based on the results of the investigation conducted previously. Subsequently, actors match every function with certain desired requirements and user groups. Consequently, the results can show a user group and its desired requirements provided by a specific function, functions needed by a specific user group, and functions that fulfill certain desired requirements. An exemplified outcome of this task is illustrated in Figure 2.

Lastly, functions are prioritized by the Analytic Hierarchy Process (AHP) method and core functions are selected as the final outcome of this stage. The AHP is a decision-aiding method developed by Saaty [39–41]. It is one of the most widely used multi-criteria decision-making tools and is an Eigenvalue approach to pair-wise comparisons. It also provides a methodology to calibrate the numeric scale for the measurement of both quantitative and qualitative performances [42]. The number of core functions can vary according to constraints such as project schedule and financial budget, and the remaining functions can be developed and added to the next version of the PSS. Through the previous steps such as investigating customer needs and desired requirements, deriving functions, and linking functions with desired requirements, participants in this stage can be regarded as experts who have sufficient knowledge about the desired requirements and the necessary functions. Thus, they can evaluate the relative importance between two functions based on their experiences when using the AHP method.

User context & DR* / Functions	User group 1								
	Context 1			Context 2			Context 3		...
	DR 1-1	DR 1-2	...	DR 2-1	DR 2-2	...	DR 3-1	DR 3-2	...
Function 1	O	O			O				
Function 2				O			O		
Function 3					O		O	O	
Function 4	O			O					
⋮									

* DR: desired requirement

Figure 2. An example of a matrix for linking functions to desired requirements for each user context.

3.3.3. Service Design

The service design stage and the product development stage proceed in parallel under the respective guidance of the service provider and product partner after the second stage, idea generation and selection. In the service design stage, the service provider designs services in detail, which can be realized with the product functions derived in the previous stage.

Service dominant logic is comprised of five steps as follows: (1) as-is analysis; (2) setting service design direction; (3) creating service use-cases; (4) making service scenarios; and (5) checking feasibility. First, the service provider conducts the "as-is analysis", which analyzes the current situation of services offered without a product. The deficiencies in current services that are contrary to the ideal services and desired requirements are derived from "as-is analysis". Thereafter, the service provider establishes the direction of the service design for overcoming the gap between the current services and the ideal ones via integration with product functions. Subsequently, the service provider develops use-cases based on the design direction, which includes elements such as actors (users, service providers, and so on), product, and infrastructure (systems, networks, and so on.) as well as the relationships between elements such as information input/output and physical materials. After all the use cases have been developed, service scenarios for each user group can be created by aggregating them. During these tasks, modeling methods such as IDEF0 which is a compound acronym Icam DEFinition for Function Modeling, where "ICAM" is an acronym for Integrated Computer Aided Manufacturing and service blueprint [29] can be exploited. After the use cases and service scenarios have been developed, they are delivered to the product partner to verify the technical feasibility. Then, the service provider receives feedback on the technical feasibility of the service, and redesigns services based on this. Furthermore, the service provider should give feedback on the pilot product to the product partner.

3.3.4. Product Development

In this stage, the product partner develops the product. The product partner develops the basic design, architecture, and product specifications, and realizes the functions derived from the idea generation and selection. Once the pilot product is created, the product partner should deliver it to the service provider and modify its design, functions, and so on, according to the feedback from the service provider. In addition, once the product partner receives the use cases and service scenarios from the service provider, the product partner checks the feasibility to determine whether it is possible to realize the product functions required by the service or not. If there is a function that is impossible to realize, the product partner sends feedback so that the relevant service can be redesigned. Otherwise, the product partner modifies the functions, architecture, or specifications of the product according to the use cases and service scenarios. Effective and efficient interaction between the service provider and product partner is critical to develop a successful PSS. Thus, various iterations of feasibility checks, verifications, feedback and redesigns are inevitable while jointly developing the service and product. Once the final consensus on the service and product is achieved through these processes, the product partner manufactures the products. Finally, service-oriented PSS development is finished and launched. There are many factors to take into account when launching a service-oriented PSS. The launching stage needs to address some basic issues such as launch goal and strategy, major player and stakeholders, target customers, current market environment, and so on [43]. It is critical to carefully design a launch plan and prepare internally before a public launch. This internal preparation will address issues such as testing and validation, pricing, documentation, warranty, demos, sales tools, training for sale/channels/service/support, and so on.

4. Illustration: T Smart Learning

4.1. Introduction to the Case Companies and the PSS Development Project

The illustration in this paper is derived from a PSS development project undertaken by S Telecom in collaboration with C Learning. S Telecom is a mobile service provider in Korea, with 50.6% market share as of 2010. Since its launch on 29 March 1984 S Telecom has evolved from a first-generation analog cellular system, to a second-generation CDMA provider, and then to the world's first third-generation synchronized IMT-2000 cellular system. S Telecom also became the world's first company to commercialize HSDPA in May 2006. S Telecom provides not only mobile telecommunication services but also convergence services including media, social networking, content delivery, location-based service, platform, commerce, and a host of other options. Recently, S Telecom has been actively seeking new business opportunities to cope with B2C market saturation by developing B2B innovation models in various industry sectors, including the education industry.

C Learning is a language institute located in Korea and Canada. C Learning was founded in 1998 and offers ESL (English as a Second Language) learning services by combining self-developed programs and native English-speaking instructors. C Learning provides more than 60,000 students with unique programs based on critical thinking and cognitive language development. This is made possible by more than 1300 instructors, 390 corporate employees, and its ESL R-and-D center. Recently, the company has reached saturation in terms of the number of students it can teach due to physical space constraints. Thus, an innovative method for continuous growth is required. Additionally, the Korean Education Ministry unveiled a plan to introduce a new English aptitude test—NEAT (National English Ability Test)—that focuses on tests of speaking and writing ability, and will replace the English section of the standardized college entrance examination. Therefore, new coursework and classes to prepare for the NEAT will have to be created.

Under this background, S Telecom and C Learning signed a memorandum of understanding on developing an English learning system that uses wireless communications networks to allow students to study anywhere and anytime, keep parents up to date with students' progress, and to increase communication between the teacher and students within the classroom. The characteristics of this system as a PSS are as follows. It consists of actors (students, parents, and instructors), contents, learning-support devices, and network infrastructures. From its inception, the project considered English learning services and learning-support devices (products) simultaneously in order to create a successful PSS that can raise the effectiveness and efficiency of learning. Accordingly, many stakeholders' needs were investigated and incorporated during the development process. Furthermore, this system will only be meaningful if customer needs are fulfilled by the services or functions offered via the product. Thus, product possession itself has no meaning. In particular, product functions were developed in order to fulfill customer needs and desired requirements that were derived and analyzed from existing English learning services. These characteristics made this English learning system a service-oriented PSS.

4.2. Strategic Planning

To begin, S Telecom and C Learning analyzed the global trend and potential of the English education market, the state of affairs of the major IT players (Apple, Intel, and so on) in the education sector, and local cases of device-based learning services by mobile service providers. These analyses produced the following results: (1) English education is experiencing high growth in the global market and Asia is the most promising region; (2) the focus of English education is moving toward improving fundamental listening, speaking, reading, and writing abilities, instead of grammar and reading comprehension; and (3) key success factors for a device-based learning system involve not only fine contents but also specialized functions increase the effectiveness of education. Consequently, S Telecom and C Learning set up an objective to develop a PSS that combines an English learning service and a mobile device. The first target service was the NEAT coursework, which had already been made by the R-and-D center of C Learning. The target product was a tablet PC-like device, which supports wireless data communication and provides specialized functions for effectively improving listening, speaking, reading, and writing English abilities. In addition, they made a plan to gradually expand the target market by adding other coursework and subjects and entering global education markets such as China and Southeast Asian countries.

Next, S Telecom and C Learning set up an exclusive TFT (Task Force Team) for developing the product. After establishing the team setting, the TFT searched for various device manufacturers and software developers in order to select product partners, and contacted them based on considerations of technological competency and quality, as well as cost. Finally, the hardware and software-product partners were selected and members from these product partners joined the TFT.

4.3. Idea Generation and Selection

For idea generation and selection, the TFT thoroughly investigated customer needs and desired requirements in English education. The TFT conducted in-depth interviews with more than 20 students and parents, and 20 experts in English education such as English teachers, directors of language institutes, and coursework developers so that users' and teachers' needs for existing English learning services and ideal methods of learning English were investigated. Additionally, the TFT reviewed eight books about the theory of English learning and 11 autobiographies by people who were successful in learning English. They also benchmarked 52 on/offline learning services and 36 learning-support devices. This broad and deep investigation enabled the TFT to achieve a full understanding of the existing English education services. It is very important to devote sufficient time and effort to this kind of task, since it serves as the foundation of the following tasks.

After extensive investigations, the TFT derived device functions based on the investigation results. The needs were converted into functions via QFD methodology, and other functions were added based on the benchmarking results. In this process, there was a preliminary check of the feasibilities of the functions, especially by TFT members who joined from product partners. For example, the "eyeball tracking" function was excluded due to technical problems and cost. Finally, 149 functions were derived. Examples of customer needs and relevant functions are summarized in Table 2.

Table 2. Examples of customer needs and relevant functions.

User Group	Need	Function
Student	"Although I cannot understand what is said in class, I hesitate to ask a question." "I want learning to be more interesting." "I want more exposure to English."	Evaluating the current level, Daily test, Learning history, Learning game, Role-play, Avatar, Online community, Push contents, and *etc.*
Teacher	"I want to arouse students' interest with teaching materials made of multimedia contents such as movies, sitcoms, news, and pop songs." "In the class, it takes too much time to correct each student's speaking and writing." "I want to check homework and score exams more efficiently."	Coursework generator, Multimedia contents library, Speaking evaluation, Writing evaluation, Auto-grading, Class planner, Student profile management, and *etc.*
Parent	"I wonder my child follows the coursework well." "I want to know how much my child's achievement level is improving."	Informing of diagnosis results, Informing of progress, Informing of attitude in class, and *etc.*

The following step involves matching functions with desired requirements as well as the user context for each user group using QFD. This task was conducted through a one-day workshop attended by all members of the TFT, whereas previous tasks such as interviews, benchmarking, and function derivation were assigned to groups composed of two or three members. The TFT divided users into three groups: student, teacher and parent. For each group, the TFT analyzed user context and derived desired requirements in each context based on the investigation results (see Figures 3 and 4). Finally, 34 function sets were derived by grouping similar functions among 149 functions.

	Student									
User context & DR* / Functions	...	Speaking				...	Listening			...
		Mimicking /shadowing	Imitation/ reproduction	Present-ation	Debate		Recog-nizing	Skim-ming	Scan-ning	
Text-to-speech		O					O	O	O	
Record and play			O	O						
Partial repeat		O					O			
Memo				O	O			O	O	
⋮										

* DR: desired requirement

Figure 3. The partial outcome of linking functions to desired requirements for students' context.

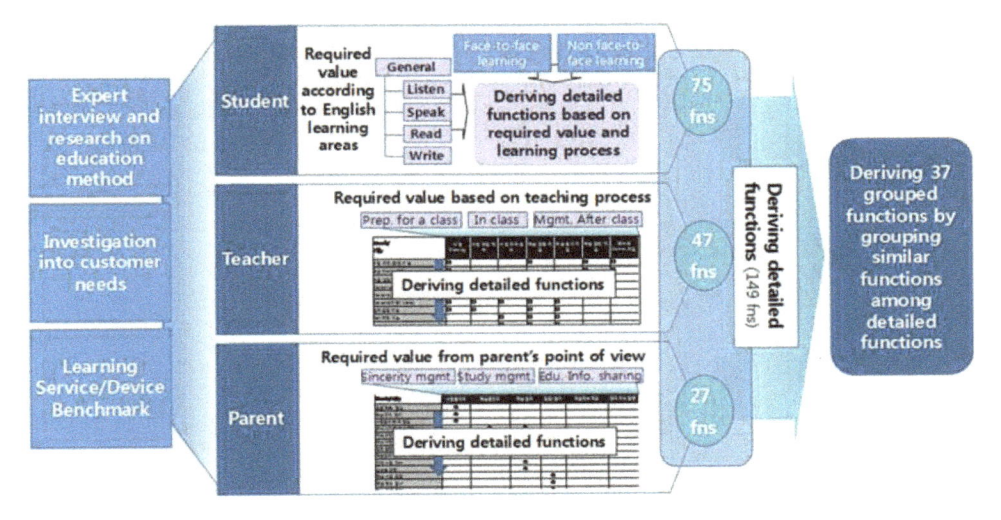

Figure 4. The partial outcome of linking functions to desired requirements for students' context.

Lastly, the TFT prioritized the function sets by the AHP method, and selected the core function sets. Since too many functions were derived, it was not reasonable to develop them all together in view of time-to-market, development cost, and quality. Thus, the TFT needed to select functions that would be developed for the first version of T Smart Learning, and the AHP method was employed for this aim. In addition, all members took an entire day to prioritize function sets as a group. The criteria for AHP were determined through discussion as follows: (1) effectiveness of learning; (2) personalized learning; and (3) competitiveness. After obtaining the weights for all criteria by pairwise comparisons, the TFT conducted pairwise comparisons between function sets for each criterion. Eventually, all function sets were prioritized and all consistency ratios were below 0.1, which means that all comparisons were consistent (see Table 3). Based on the priorities, five function sets for students were selected as core function sets. Additionally, the function sets for teachers and parents were selected as core function sets in order to cover all user groups, even though these priorities were ranked below the other function sets. In the final outcome (see Appendix 5), the core function sets included: (1) listening-specialized function set; (2) speaking-specialized function set; (3) reading-specialized function set; (4) writing-specialized function set; (5) personal care function set; (6) teacher-support function set; and (7) parent-support function set. Other function sets will be developed and added in the next version of T Smart Learning.

In this step, the AHP method was an effective means to reach a consensus on which functions would be developed first. During pairwise comparisons, the members of TFT discussed the relative importance between functions and, consequently, the consensus was built spontaneously. Thus, the AHP method served as a tool for not only prioritizing functions but also for building a consensus among TFT members.

Table 3. Priority of criteria and consistency ratio.

Criteria	Priority	Consistency Ratio for Function Sets Evaluation
Effectiveness of learning	0.5438	0.05066
Personalized learning	0.1103	0.02724
Competitiveness	0.3460	0.03084

4.4. Service Design

The TFT (excluding members from product partners) designed services in detail, which can be realized by utilizing the core functions derived in the previous stage. First, the TFT analyzed the deficiencies of the current English education services offered without a product, and derived the service design direction for each function set to compensate for the gap between the current situation and desired requirements investigated previously. Thereafter, the TFT created the service use-cases based on the design directions and developed service scenarios by aggregating use-cases.

The case of the speaking-specialized function set is as follows. The requirements for learning how to speak English are mimicking, imitation, reproduction, presentation, debate, self-check, and evaluation. In detail, students should listen to the native speaker's pronunciation and imitate it at the beginning. The next step is to practice various expressions that have similar meanings. Subsequently, it is necessary to improve the ability to organize the contents of what will be said. Finally, students will be able to make a presentation and participate in a debate with their own thoughts and opinions. In all these processes, self-check and evaluation can make learning more effective. However, there is little or no chance to speak English in reality. Moreover, students cannot find self-learning methods or receive instant feedback on their speaking abilities. Thus, the TFT established the design direction as follows: (1) providing various expressions recorded in a native speaker's pronunciation in order to allow self-practice; (2) giving instant feedback on speaking ability; and (3) offering a virtual place to communicate with colleagues via telepresence. According to these design directions, the TFT designed service use cases such as "speaking English by watching one's face via a camera in the device", "comparing one's pronunciation with a native speaker's by a record and play function", "providing a role-play service through which one can communicate with virtual characters through the device", and "providing a group discussion service via telepresence and giving instant feedback based on STT (Speech-to-Text) technology". The TFT delivered these outcomes to the product partners and received feedback from them. Subsequently, the use-cases were redesigned based on the feedback. For example, the software product partner recommended that the TFT change "giving instant feedback based on STT technology" because of the low accuracy of current STT technology. Thus, the TFT changed the concept of the feedback service from automated instant feedback to semi-automated not-instant feedback, in which manual correction by a teacher is included. The use-case of the feedback service is shown in Figure 5.

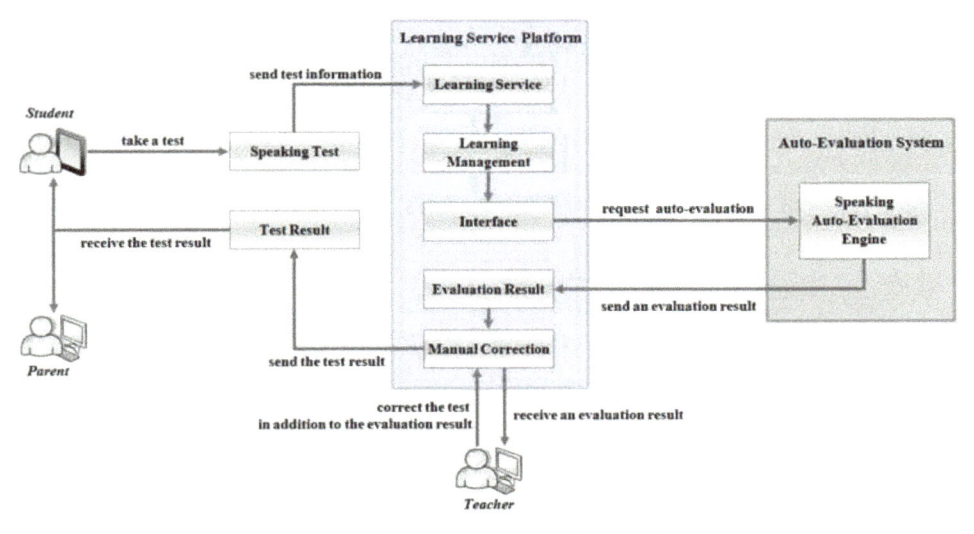

Figure 5. The use-case of the feedback service.

Finally, the TFT developed the service scenario for each user group by aggregating the service use-cases, and the partial outcome of the service scenario for the students is illustrated in Figure 6. The service scenarios were also confirmed by the product partners.

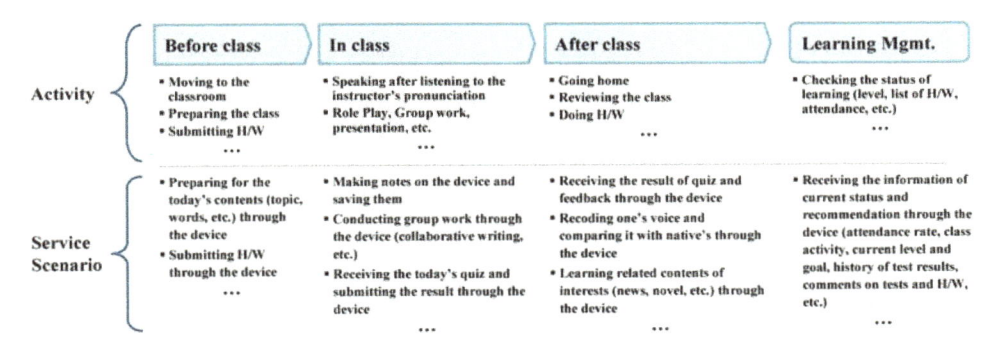

Figure 6. The partial outcome of the service scenario for the student.

4.5. Product Development

The respective hardware and software-product partners developed the hardware and software products that could realize the core functions derived in the idea generation and selection stage. During the development process, the product partners received service use-cases and scenarios from the TFT and incorporated them into the product development. Furthermore, the product partners communicated with the TFT continuously to receive feedback on the intermediate outcomes, and modified the products accordingly. The hardware product partner intended to develop a new device that specialized in learning, and the software product partner intended to develop a new software platform and related applications for the device based on Android open-source software.

However, it was hard to complete the hardware product development before the scheduled date. When considering the quality, cost, and release timing, the TFT and product partners decided to apply an existing tablet PC for the first version. Accordingly, the TFT and the hardware product partner consented to develop a learning-specialized device based on a long-term plan, whereas the software product partner developed the application launcher that would make an Android OS-based tablet PC operate as a new learning device. In this case, the application launcher can be regarded as another OS operating on top of the Android OS. While developing the software product, the software product partner improved the user interface and functions according to feedback from the TFT. Although the shape and specifications of the device are identical with the existing general-purpose tablet PC, the device with the launcher can provide an entirely new English-learning experience. In addition to the launcher, the software product partner developed a system comprised of the architecture, platform, and servers, which is indispensable for operating a service based on a mobile network and device (see Figure 7). Finally, S Telecom and C Learning launched a service-oriented PSS, T Smart Learning, on 18 July 2011, after a one month pilot test. The actual appearance of T Smart Learning is shown in Figure 8. The left figure is the main screen of T Smart Learning and the right one is the screen studying English.

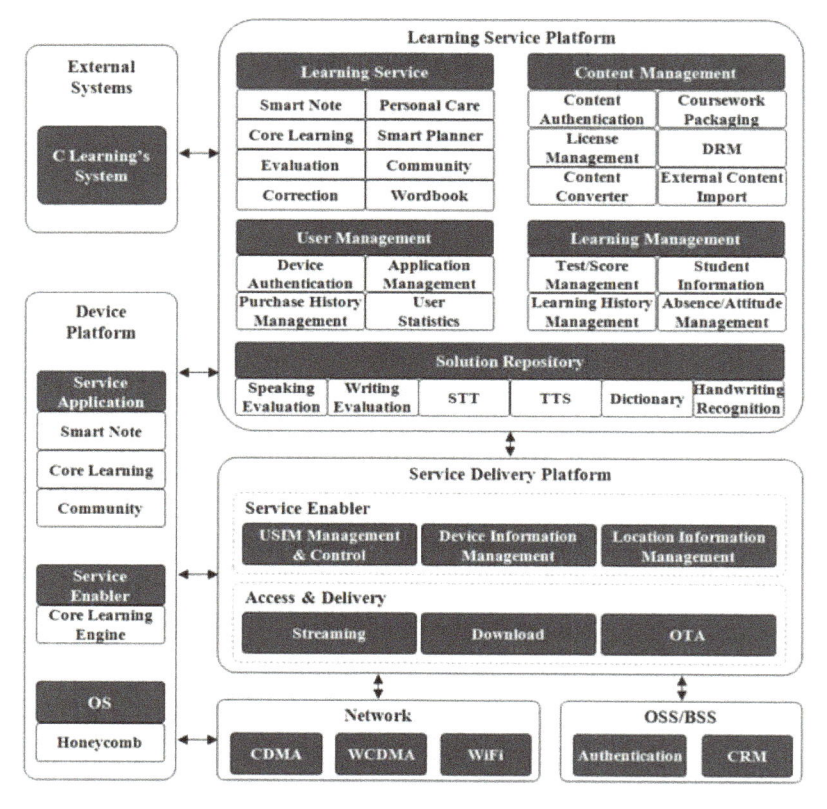

Figure 7. System architecture of T Smart Learning.

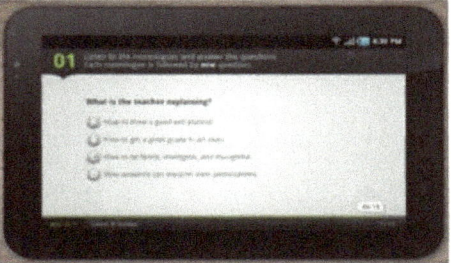

Figure 8. Actual appearance of T Smart Learning.

4.6. Discussions and Implications

The proposed framework was validated by applying it to a practical case in the illustration part. Although many cases can be utilized for complete validation, this paper performed an in-depth analysis in the T Smart Learning case to investigate the details of the framework. Consequently, the systematic approach to develop a service-oriented PSS enabled us to successfully generate creative ideas, design a service, and develop a PSS by reflecting the interaction between service providers and product partners. The most important part in the validation is how much users are satisfied with the practicality of the suggested approach. The TFT members in the aforementioned case highlighted the usefulness of four stages and techniques in each stage such as QFD and scenario analysis. In addition, active feedbacks among stakeholders could facilitate the process of developing the PSS.

However, several critical points should be considered to elevate the quality of application of the proposed approach. In the idea generation and selection stage of our case study, the TFT members of service providers had difficulty defining functions and judging their development potential. They also had difficulty separating them into hardware and software products because of the lack of knowledge and product development experience. At this time, the TFT members of the product partners played a key role in checking the feasibility of the functions and classifying them. On the contrary, the members of product partners who had a rudimentary understanding of the service gained a deeper understanding through the steps of deriving functions and conducting the AHP method, and this positively influenced the development of the requisite product in service-oriented PSS. Thus, it is definitely necessary to involve the product partners in the idea generation and selection stage.

The service providers and product partners should communicate and interact during the service design and product development stages. Through efficient and effective communication feedback is exchanged and incorporated into service design and product development. If miscommunication occurs at this point, the project team will not achieve satisfactory results. In our case, all TFT members got together and shared the progress of service design and product development once every two weeks. In spite of that, the project schedule was actually delayed due to miscommunication. Thus, it is necessary to execute more research on a systematic method for effective communication between the service design and product development teams. In this regard, Kleinsmann *et al.* [44] found factors that influence the creation of a shared understanding in collaborative new product development, and they also identified four collaboration types and their mechanisms. A similar study of PSS development would provide valuable findings and implications.

It is not easy to develop a new hardware product for service-oriented PSS. In our case, a general-purpose tablet PC was employed, contrary to the initial objective, although the hardware product partner still aimed to develop a new device that specialized in English education. Since the development of a new hardware product is highly risky in terms of cost and time, the service provider should consider customizing a general-purpose hardware product from its inception. Thus, the decision-making step on whether to develop or customize should be included in future research on the service-oriented PSS development process.

5. Conclusions

This paper proposes a service-oriented PSS development process in which the PSS development project is initiated and led by a service provider from a service-centric point of view. The proposed process, which is based on the product development process, service development process, and cases of PSS development projects, consists of four stages: (1) strategic planning; (2) idea generation and selection; (3) service design; and (4) product development. For each stage, actors and detailed procedures, including key features and useful methods, are suggested. Additionally, the real PSS development case of an English education service is introduced in detail as a demonstration of the application of the proposed process.

The contribution of this paper is that it expands the current scope of PSS research by suggesting the concept and development process of service-oriented PSS from the service provider's viewpoint, contrary to the manufacturer's viewpoint of existing studies. This can establish a foundation for research on service-oriented PSS development. Moreover, the proposed process and illustration are expected to serve as a useful guideline when service providers develop a service-oriented PSS.

However, this paper has some limitations. Firstly, the majority of the proposed process covers qualitative aspects. If more quantitative methods are added to the process, the proposed process can be made more systematic. Thus, the systematic and quantitative approach to partner selection, idea generation, service design, and collaboration with product partners are future research topics. Secondly, the case presented in this paper covers only specific industry sectors. Numerous case studies of broad industry sectors can provide us with worthwhile implications for service-oriented PSS development. In particular, cases of proven market success could confirm the validity of the proposed process. Therefore, in-depth case studies of various industries including successful cases could be another line of future research. Thirdly, since this research focuses on the PSS development process, subsequent processes such as a launching and operating process were not dealt with in this paper. Unique characteristics of PSS can be reflected to implement the details of the launching and operating processes. Thus, future research can present a complete framework of service-oriented PSS development from planning to operation by including the launching and operating process.

Acknowledgments: This work was supported by the National Research Foundation of Korea Grant funded by the Korean Government (NRF-2014R1A1A2054892).

Author Contributions: Seungkyum Kim designed the study, outlined the methodology, analyzed the data, interpreted the results and wrote the manuscript. Changho Son analyzed the data and wrote the manuscript. Byungun Yoon designed the study and wrote the manuscript. Yongtae Park implemented the research, designed the study, outlined the methodology, and helped complete the draft of this research. All authors have read and approved the final manuscript.

Conflicts of Interest: The authors declare no conflict of interest.

Appendix

Table A1. 34 Function sets and AHP results.

User Group	Function Sets	AHP Results				Note
		Effectiveness of Learning	Personalized Learning	Competitiveness	Overall Priority	
student	writing-specialized	0.05249	0.05220	0.08347	0.06317	core function
student	speaking-specialized	0.05517	0.05220	0.05839	0.05596	core function
student	listening-specialized	0.05438	0.05220	0.05839	0.05553	core function
student	reading-specialized	0.05431	0.05220	0.05839	0.05549	core function
student	personal care	0.05309	0.05220	0.05839	0.05482	core function
teacher	interaction in class	0.03939	0.05986	0.06446	0.05032	core function (teacher-support)
teacher	auto-correction	0.05693	0.04637	0.03691	0.04884	core function (teacher-support)
student	dictionary	0.05161	0.04637	0.03691	0.04595	
teacher	auto-grading	0.04297	0.04402	0.03739	0.04116	core function (teacher-support)
student	note	0.04175	0.02700	0.03615	0.03819	
student	planner	0.04283	0.01653	0.02806	0.03482	
student	diagnosis	0.02942	0.03376	0.03715	0.03258	
student	push contents	0.03615	0.01263	0.01679	0.02686	
student	contents library	0.02209	0.02926	0.03220	0.02638	
student	game	0.02837	0.03330	0.02007	0.02604	
teacher	checking homework	0.02182	0.03009	0.03117	0.02597	core function (teacher-support)
teacher	making tests	0.02755	0.01008	0.01998	0.02300	core function (teacher-support)
teacher	making teaching material	0.01824	0.03138	0.02745	0.02288	core function (teacher-support)
student	communication	0.02073	0.01957	0.02633	0.02254	
student	search	0.03144	0.01354	0.01139	0.02253	
parent	informing of diagnosis results	0.02337	0.01279	0.01139	0.01806	core function (parent-support)
parent	informing of progress	0.01537	0.02573	0.01967	0.01800	core function (parent-support)
student	counseling	0.01593	0.01276	0.02117	0.01739	
teacher	class/student management	0.01538	0.01974	0.01211	0.01473	core function (teacher-support)
teacher	communication with parents	0.01499	0.01974	0.01211	0.01452	
parent	informing of attitude in class	0.01394	0.02704	0.01072	0.01427	core function (parent-support)
parent	intimacy	0.01190	0.02276	0.01160	0.01300	core function (parent-support)
parent	education-related information	0.01226	0.01660	0.01215	0.01270	core function (parent-support)
student	synchronization	0.01073	0.01974	0.01211	0.01220	
teacher	other teacher-support	0.00889	0.02055	0.01160	0.01112	
student	help	0.01079	0.01092	0.01008	0.01056	
teacher	student control	0.00920	0.00852	0.01095	0.00973	
student	timer	0.00789	0.01206	0.01160	0.00964	
parent	nurture-related information	0.00696	0.01014	0.01139	0.00885	core function (parent-support)

References

1. Martinez, V.; Bastl, M.; Kingston, J.; Evans, S. Challenges in transforming manufacturing organizations into product-service providers. *J. Manuf. Technol. Manag.* **2010**, *21*, 449–469.
2. Goedkoop, M.J.; van Halen, C.J.G.; te Riele, H.R.M.; Rommens, P.J.M. *Product Service Systems, Ecological and Economic Basis*; Technical Report; Pre Consultants: Amersfoort, The Netherlands, 1999.
3. Baines, T.S.; Lightfoot, H.W.; Evans, S.; Neely, A.; Greenough, R.; Peppard, J.; Roy, R.; Shehab, E.; Braganza, A.; Tiwari, A.; *et al.* State-of-the-art in product-service systems. *Proc. Inst. Mech. Eng. Part B* **2007**, *221*, 1543–1552. [CrossRef]
4. Low, M.K.; Lamvik, T.; Walsh, K.; Myklebust, O. Manufacturing a green service: Engaging the TRIZ model of innovation. *IEEE Trans. Electron. Packag. Manuf.* **2001**, *24*, 10–17.
5. Alonso-Rasgado, T.; Thompson, G. A rapid design process for Total Care Product creation. *J. Eng. Des.* **2006**, *17*, 509–531. [CrossRef]
6. Aurich, J.C.; Fuchs, C.; Wagenknecht, C. Life cycle oriented design of technical Product-Service Systems. *J. Clean. Prod.* **2006**, *14*, 1480–1494. [CrossRef]
7. Tan, A.R.; McAloone, T.C.; Gall, C. Product/service-system development—An explorative case study in a manufacturing company. In Proceedings of the International Conference on Engineering Design 2007, Paris, France, 28–31 August 2007.
8. Uchihira, N.; Kyoya, Y.; Kim, S.; Maeda, K.; Ozawa, M.; Ishii, K. Analysis and Design Methodology for Recognizing Opportunities and Difficulties for Product-based Services. In Proceedings of the PICMET 2007, Portland, OR, USA, 5–9 August 2007.
9. Sakao, T.; Sandström, G.Ö.; Matzen, D. Framing research for service orientation of manufacturers through PSS approaches. *J. Manuf. Technol. Manag.* **2009**, *20*, 754–778.
10. Shimomura, Y.; Hara, T.; Arai, T. A unified representation scheme for effective PSS development. *CIRP Ann.-Manuf. Technol.* **2009**, *58*, 379–382. [CrossRef]
11. Yang, X.; Moore, P.; Pu, J.; Wong, C. A practical methodology for realizing product service systems for consumer products. *Comput. Ind. Eng.* **2009**, *56*, 224–235. [CrossRef]
12. Wong, M. Implementation of innovative product service-systems in the consumer goods industry. Ph.D. Thesis, University of Cambridge, Department of Engineering, Cambridge, UK, 2004.
13. Mont, O. Clarifying the concept of product-service system. *J. Clean. Prod.* **2002**, *10*, 237–245. [CrossRef]
14. Manzini, E.; Vezzoli, C. A strategic design approach to develop sustainable product service systems: Examples taken from the "environmentally friendly innovation" Italian prize. *J. Clean. Prod.* **2003**, *11*, 851–857. [CrossRef]
15. Tukker, A. Eight types of product service system: Eight ways to sustainability experiences from SusProNet. *Bus. Strateg. Environ.* **2004**, *13*, 246–260. [CrossRef]
16. Krucken, L.; Meroni, A. Building stakeholder networks to develop and deliver product-service-systems: Practical experiences on elaborating pro-active materials for communication. *J. Clean. Prod.* **2006**, *14*, 1502–1508. [CrossRef]
17. Tukker, A.; Tischner, U. *New Business for Old Europe: Product-Service Development, Competitiveness and Sustainability*; Greenleaf Publishing: Sheffield, UK, 2006.
18. Tukker, A.; van Halen, C. *Innovation Scan for Product Service Systems: Manual*; TNO: Delft, The Netherlands; PricewaterhouseCoopers: Utrecht, The Netherlands, 2003.
19. Suh, J.; Park, S. Service-oriented Technology Roadmap (SoTRM) using patent map for R&D strategy of service industry. *Expert Syst. Appl.* **2009**, *36*, 6754–6772.
20. Lee, S.; Kim, Y. A product-service system design method integrating service function and service activity and case studies. In Proceedings of the 2nd CIRP IPS2 Conference, Linköping, Sweden, 14–15 April 2010.
21. Chen, J.; Huang, C. A TRIZ based eco-innovation method for PSS. In Proceedings of the 16th CIRP International Conference on Life Cycle Engineering, LCE 2009, Cairo, Egypt, 4–6 May 2009.
22. Chen, J.; Li, H. Innovative design method of product service system by using case study and TRIZ model. In Proceedings of the 2nd CIRP IPS2 Conference, Linköping, Sweden, 14–15 April 2010.
23. Genrich, A.; Shulyak, L. *And Suddenly the Inventor Appeared: TRIZ, the Theory of Inventive Problem Solving*; Technical Innovation Center, Inc.: Worcester, UK, 1996.

24. Domb, E. QFD and TIPS/TRIZ. Available online: http://www.trizjournal.com/archives/1998/06/c/index.htm (accessed on 23 October 2015).
25. Yamashina, H.; Ito, T.; Kawada, H. Innovative product development process by integrating QFD and TRIZ. *Int. J. Prod. Res.* **2002**, *40*, 1031–1050. [CrossRef]
26. Uhlmann, E.; Stelzer, C. Identifiaction of the IPS2 business model in the early stage of creation. In Proceedings of the 2nd CIRP IPS2 Conference, Linköping, Sweden, 14–15 April 2010.
27. Meier, H.; Kroll, M. From products to solutions-IPS2 as a means for creating customer value. In Proceedings of the 16th CIRP International Conference on Life Cycle Engineering, LCE 2009, Cairo, Egypt, 4–6 May 2009.
28. Manzini, E.; Collina, L.; Evans, S. *Solution Oriented Partnership: How to Design Industrialised Sustainable Solutions*; Cranfield University: Cranfield, UK, 2004.
29. Morelli, N. Developing new product service systems (PSS): Methodologies and operational tools. *J. Clean. Prod.* **2006**, *14*, 145–1501. [CrossRef]
30. Schuh, G.; Gudergan, G. Service engineering as an approach to designing industrial product service systems. In Proceedings of the 1st CIRP Industrial Product-Service Systems (IPS2) Conference, Cranfield, UK, 1–2 April 2009.
31. Hauser, J.R.; Clausing, D. The house of quality. *Harvard Business Review*, May 1988; 63–73.
32. Umeda, Y.; Tsutsumida, M.; Tomiyama, T.; Tamura, T.; Fujimoto, J. Study on feasibility of service-oriented products using life cycle simulation. *J. Jpn. Soc. Des. Eng.* **2001**, *36*, 517–526.
33. Fujimoto, J.; Umeda, Y.; Tamura, T.; Tomiyama, T.; Kimura, F. Development of service-oriented products based on the inverse manufacturing concept. *Environ. Sci. Technol.* **2003**, *37*, 5398–5406. [CrossRef] [PubMed]
34. Cooper, R.G.; Edgett, S.J.; Kleinschmidt, E.J. Optimizing the stage-gate process: What best-practice companies do—I. *Res. Technol. Manag.* **2002**, *45*, 21–27.
35. Cooper, R.G.; Edgett, S.J.; Kleinschmidt, E.J. Optimizing the stage-gate process: What best-practice companies do—II. *Res. Technol. Manag.* **2002**, *45*, 43–49.
36. Brügemann, L.M. Innovation of an Eco-efficient Product-Service Combination. Master's thesis, Delft University of Technology, Delft, The Netherlands, 2000.
37. Chesbrough, H. Open innovation: Where we've been and where we're going. *Res. Technol. Manag.* **2012**, *55*, 20–27. [CrossRef]
38. Emden, Z.; Calantone, R.J.; Droge, C. Collaborating for new product development: Selecting the partner with maximum potential to create value. *J. Prod. Innov. Manag.* **2006**, *23*, 330–341. [CrossRef]
39. Saaty, T.L. *The Analytic (Hierarchy) Process*; McGraw-Hill: New York, NY, USA, 1980.
40. Saaty, T.L. Decision making for leaders. *IEEE Trans. Syst. Man Cybern.* **1985**, *15*, 450–452. [CrossRef]
41. Saaty, T.L. How to make a decision: The analytic hierarchy process. *Eur. J. Oper. Res.* **1990**, *48*, 9–26. [CrossRef]
42. Vaidya, O.S.; Kumar, S. Analytic hierarchy process: An overview of applications. *Eur. J. Oper. Res.* **2006**, *169*, 1–29. [CrossRef]
43. Soni, A.; Cohen, H. Successfully launching your product: Getting it right. *Handb. Bus. Strateg.* **2004**, *5*, 263–268. [CrossRef]
44. Kleinsmann, M.; Buijs, J.; Valkenburg, R. Understanding the complexity of knowledge integration in collaborative new product development teams: A case study. *J. Eng. Technol. Manag.* **2010**, *27*, 20–32. [CrossRef]

© 2015 by the authors. Licensee MDPI, Basel, Switzerland. This article is an open access article distributed under the terms and conditions of the Creative Commons Attribution (CC BY) license (http://creativecommons.org/licenses/by/4.0/).

Review

Designing the Business Models for Circular Economy—Towards the Conceptual Framework

Mateusz Lewandowski

Institute of Public Affairs, Faculty of Management and Social Communication, Jagiellonian University, Lojasiewicza 4, Krakow 31-348, Poland; mateusz.lewandowski@uj.edu.pl; Tel.: +48-12-664-5642; Fax: +48-12-664-5859

Academic Editor: Adam Jabłoński
Received: 12 November 2015; Accepted: 30 December 2015; Published: 18 January 2016

Abstract: Switching from the current linear model of economy to a circular one has recently attracted increased attention from major global companies e.g., Google, Unilever, Renault, and policymakers attending the World Economic Forum. The reasons for this are the huge financial, social and environmental benefits. However, the global shift from one model of economy to another also concerns smaller companies on a micro-level. Thus, comprehensive knowledge on designing circular business models is needed to stimulate and foster implementation of the circular economy. Existing business models for the circular economy have limited transferability and there is no comprehensive framework supporting every kind of company in designing a circular business model. This study employs a literature review to identify and classify the circular economy characteristics according to a business model structure. The investigation in the eight sub-domains of research on circular business models was used to redefine the components of the business model canvas in the context of the circular economy. Two new components—the take-back system and adoption factors—have been identified, thereby leading to the conceptualization of an extended framework for the circular business model canvas. Additionally, the triple fit challenge has been recognized as an enabler of the transition towards a circular business model. Some directions for further research have been outlined, as well.

Keywords: business models; circular economy; circular business model; sustainable business model; business model design

1. Introduction

Switching from the current linear model of economy to a circular one would not only bring savings of hundreds of billions US dollars to the EU alone, but also significantly reduce the negative impact on the natural environment [1,2]. This is why the circular economy (CE) has attracted increased attention as one of the most powerful and most recent moves towards sustainability [3,4]. The transition to the circular economy entails four fundamental building blocks—materials and product design, new business models, global reverse networks, and enabling conditions [5]. Switching an economy to a circular one depends, on the one hand, on policymakers and their decisions [6]; on the other hand, it depends on introducing circularity into their business models by business entities [7]. The scope of interest of this study is limited to the latter, micro-level perspective of designing circular business models.

Comprehensive knowledge on designing circular business models is needed to stimulate and foster implementation of the circular economy on a micro-level. Existing knowledge provides several well-elaborated and verified frameworks of business models, design patterns and tools to build a business model [8,9]. Although many case studies revealed several types of circular business actions or models [4,7], these models have limited transferability. There are very few studies covering, in a more comprehensive manner, how a circular business model framework should look. Previous research instead has taken the following approaches: building on a business model canvas (BMC) and classifying the product-service system characteristics according to its structure [10]; significantly reconstructing the BMC into a business cycle canvas to support practitioners in thinking in business systems and beyond the individual business model [11]; using it as a part of a bigger framework of a business model limited to eco-innovation [12]; or extending it to encompass wider social perspectives of costs and benefits [13]. Other studies provide some steps for analyzing an existing business model for potential opportunities to introduce circularity [7,14].

None of these reviewed studies have provided satisfactory answers to the following questions: How may the principles of the circular economy be applied to a business model? What components should a circular business model consist of to be applicable to every company? This study considers the circular economy as a new contribution to the development of business model theory. Because changing a company's business model into a circular one is challenging, the following research provides a conceptual framework of the circular business model to support practitioners in the transition process from linear business models to more circular ones.

The paper is structured as follows. Section 2 presents the concept of this study and methodological remarks. Section 3 identifies the specificity of circular business models according to the eight sub-domains of research in the area of business models proposed by Pateli and Giaglis [15]. Section 4 classifies the findings of the review according to the business model framework developed by Osterwalder and Pigneur [8]. Thus, the nine building blocks of a business model framework are characterized in the context of the circular economy. This section reveals the need to extend the business model framework to make it more applicable to the circular economy. Section 5 provides a proposition to address this need and presents a conceptualization of an extended framework of business model—the circular business model canvas (CBMC). Section 6 provides suggestions for future research. Section 7 presents the conclusions of the study.

2. The Method and Concept of the Study

In order to answer the questions how the principles of the circular economy can be applied to a business model, and which universally applicable components are needed for a circular business model, a narrative conceptual review has been employed.

The process was divided into three steps.

(1) Identification of the state of the art on business models in the CE (circular business models)
(2) Categorization of the initial body of literature according to the components of business model structure
(3) Synthesis and development of the framework for a circular business model

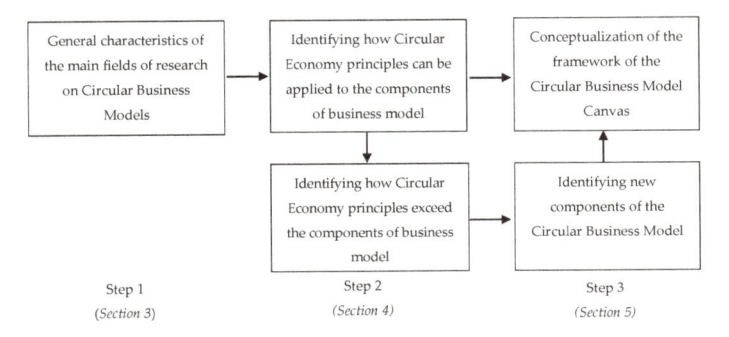

Figure 1. The Concept of Developing a Framework of Business Model for the Circular Economy.

2.1. Literature Review—Conceptual Frameworks for Categorizing the Research on Circular Business Models

This step identified the body of knowledge needed to obtain the answers for the research questions in the next steps. The following academic databases were used for the literature search: EBSCO Host, Google Scholar, Scopus, and ProQuest. Key words included variations on terms such as circular economy, business model, circular business model, sustainable business model. Then a complementary manual search was conducted on the websites of contributors to circular economy to look for other relevant papers, reports and books. Also the anonymous reviewers suggested some additional references.

This literature search generated articles on conceptualizing the state of the art on business models in the circular economy (circular business models) according to the eight sub-domains of research in the area of business models proposed by Pateli and Giaglis [15]. Those sub-domains include: definitions, components, taxonomies, conceptual models, design methods and tools, adoption factors, evaluation models, and change methodologies [15]. The research in the sub-domain of definitions concerns defining the purpose, scope, and primary elements of a business model, as well as exploring its relationships with other business concepts, such as strategy and business processes. Thus, in relation to circular business models, a wider context of the circular economy must be explained in the first place. Research on components of business models focuses on identifying its fundamental constructs and constituent elements. They are derived from the main principles of CE. Research in the taxonomies' sub-domain provides possible categorizations of circular business models into a number of typologies based on various criteria. Investigations related to the conceptual models focus on identifying and describing the relationship between the constituent elements of a circular business model, and include their graphical representation. Exploration of the design methods and tools concerns the development and use of methods, languages, standards and software to allow organizations to design, experiment, and change business models in an easy and cost-effective way into more circular business models. The research related to the adoption factors focuses on the factors that affect this change, as well as on socioeconomic implications of circular business models. The sub-domain related to evaluation models focuses on identifying criteria for assessing the feasibility, viability, and profitability of circular business models or evaluating them against alternative or best practice cases. Investigation concerning change methodologies pertain to guidelines, steps, and actions to be taken for transforming existing business models into a more circular one. Table 1 below presents an overview of this step, and the results are presented in the Section 2. This step identified the body of knowledge needed to obtain the answers for the research questions in the next steps.

Table 1. Categorization of the literature devoted to the circular economy.

CBM Research Domains	Authors
Definitions	EMF Vol. 1&2 [2,4]; Joustra *et al.* [16]; Mentink [11]; Scott [3]; Lovins *et al.* [17]; Renswoude *et al.* [7]; Linder & Williander [18]; Ayres & Simonis [19]; Renner [20]
Components	EMF Vol. 1. [4]; Renswoude *et al.* [7]; Boons and Lüdeke-Freund [21]; Laubscher and Marinelli [22]; EMF [23]; Mentink [11]; Govindan, Soleimani, & Kannan [24]
Taxonomies	Lacy *et al.* [25]; Bakker *et al.* [26]; Damen [27]; EMF Vol. 1. [4]; Lacy *et al.* [28]; WRAP [29]; Renswoude *et al.* [7]; Planing [5]; Jong *et al.* [14]; Tukker and Tischner [30]; Van Ostaeyen *et al.* [31]; El-Haggar [32]; Bakker *et al.* [33]; Ludeke-Freund [12]; Moser and Jakl [34]; Mentink [11]; Scott [3]; Bautista-Lazo [35]; Tukker [36]; EMF [6]
Conceptual Models	Mentink [11]; Wirtz [9]; Osterwalder and Pigneur [8]; Barquet *et al.* [10]; Osterwalder *et al.* [37]; Ludeke-Freund [12]; Dewulf [13]; Stubbs & Cocklin [38]; Roome and Louche [39]; Gauthier and Gilomen [40]; Abdelkafi and Tauscher [41]; Jabłoński [42]; Upward and Jones [43]; Nilsson & Söderberg [44]

Table 1. *Cont.*

CBM Research Domains	Authors
Design Methods and Tools	Joustra *et al.* [16]; Jong *et al.* [14]; Scott [3]; Renswoude *et al.* [7]; Osterwalder and Pigneur [8]; Mentink [11]; Barquet *et al.* [10]; Jabłoński [42]; Parlikad *et al.* [45]; El-Haggar [32]; Guinée [46]
Adoption Factors	Winter [47]; Planing [5]; Lacy *et al.* [28]; Joustra *et al.* [16]; Scott [3]; Parlikad *et al.* [45]; Mentink [11]; Laubscher and Marinelli [22]; EMF Vol. 1. [4]; Renswoude *et al.* [7]; Scheepens *et al.* [48]; EMF [6]; Jong *et al.* [14]; Beuren *et al.* [49]; Jabłoński [50]; Pearce [51]; Linder & Williander [18]; Parlikad, *et al.* [45]; Beuren *et al.* [49]; Jabłoński (2015); Zairul *et al.* [52]; Roos [53]; Bechtel *et al.* [54]; UNEP [55]; Besch [56]; Heese *et al.* [57]; Walsh [58]; Firnkorn & Muller [59]; Shafiee & Stec [60]
Evaluation Models	Winter [47]; Laubscher and Marinelli [22]; Mentink [11]; EMF [23]; Andersson & Stavileci [61]; Jasch [62]; Jasch [63]; Gale [64]
Change Methodologies	Scott [3]; Roome & Louche [39]; Gauthier & Gilomen [40]

2.2. Categorization of the Initial Body of Literature According to the Components of Business Model Structure

The second step identified how the idea of circular economy can be applied to each component of the business model. This approach was inspired by Barquet *et al.* [10], who used a similar one for the characteristics of product-service systems (PSS). Business model structure was defined on the basis of the business model canvas (BMC) developed by Osterwalder and Pigneur [8]. BMC was chosen due to the ease of its practical application, complexity of components, worldwide recognition, and previous contributions to the development of circular business models [10–12]. However, a relatively large proportion of the literature pointed out several ways of applying the principles of the circular economy which exceeded the existing components of the business model. Table 2 below presents an overview of this step, and the results are presented in Section 3.

Table 2. Example categorization of the literature devoted to the circular economy according to a business model structure.

BM components	Authors
Partners	Scott [3]; Joustra *et al.* [16]; El-Haggar [32]; Renswoude *et al.* [7]; Sheu [65]; Robinson *et al.* [66]; EMF Vol. 1. [4]
Key Activities	El-Haggar [32]; Scott [3]; WRAP [29]; Renswoude *et al.* [7]; Lacy *et al.* [28]; Rifkin [67]; Lacy *et al.* [25]; Joustra *et al.* [16]; EMF Vol. 3 [1]; Laubscher and Marinelli [22]; EMF Vol. 1. [4]; EMF [23]; EMF [6]
Key Resources	Planing [5]; Renswoude *et al.* [7]; Lacy *et al.* [28]; El-Haggar [32]; EMF [23]; Freyermuth [68]; Scott [3]
Value Proposition and Customer Segments	Jong *et al.* [14]; Planing [5]; Renswoude *et al.* [7]; Lacy *et al.* [28]; Parlikad *et al.* [45]; Bakker *et al.* [33]; El-Haggar [32]; Lacy *et al.* [25]; Scott [3]; EMF Vol. 1. [4]; Tukker and Tischner [30]; Tukker [36]; Laubscher and Marinelli [22]; Bakker *et al.* [26]; EMF [6]
Customer Relations	Renswoude *et al.* [7]; Recycling 2.0 [69]; Lacy *et al.* [25]
Channels	EMF [6]; Recycling 2.0 [69]; EMF [23]
Cost Structure	Laubscher and Marinelli [22]; Mentink [11]; Subramanian and Gunasekaran [70]; Sivertsson and Tell [71]; Berning and Venter [72]; Barquet *et al.* [10]
Revenue Streams	Van Ostaeyen *et al.* [31]; Renswoude *et al.* [7]; Tukker [36]
Additional Issues Related to Circular Economy	Material loops: EMF Vol. 1&2 [2,4]; Mentink [11]; Renswoude *et al.* [7]; Lacy *et al.* [28]; WRAP [29]; EMF Vol. 3 [1]; Govindan *et al.* [24]; El-Haggar [32]; EMF [23]; Freyermuth [68]; Scott [3]; Lacy *et al.* [25]; Planing [5]; Adoption factors: Planing [5]; Scott [3]; El-Haggar [32]; Laubscher and Marinelli [22]; Lacy *et al.* [28]; Joustra *et al.* [16]; Jong *et al.* [14]; Renswoude *et al.* [7]; Barquet *et al.* [10]; Mentink [11]; Guinée [46]; EMF [23]; EMF [4]; EMF [6]; Parlikad *et al.* [45]; Stubbs & Cocklin [38]; Skelton and Pattis [73]; Winter [47]

2.3. Synthesis and Development of the Framework of Circular Business Model

Pursuing better answers to the research questions resulted in undertaking step 3. This step synthesizes how the circular economy principles apply to each component of the business model, and proposes the new components of the circular business model. These components pertain to the ways in which the CE principles exceeded the popular business model framework. Additionally, advantages and disadvantages of the new framework were outlined. These results are presented in the Section 4.

3. Research on Circular Business Models—The Review

3.1. Definitions

Although it is a contemporary movement, the circular economy is based on old ideas [74]; it is thus reasonable to outline its specificity. This includes the definitions, the origins of the movement, and its main principles. CE was probably first defined and conceptualized in the Ellen MacArthur Foundations report, as *"an industrial system that is restorative or regenerative by intention and design"* [4]. This means pursuing and creating the opportunities for a shift from an "end-of-life" concept to Cradle-to-Cradle™, from using unrenewable energy towards using renewable, from using toxic chemicals to their elimination, from much waste to eliminating waste through the superior design of materials, products, systems, and also business models [4]. The circular economy becomes a new vision of the treatment of resources, energy, value creation and entrepreneurship [16].

Linder and Williander [18] define a circular business model as *"a business model in which the conceptual logic for value creation is based on utilizing the economic value retained in products after use in the production of new offerings"* (p. 2). Mentink [11] defines CE as *"an economic system with closed material loops,"* and a circular business model as *"the rationale of how an organization creates, delivers and captures value with and within closed material loops"* (p. 35). He argues that circular business models do not necessarily aim to balance ecological, social and ecological needs, in contrast to business models, although at the same time they can serve sustainability goals [11]. However, another approach is also supported in the literature. Most recently, Scott [3] provided a useful conceptualization of CE in relation to sustainability. He argues for understanding the circular economy as *"a concept used to describe a zero-waste industrial economy that profits from two types of material inputs: (1) biological materials are those that can be reintroduced back into the biosphere in a restorative manner without harm or waste (i.e: they breakdown naturally); and, (2) technical materials, which can be continuously re-used without harm or waste"* (p. 6). In turn, he defines sustainability as the capacity to continue into the long term and, at the same time, as a mechanism that enables the circular economy to work [3].

The general concept underlying the circular economy has been developed by many schools of thought, such as Regenerative Design, Performance Economy, Cradle to Cradle, Industrial Ecology, Biomimicry, Blue Economy, Permaculture, Natural Capitalism, Industrial Metabolism and Industrial Symbiosis [2,4,17,19,20]. Those schools of thought are complementary to each other and provided the foundation for the main principles of this new approach to economy [2,4,7,16]:

(1) Design out waste/Design for reuse
(2) Build resilience through diversity
(3) Rely on energy from renewable sources
(4) Think in systems
(5) Waste is food/Think in cascades/Share values (symbiosis)

This variety of concepts supports Scott's [3] approach to the relation between sustainability and circular economy.

3.2. Components

The fundamental constructs and constituent elements of circular business models can be derived from the main principles of the circular economy. In the literature, such components are understood and defined variously, for instance: the ReSOLVE (regenerate, share, optimize, loop, virtualize, exchange) framework [4,23], ways of circular value creation [7], normative requirements for business models [21], and areas for integration [22].

There are six business actions to implement the principles of the circular economy and which represent major circular business opportunities depicted by the ReSOLVE framework [23]. Regenerate signifies the shift to renewable energy and materials. It is related to returning recovered biological resources to the biosphere. Thus it aims to reclaim, retain, and regenerate the health of ecosystems. Share actions aim at maximizing utilization of products by sharing them among users. It may be realized through peer-to-peer sharing of private products or public sharing of a pool of products. Sharing means also reusing products as long as they are technically acceptable to use (e.g., second-hand), and prolonging their life through maintenance, repair, and design-enhancing durability. Optimise actions are focused on increasing the performance/efficiency of a product and removing waste in the production process and in the supply chain. They may also be related to leveraging big data, automation, remote sensing, and steering. What is important is that optimization does not require changing the product or the technology. Loop actions aim at keeping components and materials in closed loops. The higher priority is given to inner loops. Virtualize actions assume to deliver particular utility virtually instead of materially. Exchange actions are focused on replacing old materials with advanced non-renewable materials and/or with applying new technologies (e.g., 3D printing). It may also be related to choosing new products and services [23].

Renswoude *et al.* [7] identify similar ways of circular value creation, pertaining to the short cycle, where products and services are maintained, repaired and adjusted, to the long cycle which extends the lifetime of existing products and processes, to cascades based on creating new combinations of resources and material components and purchasing upcycled waste streams, to pure circles in which resources and materials are 100% reused, to dematerialized services offered instead of physical products and to production on demand.

Other studies identified four normative requirements for business models for sustainable innovation, grounded in wider concepts such as sustainable development [21]. The first is a value proposition reflecting the balance of economic, ecological and social needs. The second is a supply chain engaging suppliers into sustainable supply chain management (materials cycles). The third is a customer interface, motivating customers to take responsibility for their consumption. The fourth is a financial model, mainly reflecting an appropriate distribution of economic costs and benefits among actors involved in the business model [21]. Boons and Lüdeke-Freund [21] (p. 13) also noticed that comparable conceptual notions of sustainable business models did not exist.

Mentink [11] (p. 34) used a similar approach to the business model as Frankenberger *et al.* [75], and outlined the changes of business model components needed for developing a more circular service model, such as:

- value propositions (*what?*)—products should become fully reused or recycled, which requires reverse logistics systems, or firms should turn towards product-service system (PSS) and sell performance related to serviced products
- activities, processes, resources and capabilities (*how?*)—products have to be made in specific processes, with recycled materials and specific resources, which may require not only specific capabilities but also creating reverse logistics systems and maintaining relationships with other companies and customers to assure closing of material loops
- revenue models (*why?*)—selling product-based services charged according to their use
- customers or customer interfaces (*who?*)—selling "circular" products or services may require prior changes of customer habits or, if this is not possible, even changes of customers

Laubscher and Marinelli [22] identified six key areas for integration of the circular economy principles with the business model:

(1) Sales model—a shift from selling volumes of products towards selling services and retrieving products after first life from customers
(2) Product design/material composition—the change concerns the way products are designed and engineered to maximize high quality reuse of product, its components and materials
(3) IT/data management—in order to enable resource optimization a key competence is required, which is the ability to keep track of products, components and material data
(4) Supply loops—turning towards the maximization of the recovery of own assets where profitable and to maximization of the use of recycled materials/used components in order to gain additional value from product, component and material flows
(5) Strategic sourcing for own operations—building trusted partnerships and long-term relationships with suppliers and customers, including co-creation
(6) HR/incentives—a shift needs adequate culture adaptation and development of capabilities, enhanced by training programs and rewards

One of the most important components of circular business models is the reversed supply-chain logistics. A comprehensive review on this subject has been done by Govindan, Soleimani, and Kannan [24].

3.3. Taxonomies

In the literature, there are several propositions of how to categorize business models. Most of them are very similar and use the criterion of the source of value creation (e.g., [4,7,25]). Few authors proposed other criteria, such as sources of value in a product-service systems [5,14,30], before-the-event techniques of cleaner production [32], design strategies for product life extension [33], cycle of product/component/material circulation in material loops [5], or mixed criteria [12]. However, the typologies are somewhat overlapping, and the distinction criteria are sometimes blurred. An overview of the circular business models, systematized according to the ReSOLVE framework, is presented in Table 3.

Table 3. An overview of circular business model types.

Classification Criteria	Model	Literature Sources	Explanation	Example(s)
Regenerate	Energy recovery	Damen [27]; Lacy et al. [28]	The conversion of non-recyclable waste materials into useable heat, electricity, or fuel	Ralphs and Food 4 Less installed an "anaerobic digestion" system
	Circular Supplies	Lacy et al. [28]; EMF [23]	Using renewable energy	Iberdrola
	Efficient buildings	Scott [3]	Locating business activities in efficient buildings	Phillips Eco-Enterprise Center
	Sustainable product locations	Scott [3]	Locating business in eco-industrial parks	Kalundborg Eco-industrial Park
	Chemical leasing	Moser and Jakl [54]	The producer mainly sells the functions performed by the chemical, so the environmental impacts and use of hazardous chemical are reduced	Safechem
Share	Maintenance and Repair	Lacy et al. [28]; WRAP [76]; Bakker et al. [33]; Planing [5]; Damen [27]	Product life cycle is extended through maintenance and repair	Patagonia, Giroflex
	Collaborative Consumption, Sharing Platforms, PSS: Product renting, sharing or pooling	Lacy et al. [28]; Lacy et al. [25]; WRAP [76]; Planing [5]; Tukker [36]; Jong et al. [14]	Enable sharing use, access, or ownership of product between members of the public or between businesses.	BlaBlaCar, Airbnb, ThredUP
	PSS: Product lease	Tukker [36]; Jong et al. [14]; WRAP [76];	Exclusive use of a product without being the owner	Mud Jeans, Dell, Leasedrive, Stone Rent-a-PC
	PSS: Availability based	Van Ostaeyen, et al. [31]; Mentink [11]	The product or service is available for the customer for a specific period of time	GreenWheels
	PSS: Performance based	Van Ostaeyen, et al. [31]; Zairul et al. 2015 [52]	The revenue is generated according to delivered solution, effect or demand-fulfilment	Philips's "Pay per Lux" solution; the need for new housing model for young starters in Malaysia
	Incentivized return and reuse or Next Life Sales	WRAP [76]; Mentink [11]; Lacy et al. [25]; Damen [27]	Customers return used products for an agreed value. Collected products are resold or refurbished and sold	Vodafone Red Hot, Tata Motors Assured
	Upgrading	Planing [5]; Mentink [11]	Replacing modules or components with better quality ones	Phoneblocks
	Product Attachment and Trust	Mentink [11]	Creating products that will be loved, liked or trusted longer	Apple products
	Bring your own device	WRAP [76]	Users bring their own devices to get the access to services,	Citrix pays employees for bringing own computers
	Hybrid model	Bakker et al. [26]	A durable product contains short-lived consumables	Océ-Canon printers and copiers
	Gap-exploiter model	Bakker et al. [26]; Mentink [11]	Exploits "lifetime value gaps" or leftover value in product systems. (e.g., shoes lasting longer than their soles).	printer cartridges outlasting the ink they contain

Table 3. Cont.

Classification Criteria	Model	Literature Sources	Explanation	Example(s)
Optimise	Asset management	WRAP [76]	Internal collection, reuse, refurbishing and resale of used products	FLOOW2, P2PLocal
	Produce on demand	Renswoude et al. [1]; WRAP [76], Scott [1]	Producing when demand is present and products were ordered	Alt-Berg Bootmakers, Made, Dell Computer Company
	Waste reduction, Good housekeeping, Lean thinking, Fit thinking	Renswoude et al. [1]; Scott [1]; El-Haggar [32]; Bautista-Lazo [83]	Waste reduction in the production process and before	Nitech rechargeable batteries
	PSS: Activity management/outsourcing	Tukker [30]	More efficient use of capital goods, materials, human resources through outsourcing	Outsourcing
Loop	Remanufacture, Product Transformation	Damen [27]; Planing [3]; Lacy et al. [25]	Restoring a product or its components to "as new" quality	Bosch remanufactured car parts
	Recycling, Recycling 2.0, Resource Recovery	Lacy et al. [25] Damen [27] Planing [3]; Lacy et al. [28]	Recovering resources out of disposed products or by-products	PET bottles, Desso
	Upcycling	Lacy et al. [28] Mentink [1]; Planing [1]	Materials are reused and their value is upgraded	De Steigeraar (design and build of furniture from scrap wood)
	Circular Supplies	Renswoude et al. [1]; Lacy et al. [28]	Using supplies from material loops, bio based- or fully recyclable	Royal DSM
Virtualize	Dematerialized services	WRAP [76]; Renswoude et al. [7]	Shifting physical products, services or processes to virtual	Spotify (music online)
Exchange	New technology	EMF [6]	New technology of production	WinSun 3D printing houses

3.4. Conceptual Models

The relationships between constituent elements of a circular business model have been conceptualized in the literature. Every business model is both linear and circular to some extent [7,11]. This is because every company optimizes its processes, virtualizes products or processes (using e-mails instead of traditional letters) and/or uses some resources from material loops, and thus introduces some principles of the circular economy, albeit not necessarily deliberately. Renswoude *et al.* [7] put it differently—"100% circular business models do not exist (yet). Not creating any waste at all is difficult to achieve for physical and practical reasons (p. 2)". For this reason, the main conceptual frameworks of business models apply to the circular economy. However, some frameworks of circular business models have been developed for either type.

There are quite many conceptual frameworks of business models in general [75,77–82]. Thus, a further systematization became a reasonable direction of research. And so, there are two more comprehensive propositions, one by Wirtz [9], and one by Osterwalder and Pigneur [8]. Wirtz (2011) [9] made a systematic overview of the business model concept, and proposed an integrated business model consisting of nine partial models divided into three main components—strategic, customer and market, value creation. The strategic component comprises three models regarding the strategy (mission, strategic positions and development paths, value proposition), resources (core competencies and assets), and network (business model networks and partners). The customer and market components consist of customer model (customer relationships/target group, channel configuration, customer touchpoint), market offer model (competitors, market structure, value offering/products and services), and revenue model (revenue streams and revenue differentiation). The value creation component encompasses production of goods and services (manufacturing model and value generation), procurement model (resource acquisition and information), and financial model (financing model, capital model and cost structure model).

A more recognized and applied framework of a business model distinguishes nine building blocks [83], and is conceptualized as the business model canvas (BMC) [8]. The BMC consists of [8,10]:

(1) Customer segments that an organization serves
(2) Value propositions that seek to solve customers' problems and satisfy their needs
(3) Channels which an organization uses to deliver, communicate and sell value propositions
(4) Customer relationships which an organization builds and maintains with each customer segment
(5) Revenue streams resulting from value propositions successfully offered to customers
(6) Key resources as the assets required to offer and deliver the aforementioned elements
(7) Key activities which are performed to offered and deliver the aforementioned elements
(8) Key partnerships being a network of suppliers and partners that support the business model execution by providing some resources and performing some activities
(9) Cost structure comprising all the costs incurred when operating a business model

Most recently, value proposition design has been developed, and comprises of six building blocks, which are a detailed description of the two BM canvas blocks—value propositions and customer segments [37]. Value proposition is composed of the products and services offered to the customer, the relievers of customers pains, and the creators of customer gains pertaining to the tasks and jobs he or she needs to accomplish with the assistance of the offered product or service. Thus, on the customer's side are the jobs, pains and gains related to doing the jobs. The visualization of both canvases are presented in Figure 2.

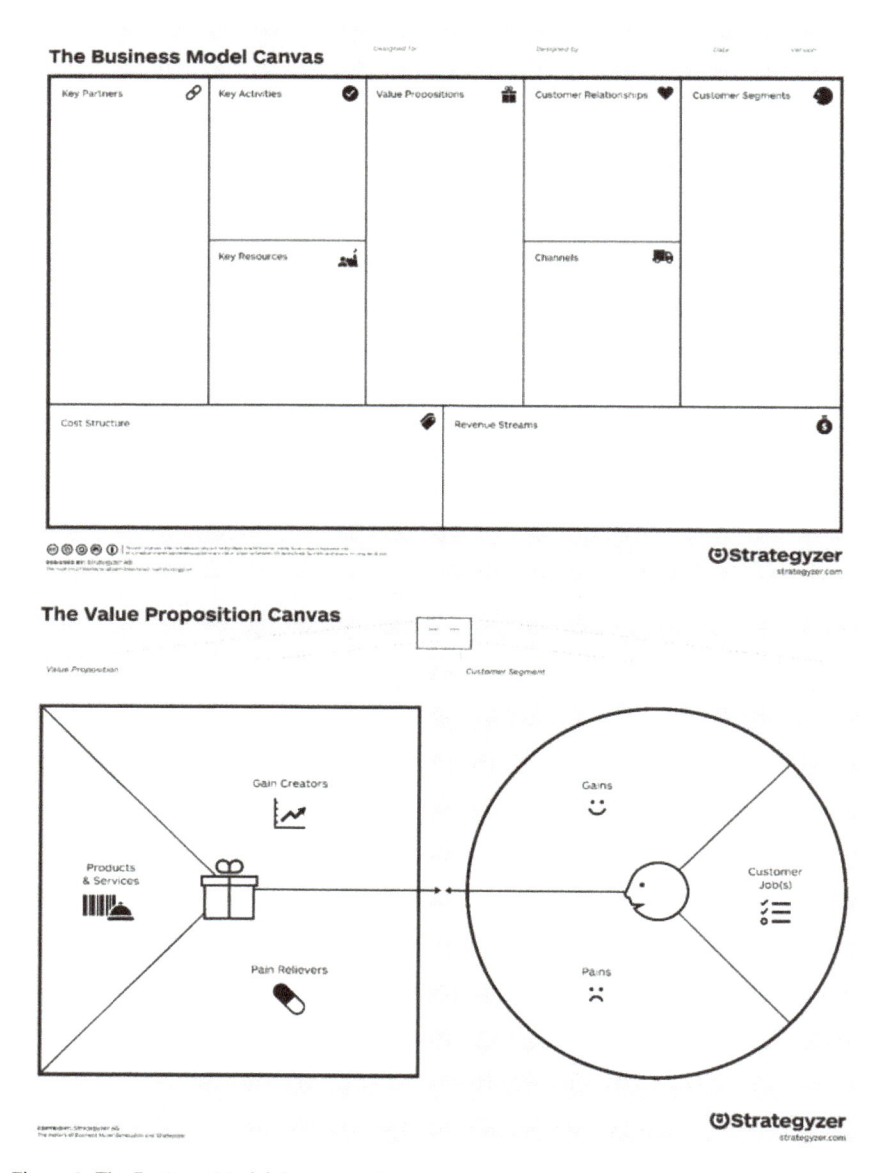

Figure 2. The Business Model Canvas and the Value Proposition Canvas. Source: Osterwalder and Pigneur [8] and Osterwalder *et al.*, (2014) [37]. Reproduced with permission from Strategyzer.com and Strategyzer AG.

The BM canvas has been recognized and used for further conceptualizations of circular and sustainable business models, such as Barquet *et al.* [10], Lüdeke-Freund [12], Dewulf [13], Mentink [11], and Nilsson and Söderberg [44]. Barquet *et al.* [10] used the BM canvas for identification and classification of the product service systems' characteristics according to a business model structure. Moreover, the authors used it as design tool for a circular business model [10]. Lüdeke-Freund [12] applied the business model canvas (BMC) developed by Osterwalder and Pigneur [8] to the context of eco-innovation. In Lüdeke-Freund's framework, the canvas is a central component, but linked with others, both preceding and subsequent. The infrastructure management (partners, resources, activities) is highly impacted by the development of marketable eco-innovations, barriers of sustainable development, and marketing eco-innovations. Thus, contextual factors are important enablers for a business model to operate in practice. On the other hand, eco-innovations create an extended customer value (a mix of customer public value, customer equity and customer value). Dewulf [13] developed an extended business model canvas with two additional components—societal costs and societal benefits. Mentink [11] developed a business cycle canvas, which applies the concept of business cycle to the business model framework. This proposition is focused on the circulation of materials in a closed loops, and thus is more useful to analyze if the company's network will support material loops. Nilsson and Söderberg [44] developed a business model canvas adjusted for the urban mining segment and evaluated the business model element differences between the traditional C and D and urban mining industry.

Some other conceptual frameworks exist in the literature related to sustainability. For instance, Stubbs and Cocklin [38] developed a case study-based conceptualization of a sustainability business model, consisting of two types of attributes—structural and cultural ones. Each type has its economic, environmental, social, and holistic characteristics. Structural attributes are depicted by:

- Economic characteristics, such as external bodies expecting triple bottom line performance, lobbying for changes to taxation system and legislation to support sustainability, keeping capital local
- Environmental characteristics, such as a threefold strategy (offsets, sustainable, restorative), closed-loop systems, implementation of services model, operating in industrial ecosystems and stakeholder networks
- Social characteristics, such as understanding stakeholder's needs and expectations, educating and consulting stakeholders

Holistic characteristics, such as cooperation and collaboration; triple bottom line approach to performance; implementing demand-driven model; adapting organization to sustainability.

Cultural attributes are depicted by:

- Economic characteristics, such as considering profit as a means to do something more ("higher purpose"), not as an end, which is also a reason for shareholders to invest
- Environmental characteristics, such as treating nature as a stakeholder
- Social characteristics, such as balancing stakeholders' expectations, sharing resources among stakeholders, and building relationships
- Holistic characteristics, such as focusing on medium to long-term effects, and on reducing consumption

Most recent contributions to conceptual models concern the dynamics between components of the business model. For instance, Roome and Louche [39] developed *process model of business model change for sustainability*, which explains how new business models for sustainability are fashioned through the interactions between individuals and groups inside and outside companies. Gauthier and Gilomen [40] analyzed transformations of the elements of sustainable business model and identified a typology of such changes (see Subsection 3.8 in this paper). Abdelkafi and Täuscher [41] developed a system dynamics-based representation of business models for sustainability. Not only has the dynamic of internal business model components been researched, but also the dynamics in relation to the business model environment. One of the key issues in this regard pertains to networks. Jabłoński [42] outlined the process of transition from an idea to the operationalization of the business model by searching for business model components from the network. However, the static approach is also being investigated. For example, Upward and Jones [43] developed the strongly sustainable business model ontology. Another approach proposed by Bautista-Lazo and Short [84] conceptualized an All

Seeing Eye of Business model, which addresses the types of waste and their potential as a profit or loss generator.

3.5. Design Methods and Tools

There are several design methods and tools for the business model in the literature. Some of them focus on enhancing the design process [3,7,8,10], and others are used in particular situations and for particular business models [32,42,46].

Joustra *et al.* [16] and Jong *et al.* [14] identified five steps to support for small and medium enterprises (SMEs) to enter the circular economy. The first two steps comprise reading about the CE, and learning about the readiness of the company, partners and stakeholders in the supply chain for CE. The next two steps suggest evaluating redesign opportunities that might bring the products into a more circular business model, and to understand the service that a company could potentially deliver and how the model needs to be redesigned to enable this. The last step tests whether the value delivered is the value that customers expect and will pay for.

Scott [3] proposed the 7-P model as a starting point toward understanding and applying the mechanism of the circular economy in a business. This model takes the practitioner's approach and describes seven main components, which can be divided into three steps. The first is to learn and understand the fundamentals of the circular economy, and what the change will concern, and decide on establishing sustainability as an objective (prepare). The next step is to organize and implement the mechanisms of the circular economy related to the process, preservation, people, place, product, and production. The last step is to enable and support implementation of CE, mainly through building teams and managing change (People).

Renswoude *et al.* [7] developed the business model scan, a methodology to enhance a transition of the company into a more circular form. It consists of six process stages about which many questions are asked. Those questions are related to value proposition, design, supply, manufacturing, use, and next life. Osterwalder and Pigneur [8] proposed five stages of business model design process, encompassing mobilize, understand, design, implement, and manage. This methodology is supported by the business model canvas (described in Section 3.4). BMC has been applied to research and design circular business models [10,11]. Jablonski [42] distinguished eleven stages of the design and operationalization of the company's technological business model embedded in the network. Parlikad *et al.* [45] identified the information requirements for end-of-life decision making and established a possible set of characteristics of a lifecycle information system to support management. They also reviewed existing product lifecycle information systems and divided them into two categories. Design/disassembly data-sharing systems encompass: Inverse Manufacturing Product Recycling Information System (IMPRIS), Recycling Passport, Products Lifecycle Management System (PLMS), Integrated Recycling Data Management System (ReDaMa). Lifecycle information monitoring systems comprises of: Information System for Product Recovery (ISPR), Life Cycle Data Acquisition System (LCDA), Green Port [45]. Cleaner production audits are undertaken to identify opportunities for cleaner production. The methodology for the cleaner production opportunity assessment has been outlined by El-Haggar [32] (p. 29), and consists of many activities related to and focused on the following: team, pre-audit, surrounding environment, operations and processes, inputs and outputs, wasteful processes, material and energy balance, opportunities, priorities, implementation, assessment, process sustainability, sustainable development. Another important method is life cycle assessment [85] which is explained as *"a tool for the analysis of the environmental burden of products at all stages in their life cycle—from the extraction of resources, through the production of materials, product parts and the product itself, and the use of the product to the management after it is discarded, either by reuse, recycling or final disposal (in effect, therefore, 'from the cradle to the grave')"* [46] (pp. 5–6). Scott [3] (p. 81) also suggests that environmental audits, such as compliance audit, waste audit, waste disposal audit, water audit, can be used. Mentink [11] discussed a few other methods and tools, such as: New Framework on

Circular Design, Practical Guide for PSS Development, Circular Economy Toolkit, Play it Forward, 4-I Framework, and Sustainable Business Model Canvas.

3.6. Adoption Factors

Factors affecting CBM adoption are mostly related to general factors [5,47], human resources [3,16,28], political system and legislation [3,6], IT and data management [3,45], and business risks [11]. There are also crucial socioeconomic implications, justifying the efforts towards CE [4,7,22], and other enablers such as leadership, collaboration, motivation through the concept itself, and customer behavior [53].

General factors encompass conditions which need to be fulfilled to secure profitability of closed circles. Winter [47] (p. 16) points out five of them: sufficiently valuable materials/products, control of product or material chain, ease of reuse, remanufacture or recycle materials/products, predictable demand for future products, keeping materials/products concentrated and uncontaminated. Planing [5], however, argued that customer irrationality, conflict of interest within companies, misaligned profit-share along the supply chain, and geographic dispersion could be the reasons for rejecting circular business models. Scheepens *et al.* [48] argue that transition to CE is impacted by different factors on several levels: societal, regulatory, services and infrastructure, and product and technology. Sivertsson and Tell [71] identified barriers to business model innovation in the agricultural context for each of the nine building blocks of the business model canvas (by Osterwalder and Pigneur [8]). Pearce identified six kinds of customers whose needs may be satisfied by the companies offering remanufactured products. These types comprise the customers who (1) need to retain a specific product because it has a technically defined role in their current processes; (2) want to avoid the need to re-specify, re-approve or re-certify a product; (3) make low utilization of new equipment; (4) wish to continue using a product which has been discontinued by the original manufacturer; (5) want to extend the service lives of used products, whether discontinued or not; and (6) are interested in environmentally friendly products [51]. Linder and Williander [18] outlined challenges regarding remanufacturing, such as: considerable expertise and knowledge of the product; efficient product retrieval; suitable types of products; risk of cannibalization if the new, longer-lasting products reduce sales of the previous products; fashion changes; a financial risk for the producer if the offer is to be rented; increased operational risk; lack of supporting law, policy and regulations; and compatibility with the business models of partners.

Regarding the role of human resources in a company shift towards the circular economy, various suggestions have been made. On the basis of successful waste elimination schemes, Scott [3] formulated general recommendations for creating teams related to team members and team size, volunteers, goals, motivation, maintaining links with organization, organizing team meetings, positive thinking, and leadership. Lacy *et al.* [28] (p. 18) identified five capabilities of successful circular leaders (business planning and strategy, innovation and product development, in sourcing and manufacturing, sales and marketing, reverse logistics and return chains). Other researchers also emphasized the role of leadership, mostly pertaining to the appreciation of the new strategic direction, understanding its benefits and risks, and the ability to establish a common understanding in the business [53,54].

Joustra *et al.* [16] (p. 11) identified eight elementary skills for any circular economy project team, such as: entrepreneurial and developing, craftsmanship aimed at product/services, systems thinking and capability of identifying causal loops, future oriented and out-of-the-box, celebrating diversity, addressing insecurities, designing circular systems, products and services, and being creative, innovative and connected. Laubscher and Marinelli [22] give some insights from the practice and emphasized the role of adequate culture adaptation and development of capabilities in a BM transformation towards CE. This can be obtained through dedicated training programs, performance and rewards schemes, personal targets and bonuses for sales managers.

Others argue that policymakers at all government levels (municipal, regional, national, and supranational) play an important role in the circular economy [3,6]. There are two broad and complementary policymaking strategies to accelerate the circular economy: fixing market and regulatory failures, and stimulating market activity by, for example, setting targets, changing public procurement policy, creating collaboration platforms and providing financial or technical support to businesses [6].

Parlikad, *et al.* [45] and Scott [3] (p. 79) argue that IT and data management systems are essential for the circular economy, because they allow to keep track of products, components and material data. This strongly supports effective reverse logistics systems, material loops (also cross-industry) and reuse of components.

Some business risks of service models (or PSS) have also been identified in the literature. They are related to the fact that (a) owning a product is preferred if the user is emotionally attached to the product or the product has an important intangible value, impacting, for instance, the owner's social status; (b) result or function-oriented services need a good explanation and description, which may increase transaction costs; (c) the service provider must predict and control the risks, uncertainties and responsibilities related to selling a result-oriented service [11,14,16]. Moreover, validating a circular business model always has a higher business risk than validating a corresponding traditional, linear business model [18].

Regarding the impact of the circular economy, there are three main winners: economies, companies and user/consumers [3,4,7,55]. CE advantages for economies are related to e.g., the impact on economic growth, material cost savings, mitigation of price volatility and supply risks, significant job growth in services, employment market resilience [4,49]. Laubscher and Marinelli [22] point that companies can gain financial and reputational value. Others argue that CE will give the companies new profit possibilities, increase competitive advantage and build resilience against several strategic challenges [4,56,57]. Detailed advantages could concern: innovation and competitive advantage, additional revenue streams, long-term contracts, customer loyalty and feedback, multiple benefits of internal resource management, and beneficial partnerships throughout the value chain [7,58–60]. Customer and user benefits mainly comprise of increased choice at lower cost; however, there are also some social benefits, like a contribution against climate change [4,52].

Importantly, adaptation factors change in time and those changes also impact the evolution of business models [50].

3.7. Evaluation Models

The criteria for assessing the feasibility, viability, and profitability of circular business models must be adjusted to the micro, meso and macro-level of implementation [47]. On the micro-level Laubscher and Marinelli [22] argue for measuring the reduced ecological footprint, direct financial value through recovery of materials and assets, and top line growth through new business models. A more extended set of key performance indicators could encompass a percentage of: revenues from repairs, reused parts, refurbished products, recycled material used product value after period X, revenue from second-hand products, times of reuse of resource, technical lifetime value of by-products, by-products used, separability of resources, toxic materials used, and products leased [11]. Anderson and Stavileci [61] proposed several criteria for evaluation of the business model's validity for the circular economy, such as: turnover possibility, margins, capital intensiveness, implementation time, dependence on supplier, possible usage of recycled materials, usage of unsustainable materials, benefits from additive manufacturing, percentage of lifecycle, product oriented, and service oriented. There are also some guidelines for accounting the costs of material flow (MFCA) [62–64].

On the macro-level, there are several measurements for three CE principles [23]. Measurements concerning the principles of preservation and enhancing natural capital by controlling finite stocks and balancing renewable resource flow, comprise degradation-adjusted net value add (NVA) as a primary metric, and annual monetary benefit of ecosystem services, annual degradation, and overall remaining stock as secondary metrics. Measurements for the principle of optimization of resource yields by circulating products, components and materials in use at the highest utility at all times in both technical and biological cycles, encompass as a primary metric GDP-generated per unit of net virgin finite material input, and product utilization, product depreciation/lifetime, and material value retention or value of virgin materials as secondary metrics. Measurements for the principle of fostering system effectiveness by revealing and designing out negative externalities, consist of cost of land, air, water, and noise pollution, as a primary metric, and toxic substances in food systems, climate change, congestion, and health impacts as secondary metrics [23].

3.8. Change Methodologies

Scott [3] (pp. 103–109) argues that basic change management theories, like the Force Field Theory, Three-Stage Approach to Change Behavior, sources of staff resistance to change, can be successfully applied to manage the transition from a linear business model towards a circular one. However, other studies provide theories more specific to CE. For example, the model of the process of changing business model for sustainability explains how new business models for sustainability are fashioned through the interactions between individuals and groups inside and outside companies [39]. Gauthier and Gilomen [40] identified a typology of business model transformations toward sustainability:

(1) Business model as usual—if there are no transformations to business model elements
(2) Business model adjustment—if marginal modifications to one element of BMs occur
(3) Business model innovation—if major BM transformations were implemented
(4) Business model redesign—if a complete rethinking of organizations' BM elements results in radically new value propositions

4. Circular Economy and the Components of Business Model

4.1. Value Propositions Fitting Customer Segments (Value Proposition Design)

The core component of the circular business model is the value proposition. Circular value proposition offers a product, product-related service or a pure service [14]. This offer must allow the user/consumer to do what is needed, reduce inconveniences which the consumer/user would experience, and provide additional benefits [37].

Circular products, although ownership-based [5], have several specific features related to the CE principles. Circular products enable product-life extension through maintenance, repair, refurbishment, redistribution, upgrading and reselling [5,7,28,33,45]. They are designed to enhance reusing, recycling, and cascading. This requires a modular design and choosing materials that allow cascading, reusing, remanufacturing, recycling, or safe disposal. Thus, such products are 100% ready to circulate in the closed material loops. Moreover, product design should allow using less raw material or energy or to minimize emissions [3,25,32]. Circular products can be also dematerialized and offered not as physical but as virtual products [4,7].

In a product-service system a company offers access to the product but retains its ownership. It is an alternative to the traditional model of "buy and own". This is a way of reducing customer pains, creating gains, and getting the jobs done through offering product-oriented services or advice, use-oriented services including product leasing, renting, pooling, and pay-per-service unit, or result-oriented services, comprising outsourcing and functional result [14,25,28,30,36]. Some examples comprise: Philips pay-per light [22] or GreenWheels' shared car use, hours of thrust in a Rolls-Royce, or "Power-by-the-Hour" jet engines [26].

Circular value propositions related to services may concern shifting their traditional form to a virtual one (e.g., virtual travel) [4,6,7].

Collaborative consumption related to product sharing/renting or product pooling can bring cost savings, services tailored for customer needs, and additional benefits. For instance, BlaBlaCar offers not only cheap transportation possibilities and route connections unavailable by public transport, but also social gains (see blablacar.com). Some other sharing-based value propositions concern sharing residence, parking, appliances/tools sharing, office, and flexible seating, which may require some specially developed platforms [4,7,28].

Usually there are some incentives offered to the users/consumers [76]: for example, buy-back programs like Vodafone—New Every Year/Red Hot [1]. In this case, incentives are a source of value for the customer (part of value proposition), and products, components or materials collected back contain a value retrieved by the company.

The value proposition must be appropriate for particular customer segments, for specific types of customers [51].

4.2. Channels

One of the strongest shifts towards a circular business model regarding channels is virtualization. This means that an organization can sell a virtualized value proposition and deliver it virtually (selling digital products, like music in mp3 format) and/or sell value propositions via virtual channels (online shops selling material products) [6]. Another possibility is to communicate virtually with the customer (e.g., using web advertisements, e-mails, websites, social media, video conferences) [23,69].

4.3. Customer Relationships

Building and maintaining relationships with customers can underlie the main principle of the circular economy—eliminating waste—twofold. Those two options encompass producing on order, and engaging customers to vote for which product to make [7]. Additionally, a switch to recycling 2.0 may enhance social-marketing strategies and leverage relationships with community partners [25,69].

4.4. Revenue Streams

Revenue streams are essentially the ways in which a company makes money. There are several circular propositions, mainly associated with the product-service systems [7,31]. The first is an input-based PSS, like pay per product or pay per service. The second is availability-based PSS, encompassing a subscription-based rental where, against a low, periodic fee, consumers can use a product or service; or a progressive purchase, where customers periodically pay small amounts before the purchase. The third is usage-based PSS like pay per use, which is a one-time payment to use a product or service. The fourth one is performance-based, like performance-based contracting. However, several performance-based PSSes are possible, like solution-oriented (e.g., selling a promised level of heat transfer efficiency instead of selling radiators), effect-oriented (e.g., selling a promised temperature level in a building instead of selling radiators), and demand-fulfilment oriented (e.g., selling a promised level of thermal comfort for building occupants instead of selling radiators) [31]. Two traditional options of revenue streams concern selling pure products or pure services [36]. Revenue streams depend on the value proposition.

Moreover, revenue streams may be related to retrieved value, generated from products, components and/or raw materials collected back. For example product components, when collected back, are resold after they were restored to "as-new" quality, or remanufactured, or used to create a new product if they carry a high value [5,25]. Despite how low or high the value, it must be sufficient to make the material loops economically reasonable. Retrieved value may also be related to energy captured from waste disposal [4].

4.5. Key Resources

The assets required to create, offer and deliver value propositions via chosen channels, to build and maintain relationships and to receive revenue flows, correspond with the principles guiding the circular economy in two major ways. One is focused on input choices and the second on regenerating and restoring the natural capital.

The input choices are related to changing input materials and products. This can be done through so-called circular sourcing, which applies the principle of using only products or materials obtained from closed material loops along four circular flows [5,7,28]. Another way to achieve this is direct substitution of resources with better-performing materials, which are "less harmful to the environment, more feasible to use and have the same or better technical requirements" [32] (p. 27). Next option is direct virtualization of materials, as for instance through digitalization [23,68].

Natural capital regeneration and restoring concerns using energy from renewable sources, land restoration or reclamation, saving water, operating in more efficient buildings, and choosing sustainable production locations like eco-parks [3].

4.6. Key Activities

The key activities which directly or indirectly lead to creating, offering and delivering the value propositions, may apply the CE principles in several ways. Some are oriented on increasing performance, product design, technology exchange, and the other on remanufacturing, recycling or even lobbying.

Increasing performance can be obtained through good housekeeping, better process control, equipment modification and technology changes, sharing and virtualization. Good housekeeping and process control involve not only optimization of the process by elimination of any fault that would result in unnecessary losses, like spills, leakage, overheating *etc.*, but also effective and efficient planning and regulating of the process to ensure optimal conditions such as temperature, pH, pressure, water level, time, *etc.* [32]. This requires, for instance, continuous monitoring and management, a regular preventive maintenance program, raising staff environmental awareness, and incentive mechanisms, and is supported by lean thinking and lean management [3,32]. Recently, another way of increasing performance has been introduced—the "bring your own device" model [76]. It assumes that users bring their own devices in order to get the access to services, and thus the quantity of products required to meet market need is being reduced. An example is Citrix where employees are paid for bringing their own computers into the company to use on the company's network for work and home [76]. Equipment modification and technology changes improve the production process or replace one with another, and in turn increase efficient utilization of raw materials, water, energy, reduce emissions and eliminatestoxic materials from production [32]. A good example is using 3D printing to produce what is needed [7]. Increasing performance may be related also with sharing and virtualizing office space through flexible seating, desk-sharing, office hoteling, tele-working, audio and video conferences, the "internet of things", big data and machine learning [23,28,67].

Appropriate product design enables using less raw material or energy, to reduce emissions and toxic materials, prolonging product life, eliminating waste before resource-life extension, and to circulate the product, components and materials in a 100% closed material loop, according to the Cradle-to-Cradle concept [1,3,16,25,32].

Moreover, sometimes lobbying for the changes of legislation and political incentives to accelerate the circular economy is necessary [3,4,6,7,22]. When a company is directly engaged in lobbying, then it becomes the key activity. Otherwise lobbying depends on third-party entities and is considered as an adaptation factor.

4.7. Key Partnerships

Cooperative networks allow businesses to receive advantages from supplies, and support a company in research, product design, marketing, office support, supply routes, financial functions, production processes, and management [3,16]. Thus, collaboration enhances obtaining key resources and performing key activities. For instance, off-site recycling is done by other parties that recycle the industrial wastes at the post-consumer stage or recycle the specific wastes, which then are sold to other industries [32]. Collaborative production, based on the cooperation in the production value chain, allows the materials to circulate in a so-called closed material loop [7]. Sheu [65] argues that collaborative relationships play an important role in the green supply chains. Robinson *et al.* [66] showed that business models for solar-powered charging stations to develop infrastructure for electric vehicles may need a strong engagement of public organizations as collaborating partners. Considering the value chain and supply chain, the more circular partners in those chains, the more circular the economy. The "butterfly diagram" developed by the Ellen MacArthur Foundation shows the key role of manufactures and recycling companies [4]. Without collaboration, achieving circularity is hardly possible [53,54]. However, regarding cooperation types, different strategies support different business models [86].

4.8. Cost Structure

The reviewed literature provided no good examples on how the cost structure can enhance implementation of CE principles. However, whenever a company decides to change the cost structure it might require further organizational changes, such as for materials, energy consumption, staff behavior *etc.*, and in turn elicit more circular changes to the business model. This process could start with the analysis of the cost structure. In this regard, cost structure-related criteria can help to evaluate efficiency of optimization policies [11,22]. Cost structure is usually mentioned when the implications and potential benefits of CE are described. It may pertain to cost savings related to PSS or reverse material flow [62–64,70], production costs in agriculture [71], costs of product development [72], or investments [10].

4.9. The Need for Additional Components of a Business Model Related to the Circular Economy

The literature review conducted allowed the identification of how the principles of the circular economy can be applied to the nine components of the business model [8]. An overview according to the ReSOLVE framework is presented in Table 4.

Table 4. How the circular economy principles apply to the components of business model.

BM Components	Regenerate	Share	Optimize	Loop	Virtualize	Exchange
Partners		X		X		
Activities	X		X	X	X	
Resources	X		X	X	X	
Value proposition and Customer segments		X		X	X	
Customer relations						
Channels					X	
Cost structure	X		X	X		X
Revenue streams		X		X		
Potential to develop the BM framework						
Take-back system				X		
Adoption factors	X	X	X	X	X	X

Note: X indicates that the circular economy principles apply to the particular component of business model.

It supports the conclusion that especially two areas related to CE should be introduced to the business model framework in order to enhance designing more circular business models. These are the take-back system [4,7,24,28] and the adoption factors [5].

5. Conceptualizing the Framework of the Circular Business Model Canvas

5.1. Key Areas of Redesigning a Business Model Framework

The conducted study revealed two additional components of the business model framework in order to develop a circular business model framework. This section continues to build on the concept of the business model canvas [8], and describes the novelties and, as a result, proposes a circular business model canvas.

5.2. Take-Back System

Material loops are the core idea of the circular economy [2,4,11]. This idea assumes that products, their components and/or materials can be cascaded (in case of biological nutrients), and reused/redistributed, remanufactured/refurbished, or recycled (in case of technical nutrients), which requires prior collecting back from the consumer and reverse logistics [4,7,24,28]. The principles of the Circular Economy applied to reverse logistics are related to take-back management, incentivized return and reuse, and collection of used products. For example I:CO is an H&M partner which collects used clothes, and Vodafone introduced the buy-back program New Every Year/Red Hot [1,76]. According to the direction of material flow in a supply chain, both forward and reverse are possible [24], but reversed logistics may require different partners, channels and customer relations, and thus a new component can be distinguished in order to differentiate the specificity of forward and reverse logistics.

5.3. Adoption Factors

Due to the various reasons for rejecting circular business models [5], a company must anticipate and counteract them. There are internal and external factors affecting adaptation of a business model to the circular economy principles.

Internal factors concern organizational capabilities to shift towards the circular economy business model. Such capabilities require intangible resources, like team motivation and organizational culture, knowledge and transition procedures. These components are based on developing human resources and team building, and the application of change management instruments [3,16,22,28,32,53], on using business models' design methods and tools [3,7,8,10,11,14,16,46], and evaluation models [11,22,23].

External factors comprise technological, political, sociocultural, and economic issues [53]. Technological issues pertain to the possibilities to use adequate IT and data management technologies to support material tracking [3,22,45] and other specific technologies e.g., recycling [53,54], monitoring legislation and political incentives [3,6,53], and if necessary lobbying for them [38,73]. There are crucial socioeconomic benefits justifying the efforts of lobbying for the changes of legislation and political incentives to accelerate CE [3,4,6,7,22]. Another two groups of factors concern sociocultural issues, like customer habits and public opinion, and economic forces like predictable demand for future products or previous difficulties of business entities in adoption of CE principles [11,14,16,47,53,54]. Although the list of various factors is much wider and open-ended, Roos [53] identified a list of questions supporting practitioners in adopting circularity into business models.

5.4. The Framework of the Circular Business Model Canvas

The circular business model canvas is extended and adjusted to the circular economy version of the business model canvas developed by Osterwalder and Pigneur [8] and others [37]. It has eleven components; however, one component encompasses three sub-components. Those building blocks allow the designing of a business model according to the principles of circular economy, and consists of:

(1) Value propositions—offered by circular products enabling product-life extension, product-service system, virtualized services, and/or collaborative consumption. Moreover, this component comprises the incentives and benefits offered to the customers for bringing back used products
(2) Customer segments—directly linked with value proposition component. Value proposition design depicts the fit between value proposition and customer segments
(3) Channels—possibly virtualized through selling virtualized value proposition and delivering it also virtually, selling non-virtualized value propositions via virtual channels, and communicating with customers virtually
(4) Customer relationships—underlying production on order and/or what customers decide, and social-marketing strategies and relationships with community partners when recycling 2.0 is implemented

(5) Revenue streams—relying on the value propositions and comprising payments for a circular product or service, or payments for delivered availability, usage, or performance related to the product-based service offered. Revenues may also pertain to the value of resources retrieved from material loops
(6) Key resources—choosing suppliers offering better-performing materials, virtualization of materials, resources allowing to regenerate and restore natural capital, and/or the resources obtained from customers or third parties meant to circulate in material loops (preferably closed)
(7) Key activities—focused on increasing performance through good housekeeping, better process control, equipment modification and technology changes, sharing and virtualization, and on improving the design of the product, to make it ready for material loops and becoming more eco-friendly. Key activities might also comprise lobbying
(8) Key partnerships—based on choosing and cooperating with partners, along the value chain and supply chain, which support the circular economy
(9) Cost structure—reflecting financial changes made in other components of CBM, including the value of incentives for customers. Special evaluation criteria and accounting principles must be applied to this component
(10) Take-Back system—the design of the take-back management system including channels and customer relations related to this system
(11) Adoption factors—transition towards circular business model must be supported by various organizational capabilities and external factors

Figure 3 below presents an overview of the circular business model canvas.

Partners	Activities	Value Proposition	Customer Relations	Customer Segments
• Cooperative networks • Types of collaboration	• Optimising performance • Product Design • Lobbying • Remanufacturing, recycling • Technology exchange	• PSS • Circular Product • Virtual service • Incentives for customers in Take-Back System	• Produce on order • Customer vote (design) • Social-marketing strategies and relationships with community partners in Recycling 2.0	• Customer types
	Key Resources • Better-performing materials • Regeneration and restoring of natural capital • Virtualization of materials • Retrieved Resources (products, components, materials)		**Channels** • Virtualization **Take-Back System** • Take-back management • Channels • Customer relations	
Cost Structure • Evaluation criteria • Value of incentives for customers • Guidelines to account the costs of material flow		**Revenue Streams** • Input-based • Availability-based • Usage-based • Performance-based • Value of retrieved resources		
Adoption Factors • Organizational capabilities • PEST factors				

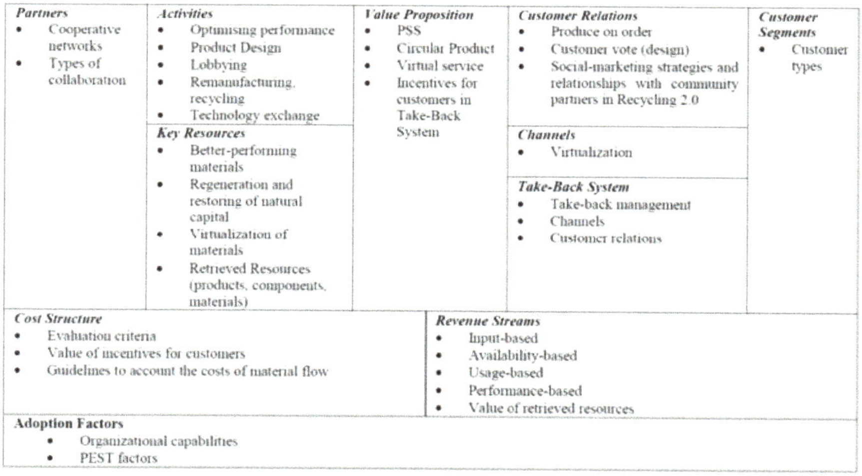

Figure 3. A framework of the circular business model canvas. Source: adapted from Osterwalder and Pigneur [8].

5.5. The Triple Fit Challenge as the Enabler of the Transition Towards a Circular Business Model

The general assumption of the business model design is that all its building blocks fit each other [8]. However, the value proposition design [37] implies that some fits are more important than others, and should be considered as the key success factors for a business model. In this regard there are three main challenges to overcome in order to enable the transition from a linear to a circular business model.

The first fit is between the value proposition, including the take-back system, and customer segments [37,51]. The second fit is between the cost structure and revenue streams. Simply the costs and revenues must be balanced, and the business model should indicate possibilities for profits [56,84]. This also pertains to other cycles of selling products (e.g., reused, recycled) [18,87]. The third fit is between the changes a company implements towards more circular business model and adaptation factors which can hinder this process (e.g., [3,6,11,16,22,50,53,56,57]).

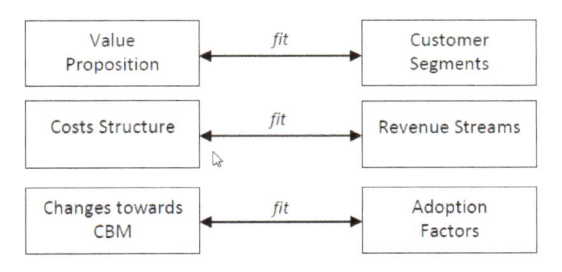

```
┌──────────────┐      fit      ┌──────────────┐
│    Value     │◄─────────────►│   Customer   │
│ Proposition  │               │   Segments   │
└──────────────┘               └──────────────┘

┌──────────────┐      fit      ┌──────────────┐
│    Costs     │◄─────────────►│   Revenue    │
│  Structure   │               │   Streams    │
└──────────────┘               └──────────────┘

┌──────────────┐      fit      ┌──────────────┐
│Changes towards│◄────────────►│   Adoption   │
│     CBM      │               │   Factors    │
└──────────────┘               └──────────────┘
```

Figure 4. The challenge of triple fit.

5.6. Advantages and Disadvantages of the Circular Business Model Canvas

The business model canvas developed by Osterwalder and Pigneur [8] can been used to design circular business models because every business model is to some extent linear and circular at the same time. This framework supports the process of designing a business model, but does not indicate how the principles of the circular economy or the business actions implementing CE are related to particular components of the business model. In turn, the ReSOLVE framework shows how the principles of the circular economy are translated into business actions implementing CE, but not in relation to business model components and design process. The circular business model canvas (CMBC) combines these two elements. There are some examples combining sustainability principles and business model components [88], albeit on a very general level and more useful for explanatory purposes than for supporting practitioners in designing business models. Hence, CBMC has some advantages as compared to the original canvas or the archetypes of sustainable business models.

Firstly, CMBC points out the ways of applying circularity to each component of the business model. As a result, it provides the entrepreneur with a selection of possibilities to be applied to one, several or all of the business model components. This supports different speeds of change—radical and incremental. Secondly, CMBC comprises and emphasizes additional components which are crucial to CE—take-back systems and adoption factors. Thirdly, CMBC indicates the three main challenges in the transition from a linear to circular business model, which the original canvas does not include. Fourthly, it combines the original components of the canvas with CE principles in one framework, which as a practical tool is easier and more user friendly than the triple-layered business model canvas (TLBMC) aimed to support the creation of sustainable business models [89].

There are also some disadvantages of CBMC. Due to its focus on CE principles, it is less useful in designing linear business models. Moreover, the new framework is also more complex, and thus more difficult to apply than the original one. Besides, this is a conceptualization, so its real usability in designing processes has yet to be empirically verified.

6. Future Research

This study was based on the literature review which implies two major limitations. First, it comprises mainly the literature related to the circular economy. Because there is some disagreement in the literature surrounding the questions whether and how circular economy and sustainability are linked and overlapping concepts [3,11], the wider literature on sustainable business models [21,41,90,91] was considered here to a lesser extent. Moreover, there is a substantial body of literature related to each school of thought underlying the circular economy, especially industrial ecology, industrial symbiosis, industrial metabolism, and cleaner production. Each and within each of them there is enough research to conduct comprehensive review studies. Govindan, Soleimani, and Kannan's [24] study is a good example of such a review. This literature was also considered here to a lesser extent, due to intentional focus on circular economy, and inclusion of those concepts in the literature on circular economy. The second limitation of this study pertains to the lack of empirical evidence; further research could therefore focus on empirical verification of the applicability of the proposed framework of the circular business model, in various business settings, especially of the new components like retrieved value proposition which requires empirical verification and further cognition. A detailed empirical investigation of the value proposition design in the context of the circular economy would be very interesting and promising. Does value proposition design need to be adjusted to the circular economy? What are the customer's pains and gains related to the circular economy and how could a fit with value proposition be achieved? In this regard, the newest book by Osterwalder *et al.* [37] provides a good starting point to consider. Another direction could explore how the three fits (in the triple fit challenge) are interrelated. Some critical success factors for circular business models could be derived from such research. A heavily underexplored area is related to applying circularity to business models of public sector organizations and also non-governmental organizations. One of many possible routes of investigation is how the public sector and NGOs may benefit from partnerships with business [66,92].

7. Conclusions

There are two very vital areas of managerial practice which have recently garnered a great deal of research interest: business models and the circular economy. This study focuses on both of them, and investigates circular business models. Not many studies have been conducted on this specific topic. Most of the studies focused on a particular type of circular business model, its specificity and context. Those models are related to various schools of thought underlying the concept of the circular economy, and they appear in the literature pertaining to sustainability, industrial ecology, cleaner production, and a closed-loop economy with different names. However, most of them can be reflected by the ReSOLVE framework developed by the Ellen MacArthur Foundation. The literature also indicated numerous adoption factors, design and managerial tools, and evaluation models needed for circular business models to operate.

Regarding the design of circular business models, existing literature identified various circular business models, few business activities pertaining to the circular economy and some guidelines how to adapt existing business model to the circular economy. Yet, those studies were mostly case-based, and provided specific business models, but with limitations in their transferability. Although existing frameworks of business models can be used to apply the principles of the circular economy, hardly any study identified how the CE principles can be applied to each component of the business model framework. Hence, there is a need for a comprehensive conceptual framework for the circular business model to support practitioners in the transition of their businesses towards circular economy.

This paper addresses the issue of designing a circular business model from the perspective of every company. It identifies how the principles of the circular economy apply to a popular business model framework, and supplements this framework with additional components relevant to the circular economy. In turn, the circular business model canvas has been developed on the basis of the business model canvas. The CBMC consists of eleven building blocks, encompassing not only traditional components with minor modifications, but also material loops and adaptation factors. The triple fit challenge to implement a circular business model has been identified as a success factor. The provided framework should assist practitioners in designing circular business models; however, it requires further examination due to limitations of this study.

The conceptual framework of the circular business model proposed in this paper contributes to the discussion on implementation of the circular economy, and supports practitioners with a tool to accelerate the transition from linearity to circularity on a micro-level.

Conflicts of Interest: Conflicts of Interest: The author declares no conflict of interest.

References

1. Ellen MacArthur Foundation. Towards the Circular Economy: Accelerating the Scale-up Across Global Supply Chains. Available online: http://www3.weforum.org/docs/ WEF_ENV_ TowardsCircularEconomy_Report_2014.pdf (accessed on 31 December 2015).
2. Ellen MacArthur Foundation. Towards the Circular Economy. Opportunities for the Consumer Goods Sector. Available online: http://www.ellenmacarthurfoundation.org/assets/downloads/ publications/ TCE_Report-2013.pdf (accessed on 31 December 2015).
3. Scott, J.T. *The Sustainable Business a Practitioner's Guide to Achieving Long-Term Profitability and Competitiveness*, 2nd ed.; Greenleaf Publishing: Sheffield, UK, 2015.
4. Ellen MacArthur Foundation. Towards the Circular Economy: Economic and Business Rationale for an Accelerated Transition. Available online: http://mvonederland.nl/system/files/media/ towards-the-circular-economy.pdf (accessed on 31 December 2015).
5. Planing, P. Business Model Innovation in a Circular Economy Reasons for Non-Acceptance of Circular Business Models. *Open J. Bus. Model Innov.* **2015**. in press.
6. Ellen MacArthur Foundation. *Delivering the Circular Economy a Toolkit for Policymakers*; Ellen MacArthur Foundation: Cowes, UK, 2015.
7. Van Renswoude, K.; Wolde, A.T.; Joustra, D.J. Circular Business Models. Part 1: An introduction to IMSA's Circular Business Model Scan. Available online: https://groenomstilling.erhvervsstyrelsen.dk/ sites/default/files/media/imsa_circular_business_models_-_april_2015_-_part_1.pdf (accessed on 31 December 2015).
8. Osterwalder, A.; Pigneur, Y. *Business Model Generation: A Handbook for Visionaries, Game Changers, and Challengers*; John Wiley and Sons: Hoboken, NJ, USA, 2010.
9. Wirtz, B.W. *Business Model Management: Design—Instruments—Success Factors*, 1st ed.; Springer Science+Business Media B.V.: Dordrecht, The Netherlands, 2011.
10. Barquet, A.P.B.; de Oliveira, M.G.; Amigo, C.R.; Cunha, V.P.; Rozenfeld, H. Employing the business model concept to support the adoption of product-service systems (PSS). *Ind. Mark. Manag.* **2013**, *42*, 693–704. [CrossRef]
11. Mentink, B. Circular Business Model Innovation: A Process Framework and a Tool for Business Model Innovation in a Circular Economy. Master's Thesis, Delft University of Technology & Leiden University, Leiden, The Netherlands, 2014.
12. Lüdeke-Freund, F. Towards a Conceptual Framework of Business Models for Sustainability. In *Knowledge Collaboration & Learning for Sustainable Innovation*, Proceedings of the ERSCP-EMSU Conference, Delft, The Netherlands, 25–29 October 2010.
13. Dewulf, K.R. Play it forward: A Game-based tool for Sustainable Product and Business Model Innovation in the Fuzzy Front End. In *Knowledge Collaboration & Learning for Sustainable Innovation*, Proceedings of the ERSCP-EMSU Conference, Delft, The Netherlands, 25–29 October 2010.
14. De Jong, E.; Engelaer, F.; Mendoza, M. Realizing Opportunities of a Circular Business Model. Available online: http://circulatenews.org/2015/04/de-lage-landen-realising-the-opportunities-of-a-circular-business-model (accessed on 31 December 2015).
15. Pateli, A.G.; Giaglis, G.M. A research framework for analysing eBusiness models. *Eur. J. Inf. Syst.* **2004**, *13*, 302–314. [CrossRef]
16. Joustra, D.J.; de Jong, E.; Engelaer, F. *Guided Choices towards a Circular Business Model*; North-West Europe Interreg IVB: Lille, France, 2013.
17. Lovins, A.B.; Lovins, L.H.; Hawken, P.; June, M.A.Y. A Road Map for Natural Capitalism. *Harv. Bus. Rev.* **1999**, *77*, 145–158. [PubMed]

18. Linder, M.; Williander, M. Circular Business Model Innovation: Inherent Uncertainties. *Bus. Strateg. Environ.* **2015**. [CrossRef]
19. Ayres, R.U.; Simonis, U.E. *Industrial Metabolism: Restructuring for Sustainable Development*; United Nations University Press: New York, NY, USA, 1994.
20. Renner, G.T. Geography of Industrial Localization. *Econ. Geogr.* **1947**, *23*, 167–189. [CrossRef]
21. Boons, F.; Lüdeke-Freund, F. Business models for sustainable innovation: state-of-the-art and steps towards a research agenda. *J. Clean. Prod.* **2013**, *45*, 9–19. [CrossRef]
22. Laubscher, M.; Marinelli, T. Integration of Circular Economy in Business. In Proceedings of the Conference: Going Green—CARE INNOVATION 2014, Vienna, Austria, 17–20 November 2014.
23. Ellen MacArthur Foundation. *Growth Within: A Circular Economy Vision for a Competitive Europe*; Ellen MacArthur Foundation: Cowes, UK, 2015.
24. Govindan, K.; Soleimani, H.; Kannan, D. Reverse logistics and closed-loop supply chain: A comprehensive review to explore the future. *Eur. J. Oper. Res.* **2014**, *240*, 603–626. [CrossRef]
25. Lacy, P.; Rosenberg, D.; Drewell, Q.; Rutqvist, J. 5 Business Models that are Driving the Circular Economy. Available online: http://www.fastcoexist.com/1681904/5-Business-Models-That-Are-Driving-the-Circular-Economy (accessed on 31 December 2015).
26. Bakker, C.A.; den Hollander, M.C.; van Hinte, E.; Zijlstra, Y. *Products That Last—Product Design for Circular Business Models*, 1st ed.; TU Delft Library/Marcel den Hollander IDRC: Delft, The Netherlands, 2014.
27. Damen, M.A. A Resources Passport for a Circular Economy. Master's Thesis, Utrecht University, Utrecht, The Netherlands, 2012.
28. Lacy, P.; Keeble, J.; McNamara, R.; Rutqvist, J.; Haglund, T.; Cui, M.; Cooper, A.; Pettersson, C.; Kevin, E.; Buddemeier, P.; *et al. Circular Advantage: Innovative Business Models and Technologies to Create Value in a World without Limits to Growth*; Accenture: Chicago, IL, USA, 2014.
29. WRAP. Innovative Business Model Map. Available online: http://www.wrap.org.uk/content/innovative-business-model-map (accessed on 4 October 2015).
30. Tukker, A.; Tischner, U. Product-services as a research field: Past, present and future. Reflections from a decade of research. *J. Clean. Prod.* **2006**, *14*, 1552–1556. [CrossRef]
31. Van Ostaeyen, J.; van Horenbeek, A.; Pintelon, L.; Duflou, J.R. A refined typology of product–service systems based on functional hierarchy modeling. *J. Clean. Prod.* **2013**, *51*, 261–276. [CrossRef]
32. El-Haggar, S. Cleaner Production. In *Sustainable Industrial Design and Waste Management: Cradle-to-Cradle for Sustainable Development*; Academic Press: Amsterdam, The Netherlands, 2007.
33. Bakker, C.; Wang, F.; Huisman, J.; den Hollander, M. Products that go round: Exploring product life extension through design. *J. Clean. Prod.* **2014**, *69*, 10–16. [CrossRef]
34. Moser, F.; Jakl, T. Chemical leasing—A review of implementation in the past decade. *Environ. Sci. Pollut. Res.* **2014**, *22*, 6325–6348. [CrossRef] [PubMed]
35. Bautista-Lazo, S. *Sustainable Manufacturing: Turning Waste Into Profitable Co-Products*; University of Liverpool: Liverpool, UK, 2013.
36. Tukker, A. Eight Types of Product Service Systems: Eight Ways To Sustainability? *Bus. Strateg. Environ.* **2004**, *13*, 246–260. [CrossRef]
37. Osterwalder, A.; Pigneur, Y.; Bernarda, G.; Smith, A. *Value Proposition Design: How to Create Products and Services Customers Want*; John Wiley and Sons: Hoboken, NJ, USA, 2014.
38. Stubbs, W.; Cocklin, C. Conceptualizing a "Sustainability Business Model". *Organ. Environ.* **2008**, *21*, 103–127. [CrossRef]
39. Roome, N.; Louche, C. Journeying Toward Business Models for Sustainability: A Conceptual Model Found Inside the Black Box of Organisational Transformation. *Organ. Environ.* **2015**. [CrossRef]
40. Gauthier, C.; Gilomen, B. Business Models for Sustainability: Energy Efficiency in Urban Districts. *Organ. Environ.* **2015**. [CrossRef]
41. Abdelkafi, N.; Täuscher, K. Business Models for Sustainability From a System Dynamics Perspective. *Organ. Environ.* **2015**. [CrossRef]
42. Jabłoński, A. Design and Operationalization of Technological Business Models. *Acta Univ. Agric. Silvic. Mendelianae Brun.* **2015**, *63*, 927–935. [CrossRef]
43. Upward, A.; Jones, P. An Ontology for Strongly Sustainable Business Models: Defining an Enterprise Framework Compatible With Natural and Social Science. *Organ. Environ.* **2015**. [CrossRef]

44. Nilsson, N.; Söderberg, V. How to Future Proof a Business Model: Capture and Capitalize Value in the Field of Urban Mining. Master's Thesis, Blekinge Institute of Technology, Karlskrona, Sweden, 2015.
45. Parlikad, A.K.; Mcfarlane, D.; Fleisch, E.; Gross, S. The Role of Product Identity in End-of-Life Decision Making. Available online: www.alexandria.unisg.ch/export/DL/Sandra_Gross/21460.pdf (accessed on 31 December 2015).
46. Guinée, J.B. Handbook on Life Cycle Assessment: Operational Guide to the ISO Standards. In *Book Review: The Second Dutch LCA-Guide*; Springer Science+Business Media B.V.: Dordrecht, The Netherlands, 2002; pp. 311–313.
47. De Winter, J. Circular Business Models: An Opportunity to Generate New Value, Recover Value and Mitigate Risk Associated with Pressure on Raw Material Availability and Price Volatility. Master's Thesis, University of Utrecht, Utrecht, The Netherlands, 2014.
48. Scheepens, A.E.; Vogtländer, J.G.; Brezet, J.C. Two life cycle assessment (LCA) based methods to analyse and design complex (regional) circular economy systems. Case: Making water tourism more sustainable. *J. Clean. Prod.* **2015**. in press. [CrossRef]
49. Beuren, F.H.; Gomes Ferreira, M.G.; Cauchick Miguel, P.A. Product-service systems: A literature review on integrated products and services. *J. Clean. Prod.* **2013**, *47*, 222–231. [CrossRef]
50. Jabłoński, A. Network Dynamics and Business Model Dynamics in Improving a Company's Performance. *Int. J. Econ. Commer. Manag.* **2015**, *3*, 1–10.
51. Pearce, J.A. The Profit-Making Allure of Product Reconstruction. *MIT Sloan Manag. Rev.* **2009**, *50*, 59–65.
52. Zairul, M.; Wamelink, J.W.; Gruis, V.; John, L. New industrialised housing model for young starters in Malaysia: Identifying problems for the formulation of a new business model for the housing industry. In Proceedings of the APNHR 2015: The Asia Pacific Network for Housing Research, Gwangju, Korea, 9–11 April 2015.
53. Roos, G. Business Model Innovation to Create and Capture Resource Value in Future Circular Material Chains. *Resources* **2014**, *3*, 248–274. [CrossRef]
54. Bechtel, N.; Bojko, R.; Völkel, R. Be in the Loop: Circular Economy & Strategic Sustainable Development. Master's Thesis, Blekinge Institute of Technology, Karlskrona, Sweden, 2013.
55. United Nation Environment Programme (UNEP). *Product-Service Systems and Sustainability*; UNEP: Washington, DC, USA, 2002; pp. 1–31.
56. Besch, K. Product-service systems for office furniture: Barriers and opportunities on the European market. *J. Clean. Prod.* **2005**, *13*, 1083–1094. [CrossRef]
57. Heese, H.S.; Cattani, K.; Ferrer, G.; Gilland, W.; Roth, A.V. Competitive advantage through take-back of used products. *Eur. J. Oper. Res.* **2005**, *164*, 143–157. [CrossRef]
58. Walsh, B. PSS for Product Life Extension through Remanufacturing. In Proceedings of the 2nd CIRP IPS^2 Conference, Linköping, Sweden, 14–15 April 2010; pp. 261–266.
59. Firnkorn, J.; Müller, M. Selling Mobility instead of Cars: New Business Strategies of Automakers and the Impact on Private Vehicle Holding. *Bus. Strateg. Environ.* **2012**, *21*, 264–280. [CrossRef]
60. Shafiee, A.; Stec, T. Gaining a Competitive Advantage with Sustainable Business—Implementing Inductive Charging using Systems Thinking, A Benchmarking of EVs and PHEVs. Master's Thesis, Chalmers University of Technology, Göteborg, Sweden, 2014.
61. Andersson, D.; Stavileci, S. An Assessment of How Circular Economy can Be Implemented in the Aerospace Industry. Master's Thesis, Blekinge Institute of Technology, Karlskrona, Sweden, 2015.
62. Jasch, C. How to perform an environmental management cost assessment in one day. *J. Clean. Prod.* **2006**, *14*, 1194–1213. [CrossRef]
63. Jasch, C. Environmental management accounting (EMA) as the next step in the evolution of management accounting. *J. Clean. Prod.* **2006**, *14*, 1190–1193. [CrossRef]
64. Gale, R. Environmental management accounting as a reflexive modernization strategy in cleaner production. *J. Clean. Prod.* **2006**, *14*, 1228–1236. [CrossRef]
65. Sheu, J.-B. Green Supply Chain Collaboration for Fashionable Consumer Electronics Products under Third-Party Power Intervention—A Resource Dependence Perspective. *Sustainability* **2014**, *6*, 2832–2875. [CrossRef]
66. Robinson, J.; Brase, G.; Griswold, W.; Jackson, C.; Erickson, L. Business Models for Solar Powered Charging Stations to Develop Infrastructure for Electric Vehicles. *Sustainability* **2014**, *6*, 7358–7387. [CrossRef]

67. Rifkin, J. *The Zero Marginal Cost Society: The Internet of Things, the Collaborative Commons, and the Eclipse of Capitalism*; St. Martin's Press: New York, NY, USA, 2014.
68. Freyermuth, G.S. Edges & Nodes/Cities & Nets: The History and Theories of Networks and What They Tell Us about Urbanity in the Digital Age. Available online: http://periodicals.narr.de/index.php/real/article/view/1576/1555 (accessed on 31 December 2015).
69. Waste Management. Recycling 2.0: Recycling Engagement and Education. Available online: http://www.cafr.org/summit/speakers/ppt/2015-06-08_11:10:00__Robinson_Susan.pdf (accessed on 31 December 2015).
70. Subramanian, N.; Gunasekaran, A. Cleaner supply-chain management practices for twenty-first-century organizational competitiveness: Practice-performance framework and research propositions. *Int. J. Prod. Econ.* **2015**, *164*, 216–233. [CrossRef]
71. Sivertsson, O.; Tell, J. Barriers to Business Model Innovation in Swedish Agriculture. *Sustainability* **2015**, *7*, 1957–1969. [CrossRef]
72. Berning, A.; Venter, C. Sustainable Supply Chain Engagement in a Retail Environment. *Sustainability* **2015**, *7*, 6246–6263. [CrossRef]
73. Skelton, K.; Pattis, A. Life Cycle Management In Product Development: A Comparative Analysis of Industry Practices Kristen. In Proceedings of the 6th International Conference on Life Cycle Management, Gothenburg, Sweden, 25–28 August 2013.
74. Pearce, D.W.; Turner, R.K. *Economics of Natural Resources and the Environment*; Johns Hopkins University Press: Baltiomre, MD, USA, 1990.
75. Frankenberger, K.; Weiblen, T.; Csik, M.; Gassmann, O. The 4I-framework of business model innovation: A structured view on process phases and challenges. *Int. J. Prod. Dev.* **2013**, *18*, 249–273. [CrossRef]
76. WRAP. Innovative Business Models. Available online: http://www.wrap.org.uk/content/innovative-business-models-1 (accessed on 31 December 2015).
77. Mahadevan, B. Business Models for Internet-Based E-Commerce: An Anatomy. *Calif. Manag. Rev.* **2000**, *42*, 55–69. [CrossRef]
78. Afuah, A.; Tucci, C.L. *Internet Business Models and Strategies: Text and Cases*, 1st ed.; Mcgraw-Hill College: Columbus, OH, USA, 2000.
79. Papakiriakopoulos, D.A.; Poylumenakou, A.K.; Doukidis, G.J. Building E-Business Models: An Analytical Framework and Development Guidelines. In Proceedings of the 14th Bled Electronic Commerce Conference, Bled, Slovenia, 25–26 June 2001.
80. Chesbrough, H.; Rosenbloom, R.S. The role of the business model in capturing value from innovation: evidence from Xerox Corporation's technology spin-off companies. *Ind. Corp. Chang.* **2002**, *11*, 529–555. [CrossRef]
81. Linder, J.; Cantrell, S. *Changing Business Models: Surveying the Landscape*; Accenture Institute for Strategic Change: Cambridge, MA, USA, 2000.
82. Al-debei, M.M.; El-Haddadeh, R.; Avison, D. Defining the Business Model in the New World of Digital Business. In Proceedings of the 14th Americas Conference on Information Systems, Toronto, ON, Canada, 14–17 August 2008.
83. Osterwalder, A.; Pigneur, Y.; Tucci, C.L. Clarifying Business Models: Origins, Present, and Future of the Concept. *Commun. Assoc. Inf. Syst.* **2005**, *16*, 1–25.
84. Bautista-Lazo, S.; Short, T. Introducing the All Seeing Eye of Business: A model for understanding the nature, impact and potential uses of waste. *J. Clean. Prod.* **2013**, *40*, 141–150. [CrossRef]
85. Buxel, H.; Esenduran, G.; Griffin, S. Strategic sustainability: Creating business value with life cycle analysis. *Bus. Horiz.* **2015**, *58*, 109–122. [CrossRef]
86. Saebi, T.; Foss, N.J. Business models for open innovation: Matching heterogenous open innovation strategies with business model dimensions. *Eur. Manag. J.* **2014**, *33*, 201–213. [CrossRef]
87. Kocabasoglu, C.; Prahinski, C.; Klassen, R.D. Linking forward and reverse supply chain investments: The role of business uncertainty. *J. Oper. Manag.* **2007**, *25*, 1141–1160. [CrossRef]
88. Bocken, N.M.P.; Short, S.W.; Rana, P.; Evans, S. A literature and practice review to develop sustainable business model archetypes. *J. Clean. Prod.* **2014**, *65*, 42–56. [CrossRef]

89. Joyce, A.; Paquin, R.; Pigneur, Y. The triple layered business model canvas: A tool to design more sustainable business models. In Proceedings of the ARTEM Organizational Creativity International Conference, Nancy, France, 26–27 March 2015.
90. Talonen, T.; Hakkarainen, K. Elements of sustainable business models. *Int. J. Innov. Sci.* **2014**, *6*, 43–54. [CrossRef]
91. Seay, S.S. How incorporating a sustainable business model creates value. *Bus. Stud. J.* **2015**, *7*, 46–61.
92. Lewandowski, M. Introduction to Academic Entrepreneurship. In *Academic Entrepreneurship and Technological Innovation*; Szopa, A., Karwowski, W., Ordóñez de Pablos, P., Eds.; IGI Global: Hershey, PA, USA, 2013.

© 2016 by the author. Licensee MDPI, Basel, Switzerland. This article is an open access article distributed under the terms and conditions of the Creative Commons Attribution (CC BY) license (http://creativecommons.org/licenses/by/4.0/).

MDPI
St. Alban-Anlage 66
4052 Basel
Switzerland
Tel. +41 61 683 77 34
Fax +41 61 302 89 18
www.mdpi.com

Sustainability Editorial Office
E-mail: sustainability@mdpi.com
www.mdpi.com/journal/sustainability

Ingram Content Group UK Ltd.
Milton Keynes UK
UKHW020724130423
420028UK00003B/14

9 783038 975601